ARTS OF THE UNITED STATES

ARTS *of the* UNITED STATES
A Pictorial Survey

WILLIAM H. PIERSON, JR.
and
MARTHA DAVIDSON, *Editors*

Based on a collection of color slides assembled by the University of Georgia under a grant by Carnegie Corporation of New York.

McGRAW-HILL BOOK COMPANY, INC.

NEW YORK   TORONTO   LONDON

ARTS OF THE UNITED STATES

PREFACE

When the *Carnegie Study of the Arts of the United States* was undertaken in 1955, even we who were to guide it were not fully aware of the range and magnitude of the endeavor. It soon became apparent that the potentials before us, such a wealth of material and scope of accomplishments, could be realized only with intellectual guidance, genuine interest, and cooperative assistance on the part of hundreds of persons and organizations. Paralleling this need, institutions of all sizes were called upon to make their contributions by providing access to works of art for photographic purposes and documentary information. These sources of assistance were of great importance as the Study developed—they came to our aid as we encountered innumerable problems and obstacles that required authoritative and, in many instances, imaginative solutions.

We wish it were possible to acknowledge our indebtedness to each individual who helped in this undertaking. Every contribution—from a single, pertinent suggestion to the almost single-handed formulation of entire sections—deserves our special recognition. Without such cooperation, this publication would not have become a reality.

We would like, however, with gratitude and deep appreciation, to acknowledge those specific contributions which were particularly essential to the life of the Study.

It was the financial support of the Carnegie Corporation of New York that brought fruition to this venture, which otherwise would have remained only an idea in the minds of many who are vitally interested in the arts of our country and their rightful place in the study and appreciation of our society and culture. We express our sincere thanks to John Gardner, President, and to the Board of Trustees for their initial concern and continued moral and financial support; to Florence Anderson, Secretary, for her untiring personal interest, which proved to be an inspiration to all of us; and to Margaret Mahoney, Associate Secretary, whose able assistance contributed greatly to the success of various aspects of the program.

With the uniqueness of the Study in mind, I personally am particularly cognizant of the debt owed to the Board of Advisors for its dedicated services, often above and beyond the call of duty. As I recall the endless hours of study that have gone into this project, I realize how very much was contributed by every member of this Board. To the Executive Secretary, William H. Pierson, Jr., who persevered through innumerable

problems and found a satisfactory solution to each; to Lloyd Goodrich, who gave us his sage counsel time after time; to Martha Davidson, who from the inception of the Study served so admirably as Coordinating Editor until, unhappily, she had to resign for personal reasons; and to Oliver Larkin and the late Tremaine McDowell, for their sound advice and encouragement, I extend profound thanks.

Of fundamental importance to our work were the distinguished scholars listed in the Contents who served as consultants and authors of the essays in this book. Each carried out the difficult assignment of making discriminating choices in selecting from all the material available the subjects to be photographed for the project and from his vast knowledge of his field the most important facts to be considered in the form of a brief essay. Their achievement speaks for itself in the pages which follow.

Only those of us who were so closely associated with this Study are fully aware of the efficient and dedicated services that were performed so ably by S. Lane Faison, Jr., who served as Executive Secretary of the Study during a four-month period while William Pierson was on leave; Charles B. Phelps, Associate Executive Secretary; Margot Archer, Associate Editor; Marion Shaw and Rachel Norton, Editorial Assistants. Their excellent work involved voluminous correspondence, communications of all types, typing, checking and rechecking manuscripts and lists, and countless other details.

At the outset it was realized that our major problem was how to provide visual-aid material of the finest quality. The solution of the technical problems involved would require imagination, resourcefulness, initiative, and good will on the part of whoever produced the actual photographs and slides. That they assume a role of responsibility was absolutely essential to the success of the Study. We, most fortunately, found the answer in Victor and Harold Sandak. These two people, together with their associates, devoted themselves wholeheartedly to this effort. Their work resulted in the establishment for this Study of the highest professional standards that are presently possible and effected the solution of processing problems that even they could not envision until they undertook the assignment.

The enthusiastic response of museums and other public and private organizations has been one of the most rewarding aspects of the Study. The contributions made by some, however, deserve our special thanks: the Whitney Museum of American Art for providing the space and objects with which the major portion of our experimental photography was carried out; the Henry Francis du Pont Winterthur Museum for the use of its photographic facilities in our first experiments with strobe light; Williams College for providing the offices in the Lawrence Art Museum where the final year of editorial work on the catalogue was accomplished and for placing at our disposal its dark room, library, and materials on American art. In addition, both the Whitney and Winterthur Museums along with the Metropolitan Museum of Art, the Museum of Fine Arts, Boston, and the Museum of Modern Art, New York, made available to us enormous portions of their collections and thus were forced to endure disrupting and costly invasions by our photographic teams for long periods of time.

Other important contributors are: the Addison Gallery of American Art; the Albright Art Gallery; the American Museum of Natural History; the Art Institute of Chicago; the Avery Architectural Library; the Bowdoin College Museum of Fine Arts; the Brooklyn Museum; the Carnegie Institute; the Chicago Natural History Museum; the Cincinnati Art Museum; the City Art Museum of St. Louis; the Cleveland Museum of Art; the Detroit Institute of Arts; the George Eastman House; the Essex Institute; the Fogg Art Museum; the Gibbes Art Gallery; the Historical Society of Pennsylvania; the Library of Congress; the Los Angeles County Museum; the Museum of the American Indian; the Museum of the City of New York; the Museum of New Mexico; the Museum of Science and Industry; Mystic Seaport; the National Gallery of Art; the New York State Historical Association; the New-York Historical Society; the New York Public Library; the Pennsylvania Academy of Fine Arts; the Philadelphia Museum of Art; the Phillips Gallery; the Shelburne Museum; the Smithsonian Institution; the Society for the Preservation of New England Antiquities; the Toledo Museum of Art; the University Museum, Philadelphia; the Wadsworth Atheneum; the Worcester Art Museum; and the Yale University Art Gallery.

In addition to these institutions, countless individuals have also played important roles in the success of the project. Those whose efforts merit special recognition are: Gilbert Ask of the Henry Francis du Pont Winterthur Museum; Henry B. Beville of the National Gallery of Art; Miss E. Boyd of the Museum of New Mexico; Mrs. Kathryn C. Buhler of the Museum of Fine Arts, Boston; E. Milby Burton of the Charleston Museum; Erwin Ottomar Christensen of the National Gallery of Art; Abbott Cummings of the Society for the Preservation of New England Antiquities; Miss Louisa Dresser of the Worcester Art Museum; Miss Dorothy Dudley of the Museum of Modern Art; William Duprey of the New York Public Library; Miss Lillian Green of the Metropolitan Museum of Art; Karl Kup of the New York Public Library; Thomas N. Maytham of the Museum of Fine Arts, Boston; Mrs. Anna C. Hunter of Savannah, Georgia; Miss Helen G. McCormack of the Gibbes Art Gallery; Miss Margaret McKellar of the Whitney Museum of American Art; Miss Dorothy C. Miller of the Museum of Modern Art; Hubert Owens of the University of Georgia; Miss Caroline Rollins of the Yale University Art Gallery; Miss Josephine Setz of the Yale University Art Gallery; Mrs. Ellen F. Shuman of the Metropolitan Museum of Art; Samuel G. Stoney of Charleston, South Carolina; Mrs. George Henry Warren of the Preservation Society of Newport County; and Mrs. Hertha Wegener of the Brooklyn Museum.

Despite the desire to express such feelings, no statement can adequately do justice to the pride which we of the University of Georgia have in presenting this illustrated guide as an integral and important part of the *Carnegie Study of the Arts of the United States*.

LAMAR DODD, Director

INTRODUCTION

A work of art is first of all a visual experience, a pattern of formal relationships evoking aesthetic as well as intellectual responses; at the same time, it is an index to cultural values, a tangible and informative symbol of man's aspirations and achievements. All too often in the past these two areas of communication and understanding have been isolated from one another, set apart by artists and educators alike so that each would seem to exist quite independently of the other. Currently, however, there is a growing tendency to evaluate a work of art as the product of all the stimuli which have brought it into being. Seen in this light, the art object takes on meaning as a cultural symbol as well as an aesthetic experience.

For many years students of civilization have used the symbolic expressions of a people as indices of their culture. More recently, anthropologists concerned with primitive peoples have made extensive use of the symbols employed in costume, the dance, music, and the visual arts. And students of contemporary civilizations are giving increased attention to the symbolic utterances of these cultures.

The study of the symbolism of a complex society is particularly difficult because modern peoples make themselves heard not only through the voice of the entire group but also through the voices of in-groups and individuals. Arduous as the task may be, anyone who would know the full range of any culture must study not only its broad patterns but also the expression of minority groups and individuals. The use of symbolic statements is further complicated by the fact that a people, a group, and an individual speak both overtly and covertly. In the search for covert meaning, students in the various fields of humanities are drawing new methods from historians, sociologists, anthropologists, and psychologists.

Students of art may protest that the use of symbols as cultural documents is a misuse of music, painting, or the dance. Students of civilization agree, of course, that the primary significance of a work of art lies within the field of that art itself. They believe, however, that it is impossible to understand a people fully without an understanding of their symbols, especially as expressed in the visual arts.

The question will be asked whether a work of art should ever be interpreted by a man who is not an expert in that field. Ideally, the person best qualified would be an individual who is a specialist both in the realm of art and in the sociological, political, and historical aspects of a given civilization. But not many teachers in the United States today have all these qualifications, and in actual practice, excellent results are being achieved by men who have a wide knowledge of civilization and only a modest one of art.

This broader approach to the arts has produced some interesting results throughout American educational circles. It is manifested at the undergraduate level by the introduction of courses in design and techniques into art history curriculums, and by integrated courses which cut across departmental lines and bring into common focus several aspects of the same culture. At the secondary level it reveals itself in expanding art programs and in a considerably greater recourse to visual-aids material, much of which is drawn from the world of art. In museums, too, a greater emphasis on education has given rise to courses for adults and children which make wide use of slides, and to many interesting audio-visual programs which are available to the public on a loan or rental basis.

A collateral development in the United States has been a more active interest in our own artistic heritage. In the past, the study of American art has received but slight attention. Indeed, if studied at all, it has often been presented as a provincial derivation of European ideas and values. When seen as part of the general development of Western art, this interpretation is correct, particularly in the seventeenth and eighteenth centuries. Seen in the framework of American history, however, American art takes on a very different meaning. It is now clear that among the complex issues involved in our national growth are very real areas of creative achievement in the arts. Recognition of this fact has opened the way for a more enlightened understanding of our struggle toward cultural maturity. At the same time, our leading role in international affairs has aroused a healthy curiosity about us in other nations; and much of this curiosity is centered upon our artistic production. Altogether this creates an unprecedented demand for a carefully selected body of visual material which will illustrate the nature and quality of American art and American civilization.

The Carnegie Study of the Arts of the United States is a project devoted to the partial fulfillment of this need. Its primary objectives have been, first, to compile a collection of material which will represent the history of American art in most of its phases from the beginning to the present, and to document each work as accurately as possible and, second, to select from this total collection approximately four thousand works to be photographed in color and reproduced in the form of high-quality color slides. These slides are intended for use in educational institutions, museums, and libraries in this country and abroad.

The Board of Advisors to the Study realized in the early stages of the planning that no group of individuals, however expert, would be able to choose material that would satisfy every requirement. The intention has been rather to achieve a balanced corpus of distinguished works of art which will provide the most authoritative and flexible teaching instrument for the greatest number of people. As far as possible, the objects chosen are representative of the highest quality in the visual arts of the United States, although some items have been included specifically for their ethnological or sociological interest. In scope, the survey extends from prehistoric times to the present day, and encompasses all the arts which could be reproduced effectively by means of color slides. Thus, stage design is included, but the animated arts—drama, motion pictures, and the dance—have been eliminated as being beyond the effective scope of a slide study.

As a preliminary guide to selection, the arts of the United States were divided into eighteen different categories, and a specialist in each area was invited to choose a stated number of objects which in his judgment would best record the developments and achievements of his field. He was further asked to select from this maximum list a minimum list of those objects which in his opinion would be indispensable to a selective coverage of his subject. The maximum lists contained more than 10,000 items; from these the works included in this catalogue were chosen.

Responsibility for the final choice of material rested with the Advisory Board. In carrying out this difficult task every effort was made to respect the lists as originally compiled by the consultants. However, circumstances necessitated considerable readjustment of most of these lists. The most formidable problem was that of achieving an over-all balance between the eighteen different categories. Each consultant, as an expert, was asked to concern himself only with his own field; it was the function of the Board to view the problem as a whole and to establish the proper relationships between the various categories of material. This required a general revamping of the individual lists; it also necessitated a certain amount of reshuffling from list to list.

Other factors entered the picture, some anticipated, others unforeseen. Many items selected no longer existed or could not be found. Some were so remote geographically that the cost of travel to reach them could not be justified. On one occasion the project photographers arrived to find the building they were to photograph a mass of smoldering ruins. In a few instances the owners would not permit their possessions to be included.

The original lists were also modified by the Board's decision to eliminate all items which were not suitable for color photography. Black-and-white line work such as architectural plans and black-and-white halftone illustrations were culled. It was felt that such material could easily be obtained in the form of inexpensive black-and-white slides. To reproduce them in a costly color technique would divert funds which could better be used in other areas. On the other hand, original architects' drawings *were* included, and some of the stage designs had to be shot from black-and-white photographs, since this was the only source from which they were available. In the photography section also, because of the nature of the material, it was necessary to photograph black-and-white prints. However, the use of color in this case made it possible to reproduce effectively the varying qualities of tone so often characteristic of fine photography.

There were also additions to the original lists. Some were substitutions; others were necessary in order to obtain a proper balance between the various categories. During the course of the study, too, an occasional new or hitherto unpublished item was brought to light which was deemed of sufficient quality to be included.

After much hard editorial work most of the lists, although modified, came into reasonably balanced relationships. Four, however, were altered so as to require explanation. In the Twentieth-century Decorative Arts category many of the objects called for were either inaccessible or could not be located. Consequently, only about 75 per cent of the selections were ever photographed. Similarly, only a part of the Alaskan section of the American Indian category had been photographed when operations had to be terminated. In the case of the Theater category, so much of the material no longer existed that it was necessary to make innumerable substitutions. These did not always conform with the consultant's original intentions. It should be emphasized, therefore, that the obvious limitations to be found in these three categories should be attributed to unavoidable circumstances and not to inadequate selection on the part of the consultants.

The fourth category, Costume, proved to be a special problem. After the selections had been made by the consultant it was found that the difficulties involved in getting original garments on appropriate models were so considerable that the task was impossible with the available time and funds. It was decided, therefore, to select a small group of items which were already well displayed and accessible to the camera, and to substitute for the rest portraits in which similar costumes were shown. For this reason, the essay on costume is illustrated largely through reference to paintings.

A difficult question encountered in selecting the material was whether or not to include works by foreign-born artists. Although it seemed desirable to maintain a consistent policy, it was not always possible. Generally speaking, however, foreign-born artists who have produced a substantial part of their work in the United States are represented. Conversely, American-born artists who spent most of their productive lives abroad have also been included. In the Theater category the situation was complicated by the fact that some of the most interesting designs prepared for the American stage have been the work of European artists. At the specific request of the consultant, therefore, a few such designs have been selected. Since the actual sets were executed by American workmen and the plays produced in this country, their inclusion seemed entirely reasonable.

The achievement of a consistent stylistic terminology appropriate to all categories of material turned out to be an illusive ideal. Until fairly recent times American art, if not altogether derived from Europe, has been closely related to its artistic developments. For the most part, therefore, stylistic terms used in relation to European art also have meaning when applied to American art. Yet there are numerous factors which complicate the issue The first is the inevitable time lag involved when stylistic ideas make their way from one geographical location to another. The delay in accepting cultural innovation of any kind, which is natural to all fringe cultures, was exaggerated in the American Colonies because of two factors: the economic and technical limitations imposed by the frontier and the difficulties of long overseas communications. As a result, the Colonies were from twenty-five to fifty years behind their mother countries in matters of artistic mode.

Another complication is the wide variety in the handling of the European styles once they reached these shores. Although the accepted terms can be applied quite readily to high-style objects, in provincial- and folk-art production the precise relationships are more blurred. Furthermore, in outlying regions older stylistic features continued in effect long after they had ceased to be popular in the centers of colonial culture. Thus the time lag becomes even further extended and the problem of terminology more complex.

The term "Early Georgian" illustrates the kind of difficulties which result when European terminology is carried over into the American field. Since most American architecture of the first half of the eighteenth century was built during the reigns of either George I or George II, the use of the phrase would seem historically correct. When considered stylistically, however, the buildings of this period have little or nothing to do with the Early Georgian architecture of England. Actually, they are in the style of a quarter to a half century earlier, that is, the Late Stuart or Wren Baroque. But this confusion is not limited to architecture nor to the Georgian period. It occurs in the other arts as well, particularly the decorative arts, and in most other periods of American artistic development down to modern times.

With respect to terminology, the American Indian section was the most involved of all. The Carnegie Study represents one of the first attempts to present Indian material as part of America's artistic heritage, and since this material is entirely indigenous there is no established European terminology to draw upon. The consultant used instead geographical and ethnological classifications, all of which have archaeological significance, but few of which are pertinent when applied to questions of style or artistic interpretation. Furthermore, not all authorities on Indian culture agree on the meaning of these terms. Some of the museums, for example, have insisted that their own terminology be employed. Unfortunately, these have not always been consistent with the classifications established by the consultant. Persons familiar with the Indian material, therefore, may find certain inconsistencies in the terms used, but until a broader understanding can be reached by experts in the field this kind of situation is unavoidable.

In editing both the slide lists and the essays it was found that several familiar stylistic terms were sometimes employed with different shades of meaning by different consultants. In spite of the extensive editorial work done on the project as a whole, each essay and each category of material remains essentially the work of a particular individual. It was never intended that the various articles should form a cohesive book. Each stands, therefore, as a thing complete in itself and should be understood as such.

The Study does not pretend that it is providing a definitive teaching instrument either in its scholarly or technical production. It is closer to the truth to say that it marks only the beginning. Like all projects of this kind, which begin in the unknown, it took shape as it grew. Unforeseen obstacles forcing changes in direction, differences of opinion leading to compromise, unexpected developments in the laboratory necessitating revisions of technical estimates—all these have conspired to alter ideals and modify objectives. Nevertheless, in working out the details of the project nothing has been spared. The highest professional standards of color photography and slide production have been employed throughout, standards which would not have been possible without the Carnegie grant. At the same time, every effort has been made to assure the highest quality of scholarship. It is the sincere hope of all members of the project that the final results will bring to teachers and students alike new dimensions of experience in the realm of American art.

CONTENTS

ARCHITECTURE OF THE
SEVENTEENTH AND EIGHTEENTH CENTURIES

HUGH MORRISON

The architecture of the colonial period is as diverse as the peoples who settled the new continent: Spanish, English, Dutch, Swedish, French, Flemish, Swiss, German, Scotch-Irish. All of these peoples, as well as wanderers from Nova Scotia and migrant planters from the West Indies, settled in various regions and left traces of their building customs.

The earliest buildings of all but the Spanish colonists were medieval in style and reminiscent of the Late Gothic houses and barns of the small towns and fishing villages of the home countries. They were extremely simple and devoid of all but an occasional bit of craftsman's ornament, for there was neither the wealth nor the skill to emulate in the Colonies the buttressed and traceried richness of Europe's Gothic cathedrals, great houses, and guild halls.

This medieval style prevailed in almost all the Colonies to the end of the seventeenth century and long after that in the frontier settlements. Simplicity and practicality were the keynotes of these Early Colonial buildings. They revealed their sturdy structure of hand-hewn framing members and delighted in the frank use of the building materials: the fine-lined clapboards of New England, the diapered brick masonry of Dutch New Amsterdam or English Maryland, the rough field stone of Pennsylvania or the Hudson Valley. They were the expression of a pioneer society, just as the eighteenth century styles, with their formal symmetry, finer materials, and delicately executed ornament, were the expression of a sophisticated and polite society.

New England possesses today a larger number of authentic seventeenth-century houses than any other region of the country. At the Pioneer Village in Salem one can see "English wigwams"—thatched roofs and plank-walled cottages, careful replicas of the first temporary shelters that were built in the first decade of settlement in New England. These soon gave way to "fair houses" sturdily framed in oak, with clapboard siding and interior pine wainscot enclosing a wall-filling of clay "cats" or sun-dried brick.

Notable among the early New England houses are the Fairbanks House at Dedham, built about 1637 and probably the oldest surviving frame house in the United States; the picturesque House of Seven Gables in Salem, begun about 1670; the Parson Capen House in Topsfield (1683); and the fine John Ward House in Salem (1684).

Fewer than a half dozen seventeenth-century brick houses survive in New England, and there is only one extant stone house: the impressive parsonage built for Henry Whitfield in Guilford in 1639. Of other types of structures, there were numerous garrisons and blockhouses; many "foursquare" meeting houses, such as the "Old Ship" in Hingham (1681); the early buildings of Harvard College (none of which survive today); and sundry town houses, schools, and mills.

New Netherland survived as a Dutch colony only from 1624 to 1664, but long after the English captured it the "Dutch Colonial" styles of the Hudson Valley, Long Island, and northern New Jersey persisted. The Dutch built in wood, brick, or stone, but they favored brick masonry, using a variety of shapes, colors, and bonds, with many curious patterns and inset glazed tiles to enliven their walls. Many seventeenth-century stone houses still survive in the valley towns such as Old Hurley, New Paltz, and Kingston.

The characteristic flared eaves of the "Dutch" style were in reality of Flemish origin, as Wertenbaker has shown, and these together with a gambrel roof of distinctive profile, first introduced about 1700, produced the well-known eighteenth-century version of the style seen in such classic examples as the Abraham Ackerman House at Hackensack (1704) and the Dyckman House in New York City (c. 1783). The widely projecting flared eaves of the latter were supported by posts to form a wide front porch. This feature was a development of the Revolutionary period and later was much used in other regions.

New Sweden was chartered in 1638, and five or six villages were established on the west bank of the Delaware River, including one on the site of Philadelphia. The colony fell to the Dutch in 1655 and in turn to

1

the English in 1664. No clearly defined "Swedish Colonial" style can be described, but the Swedes apparently contributed four features to the melting pot of
colonial architecture: the "true" log cabin, i.e., a building employing round logs, notched at the corners and
with protruding ends; the corner fireplace; a distinctive
type of gambrel roof with a very steep lower pitch; and
a three-room type of house plan which William Penn
later recommended to his Quaker settlers. Two surviving churches—the "Old Swedes" churches at Wilmington (1698–1699) and Philadelphia (1698–1700)—
though largely English in details, were built by Swedish
congregations and have a certain Scandinavian flavor.

William Penn's "Holy Experiment" saw the founding
of Pennsylvania in 1681 and its rapid growth as a
prosperous and densely populated colony. By 1750
Philadelphia surpassed Boston as the biggest city in
America. Using the native ledge stone, the colonists
evolved a distinctive regional style of great vigor. But
almost from the first, the Quaker settlers brought the
new style of London as it was rebuilt after the great
fire of 1666—symmetrical façades, classical decorative
detail, moulded cornices, sliding-sash windows, and
painted woodwork took the place of the medieval forms
that still prevailed in the older colonies of New England
and the South.

A belated medieval quality marks the "Pennsylvania
Dutch" style of the southeastern counties. Encouraged
by Penn's attractive terms to immigrants, hordes of
Germans from the Rhineland, the Black Forest, upper
Bavaria, and Saxony poured into Pennsylvania from
about 1710 on. With them they brought their crafts and
their mode of building, to form a genre style that lasted
until well after the Revolution. Notable are the great
stone and wood barns decorated by painted "hex"
symbols; the several buildings of The Cloister at Ephrata (1740–1746); and the Moravian Seminary at
Bethlehem (1773). Pioneers traveling down the valley
of Virginia carried an offshoot of this style that may be
seen in the Moravian buildings at Winston-Salem, North
Carolina.

The main tradition of the South had been established
in the seventeenth century, and it was, like New England's, the style of late medieval England. Whereas
New England's economy was largely one of villages,
seaports, and small farms, that of the South was based
almost entirely on big plantations. The plantation houses
were, in the seventeenth century, far from imposing.
They were a story-and-a-half high, had a steep-pitched
gable roof, and usually only two rooms downstairs. By
1680 a central passage separated these rooms, and in
a half dozen examples a projecting porch in front and

stair tower behind created a "cross" plan, unique to
Virginia and Maryland. Chimneys were at the ends of
the house, often projecting outside it to create a distinctive architectural feature. Both frame and brick
construction were used, but no frame house of the
seventeenth century survives today. Brick, laid in either
English bond or Flemish bond, was the favored material.

Notable examples in Virginia are the Adam Thoroughgood House near Norfolk, perhaps built as early
as 1636, and Bacon's Castle in Surry County (c. 1655).
The most evidently "Gothic" church in all the colonies
is Newport Parish Church ("Old Brick" St. Luke's) at
Smithfield, built either in 1632 or in 1682, according
to the varying testimony of different scholars.

Particularly characteristic of Maryland's early colonial houses is a delight in decorative patterns of dark-
glazed brick headers, forming diamonds, hearts, zigzags,
and even initials and dates—a fashion especially favored along the Eastern shore.

Carolina, chartered as a colony in 1663, and separated into North and South Carolina in 1711, became a
cosmopolitan area settled by English, Irish, Welsh,
Scotch, Dutch, French Huguenots, and planters from
the West Indies. Notable are three early plantation
houses: Medway (1686), built by a Dutchman; Middleburg (1699), built by a French Huguenot; and Mulberry (1714), built by an Englishman. But Charleston,
first settled in 1680, suffered a succession of disastrous
fires which have left scarcely a town house built before
1740.

Far removed from the well-populated shores of the
Atlantic was the vast and almost uninhabited wilderness of the Mississippi Valley. The French settled it
first from the St. Lawrence and Great Lakes water high-
ways with a series of forts and trading posts in the
"Illinois Country," built in the last quarter of the
seventeenth century. One of the few remaining examples of their houses is Cahokia Courthouse at
Cahokia, Illinois, built first as a residence about 1737.

But the major center of French colonial architecture
was in the lower valley. Louisiana was annexed as a
Crown Colony in 1699, with the capital first at Biloxi,
until New Orleans was founded in 1718. A few French
houses still stand in the close-packed streets of New
Orleans' Vieux Carré. The construction is usually of
cypress framing timbers, filled by unburned brick
(*briqueté-entre-poteaux*), protected by a surface coat
of stucco—which, in later years, was tinted in many
different pastel tones. Notable are Madam John's
Legacy (c. 1727) and Lafitte's Blacksmith Shop, built
after 1772.

In the quiet bayou country great live oaks festooned with Spanish moss shadow the French plantation houses, with their two-story porches (*galeries*) supported by small classic columns, their exterior stairways, and broad sheltering roofs. Such was Parlange, built in 1750 by the Marquis Vincent de Ternant.

When France lost Louisiana in the Treaty of 1763, the Spanish took over New Orleans and all territory west of the Mississippi. Though the Spanish dominion was brief (Napoleon regained Louisiana in 1801 and sold it to the United States in 1803) it left some architectural traces. The impressive Cabildo (1795) in New Orleans, weightily composed with a full panoply of baroque architectural forms, is almost a copy of the Casas Reales in Antequera, Mexico, built a few years before. This was also the period when several thousand Acadians, expelled from Nova Scotia by the British, settled in the Louisiana bayou country to reinforce its French heritage.

Longest of all the colonial styles in chronological span and widest in geographical spread was the Spanish. Lasting from the founding of St. Augustine in 1565 to the unfurling of the American flag on the Custom House at Monterey, California, in 1846, the Spanish dominion lasted almost three hundred years and spanned a continent.

Though animated at first by discovery and the lure of riches, the Spanish colonizing effort developed almost exclusively as a missionary program of civilizing and Christianizing the Indians, and its architectural achievements are best seen in the five great "mission fields": Florida, New Mexico, Arizona, Texas, and California.

Florida was the earliest. By 1593, twelve Franciscan friars had arrived, and over the years they founded some forty missions, stretching along the East Coast from St. Catherine's Island to Miami and along a westerly trail from St. Augustine to the Gulf. But except for the ruined walls of the mission at New Smyrna, virtually nothing remains—or is known—of them today. Perhaps there exists here an opportunity for historical and archaeological research. The only important Spanish building remaining in Florida is the great stone fort at St. Augustine, begun in 1672. Far greater than any of the forts built by the English or Dutch, it remains today one of America's most impressive monuments.

Years before the landings at Jamestown and Plymouth, Juan de Oñate established a mission some thirty miles north of Santa Fe on July 11, 1598, and at Santa Fe itself is the oldest building in the United States built by Europeans: the Governor's Palace, erected between 1610 and 1614. New Mexico was the earliest of the western mission fields: as early as 1626, forty-three mission churches had been built, and some 34,000 Indians had been converted. Greatest of the New Mexican missions is San Estevan, founded in 1629, high on the rugged mesa of Acoma. But many others reveal the primitive charm of rough-surfaced adobe walls and Indian craftsmanship and decoration: San José at Laguna, Santo Tomás at Trampas, or the sculptured forms of the mission church at Ranchos de Taos. The New Mexican mission churches employed no arches, vaults, or domes—probably because of the lack of skilled stone-cutters among the Indian workmen and the scarcity of wood for centering.

The mission fields of Texas and Arizona inaugurated in 1690 by the Franciscans and Jesuits, respectively, reveal a greater degree of architectural sophistication. With cruciform plans, vaulted and domed structure, and an intricate ornament of carved stone, moulded plaster, woodwork, and painting, they strove for the opulent grandeur of their baroque models in Mexico and Spain. The most impressive surviving examples are San José at San Antonio (1720–1731), the Purisima Concepción at San Antonio (1731), and San Xavier del Bac at Tucson (1784–1797).

The twenty-one missions of California's chain, extending along more than 500 miles of the old Camino Real, were founded between 1769 and 1823. They were constructed largely of adobe and brick, and few of them essayed vaults or domes. Architecturally, they lie between the primitive charm of the New Mexican missions and the baroque splendors of Texas and Arizona. But occasional portals, bell towers, patio fountains, and altar screens reveal sophisticated ambitions. Outstanding among the California missions are San Diego, first of the chain founded by the *padre presidente* Fra Junípero Serra; San Carlos Borromeo at Carmel, built 1793–1797; San Juan Capistrano, built 1797–1806 but left in ruins after the earthquake of 1812; and Santa Barbara, whose present church (the fourth on the site) was built between 1815 and 1820.

Noteworthy in California are several ranch houses and town houses built between the year of Mexico's independence (1821) and the American conquest in 1846. Good examples survive in San Diego, Santa Barbara, and Monterey.

The social setting of eighteenth-century architecture in the colonies of the Atlantic seaboard had changed markedly from pioneer days. By 1700 the region had been settled three-quarters of a century, more or less. The population was growing by leaps and bounds. All of the colonies from New Hampshire to Georgia were united under English rule. There was relative security from Indian attacks—though these were to recur at intervals through the time of the French and Indian War.

It was a society in which class distinctions were increasingly important. Wealth unimagined in the pioneer days poured into the Eastern cities, and the prosperous merchants, shipowners, and landed proprietors, together with the royal governors and their circles, formed a society which sought to emulate the manners, the costume, the culture, and the architecture of England.

The style of the eighteenth century was essentially aristocratic. Formal symmetry, rather than the accidents of internal functions or of evolutionary growth, dominated the shapes of buildings. Proportions and details were carefully studied, and the ordered rhythm of the facade compositions revealed a sophisticated new language of architectural forms.

This language was classical rather than medieval in derivation. It was a part of the revival of classical forms that had begun with the Early Renaissance in Italy some three centuries before and had developed through various phases of classical, mannerist, and baroque manipulation to form the several styles and periods of the countries of western Europe from 1500 to the late 1700s. Naturally, it was the styles of England that dominated the architecture of the English colonies.

Since the first tentative and rather naive introduction of Renaissance architectural details in the Elizabethan period, England had progressed to the more firmly ordered and discriminating classicism of the Early Stuart period (1620–1660), dominated by the work of Inigo Jones, and then to the freer, more colorful, more baroque style of the Late Stuart period (1660–1714), dominated by the work of Sir Christopher Wren and his followers.

At the time (around the year 1700) that the American colonies had achieved the wealth, the skills, and the desire for a more sophisticated and aristocratic architecture, it was this Wren-baroque style that was most modern and fashionable in the mother country and accordingly the admired model in the provinces. This Late Stuart tradition dominated the architecture of the colonies from 1700 to about 1750. It is sometimes referred to as our Early Georgian style.

England in the meantime had progressed to a stricter, more academic classicism, inspired by a revived Palladianism. Since this began at about the time George I ascended the throne in 1714 and lasted until the time of George III, who came to the throne in 1760, it may properly be called England's Early Georgian style. Its chief proponent was Richard Boyle, Earl of Burlington (1695–1753). Lord Burlington was an ardent disciple of Palladio and sponsored publication of Giacomo Leoni's magnificent edition of Palladio's *Four Books of Architecture* in 1715, as well as several buildings in the Palladian manner. There was also a revival of interest in the century-old work of Inigo Jones, who himself had been a formidable Palladian; one of Lord Burlington's protégés, William Kent, published the *Designs of Inigo Jones* in 1727. One of the most important English architects, James Gibbs, remained, however, more faithful to the tradition of Sir Christopher Wren than to the newer Palladianism. He was of very great influence in the colonies through his *Book of Architecture,* first published in 1728, the designs of which were echoed in many a fine mansion and church in the colonies.

Although Drayton Hall, South Carolina (1738–1742) was an early example, the Palladian mode did not become generally current in the colonies until about 1750. One of its most accomplished practitioners was the architect Peter Harrison (1716–1775) of Newport, Rhode Island. His Redwood Library (1748–1750) is full of details taken from the books of the Burlington-Palladio revival. Because the style flourished in the colonies after 1750, it has sometimes been distinguished as our "Late Georgian" style.

It is unfortunate that these terminologies seem to involve transatlantic contradictions. Since the Late Stuart style in England and the "Early Georgian" (1700–1750) in America are essentially one style, and since the Early Georgian in England and what has been termed the "Late Georgian" (1750–1780) in America are also essentially one style, it may eliminate confusion if we refer to the earlier style, in both countries, as the Wren-baroque, and to the later one, in both countries, as the Palladian. Some of the distinctions between them will be brought out later.

Throughout the eighteenth century, however, certain common characteristics reveal the great contrast to the medieval style of the seventeenth century. Formal symmetry and classical decorative details characterize all types of buildings. Brick became the favored material, although clapboard walls in New England and stone ones in Pennsylvania could still be found. Entrance doors were flanked by classical pilasters and topped by various shapes of pediments. Universally, the leaded casement windows of the seventeenth century were replaced by wood sliding-sash windows, which Wren had popularized in England.

The simple eaves of the seventeenth century were elaborated by mouldings, dentils, and modillions to achieve a full classical cornice. Steep-pitched roofs gave way to lower pitches, and although the gable and gambrel roof shapes were still used, the elegant regularity of the hipped roof was favored in all the finer mansions. Roof decks surrounded by balustrades (and variously called captain's walks and widow's walks in this country) became popular, and a few grand houses ventured a crowning cupola.

Inside the house, rooms became more spacious and more elegant. A central hall, running through from front to back, was dominated by a fine stairway, with the step ends visible ("open string") and adorned by panels or scrolls and with a stair rail of turned balusters. After 1730, spirally twisted balusters became very popular. Rooms were handsomely paneled or papered with imported pictorial wallpapers. Fireplaces and chimney breasts became important decorative features. Ceilings were covered by fine lime plaster, sometimes ornamented by intricate plaster reliefs. Impressive "Queen Anne" furniture pieces characterized the first half of the century; the lighter and more playful Chippendale style came in after 1750.

Perhaps the greatest contrast with the seventeenth century is in the universal use of paint and plaster, and the paint colors of the interiors were far richer than is now generally supposed: ochres, greens, blues, gray-blues, warm buffs, and rich red-browns were popular, though they gradually yielded to more classical whites and creams as the academic influence strengthened after 1750.

The Palladian style continued in use after the Revolution, with minor changes, to about 1800. But with Jefferson's design for the new Virginia capitol in 1785 and Bulfinch's return to Boston in 1786, fresh from the London of the Brothers Adam and William Chambers, new influences were at work and the Federal style was in the ascendant.

TOWN, CITY, AND PARK

All colonial communities were "planned" in a sense: the location was chosen with care, especially if the nucleus were to be a fort; lands were surveyed and allotted; sites were chosen for houses and the meeting house; and roads to outlying farm land were laid out. Yet the resultant patterns were almost invariably irregular and were altered in piecemeal fashion as the towns grew. The street pattern was not the prior determinant of town layout and growth; rather, land allotments came first, and the streets were provided, more or less haphazardly, to gain access to the land.

In a modern sense, this was not "town planning." We have come to regard a town plan *primarily* as an orderly, and usually mathematically regular, street plan designed to serve future building needs for some lengthy period of years. Such, for example, were the original plans for New Haven, Philadelphia, New Orleans, and Washington, D.C.

In discussing town plans of the seventeenth and eighteenth centuries, accordingly, it may be helpful to distinguish two broad categories: the irregular or "unplanned" town, best typified by the New England village, and the regularly planned town, such as Philadelphia.

A very large majority, perhaps ninety per cent, of colonial towns must be called "unplanned." The original town layout was based, not on a regular street pattern, but on functional factors such as military defense, agriculture, or shipping, and adaptation to topography. In all of these spheres, the colonists tended to follow the prevailing practices of the mother countries, as they did in architecture.

England's experience with this sort of problem in the first two decades of the seventeenth century came primarily in the colonization of Ulster in northern Ireland. By 1622 some fifteen towns had been established there by twelve London companies (mostly livery companies or guilds) who had obtained charters. Typically, they were tenant villages with the houses clustered about a small square or along a single street, each house with its assigned home lot. A large lot was reserved for a church, and at some distance was a stronghold—a sort of fortified courtyard which the Irish called a "bawn"—for defense against the hostile natives.

The plan of Jamestown, as Garvan has pointed out, was essentially like that of one of these Irish company towns. The London Company specified the design of the settlers' houses and stipulated the division of home lots and of additional fields outside the village. Of chief concern was the fort, or bawn, which was triangular in plan, measuring 420 feet on the side toward the James River and 300 feet on each of the shorter sides. Stout posts and planks, which stood 14 feet high and were embedded 4 feet in the ground, palisaded the sides, and the corners were fortified by circular bastions of large hewn timbers serving as artillery platforms. Within the fort were the church, two storehouses, and some row houses—perhaps some thirty-odd small dwellings, each about 16 feet square. It is interesting that the designer of the fort, Maister Edm.-Maria Wingfield, was a soldier who had seen service in Ireland.

Not dissimilar was the fort at New Amsterdam, first completed in 1626, but rebuilt in 1633–1635. There exists a letter from the English architect Inigo Jones, written in 1620, giving the Dutch East India Company (the West India Company was not formed until the following year) rather detailed instructions for the construction of a "Bawne," and it may be that this was the basis for the directions which the Company so minutely specified for the commander Kryn Fredericks, who arrived in 1625 with forty-two settlers. The design of the fort was given and so also was the layout of the nearby village with its market place, houses, schoolhouse, and church. Within the fort were a guardhouse, barracks, the governor's house, three windmills, and a large church.

At first, people lived in dugouts—holes dug into the ground and roofed over by poles and bark—but by 1628 these were being replaced by decent framed houses. By mid-century New Amsterdam had grown greatly, stretching across to the East River and northward to the wooden stockade across the island at what is now Wall Street. The street pattern was curving and irregular and penetrated deeply by the canal where Broad Street now is, as well as by various slips for docking vessels. Architecturally, it was a miniature replica of Amsterdam.

We have little precise knowledge of early Plymouth, but apparently its one main street—Leyden Street— had a row of thatched roof cottages with their own home lots guarded by a fort at some distance on the hill. Governor Bradford wrote that the fort, which was built in the summer of 1622, was

both strong and comly . . . of good defence, made with a flate rofe and batllments, on which their ordnance were mounted, and wher they kepte constante watch, espetially in time of danger. It served them allso for a meeting house and was fitted accordingly for that use.

Wethersfield, Connecticut, founded in 1633, gives a fairly typical picture of the method of town layout in New England and of its background in the mother country. The typical English agricultural village of the seventeenth century had a medieval form, based on open fields rather than the enclosed fields that were then becoming more common. It is called the "nucleated" village, because the houses and community structures were concentrated fairly compactly in a nucleus. Each house had its own home lot, rather narrow to the street but with 2 to 6 acres, affording room for the farmer to build his barn, sheds, hayricks, and other outbuildings behind the house. A sizable plot of common land was reserved in the center of the village for grazing purposes (the village "common"), and usually facing this a large plot of land was reserved for the church and the minister's house—which in New England was usually the largest and finest in town.

There was no regularity in such nuclear layouts: in New England they are all individual and different, depending on the lay of the land, the size of the original settlement, and other accidental factors. There might be a single street, or perhaps three or four converging on the common.

Outside of the village, the several square miles of a township grant were divided into tracts of meadowland, upland, marsh, or wood lot. In order that each farmer might have a fair share of good and bad lands, these tracts were divided into long narrow strips. This led to the practice known as "strip farming." Whereas in English villages these strips might average 2 rods (33 feet) in width and a furlong (660 feet) in length, they were generally much larger in New England. Indeed the famous "Long Lots" at Fairfield, Connecticut, laid out in 1682, averaged about 22 rods (363 feet) in width and extended some 10 *miles* to the Redding town line. These vast open fields were cultivated in strips and after the harvest were opened together for common grazing. The lanes and roads of such a township were originally laid out sheerly for access to the strip farms. They were thus subordinate to property divisions. They were not intended primarily for future building expansion or for travel to the neighboring town. Consequently, as population grew, they served both these latter functions poorly.

The village itself was kept compact for proximity to the meeting house and for defense against the Indians. Indeed it was necessary to forbid farmers from building far out in the countryside. Massachusetts, for instance, had many laws to prevent such dispersion. This meant small, well-knit towns and a coherent community life. Protection from the Indians was gained by building one or more "garrisons" or "blockhouses," fortresslike buildings into which the villagers could retreat when attacked. Usually built of square-hewn timbers and with an overhanging upper story, such fortified houses were particularly common in the frontier towns of Maine and New Hampshire. Gilmanton, New Hampshire, had four garrisons, one at each corner of the town.

As the practice of enclosure of the fields proceeded in England and as security permitted it in the New England colonies, the nuclear settlement gave way to the enclosed farm, an independent unit containing its own lands and farmhouse isolated from its neighbors.

In the meantime, the bigger cities grew without form

or order. Plans devised for nucleated villages, it can be seen, did not lend themselves well to urban growth. For a picture of the growing pains of the colonial metropolis, we may turn to Boston in the early eighteenth century. It was the largest city in the country, and its details may be studied in its first engraved plan—Captain John Bonner's map of 1722.

Boston doubled its population in the fifty years from 1690 to 1740. In 1742, according to the *Boston News-Letter,* it had 16,382 persons, living in 1,719 houses, many of them built of brick; 166 warehouses; 17 churches; and 5 public schools. It also had several public buildings: the Province House, the Town House, a public market, an almshouse, a workhouse, and a college in nearby Cambridge which boasted four brick buildings.

Boston's tangled network of narrow, curving streets was filled in by houses, side by side, gable end to the street, many with overhanging upper stories as in medieval England. Block interiors filled up with stables, storehouses, sheds for the servants, and privies or "houses of office."

The streets were jammed by carts, drays, hackney coaches, sleds bringing loads of firewood, and horsemen. Galloping of horses was forbidden, and carters had to lead their teams through the streets, but there were still traffic accidents. By 1717 rudimentary sidewalks were formed by setting up rows of posts in the street 8 feet from the buildings. Hanging signs were so numerous that after 1736 their use had to be curbed. Scavengers hired by the town cleaned the streets, but because of the lack of sanitary sewers slops were still thrown out the windows. In the streets were herds of "noisome swine" and hordes of "curst & unruly doggs and bitches."

But Boston widened and extended its old streets, paved the main ones by a center strip of cobblestones 24 feet wide, crowned in the middle and with gutters at the sides, to take the waste water from the numerous street-side pumps (there was no running water in houses). From 1704 to 1720 the city undertook extensive construction of subsurface storm sewers to drain streets and cellars. By 1720, reputedly, Boston had the best street system in the colonies and one far better than in most English cities.

As a great port, Boston had many wharves and docks. Long Wharf (1710–1713), a public pier, jutted far enough out into the harbor to berth thirty vessels at once, and huge warehouses accommodated their cargoes. In 1742, there were 166 wharves and docks along the bay shore. Dock Square was the center of the commercial district, and just where Damnation Alley led into it, a fine public market, Faneuil Hall, was built in 1740–1742. There were scores of taverns, inns, coffeehouses, alehouses, and "ordinaries," all carefully regulated by the town. By 1708 Boston, alone among colonial cities, had approved official names for all streets, lanes, and alleys. But we may assume that "Treamount St." (Tremont) and "Cornhill" (Washington St.) were far from adequate to the needs of their traffic burden—then as now.

Much the same was true of New York, which by 1740 had a population of 11,000—third in rank after Boston and Philadelphia. The Heeregraft, or Great Inlet from the East River, was filled up in 1675 to become Broad Street, and a public Great Dock was built in 1676; the tangled pattern of streets and alleys of old New Amsterdam was projected haphazardly beyond the stockade at Wall Street. The traffic congestion and noise problems were much the same as in Boston, but New York lagged far behind Boston and Philadelphia in its sewer construction. As a gesture to street sanitation, it did forbid the throwing of "any rubbish, filth, oyster shells, dead animal or anything like it" into the streets. The first underground public water supply system in the country was Philadelphia's, built in 1798–1800.

The regularly planned town had a long tradition in Europe. Almost invariably the plan was based on a gridiron of streets intersecting at right angles and forming square or oblong blocks of uniform size. A few score of such towns had been built in the thirteenth century, chiefly by Louis IX of France (1226–1270) and Edward I of England (1272–1307). Usually they were chartered by the king as allies in the endless conflicts with feudal nobles. The pattern for such towns (called "bastides") was found ready to hand in the remains of many a Roman castrum, or fortified camp.

The Renaissance era, with its passion for regularity and order and its absolutist governments, saw the widespread use of gridiron plans. Notable, for example, is the town of Richelieu in France, laid out in 1627. But the Renaissance and Baroque eras also used the radial type of plan, based on a central focus—usually a plaza or a royal palace—with wide avenues radiating outward like the spokes of a wheel. This type of plan permitted the control of all streets approaching the focus by artillery fire. Both types of plan had been described by the Roman writer Vitruvius.

The gardens at Versailles, which André Lenôtre laid out in the 1660s, employed many radial motives such as the *rond-point* and the *patte d'oie,* and so also did Sir Christopher Wren's plan for rebuilding London after the fire of 1666. The town, gardens, and park of

Karlsruhe, capital of the Grand Duchy of Baden, were conceived as a comprehensive radial scheme in 1715.

Perhaps the first regularly planned town in the colonies was New Haven, which was laid out by the surveyor John Brockett in 1638. It had nine very large square blocks (860 feet on a side) divided by a regular gridiron of streets. The town was not located aptly for military defense (indeed it had no walls or protecting works) nor was it designed for efficient use as a seaport. Rather, as Garvan has shown, it seems to have been controlled by Vitruvius's instructions as to town orientation—and very inappropriate they were to this particular location.

Charleston was founded in 1670 by Anthony Ashley-Cooper but was relocated and planned for its present site at the confluence of the Ashley and Cooper Rivers in 1680. Lord Ashley instructed Sir John Yeamans to divide the town "into regular streets," and the plan is of a modified gridiron type enclosed by a trapezoid of walls and bastions. Between 1700 and 1740 the city more than doubled in area and tripled in population. The first walls were demolished in 1717, and the streets were extended across the peninsula to the Ashley River. In November of 1740 a serious conflagration destroyed 334 dwellings and uncounted shops and warehouses. Thereafter the assembly required that all buildings be made of brick or stone, and Charleston has many old houses stucco-surfaced in many tints of yellow, pink, green, or blue, and topped by red roof tiles.

Two years after the planning of Charleston, William Penn made a much more ambitious plan for Philadelphia. His Surveyor General, Captain Thomas Holme, spent the summer of 1682 laying out a gridiron pattern of streets enclosing some 170 blocks and extending 2 miles east and west, between the Delaware and Schuylkill Rivers, and about 1 mile north and south. According to Penn's wish, the north–south streets were numbered and the east–west streets were named after various native trees and fruits. Five large blocks were reserved as public squares and grazing places for the cattle. The city grew rapidly, and as in Boston traffic became dense and dangerous. Speed laws against "excessive driving in any of the Streets" were passed in 1712, brick sidewalks were made, streets were paved, and underground brick sewers were laid.

The plan of Annapolis is the earliest known example in the colonies of the use of the radial principle. The city was laid out in 1694 under the direction of Governor Sir Francis Nicholson, who may have been familiar with Wren's plan for rebuilding London. The Annapolis plan is in part a gridiron layout, but its chief elements are two circles, one for the capitol, the other for the church. From these radiate diagonal arteries which intersect the gridiron streets. Essentially similar to L'Enfant's plan for Washington, it antedates the latter by almost a century.

Although New Orleans was founded by Bienville in 1718, the town plan—the now-famous Vieux Carré—was not laid out until 1721. The engineers LeBlond de la Tour and Adrien de Pauger plotted a gridiron of some eighty square blocks. In the center was the Place d'Armes, now Jackson Square, with a church, a school, and the governor's palace. Such street names as the Rue Chartres, the Rue St. Louis, Rue Dauphine, Rue Bourbon, and Rue Bienville remind us today of the town's French ancestry.

There were many other examples of gridiron plans in the colonial towns of the eighteenth century. Savannah, Georgia, for example, was laid out in 1733 with straight streets, regular blocks, and numerous public squares—a plan essentially similar to that of Philadelphia. The original portion of Alexandria, Virginia, was laid out on a gridiron plan in 1749 by the county surveyor John West. It is of some interest to note that his assistant surveyor, a young man of seventeen, was George Washington.

Without question the most ambitious as well as the most intricate city plan of the eighteenth century is that of Washington, D.C. Conceived by Major Pierre Charles L'Enfant in 1791, the plan echoes the magnificence of Europe's most impressive cities and gardens; it is a baroque concept throughout.

The plan is of the multiple-radial type, with a series of circles and squares for public buildings or important monuments and streets radiating out from these. Interconnected, these radials form major diagonal avenues, named after the thirteen original colonies and the new states of Vermont and Kentucky. Superimposed on this multiple-radial plan is a gridiron network of smaller streets, running due north–south and east–west and designated by numbers and letters.

Focal point of the whole plan is the Capitol, located on a hill about 80 feet high so as to command views from all directions. A great mall, 400 feet wide and about a mile long, was planned to connect the Capitol with the Potomac River. This focus is the hub of ten radiating streets, of which North and South Capitol Streets form the main north–south axis and East Capitol Street and the Mall form the main east–west axis. Only less important than the Capitol focus is the "President's Mansion," with seven streets and avenues radiating from it.

As in all baroque city planning, particular attention was devoted to the long vista, terminated by some important public building, fountain, or statue, and to reciprocal vistas in opposite directions. Even the "narrow" streets are of generous width (ranging from 90 to 110 feet, as contrasted, for example, with New York's ordinary cross-town streets, which are only 60 feet), and the avenues are of imperial size, ranging from 130 to 160 feet in width. This was less for any thought of the traffic they might eventually have to carry than for the sake of "grandeur and convenience," for it was intended that they be divided into "footways, walks of trees, and a carriage way."

The main purposes and principles of the Washington plan were clearly set forth as follows:

I. The positions for the different Edifices, and for the several Squares or Areas of different shapes, as they are laid down, were first determined on the most advantageous ground, commanding the most extensive prospects, and the better susceptible of such improvements as either use or ornament may hereafter call for.

II. Lines or Avenues of direct Communication have been devised, to connect the separate and most distant Objects with the principal, and to preserve through the whole a reciprocity of sight at the same time. Attention has been paid to the passing of those leading Avenues over the most favorable ground for prospect and convenience.

III. North and South Lines intersected by others running due East & West, make the distribution of the City into Streets, Squares, etce.; and these lines have been so combined as to meet at certain given points with those divergent Avenues, so as to form on the Spaces "first determined" the different Squares or Areas.

The seat of government was transferred to Washington in 1800. Since that time the city plan has not always been faithfully adhered to, but it has undoubtedly been the guiding framework in the gradual building of a city that many critics have ranked in a group with Paris and Mexico City (both also multiple radial plan types) as the three handsomest capitals in the world. Certainly there can be little doubt that L'Enfant's plan is one of the great works of art that America has produced.

ARCHITECTURE OF THE FEDERAL PERIOD AND THE NINETEENTH CENTURY

WILLIAM H. JORDY

The first four or five decades of the nineteenth century saw the final phases of the classical tradition which had dominated American architecture during the eighteenth century. If the tradition had passed through several stages during the eighteenth century, so its final decades were marked by two stylistic currents. There was, first, the continuation of the American neoclassicism, or "Federal" style, which Charles Bulfinch had introduced into the Boston area in the 1790s. During the 1820s, however, the Greek revival triumphed, although its beginnings date as early as 1798 with Benjamin Latrobe's Bank of Pennsylvania in Philadelphia. For two decades Greek revival forms went virtually unchallenged, until the publications of Andrew Jackson Downing in the 1840s brought to fruition that romantic naturalism and moralistic materialism which gradually superseded Greek taste. Thus almost a century and a half of the preeminence of classical ideals came to an end.

To the casual observer, the distinguishing aspect of the Federal style is its ornament. Ultimately derived from the tradition of Roman wall painting, the immediate sources were substantially the English carpenters' guides by Abraham Swan and William Pain. The inventiveness of Adamesque embellishment contrasted with the more canonical ornament which had characterized eighteenth-century work, based as this was on temple and monumental prototypes. Its delicacy of scale and its surface quality contrasted with the larger size and greater projection of earlier motifs. The carving of Samuel McIntire, a gifted provincial in Salem, who was influenced by Bulfinch in his later works, represents perhaps the consummate adaptation of Adamesque ornament in American domestic architecture.

If the delicacy of the ornament tended to forfeit architectural scale, this very refinement provided an intimate elegance to the spacious rooms which typified the Federal period. The architecture reflected the new ideal of an easy, if somewhat attenuated, formality in social behavior as contrasted with the more rigid etiquette of the earlier period. One can sense the desire to alloy ceremony with convenience and some degree of intimacy in Henry Sargent's paintings of Boston social life around 1810 (Museum of Fine Arts, Boston). The ample arched openings which link rooms in the Sargent canvases also appear between the front and back parlors in McIntire's Gardner–White–Pingree House (1804–1805). The most interesting Federal planning reveals this attempted harmony of ceremonial feeling and functional demands, with simultaneous aesthetic delight in spatial sequences of rooms of varying shapes —circles, ovals, and polygons adjacent to rectangles of various proportions—as in the simplified Adam plans for Bulfinch's third Otis House (1806).

Inspired by the more modest regency fronts in England, such as those by John Pinch for Cavendish Place in Bath, Bulfinch and McIntire crisply introduced large frameless windows into their tall blocks, the second-story living floor often boasting decorated iron balconies or grills in front of floor-to-ceiling fenestration. In contrast to the British work, brick walls were less frequently stuccoed, while wood often replaced brick. Shallow sunken panels sometimes appeared on the walls; but only very rarely did these panels receive the ornament which one finds in the most sumptuous Adamesque in England. The urbanity of these elevations appeared to best advantage in groups of contiguous houses such as those of the earliest portions of Beacon and Mt. Vernon Streets in Boston.

The same attenuated elegance appears in church architecture of the Federal period. The Gibbs-inspired steeple, such as the splendid but retarded example on Center Church in New Haven (1812–1814), often, but not always, gave way to the lower, more delicately proportioned cupola on David Hoadley's adjacent United Church (1814–1815). This latter building can be traced to a Bulfinch prototype similar to that so consummately represented by his Church of Christ in Lancaster, Massachusetts (1816–1817). A light linear embellishment also characterized certain public works in New York and Baltimore—notably Mangin and McComb's City Hall (1811) and Maximilian Godefroy's

Battle Monument (1815). In these centers, dominated by French émigrés, the influence was Directoire and early Empire neoclassicism rather than English regency and was at once more austere and classically more correct.

Although a substantial portion of Jefferson's architectural career was contemporaneous with those of the regency-inspired architects, his position is somewhat anomalous—conservative in certain respects and extremely liberal in others. His conservatism sprang from his intense love of the ancient past—in architecture, of the Roman past—and hence of any means by which he could identify his world with its classic precedents. Palladio dominated Jefferson's architectural thinking in the 1770s.

Jefferson's first contact with the architecture of ancient Rome was through the sixteenth-century Italian, Palladio. But as his knowledge of Roman literature increased, Palladio became a parallel rather than a primary source. Jefferson, like Palladio, learned much about Roman country life from the writings of Pliny and Varo II, and, in the arrangement of buildings and grounds, his incomparable Monticello is clearly inspired by Roman ideals. But Monticello also reflected Jefferson's eager absorption of contemporary architectural ideas, particularly those which he learned in France during his ambassadorship from 1784 to 1789. In Paris, he had experienced the conveniences of French planning. It was a lesson to which he was particularly responsive because his earliest Palladian houses in Virginia had already revealed his decided interest in freeing the plan from the compact symmetry of the traditional two-storied block in favor of a more complicated massing with a thin, spreading plan, one room in thickness. The cramming of Monticello with gadgets and the proliferation of polygonal extremities also owed much to Jefferson's French experience.

Just so, his University of Virginia in Charlottesville (1817–1826) showed the same respect for tradition radically adjusted to new functions. Here he conjured the past in his attempt to reproduce various classical edifices in the porticoes of his classroom buildings. The colonnaded walk linking the classroom structures recalled the stoa of the ancient Roman forum, while the domed library at the climax of the U-shaped complex evoked the Pantheon. The distinct separation of his complex into a series of separate though related volumes represented the culmination of Jefferson's experimentation with the complicated massing and low spread of the Roman villa. The functional monumentality of the University of Virginia—where monumentality dignified the function, while function conditioned the particular

form of the monumentality—was far more radical, far more "modern," than anything realized by the Federal architects. As a plan, it was the most searching and comprehensive solution to the problems of resident education yet produced in the western world, and along with the Declaration of Independence it stands as one of the greatest ideological masterpieces of American history.

Jefferson warmly admired the English émigré Benjamin Latrobe. Latrobe possessed the same radical and idealistic spirit as Jefferson, which inclined him toward a similar functional monumentality. Unlike Jefferson, however, Latrobe's source of inspiration was Greek architecture. He once called himself a "bigoted Greek"; but he qualified the label by using Greek forms in conjunction with the vaults and domes of Roman derivation and relating both to the demands of modern function—witness Latrobe's Bank of Pennsylvania (1798–1799) which, properly speaking, initiates the Greek revival in the United States. Here the Roman dome is combined with the Greek rectangle and, although some of the classical details were derived directly from Greek prototypes, the "Greek" quality depends far more on the breadth and massiveness of its forms.

This bold juxtaposition of solids, and the volumes they enclose, was further enhanced by Latrobe's expressive engineering. Here a professional like Latrobe could far outstrip an amateur like Jefferson. Throughout the Greek revival form, structure and function appeared significantly fused as they had never been interrelated during the colonial period. Unfortunately, however, this fusion could never be complete as long as form depended on a literal image of the Greek past, structure on an excessive nostalgia for massive lithic components, and function on the symmetrical rigor of the ancient temple.

If the Federal movement originated in New England, the Greek revival sprang from the middle Atlantic seaboard area around Philadelphia, Baltimore, and Washington, where Latrobe spent the greater part of his American career. As an engineer-architect, he personally trained Robert Mills and William Strickland, both of whom practiced in the same large manner as did their mentor. Just as Latrobe could transfer the bold simplicity of his forms in the Baltimore Cathedral (1804–1818) to canals and water systems, so Strickland and Mills were engineers as well as architects. Where their mentor had been interested in canals, significantly both Strickland and Mills turned to the railroad. The same interest in engineering infected the Greek revival architects around Boston, while Ithiel Town, who located his practice in New York and Connecticut, made his fortune on a patented bridge truss. Not until the advent of the Chicago School in the late nineteenth century was engineering again so evident in American architecture. In Chicago the union of the two fields was limited to a particular problem and so unconsciously held as an ideal that the equilibrium readily disintegrated. In his prophetic essays on architecture, Horatio Greenough celebrated the functional bias of the Greek revival. Thoreau, too, seems to have felt the emphasis on function and the large simplicities of form which characterized the period.

Meanwhile, the simplicities of Greek revival forms were easily translated into wooden equivalents. Thus, with the expansion of the frontier, the Greek revival spread in vernacular building. A final burst of creative expression appeared in the Deep South of the early nineteenth century, where newly moneyed planters in the Black Belt or along the lower reaches of the Mississippi Valley erected the white pillared mansions so irrevocably linked to plantation mythology. In the fully developed plantation house, a colonnade around four sides of the house rose as a grandiose screen in front of a double tier of porches. Low hipped roofs were often concealed behind a cornice parapet. The resulting edifice displayed a superb merger of regional preference for a shaded surround with the monumentality of the Greek revival vocabulary as it had been developed in the cosmopolitan centers of the Northeastern seaboard.

While the plantation house was developing into a grandiloquent epitome of Calhoun's plea for a "Greek democracy"—that is, one that permitted the holding of slaves—the North was abandoning the classical ideal. The picturesque assault on the Greek revival found an appropriate champion in an appropriate setting. This was the landscape architect Andrew Jackson Downing who wrote his immensely popular books in the Hudson Valley where landscape painters had earlier inaugurated a new direction in American painting. Nature rather than geometry provided the inspiration for a fresh start. The symmetrical forms set against nature gave way to asymmetrical irregularity in harmony with nature. Spatial contrasts in room planning and the projection of interior space out into nature by means of porches and bays represented a culmination in a planning development reaching back to Bulfinch and Jefferson. Stone (Downing's favorite material) was left in its natural color. Where wood was used (as was generally the case), painted surfaces in tans, ochres, and slate grays merged the building with nature.

Moral arguments, influenced generally by a religious sentimentality and specifically by Ruskinian theory, buttressed the appeal to nature. Against the Greek revival tendency to mask wood as an abstract, textureless evocation of stone, Downing called for "truth" and "honesty" in the use of materials. Stone should look like stone and wood like wood. In addition, there was a strong democratic component in this movement which was at once romantically naturalistic and morally materialistic. Man needed to consult authorities no longer. "Taste" need not depend on the mastery of rules handed down from the ancients and embalmed in copperplate. Man had only to go to nature, to consult his own deepest emotions. In Ruskin's words, architecture became an "art for all men." But this new romantic ideal also had its weaknesses. The naturalistic and moralistic sentimentality was confounded by the literary and pictorial imagination of the period. Success in conjuring a picture or a story excused all failures in form.

To be sure, the ideal of the pictorial evocation of the remote past had also motivated the Greek revival architect. The classical vocabulary of "Greek" forms, however, ensured his dominant concern with the abstract geometry appropriate to architecture, at the same time it linked the Greek revival to the eighteenth-century tradition. Moreover, the preference for the Greek style during the twenties and thirties resulted in a high level of unanimity in taste and hence provided general criteria with which to evaluate quality. Egyptoid forms and a strong undercurrent of primitive Gothic appeared beside the Greek, however, as portents of the greater eclecticism to come. Beginning with the forties, however, a burgeoning historicism combined with the picturesque taste for complicated surfaces and the new emphasis on a personalized aesthetic to topple the preeminence of Greek forms. Thus, at the very dawn of the new period, in 1840, Thomas Cole could paint *The Architect's Dream* for Ithiel Town and show the architect lounging Hamletlike atop a gigantic column lost in his meditation of a dream world of fantastic classical, Egyptoid, and Gothic structures. Similarly, the models recommended for domestic architecture by Downing were the "Italian Villa," the "Rural Gothic," and the "Gothic Manor House."

Although this sentimental eclecticism vitiated most work of the mid-century, the period nevertheless boasts much which is today interesting by virtue of the naturalistic, structural, and functional ideals inspiring it. The rural and suburban houses of A. J. Davis and Richard Upjohn in the forties and fifties show a new concern for the adjustment of the house to its natural surroundings, a feeling for human scale and comfortable planning, and—in the wooden structures particularly—the frank use of materials for their inherent qualities. In many wooden houses, built between 1845 and 1875, post and board were clearly expressed as such, and it was this expressive "honesty" which has led one twentieth-century critic to characterize them collectively as the "stick style."

The aesthetic of the stick, beginning with the advocacy of board-and-batten siding by Davis and Downing, was reinforced by the anonymous invention of the balloon frame near Chicago in the thirties. Spreading through the Midwest, an incompletely developed version of balloon construction received its first national publication in William Bell's *Carpentry Made Easy* (1857). Both the aesthetic and the constructive potential of the stick developed rapidly during the sixties, while the seventies saw something of a baroque climax in the violently picturesque manipulation of wood into harshly jagged rhythms and tall, angular silhouettes. Wooden structure penetrated to the surface of the house where it served to organize window openings; it projected from eaves as deep bracketing; it reached out toward the landscape in the "open work" of spacious porches. The brashest examples often contained an element of extravagant boldness and fantasy all too rare in other periods, as in the steamboat-inspired splendor of certain mansions along the Mississippi; or the "Saracenic" gaudery of P. T. Barnum's Iranistan in Bridgeport, Connecticut (1848; destroyed by fire 1857).

For the most lavish urban houses masonry was generally preferred to wood and stucco to brick. The Italian Villa and various Gothic styles were the favorite types for free-standing urban residences in the late forties and fifties, although they were sometimes treated with a more urbane regularity. The most significant city type recalled the *palazzo* of the Italian Renaissance, by way of the indirect influence of Sir Charles Barry's London clubs of the late thirties and early forties. John Notman's Philadelphia Athenaeum (1845–1847) represents one of the finest examples of the Barryesque *palazzo* in America.

Beginning in the fifties, the most common evocation of Italian Renaissance city palaces, however, occurred in the larger American cities in the form of long rows of "brownstones." The brick or stuccoed severity of the earlier row house gave way in the fifties and sixties to the repetitive rhythm of high flights of stairs flanked by bulbous balustrades and to ornately enframed windows and heavy projecting cornices.

The mansard has become as familiar an architectural symbol of the period as the brownstone. By the mid-sixties, indeed, the mansard and the brownstone had thoroughly coalesced, particularly in the single-family mansions. Cudell and Blumenthal's house of 1879 for Cyrus H. McCormick, the Chicago reaper king, is a fine example. More rarely, the mansard appeared on the row house. The mansard was apparently introduced into New York by Detlef Lienau about 1850—prior, incidentally, to its most prominent nineteenth-century use by Visconti and Lefuel for the new wings of the Louvre. In its bloated sumptuousness, the mansard was appropriate to both the formal tastes and the materialistic spirit of the period and led directly to the fashionable fetish for the French château as popularized in the eighties by the Vanderbilt houses on Fifth Avenue designed by Richard Hunt. The château, in turn, was cousin to the more prevalent "Queen Anne." With its bays, turrets, high roofs, and its decorated paneling suggestive of half-timbering, Queen Anne not only played a major role in the baroque phase of the stick style but also made a street like Commonwealth Avenue in Boston the picturesque antithesis of the sober regularity of the earlier fronts on Beacon Hill.

So much for mid-century house design. Insofar as commercial and monumental structures were built of traditional materials during the middle decades of the century, these reflected the same influences which prevailed in the more lavish urban residences. As in the best domestic building, so the most interesting commercial and monumental buildings were those permeated with an idealism distilled from the "truth to nature" theme. From the late forties and fifties, for example, one thinks of Upjohn's adaptation of the Italian Villa for municipal uses as in his City Hall for Utica, New York (1852–1853) or the austerity of the so-called "Norman" or "Lombard" Smithsonian Institution for Washington (1852) by James Renwick. All were essentially simple stone or brick blocks, still possessing the Greek revival sensibility for stripped form. But they were vertical in feeling by virtue of their wall arches, their tall, round-arched windows, and their slender campaniles. Because of its economy and simplicity, the brick "Lombard" style and even simpler derivations from it became the principal mode of building for industrial architecture from about 1850 to the turn of the century.

Renwick and especially Upjohn built the finest churches of the forties and fifties. Influenced by Pugin and the Ecclesiologist movement in England, both created churches in which a carefully considered "Gothic" detail was traced with feeling for delicate scale upon an essentially mural structure. Their most ambitious churches, like Upjohn's Trinity and Renwick's Grace Churches in New York, both completed in 1846, boasted plaster vaulting imitative of the Gothic.

Upjohn's masonry churches in less cosmopolitan centers recalled the English village church with a low moulded silhouette for chancel and nave piling up toward an asymmetrically placed spire. On the interior, they displayed handsome wooden timber construction for piers and roofs.

The country churches of Upjohn anticipated the High Victorian Gothic ecclesiastical work of such men as Leopold Eidlitz, Ware and Van Brunt, the Potters, and Richardson. In these the "Gothic" or "Romanesque" forms were used very freely with a coloristic complex of stone, brick, tile, slate, and dark-stained wood. The "pictorial" recall of specific medieval structures which characterized the ecclesiastical work of Upjohn and Renwick gave way in the sixties and seventies to a freer, more creative eclecticism. The arrogant "honesty" of Ware and Van Brunt's Memorial Hall at Harvard (1871–1874), with its strident use of contrasting materials, comprised the perfect monumental counterpart to the stick-style house of the same decade. Just so, in commercial work of the sixties and seventies, Richard Hunt's Tribune Building in New York (1873–1875) might be compared to domestic Queen Anne. One thinks, too, of the remarkable buildings by Frank Furness in Philadelphia, inspired (as was Memorial Hall) in part by the ideas of Ruskin and in part by those of Viollet-le-Duc. Creating violent changes of scale and abrupt juxtapositions, Furness's forceful buildings represent the very epitome of that vehement originality so highly prized during the third quarter of the century and so greatly condemned at its end.

The towering genius in the monumental masonry tradition, however, was Henry Hobson Richardson, whose most mature production was crowded into a mere nine years between 1877 and his early death in 1886. His use of round arches and the vigor of his masonry walls were only superficially related to Romanesque architecture in which he sensed a kindred feeling for the massive grandeur that he sought in his own buildings. In his Ames Gate Lodge in North Easton, Massachusetts (1880–1881) he piled up boulders into a low, broad hillock punched with the deep shadow of his long bands of windows. Finally, in the Marshall Field Wholesale Store in Chicago (1885–1887), he articulated a rugged granite block wholly in terms of the relation and size of its windows and of the magnificent scale of the masonry. If this was picturesque, it was also in spirit Renaissance—more so, indeed, than the literal use which McKim, Mead and White made of the Cancelleria for Henry Villard's residence in New York two years earlier in 1883.

Richardson also played a cardinal role in the forma-

tion of the second major wooden style to influence suburban domestic building in the nineteenth century. By the mid-seventies the so-called "shingle style" began to emerge from, and simultaneously to react against, the preceding "stick style." An early building in the shingle style was Richardson's Watts Sherman House in Newport, Rhode Island (1874). This house reflected contemporary Queen Anne work in England, especially that of Norman Shaw, although Richardson's work was very largely an independent development. Instead of stressing the staccato linearity of the stick, Richardson covered the big volumes of his exteriors with a soft, flickering surface of wooden shingles. He reduced the petty variety of the picturesque silhouette to a few large elements boldly related to one another; he grouped windows and bays into long rhythmic horizontals set against the verticality of the silhouette; he rearranged the congeries of irregular cubicles in picturesque planning to create a central space in the ample "living hall" with subordinate rooms forcefully related to the core space by means of wide, horizontal openings on axis. In short, he retained the freedom of the picturesque but invigorated this freedom by reconciling it to a large architectonic sense of order.

The eighties saw the culmination of the development. Some of the shingle-style houses of this decade are among the masterpieces of domestic architecture produced anywhere in the nineteenth century, especially some of the early works of McKim, Mead and White (the Cyrus McCormick House in Richland Springs, New York; the Isaac Bell House in Newport; and the William Low House in Bristol, Rhode Island; 1880–1881, 1882–1883, and 1887, respectively). Unfortunately, the abstract quality of these houses was never sufficiently appreciated by their creators. An aura of eclecticism lingered, physically in some of the detailing, psychically in the associative attitudes with which both architects and their clients viewed them. (Witness, for example, the contemporaneous "Queene Anne" label.) Hence the discipline of a growing academicism readily upset the creative reconciliation of discipline and freedom implicit in the shingle style of the eighties. Frank Lloyd Wright in the first two decades of the twentieth century, however, would sense the architectural potential of the shingle style, and to a much less extent so would a group of architects around him in Chicago and an independent group on the West Coast.

The forthright expression of wood and stone found in much of the best of the nineteenth-century architecture also appeared in the finest folk building. Folk building—that is, building either by nonprofessionals or by self-taught and tradition-taught artisans—was particularly significant in a century when professionals were few and communication less dominated by metropolitan conditioning than it now is. As in the other arts, we are just beginning to discover the bold proportions, the direct handling of materials, and the frequent fantasy in the best folk architecture of the period. To the modern eye, certainly the big barns of the period provide one of the most sympathetic of building types, while at the opposite expressive extreme the wooden "Gothic" houses in certain Rocky Mountain mining towns or the "steamboat houses" erected near New Orleans are delightfully fanciful. From forms suggestive of vigorous function to those which are unabashedly fantastic, this is the range of the best of folk building.

The buildings in both the mill town and the utopian community show a simplicity and vigor which, even late in the century, relate them to the Greek revival rather than to the picturesque tradition. Some of the mill buildings themselves are especially magnificent in the rugged boldness of the big block repeatedly punched by windows, where aesthetic quality inheres in the directness with which materials were used and in the justness of the relationship of wall to opening. The early mills were of wooden construction, the walls dominant, the windows relatively small. By 1815, however, masonry walls in brick (Massachusetts) or stone (Rhode Island) had replaced wood. In the mid-century (especially in the sixties and after), with the development of a hard brick capable of withstanding the heavy loads of the mill machinery, this new material became dominant. After the Civil War the improved brick permitted the construction of the pier-and-spandrel wall, where the vertical brick piers rose through the structure to support the lateral beams within. With this system of isolated supports, the interval between the piers could be opened much more widely to windows with a nonstructural brick spandrel panel beneath. The result, by about 1885, was a tense alternation between thick and thin, between the verticality of the layer of the piers and the horizontality of the layer of the spandrels. Throughout the century the pier-and-spandrel wall remained the fixed standard in mill construction, until the advent of the reinforced concrete frame in the twentieth century. And throughout the period, the demand for inexpensive, sturdy, functional buildings largely freed mill construction from the "architect's dream" of stylistic fantasy which haunted more pretentiously "architectural" building types. The best of them are certainly among the most impressive monuments of the century.

Rather surprisingly, the heavy timber construction of the mill interior was favored in this country until after the turn of the century. Such engineering conservatism contrasted strongly with the more venturesome use of cast and wrought iron in the interiors of English mills. Metal appeared in American factories for columns occasionally and as hardware for the basic timber construction; but American fire insurance companies favored the certain risks of heavy timber construction (termed "slow burning construction") to the uncertain risks of metal.

Although iron was rather disappointingly absent in mill construction, this new material was extensively used during the first half of the century, especially by the Greek revivalists. These architects employed iron for ornamental work, for construction which was mostly concealed, and for fireproofing which proved to be illusory before metal was "fireproofed" by a covering of terra cotta in the seventies. Compared to developments in England, however, American use of iron seems singularly timid until the bold exploitation of the cast-iron front in the late forties.

Although the belief that James Bogardus was the first to use cast iron on a large scale for such open fronts is now questioned, he was among the pioneers. The only Bogardus building still extant in New York City is a store block built for Edgar H. Laing at the corner of Washington and Murray Streets (1848), now in a dilapidated condition in the center of the produce area. His famed Harper and Brothers Building (1854) and his cast-iron façades for his own factory (1848–1849), both in New York City, are preserved only in prints. Many cast-iron buildings by Bogardus's competitors exist, however, in the older business districts of American cities. The splendid Haughwout Block which still stands in New York was designed by W. J. Gaynor in 1857 and fabricated to specification by one of Bogardus's major competitors, Daniel Badger. The more pretentious cast-iron structures often revealed this division of labor between designer and founder. The Haughwout is especially interesting as one of the earliest business structures to boast a passenger elevator. This invention, which apparently dates from the early fifties, would be instrumental for the achievement of the "skyscraper" altitudes in business buildings at the end of the century.

Bridges made bold use of metal, particularly after the middle of the century. Among the finest in America was the first major bridge across the Mississippi, at St. Louis, designed by James Eads (1868–1874). With his first wire-cabled suspension bridge across the Monongahela at Pittsburgh (1845–1856), John Roebling entered upon a bridge building career which culminated in his Brooklyn Bridge. Begun in 1867 and destined to be completed by his son Washington only in 1883, this is one of the great bridges of the world and of all American engineering works the one which has inspired the most affection. Its massive stone piers proclaim the capacity of stone to withstand enormous loads in compression and contrast magnificently with the revelation of the tensile strength of the cable supports.

The culmination of the use of metal in American architecture occurred in the "Chicago School" of skyscraper construction in the eighties and nineties. As finally developed by the late eighties, the Chicago tall office building depended for its support on a steel frame, lightly clad with a coating of hollow tile for fireproofing. Exterior sheathing of structural terra cotta or masonry served no supporting purpose but merely assisted in protecting the frame and provided the "architecture." In the eighties and nineties "architectural" additions to the frame were so minimized as to make of Burnham and Root's Reliance Building (the first four stories in 1890, the remainder in 1895) virtually a frame infilled with the widest possible windows. The openness of the two glass-and-metal walls fronting on a major downtown intersection prophesy a similar aesthetic in these materials after World War II.

If the spindly boldness of the Reliance, S. S. Beman's Studebaker Building (1895), or the more refined and at the same time more highly standardized versions of minimal Chicago construction by Holabird and Roche are characteristic of the most doctrinaire skyscrapers of the Chicago School, these are not quite the aesthetic masterpieces.

The masterpieces of the Chicago School are four: John Wellborn Root's Monadnock Building (1889–1891); and three buildings designed by Louis Sullivan —the Wainwright Building in St. Louis (1890–1891), the Guaranty Building in Buffalo (1894–1895), and the Schlesinger and Mayer Department Store (1899–1904, now Carson, Pirie and Scott). Just below these four would come William LeBaron Jenney's second Leiter Store (1889–1890; now Sears, Roebuck). Root's building was the last of the tall masonry structures with walls 6 feet thick at the base. Despite its conservative construction, however, the smooth planes of the wall and the very crisp perch of the frameless windows mark its aesthetic as modern. Like the best of the mill buildings the proportion of window to wall is superb. Whereas Root expressed the identical character of the office space above the ground level by the regular rhythm of the openings in a flat wall surface made slightly undulating by bays, Sullivan achieved the same expression in his Wainwright and Guaranty Buildings by the use of the pier-and-spandrel wall. The vertical rise of the piers in front of the horizontals of

the spandrels creates an architectural textile of light against shadow, subtilized by the more delicate splintering of light over Sullivan's foliated ornament in terra cotta. The lingering sense of the massiveness of masonry in the Wainwright disappears in the Guaranty, where the brick piers give way to a terra-cotta skin completely covering the building. Surface ornament over this entire skin extends the flicker of light to the whole structure and thus further emphasizes the sense of weightlessness. Finally, in the upper stories of the Schlesinger and Mayer Store, Sullivan abandoned the play of pier against spandrel and simply stretched the thin skin of the smooth wall around the wide, horizontal "Chicago" windows, a prototype which his contemporaries had used earlier in such buildings as the Reliance but here realized by Sullivan with a consummate sense of proportion and elegant decision. A taut planarity replaced the plastic interweaving of pier and spandrel; the impartial reticulation of the steel frame with horizontality only slightly dominating verticality replaced the more expressionistic, and at the same time more arbitrary, exaggeration of the "soaring" element in the building.

One of the most familiar episodes in American architectural history is certainly that of the impact of the Columbian Exposition (1895) on the Chicago School. The classical colonnades enframing the central lagoon introduced the Middle West to academic ideals for the first time on an impressive scale. The monumentality resulted from a gentleman's agreement among professionals to cooperate toward the creation of a unified effect by agreeing to submit to rules of "good taste" derived from a great tradition. The historicism, the professionalism, the "good taste"—this largesse from the East dazzled the Western architects and made the Chicago productions appear harsh and crude. Although academic ideals made a fitful and impure appearance in the seventies, the two works which signalized the effective beginning of the movement were McKim, Mead and White's mansion for Henry Villard in New York (really several houses in a single block—1883) and the H. A. C. Taylor House in Newport (1885). The first revealed archaeological pretensions in its dependence on Letarouilly to create a small-scale version of the Cancelleria; the second represented the first major monument in the new colonial revival. Formalistic ideals replaced the romantic, rationalistic interest in nature and construction. The axis was stressed instead of the free plan. The façade house became an abstract plane for ornamental display rather than for the revelation of materials and technique; the building as a whole was created in opposition to nature, not as a projection into its environment. The Villard and Taylor houses represent the beginnings of McKim, Mead and White's career as the leading American firm in upholding the academic ideal. As early as 1887, they achieved what many believe to be their academic masterpiece—and one of the masterpieces of the entire movement—in the Boston Public Library.

With the instinctive sagacity of true genius, Frank Lloyd Wright embraced all the creative tendencies of American architecture in the eighties and nineties and fused them into that personal synthesis which has brought so much of the best of the nineteenth century to modern architecture. His own house in Oak Park (1889) clearly disclosed his absorption of the shingle style and the ideals implicit in the shingle tradition. His George Blossom House (1892), his project for the Milwaukee Library and Museum, and his elaborate scheme for the Wolf Lake Amusement Park (both in 1893) revealed his awareness of the formal lessons of the academic tradition. His James Charnley House (1891) and the W. H. Winslow House (1893) especially, among his early works, displayed the impress of Sullivan and, through the "Lieber Meister," of Richardson in their freedom from precedent (except of course, Sullivan's), their abstract geometrical massing, and their elegant decisiveness. Finally, the Chicago School of skyscraper construction reinforced Wright's intuitive awareness of the expressive possibilities in structure.

If he came to call his architecture "organic," it was far more than romantic naturalism which sustained his work. Wright disciplined the spirit of freedom implicit in his work by that vigorously abstract sense of order and geometry appropriate to great architecture. Thus in the works of roughly the first decade of his practice, he disclosed those qualities which would mature immediately after 1900 in his earliest masterpieces.

TOWN, CITY, AND PARK

By virtue of its premises, the romantic approach to nature realized some of its most complete achievements in landscape design. Here the great figure was Frederick Law Olmsted. His design in 1857 for Central Park, to which his collaborator Calvert Vaux may have contributed substantially, represented the first of the great landscape parks in the United States. It was modeled on those of Paxton in England and Alphand in France and established the basis for a series of magnificent parks which Olmsted designed for most of the largest cities in the country. Franklin Park in Boston, designed in 1885, is a later example which reveals more clearly than Central Park the typical elements in his fully de-

veloped work. His ideal was a series of parks linked by tree-lined boulevards into a "system." The boulevards were wide, paved, residential streets which ideally provided for the separation of different kinds of traffic. Eventually the Boston system of parks and boulevards was extended by a metropolitan system embracing the central city and thirty-five surrounding communities, largely as a result of the vision of the journalist Sylvester Baxter and the landscape architect Charles Eliot. This regional system complemented the city system by providing for a ring of forest retreats around the city modeled on European examples, with the Blue Hills Reservation to the south and Middlesex Fells to the north as the most sizable preserves. Linear parks stretched along the Charles and two lesser rivers draining the area. Public beaches were to be acquired along the seacoast. Boston's Metropolitan Park Commission, organized in 1893, together with the earlier Metropolitan Sewerage Commission of 1889, represented the first significant examples of metropolitan planning in this country.

Although park planning represented Olmsted's preeminent interest, he occasionally plaited real estate developments with the same curvilinear forms which he employed in his parks and in marked contrast to the rectangularity endemic to American city street patterns. By the beginning of the nineteenth century, the American urban street pattern was succumbing to the system of orthogonals of which eighteenth-century Philadelphia and Jefferson's proposed plans for Richmond and Washington, D.C., are notable harbingers. This rectangular street grid, recommended in the eighteenth century for reasons of aesthetics and convenience, was largely retained throughout the nineteenth century because of its appeal to the real estate speculator. Thus the medieval street pattern of lower Manhattan dramatically gave way to the gridiron system in the Commissioner's plan of 1810. The same contrast in street pattern appeared in the old harbor area of Boston as opposed to a nineteenth-century extension like Back Bay (1856–1900). Here, however, the boulevarded grandeur of Commonwealth Avenue revealed the inspiration of Haussmann's boulevards for Paris and provided a focus for the area, so lacking in the monotonous spread of the rectangle in the street systems of most American cities.

In planned "garden" residential developments—like A. J. Davis's Llewellyn Park in Orange, New Jersey (1852–1853) and Olmsted's Riverside, Illinois (1868–1869), two of the most significant examples of nineteenth-century suburban planning—picturesque irregularity was cultivated for predominantly aesthetic reasons. The winding streets (rather excessively so) and thread of parks in these developments complemented the contours of the land. Olmsted, however, also purposely designed the tortuous streets to discourage through traffic. A direct parkway, unfortunately never built, was to have linked Riverside to Chicago. Thus his community anticipated in a primitive manner ideal traffic patterns for residential communities developed in the twentieth century.

In contrast to the suburban retreats, the early mill towns of southern New England represented the vital juxtaposition of work and residence. Unfortunately, work hours were too long to warrant elaborate facilities for recreation beyond a rudimentary library and a lyceum in connection with the schoolhouse, although almost all of them in their earliest stages were at least surrounded by open country. Professional planners, however, never took cognizance of the mill town; on the other hand, with steadily increasing migration and an abundant supply of labor, mill owners no longer needed to provide housing for their workers. What could have been the physical setting for a humane industrial order, had its implications been developed, rotted away or, more frequently, prospered (at least until recently) into the familiar sordidness of the factory town. But remnants of the old towns remain to chide us for their neglect. One can still see the row of dormitory buildings where the "Lowell girls" lived and published their literary paper on a street that runs directly to the wall of mill buildings along the Merrimac. Or there is the sleepy town of White Rock, Rhode Island, established in 1849 with the building of the textile mill a few miles from Westerly. The awesome red-brick block of the mill in the Lombard Romanesque style dominates the town like a Renaissance palace.

The main street runs parallel to the front of the building, the company store on a transverse axis, balanced on either side by the decaying duplexes for the workers, with bunk buildings for the single workers at one end of the street and the combined schoolhouse and lyceum at the other.

Such symmetry is rarer in mill town planning than the more asymmetrical arrangements still perceptible amidst the dilapidation of the smaller Rhode Island mill towns but best seen in two towns which have miraculously preserved much of their early amenity down to the present day—Slatersville, Rhode Island, and Harrisville, New Hampshire, both built between 1815 and 1850 or 1860. In the first, rows of white wooden workers' houses surround a triangular green which is dominated in the typical New England manner by a Greek revival church. The mill is situated in the valley, immediately below the level of the town so that from the green one glimpses only its roof and belfry. In Harrisville, brick mills and workers' houses climb a winding stream bed on a series of terraces, the whole complex surrounded by mountains. Harrisville must be the most picturesque mill town extant from the nineteenth century, just as the far better known Nantucket is architecturally the most beautifully preserved of all nineteenth-century New England seaports. In comparison with the mill towns, the villages of various utopian or religious societies, like the Fourierist New Harmony in Illinois or the Rappite communities in Pennsylvania, offered few suggestions for planning. Ironically, the tightfisted, but highly moralistic, Yankee entrepreneur more or less unconsciously showed the way toward social planning better than any of the communist societies—and in some respects, better than the garden suburb planners too.

ARCHITECTURE OF THE TWENTIETH CENTURY

VINCENT SCULLY

No list of one thousand slides of American buildings constructed between 1900 and 1958 can be drawn up without several apologies. The list will by no means be complete, and one can be certain that many important buildings will, through oversight, not be represented on it. At the same time many buildings will be included which may be considered unimportant by other opinion. For these reasons it is hoped that the present list of selected buildings may be taken simply as a beginning. It should by no means be considered definitive.

Arrangement has been by architect. This system has the bad effect of splitting up any series based upon formal development or building type, but it has the advantage of leaving the material as flexible as possible for the user. Such flexibility seems of maximum importance. All of us who teach contemporary architecture do so in different ways, and it is possible that a detached observer, faced with several of our slide lists, might conclude that we were dealing with the architecture of different planets. In a sense he would be right. Underneath its massive combinations, the twentieth century is made up of many worlds, each of them inhabited by one or two people. In a list of this kind it would seem unfair to impose one such world upon many others. For this reason have been included, for example, a large number of the buildings designed by the so-called "eclectic" architects of the earlier part of the century. The world of McKim, Mead and White, Carrère and Hastings, and Bertram Goodhue is inhabited at the present time by comparatively few people; in course work, consequently, they are normally given small space. Yet the buildings are there—often large and impressive—and no outline of the period can be representative without them. Indeed it is possible that they will mean a good deal more to us within a few years as we learn to see ourselves within a larger historical context.

The present list attempts to be representative. As such it should be regarded as the raw material for a considerable number of different combinations. An examination of it by building type, for example, shows that two programs predominate: the suburban house and the large office building. In the first category every effort has been made to keep the number to a minimum, but the facts of modern architectural history act against the success of this attempt. In twentieth- as in nineteenth-century America, the single-family house has remained a primary cultural symbol, and the architects have continued to expend their best efforts upon its design. A fairly good history of the development of architecture between 1900 and the present could therefore be worked out by using a selection from among the houses included in this list.

Such concentration of effort should, however, be considered in its negative as well as its positive aspects. It should be tested in relation to human achievement in other historical periods, and it should, at least, be recognized as a modern American phenomenon, of which the general cultural implications deserve to be explored. Here the lists of seventeenth-, eighteenth-, and nineteenth-century buildings need to be used for purposes of comparison and in order to seek out the meaning of the contemporary forms. In such a search the user of these lists will be handicapped by the fact that no European buildings have been included. From a historical point of view this could be a fatal omission. It tends to make difficult the identification both of those characteristics of American domestic architecture which have grown out of a common European heritage and of those which demonstrate peculiarly American expressions and intentions.

The thinness and linearity of many of the American forms in comparison to those of Europe, for example, will be found to be a constant American characteristic from the seventeenth century onward. The flat, closed surface predominates in American work from the wooden houses of the seventeenth century, tightly sheathed as ships against the weather, through the elegant and thin details which were derived from copybooks during the eighteenth century and throughout the Greek revival, through even the tautly skeletal buildings of the stick style and the stretched shingle surfaces of the houses of the later decades of the nineteenth century. It remains a constant through all these to culminate in the tense skins of metal and glass, both in house and office building construction, which have made the American "screen wall" world famous at the present time. Neat and tidy as a sharply pressed suit, the tight American surface seems expressive of the side of American culture which is both puritan and colonial. It is indicative of that turn of mind which wishes at all costs to be proper and is at the same time determined to give nothing of itself away and to present a closed and neutral surface to the outer world. This characteristic, too, merges in its own way with the neutral anonymity and conformism of modern mass society, into which America itself, being in one sense almost without a preindustrial and predemocratic past, was naturally among the first of nations to move. So, beyond materials and beyond programs, a connection exists between, for example, the eighteenth-century Warner House at Portsmouth, New Hampshire, the Stoughton House by Richardson, and the Manufacturers Trust Building by Skidmore, Owings and Merrill. Whether of brick, wood, or steel and glass, whether opaque or transparent, the surface of these buildings is in each case treated as a closed and tightly stretched skin.

Yet the smooth façade upon the American exterior has its natural opposite which can also be traced throughout the history of American architecture from the seventeenth century onward. This opposite is the recurrent expression of a deep yearning for security, shelter, and permanence, characteristic perhaps of those voyagers who, first among Europeans, left the old, fixed ways behind them. So the seventeenth-century house shell enclosed a dark, cavelike space within it, a hollow dominated by the solid bulk and wide opening of the chimney mass with its fireplaces. So Richardson, in the nineteenth century, piled up his Romanesquoid masses of stone, penetrated by deeply engulfing arches and containing great volumes of dark interior space. All his buildings were made to look as if they had been there since time began, and all asserted that the American was in fact what he had never been: permanent upon, sheltered by, and rooted in his land. The work of Frank Lloyd Wright also partly derived from the same rich vein of mythic contact with the earth. The fire, "burning in the heart of the house," the low ceilings, the shadowy and engulfing spaces, and the heavily plastic masses of his buildings as a whole—which seem, like the paintings of Cézanne, to be celebrating the generative powers

of the earth itself—all belong to this counter tradition of longing. Here is a set of symbols which brought to light what had otherwise been hidden—like the boys' books that the most searching American novels of the nineteenth century pretended on the surface to be—beyond the proper closed façade of the puritan and colonial tradition. Wright's own constant use of non-European forms in which to couch his imagery also seems characteristic of the same rather desperate desire for rootedness.

The two elements of uneasiness and concealment have therefore been of constant importance in American creativity. The slide list must, therefore, be supplemented in every instance by relevant European material in order that the comparisons and contrasts can be made clear. For the twentieth century a small working collection of slides of prehistoric, Greek, Roman, medieval, Renaissance, Japanese, and pre-Columbian architecture will also be necessary.

The ubiquity of the suburban house in the list is balanced and complemented, as already indicated, by the number of office buildings. Between the two a general view of the potentially schizophrenic contemporary scene may begin to emerge. The houses and office buildings of the eclectic architects, though based alike upon historical precedents in detail, are so unlike in scale as to demonstrate the difficulties implicit in the integration of contemporary programs—however determined to conceal their modernity the architects may have been. The more recent contrast between an incessantly picturesque diversity in the house and a firmly mechanical determinism in the office building may indeed be a faithful image of the life of the modern commuter. It is certainly demonstrated in the work of many contemporary architects, as, for example, in that of Belluschi. It is less apparent in the buildings of Wright, Mies van der Rohe, and some others, where a rather more general view of the modern problem as all of a piece has produced certain formal and expressive relationships between building types. Thus large houses by Wright, such as "Falling Water," demonstrate a character in space and scale which is to be found both in his small houses, such as the Goetsch–Winkler, and in his office buildings, like that for the Johnson Wax Company. Through the varying shapes a common set of principles can be detected, and these demonstrate to us some of the directing impulses of twentieth-century style. Similarly, single family residences by Mies, such as the Farnsworth House, are clearly connected by common principles—differing from those of Wright—with large apartment buildings like the Lakeshore group and with his Architecture School for the Illinois Institute of Technology. Other important twentieth-century objectives can therefore be identified in Mies's work and can be understood as linking together into comprehensible patterns a great variety of contemporary programs.

Standing, however, somewhat apart from the houses and office buildings are a group of advanced engineering constructions in steel or reinforced concrete. These are usually wide spans over vast and undifferentiated interior spaces. Their incidence, and the development of the structural and plastic techniques which can create them, are on the whole uniquely modern phenomena. They deal with the emotional challenges of a peculiarly modern world of mass populations and complicated technologies. Yamasaki's Airport Terminal for St. Louis, Fuller's geodesic domes, and Saarinen's Auditorium at M.I.T., Yale Hockey Rink, and Idlewild Terminal are excellent examples. A comparison with related European material would nevertheless show that, until recently, such types have been considerably less developed in the United States than elsewhere. On the other hand, American buildings which deal directly with technical efficiency and mass production abound. The number of factories and related structures which demanded inclusion here attest to this. Taken as a group, these and the office buildings probably constitute the basic myth of the United States as it is believed to be by some Americans and most Europeans. The problem is hardly so simple or so one-dimensional, as the list itself clearly shows.

Despite all attempts at flexibility and objectivity, any list such as this should in the end make it possible for the user to illustrate the primary contributions of American architecture to contemporary world culture. Again, in order to do so, the user must bear in mind associated developments in Europe. Yet the American contribution has in fact been so important to the initiation and exploration of the modern idiom that the list can serve surprisingly well to demonstrate most of the important aspects of modern architecture as a whole. The work of most of the major modern architects is illustrated in it, with the almost solitary but critical exception of Le Corbusier. This exception is historically important because it is possible that there have been only two great phases in the development of modern architectural form: that, first in time, which was essentially created in the United States in the work of Wright and in which many European architects have participated, and, secondly, that which has slowly been taking shape both in Europe and America in the work of several architects but in which the buildings of Le Corbusier occupy a special position. The first phase can be well

illustrated or indicated here; the second can be shown only in its peculiarly American aspects.

Centuries usually make poor time divisions for historical movements. The year 1900 is no exception. While it coincides with the last of Louis Sullivan's most important buildings and with the first of Wright's mature designs, it by no means marks the beginning of the movement which each exemplifies. For the beginning one must turn to the nineteenth-century list. Here the critical date will be c. 1885–1891.

It was during these years that the experiments of the nineteenth century, both in house and skyscraper construction, created the spatial, formal, and structural types out of which twentieth-century architecture was to grow. Here a third characteristic of American thought found its expression: the theme of continuity, whereby all separate parts were to be merged into one general order through a continuous movement, which, like that of Whitman's "open road," was to sweep them all along together. Sullivan's skyscraper towers—for example, the Wainwright and Guaranty—organized clear volumes of space into precisely articulated structural cages. Doubled verticals then ascended continuously above the base, and through them wove the structural plait of the horizontal spandrels. The fate of this great type—a reticulated but vertically continuous tower which predicated the open spaces of a new kind of city in which it might stand—can be followed among the office and apartment buildings of the twentieth century. The eclectics of the early part of the century turned the cage into mass, thick or slender, made the top plastic and in this way lost volume, clarity, and any sense of generalized type. Cass Gilbert's Chrysler Building is a romantic tower in this mode. The skyscraper of the twenties, like Voorhees' Barclay–Vesey Building, became a more or less attenuated ziggurat in the densely massed groupings of New York. Later skyscrapers (such as Raymond Hood's McGraw-Hill Building) attempted to incorporate a dominant horizontal, in this way losing any expression of the structural cage or of the building as a unified vertical element. Others, like Hood's Daily News Building, accented solely the vertical cladding, handled flatly, thus losing scale and the expression of the floor levels. Some other types, like Hood's and Harrison's units for Rockefeller Center, were compressed into slabs, vertically accented and semicrenelated at the top, losing both cage and volume. By the forties, an attempt to unify the structural bay system with the "screen wall" produced Belluschi's Equitable Building, which became a cutout box without body. The suppression of the columns and the sheathing of the whole in glass created

Lever House—a cool, fragile, air-conditioned cube. But, in Mies van der Rohe's Lakeshore Apartments, the Sullivanian cage tower returned as a type. The verticals are accentuated by welded H-sections, which are close enough together to keep the viewer's eye within the building envelope—clearly read as structural cage—but far enough apart to allow the horizontal volumes of the apartment floors to be defined. Such interweaving of elements to form a clear, free-standing tower redefines that aesthetic of freedom and order which had been Sullivan's ". . . demonstration which shall be so broad as to allow of *no* exception!" Finally, Mies van der Rohe's Seagram Building, though it no longer projects its columns, makes denser and more monumental the solution of the Lakeshore Apartments. The body of the building rises vertically behind its plaza with the simple directness of the elevators inside it, and the beautiful dull bronze of its reverently assembled fabric is gathered into a sheaf of compactly massed H-sections. Standing upon its columns, like a calm presence upon its legs, the building becomes a single, integrated body.

As in his towers Sullivan had created the vertical, free-standing type, so in the Carson, Pirie and Scott store he had imagined a continuously horizontal type to bound a street or open place. Such a building can have no corner, as Sullivan understood and as many buildings in New York and elsewhere most disastrously demonstrate. Stone's Museum of Modern Art seems a successful space bounder in the continuous mode; Johnson's addition a more "classicizing," that is, fixed-unit.

In the later nineteenth-century house type, the impulse had also been toward continuity, in this case not vertical but lateral, along the contours of the land. By 1885 continuous, horizontally extended interior space had been developed in the East. By 1889 Wright had begun his domestic work in Chicago. By 1900 he had developed continuity into a full spatial and structural system; his horizontal, low-ceilinged, and compulsively extended spaces were disciplined, as in the Willitts House, by decisive cross-axial planning. The crossroad on the boundless prairie, image of endless paths of movement, now joined its own special celebration of the facts of American uprootedness to Wright's counter-images of security and permanence. From this union of emotional opposites, each developed to its fullest extent, arises the artistic greatness of Wright's achievement. Like Cézanne, as already mentioned, Wright balanced his instinct for continuity and change with a will to express the weight, solidity, and timelessness of things.

His Larkin Building and Unity Temple are excellent examples of this poignant synthesis between building mass—at once sculptural and expressive of its hollows—and the new "reality" of continuous space which he desired. Always during this period, however, Wright's compelling drive was toward more and more spatial continuity. He himself was traveling the Whitmanesque "open road," living out and finding new images for the American archetype of mobility and flight. The Robie House sums up this development, causing its brick-heavy masses to hover in long horizontals, while above them it spreads its airplane wings.

In a sense the continuity stressed by Sullivan and developed by Wright was matched in Europe by the curvilinear continuities of the Art Nouveau architects. In this way the century of science produced at its close a formal and symbolic equivalent for that revolutionary concept which the Milesian philosophers of the seventh and sixth centuries B.C.—the first scientists of all—had insisted upon as the essence of reality: the idea that the physical world was not stable or fixed but always in continuous flux and change. After 1910 and 1911, with the Wasmuth publications of those years, Wright's work itself was well known in Europe, and the user of this list should be prepared to supplement it by following the course of Wright's influence abroad and its reinterpretation in the sharper, thinner, tenser, and somewhat more bounded forms of the European designers—forms, one might add, that exhibit anew those qualities both of hardness and of modern mass anonymity which had long been endemic in America as a whole. Yet for the Europeans too, as in the cases of Mondrian and Mies van der Rohe, the concept of continuity formed the underlying objective of design. One is forced to conclude that continuity of space was the essential symbolic expression of nineteenth- and early twentieth-century belief and that such continuity was, in architectural form, developed first in the United States. This probably occurred because the United States, as the youngest segment of western civilization, was most prepared to find forms to express the new attitudes of materialistic and scientific confidence, cultural uprootedness, and indefinite expansion which characterized the first phases of the modern age.

Wright's struggle to advance the frontiers of continuous space throughout the twentieth century can be most brilliantly illustrated from the present list. His concomitant need—the balancing one mentioned earlier—to find roots for stability in more ceremonial and archaic cultures can also be seen. That the Japanese influence was first is clear, and it involved comparatively light and skeletal sensibilities. The Hickox and Willitts Houses show this, as does the interior of Unity Temple, where we may also note the possibility of a direct influence by Wright upon Mondrian's later paintings. But after his break with his essentially nineteenth-century suburb in 1910, Wright seems to have sought for inspiration among heavier, more monumental forms. Generally these were pre-Columbian, often Mayan, sometimes Mexican (A. D. German Warehouse, Barnsdall House, and the block houses of the twenties). Finally, in Wright's work of the thirties, one can note that the influence he had exerted upon Europe was in a sense returning to be reevaluated by him. His "House on the Mesa" Project of 1932 and his Usonian house types demonstrate his receptivity. His Kaufmann House of 1936 would appear to be an inspired synthesis of most of his own earlier work and of the influences he had in turn received from both European and pre-Columbian sources. His search thereafter, through hexagon and circle, was directed toward the ultimate continuities of space as created by the "reflex" (Hanna House, Madison Unitarian Church) and the curvilinear (Johnson Wax Building, Guggenheim Museum). In the end it is at Taliesin West that the symbolic implications of American mobility as a whole become most clear. It is the ultimate frontier. Grouped around the oasis, a nomad band throws up its fortifications, pitches its tents, and faces the emptiness of the desert. Inside are the deep fireplaces and the hidden gardens. But the whole is penetrated by a long axis of space—a road that moves from the entrance through the body of the building to spill out again upon the terrace, beyond which the empty spaces of the wide world lie. Deep American myths are gathered together here, in Indian-recalling forms which now seem to go, as D. H. Lawrence once put it, ". . . deeper than white America."

A great many buildings by a distinguished number of architects mirror on this list the joint influence of Wright and the European architects. Thus the general idiom of design since the later thirties can with all objectivity only be considered as a kind of "International Style," despite the fact that many architects dislike the term. Whether tending toward the greater weight and richness of Wright or the more pronounced thinness and spareness which is both American and European, most American architects have still worked in a kind of style which has been derived from both sources. Again, the basic theme of most of their work has been that of spatial flow and continuity.

The buildings of those European architects who

themselves emigrated to America during the thirties also play an important part on the list. Neutra, for example, working first with Wright, develops his own synthesis of America and Europe in California. The effect of Gropius as a teacher was especially profound in the United States during the later thirties and the forties. The buildings of Marcel Breuer continue to demonstrate the liveliest aspects of the Bauhaus tradition, while those of Gropius and his associates may reveal a somewhat more dogged and academic side (Harvard Graduate Center). In the fifties, however, the work of Mies van der Rohe and his followers would seem to be exerting a profounder influence. During this present period a large body of work indeed seems to demonstrate certain significant changes in the development of modern architecture. The most recent buildings of Mies—such as the Illinois Institute of Technology, the Farnsworth House, the Lakeshore Apartments, and the Seagram Building—have turned away from spatial continuity toward symmetrical form and a concentration upon the precisely defined structural integument. Mies has also, as already noted, insisted upon basic architectural types, each clearly separate one from the other and thus conceived in terms of modular order and stability rather than of continuity and flow. His buildings tend also to be city types, though, where possible, designed with the openness of Japanese pavilions. There is nothing suburban or, in a sense, individualized about them. The influence of these aspects of Mies's design is to be found in the work of a large number of American architects, such as Eero Saarinen, Philip Johnson, Paul Rudolph, and others. Their buildings also show a related sense of vaulted, volumetric space and sometimes of coherent single shapes derived from triangulated, space-frame structures. Such tendencies also unite architects otherwise as far apart as Louis I. Kahn and Catalano. Even at the opposite extreme of building a similar turning toward order and type can be discerned. Even the rather "naturalistic" work in wood of "Bay Region" architects such as Wurster and Esherick—work which tends to be skeletal, often gabled, spatially simple, and volumetric—demonstrates this movement. All of these related developments seem to indicate that the phase in which spatial continuity was a dominant may be coming to a close, and a new phase—which might be called that of "stability," with certain classicizing undertones —is coming into being. Other important aspects of these changes are to be found in the recent sculptural and humanistically challenging buildings of Le Corbusier, none of which, unfortunately, have as yet been constructed in the United States. Yet in Kahn's most recent work, too, the larger implications of the new concern for the building as a sculptural fabric are apparent. His buildings have only that space which is integral not only to its use but also to the structural system whereby it is made. In this way emphasis returns to the building fabric itself as a physical object, not merely a hollow container for human action. In this way the expressive range of architecture is expanded, but, most of all, the human self—concerned throughout the phase of continuity primarily with its own movement—is now presented with the building as an object outside the self: a separate, stable being existing through laws which are complementary to but not identical with those which govern men. It is probably out of this attitude of mind that the truly new forms may be expected to evolve.

This development is an outstandingly important one in terms of American culture as a whole. The thing that stands by itself, specific and unique, has always been furthest from American accomplishment, but in some ways it has been the goal of American striving. In painting and sculpture, as in architecture, the specific image, wholly and only itself, has eluded the American artist who has achieved instead his compulsive flat patterns— as in both the architecture and the painting of the colonial period and the twentieth century alike—or his images of flux and flow, as in nineteenth-century landscape and portrait painting, twentieth-century abstract expressionism, and in the house planning of both eras. Yet, counter to these accomplishments, an opposing will to find the pure, clear, and unchanging form has always been present. The portraits of Feke, Copley, and Earl, the buildings of Jefferson and of the Greek revival, even the earth images of Wright, certainly the towers of Sullivan and Mies and the creations of Kahn, show this intention. The desire is a classic one, to find the individual thing through a reverence for its own specific nature but to compact the whole of experience into a few lucid forms. For no culture earlier than that of modern America has this double desire for specialness and generalization been so difficult of fulfillment, but it seems clear that no culture after that of the Greeks has ever wanted so much to achieve it. For the Greeks it was the very sense of the instability of human life which produced the desire itself. For America, in the vastly more complicated circumstances of the mass age, the problem of resolution may appear to be almost insoluble, but the recognition of instability and the wish to draw permanent truth out of it are clearly there and would seem to be the outstanding items of

concern to both architects and planners at the present time.

TOWN, CITY, AND PARK

The development of planning and of group building projects has been inextricably bound up in America as elsewhere with the progress of building design itself. The suburbs of the nineteenth century, often carefully planned, formed the milieu in which the continuous spaces of Wright's early houses found their place. They themselves were an expression of the same American urge toward mobility and the windings of space. Radburn, New Jersey, and Greenbelt, Maryland, essentially continue their tradition in the more rationalized form which relates to the Garden City concept of Ebenezer Howard. Out of them have also grown, in the twentieth century, not only a flood of rather ill-considered suburbias but also, indeed, Wright's own Broadacre City image itself.

On the other hand, the skyscrapers of Sullivan had forced their way up against the crowded forces of other skyscrapers in the inadequately planned centers of large cities. The crowding of the city had given rise to the skyscraper itself, but the city hardly knew what to do with it once it was there. It was essentially Le Corbusier who realized that skyscrapers needed open space around them and might thus become the basic units for a city at a new scale. Since that time many American projects, from Rockefeller Center to Pittsburgh's Point Park, have demonstrated the influence of that concept, but no adequately scaled examples, re-forming the city as a whole, have as yet been carried out.

The most developed planning projects in the United States during the earlier twentieth century were in fact a kind of reaction against both the suburban tradition and the implications of the skyscraper as a "mid-space" element. The "City Beautiful" projects of the eclectic architects attempted instead to reconstitute the axes and avenues of the baroque tradition. It was the design of the "mall," as in Washington. In its own way, and masking its objectives behind popularly recognizable forms, it too was seeking a curious kind of continuity. Unlike Wright and the modern architects, however, it could not accept a Bergsonian or Milesian concept of flux as meaningful in its symbolic world. Therefore "City Beautiful" planning was generally symmetrical and had fixed conclusions at the end of its axes. Such buildings or monuments were often to be seen across a vast desert of open space—as in Burnham's sweeping plans for Chicago—and their semiclassical forms were blown up out of all proportion in order to cope with a mass ambient for which their intrinsic scale had never been intended. The governmental buildings of both Europe and America demonstrate this destruction of classicism by their very attempt to fit themselves to the expression of state power in the modern age.

At the present time, while the long phase of continuity continues to stretch out into planned or unplanned suburbs and new towns, the opening of the new phase of stability is beginning to exert an effect upon the centers of cities themselves. The impressive number of civic redevelopment projects on the planning list demonstrates this development. It is the necessary complement to that new preoccupation with designing in forms appropriate to the city which has been observed in the work of Mies, Johnson, and others. Many of these projects, such as those for Philadelphia, Detroit, and New Haven, have to do with a perfectly possible renewal of the decaying city at its center, not with a more sweeping and probably unrealizable scheme for the reconstruction of the city as a whole. The moment seems to be arriving when the present can put the past to use and when both can be made to work together toward that continuing process of organic renewal upon which the life of any city depends. The challenge as it now appears to be is posed in exact terms: between the automobile and the city—between the automobile as the culminating image of American nomadism and now obsessively decorated and loaded with loot like the yurts of the Mongols and the city as the fixed abiding place of civilized men. The lines of difference between these two opposites are more clearly drawn in America than they are anywhere else in the world. How they are reconciled may well determine the nature of human living for many centuries to come.

It was noted earlier that the basic question posed by this material involved the relative contribution of the United States to modern world culture. The material itself proposes a triple answer to that question: (1) that the phase of "continuity" in modern architecture arose largely out of early work done here and was indeed derived from deeply seated modern compulsions which were first powerful in America; (2) that, on the other hand, the United States of the thirties proved capable of embracing an international culture and in fact harbored and protected it from various totalitarian threats during that period; and (3) that in the late fifties the United States—though still often taking refuge behind its screen wall—seemed ready to couple its traditional drive toward "continuity" with new patterns and symbols of "stability." Out of such possible compacting of opposites may evolve, during the second half of the century—if we are fortunate—another of those rare unions of anxiety with courage and of mobility with permanence which have in the past produced the "classic" arts.

DESIGN AND DECORATIVE ARTS OF THE SEVENTEENTH AND EIGHTEENTH CENTURIES

CHARLES F. MONTGOMERY

COAUTHORS
FLORENCE M. MONTGOMERY
CHARLES F. MONTGOMERY, JR.

In a wilderness the basic human needs assume the greatest importance. Paramount among such needs of the early settler in America was that of security—the physical security afforded by a house which offered the actual safety of a roof and stout walls and the emotional security gained by dwelling among furnishings consisting of objects similar to those known and enjoyed in the European home. For this reason, from the time of the first settlement the colonist gave great attention to the objects with which he surrounded himself. Some of these he was able to import from the homeland; more often than not, he commissioned a local artisan or craftsman to make from wood, pewter, silver, pottery, glass, or iron the objects essential to the functions and pleasures of everyday life. On every hand we find the seventeenth- and eighteenth-century American giving vent to his aesthetic impulse in the care of fabrication, attention to decoration, and generous use of color in everyday objects, be it a chair or pottery pie plate for his home, a weather vane or chalice for his church, or a tankard or sign for his tavern.

To explain the development of an American character in these objects is a complex problem. Many forces were at work: (1) although the culture was predominantly English, continental influence exercised through émigre artisans was a factor; (2) in what was obviously a pioneer society, the primary emphasis was necessarily on utility and function; each object had to serve satisfactorily its intended use; (3) although in colonial America labor of all kinds was in demand and skilled labor was at a premium, beauty was not forgotten. Ways were found to create the beautiful with economy of time and effort, sometimes through simplification of traditional ornament and sometimes through substitution of simpler methods—for example, painting to simulate marble, marquetry, and inlay; or crewelwork to substitute for rich brocaded textiles. With simplified ornament, the appearance of the object and its beauty were often more dependent on proportion, the articulation and interrelationship of the parts, and particularly on the outline of the total mass.

American decorative arts of the seventeenth century were characterized by a continuation of the Renaissance style still popular in England. Both furniture and silver forms were robust and massive.

In furniture, case pieces were rectilinear, with harmonious subdivisions defined by ornamental spindles or mouldings. Each structural member was distinct in the over-all design, with unity attained through a symmetry, repetition, and slight variation of motif. In this essentially architectonic style, motifs such as the arch, the column, the pilaster, and the dentil were commonly used as ornament. Decoration was flat and self-contained. Surface carving, applied bosses, and split spindles, as well as painting in a restricted number of colors, were employed. Although much research remains to be done, the writer feels that the pattern for both painted and carved decoration was largely derived from the printed ornament and floriated letters of which variants were to be seen in almost every contemporary book.

Hard pine, maple, and oak were the common structural woods, and the last named was so generally used that the seventeenth century has often been called the Age of Oak. The principles involved in its use were the same for furniture, house, or ship and were well known to many of the first colonists who came to America from East Anglia, a shipbuilding center, where the crafts of joinery and woodworking were deeply rooted. The mortise and tenon were used to provide firm joints, and turning on the lathe yielded spiral, spool, and baluster shapes.

In simplest form, the chest, an essential piece of furniture in every seventeenth-century home, was a simple six-board box with hinged top and with ends extended to provide feet. Chests made before 1660 were often carved over the entire front surface, whereas later ones were embellished with split spindles, mouldings, and bosses. Two regional types of which many survive are the carved sunflower- and tulip-decorated chests of the Hartford and Wethersfield areas and the Hadley chest with its flat carved leaves, scrolls, and often the initials of the original owner. As time passed, drawers were added at the bottom to form the so-called blanket chest and, still later, the four-drawer chest approximating in form the modern bureau. Similar to chests in construction were boxes used to store books and papers; called Bible boxes, with either flat or slant tops, these were the forerunners of the earliest type of desk—a slant-top box on a turned frame, appropriately called "desk-on-frame."

The most important piece of furniture in the eyes of the seventeenth-century man was the court or press cupboard used for the storage of food and the display of prized silver and pottery. Reminiscent of sixteenth-century palace furniture, its ownership was indicative of rank in the community.

Before 1650 most households had only one or two chairs, often of large size and used by the head of the house or the guest of honor, following age-old court custom. Common types were the Brewster and Carver chairs, with vertical spindle backs, and the wainscot chair, distinguished by a paneled back and board seat. The Cromwellian chair, characterized by even knob turnings, derives its name from its widespread use in England during the Commonwealth; however, similar chairs are frequently seen in the paintings of the Dutch Little Masters of earlier date. Although slat-back chairs may have come into use slightly later than the others mentioned, many show the bold turnings, heavy members, and forthright structure indicating seventeenth-century workmanship. Whereas other chair types died with the century, the slat back became progressively lighter in appearance and persisted throughout the nineteenth century. Chair seats were usually plaited of rush or splint and cushions often used. Commoner than chairs for seating were the forms, or benches, and joined or joint stools.

Regardless of their size, tables were of trestle type or of stretcher type, such as the gate-leg.

Extant examples of seventeenth-century bedsteads are all low-post, with turned legs. High-post beds with curtains were frequently listed in American household inventories, but none are now known.

From the earliest days of colonization, the silversmith's art was practiced in America. In the absence of banks, colonists relied upon the silversmith to work their coins into useful articles, many of which were surprisingly elaborate in both form and decoration. Such pieces as tankards, spoons, and porringers often represented a substantial part of the wealth of the family. Makers' marks, owners' initials, engraved arms, or other decoration were useful for identification in case of loss or theft. The largest number of surviving seventeenth-century forms are to be found in drinking vessels for either domestic or church use, such as tankards, caudle cups, beakers, tumblers, dram and standing cups, and punch bowls. Many of them have been preserved in the churches for which they were made or to which they were later bequeathed.

The principal centers of silversmithing in seventeenth-century America were Boston and New York and, to a lesser extent, Philadelphia. As Boston was settled by the English and New York by the Dutch, differences in the cultures of these colonial towns carried over into their silver. The florid and robust quality of New York pieces is seen especially in tankards with richly engraved fronts and covers and applied foliated bands around heavily moulded bases and in great shallow drinking bowls with repoussé floral ornament separated in paneled cartouches.

Porringer handles, tankard thumbpieces, handle tips, and baluster stems on standing cups and candlesticks were cast. Other parts of the vessels were ordinarily forged and raised from ingots prepared by the silversmith.

Favored for engraved decoration were natural and stylized representations of flowers and animals, derived from such varied sources as Oriental porcelain or a Dutch book of didactic poetic fables by Jacobus Cats. Flat chasing occurs on a number of pieces, while reeding is found on others. The repoussé turkey on a caudle cup made by Robert Sanderson has the distinction of being the first domestically derived decorative device.

In 1674 the Dutch for all time relinquished possession of New Amsterdam, and the Eastern seaboard from New Hampshire to North Carolina was under the British Crown. Although the colonists were from Holland, Germany, Sweden, Switzerland, and France, as well as from England, the dominant cultural influence was British. Colonial leaders were Englishmen. Direct trade was by law confined to the mother country. But at the end of the seventeenth century England was no longer the provincial island she once had been. The taste for luxury and novelty expressed during the reign of Charles I and interrupted by the austere regime of Oliver Cromwell burst forth with renewed vitality in the Restoration of Charles II, who brought back with him tastes and styles learned during his enforced sojourn on the Continent. With the revocation of the Edict of Nantes in 1685, large numbers of Huguenot craftsmen fled France. Many went to England (more than 50,000 silk weavers, to single out one group); some came directly to America. William III, Prince of Orange, on ascending the throne in 1689, brought artists and artisans with him from Holland. All of these were dominant factors in bringing about a revolution in taste and a new style we know as William and Mary (1689–1702—dominant in America until 1725).

Baroque in character, this new style is typified by dynamic opposition and energy, curved and contorted forms, and strong contrasts of light and shade. In silver and furniture, as in architecture, plasticity and a feeling of depth and movement are achieved by broken surfaces. Bold effects are attained through the dramatic juxtaposition of solids and voids, protrusions and recessions, and the use of rich materials.

The furniture of this period is characterized by baroque details of ornament organized within a strict geometrical structure. Plain surfaces were avoided. Richly figured woods, such as burled veneers, and vine and floral painting as well as japanning, an Anglicized version of Chinese lacquer work, were employed to enrich surface effect. Heavy mouldings on case pieces, following baroque architectural practice, add weight and lend dignity to the furniture. Vigorous carving in broken S-scrolls and a variety of leg and arm supports are seen.

With the advent of the eighteenth century, some earlier types of furniture either disappeared or were modified. The contrast in size and relation of turnings was sharper and the effect more dramatic although the over-all forms were less bulky. Curved elements providing greater comfort and grace were in evidence in the back, the arms, and the feet of side chairs and armchairs. The so-called Spanish foot was introduced at this time, as were caning and chair backs with turned split spindles, called "balusters." These three elements, together with carved cresting rails, came via England from their places of origin: the Low Countries and Spain.

Also new were the fully upholstered easy chair and the day bed or couch closely related to chairs in its turned legs, stretchers, and the shape of its adjustable headrest. There was greater variety of tables in many sizes and shapes, and we note one made specifically for tea. Already the influence of Oriental imports was beginning to be felt in America.

The court cupboard and the blanket chest were superseded by the chest of drawers brightened with brass teardrop drawer pulls and chased escutcheons.

Innovations were the high chest of drawers and matching dressing tables, raised on legs turned in the shape of a trumpet or, more rarely, in spirals. First made at this time also were tall-case clocks. High-post beds were popular, furnished either with crewelwork—home-embroidered linen—hangings in exotic floral designs, or with colorful imported silk or woolen stuffs. Desks followed the sequence of development from the Bible box and the desk-on-frame to become, as it were, desks-on-chests.

Between 1700 and 1725 we find a fully developed baroque style in American silver. Gadrooning and repoussé were the principal decorative techniques. Old forms persisted in many drinking vessels, but the popularity of new beverages resulted in handsome forms for serving imported tea and chocolate. Regional differences are noted in the globular shape of teapots favored by New York makers and the pear shape current in Boston. Exhibiting greater opulence and sophistication are the monteith, the covered cup, the sugar box, and the mustard pot. Standing salts, a medieval survival, were still being made, but grafted to the older form was the new decoration of a gadrooned band. Less imposing, but more prevalent in New York, was the gadrooned trencher salt. Cast candlesticks with a variety of baluster stems and conforming bases were apparently less common than their English prototypes and are great rarities today.

Although Queen Anne died in 1714, the style which bears her name extended to 1750 in America and included English Georgian styles. Essentially baroque but more fully developed with less contortion and sharp contrast than in the previous period, the Queen Anne style is marked by organic unity. It is a fluid, curvilinear style with freedom and strength of line. Bold outlines, balance, symmetry, the subtle interplay of curves, the contrast of solid and void, the use of the naturalistic cockleshell, and borrowed Oriental forms and motifs are its hallmarks. Japanning was increasingly used for furniture decoration. Walnut was the wood most frequently employed in high-style furniture, with maple, cherry, and various other native woods also used in country regions.

Among the new furniture forms were the chest-on-chest, the upholstered stool, the fire screen, and the sofa. Cabinetmaking became a highly developed trade, and refinements as well as new details of construction are found in furniture of the period: the cabriole leg, replacing the straight turned leg, terminated in the round-pad (Dutch) foot, a pointed (slipper) foot, or the three-toed (trifid) foot; these in turn were followed by the claw-and-ball foot. Decorative motifs common to furniture of this period were scrolls, volutes, shells, arches, and S-curves. When carving occurs, it is found in symmetrical scrolls and shells on the knees of cabriole legs, chair backs and seat rails, drawer fronts, and pediments.

The transition to the curvilinear style of the Queen Anne period may be seen in certain upholstered chairs. The earlier style is still apparent in the straight lines of the frame, the rigid scrolls of the cresting rail; new are the angular cabriole legs, though still braced by stretchers. The regional character of furniture is clearly differentiated at this time and is to be found in the carving of the feet, the secondary woods used in the understructure, the shape of chair seats, the method of pinning the seat and legs together, the finials of case pieces, and often in the form of the piece and its proportions. These differences are distinguished in the tall, straight proportions and the persistence of stretchers in New England examples. New York chairs are broader and heavier, with a series of broken curves in the stiles which match the outlines of the generous splats. Philadelphia chairs exhibit greater elegance and grace of proportion than do those of other regions and often more carving.

The forms of tables became even more diverse in shape and size in this period. Dining, tea, breakfast, and card tables were a few designed for specific uses. Marble provided the colorful and handsome, as well as the practical, surface for side tables, the forerunner of the sideboard.

Desks in the Queen Anne period assumed a variety of forms, with from one drawer to four drawers or the desk-and-bookcase. In the Boston area such case pieces were sometimes decorated with line inlay and stars, fans, and even inlaid birds. Only in urban centers did the tall clock change appreciably, as in the one from Newport, Rhode Island, by James Wady, with its pedimented hoods, gilded shell, fretwork, and brass mounts and in the one from Boston by the Gawen Brown Works, brightly japanned on a rich, variegated ground color.

An English law of 1697 had far-reaching, though delayed, effect upon colonial silver designs. It raised the content from 925 to 958 parts pure silver in 1000. This purer metal was softer and the vessels less sturdy when worked into the earlier thin and ornate forms. Gadrooning and repoussé were replaced by banding and applied ornament, which strengthened the basic utensil. For beauty, greater reliance was placed on the form itself. In part, the adaptation of shapely Oriental ceramic forms lately imported served this requirement particularly in teapots, canisters, and sugar bowls.

Queen Anne silver has a vigor of line and balance that surpasses that of any other period. Such perfect, though far from static, balance can be seen especially in teapots and coffeepots. Square, hexagonal, and octagonal forms were popular; and such faceting brought out contrasts of light and shade, a primary attribute of the baroque style.

About 1750 there developed a gradual evolution in ornament which is epitomized in the Chippendale style of furniture, which takes its name from the pattern book *The Gentleman and Cabinet-maker's Director,* first published by Thomas Chippendale in London in 1754. In it are combined or included (1) the French Rococo of Louis XV, (2) the reinterpretation of Gothic elements, and (3) the English interpretations of the Chinese, all of which indicate an interest in the modern —equated with the French taste then as now—and a romantic interest in places remote in time and place. This style is marked by a dispersal of energy, outward-flowing curves, and fluid, playful surface decoration. Carving on furniture and repoussé and engraving in silver employed fanciful variations of naturalistic devices such as the rock and shell, exotic birds, flowers, and flames. Cartouches, fretwork, foliate and twined meandering sprays were common to carving, as was the tattered shell, which replaced the lobed cockleshell of the baroque.

Although pine was a favorite for carved and gilded mirrors and cherry and maple were sometimes used, rich-colored, close-grained mahogany was the favorite wood. Its strength lent itself to carving and the attenuated, sinuous ornament.

In American furniture the clearest expression of the rococo is seen in the details—the pierced cartouche and flame used as finials on case pieces and the asymmetrical shell, vine surface carving, and piercing. The straight leg and the French scroll foot favored by Chippendale over the already old-fashioned claw-and-ball foot were never so popular in America as in England.

As would be expected, in Chippendale's designs for chairs in the "Gothic" and "Chinese" taste, ogee arches and tracery are included in the former; Chinese in feeling are the colonnettes framing the mirror, the pagoda-like caps on the side chair stiles, the pierced stretcher, and the fret carving. Even though specified as Gothic or Chinese, both usually included elements of the rococo.

The highest expression of the rococo in American furniture is to be seen in Philadelphia craftsmanship, clearly manifested in the designs of an endless variety of delicately pierced and carved chair splats. Philadelphia high chests, while massive and tall, were lightened by fine carving of leaves, shells, rockwork, and fancy brasses or bronze mounts. Matching dressing tables in smaller scale continued to be made. Some marble-topped pier tables received lavish rock and shell carving on their skirts, occasionally with elements of the carving left free-standing. Although few have survived, mirrors painted white and picked out in gold were popular; they are reminiscent of the designs of Lock and Copland (London, 1750–1770), English pioneers in adapting the rococo to the needs of the carver. On the finest examples of tripod-base candlestands, fire screens, and tea tables, the knees, pedestals, and piecrust edge were intricately carved.

New York furniture is less fanciful in design and shows a closer affinity to English furniture in its broad, heavy proportions. Chair backs were wider and less intricately pierced, carving heavier and less skillfully executed, and the edges of aprons often boldly gadrooned.

Case furniture from Massachusetts is noteworthy for the use of bombé and serpentine forms; carved from solid pieces of wood, they are more closely related to French and Dutch rococo furniture than to English. Massachusetts furniture, more than that of other cabinetmaking centers, relied on such classical details as broken pediments, fluted pilasters, engaged columns, Ionic or Corinthian capitals.

Although less is known about it, fine furniture was made in the South in the rococo style. An unusual example is a table, noteworthy for its fretwork band, marble top, and unusual legs and feet set at an angle.

The greatest contribution of the American cabinetmaker is to be seen in the block-front furniture produced by the Townsend–Goddard families of Newport, Rhode Island. This distinctive American style was originated and brought to full flower by members of these Quaker families, of which no fewer than twenty members were cabinetmakers over a 100-year period. The chests, desks, and desk-and-bookcases are marked by three vigorous, broad shells at the top of nearly flat vertical panels alternately raised and recessed. Heavy blocked mouldings and ogee-bracket feet support the cases. Strongly baroque, with great emphasis on the play of light and shade across broad surfaces of dark mahogany, these Newport masterpieces were produced between 1760 and 1785, when cabinetmakers of other centers had turned to the rococo.

Contemporary with the Chippendale style, but in no way related to it, is the Windsor chair in all its variants, including the side chair, writing arm, settee, and footstool. All these were widely made for both garden and household use throughout the second half of the eighteenth century. The idea for this stick furniture, whose construction has been likened by Sigfried Giedion to that of the balloon frame in architecture, came from England; but its development here seems uniquely American. Between 1750 and 1800 the variety of forms changed but little, but the character of the turned legs and spindles became progressively more delicate with less contrast between maximum and minimum dimension of turning. After the eighteenth century, though the form persisted, it declined from the noble, well-articulated shapes to strictly utilitarian cottage furniture.

In silver the outward-flowing motion of the rococo is expressed in both form and ornament. Coffeepots and teapots, now of greater capacity, were shaped in inverted-pear and tulip forms with elaborate repoussé cartouches and delicate engraved floral ornament. Cast cabriole legs and shell feet formed the bases of chafing dishes, trays, cream pitchers, and kettle stands. Handles displayed a great variety of lively curves, both in wood and in metal. In contrast to the smooth-surfaced Queen Anne pieces, few surfaces or junctures between parts were left unadorned. Elaborate piercing is found on casters and other pieces not used for liquids. With the greater wealth of the colonists, quantities of silver were fashioned for both ornament and utility: desk-and-bookcases boasted inkstands complete with ink, sand pots, and tray; snuffers with tray were at hand for trimming taper candlesticks conveniently for writing; tea equipage included hot-water kettles, pots, pitchers, bowls, and tongs; and for the dining table—cruet stands, dish rings, baskets, and vegetable dishes. Special commissions continued to be the proud work of skilled American silversmiths. Myer Myers executed the *Four Crowns of the Law* for the Touro Synagogue, in Newport, Rhode Island; and Paul Revere fashioned a great punch bowl for the Sons of Liberty. Flaunting a liberty cap and inscribed "to the Memory of the illustrious Ninety-two" who had voted not to rescind the embargoes on English-made goods, it is one of the most beautiful and historic pieces of American silver.

Following his return from Italy in 1759, Robert Adam introduced into England a new style in architecture that was to have widespread effect on all the decorative arts. For his many commissions he insisted upon designing both exterior and interior architecture and furnishings, including plasterwork ceilings, floor coverings, furniture and upholstery, lighting fixtures, and hardware. Although his new "antique" or classical style became immediately popular, because of the strained political relations between the colonies and England, it did not reach this country until after the

Revolution and then only as interpreted through the design books of George Hepplewhite, Thomas Sheraton, and others. On its appearance, however, it gained immediate acceptance and swept aside the rococo, which had by this time acquired, in Jefferson's words, ". . . the burthen of barbarous ornaments." The classical was deemed a suitable style for the new nation. The ancients were emulated for their qualities of justice, patriotism, liberty, and industry. Men of the new nation aspired, therefore, to the ownership of objects reminiscent of Roman republicanism.

Characteristic of this period are light and delicate rectilinear forms. Contrast of geometric elements and the juxtaposition of a variety of forms and sizes to one another were basic to the style—that is, ovals to rectangles, circles to squares, large areas to small. Subtle contrasts of color and texture were employed which in furniture were achieved through the use of light and dark woods, light fabrics with mahogany, and inset glass or painted panels. The decoration was largely derived from arabesque painting found on vases unearthed at Herculaneum and Pompeii just prior to Robert Adam's visit to Italy. The urn was one of the commonest motifs; others included the anthemion, honeysuckle, bellflower, patera, swags of drapery, rinceau band, Greek key, reeding, and fluting. In America, patriotic motifs including the American eagle and symbolic figures were frequently used.

Five important schools of furniture makers and their central figures have been identified: Samuel McIntire, architect and carver of Salem; Thomas Seymour of Boston; Duncan Phyfe of New York; Ephraim Haines and Henry Connelly of Philadelphia; and the Annapolis–Baltimore group. Of these, McIntire and Phyfe employed carving, whereas the others used inlay to fine effect.

The Boston, Salem, and Baltimore furniture is of particular social interest in that it reflects the new prosperity occasioned by world-wide shipping from these ports. McIntire of Salem was, on a small scale, similar to Adam in that he worked not only with the furniture but also on the houses of the Salem merchant princes.

Completely neoclassical and new are the delicately carved ornament and the striking contrasts of wood used in the finest work of these New England centers—whether in a card table, a chest, or a graceful chair.

Neoclassical side chairs, all with straight legs, were of two principal types: some with rectangular backs composed of turned members; and others of shield-back design with splats of urns, swags of drapery, or feathers.

Today popularly known as the Martha Washington, a new variety of chair first made in this period had as its distinguishing features a high upholstered back and exposed wooden arms. Because of its comparative lightness, it was more popular than the fully upholstered easy chair.

Tall clocks were still made, but their over-all effect was lightened by inlays and the "cutout" pediments giving to the hood a filigree effect. The increasingly favored wall clock assumed two forms: the first was that of a small case mounted on a separate bracket; the second, the hanging banjo type invented by the Willards of Roxbury, Massachusetts. Looking glasses varied between the light and fanciful sorts with crests of flowers and ears of grain, often gilded and sometimes inset with painted panels above the mirror, scrolled mahogany frames with bird finials, and the circular or oval girandole type with gilt frame usually adorned with applied balls and an eagle. Several varieties of delicate furniture were made especially for women. In this category are sewing tables, ladies' dressing tables, ladies' secretaries, and small dressing glasses.

At this time furniture for the dining room received particular attention. The sideboard is an innovation, as are china cabinets, knife cases, wine coolers, and hunt boards, popular in the South. All of these pieces continued to be made into the first three decades of the nineteenth century, when they went out of fashion and the new mode became the Empire style.

The silver of the classical period has great dignity occasioned principally by the forms and the understatement of ornament. The forms are in most instances derived from classical urns, lamps, columns, and helmets. Imported ceramic forms such as Liverpool creamware pitchers and Chinese export porcelain bowls also influenced silver shapes. From whatever source, the silver objects of the time have a precise symmetry and a restraint that can only be called classic. Bright-cut engraving, beading, reeding, and channeling are the principal types of ornament. Wreaths, delicate garlands of flowers, ribbons, and bowknots are the engraved motifs of the period. Tea and coffee services, made for the first time in matching sets with cream pitchers, and sugar and waste bowls were the principal products of the silversmith.

In some other crafts, as in country cabinetmaking, chronological development of style is less apparent than in city-made products. In rural regions, old forms lingered on for long periods of time—forms so basic that to this day we have been unable to improve on them. Centuries-old elemental production methods and techniques, governed by the nature of traditional materials used, and decorative motifs found favor long after they were outmoded in urban centers in closer contact with Europe. Often naïve touches were added through the inclusion of personal inscriptions, initials, names, rhymes, mottoes. The resultant over-all effect is that of folk art in the nonacademic and highly personal combination and recombination of the very old, the old, and current elements of design.

Pewter in some form—plates, dishes, mugs, tankards, spoons, porringers, or commodes—was in use in every American household from the earliest settlement until the close of the eighteenth century. Because of the perishable nature of this soft metal (90 per cent tin) and the ready convertibility of old metal into new, there is a great scarcity of the native ware made before the Revolution, and not more than a half-dozen seventeenth-century pieces are known today.

New pewter in large quantities was imported from England, which, when damaged or worn out, was promptly melted down and reworked by American craftsmen after 1640. In that year, the first recorded pewter shop was set up in Salem, Massachusetts, and was followed soon after by pewterers in most other American centers.

Prior to 1750 pewter forms seem to have been nearly *au courant* with silver forms. After that time, pewter was replaced as the tableware of the fashionable; and for the next fifty years, only the most progressive pewterers, like William Will of Philadelphia, produced up-to-date forms. Flat-lidded early eighteenth-century-style tankards were being produced in New York in the 1790s, though possibly largely for country sale.

Bronze moulds for casting pewter were costly and hard to obtain and are believed to have passed by inheritance or sale to successive generations of pewterers. Often in most ingenious fashion the craftsman used moulds for several purposes—for example, the cover for a sugar bowl as the base of a chalice, a salt as a cover of a coffeepot, or a six-inch plate as the bottom of a flagon.

Although American pewter styles are closely related to those of silver, there were notable contributions, especially in the work of Johann Christoff Heyne of Lancaster, Pennsylvania, and Peter Young of Albany, New York. Their chalices are models of balanced strength rivaled only by the clean line of the New York- and Connecticut-made beakers. Porringers with great variety of handle design have survived and were favorites in America. Plain and flowered handles were standard in Newport, geometrically pierced handles were popular in New York, and only tab-handled basins are to be found bearing the touches of Pennsylvania craftsmen. For-

tunately, with pewter, as with silver, a large percentage of the known pieces were stamped with marks by which the makers may be readily identified.

Although pottery making has been carried on continuously in America from the middle of the seventeenth century down to the present time, few pieces made before 1750 can be identified. Quantities of red earthenware were made in Massachusetts, New York, Virginia, and New Jersey before 1685. Excavations of pottery sites indicate that earthenware baking dishes, jars, jugs, waste bowls, mugs, and pitchers were made with colored glazes, incised lines, and tooled decoration—age-old devices relied upon by potters everywhere. In Pennsylvania the German potters introduced and used widely after 1750 not only colored glazes but also the sgraffito, or scratch technique, to further enhance their wares with peafowls, flowers, figures, and homely verses.

In addition to redware, gray stoneware was also produced in quantity after 1750. Occasionally ornamented with incised line and cobalt-blue-colored motifs, these, like all pottery, relied for their appeal chiefly on their forthright lines and proportions.

In 1646 the first successful American ironworks was promoted by John Winthrop, Jr., and started by Joseph Jenks at Saugus, Massachusetts; it became one of the most up-to-date in the world and continued in operation for nearly thirty years. At the time of the restoration of the Saugus Ironworks by the American Iron and Steel Institute in 1954, many parts of pots, kettles, and other objects presumably manufactured there were excavated on the site; and, although no single piece from Saugus can be positively identified, it is believed the fireback is a product of this furnace. Elsewhere in the colonies foundries sprang up in rapid succession, many of these in New Jersey and Pennsylvania, where during the eighteenth century large amounts of raw materials were refined.

Large numbers of five- and six-plate jamb stoves, with sides and fronts often ornamented with Biblical scenes, were produced for use in Pennsylvania German homes. In 1742 Benjamin Franklin invented an open-front stove composed of cast-iron plates originally ornamented with a sun and the inscription *ALTER IDEM* ("Another like me"). Known as Franklin stoves, similar heating devices were made at many furnaces.

Although many iron and steel products were imported into the colonies, some pig iron was exported from them to Europe, as well as used widely here by the many blacksmiths who were important members of every community. They were called upon for innumerable mending operations as well as for the many, many objects of iron needed for house building and household wares: nails, latches, hinges, andirons, shovels and tongs, skillets, kettles, flippers, weather vanes, and other articles for daily use. The variety is infinite, with some regional variation, particularly in the latches for home and church—generally delicate in New England, sturdy and bold in New York and the Hudson Valley, and often suggestive in Pennsylvania of other German decoration. Throughout the first two centuries of American iron production, whether cast or wrought, to be functional was not enough; most pieces that have come down to us are beautiful as well.

Two attempts were made to establish glasshouses in early settlements at Jamestown; but these failed, as did every succeeding one until the successful enterprise set up by Caspar Wistar near Salem, New Jersey, in 1739. Although this house prospered for forty years and produced quantities of window glass, bottles of several sizes, and presumably offhand blown pieces made by the workmen for family and friends at the end of the day, no piece can be positively identified as Wistar glass today. To make such identification even more difficult, after the closing of the Wistar factory about 1780, its imported workmen are believed to have started other factories. In these, we believe, as at Wistarberg, free-blown glass objects were made, and the tradition of South Jersey blown glass, which continued into the nineteenth century, was established. Closely parallel to the continental utilization of tooled and overlaid ornament, at least one American type of decoration is believed to have evolved there—the kind known as lily pad. Many bowls, pitchers, and other household articles were made both in New Jersey and, in the nineteenth century, in New York State glasshouses, to which the style apparently spread.

In 1763 Heinrich Wilhelm Stiegel, after a successful career as ironmaster, started the first of his three glass factories, which, over the next twenty years, produced large quantities of fine table glass of three varieties—enameled, copper-wheel engraved, and pattern moulded. These wares were sent to many American cities for sale, and much documentary evidence remains concerning Stiegel's importation of the finest workmen from both England and the Continent and the manufacture and distribution of his glass. Unfortunately, as with the Wistarberg, not a piece can be positively identified as made at Manheim in his factories. However, it can be said with assurance that the glass in a few specific pieces are Stiegel type and made either at Manheim or by Stiegel workmen who went to other factories after the financial collapse of the colorful German immigrant who, at the height of his career, styled himself as "Baron."

There were other late eighteenth-century glassmaking enterprises, but by far the most important was that of John Frederick Amelung, who came from Germany and landed at Baltimore in 1784 "with 68 hands." Five months later he was offering to the public window glass, green and hollow ware from the glasshouse which he had established at New Bremen, near Frederick, Maryland. Today several dated and inscribed pieces from the "New Bremen Glass Manufactory" survive to make safe attributions on many other pieces with similar characteristics and to show the variety of forms made. These indicate the fine quality of the metal and prove that much of the Amelung glass is without peer. The shapes are aesthetically satisfactory and the execution excellent. As was the case with most American glass enterprises, Amelung's ended in bankruptcy in 1795.

DESIGN AND DECORATIVE ARTS OF
THE NINETEENTH CENTURY

G . H A Y D N H U N T L E Y

The decorative arts usually afford clearer perceptions of the development of popular taste than do such arts as painting or architecture. The fact that many of these works are ephemera, that most of them are useful objects, often necessities, aids in breaking down the common man's fear to express artistic judgment, even if that expression is manifested only by the act of choosing for purchase. For this reason, as a barometer of popular taste, the decorative arts are unsurpassed. Also because of their wide range of cost, they show the taste of all classes. Since they are not regarded too seriously as art, the decorative arts—like popular music—reflect emphatically, often almost spontaneously, both the passing and lasting interests of a period. When we contemplate the wealth of tribute paid to Zachary Taylor in textile designs and on whiskey flasks, we realize vividly how important in 1847 was our victory over the Mexicans. So, too, do the minor arts trumpet the almost unbelievably enthusiastic reception of Jenny Lind in America. These are examples of passing interests reflected primarily in subject matter. The more lasting interests generated stylistic changes. For example, early in the century our admiration for the French began to modify the British tradition which continued from colonial times. This French influence, seen in Duncan Phyfe's "Recamier" sofa, after a few years developed into the dominant "Empire" style.

In our western civilization the decorative arts of the nineteenth century did not follow clear national lines. Fads and fashions, as well as ideas and actual objects, passed frontiers freely and swiftly. Time and again where conditions were similar, men in different countries made the same invention independently. This was true not only in scientific areas but in artistic creations as well. That Winslow Homer's paintings sometimes resemble Courbet's does not necessarily signify that one artist influenced the other. The ornamental devices which we associate with Art Nouveau began to appear spontaneously and independently (so far as we know) in the late eighties in French painting, in British decorative art, and in American architectural design

and ornament. Cosmopolitanism is surely a characteristic of nineteenth-century art because many of our designers and artisans were foreigners who came to these shores already well trained in the traditions of their native lands. The Venetian brothers Rago under Stiegel, Theophile Fry and Daniel Greatbach at Bennington, Duncan Phyfe and John Belter are only a few examples of the hundreds of immigrants who designed and produced art in America. Another factor which impedes our recognition of American qualities was that in certain fields the prestige of importations so dominated the market that our designers felt compelled to imitate them. A notorious case is afforded by William Tucker's porcelain, which he seldom marked for fear that customers would spurn it as American. The public set a premium on French and English wallpaper, British textiles, and jewelry from Paris and Rome. Toys came from Germany. Even ordinary glassware, which we turned out so abundantly, had to compete with the foreign-made. Fine glassware was mostly imported.

Americans, however, had their own particular needs, traditions, and tastes which influenced even the foreign designers. For example, Fry and Greatbach, both immigrants, worked in potteries with established traditions and techniques to which they had to adapt themselves. Since their works were for the American market they had to visualize how they would be used in the American home and how they would appeal to the American housewife when displayed by the American peddler or on the shelves of the country store. Without doubt, these artists became Americans, and so, too, did their designs become American. Likewise, the influence of importations was tempered by the Americanism of the market. The consumer and the importer were selective. Not all weaves and designs of British textiles found favor. Not all patterns of English and French wallpaper came to our shores. Indeed, frequently the foreign manufacturer, after sounding out the American market, made designs exclusively for sale here. Such was the "Gaudy Dutch" dinnerware from Staffordshire. It conformed so completely to an established taste that it can have had little influence in the formation of that taste.

Elements peculiar to the way of life in America have influenced our art. Some British artisans who wrote reports on the Paris Exposition of 1867 pointed out characteristics of American products. Charles Hibbs writing on "Small Arms, etc.," reported:[1]

. . . like most American productions, they are rough, plain, and good. . . . The rough and ready way in which they cast aside old theories, the boldness with which they start out on new and untrodden paths, the entire confidence they have in themselves, and their sagacity in finding out what is to be done, and doing it—all find expression in their work.

Such observations are strongest in the realm of the machine, but Frank Jackson writing "On Design" (of the decorative arts) said:[2]

While other exhibits rest primarily upon rare and costly works, elaborated to the highest degree, this little display of the Americans rests upon humble works, proving that ordinary articles may be exalted and invested with a dignity that will entitle them to rank with the proudest achievements of industrial art.

The British artisans saw that the general characteristics which they noted—the flouting of tradition, the ingenuity, and the respect for the simple and humble—are valid for American applied art and architecture as a whole in comparison with works from Europe.

Nevertheless, even if we accept the validity of these characteristics, it is difficult to apply them for the purpose of determining whether or not a particular work is American. For one thing, to pass judgment one must know comparable objects produced elsewhere. Also there are exceptions to the rule: the intricate, methodically planned furniture of John Belter and the costly work of Tiffany and Co., to mention but two. One must know the variations of American art and make allowance for them. Furthermore, one must have a good grounding in the style of the period in which the article was produced. And this knowledge is not easily acquired, for not only is the style development of the nineteenth century extremely complicated by rapidity of change and an intricate interweaving of historical influences, but also it has been little studied.

For convenience's sake let us divide the nineteenth century arbitrarily into four periods, which we shall call the Federal (about 1800–1830), the Romantic-Eclectic (about 1830–1860), the Early Victorian

(about 1860–1880), and the Late Victorian (about 1880–1900).

While in many ways the Federal period was a continuation of the eighteenth century, it developed characteristics which mark it as an era in its own right. The gentlemanly attitude, still important in politics and social relations, had as its fitting parallel in the decorative arts the general prevalence of the workshop tradition. American culture remained closely bound to the English, and taste continued in the eighteenth-century British tradition. The exercise of taste was not difficult because the art forms were basically of classical tradition and followed classical rules. Thus in art this was a relatively conservative period. On the other hand, various forces were working to make the new nation more independent politically, culturally, and economically. These forces began to modify the cultural conservatism.

The geographical expansion into the Western Reserve and the Ohio Valley, created new centers far from the Atlantic Coast, where settlers were little concerned with European modes. The Napoleonic Wars hampered both trade and cultural exchange with Europe. In 1823 America's confidence in itself and its independence from Europe were expressed politically in the pronouncement of the Monroe Doctrine. Of necessity, the United States began to develop her own manufactures which, after a second war with England, were encouraged by the protective tariff of 1816. The completion of the Erie Canal in 1825 linked Eastern waterways with the vast network of Western lakes and rivers on which the newly invented steamboat provided convenient and cheap transportation and opened a vast new market for the nascent factories of the East. Industry responded accordingly, especially during the 1820s. Already Eli Whitney had invented the cotton gin and produced a musket with interchangeable parts. In Connecticut this method of production gave impetus to the flourishing clock industry of Eli Terry and the founding of Lambert Hitchcock's chair factory, America's first furniture factory. The creation of the city of Lowell in the twenties by one firm marked the amazing progress of the textile industry in New England.

Although we have designated the Federal as a relatively conservative period, nevertheless, when comparing the decorative arts of the beginning of the period with those of the end one notices significant changes. In the earlier work, one feels strongly the rectangularity formed by the horizontal and vertical members, relieved by delicate oval or shield forms. In the later, the rounded forms of the circle and column predominate, and curves often become bold. Outlines become more closed, and there is a noticeable trend away from the tectonic

[1] *Reports of Artisans,* London, 1867, part II, pp. 97–98.
[2] *Ibid.,* part II, p. 208.

toward a flowing, more organic organization. The use of mouldings differs: in the early part of this period they tend to frame areas and mark terminations of structural parts; in the later they frequently appear on surfaces which seem to continue under them. The delicately carved relief and flush inlays cede to bolder carving often applied above a smooth surface with which it contrasts. Ormolu is also used with similar effect.

Recurrent British influence is called to mind by the application of the terms "Hepplewhite" and "Sheraton" to many works of the Federal period—for example, the side chair by Duncan Phyfe. On the other hand the later "Recamier" sofa by Phyfe illustrates a growing French influence which made the "Empire" style of furnishings fitting accompaniments to our Greek revival homes of the twenties and thirties. The pier table (Brooklyn Museum, c. 1830) with its strong, architectural forms and the lyre clock (Brooklyn Museum, c. 1830) of freer, more decorative design exemplify the two poles of the fully developed "Empire" style.

The boldness and sureness of the American temperament appears most strikingly in works which are relatively free from the influence of European styles, such as a mahogany dining table (New-York Historical Society, c. 1810–1825), a teapot by Najah Taylor, a glass sugar bowl (Brooklyn Museum, c. 1825), and an earthenware jar (Brooklyn Museum, early nineteenth century). Although the handicraft tradition was dying out, these pieces, like the production of the Shakers, show that its products were not necessarily decadent in quality.

The Romantic-Eclectic period in America was an era of boisterous growth on all sides. Immigrants, Irish and Germans, poured into our Eastern ports where many found work in a variety of growing industries. Others pushed on to settle in the Mississippi Valley via the Erie Canal and in the 1840s by the network of railways which constantly reached farther west. The fur trade and the discovery of gold in California and the Rockies stimulated American settlement of the Far West. In commerce and in the mines fortunes were made almost overnight and often lost as quickly in brief but bitter depressions.

In the South, however, the Neoclassical period brought no industrial revolution. There princely fortunes were founded on cotton and slaves. The planters had little commerce with the North and even less sympathy with Northern ideals and interests. The contrast between Northern and Southern ways of life was no greater than many other contrasts: between reason and romanticism, between the worship of tradition and the

daring innovations of the day. It was an age of imagination and inspiration with its Poe and its Emerson. It was an age which produced a P. T. Barnum and an Abraham Lincoln.

As in the life of the times, so too in the art, contrast and diversity reigned. The hegemony of classical inspiration and the corresponding rule of taste did not go unchallenged even at its height. Gothic motives appeared in furniture and ceramics. Classic forms continued, sometimes so transformed, as in the pressed-glass dolphin candlestick (Metropolitan Museum, c. 1840), that one scarcely remembers the classical source. But the dominant revival was the rococo, admirably handled by Samuel Kirk in a teapot as early as 1828 (Brooklyn Museum, 1828). Critics of the age felt that somehow taste had vanished. Fenimore Cooper lamented that everyone thought he was a connoisseur. Reformers offered solutions to correct the situation: teach art in the schools; organize exhibitions; establish museums; study the history of art; and—in a more practical measure—go directly to nature for models of structure and ornament. The silver goblet by Hayden Brothers (New-York Historical Society, c. 1853) is an illustration of the naïve but tasteful turning to nature for ornament. From the organic, structural lessons learned from nature—which Horatio Greenough recognized in ships like the clipper *Nightingale*—came the spring iron rocking chair of Peter Cooper (Cooper Union, c. 1860), a type well adapted for factory production. But the factories found it more profitable to turn out imitations in the historical styles. Often the chief distinction between the cheap and the more expensive factory products was the amount and richness of ornament added to the basic forms. Craftsmen, such as Belter in furniture and William Gale in silver, continued to work at a high level of proficiency to fulfill the demands of a wealthy patronage.

During the thirties the stylistic trend of the late Federal period continued strongly even when clothed in Gothic trappings. At the same time, novel stylistic factors were generated under the influence of European imports of the rococo. By 1845 the rococo had gained an ascendancy which it maintained undisputed until the Civil War. Major stylistic changes were inevitable as the exuberant and fanciful motives of the style of Louis XV were adapted to modern needs, new materials, and factory production.

The S-curves of the end of the Federal period had prepared the way for the undulating lines of the new style, which also introduced a more organic relationship of parts to the whole. The raised ornament of the twenties became more raised, often even knobby, and much more profuse. In cheaper furniture, mouldings and other carved parts were machine-made and then sold to furniture makers, who glued them on.

Compared to the Federal style, forms became taller and thinner. Often a rather bulky mass rested on seemingly fragile legs. Somewhat masked by rich rococo motives with lacy perforations and projections was a strong predilection for the circular and even for closed outlines. The reverse curves were much more rounded than in eighteenth-century rococo. Exact symmetry was the rule. The most significant changes were greater slenderness, more ornament, including a multiplication of mouldings, and much rougher surfaces, often almost knobby. In flat designs this rough surface effect was achieved by pronounced shading and the use of perspective.

Color changes are so difficult to describe that only a brief statement must suffice. Ordinarily the Federal period scheme was to oppose fairly broad areas of pronounced value contrast, for example, dark brown and gold or green and white, as seen in such works as the console table attributed to Lannuier (Museum of City of New York, c. 1815–1820) or the bed carpet (Metropolitan Museum, 1809). By 1850, general effects were warmer and livelier. Tones of almost equal value, in small areas, create what might be called harmonious vibration. This is seen in the Ketterlinus calendar for 1855 (New-York Historical Society, see Visual Communications) and in the decoration of fire engines and sewing machines. In home furnishings a deep red often predominated, played off against green, gold, or brown.

The Early Victorian period in the United States actually began during the Civil War, when the production of decorative arts was limited. From about 1860 to 1867 the rococo of the previous period continued but some clear changes occurred. In color, somber tones of gray and brown took over. Forms became strongly rounded and surfaces smoother as the favorite Louis XV gave way to a classical compound of Empire, Renaissance, and baroque features.

The Civil War, as subsequent wars have done, accelerated technological developments. By 1867 the craft tradition was moribund even amongst the Pennsylvania Dutch and the Bishop Hill colonists. Factories continued to copy, or modify, handmade models from abroad or earlier times. But more and more the manufacturers, spurred on by the popular success of Charles Eastlake's *Hints on Household Taste,* turned to idioms of design which had been worked out specifically for machine production or which were inspired by the designs of machinery. The appreciation of the beauty of well-designed machines became widespread. The evi-

dence for this awareness is to be found in the literature of the World Fairs of 1867 (Paris) and 1876 (Philadelphia). But much more potent is the inarticulate evidence of the facts: first, machinery exhibits became increasingly attractive to visitors; and secondly, an understanding of the idea that "every force has its own form" led more and more to the elimination of ornament on machines and implements.

The much maligned "Eastlake Style" was a popularization of a kind of design, based on the soundest of principles, developed primarily by the School of Design in London under Henry Cole. Imported objects of the new design were certainly known long before 1872, when Eastlake's book was first published in this country. That they had affected our design is apparent in the decoration of the silver tea kettle made by Tiffany and Co. (New-York Historical Society), for presentation to the victorious yacht *Mallory* in 1862.

By about 1875 one could recognize that a new style had fully matured. Angles replaced the sinuous curves of the Romantic-Eclectic period. Designs were sometimes of simple geometric form, but more often they were a complicated combination of rectangles, acute angles, and segments of circles. Outlines were open. Asymmetry appeared, but symmetry was the rule and it was usually strongly marked. Decoration consisted of a multiplicity of small devices—stripes, diagonals, chevrons, imbrications, curls, crosses, stars, snowflakes, and desiccated flowers—which were framed in bands, rectangles, diamonds, circles, or quatrefoils. A favorite device was the V-shaped trident. Two-dimensional designs, like textiles, were flat in effect. Carving was often incised, and painted decoration was usually in silhouette without modeling or shadows. Various historical styles supplied motives, but the greatest number came from the Gothic. The Islamic and Neo-Greek were frequent substyles, and Japanese forms appeared occasionally.

In color, the grays and browns of the sixties ceded about 1870 to pastels, light neutral tones, and gold, only to be superseded about five years later by a striking use of intense colors. While walnut was the favorite wood for furniture in the sixties, light oak, often unvarnished, and maple were characteristic in the seventies. Especially in the exhibits of the Centennial Exposition of 1876 one feels the affirmation of a new confidence in the might and permanency of America in the boldness of color and decoration of the wallpaper, textiles, and jewelry, and in the strong, unashamedly utilitarian, and yet elegant, design of machines and vehicles.

Largely under the influence of British precedent, the decade of the seventies was a period when the American people became very conscious of design. Art museums began to be established and publications on art, especially in periodical form, became numerous for the first time. Practical books on how to furnish a home appeared. Textbooks for teaching design in the lower grades were published. These activities plus the great admiration for the British crafts exhibits at Philadelphia in 1876 prepared the way for developments in the succeeding period.

The achievement of the Late Victorian period may be looked on as a consummation of the entire Victorian era, for it realized the dream of a half century, the development of an original style, free—or almost free—of historical borrowing. The theories of design formulated under the Romantic-Eclectic movement, their courageous application in the Early Victorian period, at last bore their fruit.

The progress of the Arts and Crafts movement and the success of schools of design such as the Cooper Institute, made available a goodly number of artist-designers who knew the materials and processes of manufacture. This is seen in such ceramics as the Rookwood glazed earthenware vase (Brooklyn Museum, 1887) and the white earthenware vase from the Middle Lane potteries (Brooklyn Museum, 1890). The same spirit produced the woven silks of Mrs. Candace Wheeler (Metropolitan Museum, 1883–1887), unique examples of "art glass," and highly novel designs for wallpaper.

The ruling stylistic features of the eighties bring to mind the architecture of H. H. Richardson and the early work of Sullivan. Circles, spheres, and domes complemented weight-giving horizontals. Outlines became closed. Ornament, often of textural effect, tended to cover completely the simple, geometric forms without the petty subdivisions of the seventies. Surfaces often were actually textured. Colors were strong, with dark greens, browns, and autumnal shades prevailing. Dark finished woods, usually unvarnished, were much used in furniture.

In the nineties the stylistic tendencies of the previous decade tended to branch in two directions which are well known to students of architecture. In one, that which paralleled the dominant trend of the Columbian Exposition of 1893, the classic prevailed. In the other, the parallel was with the nonhistorical Art Nouveau. The stylistic characteristics of the classic are fairly obvi-

ous. Those of the more original new style emphasized the slenderness of the upright rectangle and the sinuosity of thickening and thinning reverse curves to produce lightness and nervous movement. Forms were generally closed and with crisp outlines. Surfaces tended to be smooth, shadows minimized. Occult balance, which had appeared in the Early Victorian under Japanese influence, was frequent. The adoption of other oriental devices which naturally followed is seen in the ceramic and glass vessels of the time. Decorative motives abstracted from nature often occur, notably marsh grass, iris, various species of lilies, and peacocks. Seemingly accidental forms, similar to shapes seen in the paintings of Paul Gauguin, were repeated in bands or diaper patterns. L. C. Tiffany employed controlled accidental effects in his Favrile glass bowls and vases at the turn of the century. Exotic color schemes remind one that the sobriquets of the nineties were "the Yellow Decade" and "the Mauve Decade."

No century has witnessed a greater change in the way of life than the nineteenth. Developments in the natural sciences, followed by the application of those developments in industry and transportation, changed the United States of America from a small predominantly agricultural nation, essentially colonial in outlook, to a continental empire of fantastic energy and productivity.

This change is reflected in the decorative arts. At the beginning of the nineteenth century they were the products of shop or home craftsmen who used techniques, tools, and materials that differed little from those of the Greeks and Romans. By the middle of the century the same types of wares were being produced by steam-powered machines in factories. The general aim was to reproduce the effect of handmade objects. By the end of the century the handicrafts were revived, some, like the silks of Mrs. Wheeler or the glass of L. C. Tiffany, to supply an elite market and some to be pursued primarily as hobbies in the home. The decorative arts for the great market, however, were machine-made. All too often the market and the machine operated to the detriment of design, but this was not always true. Sometimes good handicraft designs influenced commercial production, and a combination of new materials, a new mastery of old materials, and an understanding of the limitations and capacities of machines began to pave the way for a new era.

DESIGN AND DECORATIVE ARTS OF THE
TWENTIETH CENTURY

WILLIAM FRIEDMAN

Five major forces have contributed directly to the complex structure of twentieth century American design: (1) our own indigenous vernacular tradition, (2) the Arts and Crafts movement, (3) late nineteenth-century mechanical invention, engineering, and architecture, (4) Art Nouveau, (5) abstract painting and sculpture. With these should be mentioned four additional elements that have an important place in the morphology of modern design: (6) exotic, archaic, and primitive arts, (7) machine-age rationalism (*Die Neue Sachlichkeit*), (8) large-scale production and expanded markets, (9) contemporary work abroad.

At times the best aspects of all these forces are to be found fused into a relatively harmonious system of design thought and practice. Otherwise, for the most part, they have operated separately (or only in a partial synthesis) in a conflicting, and often confused, coexistence.

Tremendous activity in mechanical invention, significant developments in engineering and architecture—paralleled by the ethical zeal of the Arts and Crafts movement—were the legacy of the last half of the nineteenth century. These, in turn, were distilled, further developed, and enriched by abstract painting and sculpture from 1910 on, by *de Stijl,* Constructivism, and *Die Neue Sachlichkeit* of post-World War I Holland, Russia, and Germany—plus our own special brand of Yankee invention and ingenuity.

Less constant and continuous than these movements, turn-of-the-century Art Nouveau has nevertheless maintained an influence on the thinking of many designers and craftsmen during the past twenty-odd years. And not to be excluded in any discussion of significant forces that have been at work influencing and shaping our design consciousness are, first, the aesthetic principles and products of Oriental and other exotic cultures, especially Japanese; second, primitive cultures of every continent; and third, archaic cultures of many peoples, including the pre-Columbian of this hemisphere during their early and middle periods.

It has been stated often that modern American life is dominated by the automobile, radio and TV, the refrigerator, the washing machine, and numerous other labor-saving appliances. The roots of this present-day gadget consciousness are to be found in our mechanical inventiveness just prior to the turn of the century. In the little more than twenty years between 1893 and 1914, the type-form prototypes were established for the automobile, the airplane, the washing machine and vacuum cleaner, modern plumbing, the electric light, the phonograph, the typewriter, and the safety razor.

For the last thirteen years of that twenty-year period (1901–1914), a minor revolution in the taste of furniture and home furnishings took place—only to lose its vigor in the end. This revolution against nineteenth century overstuffiness and clutter—our version of England's Arts and Crafts movement—was led by two American disciples of William Morris: Gustav Stickley and Elbert Hubbard. Both these men were Midwesterners who had moved east to settle in upstate New York. Stickley left his native Wisconsin in 1884, while in his mid-thirties, to establish a furniture factory in Binghamton. Hubbard, from Illinois, started as a soap salesman and, with a small fortune accumulated from his business success, subsequently established his Roycrofters Press in East Aurora in 1895. Here he soon began to publish his leather-bound tracts and a magazine, *The Philistine,* which eventually achieved a circulation around 1910 of a quarter-million copies. Stickley established *The Craftsman* magazine in 1901 and later opened a showroom in New York City for the display and sale of his Craftsman furniture and home furnishings. Subsequently, his entire organization moved to New York City.

Stickley was fired with a missionary zeal to provide the working class, farm, and even middle class population with "sensible, honest, sturdy" furniture in "wholesome" Craftsman homes, based on "the big fundamental principles of honesty, simplicity, and usefulness." By 1909 several dozen large stores all over the country, including Marshall Field's in Chicago, were selling Craftsman furniture made of the characteristic dark-brown fumed oak and upholstered in black leather.

Heavy in appearance and massive without much grace, the furniture was in sharp contrast to the prevailing ornate, overstuffed articles otherwise available to the public of that and the previous generation. Spurred by Stickley's success, other manufacturers—with less lofty motives—joined the band wagon. Soon the country's retail stores and mail-order houses were flooded with "Mission" furniture as it was labeled. (The name derived from the Spanish missions of California whose furniture was supposed to have provided the design inspiration for Stickley.) Actually, this furniture represented a Grand Rapids' version of Spanish Mission furniture fused with rugged New England colonial, indigenous frontier American, Shaker, a touch of Frank Lloyd Wright, as well as of Stickley, and the English Arts and Crafts (Morris, Mackintosh, Voysey).

At this period, one development in furniture occurred that was to have far-reaching influence. This was the sectional unit bookcase produced by Globe–Wernicke of Cincinnati. Advertised nationally, by 1908 these units were stocked by 1,500 distributors in every part of the United States. The units were less heavy than most of the "Mission" furniture and were made in woods other than oak. The fronts had disappearing sliding doors of leaded glass.

By 1910 the "unit" idea was picked up by the Germans, who brought it to a high degree of development in case goods, shelves, and the like—as did the English considerably later. Unit or modular furniture, in the meantime, was forgotten here for a long period and was not revived in the furniture industry on any serious scale until after the end of World War II.

Trailing somewhat later in the footsteps of the revolution in the living room, library, and bedroom was an equally vigorous movement toward "cleaning up" the kitchen and the bathroom. The popularization of tile and other hygienic surfaces for walls and counter tops, the elimination of dirt-collecting spaces under sinks and bath tubs through the device of the "built-in" fixture, all this altered the functioning and appearance of these utility rooms by the time of the boom years following the close of World War I.

The average consumer was beginning to gain some confidence in the mechanical and visual rightness of those things that were relatively new in his environment. Articles that were not in existence prior to 1876—the telephone, the phonograph, the automobile (once it outgrew the horseless carriage stage), the electric light, the airplane—developed a design rationale of their own. There were no style precedents to follow. In the office, in the store, a new visual vocabulary was being estab-

lished, in everything from typewriters, adding machines, and dictaphones to cash registers, weighing scales, and coffee grinders.

Now, it is noteworthy that practically all these manufactured articles were of anonymous design. It is true that some so-called "art wares" were name-designed. But, in the years prior to World War I, most of these designer-craftsmen were not known to the general public. The followers of these men were, for the most part, mainly the members of the various Arts and Crafts societies around the country.

One person, however, was a household name, especially in the large urban centers of population. He was Louis Comfort Tiffany. The son of the founder of Tiffany and Company in New York, he was equally at home abroad and in the United States. At the turn of the century he was the major American link with the Art Nouveau movement in Europe, into which he entered with a great amount of creative energy. His glass and metal products—vases, bowls, lamps, and cigarette boxes—were sold in fine stores from Newark to Santa Barbara and at Maison Bing in Paris. In America his glass and lamps were merchandised side by side with Craftsman furniture, Rookwood pottery, and Lenox china.

The two movements that did concern themselves with the aesthetic problem—Arts and Crafts and Art Nouveau—did not attempt to come to grips with the machine. Both Stickley's and Tiffany's approach to design was that of the handcraftsman. Those articles that were machine-made—automobiles, kitchen sinks, and household appliances—were aesthetically unself-conscious. Whatever beauty they might possess was an unplanned by-product of doing a thing "right." In strictly mechanical things, Yankee ingenuity and skill operated with a great deal of sensitivity to the visual and tactile aspects of form. Take, for instance, the water-supply valve manufactured by the Eastwood Manufacturing Company of Belleville, New Jersey. In their advertisement in the *Hardware Dealers Magazine* for February, 1898, they were as proud of the valve handle as they were of the valve itself and its mechanical features: "Examine the handle which is also patented." And their pride was justified by their honest concern with the "feel" of the valve handle in the hand. This attention given to such refinements of detail anticipated by some forty years the pioneering work of Thomas Lamb in problems of handle design.

In the midst of the flounderings of Art Nouveau, which, in the United States, had a limited and somewhat esoteric appeal, and the gropings of the Arts and Crafts, which was making its appeal to the common man, in

Chicago in 1902 the then thirty-two year old Frank Lloyd Wright called upon Americans to understand the machine and its potentials for creating products of artistic merit. His words were an anticipation of the place the artist would assume in industry; in twenty-five years there would emerge a new professional, the industrial designer.

. . . [Artists'] tools today are processes and machines where they were once but a hammer or a gouge, as the artist is more the leader of an orchestra in which he was once a soloist. Is it not more likely that the medium of artistic expression itself has changed and broadened until a new definition and a new direction must be given the art activity of the future, and that the machine has finally made for the artist, whether he will own it yet or not, a splendid distinction between the art of old and art to come? A distinction made by the tool which frees human labor, lengthens and broadens the life of the simplest man and thereby the basis of the democracy upon which we insist.

Americans have, historically, suffered from a sense of inferiority with regard to matters of art, architecture, and design. They have sought aesthetic inspiration and satisfaction from the cultivated tradition of Europe, while neglecting to recognize the merit of things created right in their own backyard. Usually after a lag of one or two generations, however, Americans do come to appreciate those of their native geniuses whom they had discarded earlier after only a brief contact—Sullivan, Wright, Stickley, to mention a few.

The period from 1914 to 1925 was one of eclecticism in architecture, home furnishings, and the decorative arts. But, by the mid-twenties American architects and designers, as well as students who had gone abroad to study, began to return home with new stimuli. They had come in contact with Le Corbusier and the Bauhaus, with Constructivism, *de Stijl,* and other forms of abstract painting and sculpture.

In 1925, with the impact of l'Exposition International des Arts Decoratifs in Paris, American manufacturers could no longer ignore "modern" design. And five years later the Stockholm Exhibition was to exert a most forceful and telling influence on the thinking of American architects, designers, and teachers. "Modern" was definitely here to stay. This was certainly reflected in the buildings of the Chicago Century of Science and Progress Exposition of 1933 and in the products exhibited there. We may add to this the experiences of the Paris World's Fair in 1937 so that, by the time of the New York World's Fair in 1939–1940 on the eve of World War II, the design revolution was complete and irrevocable. The circle was closed, even though it had

had to make many spiral convolutions. Messrs. Sullivan, Wright, and Stickley had come home.

It should not be inferred from the foregoing, however, that the design revolution affected all levels of the population. There was, and still is, a tremendous resistance to modern design on the part of the majority of American families. The prevailing taste in the fifteen years from 1925 to 1940 was still eclectic. Reproductions of the past periods were favored, especially in furniture and home furnishings. And even worse, superficial clichés were incorporated indiscriminately in furniture and fixtures, resulting in *modernistic* skyscraper bookshelves and bulbous overstuffed *modernoid* couches and the like.

And yet, with the perspective of even a few decades, one cannot fail to be impressed with the work and vigor of those few designers and manufacturers who spearheaded the design revolution of the late twenties and through the thirties. Noteworthy among these were Buckminster Fuller with his Dymaxion house and subsequent prefabricated bathroom for the Phelps–Dodge Corporation; Percival Goodman and his interiors, special furniture, and fixtures for numerous department stores; Gilbert Rohde's furniture for Kroehler, Heywood Wakefield, Howell, Troy Sunshade, and Herman Miller; Edward Wormley's furniture for Dunbar; Russel Wright's dinnerware for Steubenville Pottery Company, his aluminum accessories and his experimental furniture for various manufacturers; George Sakier's bathroom fixtures for Standard Sanitary–American Radiator Corporation and his glassware for Fostoria; Henry Dreyfuss's refrigerator design for General Electric and his work on the development of the telephone handset instrument in collaboration with the Bell Telephone Laboratories; Archibald Welden's cooking utensils for the Revere Copper and Brass Company; as well as the work of Kem Weber, Jo Sinel, Walter Dorwin Teague, Harold Van Doren, Lurelle V. A. Guild, Raymond Loewy, Kurt Versen, and Walter Von Nessen in the development of a variety of industrial and household products.

Although working principally in the field of architecture, Richard Neutra of California has exerted an important influence on thinking and practice in the design of interiors, furniture, and household equipment. His book, *Survival through Design,* is a contribution to the understanding of biological and psychological problems in design.

Two important events in design education took place in the mid-thirties: the establishment of the Laboratory School of Design in New York and of the New Bauhaus (later renamed the Institute of Design) in Chicago.

These and other educational institutions were enriched by the arrival from abroad of Frederick Kiesler, Eliel Saarinen, Mies van der Rohe, Walter Gropius, L. Moholy-Nagy, Marcel Breuer, Josef Albers, Hilde Reiss, Antonin Heythum, and Serge Chermayeff, whose work was an immediate stimulus to the younger generation of native-born designers.

The museums of the United States are replete with the artifacts of many cultures, ancient and modern. These include painting and sculpture of the twentieth century, European and American. When it comes to American design and decorative arts since 1900, however, these are the stepchildren of the collecting world. Although it is true that a few of our art museums contain some handmade and manufactured articles of the twentieth century, the present study has brought into focus the sad neglect of this important phase of American creative activity.

This weakness in actual collecting and preservation was compensated for, at an early date, by the staging of loan exhibitions of crafts, architecture, and manufactured products. The pioneer in this activity was the Newark Library and Museum under the direction of the late John Cotton Dana who, in the years prior to World War I, held exhibitions of the ceramic wares of the State of New Jersey—bathroom fixtures, dinnerware, and building materials—of articles selected by the German *Werkbund,* and the like, an activity that has continued for almost fifty years.

Soon after the end of World War I, the Metropolitan Museum of Art in New York staged the first of an extensive series of exhibitions on architecture and design under the direction of Richard Bach with the cooperation of designers and manufacturers. Important exhibitions were held through the following years at the Philadelphia Art Alliance and at the Architectural League of New York. In 1934 the Museum of Modern Art in New York held its exhibition, Machine Art, which was assembled by Philip Johnson. This was followed at the Museum by a number of exhibitions of well-designed articles under the direction of John McAndrew and Eliot Noyes. These were augmented later by a separate program of Good Design shows staged by Edgar Kaufmann at the Merchandise Mart of Chicago. As a result of this unique relationship between a museum and a trade center, the Good Design program exerted an important educational influence on consumers, manufacturers, and retailers alike. The first museum in the United States to set aside permanent gallery space for contemporary design exhibitions was the Walker Art Center in Minneapolis, which formally established its Design program in 1944 under the direction of D. S.

Defenbacher, William Friedman, and Hilde Reiss. As part of this program, the Center constructed the second of its Idea Houses in 1947 on the grounds of the museum—the first house having been built and open for public view as early as 1941. Since then, art museums throughout the country have taken an active part in creating an understanding and acceptance of modern design by the American consumer.

The wide disparity in design quality of the products of contemporary craftsmen and industry can best be understood if we consider the diversity of the forces motivating those who are responsible for this tremendous output of production.

Well over fifty per cent of the things produced today are of poor quality: shoddy in craftsmanship, deficient in performance by youth or middle age of their life, and low in appearance value. The things of excellence are estimated to constitute an average of five per cent of the total volume of American production—in some categories as low as one-tenth of one per cent (lighting fixtures), in others as high as fifteen to twenty per cent (fabrics).

Built-in obsolescence, regrettably, is still the guiding principle in much production. Things must wear out as a result of poor workmanship. And, furthermore, things must wear out not only with respect to the durability of materials but also in terms of durability of appearance. The automobile is a good case in point; here is to be found the clue to the constant change in so many contemporary products for no technically justifiable cause but for the sake of change itself. The designs for so many good products—designs possessing some potential for refinement and improvement—are not given a chance. They are discarded much too soon to make way for newer and ever newer yearly models based upon superficial changes in "style."

One notable exception to this practice is the ordinary desk telephone. It occupies a unique position in the paraphernalia of contemporary American life. The telephone for home or office is the one consumer product that cannot be purchased. Its design is carefully controlled; only one model, duplicated by the millions (alike for laborer and tycoon), is obtainable with only the choice of a few available colors. This product is a striking example of excellence of design achieved without the wastefulness inherent in changing models every year. As Wallance points out in his book, *Shaping America's Products,* an extraordinary amount of research and study goes into the human engineering (psychophysical), as well as into the technical, production, and appearance aspects of the problem of telephone design. All of this is part of a continuing program of collaboration since 1930 between the Henry Dreyfuss design organization and the engineers and technicians of the Bell Telephone Laboratories. In the past fifty-odd years, there have been only five new models of the desk telephone: 1900, 1914, 1927, 1937, 1950.

There are numerous other instances in which manufacturers and designers today work in harmonious collaboration to produce articles of high quality. Many of these articles, such as chairs, lamps, fabrics, and dinnerware, have been in continuous production anywhere from five to twenty years or more. They have been undergoing a steady process of refinement in quality of materials as well as form, and well may be termed the "classics" of modern design.

The young designer-architects Charles Eames and Eero Saarinen, in 1940, designed some lightweight chairs of moulded laminated wood and sectional "unit" furniture that were awarded prizes that year in the Organic Design Competition of the Museum of Modern Art. Experimentation with production methods during the war years, as well as further refinements in form, resulted in the production of new Eames chairs, tables, and cabinets by Evans Products Company in 1945 and subsequently by the Herman Miller Furniture Company, which still produces them. Saarinen's further studies have resulted in the moulded plastic-shell chair covered with latex and upholstered in fabric that has been manufactured by Knoll Associates since 1948.

It is not possible to catalogue here all the things of merit that have been produced since the close of World War II. The collection of slides is, in a sense, an illustrated digest version of such a catalog. The United States need not feel inferior at all about the design of the products it makes. The designer-craftsman in small-scale studio production, and designers in collaboration with manufacturers in large-scale factory production—together with an increasingly informed consuming public—are well on the way to sharing in the benefits of their collective endeavors.

COSTUME DESIGN

LUCY BARTON

Everything connected with the early settlers of America was immigratory, including their dress. The colonists continued to depend on the Old World for whatever they wore, importing either complete garments or materials until such time as they were able to grow, spin, and weave for themselves. Even then they always imported luxury materials and current styles. In fact, this country never ceased to accept the dictates of Europe as to fashion. What then does a survey of dress in America turn out to be? It is neither a history of the craft of garment making in the New World nor a carbon copy of the history of costume in the Old. What is significant in American clothes is the way in which they reflect the changing world of these transplanted Europeans, from their first frontier existence where only the simplest necessities of clothing were made by the housewife, for everything else had come over with her or had been ordered later from "home," to present-day America where she can, if she chooses, buy everything from a department store or mail-order house "made in America by Americans."

In the years between, the arts of tailor and dressmaker flourished in American cities and were cultivated assiduously, if not so adroitly, on farm and plantation. Domestic craftsmen did their very best in the face of limitations in materials and remoteness from the centers of fashion; for to the wearer and his or her contemporaries a garment was beautiful and satisfying in proportion as it conformed to the current mode in fabric, cut, finishing, and ornamentation.

To return to beginnings: the aborigines whom our ancestors found when they came to these shores were clothed sufficiently to meet European standards of decency. But neither the Indians nor their garments were destined to play more than a minor part in the development of the New World. The colonists, still tied to the Old World, took over from the Indians only such elements as experience showed to be more practical than those which they already had. The most obvious was the moccasin, a practical footwear for both sexes, being as well suited to a woman's chores in a rough country as to a man's.

How much else colonial wives adopted from squaw dress is uncertain, but probably not very much, since their desire was always to look like women across the ocean. In this respect, it is ironic that the one authentic portrait of our one authentic American princess, Pocahontas, who became the Lady Rebekah, shows her in the costume of a gentlewoman in the reign of James I.

The woods Indians whom the early settlers encountered along the Atlantic seaboard were clad in skins, always the earliest material to be fashioned by human ingenuity into wearing apparel. Thus to the newcomers, who were not yet equipped to manufacture their own textiles, leather became extremely important. Because the men led more venturesome lives than their womenfolk, they found considerable use for Indian garments, particularly the leggings. Such borrowings as they made in the early eighteenth century are recorded in written accounts. There are few pictures. Since nobody would take pride in wearing quasi-Indian garb, an Englishman who sat for his portrait thus attired must have had a special reason for so doing. A portrait of Colonel Guy Johnson of the British Army, for instance, shows him in uniform with distinctive details connecting him with the Indians whom he led against the inhabitants of upper New York State. With his red military coat and his buff waistcoat and breeches he wears the cuffed and beaded moccasins of the woods Indian, a baldric apparently of wampum, such as the one of the Indian who stands behind him, an Indian blanket, and a headpiece (carried) of shovel shape adorned with an upright cluster of feathers. It would seem that his dress was intended to flatter his savage allies.

In connection with leather, a "truly native material," it is worthwhile to note how patriots turned to it in the last years before the struggle with England. This resulted primarily as a protest against the duties laid on woven fabrics.[1]

A very great number of the respectable tradesmen of this Town have come to a resolution to wear nothing but

[1] George F. Dow, *The Arts and Crafts of New England, 1704–1775,* The Wayside Press, Topsfield, Massachusetts, 1927, p. 183.

Leather for their Working Habit for the future, and that to be only of the manufacture of this Government.

Boston Gazette, September 24, 1764

In the next issue of the *Gazette* is the advertisement:

Adam Colson, near the Great Trees at the South End, dresses all Sorts of Skins suitable for the purpose above mentioned in the neatest and genteelist manner. . . . It is worth observing that a jacket made of Moos skin, fit for Apprentices, will wear out at least seven jackets made of Broad Cloth, and will wear handsome to the end.

Indian-inspired dress became the common garb of the white hunter and backwoodsman of the nineteenth century, heroes who are often recorded in romantic pictures of the frontier. Such is the garb of Daniel Boone as shown in Bingham's *Daniel Boone Escorting a Band of Pioneers* (City Art Museum of St. Louis), Davy Crockett, and other frontiersmen who have become part of the American legend.

The Indians, whose dress is covered in greater detail in the American Indian section of this study, were regarded as enemies by the Army and the pioneers. To white men and women their appearance was fearful But the Indian peril passed, and eventually war bonnets and tomahawks became the play-dress of many small boys. The beautiful original dress of the Pueblo Indians—still to be seen in museums and where ritual dances are performed—was not borrowed or adapted by the first Europeans in the Southwest; they kept their own Spanish costume, generally in the simple, peasant version. It remained for twentieth-century Americans to discover Indian art and find inspiration for personal adornment in its motifs.

During the eighteenth century, the nineteenth, and a part of the twentieth there were two ways of dressing, the urban and the rural. Backwoods folk, willy-nilly, adapted themselves to their environment and made use of materials at hand. Not so those colonials who dwelt in the coastal towns. They were hardly to be distinguished from their contemporaries in the Old World. Nevertheless, there was always a time lag in fashion. With the infrequent ship sailings and the long, slow crossing, styles newly introduced to Boston or New York had already become a little outmoded in London.

Naturally enough visual records of clothes worn by the colonists of the seventeenth and eighteenth centuries are restricted to the dress of the well to do: merchants of the seacoast and their ladies, and the plantation gentry of Maryland and Virginia.

Not always did the prosperous import their garments ready-made, although such merchandise is advertised in the newspapers from rather early in the 1700s. Luxury fabrics were of course brought over, but they were made up by local tailors, dressmakers, or the housewife herself. The portraits and the actual garments that have been chosen for this study bear witness to the skill of the craftsman, but at the same time they exhibit a touch of the provincial, a suggestion of the "country dressmaker." How much more chic are actual dresses of known European provenance and the apparel depicted by French and English portraitists of the same years! In American examples the details are much simpler and the handling not so clever. They could readily have been made at home or by one of those dressmakers (always "lately from London") who advertised in the New York and Boston papers. Such an advertisement, dated 1752, reads:[2]

Mary Wallace and Clementina Ferguson, just arrived from the Kingdom of Ireland, intend to follow the business of mantua-making, and have furnished themselves in London in patterns of the following kinds of wear . . .

The anonymous portrait of Thomas Van Alstyne (New-York Historical Society) shows him in a suit which was probably made about 1721, when the picture was painted. The fabric may have been imported, but there is every reason to assume that the suit itself was made-up right in the colonies. Tailors were numerous in cities like New York by the middle of the century, and they must have been flourishing during the first quarter.

Occasionally a costume will show certain local characteristics that retain some flavor of national origin. Noteworthy in this respect is the costume in the portrait of the girl said to be Magdalena Douw of Albany, painted about 1729 (Henry Francis duPont Winterthur Museum). She is wearing a sack-backed gown of rich brocade—imported of course—made in the usual eighteenth-century style, but the gown is considerably shorter in the skirt than gowns of young ladies in Europe. Her hair falls on her shoulders. The Dutch cap she is wearing would never have been seen on a Boston girl of the same date. Her impressive red shoes are a rather clumsy version of the current style in footwear; they may well have been cobbled in Albany, for shoemakers are among the earliest craftsmen recorded as working in the colonies.

Fashions in dress may often be read more accurately from a painting than from an actual garment. A portrait

[2] Esther Singleton, *Social New York under the Georges, 1714–1776*, D. Appleton & Company, Inc., New York, 1902, p. 237.

tends to epitomize a style, simply because both sitter and artist want the subject to look as modish as possible. Therefore fashionable portraits, just as fashion plates, tend to present the current ideal of beauty better than an actual garment which has had to be fitted to the wearer's figure, often less than ideal. Perhaps that is why ladies and gentlemen of Boston's wealthy merchant class, when painted by John Singleton Copley in mid-eighteenth century, look every bit as perfectly turned out as their contemporaries in England. Mr. and Mrs. Thomas Mifflin, as seen in Copley's superb portrait (Historical Society of Pennsylvania) would have been perfectly well dressed for the society of either London or Paris. A century and a quarter later the portraits of John Singer Sargent similarly set forth the fashionable ideal. In 1897 a young society couple, Mr. and Mrs. Isaac Newton Phelps Stokes (Metropolitan Museum of Art), are posing for Sargent. But here is something new; they are wearing tennis costume instead of the formal ball attire traditional for portraits. Sargent himself painted many such, but here he is recording quite a different fashion ideal for a different age—the informal shirtwaist look. Every young man and woman in America with leisure to pursue outdoor interests would aim at such smartness.

At the same time that painters were recording the latest modes with their current extravagances they also had for sitters members of that quiet, conservative, but prosperous group, the Quakers. Portraits of Quaker women show even more clearly than do surviving dresses a characteristic which is often remarked on by writers: although the Friends' dress was simple and in color subdued, the fabric was rich and the dressmaking exquisite. Consider the Hesselius portrait of Mrs. Richard Galloway (Metropolitan Museum of Art), a Quaker lady of the eighteenth century, or the unsigned portrait of Mrs. Joseph Wing of Cape Cod (Sandwich Historical Museum) in the early nineteenth. According to Gummere[3] the essentials of Quaker dress changed only in the fundamental shape: from tight bodice and bell skirt, to high waist and slim skirt, and back again to the bell shape. Certainly it is the cut of the shoulder seams and the shape of the sleeve that dates Mrs. Wing's dress as of the 1830s. These dresses are typical. They are elegantly cut in the current mode from rich silks in subdued tones and accompanied by a delicate and modest fichu and a cap of sheerest lawn. Quaker women laid stress on neatness and decorum in dress as well as in conduct.

The appearance of Quaker men is familiar to us

[3] Amelia Mott Gummere, *The Quaker, A Study in Costume*, Ferris and Leach, Philadelphia, 1901.

from history books and can be seen in Benjamin West's painting *Penn's Treaty with the Indians* (Pennsylvania Academy of the Fine Arts). Well into the nineteenth century they clung to the wide, flat-crowned hat and the straight-up-and-down coat, which had changed surprisingly little since William Penn's day. Only in neckwear and leg coverings did they conform to the changing modes.

The group whose dress shows the least change is of course the clergy. They followed in the colonies and later in the states the lead of their brothers of the cloth overseas. A portrait of John Davenport, 1670 (attrib. J. Foster, Yale Art Gallery), shows him distinguished by the neck tabs, often called Geneva bands, which are in evidence again on the Reverend Thomas Hiscox as seen in the portrait by Robert Feke (Collection Countess Lazlo Szechenyi). The Anglican or Roman collar appeared later in the century, but Geneva bands persisted and may often be seen in Protestant pulpits today.

In the course of three centuries various religious sects have formed sturdy little farming communities over the country—Mennonites, Amish, Shakers, and others. Each has some distinctive feature of dress such as hooks and eyes instead of buttons or a special head covering. But they have in common a simple and unsophisticated cut of jacket and trousers, bodice and skirt—the sort of thing that does not change appreciably from century to century. These utilitarian patterns are made up in rough, durable fabrics of dark shades—plain country dress for plain country people who distrusted elegance.

In a record of dress as one of the decorative arts it should be pointed out that the garments with which the humble clothed themselves, being designed primarily for decency and warmth, made little claim to aesthetic appeal; such clothes were discarded when they ceased to be serviceable, their ultimate destination being presumably rag carpets. In colonial times people so clad had no appeal for American artists, who painted only the prosperous and their wives. In Europe the artists of the new realistic school had been turning for models to the poor and ragged, but no painter did so here. For information about our seventeenth- and eighteenth-century common folk we must look to the written word.

From early in the nineteenth century, however, the history of America's growth can be read in genre pictures. Under a rising nationalism native painters turned to the American scene and sought to dignify the common man in the new democracy. Subjects were drawn from men and women going about their business in the hayfield and barnyard, in the little red schoolhouse, on the river. Sometimes these pictures look highly romantic, as for example George Caleb Bingham's *Fur Traders Descending the Missouri* (Metropolitan Museum of Art), but apparently some masculine attire did actually deviate thus happily from the prevailing drabness which was by the mid-sixties descending like a blight on men everywhere. The rural colored shirts and suspenders, hunting jackets, and occasional red waistcoats saved the day. Such clothes have seldom been preserved, but the memory of them is kept alive for us by Bingham, Mount, Woodville, and others. On the frontier, men imitated the Indians with their gay ornamentation of fringe, beads, and fur tails but pursued their own fancy in their choice of bright colors. A Southwestern writer has this to say about occupational dress on the frontier:[4]

. . . bragging was characteristic of the frontier, but not of all frontiersmen. It was indulged in by the more extroversive members of groups engaged in hazardous frontier occupations—keelboating, hunting, trapping, and cowboying—occupations requiring extraordinary courage as well as specialized knowledge and skills. It is significant that each group had its distinctive costume, and external badge of their calling: the red flannel shirt of the riverman, the green shirt and coonskin cap and buckskin leggings of the hunter, the similar costume of the mountain trapper, who preferred a buckskin shirt and Indian moccasins, and the hat, boots, and bandanna of the cowboy. A case can be made for the functionality of these costumes, but even functional uniforms are not voluntarily worn by men who are not pleased to have their clothes proclaim their calling. . . .

Cowboy costume is now the best known of these much-prized "uniforms." It is still to be seen both in honest use and in various "dude" travesties. Frederic Remington recorded the real cowboy dress in many pictures.

Nineteenth-century fashions for women could be represented entirely by actual garments, many of them fully documented. The examples chosen for this survey, all from the Valentine Museum in Richmond, Virginia, show a representative sequence of such dresses. The general styles followed closely the fashions current overseas and bear out the evidence of contemporary paintings. On the other hand few men's clothes have gone into museums; if too good for carpet rags, they were no doubt passed on to "the poor." Hence for a record of male dress we have to rely on the pictorial arts; for instance, in a portrait of Samuel Coates, about 1812, by Thomas Sully (Pennsylvania Hospital) and in two

paintings by John Neagle, one of the architect William Strickland (Yale Art Gallery) and the other of Pat Lyon (Pennsylvania Academy of the Fine Arts), we have a revealing contrast between the gentleman and the workingman.

And what of children all this time? In America the fashions for well-to-do children in the city or on a country estate, like those for their elders, followed the lead of Europe, where from the late fifteenth century children's clothes had been stiff, unchildlike versions of grown-up dress. In the seventeenth and eighteenth centuries youngsters were relentlessly busked and stayed and farthingaled. At least it was in such imitation adult attire that they sat for their portraits. In America no seventeenth-century childhood frocks survive, but they can be seen in such paintings as the anonymous group portrait of David, Joanna, and Abigail Mason (Collection Mrs. Paul Mascarene Hamlen). From the early eighteenth century the portrait of Eleanor Darnall painted in Maryland about 1710 by Justus Engelhardt Kühn (Maryland Historical Society) shows a child's formal attire. Although it echoes the stiff adult fashions of the reign of William and Mary, this pretty costume is nevertheless not too difficult to get around in; we may assume that Eleanor actually wore it on occasions other than portrait sittings. The same ideas applied to boys' clothes may be seen in Kühn's portrait of Henry Darnall III (also about 1710, Maryland Historical Society).

As in the mother country, boys, when they were breeched, donned suits in the general style worn by their fathers—a custom that has persisted with interruptions ever since. John van Cortlandt (Brooklyn Museum) was painted between 1720–1730 at about ten years of age. His appearance deviates from that of an adult only in the hair style: the boy's hair lies loose on his shoulders, whereas his father's would have been tied back.

Toward the end of the century a wave of dress reform swept Europe. It began with the children. For out of the educational reforms of Jean Jacques Rousseau in mid-century France had come a new conception of childhood, including children's dress. England welcomed the idea and began putting her upper-class children, so many of whom lived on country estates, into simplified dress: little girls into what amounted to a chemise with a sash and little boys into shirts and pantaloons. Such children have been immortalized by Sir Joshua Reynolds and others, including the by-then expatriate Copley (recall his painting of the daughters of George III). The English version traveled back to France and also to America. By then women were

[4] Mody C. Boatright, *Folk Laughter on the American Frontier*, The Macmillan Company, New York, 1949.

adopting it, first older girls, then younger women, and so on. In spite of the break with England, American women were still following English fashions, as portraits prove. Ralph Earl's portrait of *Mrs. Benjamin Tallmadge with her Son Henry and Daughter Maria* painted in 1790 (Litchfield Historical Society) gives a charming development of the new style (1785–1795). The relative simplicity, the round, sashed waist, the filmy fabrics in pastel tints make it very close to the still simpler version taken over from children's "reformed" dress and labeled "à l'enfance."

In nineteenth-century juvenile dress an important part was played by pantaloons. Boys continued to wear them even after the short jacket and frilled shirt went out of style and a knee-length smock came in. Little boys began to wear the tubular leg coverings while still in frocks very like those of their sisters. Features typical of children's clothing in the entire first half of the nineteenth century can be seen in a portrait of *Joseph Moore and his Family* painted by Erastus Salisbury Field about 1840 (Museum of Fine Arts, Boston). Here the younger boys wear low-cut frocks of about knee-length, from under which tubular pantalettes descend to the ankle. Their sister has somewhat longer skirts, and her pantalettes have lace trimming but are otherwise like the boys'. Her dress faithfully reflects current feminine fashions. Another interesting example of a girl's dress of the period is seen in Isaac Augustus Wetherby's portrait of Mary Eliza Jenkins (1843, Fruitlands Museum, Harvard, Massachusetts) and of a boy's clothes in Thomas Sully's portrait of a *Mother and Son* (1840, Metropolitan Museum of Art).

Small boys wore frocks until quite late in the century. A few years later a boy of four or five would be wearing a kilted skirt and a blouse with wide ruffle-edged collar. A somewhat older boy went into jacket and short pants which reflected, in general, the increasing dullness of adult male clothing. At the same time (the last three decades of the century) girls' clothes grew fussier, echoing women's gowns.

Toward the end of the century "short pants" were the correct wear for growing boys; in the early 1900s knickerbockers were the thing; suddenly long trousers came back, even for mere toddlers. During the same span of years girls' dresses continued to reflect grown-up styles but with increasing emphasis on simplicity. Today when feminine fashions practically ignore age difference, "mother and daugher" dresses often prove equally becoming to both members of the pair. And the charm is doubled.

All the way along, childhood garments even when otherwise plain were often embellished with embroidery. So were garments for men and women. But the needle crafts should have treatment in their own right, quite apart from costume, as being the chief tool of artistic expression for colonial women. Examples are still extant which include embroidery in silk floss of many colors, intricate decoration composed of drawn work and French knots, satin quilting, so popular throughout the eighteenth century and half of the nineteenth, fustian (coarse linen) embroidered in a bold design of flowers, animals, and landscape. Incidentally this kind of domestic craftsmanship should serve to contradict the prevalent notion that New Englanders were averse to personal adornment.

It is as decoration that needlework enters the picture in costume history. There are other important many-sided areas which, just as needlework, demand full and detailed treatment. A survey can only mention them in passing. "Occupational dress" is one. The subject has been touched upon in connection with frontiersmen. Such garment combinations constitute a "uniform" only by courtesy, custom having made them the usual dress. True uniforms are imposed upon the wearer by higher authority. Such are military and civic uniforms and various liveries.

Our honored military uniforms may be readily studied from actual garments in regional museums. Painters have presented them more vividly and dramatically. Fine examples are found particularly in the portraits of Stuart, Earl, Trumbull, and Peale. The familiar uniforms of the Civil War are lovingly preserved in local museums of both North and South, but paintings like Winslow Homer's *Prisoners from the Front* (Metropolitan Museum of Art) record the war in a more moving way. American cities took pride in their firemen and policemen and had them painted for posterity. Painting, lithographs, photographs—all offered channels for expressing public sentiment toward them and recognizing heroism. The story of liveries—of servants and others—may be followed in tailors' advertisements, books of etiquette, and illustrated periodicals.

The twentieth century in the world of fashion started out as a continuation of the nineteenth. Well-to-do American women continued to dress like European women of comparable means and to import gowns with "names" like Worth and Poiret. The years known as Victorian and Edwardian are the years when the *couturier's* skill reached its peak. It is axiomatic that dressmaking as a craft has flourished most vigorously during periods of artificiality, and this era was in truth artificial. Early in the period William Morris Hunt and Winslow Homer left vivid records of dress representing all walks of life, and later Sargent and other "society" portraitists recorded the most elegant styles. Many such gowns have found homes in our regional museums. The dress worn in the White House by Mrs. William McKinley in 1897 is one example. Ladies not so much in the public eye, but dressed with equal charm, grace the canvases of William Chase, Thomas Eakins, and other American painters of this pleasant era.

Ordinary women made their own clothes or relied on a dressmaker who came spring and fall and stayed a week or so to get the womenfolk all sewed up. As the century progressed and the garment industry got into its stride, more and more women turned to ready-mades. Mass-production garments are not represented in this survey, since however admirable the original design from which the master pattern was cut, the factory-made replicas no longer qualify as craftsmanship. Individually made dresses, even when cut from a pattern widely distributed, always take on something of the personality of both maker and wearer.

American fashion magazines offer a record of the styles, always international rather than purely American. In some periods fashion drawings have been excellent examples of graphic art. The same could not be said for the illustrations in mail-order catalogues. Nevertheless from the latter part of the nineteenth century until about twenty years ago these catalogues gave a more accurate picture of what upcountry women were wearing. Currently, the mail-order ladies have taken on a sophisticated urban look, and often the women who order manage to look exactly like them.

The story of dress in America up to 1914 is a leisurely one, with the swing of fashion's pendulum slow and decorous. World War I upset the rhythm. From that time on there have been innumerable changes in the social scene, practically all having some effect upon dress.

From 1914 on, the half-century brought two wars, an "incident," a "cold war," unprecedented prosperity, a cruel Depression, and the uneasy present. Change became the order of the day. Through it all, fashion arbiters in Europe continued to design. Meanwhile the clothing industry in America had become big business. Maintaining its high level of prosperity required a quick turnover through frequent and radical changes in styles. Not a difficult matter with a free-spending public already clothes-conscious and mass media at hand sure to promote the look of the moment: movies, television, and particularly advertisements, which show only well-dressed, charming people enjoying everything from soft drinks to a Mediterranean cruise.

During the years before the great wars a number of important painters took for their subjects scenes in American homes and incidentally left thereby a record of dress in that era. Comparable painters in the modern world seem to have lost interest in factual presentation of such subjects. Nowadays the changing scene, the changing dress is recorded in fashion sketches, in magazine covers and illustrations, and in advertisements—commercial art.

In American dress may be traced a record of American people, from the earliest settlers who clothed themselves to meet the rigors of the wilderness to their descendants and heritors who pick and choose from the world's luxuries for their adornment. American costume is part and parcel of American life.

GRAPHIC ARTS OF THE
EIGHTEENTH AND NINETEENTH CENTURIES

CARL ZIGROSSER

American printmaking during colonial times and during most of the nineteenth century was definitely an art for the common people. At the beginning of the century there were few if any public collections or art museums. Almost the only pictures which people saw, or came in contact with, were engravings, and they were relatively few in number. The cultural climate of the Colonies, based as it was upon that of the mother country, was not slanted to any great degree toward a pictorial or graphic tradition. Architecture and the decorative arts, the production of furniture and fine silver, flourished in the Colonies as it did in England. But even in England printmaking, as a distinctively native art, was limited during the eighteenth century largely to mezzotint, which indeed was often called "engraving in the English manner" on the continent. Mezzotint was almost entirely an art of portraiture, reproductive of painting. Thus it happened that the earliest prints made in this country were portraits. The first known print was a woodcut, crude but powerful, of the Rev. Richard Mather, made probably by the printer John Foster, about 1670. There must have been a demand for likenesses of influential divines in New England, as the mezzotints by Peter Pelham, Copley, and Jennys testify. These particular prints—executed by the artist after his own design, for, contrary to the usual practice, he was here both painter and mezzotinter—were surprisingly well done, displaying a strong sense of character, albeit sober and austere. Pelham's portrait of the Rev. Cotton Mather is generally considered the first mezzotint and framing print made in America; and it would indeed hold its own in any collection of mezzotint portraits. Somewhat more lusty and satiric in spirit is John Greenwood's original mezzotint of *Jersey Nanny*. There was apt to be more demand by numbers of people for pictures, and thus more incentive for printmaking, in the urban and middle class areas of New England than in the agricultural regions of Virginia and the South. The aristocratic owners of the plantations were more likely to satisfy their need for culture through oil paintings and direct importation from England.

Besides portraits the colonists were interested in maps and views, battles and notable events, and, as they became increasingly conscious of separation from the mother country, the memorable events of the American Revolution. When one contrasts the graphic documentation of the American Revolution with that of the French Revolution occurring but a few years later, one realizes how inadequate was the technical tradition which the American craftsmen took over from England. Amos Doolittle's engravings (based on drawings by Ralph Earl) of the battles of *Lexington* and *Concord* are absurdly crude, but they are nonetheless a part of our historic heritage. The same holds true of the earlier Johnson–Blodgett engraving of the *Battle of Lake George* and the amusing Dawkins portrayal of the *Paxton Expedition*. Perhaps the most famous of all Revolutionary prints is Paul Revere's *Boston Massacre*. Revere was a silversmith and a patriot, renowned in history and legend, but he was an indifferent engraver. It turns out that Revere copied his picture from a larger and better engraving by Henry Pelham, the only recorded impression of which is to be found in the American Antiquarian Society. Doolittle's engraving (after a drawing by Peter Lacour) of *Federal Hall and the Inauguration of Washington as President* does have considerable charm and the vividness of a contemporary rendering. With the documentation in portraiture of some of the key figures of the Revolution, such as Franklin, Washington, and Jefferson, we are on sounder aesthetic ground, for Charles Willson Peale and Edward Savage were accomplished painters as well as technically competent printmakers.

Topography, or the production of views, was an important and favored category of graphic art. The citizens of the young nation began to take pride in their country and demanded delineations of its flourishing cities and picturesque scenery. Perhaps the most impressive early enterprise of this type was the set of twenty-eight intaglio views of Philadelphia issued by William and Thomas Birch in 1800. J. L. Bouquet de Woiseri followed with an aquatint of the *First Cities of the United States* in 1810. In the prospectus to *Picturesque Views of American Scenery* (aquatints by John Hill after paintings by Joshua Shaw, 1819) the publisher wrote:

Our country abounds with Scenery, comprehending all the varieties of the sublime, the beautiful, and the picturesque in nature, worthy to engage the skill of an Artist in their delineation; and as no well-executed work of this description has ever been produced, it is confidently hoped that the present will meet with due encouragement.

The view of Lynnhaven Bay is taken from this series. The *View near Fishkill* is representative of another famous series, the *Hudson River Portfolio,* 1825, with aquatints chiefly by J. Hill after W. G. Wall. Still another work containing aquatints by Hill is the *Progressive Drawing Book* by Fielding Lucas, Baltimore, 1827. Such instructive books, of which a number were issued at this time, did much to set a standard pattern for landscape composition, since they were used not only by art students for professional training but also by amateur painters for copying.

Meanwhile, during the 1830s and 1840s, there was considerable production of excellent aquatint views of cities. Conspicuous in this field was W. J. Bennett, whose accurate and aesthetically satisfying views of New York, Boston, West Point, Baltimore, Washington, and New Orleans are justly famous. Notable, too, are the Hornor view of Broadway, 1836, J. Rubens Smith's *Franklin House, Philadelphia,* 1842, and several by Robert Havell who, having finished engraving his monumental folios of Audubon's *Birds,* settled in this country and executed charming views of Boston, West Point, and Niagara Falls. Toward the end of this period lithography began to supplant aquatint as a print medium because it was cheaper and yielded more impressions. Many fine views appeared in this medium, especially the early (1829) and impressive *Battery and New York Harbor* by Thomas Thompson, the highly finished Köllner series of *American Cities,* Henry Walton's singular views of upstate New York (*Ithaca,* for example), and New England ports by such painters as Fitz Hugh Lane and J. Foxcroft Cole. Production of good views continued into the 1860s.

The transition from specific view to generalized or idealized landscape was easy. It took place in painting with the growth of the Hudson River School. Of the three earliest leaders of the school, Asher B. Durand started out as and was for many years a professional

engraver, Thomas Doughty was an accomplished lithographer, and Thomas Cole made at least one lithograph. It may well be, as Virgil Barker has pointed out, that their early technical training may have influenced their approach to painting, leading to the elaboration of minute and out-of-scale details at the expense of a broader and more painterlike treatment of color and form. The full range of the mid-century landscape school was not reflected in prints to any large extent. Durand's engraving after Cole's painting of *Lake Winnepiseogee* of 1830 may perhaps serve as a typical example. Or possibly the original lithographs made by Thomas Moran around 1868–1869. The two states of John Sartain's engraving after Boutelle's painting *Morning, Valley of the Battenkill,* 1870, illustrate a technical point in the production of a mezzotint of the period: the first state in pure etched outline, the second with mezzotint added.

One cannot by any means ignore Audubon's monumental incursion into natural history, the four elephantine folios of *American Birds,* 1827–1838, created through an ideal collaboration of the engraver Robert Havell with the artist-naturalist J. J. Audubon. It was a unique and stupendous undertaking, this task of depicting, in natural size and in their proper setting, all the birds of America. Audubon achieved a perfect fusion of aesthetic sensibility and scientific recording. One may measure the full extent of his accomplishment and the breath-taking originality of his conception by comparing a plate of Audubon's *Birds* with similar contemporary subject matter by M. E. D. Brown and by Audubon's rival, Alexander Wilson, as engraved by Lawson. It was the activity of Wilson's partisans in Philadelphia which forced Audubon to have his work engraved in England.

Mention was made of the development of lithography in the second quarter of the nineteenth century. The first lithograph made in America was by Bass Otis, *The Mill,* and appeared in the *Analectic Magazine* in 1819. Benjamin West had already made a lithograph in England in 1801, *The Angel of the Resurrection.* Rembrandt Peale was the first artist of established reputation to take up the medium in America. His portrait of *Washington, Pater Patriae,* of 1827 is an accomplished piece of work and his landscape *Jefferson's Rock* is charming, though somewhat monotonous in tone. One may cite for their early proficiency on stone such painters as Inman, Doughty, and Thompson, and such professional lithographers as M. E. D. Brown, Newsam, Lehman, Swett, and Bufford. Two portrait collections of the 1840s are noteworthy for their originality and competent projection of character: the lithographed silhouettes, with appropriate backgrounds, by W. H. Brown (*Marshall, Randolph, Jackson,* and *Calhoun*) and the *Portrait Gallery* lithographed in Washington by Charles Fenderich (*Tyler* and *Costin*). Two other masterpieces of portraiture, though somewhat earlier and in a different medium (stipple), must not be overlooked: Longacre's engraving after Sully of Jackson and Lewis's engraving after a destroyed painting by Harding of *Daniel Boone,* this latter presumed to be the first print made west of the Mississippi.

Lithography, rapidly developing as a business as well as an art, found many commercial uses as music-sheet covers (D. C. Johnston's *Ice Cream Quick Step,* 1841, or Sarony and Major's *Christy's Melodies,* 1848), trade cards, posters, and the various job-printing commissions depicted in Bowen's *Specimens of Lithography,* 1840. Later in the century the lithographic firms turned completely commercial and no longer employed artists, with the result that their productions had none of the fascination of the earlier work as a documentation of modes and manners.

The regular mediums of engraving on metal and wood likewise continued to be in use for all manner of applied art, for trade cards (Thomas Birch, Joshua Shaw, and Baker's *Marble Yard*), posters (Farwell's *Johnson's Circus*), fashion plates (*Godey's Lady's Book*), and especially for book and periodical illustration. This last field is so vast and complicated that treatment must necessarily be summary. Typical examples are Durand's engraving after Morse of *The Wife* and Alexander Anderson's wood engraving of *Uncle Tom's Cabin.* J. G. Chapman dominated the field of illustration in the 1840s, as Darley did in the 1850s and 1860s. But the Harper Bible of 1846, celebrated as it was for its 1,400 wood engravings after Chapman, somehow has little to say to us today. Darley, on the other hand, was a talented and versatile draughtsman, the best of whose work still has an appeal in our time. Two other wood engravings may be cited: Hoppin's illustration, very much in the spirit of James Russell Lowell's *The Courtin',* and John LaFarge's imaginative and felicitous illustration of *The Fisherman and the Genie.* Toward the end of the century the perfection of photomechanical methods of reproduction supplanted old-fashioned engraving for purposes of illustration. The achievement of the school of illustrators then dominant—which was considerable and worthy of note—may best be studied in their original drawings (Abbey, Blum, Frost, Pennell, Pyle, Remington, and Vedder), rather than in their process reproductions.

The ferment and expansion of the 1830s and 1840s were reflected in prints in various other ways. The young nation was feeling its oats and took great pride in the martial and naval achievements of its immediate past. It was the period when generals became presidents: "Old Hickory" Jackson, "Tippecanoe" Harrison, and "Old Rough and Ready" Taylor. The War of 1812 was a glorious memory. Those events which could be glamorized, chiefly the naval victories, were painted by Thomas Birch and Reinagle and popularized in engravings by Lawson, Tanner, and Tiebout. *The United States Military Magazine and Record of all the Volunteers, together with the Army and Navy,* 1839–1841, serves to recall the popularity of the volunteer companies, who drilled in gorgeous uniforms and had fun in summer encampments (Huddy's *Ancient and Honorable Artillery of Boston,* and Hoffy's *Lieutenant, U. S. Navy*). The *opéra bouffe* aspect of the Mexican War is aptly characterized by Nagel's *Death of Major Ringgold* and Sarony's caricature of *The Mexican Commander.*

Along with their pride in martial achievement and in their cities and scenery, the Americans gloried in their American way of life. The genre picture became popular. Since the nation was still predominantly rural in culture, and the country was still very close to the city, much of the genre was rural in feeling. The paintings of Mount as engraved by Burt or Jones, of Bingham as engraved by Sartain or Doney, the lithographs of Lillie Martin Spencer, and later of Eastman Johnson, Durrie, Fanny Palmer, Tait, and Maurer are typical and engaging examples in this class. These, together with large patriotic prints, such as Durand's engraving of Trumbull's *Declaration of Independence,* various portraits of presidents, or Sartain's mezzotint *General Marion in his Swamp Encampment,* and together with certain sporting prints and "westerns," to be enumerated later, give a cross section of the framing prints favored by the people.

Prints were indeed popular during this period. Among the numerous factors which brought about this active interest in prints and art in general, not the least was the activity of the American Art Union from about 1844 to 1852. This organization, under the distinguished direction of William Cullen Bryant and others, bought hundreds of paintings and sculpture by American artists and distributed them to its members by lot. For an annual fee of $5 a member received an impressive engraving of some famous painting as a premium and also a chance to acquire an original painting (witness Matteson's lithograph *The Distribution of American Art Union Prizes at the Broadway Tabernacle,* December 24, 1847). At one time its membership counted 16,000 when Thomas Cole's series *The Voyage of Life* was announced for distribution. Among the premium prints issued by the society may be cited Woodville's *Mexican News,* engraved by Alfred Jones, Bingham's *Jolly Flat Boat Men,* engraved by Doney (9,666 impressions), Mount's *Farmer's Nooning,* engraved by Jones, and Darley's lithograph in illustration of the *Legend of Sleepy Hollow.* These prints often entered homes where there never had been any art before. The example of the New York society was followed by similar organizations in Philadelphia, Boston, and Cincinnati. There is no telling to what extent the movement might have expanded, if it had not come in conflict with antilottery laws. The Union was dissolved by court order in 1852.

Where the Art Union left off, private enterprise took over the task of purveying prints to the American people, with perhaps a little more emphasis on the common touch. Nathaniel Currier, his successor, Currier and Ives, Sarony and Major, Endicott and Co., the Kelloggs of Connecticut, Wagner and McGuigan, Prang and Co., Kurz and Allison, and a host of ephemeral firms issued thousands of prints and prospered. Of these, Nathaniel Currier and Currier and Ives were the most famous and enduring, both in the quality and in the quantity of their output, so much so, that the name has become a synonym for a certain class of print. The range of their subject matter is extensive and furnishes an illuminating index of the taste of the average American: historical events and portraits, landscapes and city views, sporting subjects, clipper ships, Western and Indian scenes, railroads, sentimental or fancy subjects, and comics. The heyday of their production was in the 1850s and 1860s; later their prints became routine and dull. The approach of their leading artists was essentially romantic; they were really purveyors to the American Dream. With the celebrated rural subjects of Durrie and Fanny Palmer, for example, it would almost seem as if they were imbued with nostalgic perspective at the very time they were made, a feeling of the good old days down at the farm. At their best the sentiment was genuine and not at all sentimental, as it was in most of the run-of-mill productions. But one need only compare them with Winslow Homer's wood engravings, similar in subject and equally factual in rendering, to sense the difference between healthy realism and romantic glamour. One wonders who bought the Currier prints when they were issued; could it have been the people who were born on a farm and left it to go to the city? The sporting artists, Tait, Palmer, and Maurer, were themselves keen and active sportsmen, and their pictures are filled with satisfying detail, yet they always depict the returning hunters or fishermen as loaded down with the trophies of the chase for

fireside sportsmen to dream about. Most of the Currier Western and Indian subjects were studio products, for, as far as is known, none of the artists, Tait, Maurer, or Cameron, were ever actually in the West. They projected in graphic form the American's idea of the West as the region of adventure and romance; in a sense perhaps, they even moulded the idea. For an on-the-spot recording, one turns to a group of prints and drawings, united by the common theme of the buffalo, by Audubon, Catlin, Bodmer, and A. J. Miller and especially to the Indian sketches of Catlin and Bodmer, whose work is known to have been used by the Currier designers as source material.

The tremendous interest of the American people in the expansion of their country—the Prairies and the Far West, the excitements of the Gold Rush in 1849, the development of various modes of transportation, the clipper ships, the transcontinental railroads, the Mississippi River boats, and the canals—has been dramatically and delightfully documented by Currier and Ives and other publishers. It should be emphasized that for every creditable print issued there may have been a hundred others which had little or no merit as a work of art. Lithography was a business as well as an art. Louis Maurer has revealed that even with the best of the firms, such as Currier and Ives, the work was often the product of many hands, one specialist doing backgrounds, another figure work, and the like. Publishers often copied other prints in whole or in part and were not always scrupulous about giving credit for their borrowings. The best of the Currier and Ives, however, will always have a place in any survey of American printmaking, not only for their graphic quality and historical importance but also for their romantic appeal. The charm which these works exert upon the collector today is largely sentimental and romantic, a glimpse of an ideal world, now gone forever, which indeed may never have existed but which is now definitely part of our legendary heritage.

The Civil War was well recorded by photography and by a new type of artist war correspondent—Winslow Homer, Edwin Forbes, Alfred J. and William Waud—sent to the front by the illustrated weeklies. The conflict between North and South also evoked some bitter caricature by Nast and Adalbert Volck and that curious half-fantastic half-satiric lithograph by Blythe *Abraham Lincoln Writing the Emancipation Proclamation.* The effect of the war on printmaking and art in general was harmful and, in its aftermath, disastrous. The gilded age was at hand, and a great social change was taking place. We were entering what Oliver Larkin called a "chromo civilization." It was an age of gaudy ostentation and vulgar taste in general; money-making was the ruling passion. In such an atmosphere the artist, and particularly the printmaker, was thrown back on himself. He lost touch with his public. The lithographic firms had turned completely commercial and were developing a particularly insensitive form of color printing which became known as the chromo. Engraving was relegated to mechanical bank note engraving. Etching was more or less moribund in spite of the French dealer Cadart's efforts to stimulate the interest of American artists during a visit in 1866. Wood engraving had turned into a routine reproductive craft in the service of the illustrated weeklies, where factual reporting and speed were essential. Winslow Homer, after designing a notable and quite delightful group of genre wood engravings (some of them poorly engraved) for *Harper's Weekly* in the late 1860s and early 1870s, gave up graphic art to devote himself entirely to painting.

Henceforth, the impulse to create prints had to come more or less from the artist himself. In making a so-called painter-etching, the artist had no specific market in mind; he was merely doing something to satisfy his own aesthetic impulses. To be sure, there had been some previous examples of such work. John G. Chapman, after a highly successful career as a painter and illustrator, retired to Italy and etched some intimate scenes in the Roman Campagna (*Ostia,* 1855). William Morris Hunt, back from France and his friendship with Millet, made several lithographs in the mid-1850s (*Flower Seller, Woman at Well*). J. Foxcroft Cole in 1870 made a series of pastorals in lithography, inspired possibly by the example of Charles Jacque. Dr. William Rimmer surely must have made his curious lithograph *Female Figure on a Couch,* 1859, to please himself.

Around the beginning of the 1880s, there occurred the so-called revival of etching. In 1877 the New York Etching Club was formed under the leadership of James D. Smillie (*A Fallow Field*). Similar organizations were formed in other cities. The whole movement was given active encouragement by S. R. Koehler, curator of prints at the Museum of Fine Arts and editor of the short-lived but influential *American Art Review,* 1880–1882. The organizations died out in a few years chiefly because most of the members were second-rate artists, but the idea of original etching was in the air, and more and better artists began experimenting with the medium. George Inness made his first and only etching in 1879. Stephen Parrish, the father of Maxfield Parrish, initiated Charles Platt into the craft. The latter made a number of charming, if somewhat dated, etch-

ings, and might have become one of our leading etchers if he had not given up printmaking to become a distinguished architect. Meanwhile abroad, Otto Bacher and Frank Duveneck met Whistler while they were etching in Venice. Of the two, Duveneck was an artist of greater stature and less influenced by Whistler's technique and personality. Duveneck's thirty-odd etchings place him in the front rank of nineteenth-century etchers. Some of his prints on exhibition in London were mistaken by Seymour Haden for Whistler's—it is difficult now to see just why, except for a similarity of Venetian subject matter—and became the occasion of one of Whistler's celebrated quarrels. Joseph Pennell already had quite a group of etchings to his credit when he fell under the spell of Whistler and became his acknowledged disciple.

In the 1890s a number of well-known painters tried their hand at printmaking. John Singer Sargent, at the instigation of Belleroche, made a few lithographs, including the characteristic *Young Man Seated.* Henry W. Ranger executed two atmospheric lithotints of the Seine in Paris. Arthur B. Davies, the young romantic, made a group of tenderly poetic lithographs in 1895. John Sloan began making etchings before the turn of the century, though he had not yet achieved his mature style. Incidentally, Robert Blum, back in 1885, made an etching *Scene at a Fair* which seems an anticipation of the later subject matter of Sloan and Glackens. J. H. Twachtman, probably under the prompting of his friend Weir, made a number of etchings in a delicate and sketchily calligraphic hand. J. Alden Weir, himself, had the instincts of a true graphic artist. There is a high seriousness to his finished work and an elegance, a sensitive feeling for the potentialities of the various mediums, etching, drypoint, and lithograph, and above all a projection of living personality. He might have become a major graphic artist if his eyesight had not prevented his continuing with a medium to which he had become genuinely devoted. Mary Cassatt was one of the major graphic artists of the late nineteenth century. She devoted much of her art to a sympathetic delineation of women and children without lapsing into sentimentality. Her sound draughtsmanship, her instinctive sense of style, and her technical mastery of such mediums as drypoint, soft-ground etching, aquatint, and color printing earned her the respect of Degas and the approbation of critics and collectors.

Of all the printmakers of the second half of the nineteenth century, Whistler is perhaps the best known both here and abroad, the most influential, the most prolific in quantity of prints. He has been the object of extravagant adulation and equally uncritical denigration. Some fifty years after his death, we may now strike some reasonable balance in between. For such an evaluation, there are on the credit side his pioneering discovery of the Thames and its industrial structures as aesthetic material; the distinguished and vigorous portraits of the 1860s (*Annie Haden, Fumette, Riault*); the mood and atmosphere of the Venice scenes; the delicacy and sensibility of the lithographs; the resolute fight against the anecdotal in art and for an impressionism, not of scientific color, but of exquisite taste and decorative charm. On the debit side: the sketchiness and triviality of many of his subjects, especially during the later years; the essential rootlessness of his art, for, as the expatriate par excellence, he had roots neither in his native America nor in London and Paris where he lived; and his fundamental weakness as a creator, for his power came more from taste and connoisseurship than from creative imagination.

A few foreigners have found their way into this survey—with some justification, it is believed. St. Memin is surely part of the American tradition; and Bodmer has been copied so much as to become part of it also. Included also are a group of Pennsylvania-German woodcuts and "fraktur" drawings. The people who made them were certainly American, even though their art was strongly influenced by German peasant tradition. Their baptismal certificates and religious mottoes have the intensity of feeling, the directness of expression with limited technique, the essential poetry which mark the best of true folk art.

In the final analysis, American printmaking in the nineteenth century was largely a practical or purposive art. The printmaker was useful in the community as the middleman or mediator between the painter in his studio and that vast body of unknown potential called the public. When graphic art was in a flourishing state, as it was during the second quarter of the century, the painter sometimes even painted a picture specifically for reproduction. It also happened at various times that the painter-designer and the printmaker were one and the same. Today with our high regard for originality, we set great store by such "original" graphic works, but in their day they had no such special virtue. Thus, up to the time of Whistler and his militant advocacy of art for art's sake, printmaking in America had a definite purpose and a specific use. Competent rendering of subject matter, and not pure creation, was paramount, and achievement should be judged on that basis. As far as technique was concerned, the Americans were proficient and resourceful; they did their job well and were in no sense inferior to their contemporaries in Germany,

England, and elsewhere. In other words American graphic art during the nineteenth century could hold its own in comparison with most other national schools, although it of course had special relevance for Americans as a reflection of their history and culture, just as the other schools had special meaning for their own nationals. French printmaking alone seems to have transcended national boundaries, largely because France possessed many artists of major stature at all times during the century.

Of the original etchers of the late nineteenth century, Cassatt, Duveneck, and Weir do seem to stand apart and above the rank and file. But towering above all the rest in the importance and quality of their achievement as graphic artists in the past century are three figures: Audubon, who combined art and science to produce one of the world's greatest works of ornithology; Whistler, who made a lasting contribution to etching and lithography; and Winslow Homer, whose graphic records of American life have come to possess universal appeal. In many ways Homer was the exact foil and counterpart of Whistler. Numerous parallel contrasts between the two contemporaries could be traced if opportunity and space were available. With his independence of mind and eye, Homer was one of the most original figures in American art. It is unfortunate that more was not demanded of him as a printmaker, for he had the instinct and the technical equipment of a very great graphic artist. Homer was a popular artist; and his public, unfortunately, made no great demands upon his technique. He began as an apprentice in Bufford's lithographic shop and did some commercial work there (the music sheet cover *Minnie Clyde*). The only lithographs which he made later were the six *Campaign Sketches* of 1862. It is regrettable that he did not continue with the medium, for his wood engravings lack the textural quality and autographic drawing of the lithographs. He also made six large etchings in the 1880s after his own paintings, but he did not feel at ease with the medium or the reproductive technique required. His greatest contribution to graphic art—in addition to his drawings, early and late—were the two hundred odd wood engravings which he designed (but did not cut) for various periodicals: *Harper's Weekly, Ballou's Pictorial, Appleton's Journal, Every Saturday,* and others from 1860 to 1875. The best of these are among the most charming genre pieces ever printed in America. They show the American way of life in its best light, a veritable American idyll: glimpses of the farmer at work, the sociabilities of country life, skating in Central Park, camping experiences, the Saratoga races, and the watering places—all delineated with freshness and honesty of vision, with masterly draughts-manship and compositional skill. There were memories of childhood, too, in these engravings, of simple rustic and seaside pleasures, berry picking, clambakes, and the like. In Lloyd Goodrich's words:

He expressed the grave, matter-of-fact poetry of child-hood with a simplicity that is captivating and a tenderness that is all the more poignant for being entirely uncon-scious.

After 1875 Homer devoted himself largely to a delineation of the sea—in drawings, water colors, and oil paintings.

A final word on the survey of nineteenth-century graphic art. At all times the aim has been to maintain a just proportion between the various categories of prints and to furnish worthy examples in each, in-cluding some not often considered by the art historian. And likewise, a fair representation of the various graphic mediums: engraving, mezzotint, stipple, etch-ing, aquatint, lithograph, woodcut, and wood engraving. Of all these, woodcut and wood engraving are perhaps least adequately presented in terms of quantity. The full development of the medium, however, particularly as used in illustration, the relative merits of black line versus white line, and the controversies between the Old and the New School are of interest only to special-ists.

The limitation imposed in the drawing section, to omit studies for painting, has somewhat narrowed the field and perhaps unduly stressed portraiture, nude studies, and illustration. Most of the American artists of the nineteenth century were practical people and did not often sketch for the sheer pleasure of drawing.

GRAPHIC ARTS OF THE TWENTIETH CENTURY

CARL ZIGROSSER

The progression of printmaking does not always fit into neat categories of centuries. Thus, the decisive date ushering in twentieth century art was not 1900 but 1913 on the occasion of the Armory Show in New York. The state of American graphic art in the late 1890s and early 1900s was at a low ebb. At the bottom level were innocuous landscapes and banal storytelling pictures by etchers no longer heard of. Foreign influences generally were dominant. The prints of Méryon, Haden, Cameron, Dendy Sadler, Haig, Zorn, and the American expatriates, Whistler and Pennell, were being collected. Reproductive prints were still popular, particularly wood engravings. In the Pan-American Exposition at Buffalo in 1901, half the awards went to wood engravers, Timothy Cole getting the gold medal; in the Louisiana Purchase Exposition at St. Louis in 1904 four awards were given to wood engravers compared with seven to etchers (none to lithographers), Cole again receiving a special grand prize. But by 1915 etching was definitely in the ascendant, as shown by the awards at the Panama-Pacific Exposition at San Francisco, where the prizes to etchers outnumbered those to reproductive wood engravers 35 to 4.

Etching thus became a favored medium. The subject matter in vogue was reassuring rather than challenging: patriarchal types (Cadwallader Washburn), cathedrals and other European landmarks (John Taylor Arms, Samuel Chamberlain), reminiscences of sport (Frank W. Benson). The First World War helped jolt the country out of its provincialism, or rather out of its complacent acceptance of a genteel art tradition. In a sense the war took the glamour out of Europe; it no longer was something remote and awe-inspiring where the beauty of centuries dwelt. The United States suffered less than the other nations engaged in the war and emerged with a cocky pride in its own achievements.

There were, of course, sporadic attempts to grow up even before the war. Certain etchers did actually portray American subjects: Charles Henry White, Earle Horter, or John Marin with urban views; Mahonri Young or

G. E. Burr with a background of the Southwest; Ernest Haskell with giant redwoods and California landscapes. Joseph Pennell, fresh from London triumphs, came back to America to discover the New York sky line, the "wonder of work," and the glories of the Panama Canal. More important still, such painters as John Sloan, as early as 1905, William J. Glackens in drawings, and others, somewhat later, such as George Bellows, Edward Hopper, and Glenn Coleman, rebelled against the saccharine unreality of the Academy and strove to represent graphically and vigorously what they felt and saw around them. The subject matter may not have been elegant or genteel, but at least it was a genuine and not a secondhand experience; it was vital, and had exciting aesthetic possibilities. Reginald Marsh, Raphael Soyer, Martin Lewis, and Mabel Dwight followed a little later in the same vein. They were the first modern discoverers of the American Scene.

The practitioners of other mediums began to challenge the prestige of etching. Albert Sterner, Joseph Pennell, George Bellows, and Adolf Dehn were pioneers in the rehabilitation of lithography as an artistic medium, thus rescuing it from the stigma of commercialism, which had blighted its possibilities for so long. Lithography was later to become one of the most responsive and flexible mediums for artists' use. Likewise, such artists as Rudolph Ruzicka, Rockwell Kent, J. J. Lankes, John J. A. Murphy, and, later, Howard Cook, Thomas Nason, and Paul Landacre freed wood engraving from its servitude as a reproductive medium and raised it to the dignity of an original creative vehicle.

Meanwhile exciting reports began to drift in from Paris about new and strange ways of painting and drawing. Exhibiting centers of experimental work came into being, such as Stieglitz's "291," where Marin's modern etchings were shown and likewise drawings by Weber and Walkowitz. The big Armory Show of 1913, organized by Arthur B. Davies, Walter Pach, and Walt Kuhn, put modern art dramatically on the map in this country. The innovations of the post-impressionists shocked and bewildered an unprepared public. But, equally important, the same exhibition introduced to a wider audience the work of the realists and independents who were outside the pale of the Academy and the conservative etching societies. The Armory showing stimulated and encouraged the younger artists but did not at once win over popular taste. The liberating influence of Fauvism and cubism made its way slowly against violent and scurrilous opposition. But these were not the only factors that helped to modify the taste of the time. The Jazz Age was in many ways a period of revolutionary ferment and foreign innovation. If Cézanne and Matisse and Duchamp were avant-garde, so were Russian ballet and its décor, so were peasant art and folk art and primitive sculpture in general, so was picturesque adventure in foreign lands (Rockwell Kent, George Biddle, Pop Hart, Boardman Robinson). All these influences played a part in breaking down academic standards and restrictions. By the end of the 1920s the battle for the freedom of art expression had been won.

Meanwhile the younger generation, absorbing the principles of the post-impressionists—dynamic design, accentuated three-dimensional feeling, distortion or stylization for emotive effect—embarked on an unparalleled phase of creative activity. The work of John J. A. Murphy, Charles Sheeler, Wanda Gág, Yasuo Kuniyoshi, Niles Spencer, and Stuart Davis is noteworthy in this respect, and of course many of the printmakers already mentioned continued to produce. The period was by way of becoming a golden age of printmaking. Money was plentiful, and prints by both conservative and advanced artists were actively collected. Even such generally unprofitable categories as satire and caricature found acceptance (Alfred Frueh, Adolf Dehn, Peggy Bacon).

This expansion was arrested catastrophically by the financial crash of 1929 and the resultant Depression. It wiped out the old-fashioned collector. Since the financial worth of his collection, often inflated beyond true value, was dissipated, he suffered monetary loss as well as great disillusionment. The professional printmakers, who were dependent on the patronage of the collector, likewise suffered a setback from which they never fully recovered. The young collectors, who grew up after the Depression and had the means to buy works of art, usually acquired only sufficient pictures to cover their walls. The serious collector who aimed at a full coverage of a printmaker's work was no more.

Two trends were evident during the 1930s. One of these was the revolt against the dominance of the big cities, New York and Chicago, and the emergence of regional schools. Perhaps the most publicized of such schools was the trio, Benton, Curry, and Wood; but numerous other artists, as for instance, Harry Wickey, Howard Cook, Adolf Dehn, Carol Cloar, also depicted the "American scene" without quite so much fanfare. Insofar as regionalism represented the establishment of local centers of printmaking all over the country, it was a gain to American graphic art, for it encouraged artists to make use of neglected pictorial material close to home. The other trend was the appearance of socially conscious art in urban areas where the incidence of economic depression was greatest (William Gropper, Robert Gwathmey, Louis Lozowick, Harry Sternberg). This did not prove to be a lasting influence, for it dwindled when conditions improved. The Federal Art Projects, established as relief measures during the Depression, did, however, contribute certain tangible benefits to printmaking in America, chiefly by aiding many young artists at a critical period in their careers. The list of important printmakers who received their start on the art projects is impressive (to name but a few: Max Kahn, Misch Kohn, George Constant, Louis Schanker, Lawrence Kupferman, Mitchell Siporin, Fred Becker, Russell Limbach). Another contribution was the development of new graphic techniques, such as the carbograph and the serigraph, or silk-screen stencil print (Anthony Velonis, Hyman Warsager, Leonard Pytlak, Robert Gwathmey).

The 1950s witnessed the phenomenal rise in popularity of the school of Paris among collectors, a fact which has had considerable influence on American art as well. The German expressionists, whose work began to be seen more frequently in this country, also gained in influence during this period. And it was in 1940 that the Englishman, S. W. Hayter, arrived in this country to preach his gospel of creative engraving and mixed techniques, in an abstract vein with surrealist overtones. He soon had an eager following among printmakers. He organized the group "Atelier 17," which carried on research in soft-ground textures, relief etching, and other technical innovations. Among the contemporary printmakers who at one time or other were connected with the Atelier may be mentioned: Mauricio Lasansky, Gabor Peterdi, Fred Becker, André Racz, Sue Fuller, Reginald Marsh, Karl Schrag, Ezio Martinelli, Abraham Rattner, Seong Moy, and Norma Morgan. Through his stimulus and that of his erstwhile pupil, Mauricio Lasansky of Iowa State University (who in turn has taught such pupils as Glen Alps, Lee Chesney, John Paul Jones), a new kind of print, sometimes abstract, sometimes expressionist, but always based on complex intaglio techniques, has spread like wildfire.

In the present decade print production has reached almost astronomical proportions, and it is difficult, indeed impossible, to evaluate contemporary printmaking with any degree of perspective or finality. There is a multiplicity of technique as well as of idiom. In addition to complex elaborations of the intaglio processes, combinations of intaglio and relief printing, and improvements in serigraph manipulation, new materials, plastics, have been used (cellocut by Boris Margo, lucite engraving by Harold Paris) or new pigments have been applied (encaustic colors by Milton Goldstein). Radioactive isotopes have been employed as the duplicating principle by Caroline Durieux in her electron prints. A new school of professional printmakers seems to be in the making. More and more large color prints are being made, competing in color weight and impressiveness with paintings. With their exceedingly small editions and great variation of impression, they seem to contravene the very purpose of the print as a cheap multioriginal. Designed not for the portfolio but for the wall, these abstract color patterns suggest a new decorative convention: they are richly and endlessly pleasing to the eye, but they also appeal to deep subconscious elements, thus being differentiated from the decorative prints of the past.

In many respects the prints of today differ markedly from those of the past. For one thing the printmaker of today is very conscious of his role as a creator and therefore has no qualms about breaking with tradition. With few exceptions (as for example Wengenroth or Riggs) the modern artist employs distortion, abstraction, and all the modern idioms as a matter of course. The mirror image seems to be outmoded as an aesthetic convention. The range of abstraction may vary from easily recognizable forms (as with Ben Shahn, Leonard Baskin, or Benton Spruance) to purely geometric configurations (as with Josef Albers, James Forsberg, or Stuart Davis). Most of the printmakers, however, stress, with all the emotive resources at their command, the necessity and importance of human or even moral values. In so brief an essay as this, it is impossible to appraise or to interpret mid-century print production in all its multiplicity. The one thing that is quite obvious is the complete revolution in taste which has taken place since the beginning of the century. This can be strikingly demonstrated by the following tabulations. In 1914 a yearbook by Forbes Watson came out, reproducing groups of prints by each of the following artists: Aid, Burr, Chandler, Cotton, Gleeson, Goetsch, Goldthwaite, Haskell, Higgins, Hornby, Horter, Hunt, Hurley, Levy, Lewis, MacLaughlin, Manley, Marin, Merrill, Nordfeldt, Pearson, Plowman, Reed, Stevens, Trowbridge, White, Winslow, and Mahonri Young. Quite a number of these artists are virtually unknown today, and all of them, including the early Marin etchings, are in the traditional manner. In 1936, or roughly midway in this period, the magazine *Prints* conducted an elaborate survey of the state of printmaking. In this, ten artists were rated as having the widest national acclaim in the following order: Rockwell Kent, John Taylor Arms, Kerr Eby, Frank W. Benson, Peggy Bacon, Arthur W. Heintzelman, Adolf Dehn, Thomas Nason, Wanda Gág, and John Sloan. Supplementary to this were listings in six regional groups, in which the following stood first in each: Howard Cook, Thomas Handforth, Alfred Hutty, Levon West, Emil Ganso, and Martin Lewis. There still is no hint of any of the advanced modes of expression so much in vogue today —nonobjective composition, interior movement, abstract expressionism. No similar survey exists for today; but one might venture to say that, if one were made, the following artists might find a place: Adja Yunkers, Antonio Frasconi, Misch Kohn, Leonard Baskin, Seong Moy, Fred Becker, Mauricio Lasansky, Gabor Peterdi, Harold Paris, Harry Sternberg, Armin Landeck, Karl Schrag, Max Kahn, Benton Spruance, Adolf Dehn, Stow Wengenroth, June Wayne, Sylvia Wald, and Ben Shahn. There also is a younger group of great promise, to name but a few: Milton Goldstein, Lee Chesney, Carol Summers, Rudy Pozzatti, Glen Alps, and Aubrey Schwarz. Among the talented young printmakers who unfortunately had to be omitted for lack of space should be mentioned: Edmond Casarella, Worden Day, Terry Haass, Ross Abrams, Arthur Deshaies, Irving Amen, Edward Colker, Clare Romano, Peter Takal, Louis Bunce, and André Girard. All of the above artists are orientated toward a new era.

The majority of American graphic artists are professionals, that is to say, printmaking is their major interest. One could of course name as exceptions certain of the older artists who have merited recognition for the quantity and quality of their paintings as well as their prints: John Marin, John Sloan, George Bellows, Edward Hopper, Arthur B. Davies, Rockwell Kent, Max Weber, Childe Hassam, or Lyonel Feininger (if he may be classed as American); and one could also cite Ben Shahn, Adja Yunkers, Bernard Reder, or Gabor Peterdi, among artists of today. There are still other artists whose occupation with printmaking has been more occasional, though not the less important, as with Franklin C. Watkins, Eugene Berman, Jean Charlot, Ivan Albright, Rico LeBrun, Karl Zerbe, or Abraham Rattner.

In several instances two works, early and late, by the same artist have been included in the survey to suggest the range of his achievement. The importance of John Sloan as a graphic artist, for instance, could not be demonstrated solely by his early genre etching without also submitting his later *Nude on the Stairs,* in which formal relationships are emphasized. Similar pairs of prints by Lyonel Feininger, Max Weber, Wanda Gág, and Stuart Davis are also included.

It is often asked whether there is a distinctive American style in American graphic art. In view of the multitude of racial and cultural strains that have contributed to the web of American life and in view of the profusion of individual modes of expression, it is difficult to see any unified American style in printmaking. In modern work one cannot even speak of American subject matter when so much of it is nonfigurative or abstract. In a country as big and as democratically organized as the United States, there is not unity but diversity of expression. If one cannot point to this or that work as the typical American print, or underline a single style as the dominant national expression, one can, nonetheless, discover in all of them one common

denominator, namely an American accent. This American accent is partly a matter of technical competence or resourcefulness, the "know-how," and partly a matter of the vigor and enthusiasm with which they pursue their goal. The American school of printmaking is one of the most vital and active in the world today.

The section on drawings is perforce limited. The artists of this century, unlike their colleagues of the previous era, frequently did make sketches just for the sake of drawing. Thus the section on contemporary drawings could have been expanded indefinitely. However inadequate the group is as a cross section of twentieth-century American draughtsmanship, it does present a wide variety of techniques and styles. Five are sculptors' drawings—always fascinating for their powerful grasp of form—by Gaston Lachaise, Sandy Calder, John B. Flannagan, Jacques Lipchitz, and Theodore Roszak. Two are studies for paintings by Peter Blume and Mitchell Siporin; two are illustrations by W. J. Glackens and John Sloan. Seven are by painters who loved to make drawings: Jules Pascin, Yasuo Kuniyoshi, Federico Castellón, Morris Graves, Reginald Marsh, Arshile Gorky, and Hyman Bloom.

INDIAN ARTS AND ARTIFACTS

FREDERICK J. DOCKSTADER

In any study of American culture, the arts of the several Amerindian tribes constitute the only truly native art to which the United States may lay claim. It warrants serious study on both historical and aesthetic grounds, since it not only presents the achievements of the indigenous peoples of the continent we have inherited but also allows a case study in the ability of man to live with his environment while at the same time extracting considerable beauty from his natural surroundings.

Unfortunately, this study has never been undertaken on a large scale. Such reviews of Amerindian art as have been made in the past are few and usually regional in nature. In the past half-century of American interest in public art exhibits, there have been only three devoted solely to this subject which were at all nationwide in their organization and presentation. There have, of course, been many fine shows in the various municipal museums and galleries, but these usually reflected either the interests of individual curators and directors or the interests of their respective audiences.

The reasons for this apathy are largely psychological, political, and social. The Indian way of life was at such variance with that of the white American that the latter found it almost impossible to understand the ideas, values, and aspirations held by those he regarded as untutored savages. The barrier of language only increased his difficulty. The sense of guilt for an ignoble political policy in his treatment of the Indian put the white man on the defensive, from which it was hard to retreat; hence it was easier just to salve conscience by disdaining any possible merit in Indian cultures. Victorian intolerance for non-Christian peoples inevitably led to wholesale condemnation of the "immoral and irreligious arts of such barbarians." What little appreciation did exist was usually held by individuals or small scattered groups.

As a result of such ignoring of a national resource, the extant examples of the art of the Indian are poorly representative. There is an extremely limited corpus of art in the fields of painting, textiles, featherwork, quill-

work, and articles made from other fragile materials before 1850. Even the early examples of beadwork and woodwork are rare before that date, and the vast bulk of today's specimens in the great museums date from about 1875. This means that, except for archaeological collections, almost all of the Indian art available for study represents postcontact art expressions. Therefore, the Carnegie Study material will reflect the general situation. The archaeological specimens present Indian work uninfluenced by European thought, while the ethnological section presents varieties of Indian art from approximately 1600–1950. The preponderance of the collection will date from 1850–1950 and should be examined with this dating in mind.

In all fairness, at the outset one should make the point that white students frequently find Amerindian art difficult to understand, particularly if an unwise attempt is made to translate or "interpret" that art in other than aesthetic terms. Even in the latter instance, the goal of the Indian artist often is not necessarily that of his white counterpart: different values, standards, and goals apply; and the two cultures vary tremendously.

Although this is not the place to go into Indian versus white psychology, a few comments can be presented to guide the interested person in a better comprehension of the Indian and his art world.

Basically, Indian art is regional or provincial. There is no "Indian art" for the country as a whole or for the Indian race; each geographical or tribal area has an art expression which is quite distinct from any other. Many of these differ so greatly as to present no traits in common. Others show similarities or relationships which hint at a sometime linkage. Within these areas there are, indeed, less marked differences; the Plains people, for example, while speaking various languages, maintain art and cultural traditions which are generally in common one with the other. The California tribes, likewise, share many art elements, yet there is little similarity between the art of these two Indian groups, and the different traditions can readily be identified.

Indian art is essentially a functional art. The concept of art for art's sake is an uncommon one, which has entered only in recent years. Decoration is important, and in many cases is applied lavishly, but the object remains a functional implement, and from the functional quality considerable beauty is derived, in Indian eyes. It has been only with the increasing demands of white trade that this idea has changed and has resulted in attractive but nonfunctional objects. Even the most artistically conceived effigy figures, which so move the contemporary art critic, had a fundamental ceremonial or religious purpose. It is this underlying intent that is often so difficult for us to understand today, since we know so little of the ceremonial life of the early Indian tribes.

Having ample time, the Indian artist frequently lavished many hours in the design and execution of even the most simple implement. He was as concerned with its appearance as with the way it served his needs —for, in his mind, both were evidences of good craftsmanship. Sometimes decoration was added for identification or "just for fun," but never was the basic functionality betrayed by decorative processes.

We usually think of Indian art in terms of decoration applied to a surface. While this is true in many ways, it is equally important to remember that the Indian artist had a sure eye for form. Many of the finest examples in the present collection are aesthetically pleasing simply because of their profile, sense of balance, or proportions. They have little or no applied decoration, yet to any eye they are true masterpieces of art.

The problem of symbolism is a puzzling one for most students, and it is in this field that the greatest errors are usually committed. In brief, it can be said that there is no common symbolism in Indian art. While much of the body of Indian art design is symbolic, this has been a changing process, operating inversely with the popularity of the art. What is a symbol to one Indian will not necessarily be such to another—particularly if he is from another tribe.

What is confusing to most whites is the Indian's readiness to refer to a given design as an "arrowhead," a "fish," or a "tree." Immediately this brings the concept of a symbol to the white mind, whereas what the Indian actually meant was "arrowhead-shaped," or "this design reminds me of a tree," or "it is a looks-like-a-fish design." Such terms are used descriptively, rather than as translations of symbols. True symbolism is primarily reserved for ceremonial objects and today is rarely found on secular pieces.

Designs and design elements can be regarded as traditional in various tribes in that their application and technical form are so stylized as to permit tribal, or at least a personal, identification. The more primitive the art expression, the truer the maxim. With increased intertribal contact, trading routes, and greater white influences, these traditional designs were borrowed back and forth, until today it is not uncommon, for example, to find Pueblo or Navajo designs used in Chippewa or Sioux beadwork.

The materials of Indian art expression come naturally from the environment—earth colors, vegetable dyes, wood, stone, shell, bone, and so on. Metal was little used prior to the coming of the whites, and the limited copper or lead worked in prehistoric times came from surface finds. Almost no mining was done. In some areas aniline dyes supplemented earth colors toward the end of the nineteenth century.

Beads were first made from wood, shell, bone, stone, or clay. Some copper beads were known, but the glass beads so familiar today were unknown to the Indian before traders introduced them in the late seventeenth century. Attracted by the bright colors and relative ease of use, Indian women quickly adopted them to replace the older shell beads and difficult-to-work porcupine quills but duplicated the quill techniques in design. By 1850 glass beads had become familiar to almost all tribes and were in universal use; shellwork and quillwork became practically a lost art.

Tools were simple; stone and bone for the most part supplied the Indian's needs, yet with these he managed to accomplish astonishing feats of creative beauty. From such simple tools and materials, the art evolved in simple fashion. Although many early designs appear to be involved, upon study they are revealed to be all-over or repeat patterns of a simple basic motif. With an increased technology, complicated tools gave rise to complicated designs. Today's Machine Age technology has given Indian art many complexities, often with most unhappy results.

The role of the Indian artist was quite different from that of his white counterpart. Rarely was he set apart as a special person. Usually he was regarded as a more able craftsman, but except in a few tribes this gave him no special status. In the main, each individual practiced all the art expressions of his people but, obviously, with varying success. Important ceremonial objects were frequently made by men with good, bad, or indifferent artistic abilities. While beauty played an important part in ceremonial rites, it did not in itself give power to the ritual. Power came in direct proportion to the position of the maker in the tribal religious hierarchy.

Among a few tribes, notably in the Northwest Coast area, there were professional artists who made their living by their talent. They were hired by important chiefs to aggrandize the wealth and status of these men and their families. In other tribes, some people traded the products of their craftsmanship. Beyond this, the concept of specialization was not very common to Indian culture.

A factor too often ignored in discussing Indian art is the role of the gifted individual. We do not know how extensive this was in the past, but there must have been instances where a particularly able artist strongly affected others in his own or neighboring tribes. This certainly seems true of the Mimbres people, for example. Although it is exceedingly difficult to determine how much any one individual may be credited with the development of a new art form or the renaissance of an old one, we have ample documentation which enables us to single out a few such artists: Martínez, the San Ildefonso potter and Atsidi Sani, the Navajo silversmith, are both well documented. Each was responsible for the renaissance of an old art, development of a new style, or establishment of an art which has come to be accepted as "tribal." While not many Indian artists are known by name today, there are some (most particularly in the field of water-color painting) whose careers are well known and whose work is eagerly sought by collectors. Such institutions as the Philbrook Art Center with its annual exhibitions of American Indian painting, and the many art museums holding such exhibits irregularly, have contributed tremendously to this happy situation.

The influence of non-Indians has been exerted in many ways. The early missionaries introduced new materials, tools, and particularly new designs from Europe. Indians attending convents were taught European-style textile manufactures and designing which rapidly spread throughout the Eastern Woodlands area. Later, traders brought in other materials and tools and in some instances encouraged craftsmen to make specific articles for sale. This reached the point where some traders not only specified the type of article to be made but even drew the designs for the craftsman to copy.

In more recent times, government Indian schools conducted arts and crafts classes in which Indians were taught. The results of these classes were sometimes good, sometimes bad, largely dependent upon the teacher. The work of Dorothy Dunn at Santa Fe, as a good example, gave rise to a whole "school" of Indian painting which has become so well known today that it

is now regarded as being characteristic of the area. Museum exhibits, such as the Museum of Northern Arizona's annual Hopi Craftsman show, have done much to encourage the Indian artist.

Indian art, then, is a living thing. Although the impetus of the Indian schools was dissipated with the recent abandonment of crafts teaching by the Office of Indian Education, the United States Indian Arts and Crafts Board, an independent agency, seeks to further interest through arts and crafts guilds on the several reservations. Better-quality gift shops exert their influence, and the growth of an increasingly aware public has helped to some extent in overcoming the disastrous effects of tourist traps, foreign-made "Indian" curios, and machine-stamped junk.

Turning now to a consideration of the Carnegie Study collection, we find that the material is representative of seven major art-producing areas, each of which is divided into an archaeological (to about 1500 A.D.) and an ethnological (from 1500–1950) era. It is in the former that Indian art presents the purest forms, since outside influences are minimal; here, too, specific "schools" of Indian art can best be studied, and the diverse motifs most readily identified. Some areas hint at early intertribal trade contacts, while others seem wholly isolated. It is not our province to investigate these prehistoric contacts other than to mention that many students see evidences of far-traveled contacts, such as Mexican influences in the art of the Mound Builders.

The Eastern Woodlands area is represented archaeologically by only a few examples of stonework, for all of the early "soft goods" have disappeared. There does not seem to have been the vigorous art expressions in this area, which were so remarkable in other contemporaneous sections of the country. Pottery is of low-quality clay, decorated with incised designs, and rarely ornamented. Almost no woodwork specimens have been saved, so we must turn to the historic period for any consideration of the art work. The earliest datable piece is the wampum belt exchanged at the time of the William Penn Treaty, 1682–1683. Such a belt, woven from beads made from quahog clamshells, was used in early days to bind a contract or treaty. Later Woodlands work is represented by elaborate beadwork designs on costumes and fine textiles—some woven from moose hair—of which the Oneida burden strap is a fine example. Excellent wood carving is emphasized by the imaginative False Faces Society masks of the Iroquois and Delaware peoples, as well as the beautiful wooden bowls and effigy-handled ladles. In general,

Eastern Woodlands art is characterized by lineal designs, primarily incised or painted. Elements are simple parallel patterns. Later beadwork designs followed European floral styles, bursting into a remarkable efflorescence before degenerating into the work done at Niagara around the turn of the century.

Further south, we find the most remarkable art work of all United States archaeology. The Southeastern Woodlands people developed an unparalleled wealth of carved representational art. Such masterpieces as the Etowah, Georgia, effigies in marble, the kneeling human figures and stone effigy pipes from Tennessee, prove this; the Crested Wood Duck bowl and the Squatting Man pipe from Alabama only further emphasize the point.

In ceramics, the various types of effigy and incised-design jars are testimony that here was, indeed, a great art period. There were seemingly no limits to the work of these early artists, for at Key Marco in Florida amazing painted wood sculptures have been recovered, and the engraved shell gorgets from Tennessee and Illinois indicate skills in other media. The Hopewell people in Ohio gave birth to another great aesthetic world as evidenced by the Adena Pipe, many fine effigy pipes, and the elaborately worked sheet-copper ornaments. Even sheet-mica was employed by these ancient folk, presumably cut by flint knives into beautiful forms. The Spiro Mound, in Oklahoma, also yielded great treasures, of which the effigy pieces and the wooden mask are exemplary.

Contemporary Southeastern Woodlands art is less striking, for the fire seems to have burned out. The tribes have been so widely dispersed or decimated that their present-day culture represents a mingling of many groups. Perhaps the Cherokee have remained the most homogeneous, but they, too, have retained little of their earlier artistry. Applied decorations in beadwork, basketry, and some woodwork are sorry reminders of the fantastic creations of earlier inhabitants of the region. The characteristic art form of this area is seen as a spiral, developed in linear detail, and frequently interwoven in single or double lines.

The Plains Indians attained their greatest artistic triumphs in more recent times. We cannot comment on the archaeology of this area, which was sparsely settled until the historic period, for almost nothing of an aesthetic nature has been recovered. With the buffalo and the horse as major assets, a totally new culture was developed, and Plains art came to reflect mobility. Costumes are designed to move—their decoration is meant to be seen in action. Witness the famous feather bonnet of the Sioux, so static when hung on a peg, but when worn on horseback, as intended, the bonnet comes alive, and the feathers take on a dramatic quality rarely equaled by contemporary milliners.

Costumes represented wealth and were richly decorated with beadwork. Women's dresses sometimes weighed as much as 75 pounds when completed—a far cry from the relative lightness of the old-time quilled dresses. Painted elk, buffalo, and cowhides attained a high degree of artistry among these peoples. Many of them are narrations of past exploits, tribal history, or calendar records. Other hides were made into shields and shirts, also beautifully painted. Parfleches, or carry-alls, were brightly painted and served as trunks or storage boxes for people who moved frequently and had to take all their possessions with them. Out of this painting on hides there developed a school of water-color artists which is well known today. Design elements of this area are the familiar geometric beadwork patterns, as well as a less commonly seen floral beadwork tradition which is reflective of a period when the Plains people were living closer to the Woodlands folk.

In the Far Southwest area, more archaeological work has been done than in the rest of the United States, and many fine examples of the artistry of these ancient people have been preserved, including the painted mortar from Pueblo Bonito and the ceramic products of the Mimbres people which are famous for their naturalistic, humorous qualities. That Indians have a sense of humor, often expressed in their art, is generally overlooked by non-Indians. The Hohokám peoples developed the art of etching on shell; they were the only prehistoric Indian people known to have practiced this work.

Contemporary art is equally outstanding in this area, for there has been little loss of earlier skills; indeed, many new abilities have been added to those which remained and, as a result, this section of the United States has the most vigorous Indian art actively practiced today. Almost every medium is used, and the varieties of expression are such that this paper cannot hope to deal with them in the limited space available. Suffice it to say that in the hands of its foremost practitioners, contemporary Indian art is at its best in the Southwestern United States.

The California archaeological picture is a cloudy one. The inlaid-stone and steatite implements of the Chumash, however, are of excellent quality, and it is the marvellous basketry which has done most to remove the epithet "Digger Indians" from these people. Nowhere else in the world did basket weaving reach as high a state of technical perfection as among the Indians of California and the adjacent areas. The exquisite feather baskets of the Pomo, the tightly woven Washo work, the crisp Panamint designs are masterpieces in any collection. Designs are mainly geometric, with sparing but artistic use of vegetable-dye colors.

It is in the Northwest Coast area that the greatest sculptural art is to be found from the ethnological period. Little is known of the archaeology of this section, except for some stone carving, and this is not on the scale that developed in later centuries. The people of the Washington and Oregon uplands did work in wood, basketry, and bone, as exemplified by the illustrations in this project.

But of all the tribes who gave such a rich heritage, the Haida and Tlingit Indians of southern Alaska were by any standards magnificent artists. Their carving abilities in wood, bone, ivory, and stone are thoroughly demonstrated by objects in this study. Added to the carved surfaces are pleasing designs in soft colors. The Tlingit were capable textile weavers and seem to have been more active in this field than were their neighbors. In the metal arts, again the Tlingit mastered the working of steel and copper, fashioning knives, rattles and the like from salvaged metal found on ships wrecked along the coast. They used Haliotis inlay to give rich contrasts to the base material. Northwest Coast designs are basically abstractions of human and animal forms, applied in a manner quite puzzling to more orthodox white artists. Their ability to fit designs into a given space is remarkable.

In Alaska, the Eskimo and the Alaskan Indian left many traces of archaeological artistry in carvings worked on fossil ivory, bone, and stone. This is rare, and fine examples are eagerly sought by collectors. Contemporary works in wood, stone, bone, and ivory are well known and of a quality only slightly inferior to that of their more southerly neighbors, the Tlingit and Haida carvers. The exuberant wooden masks, carved, painted, and decorated with wooden pegs and ornamentation, are used in various ceremonies. Many are not actually "worn" but are intended to be held in the hands in front of the dancer. They demonstrate the peculiar talent of the Eskimo for exotic design and occult balance. The work of these people is perhaps the closest of all Indian art to that of the surrealist artist of the European art world.

PAINTING OF THE SEVENTEENTH AND EIGHTEENTH CENTURIES

VIRGIL BARKER

Many contemporaneous drawings and paintings give much visual information, partly factual and partly fanciful, about the discovery and exploration of the regions now included in the United States of America; but these productions still remain a portion of European art which happens to have American subject matter. Art which can properly be characterized as American had to wait until after there were Americans to want it, and in consequence the earliest surviving American paintings are a few portraits done during the 1660s in Boston and New Amsterdam.

In the other and older colonies established by the Spaniards in the Far Southwest, a notable activity in art occurred under the tutelage of the Franciscan missionaries. The pictures there are religious images called santos, derivative in design and repetitious in subject. In style they are coarsely but often vigorously calligraphic. It is a matter of record that the earliest of these church images were sent from Mexico. However, by the mid-eighteenth century the demand for a larger supply led Franciscan priests to try their hand at painting and carving. After their example Spanish villagers took up the work in the medium at hand—wood, gesso, and water-soluble paints. Enough names and dates of priests and village saint makers are now known to make it perfectly clear that under no circumstances can the santos be termed the work of Indians. Even the most primitive ones retained a strong provincial Spanish flavor. Their usefulness for the devout was so great that several generations of workmen, perhaps mostly itinerant, continued producing them well into the nineteenth century.

Along the Eastern seaboard religious pictures were for several generations after settlement rejected or neglected. The settlers there, varied though they were in racial stocks and sectarian beliefs, were all Protestants from northern Europe where painting had already become secularized. Recorded facts, few in the early years but abundant by the end of the colonial period, indicate that the earliest painters, whatever the degrees

of their individual skills, practiced a method, then primarily utilitarian in character, as it had been handed down through the still existing medieval guilds.

Apparently, also, even earlier than the surviving portraits there existed a species of pictorialism in paint in the form of street signs. The artifacts themselves have almost all disappeared, being temporary by their very nature, but there is plenty of evidence concerning the important role they played in the general consciousness of colonial Americans and of the way in which they served both as incentive and as example for more than one generation of native-born painters. Throughout the period the signs were a vividly practical device for people who could not read, for in addition to their lettering they used images as secular symbols, somewhat conventionalized for easy recognition.

Throughout the period, too, the craft of sign painting was still being actively taught in London to apprentices working under the masters in the Guild of Painter-Stainers, and the demand there for such wares was great enough for it to appear unlikely that the best workmen would find it necessary to emigrate in search of work. Thomas Child (c. 1678–1706) had been a regulation apprentice and had become a master before settling in Boston by 1688; in that town until his death he performed the all-round artisan's miscellany of chores, from painting window frames to devising funeral decorations, such as escutcheons and hatchments, and lettering his sign to hang with the Guild's carved coat of arms before his shop.

In New Amsterdam an earlier settler, Evert Duyckinck the First (1621–1702), was a craftsman in glass, manufacturing it and selling it, installing it and then decorating it after it was installed in churches and public buildings. From painting on glass he extended his activities into decorative painting on fire buckets and even into portraiture. Whether he had any special training for this last activity is not recorded, but the lack of it would not have prevented his attempts from being acceptable in a small community where a specialist might be unavailable or too expensive. This first of the Duyckincks made his combination of crafts so profitable that several descendants continued the business in later shops. A definitely professional training seems possible in the case of Hendrick Couturier (?–c. 1684), for as a youth in Leyden he had studied in the Guild of St. Luke; here he is known to have made portraits of the Stuyvesants, but his principal activities were trading and holding government office.

None of these three workmen can now be convincingly connected with any existing pictures, which leaves the surviving portraits from the 1660s still anonymous. The same is true of a group in the following decade which were executed in Boston, then the most active cultural center in all the Colonies. Two Freake portraits and five of children in the Gibbs and Mason families are stylistically akin and together suggest a derivation from the style of the Tudor period. Of course, the earlier work in Old England had been, at its height, expert in craftsmanship, while the later work in New England is marked both by lesser skill and naïveté of vision. The earlier heraldic sophistication was supplanted by iconic awkwardness, a studio level of technique by the shop level of "painting in general," as later colonial advertisements often named it. Three or four portraits convincingly attributed to native-born John Foster (1648–1681) seem to be stylistically derived from English work, but Foster's painful incapacity only demonstrates how difficult it was at that time and in that place for the would-be painter to acquire his craft from the works and workmen locally available. The *Self-portrait* by Thomas Smith (active 1680–1690) combines the two-dimensional heraldic treatment of background and setting with a more pronounced modeling of head and features, which imperfectly foretells the seminaturalistic vision to come toward the second quarter of the eighteenth century.

Between 1700 and 1725 more unknowns continued the older manner with even more erratic modifications anticipating the later way of seeing. The rough strength of the so-called *Thomas Thacher* was accompanied by the more atmospherically treated Pierponts (1711), husband and wife. In New York City Gerret Duyckinck (1660–1710) approximated the studio stylism of Europe inasmuch as that could be derived from imported prints, and up in the Hudson Valley several unnamed workmen used much the same source material for coarsely animated effigies of such patroon families as the Schuylers and the Gansevoorts. In Virginia a somewhat more fluent Anonymous depicted five Jaquelins and five Brodnaxes. At Annapolis Justus Englehardt Kühn (?–1717) painted some child portraits against landscape settings, which remain as thinly unconvincing as they are decoratively ambitious. In Charleston, which was to develop the most sophisticated society in the Colonies, the first recorded woman artist, Mrs. Henrietta Johnston (?–1728/29), rather appropriately drew the first known pastels with technical timidity but also with an awareness of the courtly fashion of England.

Thus by 1725 painting had become established as a practical craft involving several kinds of decorative work and extending to the semipictorialism of the signs. Such craftsmen were called upon to limn the earliest portraits, and for these there was enough demand to enable painting to begin functioning as an adjunct to the nourishment of family affection and community tradition. This affords a parallel to the function of "edification" in contemporaneous writings: there was not yet free play of imaginative creativity, but spiritual serviceableness was directed toward right action in terms of community adjustment. Neither in painting nor in writing did the layman or the maker consider the product as primarily an aesthetic object, but in both cases the possibility of a semiaesthetic experience existed on the margin of consciousness.

By 1725, also, society in all the Colonies had assumed a fairly uniform pattern which directly affected all the arts and crafts in such a way that the middle fifty years of the eighteenth century produced a consistent and relatively brilliant collective expression. An upper class emerged everywhere—the planters in the South, the merchants in the middle region, the landowners in New York State, the merchants and small-scale industrialists in New England—who, in their economic and social dominance, assumed the role of an aristocracy in relation to the rest of the people. Their consciousness of this role was expressed in what they built and bought, in a taste quite naturally determined by a desire to adopt the fashions then prevalent in the mother country.

The immediate result was a change in artistic style which retrospectively is startling. This generation of colonials were fully conscious of the differences in appearance between a massive oak wainscot chair and an upholstered wing chair with mahogany cabriole legs, between the bleak intensity of the *Anne Pollard* (1721) and the glossy elaboration of Blackburn's *Winslow Family* (1755). But they were hardly aware that, in changing to what they thought was fashionable, they were skipping the three-century process by which all Europe had gradually changed from medieval to rococo. However, in making this extreme stylistic break with their own immediate past, they were reaffirming the continuity of culture between a colonial people and their spiritual sources.

This first instance of the power of fashion to change American taste was made possible by the coming here of relatively sophisticated workmen in all the crafts. In painting there were several portrait specialists with studio training who would undertake to depict the colonials as the aristocrats they thought they were. Yet this class character does not seem very convincing to-day because the painters themselves were clearly not good enough to become important at home; however, the relative provincialism of their technique might itself be considered suitable to the lack of cultural ease in most of their subjects. These immigrant specialists settled fairly evenly along the entire Atlantic Coast: John Smibert (1688–1751) in Boston (1729); John Watson (1685–1768) in Perth Amboy (1714); Gustavus Hesselius (1682–1755) in Philadelphia (1711); Charles Bridges (active 1735–1740) in Virginia; and Jeremiah Theüs (1719–1774) in Charleston (1739). Most of the foregoing practiced formulas which manifest no appreciable development. Smibert and Hesselius, however, not only evidence their awareness of Late Renaissance painting beyond the confines of portraiture but also manifest in some of their portrait work in this country a responsiveness to fresh experience in a mildly blunt directness absent from the work of the others.

Toward 1750 there appeared a trio of pronounced mannerists who satisfied what may have been a desire on the part of mid-century colonials for a high degree of make-believe. William Williams (c. 1710–c. 1790), actually a scene painter for the theater in Philadelphia, offered stage-set backgrounds for his portrait figures. Joseph Blackburn (active 1750–1763) itinerated through the northern towns and John Wollaston (active 1749–1767) peregrinated around the regions south of New York with considerable success. The very artificiality in the work of these late arrivals is effective testimony to their patrons' belief in the success of their class and cultural claims. Much of this work is factually erroneous, but collectively it presents a truthful report of what their subjects aspired to and is therefore culturally significant.

Meanwhile a number of native-born craftsmen had determined to become painters, and the conflicting responses between their inherited signcraft and the current portrait specialism brought about inconsistent results. Joseph Badger (1708–1765) and John Greenwood (1727–1792) were artisans whose attempts at the more sophisticated product remained technically awkward. Greenwood's robustiousness in painting matched

a strain of humor in his personality which exploded into a daring satire of *American Sea Captains Carousing,* done in Surinam after he had left this country for good. The initial awkwardness of Robert Feke (1705?–1750?) showed that from the first he was modeling himself upon the newer studio manner instead of the older workshop manner; that fact permitted his later emphasis upon rich textures and colors approaching splendor. John Hesselius (1728–1778), under the influence not of his father but of Wollaston, manifested similar tendencies with lesser feeling for sensuous beauty; and some portraits of distinction were done by John Mare (1739–?)—one of them containing an extraordinary *trompe-l'oeil* housefly. The entire body of work by the native-born painters, contrasted with the entire body of work by foreign-born ones who came here after 1700, gives evidence of their closer contact with the actualities of colonial life.

The best portraits by the colonial American genius, John Singleton Copley (1738–1815), transcend those of all other painters before the Revolution—in skill of drawing and brilliance of color, in the exploration of visual effects, in the use of artificial settings to dramatize colonial make-believe, but especially in the mastery of both constructed form and psychological intensity as the embodiment of mundane reality. In his London period, after his stay in Italy and before his late decline into insipidity, Copley created some powerful and imposing historical paintings in which his newly acquired technical suavity was still infused with his earlier semi-imaginative materialism. The soon-Europeanized Benjamin West (1738–1820) was famous throughout his long career in a way unmatched by any other colonial American, and his work ranged from the neoclassic to the fully romantic; but his influence fructified in the better work of other men, so that his historical position remains more significant than the aesthetic value of his own pictures for later times.

The years of fighting the war and then organizing the government were an interruption to all the visual arts, though perhaps least of all to painting. Through this transition time Charles Willson Peale was at work, but both the character and the dates of his best pictures place him in the following period. Peale had studied under West in London and so had Abraham Delanoy (c. 1740–c. 1790), who had little success after returning to New York in 1767. Henry Benbridge (1744–1812?) came back in 1770 with ideas like West's, but he had acquired them in Italy direct from West's own teachers there. The most interesting man whose work is clearly transitional was Matthew Pratt

(1734–1805); although he was able to paint a few portraits during these years, he also found it necessary to fall back upon painting signs. None of these is now known, but several of them were notable for their effect upon young would-be painters of the time; apparently they went beyond the earlier two-dimensional formula into a more thorough academic concept and thus may be interpreted as a flare-up of pictorialism in sign painting before the final subsidence into lettering for a now-literate people.

However, the general extension of painting beyond the limits of portraiture is documented for a half-century earlier, although surviving examples from before the Revolution are relatively few. One fragment may exist from the array of fanciful pictures on the shutters of John Watson's painting room, but no example is now known of the fanciful landscapes of Smibert's old age. The elder Hesselius is known to have painted some religious pictures, and two mythological examples have been handed down through descendants. Two such subjects, probably derived from prints, were done by Copley when a boy. Some decorative panels dated about 1715 survive from the Clark–Frankland House in Boston, and several panel paintings play an important part in an elaborately decorated room from "Marmion," a Virginia plantation home. Still in place are some very ambitious wall paintings in the Warner House, Portsmouth, New Hampshire. The foregoing are all specifically pictorial; a much larger number of non-pictorial decorations adorned less costly pre-Revolutionary homes. And the great array of advertisements by decorative painters suggests at least the beginning of a patronage which, however shallow in actuality,

promised eventual escape from the tyranny of the human face.

For the Moravians of central Pennsylvania, John Valentine Haidt (1700–1780) painted religious pictures in series as well as portraits of sectarian worthies. The German-descended Americans of that region also continued a curious craft derived from medieval manuscript illumination in their "fraktur" drawings. This racial group's inheritance in the use of striking color and freely formalized pattern was much more adequately preserved on pottery and painted chests; the pen drawing and water color practiced in the decoration of birth and marriage certificates and other documentary records is marginal to painting as an art. But many small-scale pictures were made with the technical procedure of true "fraktur," and these played a part in the rapid increase of amateur painting in the early nineteenth century.

Even so, this "fraktur" technique was less influential than the older tradition of the artisans who had originally brought painting to the Colonies. Out of that tradition, imperfectly maintained, came Winthrop Chandler (1747–1790). He painted a still life which seems to have had an illusionistic aim, landscapes conceived now with topographical accuracy and then with decorative liveliness, portraits some of which are repetitious close-ups and some of which use elaborate settings to secure boldly rhythmic patterns. In them all he manifested the inherent honesty of the basic painting craft and innate vigor of its American adaptation, which constitute something close to a subsurface continuity under the several changes of fashion on more sophisticated levels of technique.

PAINTING OF THE FEDERAL PERIOD AND NINETEENTH CENTURY

E. P. RICHARDSON

The century and a quarter between the American Revolution and the beginning of the twentieth century was a profuse, varied, picturesque, and rewarding period of American painting. The institutions of art—art schools, exhibitions, art dealers, and the journalism of art—which in the twentieth century create the patronage and the reputation of artists, were almost wholly lacking during much of the period. But the creative impulse was strong, the artistic activity great, and it extended to every part of the country.

It is a serious problem to select a list of slides which will illustrate so large and diversified an activity. I have tried to give due prominence to the figures who form the main line of artistic achievement while at the same time offering at least a sampling of the rich regional variety of American painting. Ours is a culture composed not only of geographical diversity but of many levels:

1. There are disciplined talents whose individuality of style and perception form the main stream.

2. There were artists at work all over the country in the nineteenth century who, without being notable stylists, form a major social phenomenon. They were painting portraits in settlements on the frontier before the stumps had been cleared from the streets of raw, new towns; they journeyed up and down the Atlantic Coast and the great inland rivers in search of portrait commissions or landscape subjects; they advanced beyond the frontier to paint the unconquered Indian and the wilderness as the explorers found it. These artists were seldom of the first rank, yet their mere existence in such conditions is a phenomenon of great significance and cannot be ignored.

3. There are some who might be called artist reporters, who give us an eyewitness view of our country's history in visual records of great interest to American studies.

4. There were the "untrained professionals," who were born with an endowment of talent but by the accidents of frontier life, or geographical or social distance from other artists, never attained a professional skill.

5. There were also the amateurs and the naïve, who (in periods like neoclassicism and romanticism) were carried along by the national enthusiasm for painting and made their own contribution to the story.

The American republic was born in an age saturated in the dream of classical antiquity. American painters shared the enthusiasm of their age, yet they were too remote from the collections of classical sculpture in Rome, Florence, and Paris, which were the models for European neoclassic painters, to share the archaeological and imitative aspects of neoclassicism. Only John Vanderlyn, who spent many years in Paris and Rome, was a neoclassic painter, who strove, in the European sense, to recreate in his work an ideal world of the past. The first American to study painting in Paris, he absorbed there not only the disciplined drawing and sculpturesque style but also the ambition to create grandiose historical compositions similar to those found in French neoclassic painting. There is another side to this man. Although he did his *Marius amidst the Ruins of Carthage* while living in Rome and his *Ariadne* in Paris, once out of the studio atmosphere of these centers he no longer painted classical subjects. Instead, his early portraits and his *Panorama of Versailles* show a surprising gift for romantic realism. Tragically, however, he remained convinced that he ought to paint historical subject matter and unable to do so, he sank into an old age of bitterness and frustration.

A stronger movement was neoclassic realism. Motivated by a growing nationalism, it found in the American struggle for independence the same motives of patriotism, devotion, and self-sacrifice which the French painters found in Plutarch.

John Trumbull, studying with West in London in the undogmatic English atmosphere, escaped the dogmatism of neoclassic theory on the continent. His great admiration, in fact, was Rubens, whom the French painters abhorred. In the 1780s he began a series of paintings on the decisive events of the American Revolution (the subjects chosen with the advice of Jefferson and Adams). Their luminosity, chiaroscuro, and vivid psychological force show how much he had learned from baroque narrative painting. Unfortunately, the engravings from this series did not sell and, discouraged, he dropped the project. Thus a hopeful experiment in a neoclassic painting of scenes from contemporary history came to an end. When he was commissioned to paint four of those same subjects for the Capitol in Washington twenty years later, his art had lost its sparkle. Robert Edge Pine, a good painter of the school of London, emigrated to Philadelphia to paint a series of pictures of the American Revolution but died leaving only one sketch, which was badly finished by Savage.

Gilbert Stuart was the leader in the development of a new type of American portrait. After experimenting in London with a great variety of traditional portrait types, he returned to the United States in 1792 and created a pictorial image which concentrated on the head alone. Without movement, mood, or accessory detail it was a conception which, now dulled for us by familiarity, was a decisive creation. Each of the major cities on the coast had its portrait painters in this taste: Charles Willson Peale and James Peale in Philadelphia; Stuart in Boston; Dunlap and Jarvis in New York. There were also European trained portrait painters: St. Mémin from France; Du Simitière from Switzerland; Sharples from England, all making profiles or pastel portraits in the neoclassic manner.

These neoclassic portraits are so familiar that we do not always give them the credit due to their admirable self-effacing craftsmanship. Much less well known are the American conversation pieces. On this side of the ocean James Peale, Joseph Wright, and William Dunlap represent the attractive invention of English and Dutch eighteenth-century painting.

The simple portrait was, however, the most popular form of painting. In the back country it was the staple of a number of painters who, although without sophisticated technique, achieved significant artistic results. The most notable group seems to have been active in the Connecticut Valley: Ralph Earl, William Jennys, Reuben Moulthrop, and one known only by his last name, McKay. Jacob Eichholtz is the chief example in the Pennsylvania back country. The combination of naïveté and earnest artistic feeling in the best works of these untrained professionals is extremely pleasing to twentieth-century taste.

The Neoclassical period saw a significant widening of the horizon of American art. Jeremiah Paul, John Louis Krimmel, and Henry Sargent represent the beginning of genre painting. At the same time, James and Raphaelle Peale established a form of still-life painting, based upon the example of the Dutch and Flemish early

baroque still life, which not only provided the basis of a Philadelphia school of still life but also gained wide popularity throughout the country.

Landscape also made its appearance. It was still largely topographical in spirit: the artist painted a famous sight—a town, a waterfall, a natural bridge—about which popular curiosity centered. Vanderlyn and Trumbull journeyed through the forests of New York State to paint views of Niagara Falls, which were intended to be engraved. L'Enfant left us a panorama of West Point which contains a unique view of the Continental army in camp. Two transplanted Englishmen, Groombridge and Guy, were specialists in topographical landscape, if one may term them so. Charles Willson Peale, always experimental and inventive, was the first to suggest the spirit of true landscape: an observation of a place or a phase of nature regarded as an end in itself.

This new awareness of the life of nature, which found expression in the rising interest in natural science, is also to be seen in the work of Alexander Wilson, the first important artist-naturalist of the new republic. Less well known than Audubon, his art has nonetheless the cool, crisp, objective virtues of his period.

Narrative painting of subjects, drawn from the ideal past, remained the great theme of painting in the romantic period, although style, mood, and subject matter changed from that of neoclassicism. Allston introduced the painting of dramatic, romantic subjects drawn from the Bible or from romantic literature. With these pictures, he introduced the emotional use of light and tone into American painting. His sense of the mysterious and the wonderful in human life, his power of evoking the moods of the magical and grandiose in nature gave him a special place in the rise of romantic painting. After his final return to America in 1818 his pictures were smaller and more intimate. Striking a note of brooding reverie they reflect similar qualities of mood to be found in the writings of his friends, William Ellery Channing and Washington Irving. In contrast, Rembrandt Peale adapted an essentially neoclassic style to the new romantic subject matter. The *Court of Death,* an allegory based upon a poem by the English Bishop Porteus, speaks not only for the love of melancholy that characterized the romantics but for the heroic ambitions of romanticism as well. Allston and Peale sought solutions to the most difficult problems in paintings of enormous scale. They totally ignored practical considerations such as adequate wall space for such large pictures and equated monumentality with size. A similar tendency among abstract painters today should help us to understand these motives in artists of the past. Comparable tendencies are to be found in Thomas Sully's historical mural, *Washington at the Crossing of the Delaware,* painted for the state capitol of North Carolina. Too large for any wall in the building, it is not only a narrative picture of great excellence but is also an example of the basic conflict between artistic ambition and social use that harassed the painters of this period.

Allston, Rembrandt Peale, Sully, Waldo, C. B. King, William E. West, and the miniature painter Malbone were the creators of a romantic portrait of mood, which succeeded the neoclassic style. Ruth Bascom and Eunice Pinney are the most attractive of the naïve in this generation.

The broadening and deepening sensitivity of this generation extended also to nature. Allston's landscapes of mood were outstanding examples of this time. Taking their point of departure from the landscapes of the Roman baroque (that is, of a constructed rather than a realistically observed image), they were to remain *sui generis* for a long time in American landscape. Thomas Birch, Alvan Fisher, and Thomas Doughty found their point of departure in the topographic view, developing it however in the direction of an enjoyment of nature's solitudes and a pensive enjoyment of rural scenes.

Working in a gentle and romantic mood, Rubens Peale continued the family tradition of still life into mid-century and C. B. King introduced the thematic or story-telling still life.

With his enthusiasm for the splendor and mystery of nature, John James Audubon brought a particularly romantic sense of wonder and delight to his interpretations of the wild creatures of the vast unexplored continent. His aim was to depict with scientific accuracy the birds and animals of America. But scientists have always distrusted his plates because of their subjective and dramatic qualities. Therefore, it is as a painter and poet of the wild and interpreter of the lovely and the strange in nature that his work must be understood.

The love of the past and of idealized dramatic subject matter remained strong in the second generation, which came forward about 1825–1830.

Thomas Cole made his reputation first by small landscapes which revealed to his generation the poetry of the vast, lonely continent of wilderness. But the works which made him the most popular American painter of the time were his romantic cycles. *Course of Empire* (New-York Historical Society), *Voyage of Life* (Munson-Williams-Proctor Institute), and *The Departure and Return* express the notion of the flight of time, which was the popular form of one of the great intellectual movements of the nineteenth century. History, archaeology, geology, a new awareness of the rise and decay of multitudinous forms of life (including human civilizations) profoundly altered the intellectual horizon of our world. This sense of inexorable change Cole expressed for his world in crude, sentimental, yet unforgettable images. John Quidor, on the other hand, lived imaginatively in the world of old New York as created by Washington Irving. William Page was of a much more complex mind. In his pictures an atmosphere of reverie veils not only the imagined past but also the contemporary world. Brilliant, erratic, uneven, he was an unpredictable and memorable artist. S. F. B. Morse and J. G. Chapman were by contrast skillful figure painters, capable of painting either real or imagined scenes but without the overtones which make Page interesting.

Portraiture remained the principal bread-and-butter form of painting. The country was rich in painters who could render a dignified (and in the case of Page or Morse a distinguished) portrait: Francis Alexander, Chester Harding, G. P. A. Healy, Henry Inman, John Neagle, C. L. Elliott, and William J. Hubard represent a large and varied generation of portrait painters in the major cities; Jeremiah P. Hardy, Joseph Davis, and Joseph Stock show how the practice of the back country painters varied from the poetic and the confident to the utterly naïve.

If the leader of romantic sentiment in landscape was Thomas Cole, the principal figure of romantic realism was Asher B. Durand. Landscape in this generation began to assume a dominant role in the interest of artists (if not yet in that of the public), replacing the monumental or ideal narrative as the subject matter most challenging to the imagination. Durand began as an engraver and among his earliest works was a portfolio called the *American Landscape* which appeared in 1830. In spite of the limitations of the medium, these prints revealed his early preoccupation with nature for its own sake. When, in mid-career, he turned to painting, his vision remained similarly directed and his work in oils took on a transparent romantic realism. He was not a self-conscious stylist, yet as one of the early advocates of painting out-of-doors, he was attracted by the high key of sunlight. Thus his style developed a particular luminosity.

As interest in narrative painting declined, genre painting and its allies, humorous and satirical art, became more popular. Morse, Chapman, Mount, and Bingham, in their varied ways, made this a rich and important period for genre. Mount found his subject matter in the villages of Setauket and Stony Brook on Long Island, where he had grown up. He had the temperament to see what is artistically interesting in the familiar; and though not a colorist, he was a master of the expressive movement. Through firm, convincing drawing his rustic figures are caught in a passing moment of their lives. Bingham likewise had the genius to see the artistic significance of the ordinary. His subject matter was drawn from the life of the Western rivermen and the farmers of the Western frontier. As Mount's, Bingham's original style is rooted in a vigorous draughtsmanship which is almost classic in its slightly archaic severity. His main strength, however, lies in the subtle luminosity in which he clothed his images. Brilliant yet still and soft, clear yet smoky as an autumn day, it unites his homely figures in a world of friendly but pervasive light.

The principal humorists and satirists were D. C. Johnston, T. N. Burnham, David G. Blythe, and N. E. Ferrill. Lacking the monumental qualities of Bingham and Mount, they are both boisterous and biting in their candid reflections of the common man in the common scene. Also related to genre was the interest in the frontier and the Indian, an interest which produced a large number of artist-reporters and explorers, of whom the most prominent were Catlin, Eastman, Miller and Stanley; on a far lower artistic level than Bingham and Mount, nonetheless they left important historical records.

The affinity of the romantic imagination with nature in all its forms produced a number of men who were specialists in limited fields of subject matter. Sometimes they were artists of considerable distinction. Among them were: Robert Salmon, the marine painter; James and John Bard, the ship-portrait painters; and Edward Troye, painter of horses.

As a form of popular amusement the pictorial panorama appeared to replace the traveling monumental narrative paintings of the previous generation. One surviving example is the *Panorama of the Mississippi* by John J. Egan. Also in the field of popular art, but deeper in feeling, is the work of two imaginative primitives, Edward Hicks and Erastus Salisbury Field. The former, a sign and carriage painter as well as a Quaker preacher, expressed in his naïve compositions the Friends' dream of peace and the country dweller's simple love of his native land; the latter celebrated the centennial of the republic in gentle fantasy. Yet one must add that in a deeper sense all forms of painting constituted a popular art in those years. The popular imagination of the Americans was excited and roused by life in their new world; painting, which gave them an image of themselves and their country, was widely practiced. Artists roamed the country from one end to the other. But the exciting qualities of their work derived from the imaginative exploitation of the common

scene and not from original developments in style. The Americans were in love with their country and sought to give it expression in vivid pictorial terms; and while their style was in most cases unpretentious, it was, nevertheless, surprisingly suited to the qualities of their pictorial means.

On the surface the ideals of American painting did not change at mid-century; yet certain tendencies, which we may call luminism, naturalism, and sentimentalism, became so pronounced that they worked subtle changes in the artistic climate.

Both luminism and naturalism found their natural expression in landscape painting, which was not as popular with the general public as it was with painters. Kensett, Whittredge, and Sanford Gifford are leading figures of luminism; F. E. Church of naturalism. The two tendencies were related: the luminists retained a delicate precision of drawing in their studies of light, and the best naturalists were sensitive to light. Only the less gifted, who grouped themselves under Ruskin's banner as American pre-Raphaelites, sacrificed light and air entirely in their search for exactness of delineation.

Kensett began as an engraver and carried over into his oils the clear precise drawing and careful spacing of his early training, adding to these a fine sense of aerial tone and a poetic love of solitude. Whittredge worked in a more painterly manner, but he used luminosity and aerial tone rather than line as his principal means. Gifford bathes the world in an all-enveloping unity of light and air. They are artists of quiet, delicate sensitivity. Church, on the other hand, stirred by a reading of Humboldt's *Cosmos,* endeavored to draw a picture of the heroic grandeurs of nature as they seemed in that dawn of the great age of natural science. He travelled from the arctic to the tropics, he painted the jungles, volcanoes in eruption, the aurora borealis, the vast flood of the Great Lakes pouring ceaselessly over Niagara.

Fitz-Hugh Lane, Jasper F. Cropsey, M. J. Heade, and Conrad Wise Chapman represent the variety of temperament found within these general tendencies. George Inness stands somewhat apart. He brought to American landscape the painterly ideals of the Barbizon School, striving to interpret the American landscape with the broad brush stroke and synthetic, rather than analytical, vision of the French. Albert Bierstadt also stands a little apart, not because of a conception of style but because of his subject matter: he was a specialist in the grandiose scenery of the West, giving the Americans of the East stirring images of the scenic grandeurs of the Rockies and the half-explored lands beyond.

The same tendencies appeared in genre painting, which had now usurped the former popularity of the portrait. A delicate luminism modeled upon that of the seventeenth-century Dutch gives to the work of Eastman Johnson and R. C. Woodville a greater tonal complexity; in contrast, a forthright naturalism touched with mid-nineteenth-century sentimentality marks the work of J. G. Brown, Thomas LeClear, Jerome Thompson, C. C. Ward, and T. W. Wood.

The portrait continued as an important means of artistic expression, but the influence of the daguerreotype led to certain changes in attitude. Generally it led to a sharpening of the quest for objective reality and a lessening of the traditional stylistic qualities of the earlier work. In spite of this, not all portrait painters fell under the spell of the photograph. Among those who continued to strive for a broader range of artistic values were Eastman Johnson and Thomas Hicks.

There were some other artists who, in spite of the naturalism of the times, turned for inspiration to the world of memory and dreams. George Fuller is one of these. His brooding misty figures and veiled landscapes strike the note of reverie that Allston had introduced. William Morris Hunt, though an apostle of Jean François Millet and the Barbizon School, did his most individual work in an idealized, poetic mural painting, *The Flight of Night,* for the state capitol at Albany, New York. The subject is drawn from a Persian poem about Anahita, the goddess of night, which had long haunted his imagination; it was for him a symbol of the darkness of ignorance fleeing before the light of civilization. Owing to bad planning by the contractors, the murals were ruined by dampness; the sketch, however, is preserved. The strange eccentric William Rimmer showed in his life and in his work the difficulties experienced by a subjective and visionary mind in an age of naturalism. He was a self-taught doctor and anatomist, as well as painter and sculptor. His imagination was haunted by nightmare visions which his art was often too undisciplined to express successfully, yet at his best he is an artist of power.

Painting for the popular taste continued in almost undiminished quantity. Typical of this generation are the works of George W. Morrison, Isaac Augustus Wetherby, and Ella Emory.

A dominating factor in the development of American painting during the last quarter of the nineteenth century was the attraction of Europe. New inventions—the railroad, steamboat, telegraph—made travel and communication easy; new industrial wealth awoke new ambitions in Americans. At the same time European painting was extraordinarily rich, profuse, and creative. American painters began to study and live in Europe in unprecedented numbers.

Three figures, Whistler, Sargent, and Mary Cassatt, played so conspicuous a role in European painting that they are sometimes claimed as members of the English and French Schools; they are at least evidence of a great cosmopolitanism of talent in American artists. All three had their training in Paris, which became in the eighties the art school of the whole world.

Whistler, the oldest of the three, was a perfect embodiment of the inspirations of that cosmopolitan world of art of which he was one of the creators. American by birth and in his quality of quick receptivity, European by training, he caught the first breath of that wind from the Far East which was to blow so strongly later in the century. In Paris in the early fifties he learned the rich use of oil paint and the objective spirit of Courbet's new naturalism. But he was inspired also by the soft colors and novel patterns of Japanese prints and by the cool silvery-grey tones of Velásquez. These seemingly contradictory sources he combined and refined to form his own intensely personal and decorative style.

Sargent arrived in Paris twenty years later to learn from the now forgotten Carolus-Duran the technique of the great French painter-illustrators—the instantaneous vision, the luminous style, the painterly approach, the direct stroke with the fully loaded brush—to which he added his own objective temperament. Sargent's sense of tone was superior to his control of line, so that his early works in the strong chiaroscuro of the eighties seem more felicitous than his later work in the bright palette of impressionism.

Whistler worked alternately in Paris and London; Sargent chose the latter after the furious row kicked up by his portrait of *Madame Gautreau* in the Salon of 1884; but Mary Cassatt settled down in Paris to become, at least in her art, completely Parisian. She was a figure painter who learned much from Degas and Manet; but perhaps her most interesting period came in the nineties when, inspired by an exhibition of Japanese prints in Paris in 1890, she put a vigor of outline and pattern into her color prints and her oils that make them very personal experiments in style.

Before Americans began to study in Paris, many other European cities and countries attracted them. The favorite of American art students in the seventies was Munich, where Duveneck and W. M. Chase learned their dark, rich "Munich style." Chase, however, soon abandoned this dark palette for the light blonde tones of the Paris School.

Theodore Robinson was the first American to study with Monet and to bring back to America the broken color technique of French impressionism. But the most successful American impressionist was probably Childe Hassam, who was already a good painter in the American luminist tradition before going to Paris.

A peculiar development in American impressionism was its tendency toward a muted, misty, decorative style. This was most conspicuous in painters like Dewing and Twachtman and in the later style of Wyant, Homer Martin, and Inness.

In part this can be attributed to the normal evolution of style. After the boldness and experimental vigor of the innovators, there generally follows a second generation which refines the old style and reduces it to an idiom with more decorative implications. This was conspicuously true of the American followers of the French impressionists. But there was also a mood of quietism, a phase of subtle lyricism in these painters of the close of the century which recalls the dreamlike reveries of Allston's later works and which may well be one of the recurring phases of the American imaginative life, for it is not hard to discover it again in the artists of our own century.

The main line of stylistic development in painting, whether impressionist or not, was governed by an interest in light and in the intense study of nature. Both had their roots in the art of the earlier nineteenth century and were a natural outgrowth of what had gone before. But whereas the cosmopolitan artists adopted technical solutions already arrived at in European painting, a number of painters refused to follow them. With dogged independence they set themselves to work out their own solutions, using the subjects they found around them in American life and evolving their own style out of the precedents of American luminism. At the time, this was an unpopular movement. Today its great figures, Winslow Homer and Thomas Eakins, are among the greatest names in American painting. These artists cannot be called provincials. Homer lived for twenty-two years in New York exposed to all the influences of the art world, visited Paris, and lived two years in England. Eakins studied for three years in Paris and spent a winter in Spain, both of which were decisive influences on his style. Their choice of their own subject matter in the life they knew best at home was a deliberate artistic choice, not an accident.

Homer's art falls into two periods—before and after his visit to England in 1881–1882. His early pictures are almost always small in size and large in style; their subjects are soldiers in the Civil War, people on farms, woodsmen in the forest, observed with great freshness and without sentimentality. His later oils are large, grave, and monumental in feeling, while the freshness of his early vision continues, growing more subtle and masterly, in his later water colors.

After his return from Europe, Eakins devoted his life to painting his own vision of the life of his native city, Philadelphia. He had that imaginative passion for the meaning of the real and the familiar which, in other minds, made the greatness of Whitman and of nineteenth-century science. Since Copley had left Boston, no one had turned such a penetrating eye for character on the inhabitants of an American city as Eakins now turned in Philadelphia. His scientific interests were expressed in his paintings of great surgeons in their operating theatres; his love of the life of the city in genre paintings and in his dusky, luminous landscapes. His art was one of the utmost sobriety but also of great depths of feeling. Thomas P. Anshutz, who succeeded Eakins at the Pennsylvania Academy of the Fine Arts, was an objective realist in the same tradition and a teacher of profound influence. It was characteristic of these painters that they worked in a warm, rather dark tonality with strong contrasts of tone derived from American romantic painting, rather than in the blonde tones and broken color of French impressionism.

Parallel to these independents among the figure painters was a most interesting school of still life, which grew out of the Peale tradition in Philadelphia and the teaching of the Pennsylvania Academy of the Fine Arts. Its practitioners, Harnett, Peto, and Haberle, raised the *trompe-l'oeil* to new heights of interest and artistic significance. Yet so all-pervading was the Europeanized impressionist taste at the end of the century that these artists found their audience only among the unsophisticated—businessmen, keepers of saloons, plain middle-class Americans—who liked pictures for their subject matter and their reality. The well-bred taste of the time ignored them.

The problems of light and of the observation of nature did not obliterate the inspirations of literature and history, subjective fantasy, and dream.

John La Farge was the leader of a renewed effort to create a monumental mural art in America. In Trinity Church, Boston (1876) he was collaborating with an architect of genius who wished the mural paintings to enrich the whole fabric; in his later works, La Farge usually had to work within rigid geometric forms provided him by classic revival architecture. His compositions within the unrewarding shape of the lunette are sometimes extremely ingenious and interesting; yet the architectural style of the period prevented anything like an over-all effect such as Sargent achieved in the Boston Public Library decorations. La Farge was a thoughtful

and intelligent artist, however, and the leader of an interesting period of mural painting. But it is his water
colors, his writings, and his subtle, fugitive drawings
which, to our taste at least, best express the qualities of
his unusual intelligence. Sargent's Boston Public Library decorations, on the other hand, are perhaps more
interesting for their achievement of the over-all enrich-
ment and mood of the room than for their detail; yet he
too produced something notable for its time.

Albert P. Ryder illustrated the subjective and private intelligence in art as La Farge did the public one.
Ryder's works are easel pictures, small, modest, yet
eloquent with the mysteries of the human psyche. In
the midst of New York's tumult of life, he lived withdrawn in a world of moods and memories, inspired by
music, the sea, and the night.

The memories with which Vedder worked were
racial memories, myths, legends, poetry, transmuted
by the artist's personal imagination and feeling. He
settled in Rome in 1867 for the remainder of his
life. The warm, luminous, little landscapes which
came out of his rambles in the Italian hills have almost
the transparent romantic realism of a Corot. But in
his figure subjects it is the movement of outline and
the haunted fantasy of the mood that make him
memorable.

It would be hard to find four artists more varied in
imagination and style than La Farge, Sargent, Ryder,
and Vedder. That they existed together in one generation and worked on similar problems of the imagination, is a tribute to the vitality of the ideal strain in
American painting which persisted through the period
of scientific naturalism and realism.

PAINTING OF THE TWENTIETH CENTURY

JOHN I. H. BAUR

As the twentieth century opened, American painting found itself at a low ebb. In Everett Shinn's only slightly exaggerated words:

> It had inherited a preceding drowsiness, and that virus of ease and artificiality produced in the non-resistant body a lowering of vitality and a state of staggering decrepitude. . . . Art galleries of that time were more like funeral parlors wherein the cadavers were displayed in their sumptuous coffins.

Our genre painting, once full of boisterous life, had fallen into a quagmire of sentiment. Landscape painting, in the hands of the American tonalists, was the insubstantial echo of Whistler's most insubstantial manner. The blue shadows of impressionism were already becoming an academic device. The slashing brush strokes of Sargent and the Munich School were imitated by the innumerable students of William Merritt Chase and were only slightly livelier than the neoclassical and neo-Renaissance inventions of the followers of La Farge and Kenyon Cox. While these various academic currents produced some paintings of minor interest in the work of Edmund Tarbell, George de Forest Brush, Charles Hopkinson, Gari Melchers, Cecilia Beaux, and others, they also marked a creative dead end—a final period to the long dominion of realism in our nineteenth-century art.

Two paths led out of this impasse, and both were followed by American painters, beginning early in the century. One path was the revitalization of the old realist tradition through the discovery of a new realm of subject matter and the excitement which its exploration engendered. This was the way taken by a group of artists within the small society known as The Eight—especially by Robert Henri (though more as teacher than painter), John Sloan, William Glackens, George Luks, and Everett Shinn. Guided by Henri's philosophy that art is only the tracing of life, these men, joined by George Bellows, Glenn Coleman, and other kindred spirits, turned to the vast human spectacle of New York —to its colorful immigrants and fashionable shoppers, its five-cent movies and expensive restaurants, its parks, prizefights, prostitutes, and music halls. They discovered, in short, material which had never before been systematically explored by artists, except for the pioneering efforts, on a more limited scale, of Eugene Higgins and Jerome Myers.

"The Black Gang," "the men of rebellion," as these early social-realists were called after the first (and only) exhibition of The Eight in 1908, were not at all radical stylistically. For the most part, they carried forward the dark tonality and broad brushwork of the Munich School, reinforced by Henri's admiration for Hals and Velásquez. But with their warm and genuine sympathy, their spontaneous delight in the city's human pageant, they breathed new life into the old style, which indeed was well adapted to their moods and interests. Above all, they exploded the academic belief that only "beautiful" subjects were properly the concern of the artist. In doing so, they opened the whole area of American life to the painter, though it was not until the 1930s that this fertile material was fully exploited.

The other path was more truly revolutionary. It was the two-lane highway of abstraction and expressionism, built abroad in the early years of the century but followed, almost as soon as it was opened, by a growing number of young American painters. In Europe these movements had evolved with a certain logic out of postimpressionism. In America there had been no post-impressionist movement, except for the isolated and generally misunderstood work of Maurice Prendergast, our earliest admirer of Cézanne. As a result, we leaped without transition from realism and belated forms of impressionism into the formal language of abstraction and the extreme distortions of expressionism. Small wonder that some of the first leaps were tentative or that the public reaction for many years was one of bewildered hostility.

American expressionism, before 1920, was inspired chiefly by the French Fauves. Max Weber and Alfred Maurer studied with Matisse in 1907–1908. Bernard Karfiol and Samuel Halpert followed the more conservative lead of Derain and Marquet. Charles Demuth's early water colors were perhaps the most original adaptation of Fauve influences. But the northern expressionism of Germany and Russia also had its effect on painters like Oscar Bluemner and Ben Benn.

The abstract painters were more numerous, and again the early center of influence was Paris. There Max Weber, Arthur G. Dove, Maurice Sterne, and Abraham Walkowitz were among the pioneers who experimented with personal varieties of cubism. Synchromism, an American movement almost identical with French Orphism, was founded in 1913 by Morgan Russell and Stanton Macdonald-Wright, while Patrick Henry Bruce was a direct follower of the French Orphist, Delaunay. Italian futurism entered our art in the work of Joseph Stella and had a noticeable influence on Lyonel Feininger, who was working in Germany with the *Blaue Reiter* group. In Germany, too, were Marsden Hartley and Konrad Cramer, both painting abstractly in a more expressionist vein. John Covert, trained in both Munich and Paris, contributed a few paintings and several brilliant collages before he gave up his career as an artist. After the famous Armory Show of 1913, which first introduced the modern movements on a large scale to America, many other young artists were influenced by abstraction and expressionism, including Arthur B. Davies, John Marin, Morton L. Schamberg, Charles Sheeler, Georgia O'Keeffe, Stuart Davis, Andrew M. Dasburg, and Arthur B. Carles.

While a few memorable paintings resulted from the enthusiasm of our early modernists, we did not, as Dasburg remarked, produce any movement with "the contagious force of Cubism." Indeed, the tendency of many American artists was to take certain elements from abstract art and to adapt these, on a quite conservative level, to the romantic-realism which they had inherited from Winslow Homer and Thomas Eakins. In general, they simplified their forms, suppressed detail, and worked toward more monumental and more emphatically designed compositions. The trend can be seen as early as 1910 in the work of Rockwell Kent and Guy du Bois, followed soon after by Eugene Speicher, Leon Kroll, and Kenneth Hayes Miller. It was enriched, after 1920, by a number of painters who had started as modernists but returned to more conservative paths— among them, Karfiol, Walt Kuhn, Henry L. McFee, Maurice Sterne, and Dasburg. In the late 1920s and in the 1930s the movement reached its peak with the addition of many younger painters such as Alexander Brook, Henry Varnum Poor, Isabel Bishop, Jon Corbino, Morris Kantor, Peppino Mangravite, Henry

Mattson, and a great many others. By this time, it had lost nearly all trace of modernist influence (except for occasional echoes of Cézanne and Pascin) and had become, at best, a rich and painterly style stamped by the individuality of the artist, at worst, a studio tradition of good taste and little else.

The decade of the 1920s marked, indeed, a general reaction against modernism. A few of the stronger spirits kept on their solitary ways, and there were some new recruits in Stuart Davis, Paul Burlin, Benjamin Kopman, and the young Yasuo Kuniyoshi. But, in general, American artists withdrew from their advanced positions, as if to digest what they had learned and to consolidate their gains. Perhaps the most characteristic movement of this decade was that of the so-called immaculates, which was another compromise between abstraction and native realism—this time a more radical compromise, involving extreme simplification of form and sharp-edged clarity of design, applied, for the most part, to the functional machine aspects of American civilization. It had its forerunner in Morton L. Schamberg and its leaders in Charles Sheeler, Charles Demuth, and Georgia O'Keeffe, although Demuth gave it a Dadalike twist and O'Keeffe a personal symbolism that were not typical of the movement as a whole. It was Sheeler, more than anyone else, who discovered the abstract beauty in our industrial forms, from steamships to factories, and who developed a polished semiabstract style of corresponding austerity. Late in the 1920s he was joined by several others, including Niles Spencer and, for a brief time, Peter Blume.

The economic depression, which started in 1929, seems to have been a major factor in the accelerated trend away from abstract art during the 1930s, a trend that was even more pronounced than in the preceding decade. At the same time, the Depression inspired a new social consciousness among artists, which was generally embodied in some form of expressionism, perhaps because that movement gave more scope for passionate utterance on specific subjects than did either abstraction or realism. In the work of Ben Shahn, Philip Evergood, William Gropper, George Grosz, Robert Gwathmey, and the young Jack Levine, its distortions were used as a sharp-edged weapon against privilege and social injustice. A more sober realism was also used by several artists to reveal social conditions, though in a less militant spirit. The melancholy poetry of the Soyer brothers, the Bowery and Coney Island dramas of Reginald Marsh, the street and subway scenes of Kenneth Hayes Miller and Isabel Bishop constitute an allied movement sometimes called the Fourteenth Street School.

Throughout the country there was a general trend in these years away from internationalism and toward the further exploration of the American scene. Two pioneers were Edward Hopper and Charles Burchfield, both of whom had started to record their intimate impressions of city and rural life in the early 1920s and who produced, during the next decade, some truly memorable interpretations of the moods which they sensed in their chosen subjects. A more militant Americanism, ardently promoted by Thomas Craven, appeared in the Middle West where the famous "Triumvirate"—Thomas Hart Benton, John Steuart Curry, and Grant Wood—inveighed against all European "isms" and even against the "effete" American artists of the Eastern seaboard. Regionalism became a more powerful factor in our art than at any time in the century. For a while Aaron Bohrod represented Chicago, just as Everett Spruce, to an even greater degree, imposed his personal expressionism on Texas. Everywhere the search for new aspects of America widened. Fletcher Martin painted baseball, Joseph Hirsch portrayed the businessman—two characteristic phenomena neglected before. Alexandre Hogue and William Palmer uncovered the devastation of the dust bowl, Peter Hurd the high plains and mountains of the Far West. The Federal Art Project of the WPA supported many of these artists during the Depression years, and while it prescribed no subjects or styles, much of the work done was devoted to the American scene, and the predominant manner was romantic realism, couched in a variety of painterly techniques.

In 1930, however, Grant Wood had developed, in *American Gothic* (The Art Institute of Chicago), a hard, almost photographic realism, which seems to have been the starting point for a whole new movement of minutely observed and precisely rendered pictures. Wood, himself, soon abandoned the style, but it was carried to further extremes during the 1930s by Paul Cadmus, Jared French, Andrew Wyeth, and Peter Hurd. Charles Sheeler moved in a similar direction at this time, as did Ben Shahn in a few paintings like his *Vacant Lot* (Wadsworth Atheneum). Since 1940 this extreme realism has been adopted by a group of younger painters, including George Tooker, Robert Vickrey, Stephen Greene, Bernard Perlin, and Carlyle Brown.

It has also been used, with quite different effect, by several American artists who have come under the influence of surrealism. This movement, devoted to the fantastic, the irrational, and the exploration of the subconscious mind, was born in Paris in 1924, where the expatriate American Man Ray was an early member,

as were the Europeans Yves Tanguy and Kurt Seligmann, who later settled in this country. The first surrealist exhibitions here were held in the early 1930s, and soon there were new converts, such as Walter Quirt, Federico Castellon, Kay Sage, and Leon Kelly. Orthodox surrealism, with its antiaesthetic platform and its insistence on automatism, never became a widespread movement in America. But it did affect in varying degrees many of our most gifted realists, who have used their impressive technical skills for more fantastic ends than they might otherwise have pursued. Peter Blume, Ivan Albright, Louis Guglielmi, Alton Pickens, and Lorser Feitelson have all made use of surrealist devices, although they can scarcely be called surrealists themselves.

About 1940, the tide turned again. Abstract art, which had ebbed during the preceding decade, now rose in a spontaneous wave until it became, for the first time in our history, a dominant movement in American art. One can only conjecture the causes of this change. Among them may have been the feeling that American-scene painting had exhausted its resources, together with the fact that the Second World War generated both a spirit of internationalism and, at the same time, a sense of disillusionment. The latter doubtless turned some artists toward purely aesthetic problems and others toward personal introspection—the two mainsprings of abstraction.

Whatever the causes, the portents began to appear in the late 1930s. One was the arrival in America of many outstanding European modernists, driven from their homelands by persecution or war. Several of them came from the Nazi-suppressed Bauhaus in Germany and settled here permanently, among them Josef Albers and László Moholy-Nagy, who became influential teachers. Another was the American-born Lyonel Feininger. In 1937, a group of young Americans embarked on what George L. K. Morris called "the quest for an abstract tradition" and founded the society known as American Abstract Artists. Soon many older painters who had been identified with the American scene, such as Arnold Blanch, Fletcher Martin, and Philip Guston, abandoned their various kinds of realism for a more abstract approach. By the mid-1940s, there could be no doubt that abstract art had attained a formidable impetus.

Since then, American abstract painting has followed a number of very different courses, some of them related to earlier European forms of abstraction. Thus cubism has been reexplored and reinterpreted by such painters as Stuart Davis, G. L. K. Morris, and Bradley Walker Tomlin. The geometrical severity of Mondrian and the Dutch *de Stijl* movement has had its followers here in Fritz Glarner, Ilya Bolotowsky, and Burgoyne Diller, while constructivism has affected Balcomb Greene and I. Rice Pereira. Individual European masters, particularly Picasso, Klee, and Miro, have also had a recognizable influence at various times on such dissimilar artists as Max Weber, Karl Knaths, Arshile Gorky, and many others. It must be emphasized, however, that all of the artists mentioned in this paragraph have absorbed their influences and have usually moved far from their original sources. To take a single example, Davis's staccato rhythms and strident color chords have made of cubism an entirely different kind of art, one which reflects with extraordinary perception certain aspects of American life.

Perhaps the most original, and certainly the most influential, contribution of America to international abstraction is the so-called abstract-expressionist movement, which has already had a considerable effect on European artists. It is the first American-born movement to do so. Taking elements from surrealism—particularly a certain degree of automatism and a distrust of the rational structure of cubism—the leaders of this movement have sought to express mind and being on their canvases by the spontaneous, uncalculated action of painting. (They have, for this reason, also been called the action painters.) Unlike the surrealists, they have not courted fantasy or the irrational, and their search has been both a difficult and a serious one. An important forerunner of this trend was Arshile Gorky during his late period, from about 1940 to his death in 1948. Its most controversial figure was the late Jackson Pollock, who achieved a violent intensity of expression by dripping and splattering his paint on huge canvases spread on the floor. Another leading figure is Willem de Kooning, although he has reverted more often than the rest to concrete imagery, as in his *Woman* series. In the work of Mark Rothko, William Baziotes, James Brooks, Theodoros Stamos, Franz Kline, Clyfford Still, Adolph Gottlieb, and Bradley Walker Tomlin (after c. 1946), the movement has spread through a great variety of personal styles. It has also had an interesting sequel in the very recent movement known as abstract-impressionism, in which Philip Guston is now a leading figure. As its title implies, this is a somewhat less subjective approach, in which impressions of the visual world are translated abstractly by approximately the same spontaneous technique as that devised by the abstract-expressionists. The late lily-pond paintings of Claude Monet have exercised a certain influence on this trend.

While these are the main directions of abstract art since 1940, there have also been a great many personal variations which do not fit into the well-defined trends, though they often incorporate traits drawn from several of them. Thus Attilio Salemme and Ad Reinhardt are geometrical-abstractionists though far removed from *de Stijl*. Similarly, Hans Hofmann and John Ferren are related to abstract-expressionism but seem more objective in their attitudes. Among a multitude of others who have given diversity to our abstract or semiabstract painting are Lee Gatch, Lamar Dodd, Joseph Glasco, Jimmy Ernst, John Heliker, Ralston Crawford, and Carl Morris.

Unlike abstraction, which has tended to rise and subside in distinct waves, expressionism has grown steadily throughout the twentieth century and has been, for many years, a major trend in our contemporary art. Since 1940 it has flowered with particular brilliance, partly because of the fact that several pioneer expressionists reached their fullest powers during these years. Thus both Hartley and Kuniyoshi did, without question, the finest work of their careers during the last few years of their lives, while Marin's late oils, long neglected, now begin to seem a crowning achievement. Among living artists, Weber, Shahn, Evergood, Karl Knaths, Abraham Rattner, and Karl Zerbe have richly fulfilled their early promise during this same period.

The contagious appeal of expressionism to artists of widely different temperaments is also apparent in the many new figures who have joined its ranks during the past two decades. Their variety of theme and style is impressive. They range from the ascetic New England landscapes of William Kienbusch to Hyman Bloom's exotic studies of mortality and decay, from the stark religious imagery of Rico Lebrun to William Congdon's withdrawn and twilight poetry. In the equally personal work of Franklin Watkins, Benjamin Kopman, Ernest Fiene, Ben-Zion, Jonah Kinigstein, and a great many more, the vocabulary of present-day expressionism has been notably enlarged. The socially conscious wing of the movement has also enlisted strong new recruits in such men as Gregorio Prestopino, Jacob Lawrence, and Anton Refregier. On the whole, this aspect of expressionism has mellowed and has been less militant since the passing of the Depression, though it remains deeply concerned with the relations of man to society.

Realism, particularly in its more romantic aspects, is the one formerly widespread movement which appears to have visibly dwindled in creative energy since 1940. Gone today are many of the best representational painters of the 1920s and 1930s—either literally, through death, as in the case of Kuhn and Karfiol, or because they have changed to a different idiom, as have Blanch, Guston, Adolph Dehn, and others. Those who remain have not, with some exceptions, done their best work in recent years. Nor has there been much fresh talent added, except for the relatively small group of extreme realists already mentioned. On the other hand, since 1950 portents of a new realist trend have appeared in the work of several gifted young painters who have broken their early allegiance to abstraction and moved in the direction of a Bonnardlike post-impressionism, sometimes quite highly organized, as in Grace Hartigan's painting, sometimes sketchy, sensitive, and evanescent, as in certain canvases by Larry Rivers. Whether this is the beginning of a wider movement is still difficult to say.

These are the broad currents (and some of the back eddies) of American painting in the twentieth century —seldom very distinct, frequently blending their waters, but still accounting for the main flow of creative effort in our day. No survey of the period would be complete, however, without mention of two groups of artists who have remained relatively unaffected by the battle of styles or by the dominant ideas, ideals, and enthusiasms that have been an essential part of that battle.

In one group are those scattered romantic visionaries, those poets of the inner eye, who have enriched our art in unexpected ways, sometimes with imaginative fantasy, sometimes with mystical insights. Their visions are essentially personal and distinctive, though occasionally they overlap with one another. The haunted and haunting maidens of Arthur B. Davies, Middleton Manigault, and Darrel Austin are quite unlike, but they all inhabit mysterious, unreal worlds that exist only in the artist's mind. An element of Oriental mysticism forms a tenuous link between the work of Mark Tobey and Morris Graves, who also shared at one time the technique of "white writing," long since abandoned by Graves. Both of these painters live on the Northwest Coast, which has also given us the strange imagery of C. S. Price and Kenneth Callahan. But region has little to do with art of this kind. The Middle West has nurtured Burchfield's nature fantasies and reconstructions of childhood emotions (in his very early and his late work). In the East, Edwin Dickinson's enigmatic ruins and Loren MacIver's tender poetry of the city add their own personal notes. Unlike most painters, several of these artists work in a wide variety of styles, ranging individually from abstraction, or semiabstraction, to a quite precise realism and often working in different ways at the same time. It is the mind's image

rather than the style which is paramount in their art and which gives consistency to the inconsistency of manner. Any means is justified to evoke the magic sought.

The second group outside the main currents of contemporary art embraces our so-called primitives—those generally untrained and always unsophisticated artists whose aim seems principally to record as accurately as possible familiar scenes or subjects that bear emotional significance for them. Lacking the technical means to be realists, they nevertheless create by some alchemy their moods of place and theme, realized in the instinctively decorative patterns which seem to be the natural heritage of primitive painters in all times. We tend to consider the nineteenth century as the golden age of primitive painting in America, and doubtless conditions were then more favorable to the production of a naïve art. But we have had our smaller share of gifted primitives in the twentieth century—among them John Kane, Joseph Pickett, Horace Pippin, Morris Hirshfield, and the incredibly popular "Grandma" Moses. Due partly to the liberating influence of modernism, the public taste for primitive painting is a distinctly twentieth-century phenomenon. It has also led to primitivism, that is, to the use of certain primitive devices by sophisticated painters. Sometimes this produces an engaging but rather superficial art, as in the witty designs of Lucille Corcos. Other painters, such as Shahn, Evergood, and Honoré Sharrer, have turned their primitive borrowings to more serious ends, striving for the simplicity and the uninhibited directness of expression which are among the appealing qualities in the art of children and the naïve. Somewhere between sophisticated and truly primitive art lies the work of an eccentric such as Louis Eilshemius, who, though far from untrained or unknowing, was drawn into semiprimitivism by a profound emotional crisis.

This, in most summary outline, is the main structure of twentieth-century American painting. The Armory Show, which broke the long hold of realism and romantic-realism on our earlier art, is now nearly fifty years past. Out of the energies released by that event and all it symbolized, out of the disruption of old certainties and the new uncertainties which have beset our times, has come the immense diversity of painting today. What we have lost in comfortable assurance has been made up to us many fold in the richness and extraordinary vitality of these questing years.

PHOTOGRAPHY

BEAUMONT NEWHALL

Photography came to America from France in 1839. The first news was brought by Samuel F. B. Morse, who visited Daguerre in the spring while the daguerreotype process was still the secret of its inventor. In a letter to the *New York Observer,* April 20, 1839, he described with a painter's eye the pictures which Daguerre had made; they were, he said, "Rembrandt perfected," and he held out such optimistic promises for the process that on his return to America he at once saw to it that Daguerre was elected an Honorary Member of the National Academy of Design.

The French government published Daguerre's process at an open meeting of the Academy of Science and the Academy of Fine Arts in Paris on August 19. Shortly thereafter an instruction book was printed. Morse boasted to Daguerre that as soon as the booklet arrived in America he began to make daguerreotypes. His first success, a picture of the Unitarian Church in New York City, was put on view on September 27. He admitted, however, that he was not the first; a certain D. W. Seager, he said, had already taken a daguerreotype. Within weeks others were practicing the newly discovered art, notably John W. Draper, Joseph Saxton, Robert Cornelius, Alexander S. Wolcott, and John Johnson. These pioneers worked with homemade cameras built from Daguerre's plans; they made their own materials and somehow by trial and error produced pictures.

The daguerreotype process, as Daguerre described it, consisted of polishing the silver surface of a silver-plated copper sheet 6½ by 8½ inches in size until it was mirror-bright. It was then put on top of a box containing iodine, the fumes of which reacted with silver to form light-sensitive silver iodide. The plate was exposed in a bulky box camera and afterwards developed with heated mercury, which formed a whitish amalgam in proportion to the lights and shades of the original subject. A quick wash in sodium thiosulphate removed the unaffected silver iodide, and a rinse in water completed the operation.

Although the instruction manual (which was re-printed three times in America by popular demand) fully explained the process, the skill of hand required for perfection could hardly be mastered without personal instruction. François Gouraud, Daguerre's pupil and agent for the sale of apparatus, arrived in New York on November 23, 1849, and began to give lessons. Morse and his colleagues became eager students. Gouraud traveled to Providence, Rhode Island, and Boston, where his demonstrations drew crowds of the curious.

Exposures were at first minutes long. A daguerreotype of King's Chapel, Boston, taken by Gouraud's pupil Samuel Bemis in 1840, required an exposure of forty minutes. Under these conditions portraiture was impractical. Both Morse and Draper, who claimed to have made portraits in September and October, subjected members of their family to the trial of sitting in the blazing sun with closed eyes for ten minutes or more with faces whitened with flour. Of these pioneer attempts, nothing remains. Draper sent Sir John F. W. Herschel, the British scientist, a daguerreotype of his sister on July 28, 1840, which for years was considered the first photographic portrait. Circumstantial evidence, when carefully weighed, points to the date for the production of this portrait not long before its shipment to Herschel. Unfortunately this incunabulum of photography was destroyed in an attempt to clean it in 1933.

John Johnson and Alexander S. Wolcott designed a new type of camera specifically for portraiture. Instead of a lens they used a concave mirror which formed an image much brighter than Daguerre's lens. Their first portraits, believed to have been made in October, 1839, were miniatures half the size of a postage stamp. They soon improved their camera to make pictures 2 by 2½ inches and by February, 1840, opened a studio in New York. Portraits (now in the Smithsonian Institution) by their associate, Henry Fitz, are in all probability the earliest existing portrait daguerreotypes made anywhere in the world.

In 1840 two technical improvements had been made

in the daguerreotype process which reduced exposures to seconds and made portraiture entirely feasible. Josef Petzval of Vienna designed a lens which admitted more than sixteen times the light of Daguerre's meniscus, and John Frederick Goddard of London increased the sensitivity of the daguerreotype plate by fuming it with chlorine as well as iodine. Apparatus more compact than Daguerre's was built for smaller-sized plates.

Portrait galleries now opened in every major city, and traveling daguerreotypists in carts fitted up as studios visited the smaller towns. Thousands upon thousands of portraits taken by these humble and often unknown operators exist. Usually the "one-sixth" size (2¾ by 3¼ inches) and fitted into imitation leather or plastic cases, they often have a certain naïve charm but seldom any value beyond sharp, clear-cut likenesses of forgotten ancestors.

A few daguerreotypists stand out as artists. In Boston the firm of Albert Sands Southworth and Josiah Johnson Hawes—both pupils of Gouraud—produced some of the finest portrait daguerreotypes ever made. They boasted that "one of the partners is a practical daguerreotypist" and were proud of the fact that, unlike most gallery proprietors, they did not employ operators, as cameramen were called. The portraits they made of famous men in the 1850s are outstanding in their characterization and simplicity of their composition. The firm undertook difficult, unconventional assignments: a schoolroom with teacher and pupils by "available light"; a reenactment of a surgical operation taken in the Massachusetts General Hospital; square-riggers in dry dock.

The most famous name in early American photography is that of Mathew B. Brady. In 1843, while engaged in making cases for jewelry and for surgical instruments, he offered to supply cases for daguerreotypes. A year later he opened his own daguerreotype gallery on Broadway and set about forming a "Gallery of Illustrious Americans," a part of which was published in lithographic reproduction in 1850. A quantity of portraits from Brady's collection is now in the Library of Congress. It is not clear how many of these striking and priceless portraits of great historic Americans were actually taken by Brady. It appears that he acted as a collector and historian rather than as a practical photographer, and that he commissioned portraits or purchased them from other photographers. Individual credits were not the fashion of the day.

In England, simultaneously with the announcement of the daguerreotype process, William Henry Fox Talbot published a radically different technique of photography which made use of paper negatives, from which prints could be made in any quantity. The process, known in its improved state as "calotype," was patented in the United States. Little use was made of it however, apart from an impressive set of views of New York City taken by Victor Prevost, a Frenchman who came to America as a colorist.

By the late 1850s, both the daguerreotype and the calotype processes were completely displaced by the wet collodion technique, invented in 1851 by the Englishman Frederick Scott Archer. The photographer coated sheets of glass with light-sensitive collodion immediately before using them. Because the plates retained their sensitivity while wet, photographers had to have darkrooms available wherever they went. Some fitted up wagons as field laboratories, others went to the labor of setting up light-tight tents. Bothersome as the process was, it yielded negatives of great delicacy and detail, which were printed on paper coated with albumen and silver salts and toned brown in the processing.

The glass negative, which had a whitish deposit to represent the highlights, would appear positive when backed by black. This direct positive was named "ambrotype" in America. A similar technique, which made use of sheets of iron japanned black or chocolate color instead of glass, was known as "ferrotype" or "tintype." The ambrotype, which imitated the daguerreotype in appearance and presentation, had but a short life and died in the sixties. The tintype lingered on well into the present century. It became the most popular form of picturemaking until the snapshot replaced it for informal portraits and records of good times.

Two other special applications of the collodion process met with favor in America: *cartes de visite* and stereographs. The former were portraits on mounts 2½ by 4 inches, approximately the size of a visiting card. They were taken eight at a time on a single negative with multilens camera designed by the Frenchman Adolphe-Eugène Disdéri in 1854; the process was introduced in America around 1860. The cost per picture was radically reduced by this mass production system, and portraits were sold by the thousand thousand. The *carte de visite* system was also used to multiply pictures of famous people. Slip-in albums were sold to keep them in, and soon no Victorian parlor was complete without a bulky, plush-covered book with fancy clasps alongside the stereoscope and a basket of stereoscopic pictures.

The skeleton-type viewer, which replaced the awkward box-type English viewer, was the invention of Oliver Wendell Holmes around 1863. "Stereographs," as Holmes called the twin pictures which appeared in three dimensions when seen in his viewer, were taken all over the world and sold like books by dealers. Americans excelled in stereoscopic work and pioneered in improving the technique to such a point that instantaneous photographs were taken of city streets choked with traffic and pedestrians.

The Civil War gave Mathew B. Brady his greatest opportunity to record history with the camera. He went to the front, organized teams of combat photographers, and produced the remarkable collection of several thousand *Photographic Views of the War* which were published by Anthony. The negatives of this priceless documentation are now preserved in the Library of Congress and the National Archives. The list of those who contributed to this collection is still incomplete, but the outstanding photographers were Alexander Gardner (who left Brady to establish his own collection during the war), Timothy H. O'Sullivan, and George M. Barnard. By a curious coincidence George S. Cook of Charleston, South Carolina, who had been employed in New York by Brady, became the chief combat photographer for the Confederacy. Taken as a whole, the photographic documentation of the Civil War is a landmark. No such complete pictorial record of warfare had ever been put together before. The impact of these stark images, which, as Brady stated, "present grimvisaged war exactly as it appears," has seldom been excelled even today. Unable to photograph action, Brady and his men concentrated upon the ravages of war—ruined buildings, hasty emplacements—and the men who did the fighting, posed informally outside their quarters or within fortifications. Some of the photographs of corpses lying where they fell are among the strongest indictments of war ever recorded.

It was so nearly like visiting the battlefield to look over those views [wrote Oliver Wendell Holmes on returning from the front], that all the emotions excited by the actual sight of the strained and sordid scene, strewed with rags and wrecks, came back to us, and we buried them in the recesses of our cabinet as we would have buried the mutilated remains of the dead they too vividly represented.

When hostilities ceased, America began to explore the vast and virtually unknown areas beyond the Mississippi. Photographers accompanied the official government expeditions. T. H. O'Sullivan was photographer to Clarence King's geological exploration of the fortieth parallel in 1867; in 1870 he was in Panama; and from 1871 to 1873 he explored Arizona and New Mexico territories with Lt. George M. Wheeler. His photographs of the Canyon de Chelly are memorable; his records of vanishing Indian tribes are historically and ethnologically invaluable. Alexander Gardner drove his photographic buggy across Kansas, photographing the building of the transcontinental railroad. John Wesley Powell reported his exploration of the Grand Canyon with photographs taken, for the most part, by John K. Hillers. Photographs of the Yellowstone area, taken by William Henry Jackson in 1872, were used to persuade Congress to create the Yellowstone National Park. Jackson became the chief expeditionary photographer in the country, returning summer after summer to the Rocky Mountains and the West. He packed a 20 by 24 inch view camera to mountain peaks— along with the inseparable dark tent for, like every photographer in the land, he was using the wet collodion process. Many "dry plate" techniques were proposed to simplify photography, but all proved impractical until an English physician, Richard Leach Maddox, proposed the use of gelatin for binding the light-sensitive silver salts to glass. The year of this great discovery was 1871; by 1880 the gelatin process rendered the collodion technique obsolete.

The new material could be prepared in advance and could be processed at the photographer's convenience. No longer was he chained to a darkroom. He was also able to dispense with a tripod, for gelatin plates were so much more sensitive that snapshots regularly became possible. New cameras were designed, boxlike and inconspicuous. Amateurs everywhere began to photograph people unawares with their "detective cameras." To capture swift action became their goal. As one photographer wrote in 1885:

The amateur feels a peculiar desire to "take" something, and if the "something" be an animate object unconscious of his presence so much the better, and with what a thrill does he see his first "snapshot" develop up, whether a railroad train, a trotting horse, or a man hurrying along the ground. . . .

In this very year Eadweard Muybridge repeated in Philadelphia with dry plates what he had accomplished in 1878 under a brilliant California sky with wet plates. He had photographed a horse in full gallop, in twelve successive exposures of 1/500 second each. The pictures were a revelation to the world; nobody had observed the legs of a swiftly moving animal. Muybridge was invited by the University of Pennsylvania to continue his work there and produced under the title *Animal Locomotion* a series of over 750 action photographs of all kinds of animals in motion and human figures engaged in a wide variety of action.

With the invention of the Kodak camera by George Eastman, photography entered a new era. Eastman, who began as an amateur in the wet-collodion days, opened in 1880 one of the first gelatin dry-plate factories in America. He then put on the market a roll holder for paper film, which William Henry Jackson found "a new power placed in our hands . . . whereby our labors are made sport." Eastman's invention was the Kodak (a name he coined). It was a simple box camera, loaded with enough roll film to make a hundred pictures, each 2½ inches in diameter. Anybody who could press a button could make pictures with it. When exposure No. 100 had been made, the entire camera was returned to the factory in Rochester, New York, where the film was developed and printed and returned. The Kodak was a phenomenal success. Thirteen thousand were sold during the first fourteen months of production.

Eastman clearly recognized that there were two classes of amateur photographers, the picturemakers who

devote enough time to acquire skill in developing, printing, toning, &c. [and those] who, lacking some, or all, of the requisites of the "true amateur" desire personal pictures or memoranda of their every-day life, objects, places or people that interest them in travel, &c.

He designed the Kodak for the latter. Serious amateurs began to form societies and to exhibit their work, seeking recognition for photography as an art form. The leader of this new movement was Alfred Stieglitz, and by the time the century ended, American pictorial photography had won international recognition.

As a young man Stieglitz had gone to Germany to complete his studies. His father had hoped that he would enter an engineering profession, but the sight of a camera in a dealer's window decided Stieglitz's future. He bought the camera, and went to study with Hermann Wilhelm Vogel, the brilliant photochemist whose discovery of the optical sensitizing of light-sensitive emulsions was epochal in the scientific development of photography. Vogel, however, was not merely a scientist; he had a lively interest in the arts and was deeply concerned with the advancement of artistic photography. Stieglitz could hardly have found a better teacher, for he not only acquired technical proficiency, but he came into contact with the world of art.

Back home in America in 1890, he found that the kind of artistic photography which he practiced simply did not exist. He joined The Camera Club and began to encourage his fellow members to organize exhibitions. As editor of *Camera Notes,* the club's journal, he built a newsletter into an illustrated quarterly of international scope. And he began, to the bewilderment of his fellow members, a fight for the recognition of photography as a fine art. At his suggestion, artists were invited to judge photographs at exhibitions. Soon joint exhibitions were held of the work of several camera clubs. The Philadelphia Academy was persuaded to put photographs on display in its gallery. When The Camera Club protested that the magazine *Camera Notes* did not publish the work of its own members, Stieglitz founded a new society, the Photo Secession, made up only of photographers whose chief concern was the use of the camera artistically.

In this new society, Stieglitz was greatly aided by a younger man, who was both painter and photographer, Edward Steichen. A quarterly magazine, *Camera Work,* was begun, lavishly printed on fine paper, with superb photogravures made under Stieglitz's direct supervision. The work of the Photo Secession was to be seen not only at their gallery named, after its location on Fifth Avenue, "291," but all over the world.

American photography is going to be the ruling note throughout the world unless others bestir themselves, [wrote the editor of the British *Amateur Photographer* in 1904]. Indeed, the Photo Secession pictures have already captured the highest places in the esteem of the civilised world. Hardly an exhibition of first importance is anywhere held without a striking collection of American work brought together and sent by Mr. Alfred Stieglitz. For the last two or three years in the European exhibitions these collections have secured the premier awards, or distinctions.

The triumph of the Photo Secession came in 1910, when the Albright Art Gallery in Buffalo turned its entire museum over to the Photo Secession for a great international exhibition. What is more, the Trustees purchased some of the photographs for its permanent collection and proposed to reserve one gallery permanently for photography.

To our eyes, most of the work exhibited by the Photo Secession does not resemble photography. Soft focus effects were almost invariably the rule; prints were made on textured papers; and the composition recalls the work of painters. In his own work Stieglitz had avoided this quasi imitation, and many of the photographs of Steichen and Clarence White were straightforward. But in retrospect one can only conclude that the photographers were much influenced by the prevailing painting style of the period, especially the paintings and etchings of Whistler and Japanese prints. Yet a final judgment of the Photo Secession cannot be made without considering the impact which it made on the world of art. For the first time in America, photography was given a chance to be judged as art.

In the artistic turmoil which preceded World War I, when the new aesthetics were born, photography like all the other arts went through a regeneration. Functional qualities were being explored in architecture and painting. What was the most functional way photography could be used? Since lenses can form highly detailed images which can be recorded with great fidelity by negative and print, the first criterion was to make photographs as crisp and sharp as possible. The soft focus lenses and textured printing papers so characteristic of the Photo Secession were therefore abandoned in favor of sharp-cutting anastigmats and smoothly coated printing paper. But, more important, the power of the camera to isolate details and throw emphasis on abstract pattern was given special consideration. It was felt that nature should be represented directly, even harshly, and without sentimentality. In the last two issues of *Camera Work,* 1915–1916, Stieglitz published photographs by Paul Strand which differed markedly from what he had published in earlier issues. They included close-ups of people taken without their knowledge which were brutally direct and photographs in which pattern dominated: circles of stacked-up sewer pipes, a barn seen across the shimmering white pickets of a fence. Stieglitz's own photographs showed a new approach in their almost relentless concern with the exact image and recalled the work he had done as a student. Charles Sheeler, the painter, used the camera to explore American forms which had escaped the attention of artists and in 1915 photographed Pennsylvania barns so that their stark forms took on an almost majestic quality. After the war Steichen, who had turned his photographic talents to the service of his country in the Air Corps, changed his style completely.

There were others who were forging a photographic style which however new it may have appeared was a return to tradition. Edward Weston, whose portraits and pastoral studies had earned him an international reputation, put aside his expensive soft focus lens for a modest rapid rectilinear lens which gave highly detailed negatives which he printed on glossy paper. He chose a camera which made negatives 8 by 10 inches in size for most of his work and made the prints the exact size of the negatives, thus avoiding the loss of detail caused by enlarging. Because he almost invariably used the lens setting technically known as f/64, some of his friends informally organized a society which they called "Group f/64" in recognition of the most conspicuous characteristic of Weston's technique.

But the magnificent images which, year in and year out for over thirty years, Weston has been producing can neither be explained nor appreciated by a mere description of his camera technique. His attitude toward photography has been highly stimulating. If a photograph is to have maximum effect, it must be made as directly as possible. The photographer must be so familiar with his camera, lens, and light-sensitive materials that he can actually previsualize the finished photograph even before he releases the shutter. The large camera, with its ground glass on which the image can be composed before the sensitive plate is exposed, is, therefore, an integral part of Weston's way of working. Furthermore, no part of the negative should be wasted, and the final print should represent exactly what was seen in the ground glass.

At the same time that Weston was working out his style in the 1920s, another American resident in Paris was developing quite a different approach to the photographic medium. Man Ray, a painter, found that photographic materials could be used without a camera to record light modulations. By simply placing objects directly on sensitized paper in dim light and then exposing the arrangement to strong light, abstract designs of a stimulating sort were easy to produce. Man Ray named these abstractions "rayographs." (Independently, in Germany, another painter, László Moholy-Nagy, was working along identical lines.) Man Ray also discovered that camera images could be distorted. By exposing the negative to white light during development, contours of objects appeared to be surrounded by dark lines in the print. No manual work was involved in this photochemical reaction, known in scientific laboratories as the Sabattier Effect. While others were simplifying and perfecting their techniques in an effort to respect the camera image, Man Ray was deliberately distorting it. He argued that "the ensuing violation of the medium employed is the most perfect assurance of the author's convictions."

We should note that all the photographers we have discussed, despite their differences of opinion, had one thing in common: they refused to interfere in any manual way with the photographic process. "Purist" was a word often used to describe Weston and his friends, usually by their critics. Those photographers who still followed the style made popular by the Photo Secession carried the so-called "control processes" to an excess. Negatives were made on paper so that unwanted areas could be hidden beneath smootches of soft pencil or charcoal. An ingenious and thoroughly antiphotographic technique named bromoil enabled the photographer to create a positive image in ink by brushing pigment into a gelatin relief formed from the negative. The result resembled neither a photograph nor a drawing.

The best experimental work of this period was summarized in the international "Film und Foto" exhibition held in Stuttgart in 1929. Both schools of modern photography were represented. Edward Weston contributed a foreword to the catalogue, as well as a large collection of his photographs, and the abstract experiments of Man Ray were featured.

Alfred Stieglitz stood aloof from the turmoil of the purists and abstractionists. He continued to photograph with more intensity than ever before. His most notable work includes a series of powerful images of New York City, seen mostly from the windows of his hotel room or the gallery which he named "An American Place." Because his photographs of people were so intense, it was said that he had an hypnotic effect on his sitters. To disprove this, he began to photograph clouds, using the simplest of cameras and techniques. Stieglitz called these 4 by 5 inch photographs "Equivalents," because they mirrored his thoughts and were equivalent to his feelings. Besides photographing, Stieglitz showed paintings in his gallery and occasionally photographs. In 1936 he presented the work of Ansel Adams, a newcomer from California.

Adams was already in command of a brilliant technique. Like Weston, he had the greatest respect for the camera image and insisted upon the utmost clarity and detail. His favorite subject matter has always been the natural scene, and over the years he has become the greatest landscape photographer of all time. But he is such a versatile cameraman and has produced outstanding photographs in so many fields, that it would be a mistake to qualify his production. The great lesson of his photography lies in his attitude of humble sympathy toward the subject. He prefers to call his photographs "interpretations of the natural scene." For Adams, nature is not a vehicle for the expression of personal emotions nor is it a place where he seeks stimulating forms. The world of nature is a wondrous place which it is his pleasure to show to others. Form is always present in an Adams photograph, but it is never allowed to overshadow the content, and when he photographs a locality or a mountain, it is always a specific locality or a specific mountain. A gifted teacher and writer, Adams has had a great influence upon younger workers. His technical manuals are standard texts. He has made a notable contribution to the problem of reproducing photographs. Anxious to get his photographs as widely distributed as possible, he has in cooperation with

photoengravers and printers succeeded in reproducing in printer's ink photographs which will bear comparison with the originals in their delicacy and richness.

In the years following World War I Edward Steichen, after having renounced the style which made him famous, was photographing people in his studio, using artificial lighting in a bold and original way. The portraits which he took for the Condé Nast publications *Vogue* and *Vanity Fair* were far removed from traditional portraits. They were clean and direct, unretouched and unsentimental. Of them Carl Sandburg has written:

Now he was producing that remarkable album of days and people, puppets and miracle children, which has been the outstanding feature of the Vanity Fair magazine. They march across its pages, a fascinating parade of actors, singers, playwrights, authors, dancers, vaudevillians, prize fighters, performers of stunts and creative artists. We would give much for a like record out of a civilization of a hundred or a thousand years ago.

The portraits, and the fashion photographs which Steichen was making at the same time, set a style which has been followed ever since. When World War II broke out Steichen, already retired from commercial photography, volunteered and became head of combat photography for the Navy, directing, often on the spot, a moving pictorial history of operations, told in terms of individuals.

Improvements in technique introduced in the 1930s greatly broadened the scope of photography. Highly sensitive films, lenses with greater light-passing power than were known before, and the wholly new electric flashbulb and electronic flash opened new possibilities. Action could now be photographed almost anywhere. The beauty of the split second, photographed in meticulous detail, was explored both in the scientific laboratory and in the studio, as in the brilliant dance interpretations of Barbara Morgan.

During the great financial Depression photographers, like artists in all fields, felt the need of turning their talents to social problems. "Documentary photography," despite its name, was a concept rather than a definition. The recording of events had been undertaken almost since the beginning of photography and these results are, of course, literally "documents" if they are supported by data of time, place, and circumstance. But by "documentary photography" was meant something more than recording. What had been learned through the aesthetic of pure photography was brought to bear on the problem of interpreting the social scene in such a way that all citizens could grasp the plight of the unfortunate. The innate power of the camera to produce believable, convincing records was all important, but of even greater importance was the imagination of the cameraman and his ability to vivify facts.

The most notable work in this field was done for the United States government, particularly the Farm Security Administration, under the direction of Roy E. Stryker. Of the group that reported to the American people on the life of the share croppers and the devastation of the dust bowl, Walker Evans, Dorothea Lange, and Arthur Rothstein are outstanding. With sharp, clean photographs which were almost clinical in their directness, Walker Evans produced a moving record of the conditions of rural America—towns, habitations, farms, and the people who worked them. Dorothea Lange concentrated upon the people, photographing them with sympathy and simplicity.

A new type of picture magazine appeared in 1936. There had been illustrated magazines before, but *Life* and *Look* brought special focus on photography and commissioned pictures for its pages. Of the original four photographers on *Life's* staff, three were specialists in the use of the miniature camera, which was just gaining popularity at the time. Alfred Eisenstaedt, Peter Stackpole, and Thomas D. McEvoy used the so-called "candid camera" to bring back photographs which were lifelike because they were unposed and taken on the spot. The fourth of *Life's* first staff photographers, Margaret Bourke-White, had been specializing in taking industrial photographs for the magazine *Fortune*. *Life's* first cover was her striking photograph

of a dam, but of greater significance was the warm human-interest picture essay which she did at Fort Peck, Montana, the boom town where the men who built the dam lived with their families. It was *Life's* first "picture essay."

Instead of taking a number of single photographs, as is customary in newspaper photography, magazine cameramen take a great many pictures, covering the subject from many angles, so that the editors will have a large selection from which to make a layout with a definite continuity. The putting of words with photographs is one of the chief problems of the photo editor. If the photographs merely illustrate the text, they are not being used to fullest advantage; if the words repeat what can be seen in the pictures, they are superfluous. A good picture story is a skillful combination of words and pictures. The creative editing of photographs in this way is a significant recent development, not only in magazines, but also in books.

It is obvious that exigencies of time and local circumstances do not always permit those photographers who work for the publications to produce their finest work. Yet memorable photographs have been taken, which have more than topical value. Alfred Eisenstaedt's series of portraits of celebrated Englishmen, W. Eugene Smith's picture essay on a Spanish village, Margaret Bourke-White's low-level aerial photographs of America, to name but a few, show the heights to which the picture essay can rise.

Photography is in the ascendancy. In little more than a century it has grown to become the typical twentieth-century visual medium. We are just beginning to learn its aesthetic potentials.

SCULPTURE OF THE SEVENTEENTH, EIGHTEENTH, AND NINETEENTH CENTURIES

GEORGE HEARD HAMILTON

Although monumental sculpture, in the traditional sense of the term, was not created in this country until after 1800, sculpture of another sort had appeared with the very foundation of the colonies along the Eastern seaboard. In articles of daily use, especially the wooden bowls and other domestic utensils, in tools and primitive machines, and somewhat later in shop signs, weather vanes, furniture ornaments, and decorative ship carving, the early settlers worked their materials with a sure sense for the plastic three-dimensional character of forms in space. As "folk art" such objects are now much prized, although often more for their sociological than artistic value. They must not be underrated, however, for in a real sense through such objects a feeling for sculpture was later kept alive throughout the nineteenth century when the influence of transient and conflicting tendencies—neoclassical, romantic, and realistic—frequently vitiated the professional artists' attempts to create sculpture for a newly self-conscious national culture. Until well into the twentieth century, in rural areas, the wood carver and blacksmith continued to make such objects as decoys, weather vanes, or carnival animals which, anonymous and even stylistically anachronistic, are nonetheless truly sculptural.

The selection of examples of folk art in this collection demonstrates the continuity, variety, and unusual artistic quality of this tradition. It begins with a group of gravestones, made between 1680 and 1795 and typical of innumerable others to be found in the older New England cemeteries. Their authors, as likely as not, were not exclusively stone carvers but combined this practice with other trades. In almost every case a striking discrepancy is apparent between the skillful, often elegant lettering and the cruder treatment of the floral or figural ornament surmounting the inscription. The latter elements were probably copied from engraved title pages and other decorative ornamentation of contemporary books, where the treatment often was equally commonplace or confused and would have presented difficulties of translation into another material.

The portrait heads on the later tombstones are among the earliest examples of sculptural portraiture in this country. The bold incisive rendering of heads and faces often conveys a surprising degree of individual characterization.

The signs swinging above shop doors in the early cities and towns would have provided a rich repertory of sculptural objects had they been preserved in sufficient quantity. The few remaining examples were almost all made after 1800 but undoubtedly they continue the earlier tradition. The Felon from a Rhode Island jail, the Navigator from New Bedford, and the bust of Benjamin Franklin, in which it is tempting to see an early bookseller's sign, are particularly engaging examples of this craft. After 1850, with increasing public literacy, lettered signs replaced the older three-dimensional symbols, except for the familiar tribe of cigar-store Indians. The later and more familiar examples were on the whole dull replicas of a stock type, but among the earlier ones are certain figures which reveal unusual sensitivity in handling the full-length, and often almost life-size, figure in wood.

In contrast to the innumerable examples of folk carving which must have been created throughout the colonies before 1800, there was never more than a scant handful of monumental figural sculpture and those few examples were imported from abroad. The largest and most impressive seems to have been the gilt-bronze equestrian figure of George III which stood on Bowling Green in New York. This was apparently a quite unexceptional example of late eighteenth-century English sculpture, to judge by the few scraps retrieved after the group was melted down at the outbreak of the Revolution. The damaged remains of a full-length figure of William Pitt by Joseph Wilton, which once stood in Charleston, South Carolina, have been preserved, but Wilton's work is better seen in the intact but undistinguished figure of Lord Botetourt at Williamsburg. These three figures are best classed as journeyman work, no worse and no better than countless similar

European figures of the time. The sculptors commanded with modest skill the stylistic repertory of baroque art, but their works are part of the over-all decorative tendency of the age rather than individual pieces of quality.

The downfall of British power in this country coincides with the decline of baroque art throughout the Western world. When the founders of our republic considered what forms they should choose for the necessary images of republican liberty, whether in architecture, painting, or sculpture, they looked beyond the declining baroque toward the new stylistic impulses of neoclassicism. Thus the first major work of architecture created in the new republic, the capitol for the state of Virginia in Richmond, was designed by Thomas Jefferson as an enlarged replica of a Roman temple. Similarly the statue of Washington by Jean Antoine Houdon, commissioned by the state of Virginia to adorn the state house, announces the nascent neoclassicism in the majestic pose, the stiff costume and the symbolic values of plow and fasces. A more thoroughly classical treatment of Washington was achieved by Houdon's great Italian contemporary, Antonio Canova, whose Washington, seated in classic pose and clad in Roman armor, stood in the state house at Raleigh, North Carolina, until destroyed by fire in 1831.

At this point we may observe a significant change, not only in the style of American sculpture but also in the materials out of which it was made. By far the greater amount of folk sculpture had been created in wood, in the more easily worked metals, and the softer stones. Early nineteenth-century taste preferred marble above all other materials, and, to coin a phrase, we may say that the Age of Wood was supplanted by the Age of Stone. An important transitional artist, one who was America's first native sculptor of unusual talent, was William Rush of Philadelphia. Like others before and after him he had emerged from the craft of carving; much of his early work consisted of figureheads and other ornamentation for the ships which sailed from Philadelphia. Rush, however, became known for his allegorical figures for the public buildings of Philadelphia, such as the *Charity* and the *Water Nymph and Bittern*. In these, and in his Washington, carved about 1814 but based on earlier studies from life, he worked within the late baroque tradition, but he attacked his wood with an energy and individuality unknown to the anonymous folk artist. His origin and training are obscure but his vigorous *Self-Portrait* (Pennsylvania Academy of the Fine Arts) and the delightful head of Elizabeth Rush (Philadelphia Museum of Art) indicate that he must have known something of late eighteenth-

century European sculpture, especially the work of Houdon, if not in actual examples then through engravings.

The beginning of monumental marble sculpture can be dated to 1824. In that year both John Frazee, a mason, and Hezekiah Augur, a furniture carver, are said to have created the first marble busts ever made by an American. Augur's, which was a copy of the head of the *Apollo Belvedere,* now lost, was made with the help of a carving machine invented by S. F. B. Morse, whose plaster statuette of the *Dying Hercules,* a study for his painting of the same title, was an early instance of the taste for things classic. Augur's bust is now lost, but Frazee's portraits are unusually competent for a craftsman who had had no professional training. But brilliant as these isolated efforts were, their authors could not prosper without further professional experience which was unavailable in this country. Frazee continued to make competent portrait busts, but Augur's subsequent works, the heroically intentioned but actually diminutive companion figures of *Jephthah and His Daughter* and the coarse bust of Professor Alexander Fisher (it was carved after the subject's death from the portrait by S. F. B. Morse and so "works" from only one angle!), all too apparently exceed the measure of his skill. Both are now shown at the Yale University Art Gallery.

There was no other solution of this problem but to study abroad, more especially in Italy where the craftsmen were available to translate into marble the sculptors' plaster images and where the lingering spell of Canova (who had died in 1822) was perpetuated in the neoclassic sculpture of the Danish master, Bertel Thorwaldsen (1770–1844), the most prominent of contemporary sculptors then living in Rome. There, and in Florence, in the colonies of English and American painters and poets, the American sculptors mastered the technical demands of their profession and absorbed the prevailing neoclassic aesthetics and subject matter. Soon considerable quantities of marbles were shipped home. If they have for the most part disappeared from the drawing rooms they originally adorned into the basements of our museums and historical societies, they deserved their fate. By and large they were skillful but uninspired variations on a few mildly mythological themes; even the portraits of living sitters almost always were empty of life and characterization. If we now call them to mind, it is less as objects of intrinsic artistic worth than as documents in the development of our American awareness of aesthetic significance.

One of the first and by far the most notable of the works created in Italy by American sculptors was

Horatio Greenough's colossal seated figure of George Washington, commissioned by Congress and intended to adorn the east lawn of the Capitol. When it finally arrived in 1841 it was greeted with derision and a few decades later was removed to a forgotten hall in the Smithsonian Institution. Yet those who seek it out cannot but be impressed by its solemn monumentality. However ridiculous to the eyes of our ancestors may have appeared this image of Washington in the pose and scanty costume of the Olympian Zeus, it is still the most exalted conception of that hero which any American artist has created. As Greenough himself declared, in words which are characteristic of the man who first detected the functional beauty of our traditional tools and machines and clipper ships: "In nakedness I behold the majesty of the essential, instead of the trappings of pretension." Although the reliefs on the side of the throne were probably only modeled by Greenough, they are exceptionally delicate in design and execution and probably the finest examples of neoclassic sculpture in this country.

The most gifted of this first generation of sculptors working abroad was Thomas Crawford who had been one of Thorwaldsen's last pupils. His bronze statue of Beethoven is an awkward but convincing expression of a romantic concept of personality executed in the prevailingly classic technique. Crawford's most important commissions were for the Capitol in Washington, for which he created the huge figure of Liberty on top of the dome, designed the first pair of bronze doors for the rotunda (completed after his premature death by Randolph Rogers), and commenced the pedimental sculpture for the Senate wing. This, the first large-scale pediment designed by an American, is a curious attempt to combine American subjects and symbols with classic forms. The best known figure is the seated Indian chief mourning the end of his people, but the woodsman, the figure of Liberty, and others are important if unrecognized additions to the iconography of Americana. The pediment as a whole should be compared, iconographically and artistically, with Greenough's *Rescue* on the steps of the Capitol. The melodramatic subject, a pioneer saving his wife and child from a murderous attack by an Indian, is treated in a confused late baroque manner.

The most famous of all American sculptors during these middle years was Hiram Powers. During his long residence in Florence he was visited by most American notables of the age, and of many he created portrait busts. None surpassed, however, his early portrait of Andrew Jackson which was modeled in Washington in the President's study before Powers went abroad.

Powers gained an international reputation in 1851 when his *Greek Slave* was shown at the Crystal Palace Exposition. His slick idealization of this passionless figure captured the imagination of the public, but it is artistically inferior to his other standing figure, the *California* (Metropolitan Museum of Art), which seems now a more searching attempt to incorporate certain psychological values within the prevailing concept of the classic nude. A similar feeling for the poetry of classic forms, particularly in their tragic aspect, distinguishes the few completed sculptures of William Rimmer, the self-taught Boston physician. The muscular and formal tensions in his *Falling Gladiator* and *Dying Centaurs* belie their comparatively small scale.

None of the remaining sculptors of the neoclassic generation rose above mediocrity, but their works are still of interest to the social and literary historian. Randolph Rogers, W. H. Rinehart, and Erastus Dow Palmer were among those who enjoyed large reputations in their day. William Wetmore Story was even less competent than most, but his life and friendships during his long residence in Italy merited the attention of Henry James, whose biography of the sculptor is as important a source of information for the artistic ideals of the time as Hawthorne's *Marble Faun* is useful as an interpretation of artist life in Rome.

There is little American sculpture that can accurately be described as romantic, so tenacious was the neoclassic mode and so suddenly was it overwhelmed, in the 1860s and 1870s, by a more realistic attitude toward subject matter and a new treatment of material. There is a dash of quixotic personality in Clark Mills's equestrian monument of Jackson in Washington and a romantic attitude toward episode in John Rogers's early groups, such as *One Last Shot*. But interest in a more searching realism soon appeared in Henry Kirke Brown's equestrian Washington in Union Square, New York. This is not only more technically competent than Mills's work, but the idealization of Washington's character is equally balanced by the realistic treatment of man and horse. For such sculpture, bronze was the preferred medium and remained for the rest of the century the material in which the finest works were created. A curious transitional group, marking a technical and stylistic point midway between the Stone Age and the Bronze Age, was Thomas Ball's *Lincoln Freeing the Slaves* (Lincoln Park, Washington, D.C.). Although the subject and the modern costume were in one sense realistic, the composition stresses a romantic concept of personality expressed in forms which are still treated with the surface smoothness of neoclassicism.

The most successful of the completely realist works was possibly J. Q. A. Ward's statue of Henry Ward Beecher. Here the man is seen as he was in life, with no detail of feature or costume omitted. That the work survives such unsparing presentation must be due to the sculptor's sympathy for his subject, since nowhere else did Ward achieve such mastery.

With the passing of the Age of Stone, Rome also passed as a center of interest for young Americans who wanted to study abroad. After 1860 Paris attracted more and more artists until it became the principal center for study in Europe, a position it enjoyed until the end of the Second World War. Its prominence was due both to the traditional excellence of the technical instruction offered by the École des Beaux-Arts and to the overwhelming activity and international prestige of the great French sculptor, Auguste Rodin. Indeed, from about 1885 onward scarcely any prominent sculptor can be completely understood except as he absorbed or rejected Rodin's teaching or example. America's finest sculptor of the last half of the century was French by descent and thoroughly disciplined by study in Paris. Augustus Saint-Gaudens was an exact contemporary of Rodin, and we may well study the impressionistic play of light and shade over the carefully worked surfaces of his bronzes with Rodin's teaching in mind.

But Saint-Gaudens was an imitator of no one, and more than most sculptors of his period he caught and preserved a certain authentic American quality in his many works. It is difficult to describe, but perhaps we find it in his unflinching portraiture, as direct and convincing as Thomas Eakins's, in his unfailing and inevitably only partially successful desire to combine, as he said, "the real with the ideal," so characteristic of the literary aspirations of his generation, or, finally, in his masterly creation of a series of sculptural images of our greatest public figures. To no other sculptor, or even painter, of the period are we indebted for such noble and convincing presentations as those of Captain Shaw (The Common, Boston), Admiral Farragut (Madison Square, New York City), General Sherman (Central Park, New York City), or Abraham Lincoln (Lincoln Park, Chicago). No matter how minutely realistic his detail and treatment of surface might appear, each work as a whole was always illumined with a sense of poetry that never broadened into sentimentality. The Lincoln of 1887 is an early and noble example of his ability to project an image of intense symbolic power through a technique that seems superficially concerned only with visual matters. Although Saint-Gaudens himself was never satisfied with the contrast between the realism of Captain Shaw and his troops and the idealism of the figure of Victory floating above their heads, the juxtaposition of the two elements is truly in the American vein; it is like a plastic translation of the similar shock of metaphors in Emerson's poetry. Later, in the Adams Memorial he created the most moving and symbolic sculpture that America had yet, perhaps even has yet, seen. It is all the more effective in that the commission required the sculptor to create a spiritual tomb figure which would nevertheless be devoid of any specific religious inconography.

The influence of Paris, in a more academic sense, appeared in the work of Saint-Gaudens's younger contemporaries. They were aware of Rodin, to be sure, but they preferred a more traditional technique and more conservative subject matter, just as in poetry public taste exchanged the harsh accents of Emerson for the sweeter harmonies of William Vaughn Moody. Throughout his long career Daniel Chester French continued, in a minor mood, Saint-Gaudens's blend of realism and idealism, but he did this with more manner and with less power. In his early *Minute Man* (Concord, Mass.), a colonial soldier in the stance of *Apollo Belvedere,* he combined neoclassic and realistic elements in such a way that the statue caught the public's eye as an acceptable symbol of our revolutionary history, but he was at his best in more completely ideal figures. The exceptionally colossal but only temporary figure of the Republic at the World's Columbian Exposition of 1893 deserved a more durable existence, but its best qualities were perpetuated in the *Alma Mater* at Columbia University.

If the history of earlier American sculpture contains fewer uncontested works of artistic quality than those in American painting and architecture, it does not deserve the indifference with which most students of American art have regarded it. The discerning eye every now and again will find unsuspected pleasures, perhaps most often among the folk arts, but not infrequently among the neoclassic marbles and the realistic bronzes. And, for the historian of ideas, American sculpture is rich in unexploited aspects of our experience. The iconographer of our liberties will find significant variations in the treatment of our heroic personalities, of Washington and Lincoln especially. The historian of taste can chart, as well in sculpture as in painting, our first native abilities, our subsequent dependence upon European standards of technique and interpretation, and finally our gradual emergence as a nation gifted with sculptors of the first rank.

SCULPTURE OF THE TWENTIETH CENTURY

A N D R E W   C A R N D U F F   R I T C H I E

Assisted by Eleanor Barton

"America was sculpturally a European province during the Nineteenth Century," writes Joseph Hudnut in 1929 in his *Modern Sculpture,* and in a small page and a quarter summarizes the several influences—romantic, classical, and exotic—that were reflected in the current sculpture of the day. Hudnut closes his brief account with a plea to architects to recognize their need for sculpture in and on their buildings. "What is necessary," he concludes, with a slap at "the stark architecture of our new buildings," is a return to that tradition of the ancient world "which united sculpture and architecture within the limits of a single art."

The plea has gone almost unheard, and this need has not been recognized by most modern architects until recently. As a result, except in academic government or public buildings, the American twentieth-century sculptor has rarely had an opportunity to share with an architect in the creation of a building. He may have been invited to "decorate" a blank wall after a building had been conceived and built, or an architect may have induced a client to buy an existing piece of sculpture to enhance an entrance lobby or a court, but even these uses of sculpture by modern architects have been rare. Whether from timidity, puritanism, fear of competition, or, more validly, the belief that a well-designed building should be sufficient unto itself, most modern architects have been unable or unwilling to make more than a superficial use, if any, of their sister craft.

All of this is by way of introduction and to explain the grim truth that from the death of Saint-Gaudens in 1907, almost until today, the struggle of the non-academic American sculptor to keep alive, far less to create, has been intense. This struggle must explain in part why so few would-be sculptors from the first decade of the century until the end of World War II have been able to rise above the mediocre and the imitative. The few who succeeded during this period in achieving a high degree of expressive individuality and eminence can almost be counted on two hands. Since the war this number has fortunately been increased by

others whose tentative earlier experiments have now borne fruit in works of greater assurance and interest and a group of younger sculptors of apparent promise.

Since Saint-Gaudens there have been, broadly speaking, two kinds of sculptors in America: one following the French Beaux-Arts, neoantique tradition; the other experimenting with new forms and techniques associated with the great new revolutions in modes of painting—Fauve, expressionist, cubist, constructivist, surrealist, and abstract. Depending upon one's point of view, these two kinds of sculptors have been called reactionary and advanced guard or traditionalist and experimentalist. Of course some traditionalists have turned experimentalists, and occasionally an experimentalist has turned traditionalist. On the whole there has been a fairly clearly defined and determined old guard that has steadily resisted the encroachments of any new developments in sculpture while the more experimental sculptors have very gradually developed their powers and accomplishments. This more advanced group has, in the second half of the twentieth century, reached the point of achieving an international reputation. Such international success, together with some signs of a change in the national attitude toward sculpture, may ultimately help to make possible that collaboration between architecture and sculpture so briskly championed by Hudnut. In any case it is already clear that, despite innumerable and sometimes unnecessary obstacles, American sculpture of the twentieth century will not justly be dismissed by future historians of art as provincial.

The leading exponent of the old guard and its most influential force is Paul Manship, who exhibited first in New York in 1913. This was the very year of the famous Armory Show which did so much to open the eyes of so many American artists to revolutionary movements in art abroad. Since that date the battle has been joined between Manship and his followers in the National Sculpture Society and the army of rebels sometimes loosely organized in an association such as the Sculptors Guild, more often fighting alone for some nonacademic style or for individuality of expression.

Compared with his strong predecessor Saint-Gaudens, Manship refined and sweetened his neoclassic inheritance. His *Dancer and Gazelles* in the Toledo Museum of Art is representative of his highly linear, decorative treatment of forms.

Manship's technically accomplished, eclectic art may demonstrate qualities cherished by our conservative sculptors in 1960 as in 1900. Generally competent, they are seldom gifted with great creative strength or imagination. A more independent and interesting member of the older generation of sculptors who continued in action in the first part of the twentieth century was George Gray Barnard, who dared to conceive vast heroic programs in sculpture and to emulate Michelangelo and Rodin. If the results, as seen in his groups for the capitol, Harrisburg, Pennsylvania, fall far short of his own ideals, at least they represent the vigorous effort of a man whose genuine sympathy for bold creative expression may be seen in his collection of medieval sculpture (now the nucleus of The Cloisters, New York City).

Two of our most important experimental sculptors were born in Europe. Gaston Lachaise (1882–1935) began working for Manship and other sculptors, executing details on their work which they left to him to complete. Born in France and trained in Paris at the Académie des Beaux-Arts, Lachaise came to America in 1906. His first independent exhibition did not take place until 1918. In the interim, while working for others, he developed an individual style of his own. His sculptural obsession, like Maillol's, was the female nude, a woman who was the mother of all men—broad-hipped, narrow-waisted, and full-breasted, a vigorous and heroic conception. His *Standing Woman* (Whitney Museum of American Art) is almost elegant in her poised balance of torso on delicate leg and toe by comparison with the massive, earthy weightiness of his *Standing Woman* in the Museum of Modern Art. Although born abroad, Lachaise spent most of his creative life in America and we may therefore claim him as an American sculptor and certainly among the greatest we have produced on these shores.

William Zorach, who was born in Lithuania in 1887 but completely trained in America, has sustained for decades the contemporary spirit in art newly generated by the Armory Show. He began work in Cleveland as a lithographer, studying at night at the Cleveland School of Art. In 1908 he entered the National Academy of Design, New York, where he spent two years. Following this he worked in Paris for two years and in 1913 exhibited in the Armory Show. Up to this point Zorach had concentrated on painting. Later he turned to sculp-ture and, self-taught, exhibited first as a sculptor in 1924. Since that date his reputation has risen steadily. While Lachaise in the Beaux-Arts technical tradition was principally a modeler in plaster and clay, Zorach, responding to a more contemporary, puristic emphasis upon direct carving in stone and wood, has remained a carver all his life. His sculptures, such as the *Mother and Child* (Metropolitan Museum of Art) and the *Head of Christ* (Museum of Modern Art) have a monumental scale and formal density only possible in the direct cutting of the marble block by the artist himself. Consequently they have an elemental force that academic journeyman stonecutters' sculptures always lack.

During the twenties and thirties a number of American sculptors of considerable power and talent came or began to come to creative maturity. Continuing in the direct stonecutting tradition of Zorach, John Flannagan turned to field stone and, like Henry Moore, his contemporary in England, sought to aid the found stone to express the forms latent in it. This rather pantheistic approach is in contrast to carving cut stone coming from the quarry. Flannagan's life was short and tragic, but what he did produce is often charged with considerable native poetic imagination. His gravely serious *Mother and Child* (Fogg Art Museum, Harvard University) presents a poignant contrast to his finely observed mountain goat appropriately entitled *Figure of Dignity* (Metropolitan Museum of Art).

Spanish-born José de Creeft has also profited by the discipline of working directly with his materials and has produced in such works as the greenstone *Cloud* (Whitney Museum of American Art) or the hammered lead *Saturnia* (Museum of Modern Art), sculpture of great sensitivity, elegance, and power. A perceptive understanding of both his subject and medium lends great conviction to his finely modeled head *Himalaya* (Whitney Museum of American Art), with its dextrous and skillful working of the lustrous surface of the lead.

By contrast with these carvers two other sculptors who came into prominence in the late twenties and early thirties, Calder and Noguchi, reflect in their beginnings the strong influence of the school of Paris. Isamu Noguchi, born in Los Angeles of Japanese parents, went from the East Side Art School in New York to Paris where he worked under Brancusi in 1927 and 1928. His *Kouros* (Museum of Modern Art, 1945) has the precise hieratic purity of Brancusi's stone and metal sculpture which has remained the chief inspiration in Noguchi's otherwise highly personal art. In 1929–1931 and again in 1949–1950 he traveled in the Far East and studied in Japan under some of their expert ceramicists; the result is a series of terra cottas of an extraordinary range of imagery and wit. *Even the Centipede* of 1952 (Museum of Modern Art) is one of his most interesting productions in this fired-clay medium.

Alexander Calder, son of an architectural sculptor of considerable repute, also went to Paris in the late twenties and there came under the influence of the constructivist painter Mondrian and the surrealist Miro, among others. Combining both these sources of inspiration with his own Yankee ingenuity, humor, and engineering skill, he practically invented a new form of mobile sculpture which, however much it has been imitated since, continues to be one of the most original expressions of any contemporary American artist. He has wisely never imitated himself and has developed steadily from such witty simplifications as *The Hostess* (Museum of Modern Art) through the early mobiles run by motors to the series of compositions truly mobile in their delicate balance and response to the slightest breath of air. While the subtly changing patterns created by these mobiles have continued to enchant imitators, Calder himself has moved on to a new simplicity and breadth in such monumental "stabiles" as *Spiny* (Nelson Rockefeller Collection).

Another sculptor intimately involved in the school of Paris was Elie Nadelman, an attractive and puzzling figure. Born and trained in Poland, Nadelman worked in Paris in the crucial years from 1903–1914 and in America from 1915 until his death in 1946. Both in Paris and in New York, Nadelman's life ranged from a deliberately solitary existence to periods of vast success and popularity. His reputation has been equally varied: he has sometimes been considered merely a facile talent whose work would prove as ephemeral as the fashions he recorded and influenced, sometimes highly valued for his thoughtful analytical approach to basic sculptural problems. Almost forgotten in the virtual seclusion of his last years, Nadelman's work is attracting a remarkable posthumous fame. His varied experiments, from the smooth flow of volumes of the *Man in the Open Air* (Museum of Modern Art) to the metallic tension of the *Wounded Bull* (Museum of Modern Art), reveal a highly personal style and suggest the independence and interest of his theories about sculpture.

Despite the marked differences between the individual styles of these artists, all their work reveals a common feeling for the special properties of different media: stone, wood, and metal. This same feeling may be observed in the sculpture of a number of younger artists active in the twenties and thirties whose direct working with various materials seems one of the most significant developments of the period, since it led to a

new freedom and a new integrity. The actual manipulation of traditional materials led to experiments with such new media as glass and plastics and the use of such new techniques as welding and opened thereby a whole range of expressive possibilities. The respect for the particular nature of a chosen material brought a freshness and originality long absent from more imitative works which had relied too heavily on mechanical methods of production. Hundreds of nineteenth- and early twentieth-century examples that still haunt the museums, parks, public squares, and buildings of both Europe and America show, by the contrast of their lifeless quality with the great vitality of the modern examples, the lively potentials of the new approach.

During the thirties an event of great significance for sculpture, as for all the arts, was the encouragement and assistance given by the Federal government to meet the desperate situation of the years of the Depression. The ruling that structures under the Public Buildings Administration were to be decorated with sculpture only through open competition, the projects assigned to needy sculptors, and work made possible by the sponsorship of the WPA all meant a new recognition of sculpture in general and an invigorating chance for new talents in particular. Chaim Gross, Raoul Hague, Concetta Scaravaglione, and Milton Hebald are among the many sculptors who shared in this astonishingly well-conceived and still underestimated government program.

These and other sculptors who began work during the years of the Great Depression did not come into full maturity until the period of the Second World War and immediately thereafter. Their first work, understandably, had often a bitter flavor of social consciousness and criticism of the established order. Minna Harkavy's *American Miner's Family* is a tribute to the often miserable and tragic fate of these underground workers. David Smith's *Medals of Dishonor* are further evidence of the impact of the times on a deeply sensitive artist. On the other hand, some sculptors like Theodore Roszak responded to the social and economic upheaval of the thirties by attempting to express their sense of order and perfection in exquisitely assembled metal constructions.

The war, however, with all its international implications, unquestionably served to temper this almost parochial spirit of American social malaise and to forge a new understanding of our own problems as universal ones. In the postwar years, for the first time in the history of American art, one can really begin to point to a *group* of American sculptors of international stature. The leading characteristic of this group is its common acceptance of metal as a medium, brazing and welding as a technique, and painterlike "drawing in space" as a style dividing space by means of cut steel sheets or exploring and enclosing it by linear drawing in rod and wire. The cubist collage, the experiments of Russian and Dutch constructivists, and of Picasso, Gonzalez, Miró, and the surrealists have all been fuel for this new group's fire.

The oldest in point of accomplishment and originality is David Smith, who freely admits his youthful debt to the Spanish metal sculptor Gonzalez. In the course of an extraordinarily prolific and creative career he has, however, explored more territory in this new realm of welded sculpture than any of his contemporaries. Furiously inventive, antitasteful, searchingly experimental, he has not been afraid to suffer defeat, even while he has achieved many victories, in his determined search for perhaps the most complex and startling imagery in modern sculpture. His *Hudson River Landscape* is magnificently lyrical, his *Sitting Printer* is witty, and his *Blackburn—Song of an Irish Blacksmith* is a joyous tribute to the hammer and anvil. The range of Smith's expression, demonstrated by even these few works, is a measure of the richness of his sensibilities and the energy of his hand and mind.

Under the impact of World War II Theodore Roszak, who, as noted above, began as an optimistic-constructivist, turned to an expressionist imagery in metal to project his emotional reaction to the dislocation of man and society under the stress of battle in powerful and moving forms. His *Spectre of Kittyhawk* is perhaps his best sculptural statement of the disillusionment attendant upon the frightful bombarding use that had been made of the Wright brothers' flying machine.

Seymour Lipton, on the other hand, after long years of agonized representation of the forces of good and evil, again under the stress of war, turned around 1950 to hopeful processes of regeneration as displayed in blooming plants. Combining these with shell and machine forms he has produced some of the most delicate and yet powerful sculptures of today.

Herbert Ferber has also turned to abstractions derived from flame and plant forms, and in his *"and the bush was not consumed"* for the façade of the synagogue in Millburn, New Jersey, has created one of the most striking religious sculptures to be seen in this country.

The work of three younger members of this middle generation may illustrate the wide variety of interests animating sculptors today and the boldness with which different techniques and media have been used to meet radically different needs.

Richard Lippold has adapted the great geometrical-constructivist tradition to his own lyrical and decorative purposes. In the silver *Full Moon* at the Museum of Modern Art and the golden *Sun* at the Metropolitan Museum of Art, he has presented us with two wire inventions of a dazzling brilliance of technical execution and jewel-like elegance.

David Hare, for his part, has extended in a most personal way the surrealist tradition of dream-induced images. Lately, by inventing a process of casting in light, thin skins of metal (so thin, in fact, that the metal sheath is broken in passages), he has been able to suggest the transience and decay of human flesh in a most moving manner.

Ibram Lassaw's welded bronzes use all the resources of different colors and textures of varied metals to suggest ever-changing patterns of space held suspended in intricately constructed cages. His *Kwannon* is a typical example in its deftly controlled balance of interweaving irregular bars of metals welded to create a shimmering vibration of light. For the monumental demands of architectural sculpture Lassaw used a simpler design of large, sweeping, curvilinear forms in *Pillar of Fire* (Temple Beth-El, Springfield, Massachusetts), an instance (with Ferber's) of the effective way in which modern sculpture can be used in the service of religion as well as of modern architecture.

The achievements of two sculptors still in their thirties may suggest reasons for hope that the present vitality of sculpture in America will continue in the next decades. Leonard Baskin, already recognized as one of the most accomplished graphic artists of our day, has lately turned to sculpture and in such a sensitive, simplified figure as the *Man with Dead Bird* shapes a deeply felt and haunting presence. The tragic tensions of this form contrasts sharply with the truly delightful *Bird Woman* by Dimitri Hadzi. The surprisingly gay, swift movements of the birds wheeling about the strong turning figure of the woman show Hadzi's meticulous workmanship and his ability to deal easily with problems both of form and of movements in space. Hadzi, one of the younger American artists who has profited from years of work in Rome, has recently produced sculpture of real strength and high seriousness in his series of *Helmets, Shields,* and studies for a memorial to the victims of Auschwitz.

One phenomenon which merits some attention in any survey, however brief, of twentieth-century sculpture in America is the increasing importance of the activity of women as sculptors. Earlier in the century Malvina Hoffman and Anna Hyatt Huntington were always cited as exceptional figures and their technical competence so highly praised that one detects in their critics a John-sonian note of surprise that they could do it at all. Such a special judgment would be totally irrelevant for the number of able women sculptors of recent decades whose work is well able to stand on its own merits and presents a variety of accomplishments. E. L. Davis's special feeling for the range of potentials of wood as a medium may be shown by the contrast between the smooth, rounded forms of her *Cosmic Presence* and the tensed planes of the gaunt head of a *Red Army Soldier*. Berta Margoulies in *Mine Disaster* conveys the painful tension of a waiting group by boldly simplifying her frightened staring figures and pressing them tightly to-gether. The interest of modern sculptors in space as well as form is reflected in the *String Construction* of Sue Fuller and the distinguished bronzes by Mary Callery. Callery's structural daring may be seen in *Amity* and the *Composition of Birds* which exploit the molten nature of bronze to shape forms so attenuated that they seem held in existence by tensile strength alone and yet by just the slightest and most skillful modulations also seem firm and perfectly poised crea-tures.

Almost a phenomenon in himself, Jacob Epstein has been one of the dominant figures in twentieth-century sculpture, but credit for his work should fairly be given to England, his home for over half a century. Born of Polish parents in New York in 1880, Epstein studied with George Gray Barnard, attended the École des Beaux-Arts in Paris, and in 1906 settled in England, ultimately becoming a British citizen. His style has al-ways varied from the elaborate impressionist treatment of surfaces in his forcefully modeled bronzes to the monumentally conceived, bold, simple forms of his stone carvings. *Oriel Ross* is one of a long series of dis-tinguished bronze portraits in which the characteriza-tion is animated by the play of light over the many facets of the surface. Epstein's drastic reduction of forms to the simplest essentials in his early *Mother and Child* adumbrates the primitive strength and force of his later carvings, heroic in both scale and conception. The storm of controversy which has been the public re-sponse to most of Epstein's major carvings has at last abated and his commanding position in the art of the twentieth century has now been generally recog-nized.

If Britain should justly receive credit for Epstein's work it is equally important to observe that almost every country in Europe has contributed sculptors to America in the twentieth century as well as acting as chief forma-tive influences on many of our native-born sculptors. This new reciprocal relationship, constituting a lively exchange of ideas and persons rather than the nine-teenth-century provincial dependence on Europe, has unquestionably been a major factor in the growth of our sculpture toward an international status.

Therefore, before concluding, mention should be made of other great foreign-born and foreign-trained sculptors who have been resident in America for many years and who have left their imprint upon the American tradition. Archipenko, the Russian cubist who made original researches into concave and convex forms, has made a permanent contribution to modern sculpture everywhere. Naum Gabo, another great Russian and a pioneer constructivist, has explored all the fascinating possibilities of plastic as a medium and has profoundly influenced younger sculptors like Lippold. Finally, Jacques Lipchitz, one of the great sculptors of our time, has been on these shores since 1941. The example of his poetic fire, his creative energy, and his all-round mastery of the arts of carving and modeling, in the Rodin, cubist, and expressionist traditions, has left and will continue to leave an incalculable impression upon sculpture in America.

STAGE DESIGN

DONALD OENSLAGER

Before 1915 our theatre programs rarely included "Settings Designed by" for the good reason that our theatre never had known of a "stage designer." In New York it was customary for a manager to call on a scenic studio to provide his scenery. Scenery was designed and painted by the scenic artist and delivered to the theatre. Theatres in other cities boasted of resident scenic artists, who painted scenery backstage as the local theatre season progressed. This was the time-honored scenic practice of our theatre fifty years ago. Indeed, the earlier theatres of Boston, Philadelphia, New Orleans, and San Francisco had established this tradition.

Our eighteenth- and nineteenth-century American theatres were patterned on the plan of the English playhouse. In 1752 Lewis Hallam was the first of many English actors and managers to bring English companies to the New World, and he found our theatres with boxes and balconies and the proscenium frame with doors, just as he had known them in London. The scenes were the same stock wings and borders that more frequently than not bore only a casual relationship to the plays they embellished. Those sixty-four plays that were presented in the first six months of New York's new John Street Theatre (1767) must have taxed the limited stock of painted wings stored in the playhouse's scene dock, as well as the imagination of the limited audience that saw them. Our modest early American theatres boasted of few scenic artists. Journeyman painters and traveling artists indulged in painting scenery—"American Primitive" we call it today. Major John André applied his talent for painting to scenery used for the entertainment of General Howe in Philadelphia. William Dunlap, producer, playwright, historian, and painter extraordinary, recorded the scenery for the first American comedy, Royall Tyler's *The Contrast,* in 1787 at the John Street Theatre.

For a hundred years there was no apparent advance from a colonial to a Federal style of scenery. Settings continued to adhere to an artificial, purely theatrical, and romantic formula garnished with archaeological overtones. The character and the intention of scenery remained surprisingly constant, whether it served a mid-nineteenth-century Davy Crockett melodrama, Edwin Booth's *The Winter's Tale* (1864), an extravaganza like *The Black Crook,* Steele Mackaye's *Anarchy* (1887) with its "heroic frescoes" and "living pictures," Augustin Daly's *A Midsummer Night's Dream* (1888), or the ubiquitous vaudeville theatre with a palace scene painted by the mail-order Lee–Lash Studios.

By the turn of the century, however, our settings reflected the naturalistic trends of the European theatre. In 1898 the scenic artist, L. W. Seavey, provided an impressive series of archaeological backgrounds to match Ada Rehan's "beautiful simplicity and matchless eloquence" as Portia in Daly's production of *The Merchant of Venice.* In 1899 Frank Gates painted splendid photographic scenes for Mrs. Fiske's *Becky Sharp.* For the world premiere of *The Girl of the Golden West* in 1910, the Metropolitan Opera imported the painted scenes of our own golden west from a studio in Italy! But there was a fresh breeze astir in our visual theatre. That same year Winthrop Ames, a producer of impeccable taste, used E. Hamilton Bell as his art director and obtained highly imaginative scenes for *The Blue Bird* from Unitt and Wickes Scenic Studios. That season America applauded Max Reinhardt's brilliant use of color and design in his production of *Sumurun.* Joseph Urban imposed his modern Viennese style on opera in Boston. Livingston Platt brought stylization to Margaret Anglin's productions of Shakespeare, and Pavlova revealed to America the brilliant style of Léon Bakst. In 1913 in Cambridge Sam Hume organized a provocative first exhibition of the new stagecraft of leading artists of the European theatre and also of aspiring young artists of the American theatre. Gradually we became exposed to the New Movement in the theatre. Creating scenes for this theatre was developing more and more into a one-man job, and within a few years, stage designing was to become a recognized and independent profession.

Today every department of the professional theatre is unionized. Stage design is no exception. There are approximately 500 members in the Scenic Artists Union. Of this total membership approximately 110 members are scenic artists and 350 are scene designers working in the theatre, motion pictures, and television. No artist may design settings for the professional theatre unless he belongs to this Union. While Vertes, Eugene Berman, Marc Chagall, Pavel Tchelitchev, and Isamu Noguchi are essentially painters, only occasionally designing settings for opera and ballet, they are members of the Union. On the other hand, Boris Aronson is a painter who devotes most of his talent to the theatre. There is no apprentice system for stage designers. The young designer must enter the Union as a practicing designer. Admission is by examination and payment of a substantial initiation fee. Formal Union contracts are required between the designer and the producer. There is a minimum fee scale. High standards of craftsmanship and execution are maintained, and the Union protects the rights and privileges of its members.

The American stage designer is accustomed to work in every medium of theatrical expression—comedy, tragedy, opera, musical, ballet, motion pictures, and television. He must design in many styles, working on one production as a realist or a surrealist, on another as an impressionist or an expressionist, or in another one of many contemporary styles. Almost every stage designer believes his function is to allow the play or the book to design his scenes. He is a sympathetic instrument of expression who attempts, with his own imagination, to envision on the stage the setting that is in the mind's eye of the playwright.

The stage designer is essentially an artist-craftsman. He must possess many facets: a thorough knowledge of architecture and painting, a taste for the decorative arts of all periods, and an understanding of many crafts. He is at once a woodworker, a florist, a weaver, a dressmaker, a jeweler, an upholsterer.

Designing is the happiest and briefest portion of the designer's work. Before he can arrive at the actual design, he plots the ground plan. He anticipates for the director all of the movement that will take place in the set—entrances, exits, and levels arranged in relation to furniture and properties. From the ground plan the designer visualizes the elevations of the setting. This process establishes the actual design for the scene. Construction problems and mechanical methods of shifting multiscene plays also affect his design, as well as transportation problems—for no piece of scenery can be constructed larger than 5 feet 9 inches wide because the doors of all railroad baggage cars admit nothing broader than this dimension.

The designer supervises the execution of his designs for the producer. Consequently, he must work practically in terms of dollars and cents, feet and inches, minutes and hours. He makes sketches and models and drafts all scale drawings for the builder. He prepares the painter's elevations for the scenic artist. He obtains for the producer cost estimates. For a multiscene play he must consider the time and cost of shifting scenes to keep running expenses within a budget. He finds or devises all of the properties of the production—snakes that perform, a liquor bottle that speaks, a mummy case of a specific size. He coordinates sound effects—anything from a chair squeak to an elephant's trumpet to an earthquake. He contrives special effects—a football routine, a ship passing through the Panama Canal locks, moonrises, sunsets, hurricanes. He plans the light plot and conducts both lighting and scenic rehearsals. The opening night of the production is the designer's farewell, for only then are his responsibilities to the producer terminated.

Disparate forces have contributed to the visual vitality of our mid-twentieth-century theatre. Before World War I, producer David Belasco was monarch of all the realism he could survey. For the realistic scene of *The Return of Peter Grimm,* he might better have commissioned the gifted scenic artist Ernest Gros to import an actual Dutch interior and install it on his stage complete with Dutch rain and a view of a windmill turning outside the window. In lighting *Chantecler,* Maude Adams achieved the golden verisimilitude of an actual sunrise in a deep forest glade. But such wizardry could only lead to a hopeless dead end of literal reproduction. At that time Gordon Craig and Adolphe Appia, iconoclasts, reformers, and self-proclaimed prophets of the New Movement in the European theatre, were assaulting the false façades of photographic realism. Their creative writing and inspired designs for scenes gave impetus to young directors and designers in Europe and America, whose experimental work was to lift the theatre from its realistic doldrums and chart a new course for the drama.

Chroniclers of the theatre mark the date January 27, 1915, as the beginning of a new visual era of the American stage. In Wallack's old theatre at Broadway and 31st Street the curtain rose on Robert Edmond Jones's setting for Harley Granville-Barker's production of *The Man Who Married a Dumb Wife.* Here was a stylized setting which, through muted tones and bold design, imaginatively evoked medieval France without benefit of realism. Kenneth MacGowan wrote "this setting in his early manner is instinctive with all the essential character of his art; its unity, its economy, its coherence and appreciation of theatrical qualities." Arthur Hopkins at once was sympathetic to Jones's original selective sense of theatre, and, henceforth, working together, they inaugurated a long and distinguished association. That same year a group of malcontents called the Washington Square Players invited Lee Simonson to design the settings for Andreyev's *Love of One's Neighbor* at the old Band Box Theatre on 57th Street. The Theatre Guild emerged from this group, and Mr. Simonson, as designer-in-chief of the Theatre Guild, created a notable series of visual productions. Claude Bragdon applied principles of dynamic symmetry in designing his simplified scenes for Walter Hampden's *Hamlet*. At the same time Joseph Urban and Norman Bel Geddes were tearing down, not only the traditional decoration from the old theatres, but also the proscenium arch itself. Circuses, stables, and ballrooms were converted into experimental theatres. In 1919 through the urgency of Otto Kahn, Mr. Bel Geddes designed *La Nave* for the Metropolitan Opera, which was the first of a long line of exciting productions in his notable career. These dedicated young American designers had become infected with the contagious air of the New Movement, and each brought into focus his vision of the American scene. The accomplishments of all these designers established the profession of stage design in New York.

Joseph Urban had been called from the *Wiener Werkstätter* as designer to the Boston Opera House and subsequently to the Metropolitan where he established new scenic standards for the production of opera. He also revitalized the New York musical stage with his opulent collaborations with Florenz Ziegfeld. So, too, did young James Reynolds, who was bestowing glamour on John Murray Anderson's *Greenwich Village Follies*. Added stimulus came from many designers who were attracted to Broadway's lights from insurgent Art Theatres in many parts of the country. Among these were Raymond Sovey, Rollo Peters, and Woodman Thompson. From Europe, too, many designers stamped their influence on the Broadway theatre. The list includes Boris Anisfeld, Nicholas Roerich, Mstislav Dobujinsky, and Serge Soudeikine, all artists from Russia; Herman Rosse from Holland; Richard Rychtarik and Jonel Jorgulesco from Central Europe; and Frederic Kiesler from Vienna.

Immediately after the First World War, our theatre was unashamedly stimulated by an invasion of foreign-theatre troupes. From Russia came Diaghilev's Ballet, Stanislavsky's Moscow Art Theatre, Dantchenko's Moscow Art Theatre Musical Studio. From Germany Reinhardt brought his repertory of classics, which revealed his unhackneyed and varied idioms of production and his genius for fusing actors, scenery, mechanics, and lighting into a composite dramatic entity. Mei Lan Fang wafted his Chinese Theatre with all its beauty from Peking. There were ballet and theatre companies from France, England, Sweden, and Italy. All submerged us in a tidal wave of stylistic wonder. If ever our theatre was an "imaginary invalid," it was then. Each troupe administered to us its own peculiar antidote for the old realism. We were delighted with the cure, even if our theatre did suffer a rash of German expressionism and symbolism immediately followed by an attack of Russian constructivism.

What became of the avant-garde style of our scenes of thirty years ago? It bristled with pictorial overtones of Freud, machine worship, and futuristic art. Typical productions were Mordecai Gorelik's *Processional*, Robert Edmond Jones's *Macbeth*, Woodman Thompson's *God Loves Us*, Lee Simonson's *From Morn to Midnight* and *The Adding Machine*, and my own *Pinwheel*. For a time the emphasis on the visual theatre seemed on the verge of smothering the drama it clothed. Most of those fireworks have vanished from our stage with the passing of the scene itself. All that pulsing theatre receded and became obscured in the enveloping reality of a national depression and a global war.

Many off-Broadway experimental theatres were formed during that period. Those theatres became the early proving ground for the talents of young playwrights, actors, directors, and designers. There was unselfish unity of purpose among such off-Broadway groups as the Theatre Guild, the Neighborhood Playhouse, the New Playwrights, the Provincetown–Greenwich Village group, and Boleslavsky's Laboratory Theatre. These theatres produced the works of young American dramatists and the best contemporary European plays, investing them with imaginatively and economically designed and lighted productions. All this burgeoning off-Broadway theatre released young design talent into the professional Broadway theatre. Among them were Jo Mielziner, Mordecai Gorelik, Cleon Throckmorton, Aline Bernstein, and myself.

Then followed the Depression years with the WPA theatre offering a redoubtable program of varying productions which revealed the challenging work of young designers like Howard Bay and Nat Karson. In the later post-Depression gold-rush years the studios were always crowded. The second floor of Bergman's scenic studio on 39th Street was the informal roost for many designers, among them Albert Johnson, Lee Simonson, Norman Bel Geddes, Jo Mielziner, Raymond Sovey, and Stewart Chaney. Bobby Jones held court in his cubbyhole studio high up in the paint loft. Scenery came in from the sidewalk virgin-white and was hauled out "done" with frightening speed and a "Bergman bath."

Against this varied backdrop of many currents, what visual trends do we observe today in our changing theatre? We must first look to the playwrights, for today they create the conventions of our theatre practice tomorrow. Sometimes the playwright, even before completing his script, invites the visual collaboration of the designer to help establish his scenic pattern. He welcomes ideas of scenic solutions for suggesting changing locale and mood. One type of setting, which possibly points in a new direction, presents a fourth-dimensional quality with a skeletal arrangement of scenes utilizing semitransparent or solid walls. Light pursues the action of the play from one scene to another and focuses on the dramatic action without actual change of scene. Such a design Boris Aronson realized for Frances and Albert Hackett's *The Diary of Anne Frank* and Arthur Miller's *A View from the Bridge*. Howard Bay utilized the same principle in his design for *The Desperate Hours*. George Jenkins, in his use of flexible platforms with indicative scenes, achieved a swift-flowing pace to match the fluid style of Maxwell Anderson's *Lost in the Stars*. Lemuel Ayers designed a compelling scene of surrealist fantasia on a ramped stage for Tennessee Williams's macabre *Camino Real*. In Arthur Miller's *Death of a Salesman*, Jo Mielziner provided a simultaneous X-ray picture of the inside and the outside of the Salesman's house. In *Coriolanus*, using a space stage, I attempted to speed forward and highlight the action of Shakespeare's drama with mobile light.

The stage designer approaches Thornton Wilder's *Our Town* or Maxwell Anderson's *Joan of Lorraine* with an entirely different attitude. These plays require no scenery—only the bare walls of the stage. For these plays, mobile lighting becomes the motivating force of the designer's contribution. Another style of production without scenery has become fashionable—a dramatic presentation of Stephen Vincent Benet's poem, *John Brown's Body*, or of Herman Wouk's novel, *The Caine Mutiny*. On a stage a few chairs, a bench, a table before plain curtains provide adequate background without implying economic limitations. The theatre-in-the-round with the audience seated in arena fashion around a central acting area has found groups of adherents. While the aesthetic intention of this pseudo-Greek theatre form is to intensify the relationship between actor and audience, it is generally a makeshift formula born essentially of economy.

A noteworthy fusion of all the artistic elements of the theatre is to be found in much of our contemporary ballet and musical theatre. The Ballet Theatre and the New York City Center Ballet have discovered highly original directions, in which costumes and scene design are closely integrated with music and imaginative choreography. In the field of the Broadway musical theatre a vigorous welding and blending of all the parts is abundantly evident in the collective efforts of author, composer, director, choreographer, and designer. Jo Mielziner, Lemuel Ayers, Oliver Smith, Raoul du Bois, and Cecil Beaton are but a few who have, in exercising their own fancy-free talents, helped to enrich and convert this form of theatre into a highly evocative pioneering adventure in the modern theatre.

Already a gifted group of young designers are making their talents felt in the contemporary theatre. Eldon Elder, Charles Elson, William and Jean Eckart, Ralph Alswang, Ben Edwards, Leo Kerz, and Peter Larkin each contributes a potential style with his own personal approach toward design in the theatre. Each realizes, too, that designing for the Broadway theatre does not grow easier over the years. From the beginning it has grown continually harder—more of a commercial enterprise and an entertainment business, more full of shortcuts and greater pressures, more impersonal with its how much for how few dollars and hours. Notwithstanding, designing settings remains an alluring profession of counterfeit wonder and artifice, even though the theatre yearly continues to contract into a smaller institution with fewer productions in fewer theatres.

Even the busiest stage designers' works do not always reach the stage of a theatre. These are his own projects, his dreams for the theatre. The malcontent designer finds pleasure in making projects which he designs for himself as producer and also as audience. These projects are ideas for productions: experiments in forms and styles of scenery and of new directions in lighting which are not demanded by the average production which the designer is asked to devise for Broadway. A few such projects are Robert Edmond Jones's designs for Shelley's *Cenci*, Norman Bel Geddes's model for a production of Dante's *Divine Comedy*, Jo Mielziner's model for *Faust*, and my own designs for *Hamlet*. Such dreams may communicate ideas to a director, a young playwright, or a new producer for the newer freedoms of tomorrow's theatre. That is what the stage designer of today cares about and is looking for, believing with Gordon Craig that the "big Dream recurs again and again till it becomes in years the reality."

VISUAL COMMUNICATIONS

MILDRED CONSTANTINE

Benjamin Franklin's "Join, or Die" on the masthead of a newspaper in 1754 and Alvin Lustig's "The Language of Advertising" cover of *Fortune* magazine in 1952 reflect the conditions of their respective eras. All graphic design records, with printed word and image, the experience and attitudes of a time. This essay is concerned with the aesthetic evolution of graphic communication from the untutored traditional forms of "folk art" to the most sophisticated expressions of modern art.

The various forms of graphic communication are advertisements, magazine covers, cartoons, caricatures, book jackets, greeting cards, sales and information brochures, booklets, catalogues, record-album covers, sheet-music covers, direct mail announcements, comic strips, illustrations, signs, billboards, and posters. (Graphics in motion conceived for movie titles, television, and electric signs are not included in this section but are of importance and interest for future study in this field.) The function of these different graphic media is to communicate values through a potent harmony of typographic, abstract, and pictorial elements. In this study an historical approach to the development of graphic design in the United States has been followed. However, emphasis has been placed on those periods (from the 1880s to the present) when the designer, stimulated and directed by the painters, sculptors, and architects who had initiated new forms and by technological advances in the craft of printing, had a wider range of possibilities.

Only recently has graphic material of this nature been the concern of institutions devoted to art. The historical societies and libraries which normally collect and house such work regard them merely as social documents. The present selection, on the contrary, has been made solely on the basis of artistic excellence.

The predecessors of our posters, brochures, and electric signs are the stone tablets (Hammurabi Code) of the ancient Middle East and the painted announcements on walls in Greece and Rome. Hanging signs and written and drawn handbills appeared throughout Europe before the advent of printing. These and public announcements with descriptive illustrations—the on-the-spot pictures from the journals of explorers and mariners—were all exported from Europe to the United States along with other products.

The announcement of auctions and markets, the broadsides and trading cards, which sometimes were accompanied by crude woodcuts or engravings, were like book pages with explanatory remarks. In a sense these were the beginnings of advertising in the American colonies. Although numerous engravings appeared as early as 1730, they were mostly scenic views, cartographic studies, and portraits. During this period picturemaking was the work of European-trained immigrants or native-born Americans who had learned their trade from books, prints, and paintings brought over from Europe. As Holger Cahill has pointed out, "It is often hard to draw a dividing line between the art of the common man and that of the professional."

The colonist's concern with urgent political and social problems was expressed more in literary than in pictorial terms. However, Benjamin Franklin in a pamphlet written and printed in 1747 used an engraving (attributed to him) to symbolize a political situation. But it was the "Join, or Die" symbol used on the masthead of the *Pennsylvania Gazette* on May 9, 1754, whose impact, both graphic and political, marks the introduction of this method of visual communication in the United States. This grim dismembered snake, accompanied by a terse slogan, provided an allegorical symbol whose cartoonlike character made the political and moral issue more immediate than did the rhetoric of the period. The linear quality of the drawing, without embellishment or background, is reminiscent of German engravings and woodcuts of the sixteenth century.

As William Murrell has pointed out, this symbol and a later one from the *Boston Gazette* were used repeatedly in cartoons dealing with different phases of the Revolutionary struggle. Although the later years of the eighteenth century evoked pictorial satires and cartoons by such men as Franklin and Paul Revere, no one symbol had the lasting impact of "Join, or Die." We have only to recall the "V" of World War II to realize the all-pervasive qualities of a symbol.

The early part of the nineteenth century produced many signed prints relating to the current themes of work, legislation, and migration by native craftsmen who were stimulated by the acceptance of their work by publishers and the general public. Much of it is important only for the information it contained. Of more aesthetic interest is the work of Elkanah Tisdale which appeared not only in newspapers and broadsides but also in the poem *M'Fingal*. Tisdale is the designer of the famous "Gerrymander" cartoon (1821), a meaningful drawing with graphic vitality. Political commentary continued with such cartoons as the "Death of the Embargo" (1814), an efficient but academic drawing by Alexander Anderson and John Wesley Jarvis.

Two charming and stylistically individual examples of graphic illustration by unknown artists give some indication of a wider interest both in leisure-time activity and in the manners and morals of our society. The popularity of dancing led to engravings instructing in the etiquette and new steps of social dancing. A page from the *Port Folio*, a magazine published in Philadelphia in 1817, describes the social amenities and postures of the dance and also uses words to repeat its message. It is a pattern of light, linear forms which today suggest both cave painting and the drawings of Thurber in directness, awareness, humor, and economical expression of movement.

Traveling circuses were common in the United States in the early days of the nineteenth century. Before the flamboyant Barnum and Bailey posters appeared, a typical broadside advertising a traveling troupe of acrobats was made from a wood block (c. 1818). Its drawing is representational but not literary, and no caption is used.

With the introduction of lithography in 1801, book and magazine illustrations increased in number and variety. The continuing interest in the acts and policies of the government resulted in lithograph cartoons printed on single sheets of paper and sold to the general public. The numerous comic almanacs of the 1830s and 1840s published jokes and crude pictures, mostly in woodcut, which sometimes were more direct and humorous than the text. Caricatures which appeared in *The Crockett Almanac* were typical in that they possessed great vigor but little graphic subtlety. Certainly Henry Stephen's "Giraffe" from *The Comic Natural History of the Human Race* was more personal and creative. The California gold rush inspired a kind of pictorial ballad, crudely cut and colored, which served as advertisements encouraging migration, prospecting,

and such social manifestations of the period as the gambling saloon.

During the pre-Civil War period, some graphic vitality was to be found in cartoons, illustrations, and caricatures. Advertisements looked like pages of an illustrated Montgomery–Ward catalogue or a newspaper complete with headlines and leads. Two sheet-music covers are notable exceptions, one by James McNeill Whistler (1852), the other by Winslow Homer (1856). Although pictorial and typographic posters appeared during the Civil War, it was Mathew Brady's photographic reportage and Winslow Homer's stirring drawings that supplied the graphic images of that historic event.

The field of political cartooning in America grew in the 1850s. Artists with real enthusiasm, like Thomas Nast, Joseph Keppler, and Frank H. K. Bellew, collaborated with literary men who were often personal friends. Their publishers not only gave them freedom of taste and judgment but also encouraged their spontaneous graphic thinking as visual complements to an editorial point of view.

Harper's Weekly, Frank Leslie's Illustrated Newspaper, Vanity Fair, and *Puck* treated significant events and prominent people. Graphic reporting became less descriptive and more integrated through thoughtful composition and graphic interpretation.

Joseph Keppler produced comic drawings of keen insight in St. Louis for his short-lived papers, *Die Vehme* and *Puck,* before going to New York, where in 1876 he founded a new German-language *Puck* and, a year later, an English one. In both of these, Keppler and his staff (including Bernard Gillam) gave freely of humor and biting judgment for many years. Keppler's ideas were often prophetic, though they lacked subtlety and concentrated intensity.

Thomas Nast, however, was the first to move away from the complicated allegorical drawing and the central cartoon surrounded by a number of smaller ones. His drawing, stripped of irrelevant detail, suggests the single-mindedness of a crusader. The forceful simplicity evident in such famous cartoons as "Let us Prey" made Boss Tweed say, "I do not care what they print about me, most of my constituents can't read, but them damn pictures!"

Nast, who had studied drawing and painting, was capable of inventing a symbol and with its repeated use could suggest a thought without the use of a label. Indeed, he created the tiger, the elephant, and the donkey as political symbols of Tammany Hall, the Republican and Democratic parties. Nast's ability to caricature a figure with harsh truthful distortion is a form of editorializing. His drawing was designed for wood engraving and indicates an awareness of the capacities of this medium to reproduce clear line and tonal values.

P. T. Barnum developed techniques in his circus posters for recruiting a mass audience. These flamboyant "commercials" yielded nothing in the way of noteworthy design. The same graphic attitude was soon adopted for advertisements of patent medicines, soaps, collars, and other products. While they produced the prototype of the "Arrow Collar" look and the "Gibson Girl," they did little to advance the aesthetic of advertising and editorial art.

An invention of printing from stone, patented in London by Aloys Senefelder (German) in 1801, was to have an enormous impact on graphic design. Although its early use was for the reproduction of precise lines that imitated drawings, the French Jules Chéret, working in England from 1856–1866, developed and refined the technique of color lithography in a manner characterized by movement, by imaginative use of bright colors, and by a decorative flatness of treatment which were in the spirit of Art Nouveau and which foretold the manner of Lautrec. Since this new technique permitted fluid use of colors, freedom from muddy tones and tints, and did not impose the limit of size, it found immediate response among the artists in France. Chéret himself, more a technician than an artist, utilized the possibility of full-scale drawing, but his elaborate compositions imitated paintings. It remained for Henri de Toulouse-Lautrec's vital style of drawing, dramatizing the single figure by full-scale continuous line, shading and fusing the background, to bring the poster into its own as a work of art.

The first break with traditional forms appeared in the 1880s and 1890s. Art Nouveau was influencing all art forms throughout France, England, and Germany and began to affect the visual arts in America too. Cartoons and posters advertising newspapers and magazines appeared by such designers as Will Bradley, Arthur W. Dow, Edward Penfield, and Louis J. Rhead. These are almost all fundamentally decorative but far removed from the embellishments of the early nineteenth century. The characteristic asymmetrical design, curvilinear ornamentation, precise but sinuous line with cool large areas of flat color stemmed from the work of Beardsley, Crane, Toorop, and, of course, Lautrec and Steinlen. An example is the "Inland Printer Christmas 1895" advertisement by Will Bradley. Its black and green floral over-all background with diagonal emphasis sets off the two figures. Flat areas of red and white, the flowing lines of the robes against the diagonal background, and the bare outlines of face and features make

a harmony of linear rhythms. The two lines of text, above and below the pictorial elements, serve as roof and ground to the composition.

Although the first decade of the twentieth century produced cartoons, illustrations, advertisements, and posters of great variety, it was not until the prewar period, 1912–1917, that a powerful editorial graphic imagery reappeared. This time it was not reportage but social realism presented with precision and bite, creating a disquieting atmosphere. Work by Boardman Robinson, Art Young, John Sloan, Robert Minor, and George Bellows became familiar to the public through the appearance of *The Masses,* with an art editorial board consisting of Young and Sloan, as well as Maurice Becker and Alice Beach Winter. Concerned as it was with presenting the "convincing touch of truth and genius" in its editorial policy and hampered by the reticence of advertisers, the sharp, unregimented cartoons won an audience. *The Masses* however had internal financial difficulties and ceased publication only to emerge anew in 1926 with some of the old familiar names, as well as the names of such newcomers as Joseph Freeman, Egmont Arens, Hugo Gellert, and Louis Lozowick.

Outstanding for graphic power in expressing the antimilitarism of the period is Robert Minor's "At Last a Perfect Soldier." This drawing recalls the savage humor of George Grosz. Although the painters and graphic artists were united in a spirit of realistic social commentary, their work remained individual in aesthetic and technique.

After the entry of the United States into the war, a prodigious amount of posters and cartoons yielded little of artistic validity with the notable exception of two posters: Joseph Pennell's alarming image of the bombing of New York Harbor and the compelling pointing finger of James Montgomery Flagg's "I want You." In the postwar period, the signing of the Versailles Treaty provoked a monumental and prophetic cartoon by Boardman Robinson, the stark drawing bringing to mind something of Käthe Kollwitz.

The 1920s can be characterized by juxtaposing two points of view: the gay, the witty, often elegant satire of the *New Yorker* and *Life* magazine and the relentless hammering at economic inequality of the *New Masses* and the *Daily Worker.* John Held, Jr.'s "Teaching an Old Dog New Tricks," William Gropper's "The Noble Senator," Art Young's "The Great Inferno," Stuart Davis's cover for the *New Masses,* all done in 1926, suggest the period's diversity of subject matter and its equally diverse styles. Mention should be made here of the rise of the comic strip which was in effect an outgrowth of the comic illustrations and cartoons (Keppler, for example; Davenport, Opper in the 1900s, etc.). During the 1890s the first strip to appear in American newspapers was R. F. Outcault's "Hogan's Alley," followed by such favorites as Rudolph Dirks's "Katzenjammer Kids" (inspired by an earlier German strip), and Fontaine Fox's "Toonerville" characters. Among our national favorites is George Herriman's subtle, ironically humorous "Krazy Kat" (1911–1944). Herriman used the cat and mouse to satirize humans and expressed their plight and love with compassion and sympathy. His use of *non sequitur* backgrounds gave visual excitement to the play enacted. Rube Goldberg's irrational "scientific" projects were wonderfully expressed through detailed drawing. The Goldberg "Crazy Inventions," published first in 1910, became the popular fantastic art of our country. The comic strip, a combination of humorous drawing and humorous statement, started as a single narrative. In its development, it stimulated awareness through laughter and ridicule, and today it not only reflects public tastes and interests but often creates them.

The sprawling efforts in design and communication up to this period were influenced by the tremendous changes in all the arts, beginning in Europe in the postwar period and affecting the United States in the late 1920s. Fundamental changes in visual forms began with Art Nouveau movement at the turn of the century followed by cubism, futurism, and surrealism. The relation between these styles in painting, sculpture, architecture, and design did not seem to appear either as a simultaneous expression or as a direct influence on individual works but rather as a tendency formed by the inventions and discoveries of the time.

The important schools of *de Stijl* and suprematism, fused in the atmosphere of the Bauhaus, affected design throughout Europe and slowly found an audience among artists and designers in the United States. The *de Stijl* movement, which flourished in Holland from 1917 to 1932, developed a unifying concept for all the arts of rectangular forms, asymmetrically separated volumes, and clear, flat colors. Having particular meaning for the graphic designer in his handling of typography, the discipline reduced compositions to fewer colors, allowed the surface of the picture plane to become an important element, and revolutionized the graphic arts by the discovery of the positive value of empty space.

The Bauhaus disciplines, with common points of view for artist, architect, and designer, produced a vocabulary and grammar which have shaped our cultural patterns for more than thirty years. Alfred Barr has called the Bauhaus "the one school in the world where modern problems of design were approached realistically in a modern atmosphere." The recognition of a future involved primarily with industry, mass production, and the machine helped to develop a new aesthetic.

Ideas and directions in new typography came from various sources: László Moholy-Nagy said that typography must be ". . . clear communication in its most vivid form. . . . clarity must be stressed for clarity is the essence of modern printing in contrast to ancient picture writing. . . . a new typographic language must be created, combining elasticity, variety and a fresh approach to the materials of printing." Herbert Bayer, working and teaching in the Bauhaus in 1925, sought a rationalization of writing and printing, substituting the roman and sans-serif letters for the archaic Gothic form. In his search for "universal type," he created letter design based on three fundamental forms —arcs, angles, vertical and horizontal lines—and dropped all capital letters from the alphabet. The appearance in 1927 of Paul Renner's "Futura" type face, widely used in Bauhaus and *de Stijl* publications, provided a basic alphabet for modern graphic design.

These influences, together with many forms of painting and sculpture, directly affected the appearance of graphic design. The geometric stylization of animate and inanimate forms found in the paintings of Le Corbusier and Amedée Ozenfant is evident, particularly in the work of A. M. Cassandre and Jean Carlu. Both artists worked for many years in the United States and together with E. McKnight Kauffer, an American who had worked in England during the late twenties, they had enormous influence on United States design. (See the posters of Kauffer, the *Fortune* cover of Semenoick, the advertisements of Erik Nitsche, Paul Smith, and Lester Beall, as well as Beall's posters for the Rural Electrification Administration.) Herbert Matter's "4-Story Groceries," an advertisement for the Container Corporation of America, owes much to futurism with its visualization of patterns of movement. Paul Rand's 1939 cover for *PM's Guide to the New York World's Fair* utilizes geometric asymmetry with great effect; the Ladislav Sutnar catalogue page for Sweet's catalogue (1944) employs functionally logical principles of abstract design which lend greater legibility to its message.

Erik Nitsche's 1947 "Subway Poster" as well as his 1956 "General Dynamics" series and Robert Jones's album cover for *Mood Ellington* (1948) are excellent applications of abstract geometric form. In the Nitsche posters, the free use of oblique lines in composition suggests sweeping movement and endless space. The diagonals function as a light and open background for the right-angle regularity of the typographic layout.

The abstract and organically stylized forms of Hans Arp and Joan Miró and the movement implicit in their designs provided a fertile field for jacket designs, advertisements, music-album covers, and show windows. Alex Steinweiss's *Boogie Woogie* album cover, Lester Beall's cover designs for Sterling Engraving Company and Abbott Laboratories all use the exaggerated fluidity of shape and position for effect.

The incongruity and fantasy of surrealism and its shock of the unexpected make a perfect device for graphic impact. René Magritte's painting, *The False Mirror,* which portrayed the eye as a single feature isolated from its context, influenced such works as Cassandre's "Watch the Fords Go By" (1938) and William Golden's CBS television symbol used in network identification (1952). This isolation in an unexpected setting is also deftly employed by Herbert Bayer in his book jacket, "Can Our Cities Survive" (1942), and by Charles Eames's Christmas card of 1948.

The influence of the collages of Pablo Picasso, Georges Braque, and Kurt Schwitters and the design possibilities of nonpictorial material also have been thoroughly exploited. Photographers like Herbert Matter and Leo Lionni also have made use of overlapping transparent planes to create a fluid sense of space, inspired by the masterpieces of modern architecture.

Post-World War II saw a rise in the use of graphic design for commercial and institutional advertising. The development of the advertising agency and market research encouraged the use of graphics for all purposes. Young talent appeared along with the experienced designers, but there have been no innovations.

Looking at American newspapers, magazines, billboards, and the other graphic media from 1945 to the present and comparing them with those of the eighteenth and nineteenth centuries and the first decades of the twentieth, many observations are pertinent. No one of our current overwhelming problems has produced any memorable visual commentary in either social or political cartoons or caricatures. Of course, the comic strip, animated film cartoon, and television have conditioned people to a different kind of symbolism, but the work of a few brilliant men indicates that the cartoon of social commentary has not lost its impact.

Daniel Fitzpatrick, working for the *St. Louis Post-Dispatch,* carries on the tradition of a political cartoonist's crusading spirit with symbol, lucid drawing, and the briefest caption.

Robert Osborn's graphics appearing in *PM, New Republic, Industrial Design, Scope,* and in advertisements in the *New Yorker* are storms of protest drawn with boldness and rapid sweep of line. His caricatures are very personal statements from the artist which elicit real audience participation from the viewer ("Who Goes There," 1955).

Saul Steinberg, like Klee a master of the wandering line, uses a marvelous wordless calligraphy for many purposes. Whether it is a series of ads for the Simplicity Pattern Company (1956) or a cartoon for the *New Yorker* (1949), his humor emerges as a combination of satire and poetry and thus remains memorable. The meaning of a Steinberg cartoon goes far beyond the illustration image. It lies in the linear collage which Steinberg makes of idea and story, *objet trouvé,* and architecture, embodying his comment on the moods and intentions of our time.

Posters produced during the World War II period and thereafter indicate that this form of communication has begun to enjoy a new kind of patronage. They are produced more for ideas and are related more to the institutional attitudes of perceptive clients and less to selling single products. They are designed for rapid reading, employing sparse typography and symbols which work as signals for description and recognition. The hammering impact and soapbox tactics, although still evident in other forms of visual communication, are outmoded here. For example, a series which merits attention and indicates the direction of the modern poster in the United States consists of posters which the *New York Times* produced especially for the audiences in subway stations and railroad stations. In the entire series, no pictorial image is used; the slogan and the name of the newspaper are the only subject matter. The common spirit underlying the series is projected through variations in typography and abstract rhythmic patterns. (See the George Krikorian and Kenneth Haak posters.) When pictorial images are employed in posters they range from the sharp focus and precise representation of the Levy's Rye Bread poster by Robert Gage to the expressionist image of Saul Bass's movie poster, "Man with the Golden Arm."

Book jackets, covers of record albums, and advertisements in newspapers or magazines of necessity require an adjustment in scale. Whether they are pictorial, typographical, or a combination of both, they are meant to arrest, to be held in the hand, and to be studied in a more leisurely fashion. In design they are varied, influenced by painting, photography, and the structural geometric forms of architecture and engineering. There is a tremendous range; strong calligraphic line and playfully animated treatment of letter forms, often entertaining in effect, distinguish the brochures and advertisements of Ben Shahn who is also a painter and muralist. ("The Empty Studio," 1948; "Partridge in a Pear Tree," 1951; the "'52 Republican Convention," 1952.) In a series of posters which Shahn executed for the War Production Board and the CIO, he uses a more painterly idiom of modeling ("We Want Peace," 1946). Herbert Matter, photographer and typographer, reveals a primary interest in form, texture, and movement rather than content. By means of a magic surgery he creates images of essence rather than of the thing itself. His optical effects contrast sharply with his powerful use of letter forms ("America Calling," 1941; "How to Combine Architecture, Painting, Sculpture," 1951; advertisement for Knoll, 1956). Leo Lionni approaches his design problems each time with fresh ingenuity. His skill and sophistication are never limited to a set style. He deftly employs the special character of a line ("Which Way Out," 1956) or a surprising logic of juxtaposition for emphasis and authority ("Eight Automobiles," 1951; "World of Modern Art," 1954).

In a field so thoroughly standardized as design and printing is in the United States today, it is encouraging that more and more clients are putting this work into the hands of trained and capable designers. A freer range is permitted the designer in the materials used and in the techniques employed to create new expressions. His work competes for public interest and helps to project visual aspects of his client's products. Consider the corporate image inspired by the *Terapia* covers of Will Burtin which employ heavy embossing and relate letter forms to geometric design demonstrating the value of the printed word in an almost architectural setting. Another kind of image is created for the Strathmore Paper Company by a brochure in which Burtin adds another dimension to graphic design by puncturing all the pages (the punctured-page device was used earlier by Bauhaus students), thus obtaining additional spatial depth and permitting the complex colors to be viewed as a single design.

A survey of the most recent work in this section reveals an active interest in typography and letter forms. Two designers whose interests convey very different spirits are Alvin Lustig and Paul Rand. Lustig's work, relying primarily on exploiting the shapes of letters, their placement, the paper surface and texture, gains effect from an exquisite, almost fussy, kind of relationship which is enhanced by a cool color scheme. His cover for the Vivaldi record album (1953), for instance, uses nervous angularity of design to suggest the composer's baroque orchestration. Rand, on the other hand, remains devoted to primary colors and symbolic geometric forms. He orders his space and distributes his materials to predetermine eye movement, using contrasting and isolated letters like heraldic devices.

Graphic design—a new art which has importance to contemporary thought and activity—has produced only a few individual designers of great merit. But there is today a general standard of excellence, parallel with a growing use. The early craftsmen who cut or engraved designs had little creative intention. Today's designer, schooled in the complex technical details and more familiar with the art of the past and the present, is better equipped. The training of the graphic designer, in both the techniques and art of this field of communication, is today the concern of such schools on the university level as Yale, Harvard, and the Institute of Design in Chicago, and his work is collected by those institutions concerned with the qualitative selection and evaluation of works of art.

Note: The color slides described in the following catalogue may be obtained from Sandak, Inc., 39 West 53d Street, New York 19, New York.

CATALOGUE

THE TECHNIQUE OF PHOTOGRAPHY AND SLIDE PRODUCTION

From the beginning a major concern of the Carnegie Study has been to provide a continuing source of reasonably priced color slides of the highest possible quality. Thus the question immediately arose as to what technique of slide making would best achieve this objective. A preliminary survey revealed that at the time there were two methods of color photography and slide production in common use among makers of art color slides. The first was to take the camera directly to the object and there, on the spot, make as many slides as needed. From the point of view of quality this technique was the more reliable, but it presented a serious difficulty for this project; there was no sure way of determining in advance exactly how many slides would be required. Once the original inventory was exhausted, it would be necessary, if a continuing supply were to be maintained, to take the camera back to the object. However, such a procedure would be prohibitively expensive and would also become a recurring source of nuisance for museum directors and private owners alike.

The second technique was to make a master slide of each object by direct photography and to have that master slide reproduced in quantity by a duplicating process. This method could be used to turn out slides in great quantities at a minimum cost. An objection, however, was the poor quality which would inevitably result. Although marked improvements have been made in recent years, there seemed to be no duplicating process which could faithfully reproduce the original with consistent and predictable results.

To resolve this problem it was decided to conduct a series of experiments. Several objects presenting various color, texture, and lighting problems were photographed under controlled conditions. In making these photographs every well-known American color film was used. The resulting transparencies were first processed and subsequently duplicated by several carefully selected laboratories. Then came the critical tests. Both the original transparencies and the duplicates were projected immediately beside the objects themselves. By using identical projectors and controlled lighting of the objects it was possible to make a thorough comparative check of the various films and duplicating methods. The results were as diverse as the films, the techniques, and the laboratories involved. The actual slides reviewed numbered in the hundreds, and the lack of any consistent results proved conclusively that neither direct photography nor the duplicating process offered any possibility of achieving the high standards established for the project.

The answer to this apparently insoluble problem was found by turning to a completely different technique —the color negative. The negative process has been used in the motion picture industry since the first days of color film and has been widely employed in the field of professional color photography for some years. More recently it has appeared in Europe as a means of producing art color slides, and it is currently gaining popularity in this country for the same purpose.

New types of color negative film now available are not only moderately high speed and fine grain, they also have wide latitude and excellent color characteristics. One in particular is balanced for flash and can thus be used with stroboscopic light. This presents numerous advantages. A large professional strobe unit is capable of delivering sufficient quantities of illumination to make possible the exposure times called for in the specifications of the film. In addition, the amount of illumination is exactly the same with every flash. Consequently, accurate exposure indices based upon distance ratios of light source to object can easily be established, thus assuring constant exposure results. But even more important, the color balance of a strobe flash is virtually the same as daylight. Accordingly, the two can be used in combination without any disturbance of the color balance in the negative. For certain types of architectural photography this opens wide possibilities, particularly in many contemporary interiors where large areas of glass are involved and the exterior virtually becomes a part of the interior.

Perhaps the greatest advantage gained from the use of the color negative is the diversity of technical control which it permits both at the camera and in the laboratory. Because of the film's wide latitude, an elastic interpretation of exposure is possible, and the way is opened for a more immediate and subtle relationship between the film and the object being photographed. In photography in the round, for example, where strong contrasts of light and shade are involved, details in one area can be brought out without sacrificing details in the other. By adjusting the relationship between the exposure time at the camera and the development of the film, it is possible to control both the density and contrast of the finished negative. In addition, the printing of the positive transparency from the negative offers other areas of control. Here the density of the finished print can be increased or decreased simply by changing the amount of light which passes through the negative. Also, the color balance of the prints can be adjusted by adding filters to the printing-light source. Finally, it is possible to frame the image appropriately to the slide shape.

Also important to the achievement of high quality was the Board's decision to work entirely with 4×5 cut film. This not only facilitated handling, identifying, and filing of the negatives, but it also made possible a more flexible camera technique. In the past, one of the principal drawbacks to the use of the 2×2 slides has been the limitations of the 35-mm camera. The small size of the image makes accurate focusing and framing difficult, and with the fixed lens there is no way to correct for perspective distortion. However, by working in the larger size it became possible to employ the finest view cameras with every kind of swing and focusing mechanism.

One additional refinement that is to be derived from the use of 4×5 cut film is the introduction to the finished slide of a built-in black border around paintings. Because very few paintings conform in shape exactly to the proportions of the camera image, photographs of paintings made on standard reversal films frequently show sections of frame or background around the picture. In order to eliminate this it has been necessary in the past to black out the unwanted areas with a mask or tape. However, when the color negative is used, a system of double exposure will print a black border directly on the slide itself. Since this is done on the 4×5 negative before printing, it can be accomplished with greater accuracy, and the danger of serious cropping of the picture is eliminated.

All of these areas of control have given to the project the one thing it sought above all else—predictable results. It is now possible to establish and maintain standards, and slides of identical quality can be produced at any time, in any size, and in any quantity. Furthermore, each of these slides is an original in exactly the same sense that a slide produced by direct photography with a reversal film is an original. But with respect to this point, a word of explanation is in order.

When a person refers to a slide as an "original," he generally means that it is a positive transparency made by original photography directly from an object. It is thus distinguished from a "duplicate," which is made by rephotographing the original transparency rather than the object itself. The film used for both the original and the duplicate is called a reversal film because in each case the resulting photograph is a positive rather than a negative. What most people do not realize is that a positive transparency made with a reversal film *does have a negative*. If a reversal film is taken from the tanks at one of the early stages in the development process, it will seem to be a kind of greyish negative. In order to activate the film for the final print this negative is exposed to light. It is then bleached away, and the positive is developed. In other words, in the reversal technique the negative is built into the film and in the process of development is destroyed. Consequently, there is no surviving negative from which additional prints can be made. If more slides are required, they must be provided by a duplicating method using a similar reversal film with the subsequent loss of a second negative. It is precisely because of this that duplicates are not, and never can be, as good in quality as the original.

When a color negative material is used, the negative is not destroyed but becomes, in effect, the original photograph. Just as with a black-and-white negative, it can be filed away to be used over and over again, and every slide made from that negative is an "original" in exactly the same sense that every slide made by direct photography with a reversal film is an original.

Although the efforts of the Carnegie Study have been directed entirely toward the production of color slides, the advantages to be gained from the color negative are by no means limited to this medium. Persons familiar with the problems of color reproduction know only too well that one of the great drawbacks to the use of color photography for works of art is the fact that in a reversal film there is no surviving negative. Thus, every time color work is called for it is necessary to go back to the object with the camera. With the color negative this is not the case. Once files of negatives have been built up, they can be used for all types of reproduction. The color negative can be used to produce excellent color prints by photo-projection methods; it can also be used to produce high-quality transparencies in any size and for any purpose. Recent attempts have demonstrated the feasibility of making color separation positives directly from the color negative, thus eliminating the intervening steps of making a color transparency and a color separation negative. Finally, by using a panchromatic paper the color negative can be employed to make excellent black-and-white prints.

The Study also wished to produce all the slides mounted in glass ready for projection. However, the number of slides envisaged would amount to hundreds of thousands, and the achievement of this aim at first seemed doubtful. To settle the question, extensive research was carried out that led to the development of several mechanical techniques which produce the slides mounted between glass in a new type of plastic binder upon which it is possible to print the complete documentation.

In assessing and using the Carnegie slides it should never be forgotten that the color slide is not, and never can be, a substitute for an original work of art. It is first of all a completely different medium. Light projected through a transparent film onto a flat screen can never reproduce the sense of weight, density, surface, and dimensionality which one experiences when seeing an object in space with air around it. Nor does any color film, negative or otherwise, have the latitude to record the myriad nuances in tone which excite the human eye when light reveals the world of substance and color. No transparency, however high in quality, can be more than an approximation of the object seen. The Carnegie slides have been tested and screened to the point where the vast majority of them approach within narrow tolerances the highest potentials of the medium. In some instances technical complications beyond laboratory control made it impossible to meet these high standards, and as a result a number of slides were eliminated. However, some of the items in the substandard group were works of considerable artistic importance, and a few have been retained. It was felt that they would be useful at least until such time as the objects can be rephotographed and new slides produced. The discerning user will be quick to discover those slides which fall into this category but will also, it is hoped, understand the reason for their inclusion.

The color negative technique has opened up new pos-

sibilities in the production of art color slides. In summary, the most important of these is the control of the density and color balance in the printing of the slides. With reversal films no such control is possible, since both developing and printing are entirely mechanical and the finished result can be varied only at the camera itself. With the negative film, however, the laboratory technician can make a wide range of adjustments. Thus, the finished slide is no longer a foregone conclusion locked in the mechanism of the developing equipment. It is, instead, a product of the eye and the mind, and with this introduction of the human element the process becomes subject to the imagination with all its exciting potentials and lurking pitfalls. Several problems associated with the color negative have been complex and baffling and have frequently required the discrimination and judgment of the art expert as well as the laboratory technician; for some of these problems satisfactory solutions have yet to be found. Nevertheless, the advantages of controlled printing conspicuously outnumber the difficulties. In general, the quality of the Carnegie slides holds great promise for the future and more than justifies the Board's decision to seek a solution to its basic problem in the unexplored potentials of the color negative.

THE USE OF THE CATALOGUE

There are two methods of using the catalogue: first, through the organization of the material itself, and second, through the Subject–Artist Index that appears at the end.

The catalogue is divided into nine major categories of subject matter arranged in alphabetical order. Five of these are further divided chronologically making a total of seventeen. They are: *Architecture: Seventeenth and Eighteenth Centuries, Architecture: Federal Period and Nineteenth Century, Architecture: Twentieth Century; Design and Decorative Arts: Seventeenth and Eighteenth Centuries, Design and Decorative Arts: Nineteenth Century, Design and Decorative Arts: Twentieth Century; Graphic Arts: Eighteenth and Nineteenth Centuries, Graphic Arts: Twentieth Century; Indian Arts and Artifacts; Painting: Seventeenth and Eighteenth Centuries, Painting: Federal Period and Nineteenth Century, Painting: Twentieth Century; Photography; Sculpture: Seventeenth, Eighteenth, and Nineteenth Centuries, Sculpture: Twentieth Century; Stage Design;* and *Visual Communications.*

The eighteenth category, *Costume,* appears as the final subdivision of *Design and Decorative Arts: Nineteenth Century.*

Each item has a catalogue number, which appears at the upper left of each entry. In the Subject–Artist Index, reference is made to this catalogue number and not to page number.

The number which appears at the lower right of each entry is the negative number and should be used when ordering slides.

In general, material is arranged alphabetically according to artist. The following are exceptions:

Architecture: Seventeenth and Eighteenth Centuries

This section has been divided into two parts: *Architecture* and *Town, City, and Park*.

There are three major classifications of the material in the first category. They are: *Early Colonial*, which corresponds to the seventeenth century; *Late Colonial*, which covers the period from approximately 1700 to the Revolution; and *Post Colonial*, which includes the years from the Revolution to approximately 1800. The Post Colonial period overlaps with the Federal period, the first division of *Architecture: Federal Period and Nineteenth Century*. However, the buildings included in Post Colonial are those which are more closely related to the Late Colonial style than to the new ideas of the Federal style.

Under each of the above major sections the material is divided according to the nationality of the various colonies. In the English colonies further distinction is made between the Middle Atlantic, New England, and the Southern states. Beneath the Colonial division, items are arranged according to state. The individual buildings are then listed alphabetically, those for which the designer is unknown as anonymous, and the rest according to architect or designer.

Architecture: Federal Period and Nineteenth Century

The first part of the material in this category is divided into three stylistic sections:

Federal, which includes primarily those examples which represent the American version of English neoclassicism; *Romantic Classicism*, which includes those works directly inspired by classical antiquity (e.g., the Greek revival); *Romantic Eclecticism*, which includes all romantic revivals of the nineteenth century up to and including the Victorian era.

The second part contains three technological divisions: *Iron and Wood Construction, Practical Building,* and *The Skyscraper*.

Under all the above divisions the anonymous works are listed geographically according to state. After this

the buildings are listed alphabetically according to architect.

The third part, *Architectural Reform and Innovation*, contains the works of the three principal architects of the late nineteenth century: *Henry Hobson Richardson, Louis Sullivan,* and *McKim, Mead and White*. The work of McKim, Mead and White is further divided into *Shingle Style* and *Academic Reaction*. The later work of McKim, Mead and White and the early work of Frank Lloyd Wright are all included in *Architecture: Twentieth Century*.

Town, City, and Park is arranged geographically according to state. Within the geographical subdivision the items are listed alphabetically according to subject.

Architecture: Twentieth Century

The material in this category is arranged alphabetically according to architect. Most city-planning material has been incorporated directly into the main body of the category. Certain items, however, not closely associated with architecture as such have been grouped at the end under two subdivisions. They are: *Community Planning* and *Engineering and Traffic Control*.

Design and Decorative Arts: Seventeenth and Eighteenth Centuries

With the exception of the Spanish Colonial objects that are listed under *Miscellaneous*, the major divisions of this material are technological as follows: *Furniture, Silver, Pewter, Glass, Earthenware, Iron and Metals, Textiles, Wood,* and *Miscellaneous*.

Under the above divisions the arrangement is chronological according to period and style.

Design and Decorative Arts: Nineteenth Century

The major divisions of this material are technological as follows: *Ceramics, Furniture, Glass, Interiors, Iron Work, Jewelry, Machines, Silver, Textiles, Transportation, Wallpaper,* and *Miscellaneous*.

Within the above sections anonymous works are listed first, alphabetically arranged according to object type. The works by known makers follow, listed alphabetically according to maker. The only exception to this is anonymous furniture, which is broken down as follows: *Missouri-German, Pennsylvania Dutch, Pioneer,* and *Shaker*. Under these divisions the material has been arranged by object type.

The *Costume* category forms the final subdivision of *Design and Decorative Arts: Nineteenth Century*.

Graphic Arts: Eighteenth and Nineteenth Centuries

Works are listed alphabetically according to subject under graphic artists.

In all instances where a work listed is a reproduction by some graphic process of a painting, the item is still identified by the name of the graphic artist. The name of the painter is included but is secondary to that of the graphic artist. Direct reference to paintings reproduced by graphic processes can be found in the Artist–Subject Index.

Design and Decorative Arts: Twentieth Century

The major divisions of this material are technological as follows: *Appliances and Tools, Communication, Crafts, Fabrics, Furniture, Household Equipment and Accessories, Lamps, Flatware, Stemware, and Tableware, Toys, Transportation,* and *Miscellaneous*.

Under the above sections objects are arranged according to designer or maker. Works by the same designer are then listed alphabetically according to object type.

Indian Arts and Artifacts

There are two major divisions of material in this category: *Prehistoric* and *Historic*. Entries are next arranged by area and then by tribe.

Painting: Seventeenth and Eighteenth Centuries

There are two major divisions of material in this category: *Eastern Colonial* and *Spanish Colonial*. Entries are then arranged alphabetically according to artist, with anonymous works coming first. Works by the same artist are then arranged alphabetically according to subject. If portraits are included as well as topical subject matter, the portraits are grouped last and arranged alphabetically by the name of the sitter.

Painting: Federal Period and Nineteenth Century

There are two major divisions of material in this category: *Primitive* and *Professional*. Entries are then arranged alphabetically according to artist, with anonymous works coming first. If portraits are included as well as topical subject matter, the portraits are grouped last and arranged alphabetically by the name of the sitter.

Sculpture: Seventeenth, Eighteenth, and Nineteenth Centuries

There are three major divisions of material in this category: *Folk, Spanish Colonial,* and *Professional*. Entries in each division are arranged alphabetically according to artist.

ABBREVIATIONS

The abbreviations listed below are only those which may not be self-evident. The list does not, therefore, include all the contributing institutions.

Acc.	accession
act.	active
Add.	addition
Addison Gall.	Addison Gallery of American Art, Phillips Academy, Andover, Mass.
aft.	after
Albright Gall.	Albright Art Gallery, Buffalo, N.Y.
Am. Antiq. Soc.	American Antiquarian Society, Worcester, Mass.
Am. Mus. Nat. Hist.	The American Museum of Natural History, New York, N.Y.
Anon.	anonymous
aqua.	aquatint
Arch.	architect
Ariz. State Mus.	Arizona State Museum, Tucson, Ariz.
attr.	Attribution; attributed
Avery Lib., Columbia U.	Avery Architectural Library for Advanced Research, Columbia University, New York, N.Y.
b. & w.	black and white
bef.	before
Bldg.	building
Boston Mus.	Museum of Fine Arts, Boston, Mass.
Butler Art Inst.	Butler Institute of American Art, Youngstown, Ohio

c.	circa	fac.	façade
C.	century	fig.	figure
Calif. Palace Legion of Honor	California Palace of the Legion of Honor, San Francisco, Calif.	fl.	floor
		Fogg Mus.	William Hayes Fogg Art Museum, Harvard University, Cambridge, Mass.
Canajoharie Lib. Art Gall.	Canajoharie Library and Art Gallery, Canajoharie, N.Y.		
Carnegie Inst.	Carnegie Institute, Department of Fine Arts, Pittsburgh, Pa.	Ford Mus.	Henry Ford Museum and Greenfield Village, Dearborn, Mich.
Carnegie Mus.	Department of the Museum, Carnegie Institute, Pittsburgh, Pa.	Freer Gall. Art	Freer Gallery of Art, Smithsonian Institution, Washington, D.C.
Carolina Art Assoc., Gibbes Art Gall.	Carolina Art Association, Gibbes Art Gallery, Charleston, S.C.	gen.	general
		Gardner Mus.	Isabella Stewart Gardner Museum, Boston, Mass.
Charleston Mus.	Charleston Museum, Charleston, S.C.	Grand Rapids Mus.	Grand Rapids Furniture Museum, Grand Rapids, Mich.
Clark Art Inst.	Sterling and Francine Clark Art Institute, Williamstown, Mass.		
		H.	height
cm.	centimeter	Hackley Art Gall.	Hackley Art Gallery, Muskegon, Mich.
Co.	County; Company		
col.	colored	Harwood Fdn.	Harwood Foundation of the University of New Mexico, Taos, N. Mex.
Coll.	collection		
College William and Mary	College of William and Mary, Williamsburg, Va.	hist.	historical
Colorado Springs Fine Arts Center	Colorado Springs Fine Arts Center, Taylor Museum, Colorado Springs, Colo.	Hist. Soc. Pa.	Historical Society of Pennsylvania, Philadelphia, Pa.
Columbus Gall.	The Columbus Gallery of Fine Arts, Columbus, Ohio	incl.	Including; included
		Inst.	Institute; Institution
conj.	conjectural	int.	interior
Cooper Union Mus.	Cooper Union for the Advancement of Science and Art, Museum for the Arts of Decoration, New York, N.Y.	Joslyn Art Mus.	Joslyn Art Museum, Joslyn, Nebr.
		L.	length
		Lawrence Art Mus.	Lawrence Art Museum, Williamstown, Mass.
Cranbrook Inst. Sci.	Cranbrook Institute of Science, Bloomfield Hills, Mich.	Lib.	library
		lith.	lithograph
d.	pence; died	Lyman Allyn Mus.	Lyman Allyn Museum, New London, Conn.
D.	diameter		
Dartmouth College Mus.	Dartmouth College Art Gallery and Library, Hanover, N.H.	Mem.	memorial
		Marine Hist. Assoc.	Marine Historical Association, Mystic, Conn.
Des.	designer; designed by	Mariners Mus.	Mariners' Museum, Newport News, Va.
demol.	demolished		
det.	detail	Maryland Hist. Soc.	Maryland Historical Society, Baltimore, Md.
Detroit Inst.	The Detroit Institute of Arts, Detroit, Mich.	Mass. Hist. Soc.	Massachusetts Historical Society, Boston, Mass.
de Young Mem. Mus.	M. H. de Young Memorial Museum, San Francisco, Calif.	Met. Mus.	The Metropolitan Museum of Art, New York, N.Y.
div.	division	Minn. Inst.	Minneapolis Institute of Arts, Minneapolis, Minn.
drpt.	drypoint		
dwg.	drawing	Missouri Hist. Soc.	Missouri Historical Society, St. Louis, Mo.
Eastman House	George Eastman House, Rochester, N.Y.	Morgan Wesson Mem. Coll. Fine Arts	The Morgan Wesson Memorial Collection of the Springfield Museum of Fine Arts, Springfield, Mass.
elev.	elevation		
engr.	engraving		
entr.	entrance	Munson-Williams-Proctor Inst.	Munson-Williams-Proctor Institute, Utica, N.Y.
Essex Inst.	Essex Institute, Salem, Mass.		
etch.	etching		
ext.	exterior		

Mus. Am. Indian	Museum of the American Indian, Heye Foundation, New York, N.Y.
Mus. Art, Princeton	The Art Museum, Princeton, N.J.
Mus. Mod. Art	Museum of Modern Art, New York, N.Y.
Mus. N. Mex.	Museum of New Mexico, Santa Fe, N. Mex.
Mus. Primitive Art	The Museum of Primitive Art, New York, N.Y.
Nat'l Coll. Fine Arts	National Collection of Fine Arts, Smithsonian Institution, Washington, D.C.
Nat'l Gall. Art	National Gallery of Art, Smithsonian Institution, Washington, D.C.
n.d.	no date
N.E.	New England
Nelson Gall.	William Rockhill Nelson Gallery of Art—Atkins Museum of Fine Arts, Kansas City, Mo.
Newark Mus.	Newark Museum Association, Newark, N.J.
New Britain Mus.	New Britain Museum of American Art, New Britain, Conn.
N.Y. State Hist. Assoc.	New York State Historical Association, Cooperstown, N.Y.
N.Y. Hist. Soc.	New York Historical Society, New York, N.Y.
o.c.	oil on canvas
Ohio State Mus.	Ohio State Museum, Columbus, Ohio
Pk.	Park
pl.	place; plan
Pa. Acad.	Pennsylvania Academy of the Fine Arts, Philadelphia, Pa.
Peabody, Phillips Acad.	Robert S. Peabody Foundation, Phillips Academy, Andover, Mass.
Peabody Mus., Harvard U.	Peabody Museum of Archaeology and Ethnology, Harvard University, Cambridge, Mass.
Peabody Mus., Salem	Peabody Museum of Salem, Salem, Mass.
Peale Mus.	Peale Museum, Baltimore, Md.
Phila. Mus.	Philadelphia Museum of Art, Philadelphia, Pa.
Philbrook Art Center	Philbrook Art Center, Tulsa, Okla.
Phillips Coll.	The Phillips Collection, Washington, D.C.
Portland Art Mus.	Portland Art Museum, Portland, Ore.
q.	quarter
reconstr.	reconstruction; reconstructed
Rhode Island Hist. Soc.	Rhode Island Historical Society, Providence, R.I.
Rhode Island Mus.	Museum of Art, Rhode Island School of Design, Providence, R.I.
Rochester Mem. Art Gall.	Rochester Memorial Art Gallery, University of Rochester, N.Y.
Rockefeller Folk Art Coll.	Abby Aldrich Rockefeller Folk Art Collection, Williamsburg, Va.
s.	shilling
Sc.	scene
Shelburne Mus.	The Shelburne Museum, Shelburne, Vt.
Smith Art Mus.	George Walter Vincent Smith Art Museum, Springfield, Mass.
Soc.	Society
Southwest Mus.	Southwest Museum, Los Angeles, Calif.
SPNEA	Society for the Preservation of New England Antiquities
Springfield Mus. Fine Arts	Springfield Museum of Fine Arts, Springfield, Mass.
Stovall Mus. Sci. & Hist., U. Okla.	Stovall Museum of Science and History, University of Oklahoma, Norman, Okla.
Syracuse Mus.	Syracuse Museum of Fine Arts, Syracuse, N.Y.
Taylor Mus., Colorado Springs	Taylor Museum, Colorado Springs Fine Arts Center, Colorado Springs, Colo.
Toledo Mus. Art	Toledo Museum of Art, Toledo, Ohio
U.; Univ.	University
U. Colo. Mus.	University of Colorado, Fine Arts Gallery, Boulder, Colo.
U. Texas	University of Texas, Austin, Tex.
University Mus.	University Museum, The University of Pennsylvania, Philadelphia, Pa.
Virginia Mus. Fine Arts	Virginia Museum of Fine Arts, Richmond, Va.
W.	width
Wadsworth Atheneum	Wadsworth Atheneum, Hartford, Conn.
Walker Art Center	Walker Art Center, Minneapolis, Minn.
Walters Art Gall.	Walters Art Gallery, Baltimore, Md.
Warner House Assoc.	Warner House Association, Portsmouth, N.H.
Wash. State Mus.	Washington State Museum, Seattle, Wash.
w.c.	water color
Whitney Mus.	Whitney Museum of American Art, New York, N.Y.
Winterthur	The Henry Francis du Pont Winterthur Museum, Delaware
Worcester Art Mus.	Worcester Art Museum, Worcester, Mass.

ARCHITECTURE OF THE
SEVENTEENTH AND EIGHTEENTH CENTURIES

HUGH MORRISON

EARLY COLONIAL

ENGLISH (NEW ENGLAND): CONNECTICUT

1. ANON.
Henry Whitfield House,
1639-40. Guilford, Conn. Ext.   AA 44

     2. ——. Ibid. Great Hall.   AA 45

3. ANON.
Stanley-Whitman House,
c. 1660. Farmington Mus., Farmington, Conn.
Fac.   AA 29A

     4. ——. Ibid. Ext.   AA 29

MAINE

5. ANON.
McIntire Garrison House,
1640-45(?). Scotland District, York, Maine. Ext.
Property of Alice R. McIntire.   AA 5

MASSACHUSETTS

     6. ANON.
     Aptucxet Trading Post, Bourne, Mass.,
     1627, reconstructed 1930. Bourne Hist. Soc.,
     Mass. Ext.   AA 15

7. ANON.
John Balch House,
1638(?) and later. Beverly (448 Cabot St.), Mass.
Ext. Property of Beverly Hist. Soc.   AA 7

     8. ANON.
     Parson Capen House,
     1683. Topsfield, Mass. Ext.   AA 30

9. ——. Ibid. Entr. hall.   AA 31

     10. ——. Ibid. Parlor.   AA 33

11. ANON.
Jethro Coffin House,
1686. Nantucket, Mass. Ext. Property of
Nantucket Hist. Soc.   AA 43

     12. ANON.
     Fairbanks House,
     c. 1636. Dedham, Mass. Ext. from SE.   AA 19

13. ANON.
Fairbanks House,
c. 1636. Dedham, Mass. Ext. from NW.   AA 20

     14. ———. Ibid. Int. det. of roof truss.   AA 18

15. ANON.
*Reproduction of typical 17th C. "hall" from
house in Ipswich,*
n.d. Antiquarian Soc., Concord, Mass. Living
room and dining room.   AA 24

     16. ANON.
     Old College, Harvard,
     1638-42, demol. 1678. Cambridge, Mass. Conj.
     dwg. c. 1936, by SHURTLEFF, Harold R.
     Coll. Harvard U.   AA 12

17. ANON.
Hathaway (Old Bakery) House,
1682. On grounds of "House of Seven Gables."
Salem, Mass. Ext.   AA 6

     18. ANON.
     An English Wigwam,
     ext. reconstruction of pioneer Salem. As of 1630.
     Salem, Mass.   AA 1

19. ANON.
A Cottage,
ext. reconstruction of pioneer Salem as of 1630.
Salem, Mass.   AA 2

     20. ANON.
     Paul Revere House,
     c. 1676. Boston (19 North Sq.), Mass. Ext.
     Property of Paul Revere Mem. Assoc.   AA 35

21. ANON.
Scotch-Boardman House,
1686. Saugus, Mass. Gen. view. Property of
the Soc. for the Preservation of N.E. Antiquities. AA 28

     22. ANON.
     Old Ship Meeting House,
     1681, add. 1731, 1755. Hingham, Mass.
     Ext.   AA 9

23. ———. Ibid. Int.   AA 11

     24. ANON.
     Sweatt-Ilsley House,
     c. 1690. Newbury Old Town (4 High Road Inn),
     Mass. Fireplace. Property of the Soc. for the
     Preservation of N.E. Antiquities.   AA 37

25. ANON.
Capt. John Turner (Seven Gables) House,
c. 1668. Salem, Mass. Ext. from SE.   AA 39

     26. ———. Ibid. Ext. from SW.   AA 40

27. ANON.
John Ward House,
1684. Salem, Mass. Ext. Property of Essex
Institute.   AA 36

28. ANON.
Whipple House,
1639(?). Ipswich, Mass. Ext. front. Property of
Ipswich Hist. Soc.   AA 27

29. ———. Ibid. Ext., rear.   AA 27A

30. ANON.
Old Wind Mill,
1746. Nantucket, Mass. Ext.   AA 16

31. JOY, Thomas.
First Town-House, Boston,
1656, burned 1711. Conj. dwg. ink, by Charles
A. Lawrence, 1930. Coll. Bostonian Society,
Mass.   AA 14

NEW HAMPSHIRE

32. ANON.
Richard Jackson House,
1664. Portsmouth, N.H. Fac. Property of Soc. for
the Preservation of N.E. Antiquities.   AA 3

RHODE ISLAND

33. ANON.
Eleazer Arnold House,
1687. Lincoln, R.I. Ext. Property of the Soc. for
the Preservation of N.E. Antiquities.   AA 41

34. ———. Ibid. Hall.   AA 42

ENGLISH (SOUTHERN): MARYLAND

35. ANON.
Make Peace,
1663. Somerset Co., Md. Ext. showing black
diapering.   AA 101

36. ANON.
Resurrection Manor,
c. 1653. St. Mary's Co., Md. Fac.   AA 106

37. ANON.
Old State House,
1676, reconstr. 1934. St. Mary's City, Md. Ext.   AA 103

38. ———. Ibid. Assembly Room.   AA 104

SOUTH CAROLINA

39. ANON.
Medway Plantation House,
1686; later additions. Mt. Holly, S.C. Ext.
Property of Mrs. Sidney J. Legendre.   AA 111

40. ANON.
Middleburg Plantation House,
1699. Huger, S.C. Ext. Property of Mr. & Mrs.
Edward von S. Dingle.   AA 112

41. ANON.
Mulberry Plantation House,
1714. Moncks Corner, near Charleston, S.C. Ext.
Property of Mr. & Mrs. G. Everett Hoyt.　　AA 113

　　42. ——. Ibid. Corner pavilion.　　AA 114

43. ——. Ibid. SE bedroom, 2nd floor.　　AA 116

　　VIRGINIA

　　44. ANON.
　　Bacon's Castle (Arthur Allen House),
　　1655. Surry Co., Va. Fac.　　AA 93

45. ——. Ibid. View from side showing
chimneys and gable.　　AA 94

　　46. ANON.
　　Ludwell-Paradise House Kitchen,
　　1717. 17th C.-type residence (restoration).
　　Colonial Williamsburg, Va. Ext.　　AA 84

47. ANON.
Repiton Brick Office,
early 18th C.- or 17th C.(?)-type bldg.
(restoration). Colonial Williamsburg, Va. Ext.　　AA 85

　　48. ANON.
　　St. Luke's Church,
　　or "Old Brick Church", (originally Newport
　　Parish Church), 1682. Smithfield, Isle of Wight
　　Co., Va. Ext. from SW.　　AA 98

49. ——. Ibid. Ext. from SE.　　AA 99

　　50. ——. Ibid. Int. toward altar.　　AA 100

51. ANON.
Adam Thoroughgood House,
c. 1636-40. Princess Anne Co., Va. Ext.　　AA 90

　　52. ——. Ibid. Ext. chimney.　　AA 91

　　DUTCH: NEW YORK

53. ANON.
Fort Crailo,
foundations 1642(?); rebuilt in 1704(?) and
recently restored. Rensselaer, N.Y. Fac.
Property of the State of New York.　　AA 48

　　54. ——. Ibid. Parlor.　　AA 49

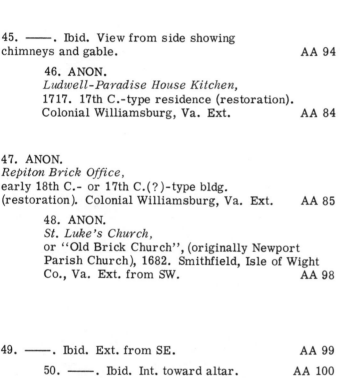

55. ANON.
City Tavern, New Amsterdam, N.Y.,
1641-42, hand-colored, enlarged photostat from
lithograph 1867 after original drawing 1679-80 by
DANCKAERTS, Jasper & SLUYTER, Peter. N.Y.
Hist. Soc.   AA 47

> **56. ANON.**
> *Old Stone House at Gowanus,*
> 1699; re-erected 1934. Brooklyn (Prospect Park
> W & 5th St.), N.Y. Ext.   AA 57

> *SWEDISH: PENNSYLVANIA*

57. ANON.
John Morton Birthplace
(log cabin), 1654, 1698, 1806. Prospect Park, Pa.
Ext.   AA 73

LATE COLONIAL
ENGLISH (NEW ENGLAND): CONNECTICUT

> **58. ANON.**
> *Connecticut Hall, Yale U.,*
> 1750-52; dormer windows added 1796-97. New
> Haven, Conn. Ext.   AA 286

59. WOODRUFF, Captain Judah.
Congregational Meeting-House,
1771. Farmington, Conn. Ext.   AA 278

> *MASSACHUSETTS*

> **60. ANON.**
> *Richard Derby House,*
> 1762. Salem (Derby St.), Mass. Ext.   AA 294

61. ANON.
Hollis Hall, Harvard,
1762-63. Cambridge, Mass. Ext.   AA 295

> **62. ANON.**
> *Jeremiah Lee House,*
> 1768. Marblehead (161 Washington St.), Mass.
> Ext.   AA 296

63. ——. Ibid. Entr. hall.   AA 297

> 64. ——. Ibid. Banquet room.   AA 298

65. ANON.
The Lindens (Hooper, Robert "King" Mansion),
1754, Danvers, Mass. Moved to Washington, D.C.,
1937. Ext. Owned by Mrs. George Maurice
Morris.   AA 287

> 66. ——. Ibid. Entr. hall.   AA 288

67. ——. Ibid. Parlor.   AA 290

> **68. ANON.**
> *The Royall House,*
> east fac., 1733-37; west fac. and chimneys 1747-
> 50. Medford (15 George St.), Mass. East fac.
> Property of the Royall House Assoc.   AA 282

69. ANON.
The Royall House,
east fac., 1733-37; west fac. and chimneys 1747-
50. Medford (15 George St.), Mass. West fac.

AA 283

    70. ——. Ibid. Entr. hall.   AA 284

71. ——. Ibid. Great chamber, second story.   AA 285

    72. ANON.
Second Town-House (Old State House),
1712-13; rebuilt 1748; restored 1881-82. Boston
(Court and Washington Sts.), Mass. Ext.   AA 280

73. ANON.
John Vassall (Longfellow) House,
1759; piazzas added later. Cambridge (Brattle
St.), Mass. Fac.   AA 291

    74. BLANCHARD, Joshua.
Thomas Hancock House, Boston,
1737-40. Replica, 1925-26. N.Y. State Hist.
Assoc., Ticonderoga, N.Y. Fac.   AA 256

75. HARRISON, Peter (1723-1805).
King's Chapel,
1749-54; Ionic portico by Thomas Clement
1785-87. Boston (Tremont & School Sts.), Mass.
Ext.   AA 261

    76. ——. Ibid. Toward altar.   AA 262

77. ——.
Christ Church,
1759-61; nave lengthened by two bays 1857.
Cambridge (Garden St.), Mass. Ext.   AA 263

    78. ——. Ibid. Int.   AA 264

79. LEVERETT, J. & WADSWORTH, B.
Massachusetts Hall, Harvard,
1718-20. Cambridge, Mass. Ext.   AA 268

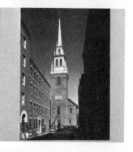

    80. PRICE, William.
Christ Church (Old North),
1723. Boston (193 Salem St.), Mass.
Ext.   AA 273

81. ——. Ibid. Int.   AA 274

    82. SMIBERT, John.
Faneuil Hall,
1740-42; enlarged 1805-06 by Charles Bulfinch.
Boston (Market St. & Dock Sq.), Mass.
Ext.   AA 275

83. SMIBERT, John.
Holden Chapel, Harvard,
1742-44. Cambridge, Mass. Ext.   AA 276

      84. TWELVES, Robert.
      Old South Meeting House,
      1729-30. Boston, Mass. Ext.   AA 277

    NEW HAMPSHIRE

85. ANON.
McPhedris-Warner House,
1718-23. Portsmouth (150 Daniel St.), N.H. Ext.   AA 281

      86. ANON.
      Wentworth-Gardner House,
      1760, Portsmouth, N.H. Fac.   AA 292

87. ——. Ibid. Det., doorway.   AA 293

    RHODE ISLAND

      88. ANON.
      Old Narragansett Church (Episcopal),
      1707. Wickford (62 Church Lane), R.I. Fac.
                            AA 382

89. BROWN, Joseph.
University Hall, Brown University,
1770-71. Providence, R.I. Ext.   AA 259

      90. ——.
      Old Market House (now Architectural School,
      Rhode Island School of Design),
      1773. Providence (Market Sq.), R.I. Ext.
                            AA 259A

91. ——.
First Baptist Meeting-House,
1774-75. Providence, R.I. Ext.   AA 257

      92. HARRISON, Peter (1723-1805).
      Redwood Library,
      1748, additions 1858, 1875, 1913 and restored
      1915. Newport, R.I. Ext.   AA 260

93. ——. Ibid. Fac.   AA 260A

      94. ——.
      Touro Synagogue,
      1759-63. Newport, R.I. Det., Ark of the Covenant.
                            AA 266

95. ——.
The Brick Market,
1761-72; restored 1928-30. Newport, R.I. Fac.   AA 267

      96. MUNDAY, Richard.
      Trinity Church,
      1725-26; spire 1741, lengthened by 2 bays 1762.
      Newport, R.I. Ext.   AA 269

97. MUNDAY, Richard.
Trinity Church,
1725-26; spire 1741, lengthened by 2 bays 1762.
Newport, R.I. Pulpit.   AA 270

     98. ——. Ibid. Int. from balcony toward altar.
                                       AA 270A

99. ——.
Old Colony House,
1739-41. Newport, R.I. Fac.   AA 271

     100. ——. Ibid. Senate room.   AA 272

ENGLISH (SOUTHERN): MARYLAND

101. ANON.
Brice House,
c. 1740. Annapolis (42 East St.), Md. Ext.   AA 234

     102. ANON.
     Chase-Lloyd House,
     1769-71. Annapolis (22 Maryland Ave.), Md. Ext.
                                         AA 235

103. ——. Ibid. Int. doorway.   AA 236

     104. ANON.
     Montpelier,
     1751, wings added c. 1770. Prince George's
     County, Md. Ext.   AA 229

105. ANON.
Tulip Hill,
c. 1756. Anne Arundel County, Md. Gen. view.   AA 230

     106. ANON.
     Whitehall,
     c. 1764-68, wings c. 1793. Anne Arundel County,
     Md. Fac. Property of Charles Scarlett, Jr.
                                         AA 232

107. ——. Ibid. Great hall.   AA 233.

     108. BUCKLAND, William.
     Hammond-Harwood House,
     1773-74. Annapolis, Md. Ext.   AA 237

109. ——. Ibid. Det. front door.   AA 238

     110. ——. Ibid. Det. dining room.   AA 239

NORTH CAROLINA

111. HAWKS, John.
Governor Tryon's Palace,
1767-70. New Bern, N.C. Central bldg., N. fac.   AA 253

112. ——. Ibid. N. fac. showing dependencies
and sentry boxes.   AA 255

113. ——. Ibid. Dining room.   AA 254

SOUTH CAROLINA

114. ANON.
Drayton Hall,
1738-42. Near Charleston, S.C. W. fac.   AA 240

115. ——. Ibid. E. fac.   AA 240A

116. ANON.
Hampton Plantation,
1735, 1757; portico, 1791. Hampton (on Wambaw
Creek near the Santee), S.C. S. Fac. Owned by
Dr. Archibald Rutledge, McClellanville, S.C.
   AA 242

117. ANON.
Ralph Izard House,
c. 1757. Charleston (110 Broad St.), S.C. Ext.   AA 249

118. ANON.
Pompion Hill Chapel,
1763. Pompion Hill, S.C. Ext.   AA 247

119. ANON.
St. James' Church,
1711. Goose Creek, S.C. Ext.   AA 243

120. ANON.
St. James' Church,
1768. Santee, S.C. Ext.   AA 244A

121. ANON.
St. Michael's Church,
1752-61. Charleston, S.C. Ext.   AA 245

122. WAITE, Ezra (joiner and carver).
Miles Brewton House,
1765-69. Charleston (27 King St.), S.C. Ext.
Owned by the Misses Susan Pringle Frost and
Rebecca Motte Frost.   AA 250

123. ——. Ibid. Det. of portico wood-carving.   AA 251

VIRGINIA

124. ANON.
Brafferton Hall, College of William and Mary,
1723. Williamsburg, Va. Ext.   AA 198

125. ANON.
Brandon,
c. 1765. Prince George Co., Va. Ext. Owned by
Mrs. Robert W. Daniel.   AA 226

126. ANON.
Christ Church,
1767-73; tower and cupola, 1818. Alexandria, Va.
Ext.   AA 384

127. ——. Ibid. Int.   AA 385

128. ANON.
Christ Church,
1732. Lancaster Co., Va. Ext.   AA 211

129. ——. Ibid. Int.   AA 212

130. ANON.
Gunston Hall,
1755-58. Fairfax Co., Va. Porch.   AA 213

131. ——. Ibid. Chinese Chippendale room des.
by BUCKLAND, William.   AA 214

132. ——. Ibid. Palladian room des. by
BUCKLAND, William.   AA 215

133. ANON.
Pohick Church,
1771-72. Fairfax Co., Va. Ext.   AA 224

134. ——. Ibid. Int.   AA 225

135. ANON.
Stratford, Lee Mansion,
1725-30. Westmoreland, Va. Ext. from S.   AA 199

136. ——. Ibid. Ext. from W.   AA 200

137. ANON.
Wren Building, College of William and Mary,
1716-1859. Williamsburg, Va.   AA 185

138. ——. Ibid. Great hall.   AA 187

139. CARY, Henry (Overseer).
Capitol,
1701-05, reconstructed 1928-34. Colonial
Williamsburg, Va. S fac.   AA 188

    140. ——. Ibid. Council Chamber.   AA 190

141. ——.
Governor's Palace,
1706-20, reconstructed 1928-34. Colonial
Williamsburg, Va. View from SE.   AA 191

    142. ——. Ibid. Main gateway.   AA 192

143. ——. Ibid. N end of ballroom wing,
1749-51, reconstructed 1928-34.   AA 194

    144. ——. Ibid. Supper room, in the ballroom
wing.   AA 195

145. SPOTSWOOD, Alexander (?).
Bruton Parish Church,
1711-15; tower spire, 1769. Williamsburg, Va.
Ext.   AA 196

    146. ——. Ibid. Int.   AA 197

147. TALIAFERRO, Richard (?).
Westover, Byrd Mansion,
c. 1730-34. Charles City Co., Va. Entr. N fac.
                                                 AA 202

    148. ——. Ibid. S fac.   AA 203

149. ——. Ibid. Entr. hall stair.   AA 205

    150. ——. Ibid. Det. hall ceiling.   AA 204

151. ——.
Carter's Grove,
1750-53, James City Co., Va. Entr. N fac.   AA 206

    152. ——. Ibid. Garden and S fac.   AA 207

153. TALIAFERRO, Richard (?).
Carter's Grove,
1750-53. James City Co., Va. N side of entr. hall.　　　　　　　　　　　　　　　　AA 209

　　　154. ——. Ibid. S side of entr. hall.　　AA 210

155. ——. Ibid. Det. balustrade, treads.　AA 208

　　　156. WASHINGTON, George (1732-99).
　　　Mount Vernon,
　　　1757-87. Fairfax County, Va. W fac.　AA 220

157. ——. Ibid. N end & arcade.　　　　AA 221

　　　158. ——. Ibid. Dining room, showing fireplace.
　　　　　　　　　　　　　　　　　　　　AA 222

ENGLISH (MID-ATLANTIC): DELAWARE

159. ANON.
William Corbit House,
1772-74. Odessa, Del. Ext.　　　　　　AA 322

　　　NEW JERSEY

　　　160. SMITH, Robert & SHIPPEN, William.
　　　Nassau Hall,
　　　Princeton U., 1754-56, engr. by DAWKINS, Henry,
　　　1764. Princeton, N.J.　　　　　　AA 323

　　　NEW YORK

161. ANON.
Sir William Johnson House,
1762. Johnstown, N.Y. Fac.　　　　　AA 333

　　　162. ANON.
　　　King's College (later Columbia U.),
　　　1760. New York, N.Y. Original bldg. engr. by
　　　TIEBOUT, Cornelius (c. 1773-1832) for "New
　　　York Magazine," May 1790. 8" x 4½". N.Y. Hist.
　　　Soc.　　　　　　　　　　　　　　AA 326

163. ANON.
Madame Jumel (Morris) Mansion,
1765. New York (Jumel Terrace & 168th St.),
N.Y. Ext.　　　　　　　　　　　　　AA 331

　　　164. ANON.
　　　Philipse Manor Hall,
　　　c. 1720. Yonkers (Warburton Ave. & Dock St.),
　　　N.Y. S fac. American Scenic & Historic
　　　Preservation Soc.　　　　　　　AA 327

165. ——. Ibid. E front, N wing, c. 1745.　AA 328

　　　166. McBEAN, Thomas.
　　　St. Paul's Chapel,
　　　1764-66; L'ENFANT, Pierre Charles (?), spire
　　　and portico, 1794-96. New York, N.Y. Ext.
　　　　　　　　　　　　　　　　　　　AA 324

167. McBEAN, Thomas.
St. Paul's Chapel,
1764-66; L'ENFANT, Pierre Charles (?), New York, N.Y.
Int.   AA 325

PENNSYLVANIA

168. ANON.
John Bartram House, Fairmount Park,
1730-31; remodelled 1770. Philadelphia, Pa.
Ext.   AA 309

169. ANON.
Cliveden, The Chew House,
1761-62. Germantown, Pa. Ext. Property of
Samuel Chew.   AA 313

170. ANON.
Green Tree Inn (Daniel Pastorius House),
1748. Germantown, Philadelphia, Pa. Ext.
                                                        AA 310

171. ANON.
Letitia Street House, Fairmount Park,
1703-15. Philadelphia, Pa. Ext.   AA 301

172. ANON.
Moore Hall,
aft. 1722. Phoenixville, Pa. Ext.   AA 306

173. ANON.
Mount Pleasant, Fairmount Park,
1761-62. Philadelphia, Pa. Main house and
dependencies.   AA 311

174. ——. Ibid. Int.   AA 312

175. ANON.
Steadman-Powel House,
1768. Formerly Phila., Pa. Room. Met. Mus.
#18.87.1-4   Rogers Fund, 1918.   AA 315

176. ANON.
Stenton (James Logan House),
1728. Germantown, Pa. Fac.   AA 308

177. ANON.
Waynesborough,
1724; 1740. Paoli, Pa. Ext. Property of William
Wayne.   AA 307

178. HAMILTON, Andrew & WOOLLEY, Edmund.
Independence Hall,
1732-53 & later. Philadelphia, Pa. S fac. AA 316

179. ——. Ibid. N fac.   AA 317

180. ——. Ibid. Assembly Room.   AA 318

181. HAMILTON, Andrew & WOOLLEY, Edmund.
Independence Hall,
1732-53 & later. Philadelphia, Pa. From central
hall through arches into Supreme Court Chamber.
AA 319

182. KEARSLEY, John (?).
Christ Church,
1727-44; steeple 1754. Philadelphia, Pa. Ext.
AA 320

183. ——. Ibid. Int.   AA 321

184. KIRK, John (Master Mason).
Graeme Park,
1721-22. Horsham, Pa. Ext.   AA 304

185. ——. Ibid. Drawing room, showing
fireplace.   AA 305

SPANISH: ARIZONA

186. ANON.
San Xavier del Bac,
mission church, 1783-97. Tucson, Ariz. Ext.
AA 142

187. ——. Ibid. Fac.   AA 143

188. ——. Ibid. Churrigueresque portal. AA 144

189. ——. Ibid. W tower and supporting
buttresses.   AA 145

190. ——. Ibid. Int.   AA 146

CALIFORNIA

191. ANON.
Capilla Real (Royal Presidio Chapel, San Carlos Church),
1794. Monterey, Calif. Fac.   AA 153

192. ANON.
Castro House,
1838. San Juan Bautista, Calif. Fac.   AA 165

193. ANON.
Thomas Oliver Larkin State Historical Monument,
1834. Monterey, Calif. Ext. corner view.   AA 166

194. ——. Ibid. Ext. from garden.   AA 167

195. ANON.
Old Pacific House,
1847. Monterey, Calif. Ext., corner view.   AA 161

    196. ANON.
    San Diego de Alcala,
    1808-13; restored 1931. San Diego, Calif. Fac.
    and campanario.   AA 149

197. ANON.
Santa Inez Mission,
1804. Solvang, Calif. Ext.   AA 162

    198. ——. Ibid. Courtyard facing church and
    convento.   AA 164

199. ——. Ibid. Nave and sanctuary. Ceiling
original 1814; reredos by Indian artists 1824.   AA 163

    200. AGUILAR, Isidoro (Master Mason).
    Mission San Juan Capistrano,
    1797-1806. San Juan Capistrano, Calif. Ruins
    of chapel.

        AA 154

201. ——. Ibid. Garden court showing
campanario (1813) at right, monks' quarters and
kitchen behind at left.   AA 155

    202. ——. Ibid. View down south corridor of
    rear (large) garden court.   AA 155B

203. PADRE ANTONIO PEYRI.
San Luis Rey Mission,
1811-15. San Luis Rey, Calif. Fac.   AA 159

    204. PADRE RIPOLO.
    Santa Barbara Mission,
    1815-20; restored 1925. Santa Barbara, Calif.
    Fac.   AA 156

205. RUIZ, Manuel Estevan (Master Mason).
San Carlos Borromeo Mission,
1793-97. Carmel, Calif. Fac. & garden court.   AA 152

    206. ——. Ibid. Bell tower.   AA 152A

FLORIDA

207. ANON.
Castillo de San Marcos (Fort San Marco),
1672-1756. St. Augustine, Fla. Approach:
barbican, moat, drawbridge, and gate.   AA 118

    208. ——. Ibid. Courtyard, looking down from
    the artillery platform.   AA 119

209. ANON.
Palace of the Governors,
1610-14; additions made aft. 1680 & 1692. Santa
Fe, N. Mex. Ext.   AA 121

> **210. ANON.**
> *San Estevan Mission,*
> 1629-c. 1642, Acoma, N. Mex. Ext.   AA 122

211. ——. Ibid. Church and pueblo complex.   AA 123

> **212. ANON.**
> *St. Francis of Assisi Mission,*
> 1772. Ranchos de Taos, N. Mex. Fac.   AA 131

213. ——. Ibid. W end, facing E.   AA 132

> **214. ANON.**
> *San Jose Mission,*
> 1699-1706. Old Laguna Pueblo, N. Mex. Fac.
>   AA 126

215. ——. Ibid. Nave.   AA 127

> **216. ——. Ibid. Sanctuary and altar.   AA 128**

217. ANON.
San Jose de Gracia Mission,
c. 1760. Trampas, N. Mex. Ext.   AA 129

> **218. ——. Ibid. Altar, 1865-67.   AA 130**

219. GALLEGOS, Celso (1857-1943).
Fogón
(fireplace), adobe. Santa Fe, N. Mex. Property
of Mrs. Lois Field.   AA 167A

> *TEXAS*

> **220. ANON.**
> *The Álamo (San Antonio de los Álamos),*
> founded 1718; built 1744-57. San Antonio, Tex.
> Fac.   AA 133

221. ANON.
Palace of the Governor,
1749. San Antonio (Military Plaza & West
Commerce), Tex. Fac.   AA 134

> **222. ——. Ibid. Living room to patio.   AA 135**

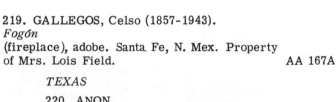

223. ANON.
San Jose y San Miguel de Aguayo Mission,
1720-31. San Antonio, Tex. Ext.　　　　AA 136

224. ——. Ibid. Det., main portal, sculpture by
HUIZAR, Pedro.　　　　AA 137

225. ——. Ibid. Det., baptistery window,
sculpture by HUIZAR, Pedro.　　　　AA 138

226. ——. Ibid. Int., baptistery.　　　　AA 139

227. ——. Ibid. Det. of flying buttresses.　　AA 139A

228. ANON.
*Nuestra Senora de la Purisima Concepcion de
Acuna Mission,*
1731- . San Antonio (Mission Rd. & Mitchell),
Tex. Ext.　　　　AA 140

229. ANON.
San Francisco de la Espada Mission,
1731. San Antonio (Espada Rd.), Tex. Ext., main
portal.　　　　AA 141

FRENCH: ILLINOIS

230. ANON.
Cahokia Courthouse,
c. 1737; reconstructed 1939. Cahokia, Ill.
Ext.　　　　AA 169

LOUISIANA

231. ANON.
The Cabildo,
1795; mansard roof 1850's. New Orleans (St.
Peter & Chartres Sts.), La. Ext.　　　　AA 184A

232. ANON.
Homeplace Plantation (Keller Mansion),
1801. Hahnville, St. Charles Parish, La. Ext.
Property of Hubert Keller.　　　　AA 179

233. ——. Ibid. Det. of porch.　　　　AA 180

234. ANON.
"Lafitte's Blacksmith Shop" (J. P. Lafitte House),
between 1772-91. New Orleans (St. Philip &
Bourbon Sts.), La. Ext.　　　　AA 174

235. ANON.
*"Madam John's Legacy" (Capt. Jean Pascal
House),*
c. 1727. New Orleans (6 Dumaine), La. Ext.　　AA 171

236. ANON.
Parlange Plantation,
1750. Pointe Coupée Parish, Mix, La. Fac.
Property of Mrs. Walter Charles Parlange.
　　　　AA 176

237. ANON.
Parlange Plantation,
1750. Pointe Coupée Parish, Mix, La.
Drawing room. Property of Mrs. Walter Charles
Parlange.   AA 177

MISSISSIPPI

238. ANON.
Connelly's Tavern,
bef. 1800. Natchez, Miss. Fac.   AA 182

239. ——. Ibid. Int.   AA 183

DUTCH: NEW JERSEY

240. ANON.
*Jacobus Demarest House (now Englewood Public
Library),*
bef. 1720. River Edge (Kinderkamack Rd.), N.J.
Ext.   AA 65

241. ANON.
Old Tennent Church,
1751. Tennent, N.J. Ext.   AA 70

242. ANON.
Vreeland House,
wing c. 1786; main house 1818. Leonia
Borough (125 Lake View Ave.), N.J. Ext.   AA 69

243. ANON.
Roelof Westervelt House,
1798. Tenafly, N.J. Main house, ext. Property
of George Price.   AA 63

244. ——. Ibid. Wing, 1745. Ext.   AA 64

NEW YORK

245. ANON.
Dyckman House,
c. 1783. New York (Broadway & 204th St.), N.Y.
Ext.   AA 66

246. ——. Ibid. Parlor.   AA 68

247. ANON.
First Dutch Reformed Church,
1784 (remodeled later). Fishkill (Main & Broad
Sts.), N.Y. Ext.   AA 71

248. ANON.
Freer House,
1720. New Paltz (98 Huguenot St.), N.Y.
Fac. Property of Huguenot Society of
New Paltz.   AA 55

249. ANON.
Abraham Hasbrouk House,
c. 1717. New Paltz (92 Huguenot St.), N.Y. Gen.
view. Property of Huguenot Society of New
Paltz.   AA 56

250. ANON.
Leendert Bronck House,
c. 1738, W. Coxsackie, N.Y. Ext. Maintained by
Greene County Hist. Soc.   AA 51

GERMAN: PENNSYLVANIA DUTCH

251. ANON.
The Cloister,
1740. Ephrata, Pa. The Saal, ext.   AA 80

  252. ——. Ibid. Int. of chapel.   AA 81

253. ——. Ibid. The Saron, 1742-43. Ext.   AA 82

  254. ANON.
  "Hex" barn,
  n.d. Berks County, Pa. Ext.   AA 79

255. ANON.
"Hex" barn,
n.d. Oley Valley Farms, Pikeville, Pa. Ext.   AA 78

  256. ANON.
  Sisters' House,
  Moravian Seminary, 1773. Bethlehem, Pa. Ext.
          AA 83

257. ANON.
Georg Müller House,
1752, Milbach, Pa. Ext.   AA 76

  258. ——. Ibid. Two rooms re-erected in Phila.
  Mus. Hall.   AA 77

SWEDISH: DELAWARE

259. ANON.
Holy Trinity ("Old Swedes") Church,
1698-99; S porch 1749; tower & belfry 1802.
Wilmington, Del.   AA 72

  ### PENNSYLVANIA

  260. ANON.
  Gloria Dei ("Old Swedes") Church,
  1698-1700. Philadelphia (929 S. Water), Pa. Ext.
          AA 74

261. ——. Ibid. Int.   AA 75

POST COLONIAL
  ### MASSACHUSETTS

  262. ANON.
  Rocky Hill Meeting-House,
  1785. Amesbury, Mass. Gen. view. Property of
  the Soc. for the Preservation of N.E. Antiquities.
          AA 300

  ### NEW HAMPSHIRE

263. ANON.
Dartmouth Hall,
1784-91; rebuilt after fires 1904, 1935. Hanover,
N.H. Fac.   AA 299

  ### RHODE ISLAND

  264. ANON.
  John Brown House,
  1786. Providence (Power St. at Benefit), R.I. Ext.
          AA 366

265. SLATER, Samuel.
Old Slater Mill,
1793. Pawtucket, R.I. Ext.   AA 381

SOUTH CAROLINA

266. ANON.
William Gibbes House,
c. 1779. Charleston (64 S. Battery St.), S.C. Ext.
                                          AA 252

VERMONT

267. ANON.
Rockingham Meeting House,
1787; restored 1907. Rockingham, Vt. Ext.   AA 380A

268. ANON.
General John Strong House,
1796-98. Addison, Vt. Fac. Property of the DAR.
                                          AA 388

VIRGINIA

269. ANON.
James Semple House,
1780. Williamsburg, Va. Ext.   AA 228

ENGLISH (NEW ENGLAND): CONNECTICUT

270. BROCKETT, John. *Gridiron plan of New Haven, Conn.,* 1638, dwg. by WADSWORTH, James, 1748, ink on paper backed with fabric, 18" x 24½" (copy, paper water-marked 1794). Yale U. Library.   #2235.5   CPA 6

MASSACHUSETTS

271. *Boston, Massachusetts,* 1722, dwg. by BONNER, John, engr. by DEWING, Francis, with alterations to 1769, 17" x 23½". Plan. Mass. Hist. Soc.   CPA 3

272. ——. Ibid. plan, det.   CPA 3A

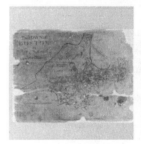

ENGLISH (SOUTH): GEORGIA

273. OGLETHORPE, James Edward (?) (1696-1785). *Savannah, Ga.,* 1733, engr. by FOURDRINIER, Pierre, $21^{14}/_{16}$" x $15^{13}/_{16}$". Stokes Coll., N.Y. Pub. Lib. View.   CPA 12

SOUTH CAROLINA

274. *Charleston, S.C.,* 1704, engr. by AKIN, James, $11^{6}/_{16}$" x $9^{2}/_{16}$". Map Div., N.Y. Pub. Lib. Plan.   CPA 4

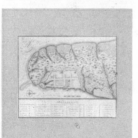

275. NEWMAN, George (?).
Middleton Place gardens,
c. 1755; redesigned 1840's. St. Andrews Parish, near Charleston, S.C. Property of John Julius Pringle Smith.   CPA 33

VIRGINIA

276. *Jamestown, Va., The Town near the Church,* c. 1617-20, a conjectural reconstruction, oil on masonite panel, 4' x 8', 1957, by KING, Sidney E. Coll. S. E. King & Paul Hudson, Jamestown Island, Va.   CPA 5A

277. ANON.
Stratford, Lee Mansion,
c. 1725-30. Westmoreland Co., Va. Formal gardens.   CPA 26

278. ROBINSON, Thomas (attr.).
Westover, Byrd Mansion,
c. 1730-34. Charles City Co., Va. Entr. gates.
                                          CPA 23

279. SHURCLIFF, Arthur A. (until 1941),
HOPKINS, Alden (1941-).
Garden, Bryan House,
Colonial Williamsburg, Va.   CPA 19

> 280. ——.
> *Garden, Christiana Campbell's Tavern.*
> Colonial Williamsburg, Va.   CPA 17

281. ——.
Garden, Alexander Craig House,
Colonial Williamsburg, Va.   CPA 16

> 282. ——.
> *Governor's Palace,*
> formal garden. Colonial Williamsburg, Va.
> Toward Palace.   CPA 22

283. ——. Ibid.
Palace Green.   CPA 20

> 284. ——. Ibid. View from roof.   CPA 21

285. ——.
Garden, Maupin-Dixon House.
Colonial Williamsburg, Va.   CPA 18

> 286. WEST, John.
> *Alexandria, Va.,*
> 1749, dwg. by GILPIN, George, engr. by CLARKE,
> Thomas, 1798, 23½" x 18½". Lib. of Congress.
> Plan.   CPA 1

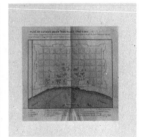

DUTCH: NEW YORK

287. *New Amsterdam (New York).* Dwg. by
FREDERICKS, Kryn (?), 1626-28, 3⅛" x 4⅞".
N.Y. Hist. Soc.   CPA 8

> *FRENCH: LOUISIANA*
>
> 288. de la TOUR, Leblond & de PAUGER,
> Adrien.
> *Plan de la ville de la Nouvelles Orleans...1723*
> (laid out 1721). Ayer Coll., Newberry Library,
> Chicago. Plan of Vieux Carré.   CPA 7

ARCHITECTURE OF THE FEDERAL PERIOD AND THE NINETEENTH CENTURY

WILLIAM H. JORDY

FEDERAL
> *ANONYMOUS (alphabetic listing by states)*
>
> > *DELAWARE*

289. ANON.
George Read II House,
1797-1801. New Castle, Del. Gen. view.   AB 778

> 290. ——. Ibid. Archway, det.   AB 779

291. ANON.
George Read II House,
1797-1801. New Castle, Del. Mantel, det.   AB 780

MAINE

292. ANON.
Nickels-Sortwell House,
1807-12. Wiscassett, Maine. Ext.   AB 716

MARYLAND

293. THORNTON, Wm. (?), (1759-1828).
Homewood, Charles Carroll IV House,
1801-03. Baltimore, Md. Ext.   AB 762

MASSACHUSETTS

294. ANON.
Christopher Gore House,
1806. Waltham, Mass. Ext., garden side.   AB 51

295. ——. Ibid. Entr. side.   AB 52

296. ——. Ibid. Oval dining room.   AB 53

OHIO

297. ANON.
Congregational Church,
c. 1840. Tallmadge, Ohio. Ext.   AB 58

298. ——. Ibid. Belfry.   AB 59

PENNSYLVANIA

299. ANON.
Pennsylvania Hospital,
1796, Philadelphia, Pa. Fac.   AB 777

300. ANON.
Eagle Hotel,
1826. Waterford, Pa. Ext.   AB 329

301. ANON.
The Woodlands,
1788-89, Philadelphia, Pa. Fac.   AB 776

RHODE ISLAND

302. ANON.
Thomas Poynton Ives House,
1806. Providence (66 Power St.), R.I. Fac.
          AB 56

SOUTH CAROLINA

303. ANON.
William Drayton House,
1820. Charleston (6 Gibbes St.), S.C. Porch fac.
Property of Mr. & Mrs. Hugh C. Lane.   AB 61

304. ANON.
Nathaniel Russell House,
bef. 1809. Charleston (51 Meeting St.), S.C. Fac.
Property of Historic Charleston Foundation.
          AB 64

305. ANON.
Nathaniel Russell House,
bef. 1809. Charleston (51 Meeting St.), S.C. Det.
door and wrought iron balcony. Property of
Historic Charleston Foundation.   AB 66

     306. ——. Ibid. Garden side.   AB 65

307. ——. Ibid. Stair hall.   AB 62

     308. ——. Ibid. Oval room, 2nd fl.   AB 67

VERMONT

309. ANON.
Early 19th C. House,
Vergennes, Vt. Ext., fanlight door. Property of
David Aubin.   AB 667

     310. ANON.
     Stone House,
     early 19th C. Orwell, Vt. Ext. Property of
     G. A. Leonard.   AB 704

ARCHITECTS (alphabetic listing)

311. BELCHER, S. (1799-1849).
Congregational Church,
1816-1817; destroyed by fire 1907; rebuilt by
GREEN, 1909. Old Lyme, Conn. Ext.   AB 25

     312. BENJAMIN, Asher (1773-1845) & TOWN,
     Ithiel (1784-1844).
     Center Church,
     1812-14. New Haven (Temple St. on the Green),
     Conn. Ext.   AB 26

313. ——. Ibid. Det. steeple.   AB 28

     314. BULFINCH, Charles (1763-1844).
     1st Harrison Gray Otis House,
     1795-96. Boston (141 Cambridge St.), Mass. Gen.
     view.   AB 741

315. ——. Ibid. Stair hall.   AB 742

     316. ——. Ibid. Dining room mantel.   AB 743

317. ——.
Harrison Gray Otis House (No. 2),
1800. Boston (85 Mt. Vernon St.), Mass. Fac.   AB 29

     318. ——.
     Harrison Gray Otis House (No. 3),
     1806. Boston (45 Beacon St.), Mass. Fac.   AB 30

319. BULFINCH, Charles (1763-1844).
Larkin-Rice House,
1815. Portsmouth (180 Middle St.), N.H. Fac.   AB 70

   320. ——.
   First Church of Christ (Old Meeting House),
   1816-17. Lancaster, Mass. Ext.   AB 75

321. ——. Ibid. Belfry.   AB 74
   322. ——. Ibid. Int. toward pulpit.   AB 75A

323. ——. Ibid. Pulpit.   AB 75B
   324. ——.
   Old State House,
   1793-96. Hartford, Conn. Fac.   AB 744

325. ——.
State House,
1795-98. Boston (Beacon St.), Mass. Fac.   AB 774

   326. ——. Ibid.
   Old Senate Chamber,
   1795-98. Int.   AB 33

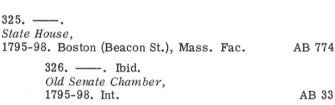

327. ——. Ibid.
House of Representatives.
Chamber.   AB 775

   328. ——. Ibid. Chamber ceiling.   AB 32

329. ——.
U.S. Capitol: East Front,
c. 1818, w.c. dwg. by DAVIS, A. J. (?),
12 ¾" x 49 ½". Lib. of Congress.   AB 35

   330. ——.
   Bulfinch Hall, Phillips Academy,
   1818. Andover, Mass. Ext.   AB 76

331. FILLMORE, Lavius (1767-1812 ?).
General Samuel Strong House,
1796. Vergennes, Vt. Fac. Property of Mrs.
Samuel Wagstaff.   AB 700A

   332. ——.
   First Congregational Church,
   1806. Bennington, Vt. Ext.   AB 700

333. HOADLEY, David.
United Church (also called North Church),
1814-15. New Haven (Temple St. on the Green),
Conn. Ext.   AB 36

334. ——. Ibid. Toward pulpit.   AB 38

335. ——. Ibid. Det. of ceiling.   AB 37

336. HOBAN, James (1762-1831).
The White House,
1815, Washington, D.C. North fac.   AB 745

337. ——. Ibid. South fac.   AB 746
338. ——. Ibid. Det. East fac.   AB 752

339. ——. Ibid. Entr. hall.   AB 748
340. ——. Ibid. Entr. hall, det.   AB 749

341. ——. Ibid. Oval Room. Restoration by
McKim, Mead and White.   AB 747

342. ——. Ibid. East Room. Restoration by
McKim, Mead and White.   AB 751

343. McINTIRE, Samuel (1757-1811).
Peirce-Nichols House,
c. 1782. Fence, 1801. Salem (Federal St.), Mass.
Ext. Property of Essex Institute.   AB 755

344. ——. Ibid. East parlor, remodeled 1801.
Door.   AB 756

345. ——. Ibid. East parlor, mantel, det.   AB 757

346. ——.
The Assembly House,
c. 1796. Salem (138 Federal St.), Mass. Fac.
                                            AB 758

347. McINTIRE, Samuel (1757-1811).
Pingree House,
1804-05. Salem (128 Essex St.), Mass. Fac.
Property of Essex Institute.   AB 44

    348. ——. Ibid. Main doorway, det.   AB 45

349. ——. Ibid. 1st fl. plan.   AB 42

    350. ——. Ibid. Entr. hall.   AB 43

351. ——. Ibid. Front parlor.   AB 41

    352. ——. Ibid. Parlor, double door, det. AB 46

353. ——. Ibid. Parlor mantel, det.   AB 40

    354. MANGIN, Joseph-Francois (act. 1794-1818)
    & McCOMB, John, Jr., (1763-1853).
    City Hall,
    1811, New York, N.Y. Gen. view.   AB 48A

355. ——. Ibid. Rotunda stairway.   AB 47

    356. ——.
    City Hall, New York City,
    1826, dwg. by WALL, W. G., engr. by HILL, J.,
    col. aquatint, 16.15" x 27.13". Ext. Mus. City
    N.Y.   AB 48

357. RAMÉE, Joseph Jacques (1764-1842).
Union College,
1813, w.c. College Archives, Union College,
Schenectady, N.Y. Site plan.   CPB 12

    358. ——. Ibid. Central complex, gen. view.
                                CPB 11

359. THORNTON, William (1759-1828).
The Octagon (John Tayloe residence),
1798-1800. Washington, D.C. (18th St. bet. E & F
Sts.). Fac. Property of American Inst. of
Architects.   AB 759

    360. ——. Ibid. 1st and 2nd fl. plans, dwg.
    directed by BROWN, Glenn, 11¾" x 18".   AB 760

361. THORNTON, William (1759-1828).
The Octagon (John Tayloe residence),
1798-1800. Washington, D.C. Entr. hall. AB 761

   362. ———.
   U.S. Capitol: East Elevation,
   1794, wash dwg., 14" x 23¾". Lib. of Congress.
                       AB 50

ROMANTIC CLASSICISM
   ANONYMOUS (alphabetic listing by states)
     CONNECTICUT

363. ANON.
Congregational Church,
1838. Madison, Conn. Fac. AB 710

     GEORGIA

   364. ANON.
   Henry Grady House,
   1845. Athens (634 Prince Ave.), Ga. Ext. AB 732

365. ANON.
President's House,
1854-55. University of Georgia, Athens. Ext. AB 733

   366. ANON. (poss. CARTER, Elias).
   Ralph Small House,
   early 1830's. Macon (156 Rogers), Ga. Ext.
                       AB 143

     LOUISIANA

367. ANON.
Oak Alley,
1830-1836; 1837; 1839. Vacherie, St. James Parish,
La. Gen. view house and drive. Property of Mrs.
Andrew Stewart. AB 153

   368. ———. Ibid. Fac. AB 154

369. ———. Ibid. Ext. side view. AB 154A

   370. ANON.
   Evergreen Plantation,
   c. 1830, Wallace, La. Ext. AB 737

     MASSACHUSETTS

371. ANON.
Greek Revival House,
c. 1850. Wellfleet, Mass. Fac. AB 705

   372. ANON.
   Greek Revival House,
   c. 1850. Eastham, Cape Cod, Mass. Ext. AB 707

     MISSISSIPPI

373. ANON.
D'Evereux,
1840. Natchez, Miss. Ext. Property of Miss
Myra Virginia Smith. AB 720

   374. ———. Ibid. Parlor. AB 721

375. ANON.
Stanton Hall,
1851. Natchez, Miss. Ext. Property of
Pilgrimage Garden Club. AB 726

376. ——. Ibid. Ext. det. iron work balcony.
AB 725

377. ——. Ibid. Double salon. AB 724

378. ANON.
Dunleith,
1847. Natchez, Miss. Ext. Property of Mr. &
Mrs. Leslie Carpenter. AB 722

379. ——. Ibid. Entr. hall. AB 723

NEW YORK

380. ANON.
Utica Insane Asylum (now Utica State Hospital),
1838. Utica (Court St.), N.Y. Ext. AB 155

OHIO

381. ANON.
Wooster-Boalt House,
1848. Norwalk (114 W. Main St.), Ohio. Ext.
Property of Mrs. Inez Overhuls. AB 161

PENNSYLVANIA

382. ANON.
Picnic House, the William Croghan House,
c. 1835. Pittsburgh, Pa. Det. ballroom entr.
AB 150

383. ——. Ibid. Det. ballroom frieze. AA 150A

384. ——. Ibid. Det. ballroom mantel. AB 149

385. ——. Ibid. Ballroom ceiling decoration. AB 146

386. ANON.
Fatlands,
1845, Audubon, Pa. Ext. AB 160

RHODE ISLAND

387. ANON.
Chestnut Hill Baptist Church,
1838. Exeter, R.I. Fac. AB 333

388. ANON.
Church,
c. 1840. Slatersville, R.I. Ext. AB 334

389. ANON.
Block of Stores,
c. 1855. Slatersville, R.I. Fac.   AB 335

VERMONT

390. ANON.
Congregational Church,
c. 1840. Charlotte, Vt. Ext.   AB 701

391. ANON.
Congregational Church,
c. 1840. Orwell, Vt. Fac.   AB 668

ARCHITECTS (alphabetic listing)

392. DAVIS, Alexander Jackson (1803-92).
John C. Stevens House (?),
1845. New York (College Pl. & Murray St.), N.Y.
Double parlor, w.c. by DAVIS, 13¼" x 18⅛".
N.Y. Hist. Soc.   AB 102

393. GALLIER, James, Sr., (1789-1868).
Pontalba Bldg.,
1851. New Orleans (Jackson Sq.), La. Ext.   AB 179

394. GALLIER, James, Jr. (?).
Belle Hélène,
mid-19th C. Geismar, Ascension Parish, La.
Ext. corner view.   AB 735

395. GODEFROY, Maximilian (c. 1770-c. 1837).
Unitarian Church,
1817-18. Baltimore (Franklin and Charles Sts.),
Md. Fac.   AB 103

396. ——. Ibid.
Dwg. GOODACRE, W., engr. Fenner Sears
& Co. engr., 4 x 6. Enoch Pratt Free   AB 104
Library, Baltimore. Int.

397. GRAFF, Frederick.
Fairmount Waterworks Pumping Station
(Aquarium), 1819-22. Philadelphia (Fairmount
Park), Pa. Gen. view. Philadelphia Museum of
Art in background.   AB 105

398. GREENE, Phillip (?).
Mrs. F. J. Dodd House,
1845, La Grange (1103 Vernon St.), Ga. Fac.
                                                    AB 731

399. HOOKER, Philip (1766-1836).
Hyde Hall,
1833; entr. added. Cooperstown, N.Y. Ext.
Property of Thomas Clarke.   AB 108

400. JAY, William (act. 1817-24).
Owens-Thomas House,
1816-19. Savannah (124 Abercorn St.), Ga. Fac.
                                                    AB 727

401. ——.
Scarbrough House,
c. 1820. Savannah (West Broad St. bet. St.
Julian & Broughton), Ga. Fac. Property of Board
of Education, Savannah, Ga.   AB 728

402. JEFFERSON, Thomas (1743-1826).
Monticello,
1768-c.1784; 1793-1809. Charlottesville, Va.
Gen. view of E front.   AB 1

403. JEFFERSON, Thomas (1743-1826).
Monticello,
1768-c.1784; 1793-1809. Charlottesville, Va.
Gen. view from NE.   AB 10A

    404. ——. Ibid. W (garden) fac.   AB 10

405. ——. Ibid. Ext. through portico. Law
office in distance.   AB 9

    406. ——. Ibid. Servants' quarters, incl.
dependency.   AB 7

407. ——. Ibid. Entr. hall, mezzanine balcony.   AB 8

    408. ——. Ibid. Det. mezzanine entablature
and door; entr. hall.   AB 5

409. ——. Ibid. Int. stairs.   AB 2

    410. ——. Ibid. Drawing room.   AB 6

411. ——. Ibid. Dining room toward tea
room.   AB 4

    412. ——. Ibid. Wedgewood fireplace in dining
room.   AB 3

413. ——. (attr.).
Bremo,
1815-19. Fluvanna Co., Va. Entr.   AB 15

    414. ——. Ibid. Gen. view, river front.   AB 16

415. ——.
University of Virginia,
1817-26. Charlottesville, Va. BOHN engr. Entire
complex from hilltop as it appeared after addition
of Robert MILLS' Rotunda "Annex", 1853.   AB 18

    416. ——. Ibid. Jefferson dwg. #9.
Rotunda Elevation in Circle,
n.d., 9   x 8 ¾ . Coll. U. of Va. Lib.   AB 18B

417. JEFFERSON, Thomas (1743-1826).
University of Virginia,
1817-26. Charlottesville, Va. Jefferson dwg.#10,
Rotunda Plan,
1st fl., n.d., 12" x 8½". Coll. U. of Va. Lib.　　AB 18C

 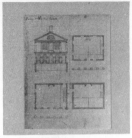

418. ——. Ibid. Jefferson dwg.#19,
Pavilion VII,
n.d., 11½" x 8¾". Coll. U. of Va. Lib.　　AB 18D

419. ——. Ibid. W lawn toward rotunda.　　AB 17

420. ——. Ibid. Rotunda from lawn; restored
1898.　　AB 20

421. ——. Ibid. Pavilions II & IV & connecting
arcade.　　AB 19

422. ——. Ibid. Pavilion IX.　　AB 21

423. ——. Ibid. Pavilion I, det. cornice &
capital.　　AB 21A

424. ——. Ibid. W range of professors'
residences and dormitory arcades.　　AB 13

425. ——. Ibid. Det. of serpentine wall.　　AB 21B

426. ——, & HOPKINS, Alden (Landscape
Architect). Garden behind Pavilion V.　　AB 12

427. ——, with CLERISSEAU, Charles-Louis.
Capitol,
1785-89. Richmond, Va. Gen. view.　　AB 753

 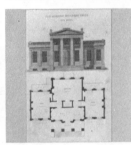

428. LAFEVER, Minard (1798-1854).
Country Villa,
1833, design, elevation, & plan from "Modern
Builder's Guide ..." New York, Sleight, Collins &
Hannay, Avery Lib., Columbia U.
#AA 606　　L13　　AB 110

429. LAMB, James (attr.).
Brookside, Wilcox-Cutts House,
1843, Orwell, Vt. Ext. Property of Robert
Granger.　　AB 111

430. LATROBE, Benjamin Henry (1764-1820).
Bank of Pennsylvania,
1799-1801, w.c., 10¼" x 18". Maryland Hist. Soc.
　　AB 113

431. LATROBE, Benjamin Henry (1764-1820).
Pittsburgh Arsenal, Proposed Central Bldg.,
1814, w.c., 10½" x 13¾". Lib. of Congress.   AB 112

    432. ——.
    Baltimore Cathedral (The Basilica of the Assump-
    tion of the Blessed Virgin Mary),
    1804-c.1818. Baltimore, Md. Ext.   AB 119

433. ——. Ibid. W.c., c. 20" x 30". Section
through nave.   AB 120

    434. ——. Ibid. Nave & choir.   AB 121

435. ——.
U.S. Capitol: East Front
bef. 1812, engr. by DETOURNELLE, 4" x 9".
Lib. of Congress.   AB 116

    436. ——.
    Senate Rotunda, U.S. Capitol,
    1809-c. 1814; rebuilt c. 1816. Washington, D.C.
    Int. showing tobacco capitals.   AB 117

437. ——.
Old Supreme Court Room (later Law Library);
U.S. Capitol,
c. 1808. Washington, D.C. Int.   AB 118

    438. MILLS, Robert (1781-1855).
    Fireproof Bldg.,
    1822-27. Charleston (100 Meeting St.), S.C. Ext.
    Property of Charleston Co., Headquarters of S.C.
    Historical Society.   AB 202

439. ——. Ibid. Int., stairway.   AB 203

    440. ——.
    Treasury Bldg.,
    1836-42. Washington, D.C. (Pennsylvania Ave.).
    Ext., view of colonnade.   AB 125

441. ——.
Washington Monument,
1815. Baltimore (Mt. Vernon Place), Md. Gen.
view.   AB 124

    442. ——. Ibid. Det. base.   AB 123

443. MILLS, Robert; continued by IVES, J. C.;
completed by CASEY, T. L.
Washington Monument,
1833-84. Washington, D.C. Gen. view at night.   AB 122

    444. PARRIS, Alexander (178?-1852).
    Hugh McLellan House (McLellan-Sweat House),
    1800. Portland (Spring & High Sts.), Me. Ext.
    Property of L.D.M. Sweat Museum.   AB 739

445. PARRIS, Alexander (178?-1852).
Sears House (now Somerset Club),
1816. Boston (Beacon St.), Mass. Fac.   AB 128

446. ——.
Quincy Market,
1825. Boston (Commercial & Market Sts.),
Mass. Ext.   AB 127

447. ——. Ibid. Lith., PENDLETON after
DAVIS, A. J., 1825. Coll. Second Bank-State
Street Trust, Boston, Mass.   AB 126

448. POLLARD, Calvin (1797-1850).
Elevation of Parlor Door,
c. 1830, design, w.c., 18½" x 13½". N.Y. Hist.
Soc.   AB 130

449. STRICKLAND, William (1788-1854).
Second Bank of U.S., later Customs House
(Independence National Historical Park), 1818-24.
Philadelphia (420 Chestnut St.), Pa. Fac.   AB 135

450. ——. Ibid. Ext., w.c. by DAVIS, A. J.
Davis Coll., Avery Lib., Columbia U. # 15
AB 137

451. ——. Ibid. Banking room.   AB 134

452. ——.
U.S. Naval Home,
1826-33. Philadelphia (Grays Ferry Rd. at 24th
St.), Pa. Fac.   AB 138

453. ——. Ibid. Central portico.   AB 138A

454. ——.
Philadelphia Exchange,
1832-34. Philadelphia (Third, Walnut & Dock
Sts.), Pa. Portico & tower.   AB 133

455. ——.
Belmont (now Acklen Hall),
Belmont College, 1850. Nashville, Tenn. Fac.   AB 139

456. ——. Ibid. Stairhall.   AB 142

457. ——. Ibid. Ballroom.   AB 140

458. ——.
Capitol,
1845-59. Nashville, Tenn. Gen. view.   AB 209

459. TOWN, Ithiel (1784-1844);
State Capitol,
1833-40. Raleigh, N.C. Ext.   AB 734

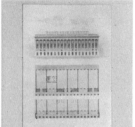

 460. —— & DAVIS, Alexander Jackson (1803-92);
 HOADLEY, David (Builder).
 Russell House (now Honors College, Wesleyan U.),
 1828-30. Middletown, Conn. Ext. AB 225

461. —— & ——. Ibid. Double parlor. AB 224

 462. —— & ——.
 Lafayette Terrace or Colonnade Row, New York,
 1836. Plan & w.c. by DAVIS. Davis Coll., Avery
 Lib., Columbia U. #R 2-6 CPB 21

463. —— & ——.
Lafayette Terrace,
1836. New York (428-434 Lafayette St.), N.Y.
Fac.   CPB 22

 464. WALTER, Thomas Ustick (1804-87).
 Girard College,
 c. 1833-47, engr. by GRAHAM, A. W., 19⁵⁄₁₆ " x
 11¹⁴⁄₁₆". Gen. view. Stokes Coll., N.Y. Pub. Lib.
            AB 151

465. ——. Ibid. Founders' Hall. Ext., oblique
view.   AB 164

 466. ——. Ibid. Int. det. showing Ionic order.
            AB 162

467. WARREN, Russell & BUCKLIN, James.
Arcade,
1827-29. Providence (Westminster to Weybosset
Sts.), R.I. Ext.   AB 167

 468. ——. Ibid. Int.   AB 166

469. WOOD, A. T.
Customs House,
1849-c. 65. New Orleans (Canal St.), La. Int. AB 171

 470. ——. Ibid. Int. det. AB 170

ROMANTIC ECLECTICISM
 ANONYMOUS (alphabetic listing by states)
  CALIFORNIA

471. ANON.
Zanetia House,
c. 1813. San Juan Bautista, Calif. Ext. AB 682

 472. ANON. (Built by Newsom & Co.)
 Carson House,
 1886. Eureka, Calif. Fac. Property of the
 Ingomar Club.   AB 385

473. ANON. (Built by Newsom & Co.)
Carson House,
1886. Eureka, Calif. Dining room. Property of
the Ingomar Club.   AB 386

474. ANON.
Builders' Houses,
c. 1885. San Francisco (1752-1760 Bush St.),
Calif. Ext.   AB 678

COLORADO

475. ANON.
House in Western Mining Town,
n.d. Black Hawk, Colo. Fac.   AB 324

LOUISIANA

476. ANON.
Afton Villa,
1849. St. Francisville, La. Ext. Property of
Wallace Percy.   AB 651

MASSACHUSETTS

477. ANON.
Mansard Cottage,
c. 1875. Eastham, Cape Cod, Mass. Fac.   AB 708

MAINE

478. ANON.
Wedding Cake House,
n.d. Kennebunkport, Maine. Ext.   AB 719

UTAH

479. ANON.
Mormon Tabernacle,
1853-93. Salt Lake City, Utah. Ext.   AB 711

VERMONT

480. ANON.
Italian Villa House,
1870. Vergennes (16 Main Street), Vt. Ext.
Property of Herrick Stevens.   AB 666

481. ANON.
Eagle Inn,
n.d. Orwell, Vt. Ext.   AB 669

WISCONSIN

482. ANON.
Octagon House,
c. 1855. Watertown, Wisconsin. Ext.   AB 384

ARCHITECTS *(alphabetic listing)*

483. AUSTIN, Henry (1804-91).
Norton House,
c. 1849. New Haven (Hillhouse Ave.), Conn. Ext. AB 353

484. ——. Ibid. Fac. Dwg. by AUSTIN. Yale U.
Library.   AB 352

485. ——.
Morse House
(Victoria Mansion), 1859. Portland (Park &
Danforth Sts.), Maine. Ext.   AB 717

486. ——. Ibid. Hall.   AB 718

487. CARRÈRE and HASTINGS.
Ponce de Leon Hotel,
1885-88. St. Augustine, Fla. Ext. view from
central court.   AB 494

489. DAVIS, Alexander Jackson (1803-92).
Design for Glen Ellen,
house for Robert Gilmore, Jr., 1832, near
Baltimore, Md., w.c. on paper, 15⁵⁄₁₆" x 8½". Two
ext. elev. and plan. Met. Mus.   #24.66.17
Dick Fund, A. J. Davis Coll., 1924.   AB 243

490. ——.
Llewellyn Park, Cottage,
c. 1860. Orange, N.J. Ext.   AB 272

491. ——. Ibid. Gatehouse, 1853-69. Gen. view. CPB 43

492. ——.
John Munn House (now Dowling Hospital),
1854. Utica (Rutgers St. & Howard Ave.), N.Y.
Ext.   AB 356

493. DOWNING, Andrew Jackson (1815-52).
A Cottage in the Bracketted Style, design V
from "Cottage Residences; ..." New York
London, Wiley & Putnam, 1842. Avery Lib.,
Columbia U.   #AA 7120   D 7521   AB 244

494. ——.
A Villa in the Italian Style
from "Cottage Residences; ..." New York &
London, Wiley & Putnam, 1842. Avery Lib.,
Columbia U.   #AA 7120   D 7521   AB 357

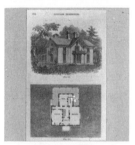

495. ——; des. DAVIS, A. J. (?).
A Cottage in the English or Rural Style
from "Cottage Residences; ..." New York & London,
London, Wiley & Putnam, 1842. Avery Lib.,
Columbia U.   #AA 7120   D 7525   AB 245

496. ANON. (Inspired by DOWNING, A.J.)
Oakes Angier Ames House,
1854. North Easton, Mass. Ext.   AB 257

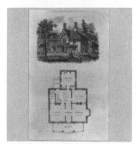

497. ANON. (Inspired by DOWNING, A.J.)
Gothic House,
wood version, c. 1845-50. Salem (260 Lafayette
St.), Mass. Fac. Property of M. Brooks.   AB 642

498. FURNESS, Frank (1839-1912).
Pennsylvania Academy of the Fine Arts,
1871-76. Philadelphia (Broad & Cherry Sts.), Pa.
Ext.   AB 363

499. ——.
*Provident Trust Co. (now The Philadelphia
National Bank),*
1879. Philadelphia, Pa. Ext.   AB 364

500. GODEFROY, Maximilian (c.1770-c.1837).
Chapel for St. Mary's Seminary,
1806, engr. 20¾" x 17½". Baltimore (Paca near
Franklin St.), Md. Ext. Maryland Hist. Soc.
                                                  AB 246

501. GODEFROY, Maximilian (c. 1770-c. 1837).
Chapel for St. Mary's Seminary,
1806. Baltimore (Paca near Franklin St.), Md.
Int. toward altar. AB 247

502. HAVILAND, John.
Eastern State Penitentiary,
1823-29. Philadelphia (Fairmount Ave. at 21 St.),
Pa. Ext. AB 107

503. HUNT, Richard Morris (1827-95).
Chateau sur Mer (William S. Wetmore House),
1872, Newport, R.I. Ext. AB 405

504. ——. Ibid. Morning room. AB 367

505. ——. Ibid. Morning room, toward
fireplace. AB 368

506. ——. Ibid. Det. mantel of morning room.
AB 366

507. ——.
Breakers,
1892. Newport (Ochre Point Ave.), R.I. Ext.
from seaside. AB 497

508. ——. Ibid. Central hall from balcony.
AB 496

509. ——. Ibid. Billiard room. AB 498

510. ——.
Belcourt (O. H. P. Belmont House),
1894. Newport, R.I. Ext. AB 709

511. ——.
Biltmore,
1895. Asheville, N.C. Fac. AB 536

512. ——.
Tribune Bldg.,
1873-75. New York (fronting on City Hall Park),
N.Y. Ext. AB 369

513. LEE, Francis D.
Unitarian Church,
1852-54. Charleston (4 Archdale), S.C. Nave. AB 252

514. ——.
*Farmers' and Exchange Bank (now Commodore
Chester H. Taylor Nautical Academy),*
1853-54. Charleston (141 East Bay), S.C. Fac.
AB 370

515. LEE, Francis D.
Farmers' and Exchange Bank (now Commodore
Chester H. Taylor Nautical Academy).
1853-54. Charleston (141 East Bay), S.C. Int.   AB 370A

516. NOTMAN, John (1810-65).
Athenaeum,
1845-47. Philadelphia (219 S. Sixth St.), Pa. Fac.
AB 374

517. O'CONNOR, P. J.
#15 Fire House,
1885. San Francisco, Calif. Ext.   AB 679

518. POTTER, Edward Tuckerman (?-1904).
Nott Memorial Library,
1858-76. Union College, Schenectady (800 Union
St.), N.Y. Ext.   AB 380

519. REID, James W. and Merritt.
Hotel del Coronado,
1887-88. Coronado, Calif. Ext.   AB 671

520. ——. Ibid. Ext., inner garden court.
AB 672

521. ——. Ibid. Int., bar.   AB 673

522. ——. Ibid. Dining room.   AB 674

523. ——. Ibid. Dining room.   AB 675

524. RENWICK, James (1818-95).
Grace Church,
1845-46. New York (Broadway and 10th St.), N.Y.
Ext.   AB 253

525. ——.
St. Patrick's Cathedral,
1858-79. New York, N.Y. Ext. from above.   AB 740

526. ——. Ext.   AB 740A

527. ——.
Smithsonian Institution,
1846-55. Washington, D.C. Entr. det.   AB 255

528. SLOAN, Samuel.
Longwood,
1860. Natchez, Miss. Ext. Property of Mrs.
James H. Ward, Mrs. R. L. Blanchard & Mrs.
Leslie K. Pollard.   AB 381

529. STURGIS, Russell (1836-1909).
Farnum Hall, Yale U.,
1868. New Haven, Conn. Gen. view from the
Green.   AB 640A

*530. TOWN, Ithiel (1784-1844).
Yale College Library (now Dwight Chapel),
1842. New Haven, Conn. Ext.   AB 715

531. UPJOHN, Richard (1802-78).
Kingscote,
1838. Newport (Bellevue Ave.), R.I. South fac.   AB 261

532. ——. Ibid. Oblique view.   AB 259

533. ——. Ibid. Entr. hall toward door.   AB 262

534. ——. Ibid. Double parlor.   AB 258A

535. ——.
First Parish Congregational Church,
1845-46. Brunswick, Maine. Ext.; spire
destroyed.   AB 282

536. ——. Ibid. Nave.   AB 281

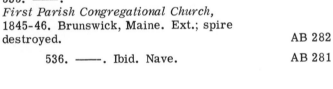

537. ——.
Trinity Church,
1846. New York (Broadway at Wall St.), N.Y.
¾ view from SW.   AB 266

538. ——. Ibid. Ext. det.   AB 263

539. ——. Ibid. Pulpit.   AB 265

540. ——. Ibid. Int.   AB 264

541. ——.
St. Luke's Church,
1857. Clermont, N.Y. Ext.   AB 269

542. ——.
City Hall,
1852-53. Utica, N.Y. Ext.   AB 387

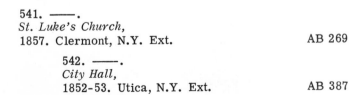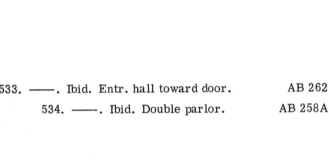

---

*There is evidence to indicate that the Yale College Library may
have been designed by Henry Austin and not Ithiel Town.

543. UPJOHN, Richard (1802-78).
Gate House, the Greenwood Cemetery,
1861. Brooklyn (5th Ave. & 25th St.), N.Y. Ext.   AB 270

  544. UPJOHN, Richard M. (1828-1903).
  State Capitol,
  1878. Hartford, Conn. Ext.   AB 703

545. VALSON, Maximilian.
San Francisco Plantation,
1849. Garyville, La. Ext.   AB 736

  546. VAUX, Calvert (1824-95).
  Family Cottage in the Mountains and Plan of
  Principal Floor,
  dwg. from "Villas and Cottages ...," New York,
  Harper & Bros., 1857. Avery Lib., Columbia U.
  #AA 7120   V 46   AB 431

547. WALTER, Thomas Ustick (1804-87).
United States Capitol Dome,
1856-63. Washington, D.C. Ext.   AB 390

  548. WARE and VAN BRUNT.
  Memorial Hall, Harvard U.,
  1871-74. Cambridge, Mass. Ext.   AB 434

549. ——. Ibid. Dining room.   AB 432

  550. ——. Ibid. Dining room, det. wood
  construction.   AB 432A

551. WOOD, James.
Tampa Bay Hotel (now University of Tampa),
1884-91. Tampa, Fla. Ext.   AB 729

  552. ——. Ibid. Main entr.   AB 730

IRON AND WOOD CONSTRUCTION
  ANONYMOUS (alphabetic listing by states)

  CALIFORNIA

553. ANON.
Conservatory, Golden Gate Park,
c. 1879. San Francisco, Calif. Ext.   AB 680

  LOUISIANA

  554. ANON.
  La Prete House (The House of the Turk),
  1835. New Orleans (Orleans & Delphine Sts.), La.
  Ext.   AB 299

  MARYLAND

555. ANON.
Cast Iron Bldg. (now Robins Paper Co.),
c. 1870. Baltimore (308-314 West Pratt St.), Md.
Fac.   AB 306

  UTAH

  556. ANON.
  Z.C.M.I. Department Store,
  1868. Salt Lake City, Utah. Fac.   AB 305

557. BELL, William.
Diagram for Balloon Frame,
pl. VI, from "Carpentry Made Easy; or, The
Science and Art of Framing on a New and
Improved System ...," Phila., J. Challen & Son,
1858. Avery Lib., Columbia U.   # AA 3120   B 41   AB 288

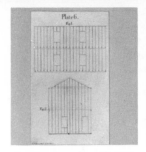

558. BOGARDUS, James (1800-74).
Cast Iron Bldg.,
1848. New York (Washington & Murray Sts.), N.Y.
Det. of windows above first fl.   AB 289

559. ———.
Harper and Brothers Bldg.,
1854, w.c., 22" x 28". New York, N.Y. Coll.
Harper & Bros. Ext.   AB 290

560. CARSTENSEN & GILDEMEISTER.
Crystal Palace, Exposition of 1853, Bryant Park,
lith. by PARSONS, C.; printed by Endicott & Co.,
N.Y., 20½" x 13½". J. Clarence Davies Coll.,
Mus. City N.Y.   # 29.100.2391   Int.   AB 650

561. DAVIS, Alexander Jackson (1803-92).
Board and Batten Farmhouse
from "Rural Residences, etc.," New York, 1837.
A. J. Davis Coll., Avery Lib., Columbia U.
AA 3120   B41   AB 312

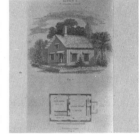

562. DOWNING, Andrew Jackson (1815-52).
A Laborer's Cottage,
design I, from "The Architecture of Country
Houses; ...," New York, D. Appleton & Co., 1850.
Avery Lib., Columbia U. # AA 7120 D 75 AB 293

563. ———.
Vertical Boarding with Different Forms of Batten,
diagram, fig. 1, from "The Architecture of Country
Houses; ...," New York, D. Appleton, 1850. Avery
Lib., Columbia U.   # AA 7120   D 75   AB 313

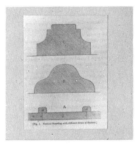

564. ———.
Cottage Window,
elevation with surrounding wall, fig. 8 from
"The Architecture of Country Houses; ..." New
York, D. Appleton, 1850. Avery Lib., Columbia U.
AA 7120   D 75   AB 313A

565. EADS, James Buchanan (1820-87).
Eads Bridge,
1868-74. St. Louis, Mo. Gen. profile of entire
bridge.   AB 295B

566. ———. Ibid. View from below showing metal
structure of a single span.   AB 294

567. GAYNOR, J. P.
Haughwout Bldg.,
1857. New York, N.Y. Ext.   AB 291

568. MIX, E. Townsend.
Northwestern Guaranty Loan Co. (now Metro-
politan Insurance Bldg.)
1890. Minneapolis, Minn. Ext., oblique view.
                                              AB 611

569. ———. Ibid. Int. court viewed from above.   AB 609

570. ———. Ibid. Int.   AB 610

571. MIX, E. Townsend.
Northwestern Guaranty Loan Co. (now Metro-politan Insurance Bldg.),
1890. Minneapolis, Minn. Int. det. elevator cage
& iron balcony railings.   AB 612

572. ROEBLING, John & WASHINGTON, A.
Brooklyn Bridge,
1867-73. New York, N.Y. Gen. view.   AB 297

573. ———. Ibid. Det. tower & cables.   AB 296

574. SMITH, Marcus DeF.
West Cornwall Covered Bridge, formerly Hart's Bridge,
spanning Housatonic River, 1841. West Cornwall,
Conn.   AB 337

575. STARBUCK IRON WORKS (Troy, N.Y.),
Bidwell Bar Suspension Bridge,
1856. Oroville, Calif.

 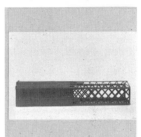

576. TOWN, Ithiel (1784-1844).
Model of Lattice Truss,
1928, made by Yale engineering students. (Model
of original bridge at Whitneyville, 1823, patent
1820). New Haven, Colony Historical Society,
Conn.   AB 293A

577. U.S. ARMY ENGINEERS.
Fort Point (also called Fort Winfield Scott),
1857. Presidio, San Francisco, Calif. View from
roof with courtyard.   AB 676

 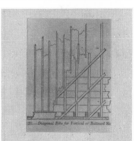

578. WOODWARD, George E. (1829-1905).
Diagonal Ribs
for Vertical or Battened Siding, fig. 120 from
"Woodward's Country Homes ...," New York, Geo.
E. & F. W. Woodward, 1865. Avery Lib.,
Columbia U.   # AA 7120   W 872   AB 309

579. WYMAN, George Herbert.
Bradbury Bldg.,
1893. Los Angeles (3rd St. & Broadway), Calif.
Int.   AB 613C

580. ———. Ibid. Int., closer view of elevators.
                                             AB 613B

581. ———. Ibid. Int., metal stairway.   AB 613

582. ———. Ibid. Det., metal elevator and
balcony.   AB 614B

PRACTICAL
     ANONYMOUS (alphabetic listing by states)
     CALIFORNIA

583. ANON.
Livery Stable,
c. 1873. San Juan Bautista, Calif. Fac.   AB 681

     COLORADO

584. ANON.
Téller House,
n.d. Central City, Colo. Ext., lower floors.
                                             AB 713

585. ANON.
Hardware Store,
n.d. Central City, Colo. Fac.   AB 714

CONNECTICUT

586. ANON.
Tobacco Barn,
n.d. South Windsor, Conn. Side.   AB 326

MASSACHUSETTS

587. ANON.
Union Wharf Warehouse,
1846. Boston (Commercial St.), Mass. Ext.   AB 301

PENNSYLVANIA

588. ANON.
Economy (Rappite Community), Storehouse and
Granary,
1826. Ambridge, Pa. Gen. view.   AB 330

589. ———. Ibid. Det. stone wall, half-timbering
of granary.   AB 331

590. ANON.
Pennsylvania Fire Insurance Co.,
1838. Philadelphia (508-510 Walnut St.), Pa. Ext.
                                                AB 156

RHODE ISLAND

591. ANON.
Lippitt Mill,
1809. Lippitt, West Warwick, R.I. Ext.   AB 298

592. ANON.
White Rock Mill,
1849. Westerly, R.I. Ext.   AB 304A

593. ALLEN, Zachariah.
Industrial Tool and Machine Co., Inc. (formerly
Bernon Mill),
1853; mansard story added later. Georgiaville,
R.I. Ext.   AB 304

SKYSCRAPER
(alphabetic listing by architects)

594. BEMAN, Solon Spencer (1853-1914).
Studebaker Bldg.,
1895. Chicago (629 S. Wabash Ave.), Ill. Ext.
                                                AB 601

595. ———. Ibid. Det. of fenestration.   AB 602

596. BURNHAM and ROOT.
Monadnock Bldg. (north half),
1889-91. Chicago (53 W. Jackson Blvd.), Ill. Ext.,
view from N end.   AB 603

597. ———. Ibid. Det. of fenestration.   AB 604

598. ———.
Reliance Bldg.,
1890-95; original design (4 stories) by ROOT,
1890; terra cotta sheathing by ATWOOD, 1895.
Chicago (32 North State St.), Ill. Ext.   AB 605

599. BURNHAM, D. H., & CO,
Flatiron Bldg.,
1902. New York (Fifth Ave. & 22nd St.), N.Y. Ext. AB 763

> **600.** HOLABIRD & ROCHE.
> *Champlain Bldg. (now Powers Bldg.),*
> 1903. Chicago (37 S. Wabash), Ill. Ext.   AB 765

601. ——.
McClurg Bldg. (now Crown Bldg.),
1899-1900. Chicago (218 S. Wabash), Ill. Ext.   AB 764

> **602.** HOLABIRD and ROCHE; SULLIVAN, Louis
> (1856-1924).
> *Gage Group,*
> 1898. Chicago (24 & 18 S. Michigan Ave.), Ill. Fac.
>   AB 607

603. JENNIE & MUNDIE.
*Chicago National Bank Bldg. (now Downtown
Parking Stations, Inc.),*
1900. Chicago (121-27 W. Monroe), Ill. Det.   AB 766

> **604.** JOHNSTON, William L.
> *Jayne Bldg.,*
> 1849, engr., 15½" x 21¾". Library Co.
> Philadelphia. Ext.   AB 608

ARCHITECTURAL REFORM AND INNOVATION

605. RICHARDSON, Henry Hobson (1838-86).
Watts Sherman House,
1874. Newport (Shepard Ave.), R.I. Fac. Property
of the Baptist Home for the Aged.   AB 439

> **606.** ——. Ibid. Ext., front entr. & gable.
>   AB 438

607. ——. Ibid. Ext., south side.   AB 442

> **608.** ——. Ibid. Fireplace in living hall,
> designed by Stanford White.   AB 443

609. ——. Ibid. Library, designed by Stanford
White (bef. 1881).   AB 473

> **610.** ——.
> *Ames Gate Lodge,*
> 1880-81. North Easton, Mass. S fac. to show
> stone versus projecting wood and tile roof.
> Property of John Ames, Sr.   AB 449

611. ——. Ibid. N. fac.   AB 448

> **612.** ——. Ibid. N fac. diagonally along wall
> right of entr. tower.   AB 450

613. RICHARDSON, Henry Hobson (1838-86).
Percy Brown House,
1881-82. Marion, Mass. Ext.   AB 452

614. ——.
M. F. Stoughton House,
1882-83. Cambridge (Brattle St.), Mass. Ext.
          AB 454

615. ——.
R. T. Paine House,
1884-86. Waltham (577 Beaver St.), Mass. Ext.
Property of Theodore Stores, Boston.   AB 458

616. ——. Ibid. Int. det. of staircase.   AB 457

617. ——.
J. J. Glessner House,
1885-87. Chicago (Prairie Ave.), Ill. Ext.   AB 460

618. ——.
Trinity Church,
1873-77. Boston, Mass. Ext.   AB 436

619. ——. Ibid. Ext. from E.   AB 437

620. ——. Ibid. Int.   AB 435

621. ——.
Ames Free Library,
1877-79. North Easton, Mass. Ext.   AB 444

622. ——. Ibid. Reading room fireplace.
          AB 445

623. ——. Ibid. Int. from balcony at west end
of stacks looking toward entr.   AB 446

624. ——.
Sever Hall, Harvard U.,
1878-80. Cambridge, Mass. Ext. Street side.
          AB 475

625. ——.
Crane Memorial Library,
1880-83. Quincy, Mass. Ext.   AB 451

626. ——.
Boston and Albany Station,
1881-84. Chestnut Hill, Mass. Ext.   AB 453

627. RICHARDSON, Henry Hobson (1838-86).
Austin Hall,
Harvard University,
1881-83. Cambridge, Mass. Fac.   AB 485

    628. ——.
    Allegheny County Buildings,
    1884-86. Pittsburgh, Pa. Gen. view.   AB 487

629. ——. Ibid. Gen. view with
Court House and *Jail.*   AB 487A

    630. ——. Ibid.
    Court House and *Courtyard.*   AB 455

631. ——. Ibid.
Jail.
Ext. det. door.   AB 456

    632. SULLIVAN, Louis (1856-1924).
    Troescher Bldg. (later Daily Times Bldg.),
    1884. Chicago, Ill. Fac.   AB 569

633. ——.
Auditorium,
1887-89. Chicago (Michigan Ave. at Congress),
Ill. Gen. view.   AB 571

    634. ——. Ibid. Ext., det. of tower.   AB 570

635. ——.
Getty Tomb,
1890. Chicago (Graceland Cemetery), Ill. Gen.
view.   AB 573

    636. ——. Ibid. Det., portal with voussoirs of
    arch above.   AB 574

637. ——.
Wainwright Bldg.,
1890-91. St. Louis (7th & Chestnut Sts.), Mo.
Gen. view.   AB 590

    638. ——. Ibid. Cornice det.   AB 577

639. ——.
Wainwright Tomb,
1892. St. Louis (Bellefontaine Cemetery), Mo.
Fac.   AB 578

    640. ——. Ibid. Det., oblique view of molding.
                                   AB 593B

641. SULLIVAN, Louis (1856-1924).
Guaranty Bldg. (now Prudential Bldg.),
1894-95. Buffalo (Church & Pearl Sts.), N.Y.
Fac.   AB 581

    642. ——. Ibid. Ext. det. cornice.   AB 580

643. ——. Ibid. Det. corner of building showing
first two floors.   AB 579

    644. ——.
Schlesinger and Meyer Dept. Store (now Carson,
Pirie, Scott),
1899-1904; addition 1906. Chicago, Ill. Entr.
corner.   AB 583

645. ——. Ibid. Det. ornament over entrance. AB 582

    646. ——. Ibid. Det. window wall.   AB 584

647. ——.
The Security Bank,
1907-08; Owatonna (W. Broadway & N. Cedar),
Minn. Ext.   AB 767

    648. ——. Ibid. Ext. det.   AB 768

649. ——.
St. Paul's Methodist Church,
1910-12. Cedar Rapids (14th St. & 3rd Ave. SE),
Iowa. Ext.   AB 769

    650. ——.
Merchants' National Bank (now Poweshiek
County Bank),
1914. Grinnell (Broad & Fourth Ave.), Iowa.
Ext.   AB 770

651. ——.
People's Savings and Loan Assoc. Bank,
1917-18. Sidney, Ohio. Ext., oblique view.   AB 771

    652. ——. Ibid. Det., portal.   AB 772

653. ——.
Farmers and Merchants Union Bank,
1919. Columbus, Wis. Ext.   AB 773

    SHINGLE STYLE

    654. McKIM, MEAD and WHITE.
Kingscote,
1880. Newport (Bellevue Ave.), R.I. Dining room
designed by WHITE, Stanford, and added to
UPJOHN's structure.   AB 508

655. McKIM, MEAD and WHITE.
Kingscote,
1880. Newport (Bellevue Ave.), R.I. Dining
room, view toward fireplace.   AB 509

     656. ——.
     Casino,
     1880-81. Newport, R.I. Fac.   AB 544

657. ——.
Tilton House,
1881-82. Newport, R.I. Entr. hall toward
stair.   AB 517

     658. ——. Ibid. Dining room.   AB 515

659. ——.
Isaac Bell House,
1882-83. Newport (Bellevue Ave.), R.I. Ext.   AB 501

     660. ——. Ibid. Entr. hall fireplace nook.
                               AB 500

661. ——.
R. W. Goelet House,
1882-83. Newport, R.I. Ext. from sea-side.   AB 511

     662. ——.
     William Low House (now Paul C. Nicholson, Jr.,
     House),
     1887. Bristol, R.I. Ext. from sea-side.   AB 510

663. STEVENS, John Calvin (1855-1940).
James Hopkins Smith House,
1885; enlarged 1900. Remodeled by KIMBALL,
Richard, 1945-46. Falmouth Foreside, Maine.
Ext. Property of Charles Shipman Payson.   AB 529

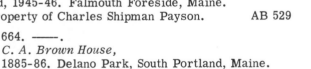

     664. ——.
     C. A. Brown House,
     1885-86. Delano Park, South Portland, Maine.
     Ext. Property of Mrs. Charles L. Donahue.
                              AB 529A

ACADEMIC REACTION

665. McKIM, MEAD and WHITE.
Ross Winans House,
1882. Baltimore, Md. Ext.   AB 521

     666. ——.
     Henry Villard Houses,
     1883. New York (451 Madison Ave.), N.Y. Ext.
                              AB 518

667. ——.
Boston Public Library,
1887. Boston, Mass. Fac.   AB 502

     668. ——. Ibid. Courtyard.   AB 505

669. McKIM, MEAD and WHITE.
Boston Public Library,
1887. Boston, Mass. Reading room.   AB 506

    670. ——.
    University Club,
    1900. New York (5th Ave. at 54th St.), N.Y. Ext.
                                       AB 523

671. ——. Ibid. Library.   AB 522

    672. ATWOOD, Charles B. (1849-95).
    *Columbian Exposition Art Bldg. (now Rosenwald
    Museum of Science and Industry),*
    1893. Chicago, Ill. Ext.   AB 738

673. BROWN, A. Paige and MERCHANT,
William G.
Ferry Tower,
1896. San Francisco (Market St.), Calif. Ext.   AB 670

    674. SMITHMEYER & PELTZ.
    Library of Congress,
    1888-97. Washington, D.C. Ext.   AB 382

675. ——. Ibid. Entr. hall.   AB 383

STRIP IN NO: 1 REPRO HEAD ON THIS LINE

    CALIFORNIA

    676. *Sacramento City, Calif.,*
    1849, col. lith, by COOPER, C. J. Stokes Coll.,
    N.Y. Pub. Lib. View.   CPB 33

    CONNECTICUT

677. *Yale College and New Haven Green,*
1839. Sepia and gouache by BARTLETT, W. H.
Stokes Coll., N.Y. Pub. Lib. Gen. view.   CPB 23

    WASHINGTON, D.C.

    678. *View of the Old Capitol from the Portico of
    the Executive Mansion,*
    1840, engr. by BARTLETT, William H.,
    7" x 4⁷/₈". Lib. of Congress.   CPB 24

679. *View of Washington,*
c. 1851, col. lith. by SACHSE, Edward, 27⁴/₁₆" x
17¹⁵/₁₆". Stokes Coll., N.Y. Pub. Lib.   CPB 35

    680. *View of Washington, D.C. with Projected
    Improvements,*
    1851, col. lith. by SMITH, Benjamin F., Jr.
    42¹⁵/₁₆" x 24¹⁰/₁₆". Stokes Coll., N.Y. Pub. Lib.
                                           CPB 36

    ILLINOIS

681. BEMAN, Solon Spencer.
Pullman Workers' Houses,
1879-84. Chicago (S. Champlain & 112th St.), Ill.
Ext.   CPB 66

    682. OLMSTED, Frederick Law., Sr. (1822-1903)
    (Landscape Arch.).
    Map of Riverside,
    Riverside, Ill., 1869, India ink & w.c. Map Room,
    N.Y. Pub. Lib.   CPB 61

LOUISIANA

683. *The City & Suburbs of New Orleans,*
1815, col. engr. by ROLLINSON, William, 30⁹/₁₆"
x 18¹¹/₁₆". Stokes Coll., N.Y. Pub. Lib. Map.   CPB 13

MASSACHUSETTS

684. GILMAN, Arthur.
Back Bay Area, Boston,
1857(?). Boston Athenaeum. Gen. view.   CPB 40

685. *Louisberg Square,*
1834-47. Boston (Mt. Vernon to Pinckney St.),
Mass. Gen. view.   CPB 20

686. *View of Lowell, Mass.,*
1833, col. lith. by FARRAR, A. E., 23¹¹/₁₆" x
14⁷/₁₆". Stokes Coll., N.Y. Pub. Lib.   CPB 19

687. *Nantucket, Mass.,*
c. 1820-50. Main St. near Pleasant St.
Looking E.   CPB 15

688. ——. Ibid. Main St. at Walnut Lane.
Looking E.   CPB 15B

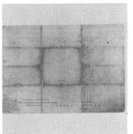

689. *Williamstown, Mass. ... from Stone Hill,*
c. 1855, col. lith. by YEOMANS, George. 26⁶/₁₆"
x 15¹⁴/₁₆". Stokes Coll., N.Y. Pub. Lib.   CPB 47

MICHIGAN

690. WOODWARD, Judge A. B. (?).
Plan of the City of Detroit, Mich.,
1807; a radial plan, only a few streets realized.
Dwg. by HULL, Abijah. Detroit Hist. Soc.   CPB 8

NEW HAMPSHIRE

691. *Harrisville, N. H.,*
1818-c.1850. Mill town. View over pond.
Chapel (left) 1840, *Church* (right) 1843.   CPB 14C

692. ——. Ibid. Gen. view from pond.   CPB 14D

693. ——. Ibid. Gen. view.   CPB 14B

694. ——. Ibid. Mill, 1822.   CPB 14E

695. ——. Ibid. Supervisor's house. Ext.   CPB 14

696. *Orford, N.H.,*
early 19th C. Street view.   CPB 2A

NEW YORK

697. *Map of Manhattan,*
1810, engr., 91$^{1}/_{16}$" x 24$^{6}/_{16}$", N.Y. State Board of
Commissioners. Eno Coll., N.Y. Pub. Lib.   CPB 10

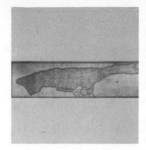 

    698. *View Broadway & Proposed Elevated*
    Railway,
    1848, col. lith., RAYNER, R. J., 24$^{4}/_{16}$" x 19$^{6}/_{16}$".
    Stokes Coll., N.Y. Pub. Lib.   CPB 28

699. NOWLAN, Samuel B. B. (Civil Eng.).
Proposed Arcade Railway under Broadway;
View near Wall St.,
c. 1870, col. lith. Stokes Coll., N.Y. Pub. Lib.   CPB 62

    700. OLMSTED, Frederick Law, Sr. (1822-1903)
    (Landscape Arch.).
    View of Central Park (toward Mall) from Water
    Terrace, New York, N.Y.,
    c. 1875, col. lith. by BACHMANN, John. Stokes
    Coll., N.Y. Pub. Lib.   CPB 63

701. ——.
Martel's New York Central Park,
1863, col. lith. Stokes Coll., N.Y. Pub. Lib.   CPB 57

    702. *View, Poestenkill, N.Y.,*
    c. 1860-70, lith. by HIDLEY, J. H. Stokes Coll.,
    N.Y. Pub. Lib.   CPB 56

NORTH CAROLINA

703. OLMSTED, Frederick Law, Sr. (1822-1903)
(Landscape Arch.).
Biltmore, Shrub Garden,
1895. Asheville, N.C.   CPB 132A

    704. ——. Ibid.
    Walled Garden,
    view toward greenhouse.   CPB 132

705. ——. Ibid.
Italian Garden.   CPB 132B

    ## OKLAHOMA

    706. *View, Oklahoma City, Indian Territory,*
    Okla.,
    1890, col. lith. by FOWLER, T. M. Stokes Coll.,
    N.Y. Pub. Lib.   CPB 70

PENNSYLVANIA

707. RAPP, George & Frederick (Founders).
Map of the Land of the Harmony Society, Beaver
County,
col., 1854, 73½" x 45½". Old Economy, Ambridge,
Pa.   CPB 105

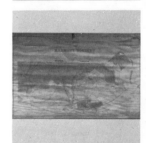 

    708. VARLÉ, P. C.
    Map of Philadelphia
    (showing proposed extensions west of Schuylkill),
    1802, engr. Stokes Coll., N.Y. Pub. Lib.   CPB 7

RHODE ISLAND

709. *Cliff Walk,*
late 19th C. Newport, R.I.   CPB 3

    710. *White Rock,*
    1849. Near Westerly, R.I. View of mill houses.
    CPB 31

ARCHITECTURE OF THE TWENTIETH CENTURY

VINCENT SCULLY

711. AECK, Richard L. ASSOC. (1912-   ).
Football Stadium,
Henry Grady High School, 1948. Atlanta (14th St.
& Blvd., N.E.), Ga. Gen. view.   AC 4

    712. ——.
    Coliseum,
    Georgia Institute of Technology, 1956. Atlanta,
    Ga. Ext.   AC 4A

713. AIN, Gregory (1906-   ).
Cooperative Apartments
(10 units), 1938. Los Angeles (2839 Avenel St.),
Calif. Front, showing garage under apartments.   AC 6

    714. ——. Ibid. Terrace of one unit.   AC 6A

715. ANDERSON and BECKWITH.
Swimming Pool,
Massachusetts Institute of Technology, 1940.
Cambridge, Mass. Int.   AC 8

    716. ARMSTRONG, Harris (1899-   ).
    American Stove Co. Bldg.,
    1948. St. Louis (S. Kingshighway), Mo. Ext.
    Property of Teamsters Union, Joint Council #13.
                                                  AC 9

717. ASHEN and ALLEN.
Chapel of the Holy Cross,
1955-56, reinforced concrete. Sedona, Ariz.
Ext. toward canyon wall.   AC 1003

    718. THE ARCHITECTS COLLABORATIVE.
    Graduate Center,
    Harvard University, 1950. Cambridge, Mass.
    Gen. view.   AC 130

719. ——. Ibid. Det. court colonnades.   AC 131

    720. ——. Ibid. Int. Harkness Commons. AC 132

721. ——. Ibid. Int. ramp & screen.   AC 132A

    722. BACON, Henry (1866-1924).
    Lincoln Memorial,
    1915. Washington, D.C. Ext.   AC 10

723. BAKEWELL, J. and BROWN, A., Jr.
City Hall,
1915. San Francisco (Market & Van Ness), Calif.
Fac.   AC 11

724. BARNEY, KASTNER & STONOROV.
Carl Mackley Houses,
c. 1935. Philadelphia (M and Bristol Sts.), Pa.
Gen. view.   CPC 232

725. BARTHELME, Donald (1907-   ).
West Columbia Elementary School,
1952. West Columbia, Tex. Ext.   AC 13

726. ——. Ibid. Class room.   AC 14

727. BELLUSCHI, Pietro (1899-   ).
McLoughlin Heights,
1942. Vancouver, Wash. Gen. view.   AC 22

728. ——.
Central Lutheran Church,
1951. Portland (2104 NE Hancock), Ore. Ext.
                                        AC 28

729. ——. Ibid. Int.   AC 29

730. ——.
Zion Lutheran Church,
1950. Portland, Ore. Bell tower.   AC 25

731. ——. Ibid. Int.   AC 26

732. ——.
Equitable Savings & Loan Assoc.,
1948. Portland (421 SW 6 Ave.), Ore. Ext.
                                        AC 16

733. ——. Ibid. Structural det.   AC 17

734. BERNARDI, Theodore C. (1903-   ).
Theodore Bernardi House,
1951. Sausalito (99 Miller Lane), Calif. Ext.
                                        AC 494

735. ——. Ibid. Living room.   AC 493B

736. BORN, Ernest (1898-   ).
Esther and Ernest Born House,
1950. San Francisco (2020 Great Highway), Calif.
Living room, fireplace area.   AC 1004

737. BORN, Ernest (1898-   ).
Esther and Ernest Born House,
1950. San Francisco, Calif. Living room from
balcony.   AC 1005

    738. BOSTON CENTER ARCHITECTS.
    Proposed Back Bay Center Development:
    Model, 1953. Boston, Mass. Coll. R. M. Bradley
    & Co.   CPC 33

739. BOSWORTH, Welles (1869-?).
American Telephone & Telegraph Co. Bldg.,
1915. New York (195 Broadway), N.Y. Ext.   AC 30

    740. BRAGDON, Claude (1866-1946).
    N.Y. Central R.R. Station,
    1912-14. Rochester, N.Y. Int.   AC 31

741. BREUER, Marcel (1902-   ).
Geller House,
Lawrence, L.I., N.Y. Entr. side.   AC 41

    742. ——. Ibid. Garden side.   AC 41A

743. ——.
Preston Robinson House,
1947. Williamstown, Mass. Ext.   AC 47

    744. ——. Ibid. Terrace.   AC 48

745. ——. Ibid. Living room.   AC 48A

    746. ——.
    Harry A. Caesar House,
    1952. Lakeville, Conn. Ext. Property of Indian
    Mountain School.   AC 50

747. ——.
Dormitory,
Vassar College, 1951. Poughkeepsie, N.Y. Ext.   AC 49

    748. ——.
    Public Library,
    1953. Grosse Pointe (Kercheval Ave. & Fisher
    Rd.), Mich. Ext.   AC 51

749. BURKET, Rhees E. (1899-   ).
Kensington Junior High School,
1938. Kensington, Md. Ext.   AC 52

    750. BYRNE, Barry (1892-   ).
    St. Columba Catholic Church,
    c. 1950. St. Paul, Minn. Ext.   AC 55

751. BYRNE, Barry (1892-   ).
St. Francis Xavier Catholic Church,
c. 1950. Kansas City (1001 E. 52nd St.), Mo. Ext.   AC 57

752. CALLISTER, Charles Warren (1918-   ).
T. Carson O'Connell House,
1954. San Rafael (335 Highland Ave.), Calif. Ext.
AC 1008

753. ——. Ibid. Living room.   AC 1006

754. ——. Ibid. Living room from balcony.
AC 1007

755. ——.
Christian Science Church,
1951. Belvedere, Calif. Ext.   AC 1010

756. ——. Ibid. Ext. corner det.   AC 1009

757. ——. Ibid. Entr. foyer.   AC 1012

758. ——. Ibid. Int.   AC 1011

759. CARRÈRE and HASTINGS.
Woolsey Hall & Commons,
Yale University, 1901-02. New Haven, Conn. Ext.
AC 58

760. ——.
Public Library,
1905. New York, N.Y. Gen. view.   AC 60

761. ——. Ibid. Rear view.   AC 61

762. ——.
Carnegie Institute,
1909. Washington, D.C. (1530 P St., N.W.). Ext.
AC 63

763. CATALANO, Eduardo (1917-   ).
Catalano House (now Ezra Meir House),
1954. Raleigh (Catalano Dr.), N.C. Ext.   AC 64

764. CLARK, CLAVAN, RICHARDSON, GROVE,
ELSEN.
Stuyvesant Town,
1947. New York (East River Dr. & Ave. C.), N.Y.
Gen. view.   CPC 190

765. COLLEY and KEIWITT.
Memorial Coliseum,
1954. Corpus Christi (400 Shoreline Dr.), Tex.
Ext.   AC 66A

    766. ——. Ibid. Int.   AC 66

767. COCKE, FORD; BERGER, A. & M.;
WURSTER, W. W. (Consultant).
Trinity University,
1951. San Antonio (715 Stadium), Tex. Gen. view.
                                         CPC 267

    768. ——. Ibid. View toward student union.
                                         CPC 268

769. COOLIDGE and CARLSON.
West Hill Place,
1915. Boston (22 Embankment Rd.), Mass. Court.
                                         CPC 28

    770. COOLIDGE, SHEPLEY, BULFINCH and
    ABBOTT.
    Cornell Medical Center,
    1932. New York (69th St. & York), N.Y. Ext.
                                         AC 67

771. CORBETT, Mario Francis (1901-   ).
Moritz Thomsen House,
1952. Vina, Calif. Ext.   AC 69

    772. ——. Ibid. Int.   AC 68

773. CRAM, GOODHUE and FERGUSON.
Administration Bldg.,
Rice Institute, 1909-12. Houston, Tex. Ext.   AC 109

    774. CRET, Paul Phillipe (1876-1945).
    Pan American Bldg.,
    1912-13. Washington (17th St. & Constitution
    Ave.), D.C. Ext.   AC 72

775. ——.
Institute of Arts,
1927. Detroit, Mich. Fac.   AC 74

    776. ——.
    Folger Shakespeare Library,
    1929-32. Washington (20 E. Capitol), D.C. Ext.
                                         AC 73

777. ——.
Federal Reserve Bldg.,
1935. Washington (20/21st Sts. & Constitution
Ave.), D.C. Fac.   AC 75

    778. DAILEY, Gardner A. (1895-   ).
    U.S. Merchant Marine Cadet School (now San
    Mateo Junior College),
    1942. San Mateo, Calif. Ext.   AC 77

779. DAILEY, Gardner A. (1895-   ).
*U.S. Merchant Marine Cadet School (now San
Mateo Junior College),*
1942, San Mateo, Calif. Classrooms.   AC 1013

    780. ——.
    *American National Red Cross, Pacific Area
    Office,*
    1950. San Francisco (1550 Sutter), Calif. Ext.
                                        AC 78

781. ——. Ibid. Int.   AC 79

    782. DeMARS, Vernon (1908-   ).
    DeMars House,
    1950. Berkeley (240 The Uplands), Calif. Ext.
                                        AC 1015

783. DeMARS and CAIRNS.
Agricultural Workers' Community,
1936-37. Chandler, Ariz. Back view of row
house.   CPC 51B

    784. DOW, Alden B.
    John Whitman House (now John Van Stirum House),
    1935. Midland (2407 Manor Drive), Mich. Ext.
                                        AC 81

785. EAMES, Charles (1907-   ).
Charles Eames House,
1949. Pacific Palisades (203 Chautauqua Blvd.),
Calif. Ext.   AC 82

    786. ——. Ibid. Living room.   AC 83

787. EGGERS and HIGGINS.
Triboro Hospital,
1941. Jamaica, N.Y. Ext.   AC 84

    788. ELLWOOD, Craig (1922-   ).
    Victor Hunt House,
    1957. Malibu (24514 Pacific Coast Highway),
    Calif. Ext. from highway showing pier supports.
                                        AC 1016

789. ——. Ibid. Ext. from beach.   AC 1018

    790. ——.
    Frank Pierson House,
    1955. Malibu (24554 Malibu Road), Calif. Fac.
                                        AC 1019

791. ESHERICK, Joseph (1914-   ).
Hans Bergin House,
1953. Kentfield (7 Treetop Way), Calif. Ext.   AC 86

    792. ——. Ibid. Living room from deck.   AC 87

793. ESHERICK, Joseph (1914-   ).
John Dern House,
1951. Redwood City (950 Palomar Dr.), Calif.
Ext. from below.   AC 88

      794. ——. Ibid. Ext., close view.   AC 90

795. FLAGG, Ernest (1857-1947).
Singer Bldg.,
1908. New York (149 Broadway), N.Y. Ext.   AC 91

      796. FRANKLIN, KUMP and ASSOC.
      City Hall,
      1941. Fresno, Calif. Fac.   AC 92

797. FULLER, Buckminster P.
Ford Rotunda Octet Truss Dome,
1953. Detroit, Mich. Int. Looking into dome 130'
above floor.   AC 94

      798. ——.
      Accordion Truss (Geodesic Dome),
      Northland Center, 1954. Detroit, Mich. Ext.
                                             AC 95

799. ——. Ibid. Int.   AC 95A

      800. FUNK, John (1908-   ).
      Marvin L. Heckendorf House,
      1939. Modesto (215 E. Patricia Lane), Calif. Ext.
                                             AC 97

801. ——.
Otto Maenchen House,
1954. Berkeley (Greenwood Common), Calif.
Garden court.   AC 1020

      802. GANSTER and PEREIRA.
      Lake County Tuberculosis Sanatorium,
      1940. Waukegan (2400 Belvedere St.), Ill. Ext.
                                             AC 98

803. GILBERT, Cass (1859-1934).
Woolworth Bldg.,
1911-1913. New York (233 Broadway), N.Y. Ext. AC 100

      804. ——.
      U.S. Supreme Court Bldg.,
      1935. Washington (2nd St. & Constitution Ave.),
      D.C. Ext.   AC 102

805. GILL, Irving (1870-1936).
G. W. Marston House,
1904-05. San Diego (3525 7th Ave.), Calif. S. Fac.
                                               AC 1022

      806. ——.
      Melville Klauber House,
      1907-10. San Diego (3060 6th Ave.), Calif. Fac.
                                             AC 103

807. GILL, Irving (1870-1936).
Melville Klauber House,
1907-10. San Diego (3060 6th Ave.), Calif. Entr.
Hall & stairway.   AC 104D

    808. ——. Ibid. Dining room.   AC 104

809. ——. Ibid. Second floor, hall & stairway. AC 104C

    810. ——.
    Walter Luther Dodge House (now Los Angeles
    Trade-Technical Jr. College of Household Service),
    1916. Hollywood (950 Kings Rd.), Calif.
    Ext.   AC 1023

811. ——.
First Church of Christ, Scientist,
1931. Coronado, Calif. Ext.   AC 1021

    812. GOFF, Bruce.
    Joseph Taylor House,
    1948-49. Norman (701 W. Brooks St.), Okla. Ext.
                                        AC 105A

813. ——. Ibid. Int., looking down ramp.   AC 105B

    814. ——. Ibid. Int., looking back toward ramp.
                                        AC 105C

815. GOODHUE, Bertram Grosvenor (1869-1924).
First Baptist Church,
1912. Pittsburgh (Bellefield Ave. & Bayard), Pa.
Ext.   AC 111

    816. ——.
    California Tower (now Museum of Man),
    San Diego Exposition, 1915. San Diego (Balboa
    Pk.), Calif. Fac.   AC 114

817. ——.
Aviary,
San Diego Exposition, 1915. San Diego (Balboa
Pk.), Calif. Ext.   AC 1024

    818. ——.
    General Store,
    1917. Tyrone, N. Mex. Fac.   AC 112

819. ——.
State Capitol,
1916-28. Lincoln, Nebr. Fac.   AC 115

    820. GOODHUE, Bertram Grosvenor (1869-1924),
    with WINSLOW, Carleton M. (1919-   ).
    Public Library,
    1927. Los Angeles (630 W. 5th St.), Calif. Fac.
                                        AC 118

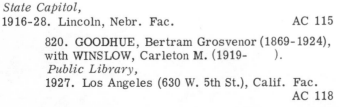

821. GOODWIN and STONE.
Museum of Modern Art,
1939. New York (11 West 53rd St.), N.Y. Ext.   AC 119

    822. GREENE, C. S. (1868- ?) and
GREENE, H. M. (1870- ?).
Blacker-Hill House,
1907. Pasadena (1177 Hillcrest), Calif. Ext.
                                        AC 120

823. ——. Ibid. Hall entr. & stairway.   AC 121

    824. ——. Ibid. Stair well, balustrade & stained
glass window.

825. ——.
David B. Gamble House,
1909. Pasadena (4 Westmoreland Pl.), Calif.
Fac.   AC 122

    826. ——. Ibid. Oblique view.   AC 122A

827. ——. Ibid. Ext. det. of balcony.   AC 123

    828. ——. Ibid. Close view of wood balcony con-
struction.   AC 123D

829. ——. Ibid. Dining room.   AC 122B

    830. ——.
Pratt House,
1909. Ojai, Calif. Ext. Property of Mr. & Mrs.
Harley Culbert.   AC 124

831. ——.
Thorson House (now Sigma Phi House),
1909. Berkeley, Calif. Ext.   AC 1025

    832. ——.
Prentiss House (now Tuthill House),
1912. Pasadena, Calif. Front view.   AC 125

833. ——. Ibid. Garden court.   AC 125A

    834. GROPIUS, Walter (1883-   ) and BREUER,
Marcel (1902-   ).
Walter Gropius House,
1938. Lincoln, Mass. Entr.   AC 33

835. GROPIUS, Walter (1883-   ) and BREUER,
Marcel (1902-   ).
Walter Gropius House,
1938. Lincoln, Mass. Entr. det.   AC 33A

    836. ———. Ibid. South view.   AC 34

837. ———.
Mrs. Henry G. Chamberlain House,
1940. Wayland, Mass. Ext.   AC 43

    838. ———.
    Aluminum City Terrace Housing,
    1942. New Kensington, Pa. Gen. view.   AC 39

839. HARRIS, Harwell Hamilton (1903-   ).
House in Fellowship Park,
1937. Los Angeles (2311 Fellowship Parkway),
Calif. Ext., view from above. Property of Mr.
& Mrs. Fritz Meier.   AC 134

    840. ———. Ibid. Ext.   AC 134C

841. ———. Ibid. Int.   AC 134B

    842. ———.
    Weston Havens House,
    1940. Berkeley (255 Panoramic Way), Calif. Ext.
    NW corner.   AC 136C

843. ———. Ibid. Deck.   AC 136B

    844. ———. Ibid. Court.   AC 136D

845. ———. Ibid. Living room.   AC 137

    846. ———.
    Ralph Johnson House,
    1949. Los Angeles (10261 Chrysanthemum Lane),
    Calif. Ext.   AC 138

847. ———. Ibid. Int. from entr. hall looking
toward dining room & terrace.   AC 138B

    848. ———. Ibid. Living room.   AC 138C

849. HARRISON, Wallace Kirkman (1895-   ).
United Nations Bldgs.,
1949. New York (E. 42nd St.), N.Y. View of
entire complex from E.   AC 140

    850. ——. Ibid. Ext. from N.   AC 141A

851. ——. Ibid. Ext. from NW.   AC 141B

    852. ——. Ibid. Glass wall of Secretariat.
                                            AC 142

853. ——. Ibid. Assembly, main auditorium.   AC 143

    854. HARRISON and ABRAMOVITZ.
    Aluminum Co. of America Bldg.,
    1950. Pittsburgh (Smithfield & 6th St.), Pa. Ext.
                                            AC 144

855. ——. Ibid. Ext. lower part.   AC 144A

    856. ——.
    Sophronia Brooks Hall Auditorium,
    Oberlin College,
    1953. Oberlin, Ohio. Ext.   AC 146

857. ——.
Three Faiths Chapel,
Brandeis University,
1954. Waltham, Mass. Gen. view.   AC 316

    858. HELMUTH, YAMASAKI and LEINWEBER.
    (Engineers: Becker, Roberts & Schaefer).
    Airport Terminal Bldg.,
    1954. St. Louis, Mo. Ext.   AC 499

859. ——. Ibid. Ext. at night.   AC 499A

    860. ——. Ibid. Int., diagonal view.   AC 500

861. ——. Ibid. Int., lateral view.   AC 500B

    862. HOFFMAN and CHALFIN.
    Vizcaya (now Dade County Art Museum),
    1916. Miami, Fla. Ext. and gardens.   CPC 143A

863. HOOD, Raymond (1881-1934).
McGraw-Hill Bldg.,
1929-30. New York (330 W. 42nd St.), N.Y. Ext.   AC 152

864. HOWARD, John Galen (1864-1931).
Gregory House,
1903. Berkeley (Greenwood Ter.), Calif. Ext.
from ter. Property of William Wilson Wurster.
AC 160

865. ——.
Hearst Memorial Mining Bldg.,
University of California,
1907. Berkeley, Calif. Fac.   AC 1026

866. HOWE, George (1886-1955).
Fortune Rock House,
1939. Somesville, Maine. Ext. Property of Clara
Fargo Thomas.   AC 166

867. ——. Ibid. Det. of cantilever.   AC 166A

868. HOWE and LESCAZE.
The Philadelphia Saving Fund Society,
1932. Philadelphia (1212 Market St.), Pa. Ext.
AC 162

869. ——. Ibid. Ext. det.   AC 163

870. ——. Ibid. Banking floor.   AC 164

871. HOWELLS and HOOD
Chicago Tribune Bldg.,
1924. Chicago (435 N. Michigan), Ill. Ext.   AC 151

872. ——.
Daily News Bldg.,
1930. New York (220 E. 42nd St.), N.Y. Ext.
AC 153

873. HOYT, Burnham (1887-   ).
Red Rocks Amphitheatre,
1944. Denver, Colo. View from stage.   AC 169

874. ——. Ibid. View from top of amphitheatre.
AC 169A

875. ——. Ibid. Stage.   AC 169B

876. HUNT, Myron (1868-1952) and GREY,
Elmer.
Polytechnic Elementary School,
1907. Pasadena (1030 E. Calif. St.), Calif. Ext.
AC 1027

877. JOHNSON, Philip (1906-   ).
Johnson House,
1949. New Canaan (Ponus St.), Conn. Glass house
& guest house. Gen. view.   AC 172

    878. ——. Ibid. Ext. of glass house.   AC 172A

879. ——. Ibid. Ext. of glass house, night
view.   AC 173A

    880. ——. Ibid. Int. of glass house.   AC 173

881. ——. Ibid.
Guest House,
1954. Int. Wire sculpture by LASSAW, Ibram.   AC 174

    882. ——.
    Rockefeller Guest House,
    1950. New York (52nd St.), N.Y. Living room with
    court. Property of Mus. Mod. Art.   AC 176

883. ——.
Richard Hodgson House,
1951. New Canaan (Ponus St.), Conn. Ext.   AC 178

    884. ——.
    Wiley House,
    1952-53. New Canaan (Sleepy Hollow Rd.), Conn.
    Ext. from upper level.   AC 179

885. ——. Ibid. Ext. from lower level.   AC 179A
    886. ——. Ibid. Living room.   AC 181

887. ——. Ibid. Living room toward kitchen
area.   AC 181A

    888. ——.
    Davis House,
    1953. Wayzata, Minn. Ext.   AC 182A

889. ——. Ibid. Living room, dining room &
court.   AC 183

    890. ——.
    Synagogue,
    1954-55. Portchester, N.Y. Ext.   AC 185

891. JOHNSON, Philip (1906-   ).
Synagogue,
1954-55. Portchester, N.Y. Main hall.   AC 186

892. JONES and EMMONS.
Emmons House,
1955-56. Pacific Palisades (661 Brooktree Rd.),
Calif. Garden court.   AC 1028

893. KAHN, Albert (1869-1942), with WILBY.
Third Ford Factory,
1910-17. Highland Park (Woodward Ave. &
Manchester St.), Mich. Ext.   AC 187

894. ———. Ibid. Int.   AC 188

895. ———.
Ford Motor Co. Administration Bldg.,
1928. Dearborn, Mich. Ext.   AC 189A

896. ———.
Dodge Truck Plant, Chrysler Corp.,
1938. Warren Township (Mound Rd.), Mich. Ext.
          AC 191

897. ———. Ibid. *Final Inspection and Repair
Area.* Int.   AC 192

898. ———.
Burroughs Adding Machine Co.,
1938. Plymouth, Mich. Ext.   AC 193

899. ———.
Willow Run Ford Factory,
1942. Willow Run, Mich. Ext.   AC 196

900. KAHN, Ely Jacques (1884-   ).
Municipal Asphalt Plant,
1944. New York (East River Dr. at E. 90th St.),
N.Y. Ext.   AC 197

901. ———.
2 Park Avenue Bldg.,
1927. New York, N.Y. Gen. view.   AC 198

902. KAHN, Louis L. (1901-   ).
Art Gallery—Design Center,
Yale University, 1951-53. Ext.   AC 200A

903. ———. Ibid. Int.   AC 200

904. KOCH, Carl (1912-   ).
Koch House (now A. G. Hill House),
1940. Belmont (77 Snake Hill Rd.), Mass. Ext.
          AC 204

905. KOCH, Carl.
Koch House (now A. G. Hill House),
1940. Belmont (77 Snake Hill Rd.), Mass. Ext.,
side view.   AC 204A

*906. KOCH and ASSOC.
"Techbuilt" Stoddard House,
1953. Williamstown, Mass. Ext.   AC 207

907. ——. Ibid. Int.   AC 207A

908. ——.
Apartment House,
1950. Cambridge (100 Memorial Drive), Mass.
Ext.   AC 209

909. KUMP, Ernest J. (1911-   ).
San Jose High School,
1952. San Jose, Calif. Administration wing.   AC 211A

910. ——.
Las Lomas High School,
1950. Walnut Creek, Calif. Ext.   AC 1053

911. KUMP and FRANKLIN.
Acalanes Union High School,
1940-41. Lafayette, Calif. Gen. view.   AC 215A

912. ——. Ibid. Ext., det.   AC 215

913. ——. Ibid. Classroom.   AC 214

914. LADD, Thornton (1924-   ).
Lillian B. Ladd House,
1949. Pasadena (1280 Glen Oaks), Calif. Entr.
court, main house on right.   AC 1029

915. ——. Ibid. Dining room from garden.   AC 1032

916. ——. Ibid. Water garden & study.   AC 1031

917. ——. Ibid. Pool & lanai.   AC 1030

918. LESCAZE, William (1896-   ), with
HEITSCHMIDT, Earl T. (1894-   ).
CBS Bldg.,
1937-38. Hollywood (Sunset Blvd.), Calif.
Ext.   AC 218

_____
*Carl Koch Assoc.: Robert Woods Kennedy (1911-   ). Carl
Koch (1912-   ). Vernon DeMars (1908-   ). Ralph Rapson
(1915-   ). William Haskins Brown (1910-   ).

919. LYNDON, Maynard (1907-   ).
Vista Elementary School (now Santa Fe),
1950. Vista, Calif. Gen. view.   AC 220

    920. ——. Ibid. Covered walk.   AC 220B

921. McCORMACK, Walter R.
Cedar Central Apartments,
1936. Cleveland (2202 E. 30th St.), Ohio. Ext.   CPC 78

    922. McKENZIE, VOORHEES and GMELIN.
Barclay-Vesey Telephone Bldg.,
1926. New York (Barclay & Vesey Sts.), N.Y.
Ext.   AC 361

923. McKIM, MEAD and WHITE.
Oelrich House,
1903. Newport, R.I. Ext.   AC 221A

    924. ——.
Columbia University,
1901-06. New York, N.Y. Gen. view.   AC 223

925. ——. Ibid. Library. Ext.   AC 224

    926. ——.
Pennsylvania Railroad Station,
1906. New York (34th St. & 7th Ave.), N.Y. Ext.
          AC 226

927. ——. Ibid. Int., main Concourse.   AC 227

    928. ——.
General Post Office,
1912. New York (33rd St. & 8th Ave.), N.Y. Ext.
          AC 230

929. ——. Ibid. Int.   AC 231

    930. ——.
State Capitol,
1914. Providence, R.I. Fac.   AC 233

931. MAYBECK, Bernard (1862-1957).
David Boyden House,
n.d. Berkeley (1208 Shattuck Ave.), Calif.
Corner view. Property of Mrs. F.B.Wood.   AC 1037

    932. ——.
Denzel C. and Vida Allen House,
1900-06. Berkeley (1200 Shattuck), Calif. Street
side.   AC 1034

933. MAYBECK, Bernard (1862-1957).
Denzel C. and Vida Allen House,
1900-06. Berkeley (1200 Shattuck), Calif. Garden
side.   AC 1035

    934. ——.
    Mrs. Leon L. Roos House,
    1909. San Francisco (3500 Jackson St.), Calif.
    Ext.   AC 237

935. ——.
First Church of Christ Scientist,
1912. Berkeley (2619 Dwight Way), Calif. Ext.   AC 240

    936. ——. Ibid. Gateway.   AC 241

937. ——.
Panama-Pacific Exposition,
1914. San Francisco, Calif. Gen. view.   AC 243

    938. ——. Ibid. *Rotunda.* Det.   AC 243A

939. ——. Ibid. *Propylaeum.* Det.   AC 244

    940. ——.
    Packard Showroom (now Chrysler),
    n.d. San Francisco (Van Ness & Ellis), Calif.
    Ext.   AC 1038

941. ——.
Women's Gymnasium or Hearst Memorial
Gymnasium,
University of California,
1925. Berkeley,(Bancroft Way), Calif. Fac.   AC 1040

    942. ——. Ibid. Pool.   AC 1039

943. MENDELSOHN, Eric (1887-1953).
Cleveland Park Synagogue,
1950. Cleveland (3325 Euclid Hts. Blvd.), Ohio.
Ext.   AC 247

    944. ——. Ibid. Ext.; classrooms in foreground,
    temple in rear.   AC 247A

945. ——. Ibid. Int.   AC 246A

    946. ——.
    Leon Russell House,
    1952. San Francisco (3778 Washington St.), Calif.
    Ext.   AC 1041

947. MENDELSOHN, Eric (1887-1953).
Leon Russell House,
1952. San Francisco (3778 Washington St.), Calif.
Front entr. & patio. AC 1042

948. ——. Ibid. Rear view. AC 1043

949. MIES van der ROHE, Ludwig (1886-   ).
Promontory Apartments,
1950. Chicago (5530 S. Shore Drive), Ill. Ext. AC 260

950. ——.
Apartment Houses,
1951. Chicago (860 Lake Shore Drive), Ill. Gen.
view. AC 262

951. ——. Ibid. Det. entr. AC 263

952. ——.
Illinois Institute of Technology,
1939-56. Chicago, Ill. Gen. view. AC 248

953. ——. Ibid.
Metallurgical Research Center.
Ext. AC 250

954. ——. Ibid.
Alumni Memorial Hall.
Ext. AC 252

955. ——. Ibid.
Alumni Memorial Hall.
Ext., det. of corner. AC 253

956. ——. Ibid.
Chapel.
Ext. AC 255

957. ——. Ibid.
Chapel.
Int. AC 255A

958. ——. Ibid.
Architecture Bldg.,
Ext. AC 256

959. ——. Ibid.
Architecture Bldg.,
Lobby, lateral view. AC 257

960. ——. Ibid. Lobby, longitudinal view.
AC 257A

961. MIES van der ROHE, Ludwig and JOHNSON, Philip.
Seagram's Bldg.,
1957. New York (Park Ave. & 53rd St.), N.Y.
Ext.   AC 264

962. ——. Ibid. Ext. at night.   AC 264A

963. NEUTRA, Richard (1892-   ).
Lovell House,
1929. Los Angeles (4616 Dundee Dr.), Calif. Ext.
Property of Mr. & Mrs. Leo A. Goldberg.   AC 266

964. ——.
Warren Tremaine House,
1946. Santa Barbara (25 Moore Rd.), Calif. Ext.
from garden.   AC 1046

965. ——. Ibid. Ext. & terrace.   AC 1047

966. ——. Ibid. View from terrace into living
room.   AC 1044

967. ——. Ibid. Living room.   AC 1045

968. ——.
Experimental School,
1934-35. Bell, Calif. Ext.   AC 269

969. ——.
Amalgamated Clothing Workers' Bldg.,
1948. Los Angeles (2501 S. Hill St.), Calif. Ext.   AC 274

970. ——.
Northwestern Mutual Insurance Co. Bldg.,
1950. Los Angeles (641 S. Westmoreland), Calif.
Ext.   AC 278

971. NOWICKI, Mathew (1910-49) and DIETRICK, Wm. Henley (1905-   ).
State Fair Arena,
1953. Raleigh, N.C. Ext.   AC 281

972. PEI, I. M. (1917-   ).
Mile-High Office Complex,
1954. Denver (17th & Colton Sts.), Colo. Corner
det.   AC 1076

973. ——. Ibid. Det. vaulted vestibule.   AC 1077

974. PEREIRA and LUCKMAN.
CBS Television City,
1952. Hollywood, Calif. Ext.   AC 1048

975. PERKINS and WILL.
Drexel School,
1947. Cicero (36th St. & 54th Court), Ill. Ext.   AC 283

976. ——.
Heathcote School,
1954. Scarsdale (Palmer Ave.), N.Y. Gen. view.
AC 286

977. POLK, Willis Jefferson (1867-1924).
Hallidie Bldg. (now Atkins Clothing Co.),
1915-17. San Francisco (130-152 Sutter St.),
Calif. Fac., first floor renovated.   AC 287

978. PURCELL and ELMSLIE.
Bradley House,
1911. Wood's Hole, Mass. Ext.   AC 291

979. ——.
The Stewart Memorial Church,
1911. Minneapolis, Minn. Ext.   AC 288

980. ——. Ibid. Int.   AC 289

981. ——.
First National Bank,
1920. Adams, Minn. Ext.   AC 297

982. ——.
Second National Bank,
1924. Aurora, Ill. Ext.   AC 298

983. ——. Ibid. Fac.   AC 298A

984. PURCELL, FRIECK and ELMSLIE.
Edison Shop,
1913. Chicago (229 S. Wabash & Adams), Ill. Ext.
AC 292

985. ——.
Merchants' National Bank,
1913. Winona, Minn. Ext.   AC 293

986. REID, John Lyon (1906-   ).
Hillsdale High School,
1955. San Mateo (31st Ave. & Alameda de Las
Pulgas), Calif. Entr. to classroom wing. AC 1049

987. ——. Ibid. Court.   AC 1052

988. ——. Ibid.
Boys' Gymnasium.
Ext.   AC 1050

989. ROGERS, James Gamble (1901-   ).
Columbia-Presbyterian Medical Center,
1928. New York (Broadway & 168th St.), N.Y. Ext.   AC 299

990. ——.
Harkness Tower,
Yale University,
1931. New Haven, Conn. Gen. view.   AC 300A

991. RUDOLPH, Paul (1918-   ).
Umbrella House, Lido Shores,
1953. Sarasota (1300 West Way Dr.), Fla. Ext.   AC 301

992. SAARINEN, Eliel (1873-1950).
Cranbrook School,
1928-41. Bloomfield Hills, Mich. Ext.   AC 322

993. SAARINEN, Eliel & Eero.
*Tabernacle Church of Christ (now First
Christian Church),*
1940. Columbus (5th & Lafayette), Ind. Ext.   AC 324

994. ——. Ibid. Int.   AC 325

995. SAARINEN, Eliel & Eero; PERKINS,
WHEELER & WILL.
Crow Island Elementary School,
1940. Winnetka, Ill. Ext.   AC 327

996. SAARINEN, SWANSON & SAARINEN.
Des Moines Art Center,
1944-48. Des Moines, Iowa. Ext.   AC 307

997. ——. Ibid. Int.   AC 307A

998. SAARINEN, SAARINEN and ASSOC.
General Motors Technical Center,
1949-56. Warren, Mich. Gen. view lake front.
AC 309

999. ——. Ibid.
Service Section.
Ext.   AC 310

1000. ——. Ibid.
Design Center.
Int. staircase.   AC 311

1001. ——. Ibid.
Dome.
Ext.   AC 312

1002. ——. Ibid.
Dome.
Int.   AC 313

1003. SAARINEN, Eero and ASSOC.
Harvey Ingham Hall of Science (foreground)
and *Pharmacy Bldg.*,
Drake University, 1950. Des Moines, Iowa.
Ext.   AC 314

    1004. ——.
    Ridgewood Quadrangle,
    Brandeis University, 1951. Waltham, Mass. Gen.
    view.   AC 315

1005. ——.
Auditorium and Chapel,
Massachusetts Institute of Technology, 1954.
Cambridge, Mass. Gen. view from above.   AC 317

    1006. ——.
    Auditorium.
    Ext.   AC 318

1007. ——. Ibid. View from above.   AC 318A

    1008. ——. Ibid. Int.   AC 319

1009. ——.
Chapel.
Ext.   AC 320

    1010. ——. Ibid. Int.   AC 321

1011. SCHAITTACHER, BAKEWELL and BROWN.
Temple Emanu-El,
1925. San Francisco (Arguello Blvd. & Lake Sts.),
Calif. Ext.   AC 1054

    1012. ——. Ibid. Entr. & patio.   AC 1055

1013. SCHINDLER, Rudolph M. (1890-1953).
Ralph Walker House (now Alfonso Giella),
1937. Los Angeles, Calif. Ext.   AC 1060

    1014. ——.
    Apartments,
    1925; second story 1936; remodeled 1950.
    La Jolla (309 Playa del Sur), Calif. Ext.
                                             AC 1059A

1015. ——. Ibid. View toward garages.   AC 1059

    1016. ——.
    Falk Apartments,
    1939. Los Angeles (3631 Carnation Ave.), Calif.
    Ext.   AC 1056

1017. SCHINDLER, Rudolf M. (1890-1953).
Herman Sachs Apartments,
1927-28. Los Angeles, Calif. Ext.   AC 1057

    1018. ——. Ibid. Ext. stairway to garden.
                           AC 1058

1019. SCHMIDT, GARDEN and MARTIN.
Montgomery Ward Warehouses,
1906-07. Chicago (618 W. Chicago Ave. Bridge),
Ill. Ext.   AC 331A

    1020. SCHWEIKHER, Paul (1903-   ).
    Louis C. Upton House,
    1950. Paradise Valley, Ariz. Int.   AC 335

1021. ——.
Maryville College Chapel and Theatre,
1953-54. Maryville, Tenn. Ext.   AC 336

    1022. ——. Ibid. Court.   AC 337

1023. ——. Ibid. Int. of theatre.   AC 337A

    1024. ——.
    Josiah Willard Gibbs Physics Laboratory,
    Yale University, 1954-55. New Haven, Conn.
    Ext.   AC 338

1025. SHAW, Howard Van Doren.
Henneberry Bldg.,
1905. Chicago (1139-43 S. Wabash Ave.), Ill.
Ext.   AC 333

    1026. SHREVE, BLY, DEL GAUDIO, HOLDEN
    & LESCAZE.
    Williamsburg Houses,
    1936. Brooklyn, N.Y. Gen. view.   CPC 176

1027. SHREVE, LAMB and HARMON.
Empire State Bldg.,
1931. New York (5th Ave. & 34th St.), N.Y. Ext.   AC 339

    1028. SHURCLIFF and SHEPLEY.
    Paul Revere Mall,
    1934. Boston, Mass. View from Hanover St.
                           CPC 32

1029. ——. Ibid. View from Unity St.   CPC 32A

    1030. SKIDMORE, OWINGS and MERRILL.
    Capitol Area Improvement Project.
    Model. County Court House, Nashville, Tenn.
                           CPC 151

1031. SKIDMORE, OWINGS and MERRILL.
Recreation Bldg., Great Lakes Naval Training Center,
1942. Near N. Chicago, Ill. Ext.   AC 340

    1032. ——. Ibid. Entr.   AC 340A

1033. ——.
Owens-Corning Fiberglas Corporation,
1946-47. New York (16 E. 56th St.), N.Y. Fac.   AC 341

    1034. ——.
    Garden Apartments,
    1950. Oak Ridge, Tenn. Gen. view.   AC 342

1035. ——.
Veterans Administration Hospital,
1950. Brooklyn, N.Y. Ext.   AC 344

    1036. ——.
    Terrace Hilton Hotel,
    1950. Cincinnati (6th St.), Ohio. Ext.   AC 345

1037. ——.
Lever House,
1952. New York (390 Park Ave.), N.Y. Ext.   AC 346

    1038. ——.
    Inland Steel Bldg.,
    1954. Chicago (Dearborn & Monroe), Ill. Ext.
                                                AC 347

1039. ——. Ibid. Ext. det.   AC 347A

    1040. ——.
    Manufacturers Trust Co.,
    1954. New York (5th Ave. & 43rd), N.Y. Ext.
                                               AC 348A

1041. ——. Ibid. Ext. at night.   AC 348

    1042. STARRETT Bros. and EKEN.
    Point Park Development for Equitable Life,
    1950-   . Pittsburgh, Pa. Gen. view.   AC 244

1043. STODDARD, George Wellington (1895-   ).
Stadium Addition,
University of Washington, 1951. Seattle, Wash.
Ext., rear.   AC 1062

    1044. ——. Ibid. Det. showing spiral ramps.
                                               AC 1063

1045. THOMAS, Andrew J.
Abbott Court,
1928. Radburn, N.J. Gen. view.   CPC 252

1046. TWITCHELL, Ralph S. (1891-   ).
Miller House (now Mario Lucci House),
1947. Casey Key, Fla. Ext.   AC 303

1047. ——. Ibid. Living room.   AC 304

1048. ——. Ibid. Living room, toward fireplace.
          AC 304A

1049. TWITCHELL and RUDOLPH.
W. K. Healey House,
1950. Sarasota, Fla. Ext.   AC 306

1050. VAN ALLEN, William (1907-   ).
Chrysler Bldg.,
1930. New York (42 St. at Lexington), N.Y. Ext.
          AC 360

*1051. VARIOUS ARCHITECTS.
Rockefeller Center,
1931-39. New York (5th Ave. & 50th St.), N.Y.
Gen. view from the east.   AC 154

1052. ——. Ibid. Ext. view of plaza.   AC 158

1053. WALKER and ASSOC.
Charles Hayden Memorial Library,
Massachusetts Institute of Technology, 1949-50.
Cambridge, Mass. Ext.   AC 364

1054. WARNECKE, Carl.
Mira Vista Elementary School,
1951. Richmond, Calif. Ext.   AC 1064

1055. WARREN and WETMORE.
Grand Central Terminal,
1903-13. New York (42nd St. & Park Ave.), N.Y.
Ext.   AC 367

1056. ——. Ibid. Grand concourse.   AC 368

1057. WATKIN, William Ward (1886-1952), with
CRAM, GOODHUE and FERGUSON.
Chemistry Laboratories,
Rice Institute, 1924-25. Houston, Tex. Ext.   AC 108

1058. WEED, Robert Law and MANLEY,
Marion I., ASSOC.
Student Union Bldg.,
University of Miami, 1948. Coral Gables, Fla.
Ext.   CAC 216

*See Appendix A

1059. WEED, Robert Law and MANLEY,
Marion I., ASSOC.
Dormitories,
University of Miami, 1948. Coral Gables, Fla.
Gen. view.   AC 217

   1060. WILLIAMSON, Donald MacLean and
JOHNSON, Charles M.
Hyperbolic Paraboloid,
1957. Laguna Beach, Calif. Ext. view from
above.   AC 1065

1061. ——. Ibid. Ext.   AC 1066

   1062. ——. Ibid. Det. of footing and
buttress.   AC 1067

1063. WRIGHT, Frank Lloyd (1869-1959).
Misses Lloyd Jones' Windmill,
1896. Hillside, Spring Green, Wis. Ext.   AC 1078

   1064. ——.
B. Harley Bradley House,
1900. Kankakee (701 S. Harrison Ave.), Ill. Ext.
                                              AC 370

1065. ——.
Arthur Heurtley House (now Nick Forte House),
1902. Oak Park (318 Forest Ave.), Ill. Ext. AC 371

   1066. ——.
Ward Willitts House,
1902. Highland Park (1445 Sheridan Rd.), Ill. Ext.
Property of Harold Kerman.   AC 373

1067. ——. Ibid. Living room.   AC 373A

   1068. ——.
Susan Laurence Dana House,
1903. Springfield, Ill. Ext.   AC 380A

1069. ——. Ibid. Ext. gallery.   AC 380B

   1070. ——.
Darwin D. Martin House,
1904. Buffalo (123 Jewett Parkway), N.Y. Ext.
Property of Sebastian J. Tauriello.   AC 385

1071. ——.
Edwin H. Cheney House,
1904. Oak Park (520 N. East Ave.), Ill. Ext. AC 387

   1072. ——.
W. A. Glasner House,
1905. Glencoe (850 Sheridan Rd.), Ill. Ext.
Property of Rudolph & Elizabeth Nedved. AC 389

1073. WRIGHT, Frank Lloyd (1869-1959).
Avery Coonley House,
1908. Riverside, Ill. Ext. with pergola. Property
of S. K. Shull.   AC 398

    1074. ——. Ibid. Hall.   AC 400

1075. ——. Ibid. Living room.   AC 399

    1076. ——.
    Isabel Roberts House,
    1908. River Forest (603 Edgewood Pl.), Ill. Ext.
    Property of Warren P. Scott.   AC 401A

1077. ——. Ibid. Living room.   AC 402

    1078. ——.
    Mrs. Thomas H. Gale House,
    1909. Oak Park (6 Elizabeth Ct.), Ill. Ext.
                              AC 403

1079. ——.
Frederick C. Robie House,
1909. Chicago (5757 Woodlawn Ave.), Ill. Ext.   AC 405

    1080. ——. Ibid. Ext., det.   AC 406

1081. ——. Ibid. Ext., det.   AC 406A

    1082. ——. Ibid. Int.   AC 407

1083. ——.
Avery Coonley Playhouse,
1912. Riverside (350 Fairbanks Rd.), Ill. Ext.   AC 413

    1084. ——.
    Emil Bach House,
    1915. Chicago (7415 Sheridan Rd.), Ill. Ext.
    Property of Manuel Weiss, M.D.   AC 417

1085. ——.
Hollyhock House,
1920. Los Angeles (Sunset & Hollywood Blvd.),
Calif. Ext.   AC 424

    1086. ——.
    John Storer House,
    1923. Los Angeles (8161 Hollywood Blvd.), Calif.
    Ext. Property of Dr. & Mrs. Otto Neurath.
                              AC 428

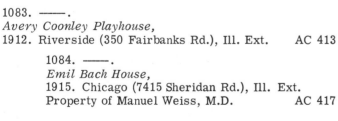

1087. WRIGHT, Frank Lloyd (1869-1959).
John Storer House,
1923. Los Angeles (8161 Hollywood Blvd.), Calif.
Int., fireplace. Property of Dr. & Mrs. Otto
Neurath.   AC 428B

    1088. ——.
    Charles Ennis House,
    1923. Los Angeles (2607 Glendower Ave.), Calif.
    Entr., uphill side.   AC 429

1089. ——. Ibid. Entr., downhill side.   AC 429B

    1090. ——.
    Samuel Freeman House,
    1924. Los Angeles (1962 Glencoe Way), Calif.
    Ext., from rear garden.   AC 430B

1091. ——. Ibid. Ext., det. of entr.   AC 430A

    1092. ——. Ibid. Living room.   AC 431

1093. ——. Ibid. Int.   AC 431A

    1094. ——.
    Richard Lloyd Jones House,
    1929. Tulsa (3700 S. Birmingham), Okla. Rear
    view from carport roof.   AC 435

1095. ——.
Malcolm M. Willey House,
1934. Minneapolis, Minn. Ext.   AC 443

    1096. ——. Ibid. Living room.   AC 444

1097. ——.
Edgar J. Kaufmann House,
1936. Bear Run, Pa. View from below waterfall. AC 446

    1098. ——. Ibid. Ext. from across glen.
                               AC 446A

1099. ——. Ibid. Ext. from bridge.   AC 447

    1100. ——. Ibid. Ext. from ent.   AC 448

1101. WRIGHT, Frank Lloyd (1869-1959).
Edgar J. Kaufmann House,
1936. Bear Run, Pa.
Ext. det. from driveway.   AC 448A

    1102. ——.
    Paul R. Hanna House,
    1937. Stanford U. (Frenchman's Rd.), Calif. Ext.
                            AC 456

1103. ——. Ibid. Patio.   AC 456A

    1104. ——. Ibid. Living room.   AC 457

1105. ——. Ibid. View from living room into
dining room.   AC 457A

    1106. ——. Ibid. Study.   AC 457C

1107. ——.
George D. Sturges House,
1939. Brentwood Heights (449 Skyeway Rd.),
Calif. Ext.   AC 467

    1108. ——.
    Lloyd Lewis House,
    1940. Libertyville (Little St. Mary's Rd.), Ill.
    Ext. Property of Mrs. Lloyd Lewis.   AC 468

1109. ——. Ibid. Ext. from below.   AC 468A

    1110. ——. Ibid. Living room.   AC 469

1111. ——.
Herbert Jacobs House II,
1948. Middleton, Wis. Ext.   AC 479

    1112. ——. Ibid. Ext. front.   AC 479A

1113. ——. Ibid. Living room.   AC 481

    1114. ——.
    David Wright House,
    1951. Scottsdale (Exeter St.), Ariz. Ext. AC 1068

1115. WRIGHT, Frank Lloyd (1869-1959).
David Wright House,
1951. Scottsdale (Exeter St.), Ariz. View from
SE with Camelback Mt. behind.   AC 1069

    1116. ———. Ibid. View from NE.   AC 1070

1117. ———. Ibid. View from ramp.   AC 1071

    1118. ———.
Taliesin I,
1911. Spring Green, Wis. Entr. loggia.   AC 411

1119. ———.
Taliesin III,
1925. Spring Green, Wis. Ext. from E, lake in
foreground.   AC 434B

    1120. ———. Ibid. West side.   AC 434A

1121. ———. Ibid. Living room.   AC 434

    1122. ———.
Taliesin West,
1938. Scottsdale (Shea Blvd.), Ariz. Gen.
view.   AC 459

1123. ———. Ibid. Terrace.   AC 460

    1124. ———. Ibid. SE side showing gong and
drafting room.   AC 460A

1125. ———. Ibid. Approach to loggia showing
office to left.   AC 460B

    1126. ———. Ibid. Approach from parking lot:
office at left, drafting room at right rear.
                                                  AC 460C

1127. ———. Ibid. Int. of drafting room.   AC 461

    1128. ———. Ibid. View through loggia toward
desert.   AC 462

1129. WRIGHT, Frank Lloyd (1869-1959).
Taliesin West,
1938. Scottsdale (Shea Blvd.), Ariz. Wright's
quarters. Int.   AC 463

    1130. ——.
    The Universalist Church,
    1906. Oak Park (Lake St. & Kenilworth Ave.), Ill.
    Ext.   AC 394

1131. ——. Ibid. Det. of pier capitals.   AC 395

    1132. ——. Ibid. Auditorium.   AC 396

1133. ——.
Unitarian Church,
1947-51. Madison (900 University Bay Dr.), Wis.
Ext.   AC 477

    1134. ——. Ibid. Int.   AC 478

1135. ——.
Hillside Home School,
1902; addition, 1956. Spring Green, Wis. Ext.   AC 378

    1136. ——. Ibid. Ext. from below.   AC 378A

1137. ——.
City National Bank Bldg. and Hotel,
1909. Mason City, Iowa. Ext.   AC 408

    1138. ——.
    A. D. German Warehouse,
    1915. Richland Center, Wis. Ext.   AC 418

1139. ——.
Johnson's Wax and Research Center,   AC 453
1936-39. Racine, Wis. Ext.

    1140. ——. Ibid.,
    Research Laboratory Tower,   AC 453A
    1948-50. Ext.

1141. ——. Ibid. Ext., night view.   AC 451

    1142. ——. Ibid. Int. office area. The Great
    Workroom.   AC 452

1143. WRIGHT, Frank Lloyd (1869-1959).
Florida Southern College,
1940-). Lakeland, Fla. Colonnades, covered
walk.   AC 471

    1144. ——. Ibid.
    Annie Pfeiffer Chapel,
    Ext.   AC 472

1145. ——. Ibid. Int.   AC 473

    1146. ——.
    V. C. Morris Store,
    1949. San Francisco (Maiden Lane), Calif. Fac.
                                                       AC 483

1147. ——. Ibid. Int. near entr.   AC 484

    1148. ——. Ibid. Int. from spiral ramp.
                                                      AC 484A

1149. ——.
Price Tower,
1955. Bartlesville, Okla. Ext.   AC 438

    1150. ——.
    Solomon R. Guggenheim Museum,
    1959. New York (5th Ave.), N.Y. Ext.   AC 475

1151. WRIGHT, Lloyd (1890-   ).
Wayfarers' Chapel,
1951. Palos Verdes, Calif. Ext.   AC 485B

    1152. ——. Ibid. Int.   AC 485

1153. WURDEMAN, Walter C. and BECKET,
Walton D.
General Petroleum Bldg.,
1948. Los Angeles (612 S. Flower St.), Calif.
Ext.   AC 486

    1154. WURSTER, William Wilson (1895-   ).
    Lawrence Halprin House,
    1952. Kentfield (15 Ravine Way), Calif. Ext.
                                                       AC 495

1155. ——. Ibid. Living room.   AC 496

    1156. ——.
    Valencia Gardens,
    1943. San Francisco (Valencia & 15th Sts.), Calif.
    First court, looking SE.   AC 490

1157. WURSTER, William Wilson (1895-   ).
Valencia Gardens,
1943. San Francisco (Valencia & 15th Sts.), Calif.
Looking NW.   AC 490A

    1158. ——.
    Schuckl Canning Co.,
    1942. Sunnyvale (182 S. Fairoaks Ave.), Calif.
    Fac.   AC 491

1159. WURSTER, BERNARDI and EMMONS.
James Kelso House,
1953. Kentfield (Vineyard Way), Calif. Entr.
Landscaping by MUNRO, Duncan.   AC 1075

    1160. ——. Ibid. Rear from pool.   AC 1074

1161. ——.
Leonard Sperry House,
1954. Los Angeles (2090 Mandeville Canyon Rd.),
Calif. Gen. view.   AC 489

    1162. ——. Ibid. Entr. at side.   AC 489B

1163. ——. Ibid. Ext. from pool toward
patio.   AC 489C

    1164. ——.
    Center for Advanced Study in the Behavioral
    Sciences, Inc.,
    c. 1954. Stanford, Calif. Entr. Court to
    Administration Bldg.   AC 1072

1165. ——. Ibid. Study wing and patio.   AC 1073

    1166. YEON, John (1910-   ).
    A. R. Wetzek House,
    1937. Portland (1061 Skyline Blvd.), Ore. Ext.
    Landscaping by YEON.   AC 501

1167. ——.
Lawrence Shaw House,
1951. Portland (12800 S.W. Goodall Rd.), Ore.
Ext.   AC 502

COMMUNITY PLANNING

    1168. *Cross-County Shopping Center,*
    1954-56. Westchester County, N.Y. Gen. view.
                           CPC 208

1169. *Edmondson Village Shopping Center,*
c. 1948. Baltimore, Md. View.   CPC 12

    1170. *Mill Valley Builders Development,*
    c. 1956. Mill Valley, Calif. View.   CPC 305

1171. GRUEN, Victor (1903-   ).
Southdale Shopping Center,
1956. Edina, Minn. Int., sidewalk cafe, shops.   CPC 308

1172. HERDING and BOYD.
Workers' Housing,
c. 1910. Phelps-Dodge Copper Co., Clarkdale,
Ariz. Gen. view.   CPC 76

1173. HILL, HOOVER, HECKLER and
KOHANKIE.
Monongahela Heights Project,
1942. Pittsburgh, Pa. Gen. view.   CPC 239

1174. KENYON, W. M. and MAINE, M. E.
Planned Mining Town,
1917. Ajo, Ariz. Gen. view.   CPC 306

1175. KETCHUM, GINA and SHARP.
Shoppers World,
1950. Framingham, Mass. Gen. view.   CPC 35

1176. SKIDMORE, OWINGS, and MERRILL.
Shopping Plaza,
1943. Oak Ridge (Jackson Sq.), Tenn. Gen. view.
                                                 CPC 219

1177. VOORHEES, WALKER, FOLEY, and
SMITH.
Fresh Meadows,
1948. New York, N.Y. Street view.   CPC 195

ENGINEERING AND TRAFFIC CONTROL

1178. *Lake Washington Floating Bridge,*
n.d. Seattle, Wash. View.   CPC 304

1179. *Pulaski Skyway,*
1930. Hudson County, N.J. View.   CPC 170

1180. TENNESSEE VALLEY AUTHORITY (with
U.S. Bureau of Reclamation).
Norris Dam,
1936. Norris, Tenn. View from below.   AC 359

1181. AMMANN, O. H. (Chief Eng.).
Bronx-Whitestone Bridge,
1939. Flushing, L.I., N.Y. View.   AC 7

1182. ——, with GILBERT, Cass (Consulting
Arch.).
George Washington Bridge (E anchorage),
1927-21. New York, N.Y. View.   AC 101

1183. APPLEGARTH, George A.
Downtown Center Garage,
1955. San Francisco (Mason & O'Farrell Sts.),
Calif.   CPC 277

1184. PANHORST, Frederick W. (Eng.).
Harbor Freeway,
1952-53. Los Angeles, Calif.   CPC 129

1185. PFLEUGER, Timothy.
Union Square Underground Parking Garage,
1942. San Francisco, Calif. Above ground. CPC 278

1186. PURCELL, Charles H., (Chief Eng.).
San Francisco—Oakland Bay Bridge,
1936. California. Cantilever overhead truss from
Yerba Buena Island to Oakland. CPC 274A

1187. ——. Ibid. View from Yerba Buena Island
to San Francisco down center of bridge. CPC 274B

1188. ——. Ibid. View of first suspension at
Yerba Buena Island to San Francisco. CPC 274C

1189. STRAUSS, Joseph B. (1870-1938) (Chief
Eng.).
Golden Gate Bridge,
1933-37. San Francisco, Calif. View from San
Francisco toward Marin County. CPC 274D

1190. ——. Ibid. View from bridge tower.
CPC 274E

1191. SKEGGS, John and BOOKER, B. W. (Asst.
Highway Engs.), PANHORST, F. W. (Structure
Designer).
Interchange Ramps,
1951-55. San Francisco, Calif. Confluence of
James Lick and Central Freeways. CPC 275

DESIGN AND DECORATIVE ARTS OF THE
SEVENTEENTH AND EIGHTEENTH CENTURIES
CHARLES F. MONTGOMERY
COAUTHORS

FLORENCE M. MONTGOMERY   CHARLES F. MONTGOMERY, JR.

SEVENTEENTH-CENTURY FURNITURE

1193. *Arm Chair,*
c. 1650, H. 45''. Pilgrim Hall, Plymouth, Mass.
#1054   DA 156

   1194. *Arm Chair,* Conn.; *Joint Stool,*
   Mass.; *Table,* R.I.; *Bench,* N.E.;
   1650-90, oak; oak; oak, maple & pine; maple &
   pine; H. 43½''; H. 22½''; L. 111½''; L. 81½''.
   Winterthur.   #53.104; #57.538; #53.47;
   #56.94.6   DA 3

1195. *Side Chair,* N.E.; *Table,* N.Y.,
1650-75; 1690-1700; maple, beech, oak; maple;
H. 35''; H. 26''. Winterthur.   #SW 3; #SW 17   DA 8A

   1196. *Table,* Mass.,
   1650-80, oak & maple with red & black, marbleized top, D. 36''. Met. Mus.   #51.12.1.   Gift
   of Mrs. J. Insley Blair, 1951.   DA 69

1197. *Trestle Table,* N.E.,
c. 1650, oak & pine, L. 146½''. Met. Mus.
#10.125.701   Gift of Mrs. Russell Sage, 1909.   DA 68

   1198. *Court Cupboard,* N.E.,
   1670-1700, oak & maple, H. 5'2''. Ford Mus.
   #36.198   DA 129

1199. *Bible Box,* Conn. Valley,
1675-1700, pine, L. 27½''. Winterthur. #54.102.2
                                           DA 8C

   1200. *Chair-Table,* N.E.,
   c. 1675, oak & pine. Met. Mus.   #10.125.697
   Gift of Mrs. Russell Sage, 1909.   DA 67

1201. *Small Chest on Frame,* N.E.,
c. 1675, painted pine, maple. Coll. C. K. Davis,
Fairfield, Conn.   DA 146

   1202. *Sunflower Chest,* Hartford, Conn.,
   1675-1700, oak, H. 38''. Winterthur.   #SW 16
                                           DA 7

1203. *Kas,* L.I., N.Y.,
c. 1675, oak & tulip poplar, H. 70½''. Winterthur.
#52.49   DA 4

   1204. *Arm Chairs,* N.Y.; N.E.;
   c. 1680; 1695; maple; ash & maple; H. 46¼'';
   H. 43¼''. Winterthur.   #SW 36; #SW 5   DA 2

1205. *Bed*, N.E.,
c. 1680-1700, oak. Met. Mus.   #53.14   Gift of
Joseph Downs, 1953.   DA 67A

    1206. *Chest,*
    1690-1700, oak, H. 35½". Nutting Coll.,
    Wadsworth Atheneum.   #1926.303   DA 144

1207. *Candlestand,*
1690-1730, walnut, H. 27". Nutting Coll.,
Wadsworth Atheneum.   #1926.524   DA 145A

    1208. *Chest,*
    1700-10, yellow pine, H. 25". Nutting Coll.,
    Wadsworth Atheneum.   #1926.296   DA 145B

1209. ALDEN, John or WINSLOW, Kenelm(?).
Cradle,
1620-50, oak & pine, H. 32½". Nutting Coll.,
Wadsworth Atheneum.   #1926.365   DA 145C

    1210. DENNIS, Thomas(?), Ipswich, Mass.
    Chest,
    c. 1675, oak, H. 30½". Boston Mus.   #29.1015
                                DA 84

1211. ——.
Chest of Drawers,
1678, oak & maple, painted, L. 45". Winterthur
#57.54.1   DA 6

    1212. ——. (attr.), Ipswich, Mass.
    Spice Chest; Beau Brummel;
    1679; 1694; oak; oak & pine, H. 16¾"; H. 19".
    Winterthur.   #57.540; #52.144   DA 1

1213. ——. (attr.), Ipswich, Mass.
Court Cupboard,
1684, oak, H. 53¾". Winterthur.   #57.542   DA 5

WILLIAM AND MARY FURNITURE

    1214. *Day Bed,* N.E.,
    1700-25, L. 68". Winterthur.   #EL 25   DA 11

1215. *Press (or Turn-up) Bed,* N.E.,
1700-25, maple, H. 86". Winterthur.   #55.783
                                       DA 14A

    1216. *Arm Chairs,* N.Y.; Pa.;
    1700-25, beech, persimmon, aspen, walnut,
    H. 44½"; H. 43½". Winterthur.   #54.516;
    #55.120
                                      DA 15B

1217. *Easy Chair,* N.E.; *Tea Table,* N.Y.;
1700-25, maple & red velvet; walnut, H. 51";
H. 27½". Winterthur.   #1R18; #53.50   DA 13

    1218. *Candlestand; Tables;* N.E.,
    1700-25, maple, H. 26½"; H. 28". Winterthur.
    #SA 35; #SW 40
                                       DA 16

1219. *Chest on Frame; Clock;* N.E.,
1700-25, red gumwood & walnut; walnut; H. 48⅝";
H. 95½". Clock brass works by WARD, Anthony.
Winterthur.   #159; #54.15   DA 10

1220. *Chest,* Guilford, Conn.,
early 18th C., painted, H. 33¼". Met. Mus.
#45.78.4   Gift of Mrs. J. Insley Blair, 1945.
                                               DA 72B

1221. *Chest,* Taunton, Mass.,
c. 1735, painted, H. 32¾", Met. Mus.   #45.78.5
Gift of Mrs. J. Insley Blair, 1945.   DA 72A

1222. *Highboy,* Mass. (prob.),
c. 1700, maple & pine. Met. Mus.   #40.37.3
Joseph Pulitzer Bequest Fund, 1940.   DA 70

1223. *Kas,* Hudson Valley,
c. 1725, tulip poplar, painted in grisaille, H. 70".
Winterthur.   DA 12

1224. *Desk,*
1700-25, burled walnut, Coll. C. K. Davis,
Fairfield, Conn.   DA 147

1225. *Secretary Desk,* N.Y.,
c. 1700, cedar with beech & walnut inlay. Mus.
City N.Y.   #45.112AC   DA 135

1226. *Oval Tavern or Tea Table; Looking Glass;*
N.E., 1700-25, maple; white pine, marbleized;
H. 25"; H. 46". Winterthur.   #54.511; #52.262
                                           DA 9

1227. *Dining Table; Arm Chair;* N.E.,
1700-25, walnut; maple, red oak, leather;
H. 27¾"; H. 47". Winterthur.   #EL 30; #1S25 DA 15A

1228. *Dressing Table; Side Chair;* Pa. (prob.),
1700-25, American beech, H. 29¼"; H. 46½".
Winterthur.   #54.521; #54.519   DA 14B

QUEEN ANNE FURNITURE

1229. *High-post Bed,* R.I.,
1735-50, maple & mahogany, H. 8'. Winterthur.
#55.793   DA 22A

1230. *Bed,* N.E., c. 1750, black birch & soft pine,
H. 85";
Side Chair, (GAINES, John, attr.), 1720-40,
maple, H. 41". Winterthur.   #57.780; #2A22
                                           DA 19

1231. *Side Chair,* Conn.,
c. 1725, cherry, upholstered in red moire,
H. 43½". Winterthur.   #SAA9   DA 18B

1232. *2 Chairs; Stool,* SAVERY, William (prob.);
Dining Table; Looking Glass; Phila.; N.Y.; Va.;
c. 1725-50, walnut, H. 45¼"; H. 17"; H. 30½";
H. 16"; W. 60". Winterthur.   #E921; #EQ17;
#EQ5; #EQ8; #EQ32   DA 25

1233. *Arm Chair,* Phila.,
1740-50, walnut, H. 46". Winterthur.   #EQ30   DA 17

    1234. *3 Side Chairs,* N.Y.; Newport, R.I.; Phila.;
    c. 1730-50; 1740-50, walnut, H. 38½"; H. 39";
    H. 42½". Winterthur.   #EV6; #3F36; #ER12

                            DA 24

1235. *High Chest,* Mass.,
1725-50, burled walnut and pine, H. 71".
Boston Mus.   #29.849   DA 86

    1236. *Chest on Chest,* Conn.,
    1730-50, cherry, H. 91½". Winterthur.   #2D7
                      DA 26

1237. *Highboy,* Hartford Area, Conn.,
1735-50, painted wood, H. 61¼". Winterthur.
#54.507   DA 174

    1238. *Grained Highboy,* Guilford, Conn.,
    c. 1750, painted designs, H. 64". New Haven
    Colony Hist. Soc.   DA 178

1239. *Secretary Desk-Bookcase,* Mass.,
1720-30, walnut, inlaid, H. 88½". Boston Mus.
#39.176   DA 85

    1240. *Desk on Frame,* Boston,
    1725-50, walnut, inlaid, H. 42". Winterthur.
    #SAA7   DA 18A

1241. *Desk on Frame; Arm Chair,* Pa.,
1740-50; 1735-50, walnut; walnut with leather,
H. 38½"; H. 41¾". Winterthur.   #1H48; #1H57
                            DA 28

    1242. *Desk; Easy Chair,* R.I.; N.E.,
    1740-50; 1725-50, maple, H. 41½"; H. 47".
    Winterthur.   #3F10; #2A8   DA 22

1243. *Desk,* N.E.,
c. 1750-70, slant-lid, mahogany on frame,
H. 41¾". Boston Mus.   #36.34   DA 185

    1244. *Sofa or Settee,* Phila., Pa.,
    c. 1740, walnut. Met. Mus.   #25.115.1
    Rogers Fund, 1925
                      DA 71

1245. *Card Table,* N.E.,
c. 1740, walnut, needlework top, H. 27". Boston
Mus.   #46.1256   DA 184

    1246. *Looking Glass; Dressing Table;* Phila.
    (prob.); Md.;
    1730-50; 1725-50, walnut, H. 48"; H. 31".
    Winterthur.   #3F4; #EF22   DA 21

1247. *Mixing Table*, N.E.,
1725-50, mahogany & marble, H. 27¼".
Winterthur.   #57.718   DA 20

 1248. PEARSON, Isaac; WADY, James; BROWN,
Gawen, N.J.; R.I.; Boston,
3 Tall Clocks,
1723; c. 1750; walnut; maple-japanned, H. 80½";
H. 98¼"; H. 93". Winterthur.   #52.252; #233;
#58.96.3   DA 27

1249. PIMM, John, Boston.
High Chest of Drawers,
1740-50, maple & pine, japanned decoration,
H. 86". Winterthur.   #57.1084   DA 23

ROCOCO FURNITURE

 1250. *Bed,* Charleston, S.C.,
1760-95, mahogany, H. 7'3". Winterthur.
#55.799   DA 30

1251. *Arm Chair,* Pa.,
1750-80, ash, hickory, maple, H. 43".
Winterthur.   #BQ46   DA 165

 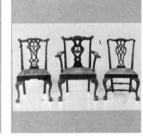

 1252. *2 Chairs; Arm Chair,* Phila.; Mass.; N.Y.,
1750-75, 1760-80; 1765-75, mahogany, H. 38";
H. 36½"; H. 38½". Winterthur.   #52.240.1;
#3A14; #SB40   DA 33

1253. *Chair,* Phila.,
1760-70, mahogany, H. 37⅞". Winterthur.   #EC50
                                      DA 34A

 1254. *Chest of Drawers,* Mass.,
c. 1760, mahogany, H. 33⅞". Boston Mus.
#41.578   DA 87

1255. *Chest of Drawers,* Newport, R.I.,
1765-75, mahogany, H. 34¼". Winterthur.   #3A2
                                      DA 32

 1256. *Chest on Chest,* Newport, R.I.,
1765-80, mahogany, H. 96". Winterthur.
#57.1394   DA 38B

1257. *Chest on Chest,* Mass.,
1770-85, curly maple, H. 86". Winterthur.
#3B46   DA 38

 1258. *High Chest of Drawers,* Phila.,
1775-90, mahogany, H. 90". Winterthur.
#58.592   DA 39

1259. *Secretary Bookcase,*
1760-80, mahogany, H. 8'3½". Boston Mus.
#56.1194   DA 186

 1260. *Looking Glass; Side Table,* Boston(?), Mass.,
1760-70; 1750-83; mahogany, H. 81½"; W. 56¾".
Winterthur.   #EE26; #1F18   DA 29

1261. *Looking Glass*, Phila.,
1765-80, mahogany, gilt, H. 55½". Winterthur.
#52.261   DA 35B

    1262. *Sofa*, Phila.,
    1775-80, mahogany, L. 72¼". Winterthur.
    #58.593.4   DA 34B

1263. *Card Table*, N.Y.,
1750-83, mahogany, 34" sq. Winterthur.
#SB41   DA 31

    1264. *Dressing Table; Arm Chair*, Phila.,
    1769; 1760-70, mahogany, H. 28⅜"; H. 40¼" at
    arms. Winterthur.   #EC41; #56.30.1   DA 35

1265. *Pier Table*, Phila.,
c. 1765, mahogany. Met. Mus. #18.110.27
Kennedy Fund, 1918   DA 74

    1266. *Side Table*,
    1760-80, mahogany, H. 29¾". Coll. Mr. & Mrs.
    Lammot duPont Copeland, Greenville, Del.
                                           DA 131

1267. *Tea Table*, Phila.,
1750-83, mahogany, H. 28⅛". Winterthur.
#EA32   DA 34C

    1268. *Wall Bracket*, Phila.,
    1760-75, stained yellow pine, H. 16½".
    Winterthur.   #24164   DA 40

1269. COGSWELL, John (attr.), Mass.,
Secretary Desk,
1760-70, mahogany, H. 92". Winterthur.
#57.1396   DA 36

    1270. DUNLAP, Samuel, II (prob.), N.H.
    High Chest of Drawers,
    1775-90, maple, H. 83". Winterthur.   #57.1391
                                           DA 37

1271. GODDARD, John (?).
Secretary Desk and Bookcase,
c. 1759, mahogany, H. 105". Rhode Island Hist.
Soc.   DA 130

    1272. ORTES, John Baptiste.
    Armoire,
    c. 1780, walnut, H. 7'9½". Missouri Hist. Soc.
                                           DA 191

1273. RANDOLPH, Benjamin (prob.).
Wing Chair,
c. 1770, mahogany, H. 45½". Phila. Mus.
#29.81.2   DA 124

CLASSICAL FURNITURE

    1274. *Arm Chair*, N.Y.,
    1790-1800, mahogany, H. 39". Boston Mus.
    #39.139   DA 93

1275. *Arm Chair,* N.H.,
1790-1800, Sheraton style, mahogany, H. 47¼".
Met. Mus.   #10.125.313   Gift of Mrs.
Russell Sage, 1909.   DA 75

　　　1276. *Side Chair,* Phila.,
　　　1796, painted beech-wood, H. 38¾". Boston Mus.
　　　#39.108   DA 94B

1277. *Side Chair,* Baltimore; *Arm Chair,* Phila.;
c. 1800; c. 1805; mahogany, H. 37"; H. 33½".
Winterthur.   #55.770.2; #53.58   DA 44

　　　1278. *Chest of Drawers,* Mass.,
　　　c. 1795, mahogany & satinwood, L. 41".
　　　Winterthur.   #3K28   DA 48B

1279. *China Cabinet & Bookcase,* Salem, Mass.,
1790-1805, mahogany & satinwood, H. 93".
Winterthur.   #57.845   DA 49

　　　1280. *Sideboard,* Baltimore,
　　　1795-1800, mahogany, silver & glass, H. 65½".
　　　Met. Mus.   #45.77A,b   Joseph Pulitzer
　　　Bequest Fund, 1945.   DA 73

1281. *Cabinet Top Desk,*
1790-1800, mahogany & satinwood, H. 68¾".
Met. Mus.   #34.135   Fletcher Fund, 1934   DA 77

　　　1282. *Secretary,* Baltimore,
　　　1790-1810, mahogany & satinwood, H. 102".
　　　Winterthur.   #57.775   DA 43

1283. *Girandole Mirror,*
c. 1800, white pine & gilt, H. 42". Winterthur.
#57.750   DA 46B

　　　1284. *Mirror,* N.Y.; *Mirror;*
　　　c. 1800; 1800-15; 60" x 24"; 51" x 27½".
　　　Winterthur.   #57.681; #57.6.15   DA 46

1285. *Ladies' Dressing Table,*
c. 1800, mahogany & satinwood, H. 72". Maryland
Hist. Soc.   DA 132

　　　1286. *Table,* N.Y.,
　　　c. 1790, Hepplewhite, mahogany & satinwood,
　　　H. 28½". Met. Mus.   #34.147   Rogers Fund,
　　　1934   DA 76

1287. *Hunt Board,* Baltimore,
1790-1800, mahogany & satinwood, L. 46½".
Winterthur.   #57.700   DA 51

　　　1288. CHAPIN, Aaron (prob.), Conn.
　　　Secretary Desk,
　　　c. 1790, cherry, inlaid maple, H. 90½".
　　　Winterthur.   DA 47

1289. FINDLAY, John & Hugh.
Painted Bench,
1805, painted decorations, H. 33½". Lent by Mrs.
E. Venable & Mrs. H. de Roth to Baltimore Mus.
#L44.31   DA 133

1290. HOOK, William (1777- ?), Salem, Mass.
Sewing Table,
c. 1808, mahogany, H. 29". Boston Mus.
#39.555   DA 92

1291. LEMON, W. & McINTIRE, Samuel, Salem,
Mass.
Chest on Chest,
1796, mahogany, H. 102½". Boston Mus.
#41.580   DA 91

1292. McINTIRE, Samuel, Salem, Mass.
Side Chair,
c. 1795, mahogany, H. 38⅜". Boston Mus.
#39.174   DA 94A

1293. ———.
Card Table,
1790-1800, mahogany, H. 30". Boston Mus.
#23.16   DA 95

1294. ——— (attr.).
Fire Screen,
c. 1795, mahogany & gilt, H. 59½". Boston Mus.
#28.373   DA 88B

1295. ——— (attr.).
Sofa,
c. 1795, L. 6'8½". Boston Mus.   #23.21   DA 187

1296. ——— (carving attr.).
Sofa,
c. 1795, mahogany, L. 87". Winterthur.
#57.650   DA 45

1297. PHYFE, Duncan, N.Y.
Interior of Phyfe Room,
c. 1800. Winterthur.   DA 50

1298. SEYMOUR, John (act. 1790-1810), Boston.
Arm Chair,
c. 1795, mahogany, H. 38¾". Boston Mus.
#23.32/23.33   DA 89

1299. ——— (maker's label).
Lady's Desk,
1796-1805, mahogany, H. 41½". Winterthur.
#1B16   DA 42B

1300. ——— (attr.).
Wine Cooler,
c. 1795, mahogany & satinwood, H. 22¾". Boston
Mus.   #39.161   DA 88A

1301. ——— and DOGGETT, Fielding (prob.).
Dressing-Glass,
1790-1800, mahogany, satinwood & gilt, H. 30¾".
Boston Mus.   #23.20   DA 90A

1302. SEYMOUR, John and Thomas (attr.), Boston.
Settee,
1795-1805, mahogany, L. 41⅛". Winterthur.
#57.682   DA 42A

1303. SEYMOUR, Thomas, Boston.
Commode,
1809, mahogany & satinwood, H. 41½". Boston
Mus.   #23.19   DA 90B

1304. WILLARD, Simon (1753-1848), Mass.
Banjo Clock & Tall Clock,
c. 1810; c. 1800; mahogany, brass, glass;
mahogany; H. 41"; H. 91". *Tall Clock* gift of Mrs.
Charles K. Davis. Winterthur.   #57.774
                                                                 DA 41

FOLK FURNITURE

1305. *Chest,* rural Pa.,
1788, tulip poplar, H. 28½". Winterthur.   #EY
                                                                 DA 172

1306. *Group of Windsor Furniture,*
provenance varies, 1740-1800, maple, pine, tulip,
ash, etc. Winterthur.   DA 166

1307. ——. Ibid.   DA 166A

1308. ——. Ibid.   DA 166B

SEVENTEENTH-CENTURY SILVER

1309. van der BURG, Cornelis (1653-99), N.Y.
Beaker,
1685, silver, H. 8". Garvan Coll., Yale U.
#1932.100   DA 108C

1310. COWELL, William (1682-1737), Boston.
Spout Cup,
c. 1700, silver, H. 5". Coll. Llora and Mark
Bortman, Boston.   DA 100A

1311. CONEY, John, Boston.
Cup,
1700-10, added engraving on front, H. 3½".
Boston Mus.   DA 189

1312. ——.
Plate,
17th C., D. 11⅛". Boston Mus.   #31.226
                                                 DA 188

1313. ——.
Sugar Box,
c. 1690, silver, H. 4⅞". Boston Mus.
#13.421   DA 100C

1314. DUMMER, Jeremiah; SANDERSON, Robert
& HULL, John; Boston.
Basin, Standing Cup,
silver. Basin: 1695, D. 14⅞", loaned by First
Parish, Cambridge. Standing Cup: c. 1683, H. 8",
loaned by First Church in Boston, Boston Mus.
                                                 DA 98

1315. DUMMER, Jeremiah (1645-1718), Boston, Mass.
Candlesticks,
17th C., silver, H. 10¾". Yale U., Garvan Coll.
#1935.234   DA 109D

1316. ——.
Punch Bowl,
1692, silver, H. 3⁵⁄₁₆". Yale U., Garvan Coll.
#1940.55   DA 109C

1317. DWIGHT, Timothy (1654-1691/2), Boston.
Salver,
bef. 1692, silver, D. 11⅝₁₆". Boston Mus.
#31.227   DA 97C

1318. "I.B.", N.Y.
Covered Cup,
c. 1695, silver, H. 5½". Winterthur.   DA 53

1319. "H.H.", N.Y.
Tumbler Cup,
17th C., silver, H. 2 ⁹₁₆". Garvan Coll., Yale U.
#1931.141   DA 108B

1320. SANDERSON, Robert (1608-93) & HULL,
John (1624-83), Boston.
Beaker & Porringer,
silver. Beaker, 1659, H. 4", lent by First Church
in Boston; Porringer, c. 1665, D. 3¾", Boston
Mus.   #42.252   DA 97

1321. ——.
Beaker,
17th C., silver, H. 6⅜". Garvan Coll., Yale U.
#1936.139   DA 107

1322. SANDERSON, Robert, Boston.
Caudle Cup,
1675-85, silver, H. 5". Winterthur.   DA 52

1323. —— & HULL,
John (1624-83), Boston, Mass.
Coinage,
from 1652-63, silver, New Eng. s.; Willow s.;
Oak s.; Pine s.; Willow 3d.; Willow 2d.; Pine 6d. &
Willow 6d. Garvan Coll., Yale U.   DA 106

1324. —— and DUMMER, J. (1645-1718).
Dram Cups,
2nd half 17th C., silver, Garvan Coll., Yale U.
#1949.78; #1930.1395   DA 109

1325. SANDERSON, Robert (1668-80), Boston.
Tankard,
1670, silver, H. 8³₁₆". Boston Mus.   #37.263   DA 98C

1326. van der SPIEGEL, Jacobus (1668-1708), N.Y.
Tankard,
1697, silver, H. 7¾". Garvan Coll., Yale U.
#1938.15   Top closed.   DA 108

1327. ——. Ibid. Top open.   DA 108A

1328. VARIOUS MAKERS, PLACES, STYLES.
Group of Spoons,
c. 1650 to c. 1800, silver. Winterthur. Figs.
68-69; 72-73; 71-74; 75-76; 91; 77-78; 79-82
                                            DA 59

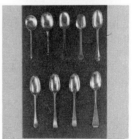

WILLIAM & MARY SILVER

1329. CONEY; WINSLOW; HURST;
Candlestick, Sugar Caster, Salt, Tankard;
c. 1700-10; H. 6⅛"; ?"; 5½". Boston Mus.
#31.217; #53.2208; #32.371   DA 99

1330. CONEY, John (1656-1722), Boston.
Chocolate Pot,
1701, silver, H. 7⅞". Boston Mus.   #29.1091
                                            DA 100B

211

1331. CONEY, John (1656-1722), Boston.
Inkstand,
early 18th C., silver, H. 4¼". Met. Mus.
#24.109.36ad   Bequest of Charles Allen Munn,
1924.   DA 80C

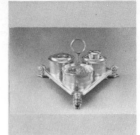

1332. ——.
Montieth,
early 18th C., silver, H. 8½". Garvan Coll.,
Yale U.   #1948.148   DA 110

1333. ——;
van INBURGH, Peter, N.Y.
Porringers,
early 18th C., silver. Garvan Coll., Yale U.
#1930.950; #1930.953; #1931.142   DA 111

1334. CONEY, John (1656-1722), Boston.
Stoughton Cup,
silver, H. 10¼". Fogg Mus.   #877.1927
                                               DA 180A

1335. ——.
Teapot,
c. 1710, silver, H. 7⅛". Met. Mus.   33.120.221
Bequest of A. T. Clearwater, 1933.   DA 80A

1336. DUMMER, Jeremiah (1645-1718), Boston.
Standing Cup & Beaker,
1701; 1705; silver, H. 7½"; H. 4⅜". Lent by
1st Church, Boston, Boston Mus.   DA 101

1337. HILLER, Benjamin, Boston.
Mug,
1714-15, silver, H. 4⅛". Lent by 1st Baptist
Church, Boston, Boston Mus.   DA 99B

1338. NYS, Johannis, Phila.
Chafing Dish,
c. 1720, silver, L. 14¾". Phila. Mus.   #111
                                               DA 121

1339. SYNG, Philip, Jr.
Baptismal Basin,
1712, silver, D. 14¾". Christ Church,
Philadelphia, Pa.   DA 154A

1340. ——.
Flagon,
1712, silver, H: 12". Christ Church, Philadelphia,
Pa.   DA 154

1341. TEN EYCK, J.; van der SPIEGEL, Jacobus,
N.Y.
Trencher Salt; Tazza,
c. 1700, silver, H. 2½"; H. 2¾". Winterthur.
Tazza #1A73   DA 54

1342. VAN DYKE, Peter (1684-1750), N.Y.
Mustard Pot,
early 18th C., silver, H. 5¼". Garvan Coll.,
Yale U.   #1930.1332   DA 111C

1343. van der SPIEGEL; SOUMAINE; VAN DYKE;
JOHNSON; FUETER, N.Y.
American Gold,
1700-84. Spoon & Bells, L. 6¹¹⁄₁₆"; teaspoons,
L. 4"; strainer spoon, L. 4½"; necklace, L. 24";
freedom box, H. ⅝"; coral & bells, L. 5¼". Garvan
Coll., Yale U.   #1947.176; #1932.101; #1930.1100;
#1942.91; #1935.242a-c; #1935.241   DA 119

1344. WINSLOW, Edward (1669-1753), Boston.
Chocolate Pot,
c. 1700, silver, H. 9⅛ . Met. Mus.
#33.120.221   Bequest of A. T. Clearwater, 1933.
                                               DA 80B

1345. WINSLOW, Edward (1669-1753), Boston.
Covered Cup,
early 18th C., silver, H. 11". Garvan Coll.,
Yale U.   #1932.47   DA 111D

    1346. ——.
    Sugar Box,
    1702, silver, H. 5". Winterthur.   DA 55

QUEEN ANNE SILVER

1347. BESLEY, Thauvet, N.Y.
Tea Caddy,
c. 1740, silver, H. 5⅝". Mus. City N.Y.   DA 137

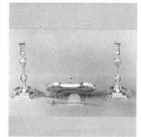

    1348. BURT, John, Boston.
    Candlesticks, Snuffer & Tray,
    c. 1725, silver. Coll. C. K. Davis, Fairfield,
    Conn.   DA 148

1349. HURD, Jacob (1702-58), Boston.
Salt Trencher,
c. 1730, silver, L. 2⅞ . Met. Mus.   43.75
Rogers Fund.   DA 82A

    1350. ——.
    Tea Kettle on Stand,
    1725-50, silver, H. 14⅜". Lent by Mrs. S.
    Cunningham, Boston Mus.   DA 102

1351. ——.
Two-Handled Covered Cup,
1744, silver, H. 15⅛". Garvan Coll., Yale U.
#1932.48   DA 112A

    1352. ——; REVERE, Paul, Sr. (1702-54), Boston.
    Sugar Bowl, Teapot; Creamer,
    1737; c. 1735; c. 1740; silver, 3¾"; 5¾"; 4⅝" .
    Boston Mus.   #42.244; #42.243; #28.45   DA 96

1353. LE ROUX, Charles (1689-1745), N.Y.
Coffee Pot,
1725-45, silver, H. 11". Garvan Coll., Yale U.
#1930.999   DA 113B

    1354. ——.
    Saltcellars,
    c. 1737, silver, H. 2½", inscribed ISA. Met. Mus.
    #35.68.2,3   Dodge Fund, 1935.   DA 82B

1355. POTWINE, John, Boston.
Flagon,
1721-37, silver, H. 13½". Garvan Coll., Yale U.
#1930.1294   DA 112B

    1356. SOUMAINE, Simeon (1685-1750), N.Y.
    Sugar Bowl,
    1725-50, silver, H. 4¼". Garvan Coll., Yale U.
    #1930.1056

1357. VAN DYKE, Peter (1684-1750), N.Y.
Teapot,
1725-35, silver, H. 8¹⁄₁₆". Garvan Coll., Yale U.
#1938.20   DA 113A

    1358. ——.
    Teapot,
    1725-35, silver, H. 7⅛". Garvan Coll., Yale U.
    #1935.230   DA 114B

ROCOCO SILVER

1359. BURT, Benjamin (1729-1805), Boston.
Teapot,
c. 1765, silver, H. 7½". Garvan Coll., Yale U.
#1930.1203   DA 115

1360. FUETER, Daniel Christian (1720-85), N.Y.
Medals,
"Montreal Medal," 1760, silver, D.1¾"; "Happy
While United," 1764, silver, D.2⅛". Garvan Coll.,
Yale U.   #1932.86; #1932.85   DA 118B

1361. HEATH, John, N.Y.
Punch Bowl,
c. 1760, silver, H. 4⁵⁄₁₆". Phillips Coll., Yale U.
#1953.10.3   DA 120

1362. KIERSTEDE, Cornelius (1675-1757), N.Y.
Bowl,
early 18th C., silver, D. 9¾".
Met. Mus.   #38.63   Lee Fund, 1938.   DA 79

1363. MYERS, Myer (1723-95), N.Y.
Cake Basket,
c. 1765, silver, H. incl. handle 11⅛", L. 14½".
Met. Mus.   #54.167   Morris K. Jesup Fund,
1954.   DA 83A

 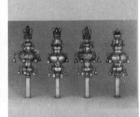

1364. ———.
Crowns of the Law,
c. 1765, silver, H. 14". Touro Synagogue,
Newport, R.I.   DA 150

1365. REVERE, Paul (1735-1818), Boston.
Punch Bowl,
1768, silver, D. 11". Boston Mus.   #49.45   DA 104

1366. RICHARDSON, Joseph.
Sugar Bowl & Teapot,
c. 1760, silver, H. 5½" & 11¼". Hist. Soc. Pa.
                                              DA 152

1367. ———.
Tea Kettle & Stand,
c. 1760, silver, H. 14½". Phila. Mus.   DA 122

1368. ———.
Vegetable Dish,
c. 1775, silver, L. 11". Phila. Mus.   #56.63.2
                                              DA 123

1369. SYNG, Philip, Jr. (1703-89).
Inkstand,
1752, silver, L. 10¼". Coll. Independence Nat'l
Hist. Park, Phila., Pa.   DA 151

1370. ———; DAVID, John, Phila.
Tankard; Sauce Boat & Cruet Stand;
1750-75; c. 1760-85, silver, H. 8⅛"; H. 4¾";
H. 10⁹⁄₁₆". Winterthur.   #1a496; #1a506;
#1a491   DA 56

1371. VAN DYKE, Richard (1717-70), N.Y.
Punch Bowl,
1740-60, silver, D. 7½". Garvan Coll., Yale U.
#1930.1203   DA 116

CLASSICAL SILVER

1372. BURT, Benjamin (1729-1805), Boston.
Tankard,
1786, silver, H. 9⅛". Boston Mus.   #36.459
                                              DA 105A

214

1373. DUBOIS, Abraham.
Tea Set,
c. 1795, silver, Garvan Coll., Yale U.
#1930.1002 A, B, C

DA 117

1374. LOWNES, Joseph (act. 1780-d. 1816), Phila.
Candlestick; Snuffers,
late 18th C., silver, H. 5⅛"; L. 9⅝". Met. Mus.
#24.109.38 a-c   Bequest of Charles Allen Munn,
1924.   DA 83B

1375. REVERE, Paul (1735-1818), Boston.
Pitcher,
1804, silver, H. 6⅝". Winterthur.   #57.858   DA 58

1376. ———.
Tea Set,
1792, silver, on deposit by Mr. & Mrs. James
Ford Bell, Minn. Inst.   #OG56.178; OG56.179;
OG56.180; OG56.181; OG56.182; OG56.183;
OG56.184; OG56.185; OG56.186   DA 153

1377. RICHARDSON, Joseph, Jr. (1752-1831),
Phila.
Bowl, Teapot, Water Pot, Creamer, Sugar, Tongs,
1791-1810, silver, H. 5¹³⁄₁₆"; 6⅜"; 5½"; 7"; 10¾";
6⅜". Winterthur.   #57.824; 57.823; 57.822;
57.826; 57.827; 57.828   DA 57

1378. ———.
Peace Medal,
1793, silver, 7¼" x 5". Coll. Llora and Mark
Bortman, Boston.   DA 118

1379. ——— & Nathaniel (act. c. 1771-91).   act.
Candlesticks,
1771-91, silver, H. 5⅜". Boston Mus.
#56.594-5   DA 105B

PEWTER

1380. DOLBEARE, John & Edmund, N.Y.;
LEDDELL, Jos. Sr. or Jr., Boston.
2 Dishes; Tankard;
c. 1700, pewter; D. 15"; D. 15⁵⁄₁₆"; H. 7".
Winterthur.   #53.179; #55.601   DA 66

1381. HEYNE, Johann Christopher, Pa.
Communion Service,
1754-80, pewter, 2 plates; beaker; chalice; flagon,
D. 6⅜"; D. 4½"; H. 10⅝"; H. 11½". Winterthur.
#ET121; #53.97a   DA 64

1382. WHITMORE, J., Middletown, Conn.;
BASSETT, F. & KIRBY, W., N.Y. City.
Three Beakers,
c. 1750-1800, pewter, H. 5⅜"; 4⅝"; H. 3½".
Winterthur.   #EV183; EV185; CK79   DA 63

1383. *Pewter in Cupboard,*
Eastern U.S., 18th & early 19th C., pewter.
Winterthur.   DA 65

GLASS

1384. ANON., N.J.; AMELUNG, New Bremen,
Md.
Sugar Bowls,
1775-1800; c. 1790-95, covered, glass.
Winterthur.   DA 62

1385. AMELUNG, New Bremen, Md.
Tobias and the Angel,
1788, flip glass, H. 11⅞". Corning Mus.
#55.4.37   DA 126A

1386. ——— (attr.).
Goblet,
c. last q. 18th C., glass, H. 10⅛". Corning Mus.
#55.4.41   DA 126B

1387. AMELUNG, New Bremen, Md.
Goblet,
1788, covered, glass, H. 11½". Inscribed. Met.
Mus.   #28.52A   Rogers Fund, 1928.   DA 78

    1388. —— (attr.).
    Masonic Firing Glass,
    1788-92, glass, H. 4⅜". Corning Mus.
    #55.4.38   DA 126C

1389. AMELUNG, Frederick, Md.
Stenger Bottle,
1792, glass, H. 7". Corning Mus.   #55.4.277 DA 126D

    1390. ——. Ibid., reverse of DA 126D. DA 126E

1391. STIEGEL GLASS WORKS, Manheim, Pa.
(prob.).
Tumbler,
c. 3rd q. 18th C., glass, H. 3⅜". Corning Mus.
#50.4.27.   DA 127B

    1392. —— (attr.).
    Bowls, Creamer, Bottle,
    c. 1764, glass. Corning Mus.   #50.4.18a;
    55.4.72; 55.4.77; 50.4.22. *Salt,* poss. New Bremen,
    Md., last q. 18th C., poss. glass-manufactory of
    John Frederick Amelung.   #55.4.274   DA 125

1393. ——.
Flip or Water Glass,
1750-75, engraved, H. 5⅞". Corning Mus.
#50.4.9   DA 127C

    1394. ——.
    Sugar Bowl,
    1764-1774, covered, glass, H. 5¾". Corning Mus.
    #55.4.69a   DA 127A

EARTHENWARE

1395. *Pitcher,*
c. 1625-53, earthenware, red-glaze, H. 11½".
Colonial Nat'l Hist. Pk., Jamestown, Va.
#J7600   DA 155

    1396. *Jug,*
    early 18th C., red earthenware, H. 9".
    Smithsonian Institution.   #392.353   DA 138

1397. ANON.; CLARK, Peter (?); VINSON,
William (?).
Jug; Vase; Pitcher;
1700-early 18th C., red earthenware; H. 8½";
H. 6¼"; H. 11". Smithsonian Institution.
#392.352; 392.393; 392.352   DA 141

    1398. *Teapot & 2 Jars,*
    1770-1800, stoneware, H. 6⅛"; H. 10¾";
    H. 11¼". Winterthur.   DA 149

1399. DANIEL BAYLEY POTTERY, Mass.
Ale Mug, Chamber Mug, Bowls, Porringer;
Wash Basin,
1764-99, red earthenware, H. 5¾"; H. 2¼";
H. 2½"; H. 3¾". Smithsonian Institution,
#391.355; 391.299; 391.304B; 392.359   DA 140

    1400. BONNIN and MORRIS.
    Sauceboat,
    1771-72, white earthenware. Brooklyn Mus.
    DA 143

1401. BONNIN and MORRIS.
Sweetmeat Dish,
1771-72, white earthenware. Brooklyn Mus.   DA 143A

1402. PAULUS, Cornelius.
Punchbowl,
1792, earthenware, H. 7". Brooklyn Mus.
#48.143   DA 142

1403. SMITH, Joseph (attr. acc. #ET86), Pa.
Group of Pottery,
1769; 1785; 1789; 1798; n.d.; (Pa. Dutch), sgraffito
& slip dec., H. 8¼"; H. 9½"; D. 13"; H. 5½";
D. 11"; Winterthur.   #ET86; ET228; ET19;
ET87; ET34   DA 60

1404. SPINNER, David.
Pie Plates,
c. 1800 (Pa. Dutch), sgraffito ware, D. 11½";
11¼". Phila. Mus.   #00-74; 00-76   DA 190

1405. WILSON, Joseph (attr.); ANON.
Deep Dish, Plate, Crock,
1764; 18th C.; early 18th C., red earthenware,
D. 11⅜"; D. 9"; H. 9½". Smithsonian Institution.
#389.335; 392.391; 392.355   DA 139

IRON AND METALS

1406. *Andirons,*
17th C., wrought iron, H. 29¾"; H. 30½".
Winterthur.   DA 171D

1407. REVERE, Paul, (1735-1818),
Boston.
Andirons (pair),
c. 1790, brass & iron, H. 21⅛". Met. Mus.
#52.77.60, 61   Bequest of Mrs. J. Insley Blair,
1952.   DA 182

1408. REVERE & Sons, Boston.
Andirons (pair),
late 18th C., brass & iron, H. 24½". Met. Mus.
#30.120.89, 90   The Sylmaris Coll. Gift
of George Coe Graves, 1930.   DA 182A

1409. *Group of Door Latches,*
style & provenance vary, late 17th & 18th C.,
wrought iron. Winterthur.   #56.58.4; 56.58.6;
56.58.2; 54.71.1; 56.58.3   DA 175

1410. *Fireback,*
1660, iron, H. 22½". Essex Inst.   #1,808
DA 169

1411. WEBB, Joseph (attr.), Mass.
Fireback,
1781, cast iron, H. 29³⁄₁₆". Winterthur.   DA 171C

1412. *Skewer Holder & Cooking Accessories,*
n.d., wrought iron. Winterthur.   #EK87;
53.173.5; 53.155.47; EK430; EK434; EK423
DA 170

1413. ANON.; LANGWORTHY, L.
Pot, iron, c. 1650, attr. Saugus Iron Works, Mass.,
D. 9½",   #EK104;
Pot with Handle, brass, 1730-40, L. Langworthy,
Newport, R.I., D. 13",   #EK459;
Kettle, copper, late 18th C., Pa., L. 24".
#55.645   Winterthur.   DA 171B

1414. *Six Plate Stove,*
c. 1760, ornamented cast iron, H. 19½".
Winterthur.   DA 171A

1415. *Group of Objects for Illumination,*
N.E., 17th & 18th C., iron. Winterthur.   #EM8;
55.604; 55.48.51; 1513; 53.158.2; 56.38.159; 4B22   DA 183

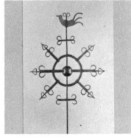

    1416. *Chandelier,*
    N.Y., 1750-75, tin, H. 29½". Winterthur.
    #56.19   DA 176

1417. *Lantern,*
Pa., 18th C., tin, 35½" x 15¼". Met. Mus.
#22.56   Rogers Fund, 1922.   DA 177

    1418. *Weather Vane,*
    N.Y., 1670, iron, H. 88". Winterthur.   DA 167

TEXTILES

1419. *Bedrug,*
Pa., 1748, hooked, wool on wool, 88½" x 80½".
Winterthur.   DA 157B

    1420. *Bedspread,*
    Boston, c. 1750, embroidered, linen,
    81½" x 113". Winterthur.   #52.358   DA 157A

1421. FOOT, Mary, Pa.
Bedspread,
1778, woven, wool, 79½" x 84". Winterthur.   DA 157C

    1422. HEWSON, William.
    Bedspread,
    c. 1800, cotton, 76" x 94". Phila. Mus.   DA 164

1423. ———.
Washington Handkerchief,
1790, cotton, 28¼" x 30¾". Winterthur.   DA 158

    1424. *Chair Seat Cover,*
    early 18th C., crewel embroidery on cotton &
    linen, 18" x 15½". Boston Mus.   #24.362
    DA 163A

1425. *Chair Seat Cover,*
3rd q. 18th C., crewel embroidery on linen,
24½" x 18". Boston Mus.   #54.113   DA 163B

    1426. *Needlework Picture,*
    mid-18th C., wool, silk, metal threads on linen,
    28½" x 25½". Boston Mus.   #47.221   DA 163

1427. *Pocketbooks,*
18th C., wool, 7¼" x 4¾", closed. Winterthur.
#3e7; SF877; SF874; 2g80; Sa9   DA 160

    1428. WALTERS & BEDWELL CO., Phila.
    Fabric,
    c. 1775, printed cotton, 35" x 61". Winterthur.
    DA 161

MISCELLANEOUS
    WOOD

1429. *Group of Objects,*
N.E., 1700-75, wood, mortar; pestle; bowl; plate;
H. 6¼"; L. 6"; D. 11¼"; D. 13½". Winterthur.
#901.25; 901.25A; 56.78.3; 54.34.3   DA 173

    1430. *Carved Codfish,*
    c. 1760, pine, L. 4' 11". Massachusetts State
    House, Boston, Mass.   DA 168

MISCELLANEOUS
    SPANISH COLONIAL

1431. *Side Chair,*
bef. 1835, pine, H. 86 cm. Mus. N.Mex.
#B fmc—83/5   DA 211

    1432. *Doors to Wall Cupboard,*
    (pair), 18th or early 19th C., pine, H. 81 cm.
    Mus. N.Mex.   DA 207

1433. *Chest* (ecclesiastical),
1st half 18th C., pine, H. 56 cm. Mus. N.Mex.
#HSNM 2519   DA 209

    1434. *Trastero* (cupboard),
    c. 1840, pine, H. 1 m. 46 cm. Mus. N.Mex.
    #L.5.58-11   DA 205

1435. *Chest,* with legs; *Shelf,* hanging,
c. 1790, pine, H. 93 cm; H. 60 cm. Cornelia G.
Thompson Coll., Mus. N.Mex.   DA 206

    1436. *Trastero* (cupboard),
    c. 1790, pine, H. 2 m. 26 cm. Mus. N.Mex.
    #B 83/69   DA 208

1437. *Chest,*
c. 1830-40, pine, lid: L. 67.5 cm; box: L. 63 cm.
Mus. N.Mex.   #L.5.58-28   DA 203

    1438. *Chest,* on legs,
    early 19th C., pine, H. 74.5 cm. Mus. N.Mex.
    #HSNM   B83/89   DA 210

1439. NEW MEXICAN GOLDSMITHS,
Gold Filigree Necklace,
1st half 19th C. Mus. N.Mex.   #A8.57-5   DA 213

    1440. *Table,*
    bef. 1840, food serving, pine, H. 29 cm. Cornelia
    G. Thompson Coll., Mus. N.Mex.   DA 201

1441. *Table,*
c. 1840-50, oblong, pine, H. 56 cm. Cornelia G.
Thompson Coll., Mus. N.Mex.   DA 204

    1442. *Sconces,*
    aft. 1840, pair with mirrors & candle brackets,
    tin, D. 59 cm; 56.5 cm. Mus. N.Mex.
    #L.5.58-9-a&b   DA 212

219

DESIGN AND DECORATIVE ARTS OF
THE NINETEENTH CENTURY

G. HAYDN HUNTLEY

CERAMICS

1443. *Jar,* R.I. (?),
early 19th C., glazed red earthenware, H. 6¼".
Brooklyn Mus.   #43.128-140   DB 16

> **1444.** *Plate,*
> 1823 (Pa. Dutch), sgraffito, green & red. N.Y.
> Hist. Soc.   DB 352

1445. BERGEY, Benjamin, Montgomery Co., Pa.
Plate,
c. 1830 (Pa. Dutch), ceramic, "pie crust" edge,
D. 13¼". Phila. Mus.   #93.218   DB 356

> **1446.** BOUGHNER, William, Greensboro, Pa.
> *Redware Jug,*
> 1849, H. 8". Smithsonian Institution.   #178.455
>   DB 22

1447. BROUWER, T. A., Jr., Middle Lane
Pottery, East Hampton, L.I.
Vase,
1890, white earthenware with metallic luster glaze,
H. 7½". Brooklyn Mus.   #44.1-24   DB 33

> **1448.** FENTON'S WORKS, Bennington, Vt.
> *Pitcher,*
> 1847-48, Parian porcelain, rose pattern, H. 10½".
> Brooklyn Mus.   #43.128-57   DB 21

1449. FURMAN, Noah, Chesequake, N.J.
Jar,
1840-56, glazed stoneware, H. 7½". Brooklyn
Mus.   #43.128-9   DB 19

> **1450.** GREATBACK, Daniel (attr.), Bennington, Vt.
> *Pitcher,*
> 1852-58, "hound handle," Rockingham ware,
> H. 12". N.Y. Hist. Soc.   #1937-599   DB 26

1451. LYMAN, FENTON & Co., Bennington, Vt.
Teapot & Creamer,
c. 1849, glazed yellow earthenware, H. 9"; H. 6½".
Brooklyn Mus.   #44.18-2; 44.18-5   DB 23

> **1452.** ——.
> *Lion,*
> 1852-58, flint-enameled earthenware, H. 10".
> Brooklyn Mus.   DB 25

1453. OTT & BREWER, Trenton, N.J.
Cup and Saucer,
c. 1882-92, "Belleek ware," porcelain. Cooper
Union Mus.   #1954-77-1   DB 29

> **1454.** ROOKWOOD POTTERY, Cincinnati, Ohio.
> *Vase,*
> 1887, glazed earthenware, H. 14½". Brooklyn
> **Mus.**   #09.888   DB 32

1455. T. C. SMITH & Sons, Union Porcelain
Works, Greenpoint, L.I.
Plate,
1877, porcelain, D. 10". Brooklyn Mus.
43.10-48   DB 28

  1456. TUCKER & HEMPHILL, Phila., Pa.
  Pitcher,
  c. 1832, porcelain, H. 8½". Brooklyn Mus.
  # 47.142   DB 18

FURNITURE
  ANONYMOUS

1457. *Arm Chair,*
N.Y. City (?), c. 1820, mahogany with brass
inlay. Mus. City N.Y.   # 43.91.13AB   DB 70

  1458. *Armchair,*
  c. 1884, H. 29½". Brooklyn Mus.   # 46.43.8
                                             DB 107

1459. *Armless Easy Chair,*
c. 1886, upholstered in velvet, deep fringe border
at bottom, H. 32½". Coll. Theodore Storer,
R. T. Paine House, Waltham, Mass.   DB 106

  1460. *Clock,*
  c. 1830, lyre-type, gilded mahogany, brass,
  H. 41". Brooklyn Mus.   # 42.278-3   DB 79

1461. *Chest of Drawers,*
c. 1820, mahogany, brass inlay. Cooper Union
Mus.   # 1926-22-90   DB 74

  1462. *Desk,*
  c. 1800, mahogany. Loaned by Pierpont Morgan
  Hamilton and Alexander Hamilton, Mus. City N.Y.
  # L246.1   DB 62

1463. *Melodeon,*
c. 1835, mahogany (?), H. 35". Brooklyn Mus.
37.144   DB 81

  1464. *Pier Mirror,*
  N.Y. c. 1800, gilt, pine & glass painting, H. 51".
  Met. Mus.   # 50.145.358   Bequest of Mary
  Stillman Harkness, 1950.   DB 60

1465. *Sofa,*
1815-20, mahogany, modern upholstery. Cooper
Union Mus.   # 1920-19-85   DB 67

  1466. *Stools,*
  N.Y., c. 1840, rosewood, needlepoint &
  upholstery. Met. Mus.   # 47.147.1, 2   Gift of
  Mrs. John C. Cattus, 1947, in memory of her
  mother, Mrs. William Gordon Ver Planck. DB 84

1467. *Table,*
c. 1820, pedestal type, mahogany & gilt. Mus.
City N.Y.   # 40.372.2   DB 75

  1468. *Card Table,*
  1830-40, Empire style, mahogany. N.Y. Hist. Soc.
  # 1945.120   DB 83

MISSOURI—GERMAN

1469. *Creole Slat-back Chair,*
c. 1800, ash & hickory, H. 33". Missouri Hist.
Soc.   DB 612

> **1470.** *Chair,*
> c. 1840, walnut & hickory, H. 26". Missouri Hist.
> Soc.   DB 611

1471. *Extension Table,*
c. 1860, walnut, H. 30". Missouri Hist. Soc.   DB 383

PENNSYLVANIA DUTCH

> **1472.** *Kitchen Cupboard,*
> 1830, wood, painted, H. 83½". Phila. Mus.
> #54.85.32   DB 355

PIONEER

1473. *Chair,*
Fredericksburg, Texas, c. 1860-70, H. 35".
Witte Mem. Mus.   #A.D. Te-Fu-2   DB 382

SHAKER

> **1474.** *Candlestand or Round Stand; Chair,*
> New Lebanon, N.Y., cherry; cherry and maple;
> H. 25¼"; H. 44". Coll. Mr. & Mrs. Edward
> Deming Andrews, New Haven, Conn.   DB 410

1475. *Side Chair,*
Lebanon, Mass., c. 1880, maple, cane seat.
N.Y. Hist. Soc.   #1945.437   DB 403

> **1476.** *Long Communal Dining Table,*
> early 19th C., L. 20'. Coll. Mr. & Mrs. Edward
> Deming Andrews, New Haven, Conn.   DB 414

1477. *Sewing Stand; Swivel Stool,*
New Lebanon, N.Y., 19th C., pine, painted red;
H. 24¾"; H. 28". Coll. Mr. & Mrs. Edward
Deming Andrews, New Haven, Conn.   DB 411

> **1478.** *Sewing Table,*
> New Lebanon, N.Y., 19th C., maple, H. 27". Coll.
> Mr. & Mrs. Edward Deming Andrews, New Haven,
> Conn.   DB 412

1479. *Trustees' Desk,*
New Lebanon, N.Y., 19th C., pine, stained with
pink wash, H. 84¾". Closed. Coll. Mr. & Mrs.
Edward Deming Andrews, New Haven, Conn. DB 408

> **1480.** ——. Ibid. Open.   DB 409

BY KNOWN MAKERS

1481. BELTER, J. H.
Settee,
c. 1855, rosewood, upholstery restored, 43" x 69".
Victorian Room, Chicago Hist. Soc.   DB 94

> **1482.** ——.
> *Center Table,*
> c. 1855, rosewood, marble top, 29½" x 40".
> Victorian Room, Chicago Hist. Soc.   DB 95

1483. BELTER, J. H.
Whatnot,
mid-19th C., rosewood, H. 69½". Brooklyn Mus.
#47.134-1   DB 89

1484. THOMAS BROOKS & Son.
Armchair,
c. 1870, walnut, H. 39½". Brooklyn Mus.
#52.120   DB 101

1485. BROOKS CABINET WAREHOUSE.
Bookcase,
rosewood, c. 1849-50. Mus. City N.Y.
#52.24.1ab   DB 92

1486. COOPER, Peter.
Rocking Chair,
c. 1860, wrought iron, painted, plush upholstery.
Cooper Union Mus.   #1938-58-1457   DB 98

1487. GRAND RAPIDS CHAIR Co., Grand Rapids,
Mich.
Secretary Bookcase,
1892, golden oak, brass fittings, H. 69". Grand
Rapids Mus.   #FG 111   DB 111

1488. HITCHCOCK (stamped).
Rocking Chair,
c. 1830, Boston style, painted and stencilled,
H. 41½". Brooklyn Mus.   #38.859L   DB 78

1489. LANNUIER, C. H. (?), N.Y. City.
Console Table,
c. 1815-20, one of a pair, mahogany & gilt.
Mus. City N.Y.   #54.207.1ab2ab   DB 68

1490. ORIOLE FURNITURE Co. Grand Rapids,
Mich.
China Cabinet,
1887, oak, brass galleries, H. 70". Grand
Rapids Mus.   DB 109

1491. BEHRENS, August H., des.
Washstand,
1890-1900, curly birch, max. H. 58½".
Washstand set: *Royal Porcelain* by MADDOX
LAMBERTON WORKS. Grand Rapids Mus.,
#FG 66; FG 42 1/8   DB 112

1492. PHYFE, Duncan, N.Y. City.
Side Chair,
1800-10, Sheraton style, mahogany, H. 33". Ford
Mus.   #29.483.49A   DB 63

1493. ——.
Side Chair,
c. 1830, mahogany, horsehair upholstery,
H. 33¾". Brooklyn Mus.   #43.23-5   DB 77

1494. ——.
Sofa,
1823, Recamier style, rosewood, gold leaf &
brass, H. 31". Brooklyn Mus.   #42.118-36
                                                   DB 76

1495. PULLMAN, George M. & A. B., Grand
Rapids, Mich.
Buffet,
1856, walnut, marble, H. 60¾". Grand Rapids
Mus.   DB 96

1496. WILLARD, Aaron, Jr. (1783-1864), Boston,
Mass.
Tall Clock,
c. 1812, mahogany, H. 99¾". Met. Mus.
#42.76.1   Joseph Pulitzer Bequest
Fund, 1942.   DB 64

GLASS

1497. *Sugarbowl,*
c. 1825, glass, blown in expanded pattern mold,
H. c.7". Brooklyn Mus. # 47.70   DB 164

   1498. *Bowl,*
   1880, glass, H. 2½". Brooklyn Mus.   # 41.833
   DB 174

1499. *Pair of Pressed Glass Candlesticks,*
c. 1840, H. 10⅜"; H. 10¼". Met. Mus.
57.131.3; 57.131.4.   Bequest of Mrs. Charles
W. Green, in memory of Dr. Charles W. Green.   DB 167

   1500. *Pitcher,*
   Saratoga, N.Y., early 19th C., green blown glass,
   H. 9¾". Met. Mus.   # 48.74   Rogers Fund,
   1948.   DB 169

1501. BOSTON & SANDWICH GLASS Co. (?).
Bowl,
c. 1830, lacy glass crossed peacock feather,
H. 2". Corning Mus.   DB 166

   1502. ——.
   Celery Vase,
   c. 1850, pressed glass, H. 10". Smithsonian
   Institution.   # 383.695   DB 170

1503. CHESTER COUNTY GLASS Co. (attr.).
Pitcher,
1857, pressed glass, H. 8½". Brooklyn Mus.
47.149-3   DB 171

   1504. NEW ENGLAND GLASS Co.
   Bowl,
   c. 1883, Amberina, blown glass, D. 8". Brooklyn
   Mus.   # 48.207-258   DB 175

1505. PHOENIX GLASS Co.
Pitcher,
1888, satin glass, H. 9¼". Smithsonian Institution.
94.501   DB 176

INTERIORS

   1506. *Drawing Room,*
   1854-56, from Milligan House, Saratoga Springs,
   N.Y. Brooklyn Mus.   DB 220

1507. *Fireplace,*
1873, marbles, iron & mosaic; mantel: L. 62"
across; fireplace: H. 46¼". Decatur Art Center,
Ill.   # 6963   DB 564

   1508. *Parlor,*
   c. 1820, from Irvington, N.J. House. Brooklyn
   Mus.   DB 217

1509. *Parlor,*
c. 1830, Empire style, from Albany, N.Y. House.
Winterthur.   DB 559

   1510. *Sitting Room,*
   c. 1884, Rockefeller House. Brooklyn Mus.
   DB 225

1511. BELTER, J. H., N.Y. City.
Victorian Parlor,
c. 1860, reconstruction. Mus. City N.Y.
#DB 92   DB 222

IRONWORK

1512. *Balcony Guard and Railing,*
1835, cast iron, H. 29". New Orleans (725
Iberville St.), La.   DB 280

1513. *Fence Railing,*
1824, cast & wrought iron. Tomb of Louise
Collin, St. Louis Cemetery #1, New Orleans,
La.   DB 277B

1514. *Fence Railing,*
1893, cast & wrought iron, H. 33". Tomb of
James Desban, St. Louis Cemetery #1, New
Orleans, La.   DB 290

1515. *Gate Ornament,*
1823, cast iron. Medelia Thomas Family,
St. Louis Cemetery #1, New Orleans, La.   DB 277A

1516. STRATTON and SEYMOUR.
Radiator,
1820-30, with statue of Temperance (?), cast iron,
black finish. Cooper Union Mus.   #1918-43-1
                                                          DB 276

JEWELRY

1517. *Bouquet Holder,*
silver-gilt with pearl handle, c. 1850. Mus. City
N.Y.   #51.71.2   DB 234

1518. *Bracelet,*
mid-19th C., gold, turquoise, pearls. Cooper
Union Mus.   #1946-50-6   DB 233

1519. *Bracelet,*
c. 1860, gold, goldstone, painted flowers. Mus.
City N.Y.   #36.276.3   DB 235

1520. *Bracelet,*
c. 1870, gold, enamel. Cooper Union Mus.
#1946-50-33   DB 237

1521. *Brooch, Earrings & Pin,*
c. 1830, gold inlaid with mother-of-pearl & paste.
Missouri Hist. Soc.   DB 569

1522. *Brooch & Earrings,*
c. 1865-70, gold, hair. Cooper Union Mus.
                                                          DB 236

1523. *Brooch and Earrings,*
c. 1880, gold. Cooper Union Mus.
#1946-50-37 A-C   DB 239

1524. *Pendant,*
c. 1875, gold, enamel, carbuncle, garnet, rose
diamonds, half pearls. Cooper Union Mus.
#1946-50-14   DB 238

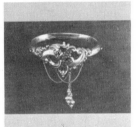

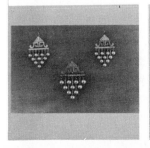

1525. *Ring,*
c. 1880, gold, turquoise. Cooper Union Mus.
#1955-95-2   DB 240

MACHINES

1526. *Fire Hose Reel,*
1838, hand-drawn. Smithsonian Institution.
#311.087   Lent by Insurance Co. of North
America.   DB 256

1527. CORLISS STEAM ENGINE Co., Providence,
R.I.
Stationary Steam Engine,
1859, flywheel 24', 300 h.p. Ford Mus.   DB 259

1528. HERRESHOFF MFG. Co., Bristol, R.I.
Stationary Steam Engine,
c. 1879. Ford Mus.   DB 265

1529. SMITH, James (painted by JOHNSON, J. H.).
Fire Engine, "Big Six",
1851, hand-pumper. Mus. City N.Y.   DB 257

1530. WHEELER & WILSON Mfg. Co., N.Y. City.
Sewing Machine with Cabinet,
1855, cast iron, steel, nickel plate, walnut. H.
closed 36¼". Grand Rapids Mus.   #FL 32
                                              DB 258

SILVER

1531. GALE, William.
Tea Service
c. 1855, silver. Naval Hist. Coll., N.Y. Hist. Soc.
                                              DB 313

1532. GARDINER, Baldwin.
Knife and Fork,
c. 1830-40, silver, Coster Crest. Mus. City N.Y.
#32.509 a-j   DB 309

1533. GORHAM.
Carafe Set,
1874, silver & glass. Mus. City N.Y.   #34.346-5 a-c
                                              DB 316

1534. ——.
Dish,
1874, pedestal foot, silver & glass. Mus. City N.Y.
#34.346.2   DB 316A

1535. HAYDEN Bros. & Co., Charleston, S.C.
Goblet,
c. 1853, silver. N.Y. Hist. Soc.   #1916.10   DB 312

1536. KIRK, Samuel.
Teapot,
1828, silver, H. 7¾". Brooklyn Mus.   #44.60.1
                                              DB 306

1537. MARQUAND & Co. (?)
Teapot,
c. 1830-35, silver. N.Y. Hist. Soc.
#1942.243 A-E   DB 308

1538. PLATT, G. W. & N. C.
Spoons,
c. 1820, silver, L. 8½"; L. 5⅝"; L. 5". Brooklyn
Mus.   #40.71-72-73; 40.66   DB 305

1539. REED & BARTON.
Spoons,
1890-1900, sterling silver, Luxembourg, Trojan &
Majestic patterns. Reed & Barton Coll., Taunton,
Mass.   DB 321

    1540. TARGEE, John.
    Pitcher,
    1813, silver, H. 13½". N.Y. Hist. Soc.   DB 303A

1541. ——.
Serving Dish,
1813, silver. N.Y. Hist. Soc.   DB 303B

    1542. TAYLOR, Najah.
    Teapot,
    c. 1820, silver, H. 11". Brooklyn Mus.
    #20.789   DB 304

1543. TIFFANY & Co.
Pitcher & Salver,
c. 1890, silver, H. 9"; D. 13". Naval Hist. Coll.,
N.Y. Hist. Soc.   DB 303

    1544. ——.
    Tea Kettle,
    c. 1862, silver, H. 9". N.Y. Hist. Soc.
    #1941.265   DB 315

TEXTILES

1545. *Bedcover or Quilt,*
1844, chintz appliqué on muslin, 73" x 73".
St. Louis Mus.   DB 610

    1546. *Blanket,*
    c. 1840, wool and cotton, twill weave, 60" x 64".
    Art Inst. Chicago.   #52.1251   DB 468

1547. *Carpet,*
c. 1854, from Milligan drawing room. Brooklyn
Mus.   DB 454

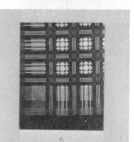

    1548. *Coverlet,*
    n.d., wool, 76" x 96". Evangeline & Benjamin F.
    Hunter Coll., Ill. State Mus.   DB 591

1549. *Kerchief for Centennial Celebration,*
1876, cotton print. N.Y. Hist. Soc.
#1944.271   DB 459

    1550. *Rug* (used as bedcover),
    1809, wool on canvas, sq. 8' 4½". Met. Mus.
    #13.207   Rogers Fund, 1913.   DB 437

1551. *Hooked Rug,*
Vermont, 1825-50, 66" x 37". Los Angeles County
Mus.   #A.2115-6   DB 442

    1552. ECONOMITES, Economy, Pa.
    Samples of Silk (4),
    1832. Art Inst. Chicago.   #52.502-52.504
                                            DB 443

1553. HULL, Evelina, Mass.
Embroidered and Painted Picture,
c. 1812, silk on silk. Met. Mus.   #39.126.1
Gift of Mrs. Joshua Marsden Van Cott, 1939.   DB 439

     1554. LADIES WORKING SOCIETY OF
     DANVILLE.
     Patchwork Quilt,
     1848, hand-embroidered silk. La. State Mus.
                                   DB 452

1555. LUSBY, Mrs. James.
Quilt,
1837-38, cotton, chintz appliqué, 114" x 109".
Smithsonian Institution.   # T 10347   DB 445

     1556. ORME, Elizabeth.
     Sampler,
     1833, silk on linen, 17¼" x 21". Smithsonian
     Institution.   # T 7319   DB 444

1557. POWELL, Mrs. Fielding Travis.
Ottoman Cover,
1855, clipped, raised wool embroidery on
broadcloth, 51" x 51". Smithsonian Institution.
T 10305   DB 455

     1558. TYLER, Harry.
     Coverlet,
     1845, wool and cotton, double weave. Smithsonian
     Institution.   # T 8897   DB 450

1559. WELLS, Margaret.
Sampler,
1809, silk on wool, 12½" x 14¼". Smithsonian Institution.
T 7892   DB 436

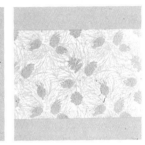

     1560. WHEELER, Mrs. Candace, des.
     Sample Textile,
     1883-87, silk weave, ground serge, overspun in
     satin weave. Met. Mus.   #28.70.6   Gift of
     Mrs. Boudinot Keith, 1928.   DB 460

TRANSPORTATION

1561. *Packet Ship, Hibernia,*
1830, New York City, from painting by WALTERS,
S., 1845. N.Y. Hist. Soc.   DB 425

     1562. McKAY, Cornelius W., East Boston, Mass.
     Schooner, Frank Atwood,
     1868-69, from painting by YORK, W. G., 1876.
     N.Y. Hist. Soc.   DB 429

1563. WESTERVELT & Sons, N.Y.
Arago, U.S. Mail Steamer,
1855, from painting by TANNEUR, Philip, oil.
Lent by John Lando, Marine Mus. City N.Y.
ML 599   DB 427

     1564. THE BREWSTER Co. N.Y. City
     Victoria,
     c. 1862, L. without shafts 138". Ford Mus.
     #30.1165.1   DB 485

1565. CUNNINGHAM, James, Rochester, N.Y.
Phaeton,
c. 1838, max. L. 217". Ford Mus.   #29.560.4   DB 483

     1566. NICHOLS, D. P. & Co.
     Hansom Cab,
     c. 1895. Chicago Hist. Soc.   # 1938.39   DB 491

228

WALLPAPER

1567. *Wallpaper,*
c. 1820, printed from woodblocks. Cooper Union
Mus.   # 1938-62-81   DB 501

    1568. PUTNAM & ROFF.
    Bandbox,
    wallpaper, c. 1820. Cooper Union Mus.
    # 1913-45-10a, b. # 33   DB 502

1569. *Bandbox,*
wallpaper, c. 1830, printed from woodblocks,
14" x 13" x 17¾". Cooper Union Mus.
1913-17-8a,b. # 53   DB 503

    1570. *Wallpaper,*
    c. 1830, printed from woodblocks, green & gray,
    13½" x 19". Cooper Union Mus.   # 1951-3-1
                                       DB 504

1571. *Wallpaper,*
1845-55, blue, white & black, 7½" x 19". Cooper
Union Mus.   # 1938-62-14   DB 505

    1572. *Wallpaper,*
    c. 1855, blue & white, 7" x 16". Cooper Union
    Mus.   # 1938-62-79   DB 506

1573. *Wallpaper,*
1860-70. Cooper Union Mus.   # 1931-45-89   DB 507

    1574. *Wallpaper,*
    c. 1870, 3½" x 8½". Cooper Union Mus.
    # 1940-90-9   DB 508

1575. *Wallpaper,*
c. 1875, 16" x 18". Cooper Union Mus.
1940-74-2   DB 509

    1576. BECKER, SMITH, PAGE & Co.
    Wallpaper,
    c. 1875, 18" x 26". Cooper Union Mus.
    #1944-47-6   DB 510

1577. *Flock Wallpaper,*
1880-90, green, 18⅛" x 27⅞". Cooper Union
Mus.   # 1937-57-2   DB 511

    1578. DRESSER, des.
    Frieze, Wallpaper,
    c. 1880, Cooper Union Mus.   # 1941-17-1
                                        DB 512

1579. ALLEN-HIGGENS Co., Mfg.
Wallpaper,
1890-1900, red moire, 18" x 19½". Cooper
Union Mus.   # 1946-57-3   DB 513

    1580. *Wallpaper,*
    1890-1900, pink, 18" x 21½". Cooper Union Mus.
    # 1946-57-4   DB 514

1581. TEMPLE, Grace Lincoln.
Wallpaper,
1890-93, light green & tan, 20" x 29". Cooper
Union Mus.   # 1938-62-59   DB 515

MISCELLANEOUS

    1582. *Lantern for Whale Oil,*
    mid-19th C., copper, brass & glass. Cooper
    Union Mus.   # 1941-98-23   DB 248

1583. *Oval Boxes,*
19th C. (Shaker), maple, pine discs top and bottom.
Coll. Mr. & Mrs. Edward Deming Andrews, New
Haven, Conn.   DB 413

    1584. GLEASON, Roswell.
    Pitcher,
    1850-60, pewter, H. 11". Brooklyn Mus.
    # 27.532   DB 339

1585. KETTERER, J.
Coffee Pot,
c. 1830 (Pa. Dutch), tin with hammered dots,
H. 12". N.Y. Hist. Soc.   DB 354

COSTUME DESIGN L U C Y   B A R T O N

    1586. ANON.
    Woman's Evening Dress,
    c. 1816, Empire style, white mull & linen.
    Costume Coll., Valentine Mus.   # 55.65 DB 600

1587. ANON.
Woman's Evening Dress,
1821, Empire style, taffeta. Costume Coll.,
Valentine Mus.   # 40.33.5   DB 601

    1588. ANON.
    Woman's Afternoon Dress,
    c. 1860, crinoline style, white India mull.
    Costume Coll., Valentine Mus.   # 49.53.1
                                              DB 602

1589. ANON.
Woman's Dress,
1869, transitional, hoop-to-bustle style, bombazine
& silk. Costume Coll., Valentine Mus.   #51.22.1
                                            DB 603

    1590. ANON.
    Boy's Dress,
    c. 1880, percale, size 3 years. Costume Coll.,
    Valentine Mus.   # 50.132.1 a, b   DB 604

1591. ANON.
Wedding Dress,
1883, bustle type, cream satin. Costume Coll.,
Valentine Mus.   # 56.67.1   DB 605

    1592. NORVALL, Carrie (1864-1939).
    Woman's Dress,
    c. 1885-90, bustle type, pink chambray. Costume
    Coll., Valentine Mus.   # 45.12 a,b,c,d DB 606

1593. ANON.
Joseph Wing,
c. 1835, o.c., 26⅞" x 21⅞". Sandwich Hist.
Mus.   DB 621

    1594. *Mrs. Joseph Wing,*
    c. 1835, o.c., 27⅞" x 21⅞". Sandwich Hist. Mus.
                                              DB 622

  *A selection of paintings relevant to costume design is to be
found in Appendix A.

DESIGN AND DECORATIVE ARTS OF THE TWENTIETH CENTURY

WILLIAM FRIEDMAN

APPLIANCES AND TOOLS

1595. DREYFUSS, Henry, des.
Bathroom Fixtures,
c. 1937, porcelain. The Crane Co., New York
N.Y.   DC 8

1596. EASTWOOD Mfg. Co., Belleville, N.J.
Valve Handle,
1898; 2½" x 4". "Hardware Dealers Magazine,"
Feb. 1898. N.Y. Pub. Lib.   DC 1

1597. HOWE, Elias.
Sewing Machine,
c. 1910, wood & metal. Mus. Science and
Industry.   #31.80   DC 3

1598. HUXTABLE, L. Garth, des., Millers Falls
Co., Greenfield, Mass.,
Hand Tools,
1957, plane, file, tool & blade; L. 11¼". Mus.
Mod. Art.   DC 16

1599. McFARLAND, D. L., des.,
Fan,
1952, plastic, swivel base; H. 14". General
Electric Co., Bridgeport, Conn.   DC 12

1600. MARKLE FEATHERLITE PRODUCTS
Corp., Detroit, Mich.
Garden Tools,
c. 1947, polished cast aluminum; L. 9¼" to
10¾". Mus. Mod. Art.   DC 9

1601. MASSELMAN, George, des., Masselman
Design Co., West Redding, Conn.
Fireplace Tool,
1953, iron; L. 36". Mus. Mod. Art.   DC 13

1602. SPILMAN, Raymond, des.
Adding Machine,
1956. Monroe Calculating Machine Co., Orange,
N.J.   DC 26

1603. TRUE TEMPER Corp., Cleveland, Ohio.
Hammer "Jet Rocket,"
1956, forged steel head, tubular steel handle and
molded rubber grip; L. 13".   DC 15

COMMUNICATION

1604. EDISON, Thomas.
Dictating Machine,
c. 1900, metal; H. 34". Mus. Science and Industry.
#43.121A   DC 2

1605. RAYMOND LOEWY Assoc., des.
Radio Receiver,
1946, metal & plastic; H. 9". Hallicrafters
Co. Mus. Mod. Art.   DC 22

1606. BELL TELEPHONE LABORATORIES.
Telephone,
1900, metal, plastic, wall type. Mus. Science and
Industry.   DC 17

1607. BELL TELEPHONE LABORATORIES.
Telephone,
1921, plastic; H. 11". Mus. Science and Industry.   DC 19

    1608. WESTERN ELECTRIC Co.
    Telephone,
    1914, plastic, metal; H. 11". Bell Tel. Pioneers
    Mus., Chicago, Ill.   DC 18

1609. ———.
Telephone,
1936-37, plastic; H. 5⅝". Bell Telephone Co.,
New York, N.Y.   DC 20

    1610. ———.
    Telephone,
    1950, plastic; H. 4¾". Bell Telephone Co., New
    York, N.Y.   DC 23

1611. DOBSON, W. A., des.
Typewriter,
1927, portable, Underwood Typewriter Co.,
Underwood Corp., New York, N.Y.   DC 5

    1612. INTERNATIONAL BUSINESS MACHINES
    Corp., New York, N.Y.
    Typewriter,
    1957, standard office model, electric.   DC 10

CRAFTS

1613. BRYNNER, Irene, des.
Necklace,
1956, gold & gold quartz; L. 18½". Coll.
Designer, New York, N.Y.   DC 65

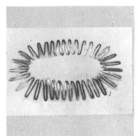

    1614. CALDER, Alexander, des.
    Necklace,
    n.d., brass, hammered; 13½" x 21". Mus. Mod.
    Art.   DC 39A

*1615. DRERUP, Karl.
Panel No. 54,
1956, enamel on steel; 11" x 11". Mus.
Contemporary Crafts, New York, N.Y.   DC 190

    *1616. GROTELL, Maija.
    Jar,
    1949, stoneware, H. 13⁷⁄₁₆". Mus. Cranbrook
    Academy of Art.   DC 46A

1617. ———.
Vases,
c. 1940, stoneware. Mus. Cranbrook Academy
of Art.   DC 46

    1618. LIPTON, Seymour.
    Eternal Light,
    1955, nickel-silver & steel; H. 12". Betty
    Parsons Gallery, New York, N.Y.   DC 36

1619. LUKENS, Glen.
Earthenware,
c. 1945. Art Dept., U. of Southern Calif.   DC 173

    1620. MAY, John, des.
    Plate, Bowl; Salt Dish; Pepper Mill;
    c. 1948, turned wood; oval 9½" x 8"; L. 11";
    D. 3"; H. 6". American House, New York, N.Y.
    DC 49

232   * Items marked with an asterisk were not selected by
    Mr. Friedman.

1621. NATZLER, Gertrud & Otto.
Ceramics,
n.d., three pieces; H. 7"; H. 2¼"; H. 2¼". Mus.
Mod. Art.   # 141.48; 352.50; 137.48   DC 38

    1622. POUSETTE-DART, Richard, des.
    Jewelry,
    1955, brass, 2 pieces, bird: L. 5"; design:
    L. 3⅞". Mus. Mod. Art.   DC 62

1623. PRESTINI, James.
Bowls,
c. 1946, wood; D. 4½" to D. 14¾". Mus. Mod.
Art.   DC 48

    1624. RENK, Merry.
    Necklace,
    1953, silver & champlevé; D. each unit 1 ½ .
    Coll. Designer, San Francisco, Calif.   DC 58

1625. SMITH, Patricia and PERCIVAL, Willa, des.
Necklace,
1954, aluminum; D. 5½". Coll. Ferdinand Boesch,
New York, N.Y.   DC 59

    1626. TIFFANY, Louis Comfort.
    Hand Mirror,
    c. 1900, peacock handle and panel, silver and
    enamel; 10½" x 5". Coll. Joseph H. Heil, New
    York, N.Y.   DC 40

*1627. ——.
Vase,
c. 1900, glass, gold iridescent, fluted; H. 3⅞".
Coll. Sarah E. Henley, Oyster Bay, N.Y.   DC 41

    1628. ——.
    Vase,
    c. 1900, glass, blue & green iridescent; H. 4⅝".
    Mus. Mod. Art.   DC 42

*1629. ——.
Vase,
c. 1900, glass, swan neck; H. 18". Coll. Edward
Wormley, New York, N.Y.   DC 43

    *1630. ——.
    Vase,
    c. 1900, glass; H. 11⅜". Ward Mount, Jersey
    City, N.J.   DC 44

1631. VOULKOS, Peter H.
Vase,
1956, stoneware; H. 30". Coll. Designer. Los
Angeles, Calif.   DC 68

    1632. WINSTON, Bob, des.
    Pendant,
    1955, silver & amethyst; 6" x 5". Coll. Designer,
    Berkeley, Calif.   DC 64

FABRICS

1633. ALBERS, Anni.
Wall Hanging,
1948, linen & cotton, handwoven; 16½" x 18½".
Mus. Mod. Art.   # 200.50   DC 70

    1634. GIRARD, Alexander, des.
    Upholstery Fabric,
    1953, 100% viscose rayon, black & white. Herman
    Miller Furniture Co., Zeeland, Mich.   # 250
                                DC 75

1635. KEPES, Juliet and Gyorgy, des.
Printed Fabric,
1949, "Linefields"; 10" x 15". Laverne Originals
Inc., New York, N.Y.   DC 71

 1636. LARSEN, Jack Lenor, des.
 Upholstery Fabric,
 1955, handwoven, leather, vinyl and nylon; 8" x
 12". Jack Lenor Larsen, Inc., New York, N.Y.
                                          DC 77

1637. LIEBES, Dorothy, des.
Sheer Textile,
1947, mohair, flax & rayon; 8½" x 11". Goodall
Fabrics, New York, N.Y.   DC 69

 1638. NICHOLS, Marie, des.
 Upholstery and Drapery Fabric,
 1954, cotton with Lurex, beige, black & gold. Coll.
 Designer, New York, N.Y.   DC 76

1639. STOUT, Pola, des.
Suiting,
1951, worsted, twill weave, spectrum colored.
Pola Stout, Inc., Brewster, N.Y.   DC 74

 1640. TILLET, D. D. and Leslie, des.
 Cotton Broadcloth,
 1949, red, screened & hand striped. Coll.
 Designers, New York, N.Y.   DC 73

FURNITURE

1641. *Dining Chair,*
c. 1900, wood. Mus. Science and Industry.   DC 78

 1642. BERTOIA, Harry, des.
 Lounge Chair,
 1953, upholstery on wire frame, metal legs;
 H. 30". Knoll Assoc., New York, N.Y.   DC 109

1643. EAMES, Charles, des.
Eames Aluminum Group,
1958, furniture, aluminum. Herman Miller
Furniture Co., Zeeland, Mich.   DC 201

 1644. ——.
 Armchair,
 1952, plastic shell, wire base; H. 31½". Herman
 Miller Furniture Co., Zeeland, Mich.   DC 97

1645. ——.
Lounge Chair; Ottoman,
1956, plywood, leather; H. 33⅜"; H. 15". Herman
Miller Furniture Co., Zeeland, Mich.   DC 113

 1646. ——.
 Low Chair,
 1946, plywood back & seat, metal legs; H. 27⅜".
 Herman Miller Furniture Co., Zeeland, Mich.
                                          DC 93

1647. ——.
Sofa,
1954, chromium, upholstered, sofa-compact;
L. 72½". Herman Miller Furniture Co., Zeeland,
Mich.   DC 111

 1648. ——.
 Storage Units,
 1949-50, plywood & metal; L. 47". Herman
 Miller Furniture Co., Zeeland, Mich.   DC 101

1649. EAMES, Charles, des.
Incidental Table,
1952, hard plastic top, folding metal legs; L. 21½".
Herman Miller Furniture Co., Zeeland, Mich.   DC 92

1650. ESHERICK, Wharton, des.-craftsman.
Telephone Table; Stool,
1956, cherry wood, rawhide seat; H. 28"; H. 17".
Private Coll., New York, N.Y.   DC 66

1651. KOMAI, Ray, des. J. G. Furniture Co.,
New York, N.Y.
Side Chair,
1949, molded plywood, metal base; H. 30". Mus.
Mod. Art.   DC 100

1652. KNOLL, Florence, des.
Cabinet,
c. 1948, wood with cane doors & metal legs,
sliding doors, walnut; H. 31". Knoll Assoc.,
New York, N.Y.   DC 95

*1653. ——.
Case Furniture,
1940, walnut, plastic & lacquer; H. 18". Knoll
Assoc., New York, N.Y.   DC 86

1654. NAKASHIMA, George, des.-craftsman.
Mira Chair,
1950, walnut. Coll. Designer, New Hope, Pa.
    DC 102

1655. ——.
Table and Chair,
1948, maple, plywood top; L. 54"; H. 28½".
Knoll Assoc., New York, N.Y.   DC 98

*1656. NELSON, George.
Chairs,
1958, plastic; H. 34"; 31¼". Herman Miller
Furniture Co., Zeeland, Mich.   DC 202

1657. ——.
Chairs,
1958, laminated birch; chair with cushion;
H. 24¾". Herman Miller Furniture Co., Zeeland,
Mich.   DC 115

*1658. ——.
Executive Swivel Tilt Chair,
1955-, H. 31". Herman Miller Furniture Co.,
Zeeland, Mich.   DC 203

1659. ——.
Chest,
1952, rosewood, aluminum & porcelain; H. 34".
Herman Miller Furniture Co., Zeeland, Mich.   DC 105

1660. ——.
Table,
1952, wood top, metal legs; L. 72". Herman
Miller Furniture Co., Zeeland, Mich.   DC 106

1661. ——.
Table,
1955, wood top, enameled metal legs; L. 60".
Herman Miller Furniture Co., Zeeland, Mich.   DC 112

1662. ——.
Mobile Table,
1950(?), enamel & plastic; H. 24½". Herman
Miller Furniture Co., Zeeland, Mich.   DC 103

1663. NEWMARCH, Billie.
Beach Seats,
1953, metal frame, colored cotton slipcover;
29" x 14". Mus. Mod. Art.   DC 108

    1664. SAARINEN, Eero, des.
    Armchair,
    1958, modeled plastic, Fiberglas, cast aluminum
    base; H. 32". Knoll Assoc., New York, N.Y.
                              DC 116

*1665. ——.
Conference Chair,
1940, molded plywood, sponge rubber; H. 31".
Knoll Assoc., New York, N.Y.   DC 85

    1666. ——.
    Lounge Chair, Ottoman,
    1948, molded plastic shell, foam rubber, iron rod
    support; H. 36"; H. 17". Knoll Assoc., New York,
    N.Y.   DC 96

1667. SAARINEN, Eero and EAMES, Charles, des.
Armchair,
1940, molded plywood, sponge rubber; H. 33".
Mus. Mod. Art.   DC 85A

    1668. STEIN, Richard, des.
    Daybed Sofa,
    c. 1946, wood frame, latex mattress. Knoll
    Assoc., New York, N.Y.   DC 91

1669. STICKLEY, L. and J. G., des.
Rocker,
c. 1910, wood, fabric. Coll. L. Thorne-Thomsen,
Lake Forest, Ill.   DC 80

    1670. WORMLEY, Edward, des.
    Long John Coffee Table,
    1946, walnut; L. 84". Dunbar Furniture Corp. of
    Indiana, Berne, Ind.   DC 107

*1671. ——.
Writing Table; Chair,
1956, walnut, fabric; L. 59"; H. 27½". Dunbar
Furniture Corp. of Indiana, Berne, Ind.   DC 81

    1672. WRIGHT, Frank Lloyd, des.
    Side Chair,
    1904, wood & leather; H. 36". Mus. Mod. Art.
                              DC 79

1673. WRIGHT, Russel.
Arm Chair,
mahogany, 1936, fur seat; H. 31". Mus. Mod.
Art.   DC 83

HOUSEHOLD EQUIPMENT AND ACCESSORIES

    1674. *Coffee Mill,*
    c. 1910, iron. Mus. Science and Industry. DC 120

1675. BINNS, Charles F., des.
Vases and Bowls,
1900-10. Stoneware. N.Y. State College of
Ceramics, Alfred U.   DC 118

    1676. CARDER, Fred., des., Steuben Glass.
    Vase,
    1929, Intarsia technique, dark blue on clear glass.
    Smithsonian Institution.   #2507   DC 122

1677. COORS PORCELAIN Co., Golden, Colo.
Chemical Porcelainware,
1910-, evaporating dishes, mortars & pestles,
beakers & small crucibles. DC 121

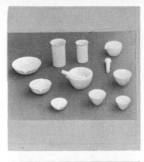

1678. CORNING GLASS WORKS, Corning, N.Y.
Double Boiler,
1948-53, ''Pyrex'' glass with plastic handle and
metal fastenings. Corning Mus. DC 139

1679. FEDERAL GLASS Co., Columbus, Ohio.
Tumbler and Old Fashioned Glasses,
four, 1900-. DC 119

1680. INGRAHAM, Elias.
Wall Clock,
1885-1915, wood; H. 14½". Mus. Science and
Industry. #52.75-87 DC 117

1681. OSTER MANUFACTURING Co., Milwaukee,
Wis.
Electric Meat Grinder,
1955, metal, white enameled; H. 12". Macy's,
New York, N.Y. DC 145

1682. PLAS-TEX Corp., Los Angeles, Calif.
Mixing Bowl Set,
c. 1955, white plastic; D. 7"; D. 8"; D. 9".
Mus. Mod. Art. DC 144

1683. POLLOCK, Dean, des.
Carving Knife,
1946-47, steel, aluminum; L. 12". Coll. Ferdinand
Boesch, New York, N.Y. DC 132

1684. SCHLUMBOHM, Peter, des. and mfg.
Coffee Maker,
1941, pyrex & birch, CHEMEX®; H. 9½".
Chemex Corp., New York, N.Y. DC 126

1685. SITTERLE CERAMICS, Croton Falls, N.Y.
Porcelainware,
1949-, pitchers. DC 53

1686. STEUBEN GLASS Co.
Vase,
1949, glass; H. 8". Corning Mus. DC 141

1687. SUNBEAM ELECTRIC Co., Chicago, Ill.
Mixmaster,
1955, metal, glass, plastic; H. 13". Macy's, New
York, N.Y. DC 146

1688. TUPPER Corp., Farnumsville, Mass.
Cocktail Shaker; Pitcher; 2 Containers,
1948-; H. 9½"; H. 5½"; H. 6" & 7". Mus. Mod.
Art. DC 140

1689. WELDEN, W. Archibald, des., Revere
Copper & Brass, Inc., Rome, N.Y.
Cocktail Shaker,
c. 1939, chromed steel; H. 11". Mus. Mod. Art. DC 129

1690. ——.
Saucepan and Lid,
1936, stainless steel, copper; H. 5½". Revere
Copper & Brass, Inc., Rome, N.Y. DC 128

1691. WESTINGHOUSE ELECTRIC Co.
Electric Hand Iron,
1955, metal & plastic. Macy's, New York, N.Y.   DC 147

LAMPS

1692. KELLY, Richard, des.
Lamp,
hanging, aluminum baffle, adjustable reel, paper
shade, 1950. Middletown Mfg. Co., Middletown,
N.Y.   DC 153

1693. MAYEN, Paul, des.
Lamp,
1951, hand-blown white lighting glass; 5" x 20".
Habitat, Inc., New York, N.Y.   DC 156

1694. NELSON, George, des.
Lamps,
1951, 7 shapes, metal frames, vinyl plastic cover.
Howard Miller Clock Co., Zeeland, Mich. DC 155

1695. NESSEN, Walter Von, des.
Lamps,
1935, metal with swinging arms. Nessen Studios,
New York, N.Y. (Table lamp not selected by
Mr. Friedman.)   DC 149

1696. NOGUCHI, Isamu, des.
Lamp Table,
1948, plastic, wood; H. 16". Knoll Assoc., New
York, N.Y.   DC 152

1697. PFISTERER, Peter. Mutual Sunset Lamp
Mfg. Co.
Floor Lamp,
1940, chromium; H. 67½". Mus. Mod. Art.   DC 151

1698. WATROUS, Gilbert, des. The Heifetz Co.,
N.Y.
Floor Lamp,
1950, brass & steel, swivel stem. Mus. Mod. Art.
DC 154

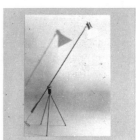

FLATWARE, STEMWARE AND TABLEWARE

1699. FORST, Florence, des.
Dinnerware,
1946, glazed earthenware. Mus. Mod. Art.   DC 175

1700. GRANT, Mary K.
Dinnerware,
1949, "Encanto," porcelain. Gladding McBean
& Co., Los Angeles, Calif.   DC 182

1701. HEATH, Edith, des.
Ash Trays, Cigarette Lighter and Jar,
1946- , stoneware. Heath Ceramics, Sausalito,
Calif.   DC 179

1702. ——.
Dinnerware,
1946- , plates, cups & saucers, stoneware. Heath
Ceramics, Sausalito, Calif.   DC 177

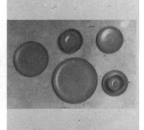

1703. ——.
Dinnerware,
1946- , serving dish, teapot, cream pitcher, cup
& saucer, stoneware. Heath Ceramics, Sausalito,
Calif.   DC 178

1704. HEDU, Jon, des., Watertown Mfg. Co.
Dinnerware,
1947, "Lifetime," molded plastic. Geo. E.
Weigle Co., New York, N.Y.   DC 180

1705. LENOX, Inc., Trenton, N.J.
Dinnerware,
1940- , porcelain. Coll. Dr. & Mrs. M. A.
McCannel, c/o Walker Art Center.   DC 172

1706. WRIGHT, Russel, des.
Dinnerware,
1946, porcelain, ovenproof, vitrified chinaware.
Iroquois China Co., Syracuse, N.Y.   DC 176

1707. ZEISEL, Eva., des., Castleton China, Inc., New
Castle, Pa.
Dinnerware,
1948, porcelain, creamer; pot; plate; H. 5½";
H. 10"; D. 8½". Mus. Mod. Art.   DC 181

1708. STARK, Frederick William, des.,
International Silver Co., Meriden, Conn.
Flatware,
1934, "Continental," silver. Macy's, New York,
N.Y.   DC 169

1709. VAN KOERT, John, des.
Flatware,
1951, "Contour," sterling silver. Towle
Silversmiths, Newburyport, Mass.   DC 183

1710. WALLANCE, Don., des., H. E. Lauffer Co.
Flatware,
1954, "Design One," stainless steel; L. 6½" to
8". Mus. Mod. Art.   DC 185

1711. SAKIER, George, des.
Stemware,
c. 1935, "Classical," pressed glass. Fostoria
Glass Co., Moundsville, West Virginia.   DC 170

 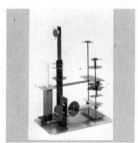

TOYS

1712. CARRARA, Arthur A., des.
Magnet Master,
1948, assembled, steel, alnico. Carradan Assoc.,
Chicago, Ill.   DC 30

1713. ——. Ibid. Unassembled.   DC 30A

1714. JAMES INDUSTRIES.
Toy—Slinky,
1948, flexible steel. Paoli, Pa.   DC 31

1715. PLAYSKOOL Mfg. Co., Chicago, Ill.
Toys,
1945, wood, push toy, pull toy, pull boat; blocks;
L. 13"; L. 3" to 11".   DC 28

1716. TOY TINKERS, Inc.
Tinkertoy,
1914- . Div. of A. G. Spalding & Bros., Inc.,
Evanston, Ill.   DC 27

TRANSPORTATION

1717. AUBURN-DUESENBERG CORD Co.,
Cord,
automobile, 1936-37, classic design, 17'2". Ford
Mus.   DC 163

1718. CADILLAC MOTOR CAR Co., Detroit, Mich.
Cadillac.
automobile, 1906, model M, light touring car.
Mus. Science and Industry.   DC 157

1719. FORD MOTOR Co., Dearborn, Mich.
Ford,
automobile, c. 1924, model T, 2 door, 5 passenger
Sedan. Ford Mus.   DC 159

    1720. ———.
    Lincoln,
    automobile, 1941, "Continental," L. 17'8". Ford
    Mus.   DC 164

1721. WILLYS OVERLAND MOTORS, Toledo, Ohio.
Willys,
1941, jeep, 10'3". Ford Mus.   DC 166

MISCELLANEOUS

    1722. HARTMANN LUGGAGE Co., Racine, Wis.
    Suitcase,
    c. 1945, leather, metal frame.   DC 187

*1723. TEAGUE, Walter Dorwin, des., Eastman
Kodak Co.
Kodak Bantam Special,
1934. Coll. Eastman House, Rochester, N.Y.   DC 21

GRAPHIC ARTS OF THE
EIGHTEENTH AND NINETEENTH CENTURIES
C A R L   Z I G R O S S E R

1725. ANON.
Adam and Eve,
c. 1820 (Pa. Dutch), col. woodcut, 7¾" x 5⅝".
Phila. Mus.   # 02.428   GB 166

    1726. ANON.
    Baptismal Certificate,
    1826 (Pa. Dutch), woodcut & stencil, 15" x 12⅜".
    Phila. Mus.   # 20.71.6   GB 168

1727. ANON.
Representation of Different Ways Leading to
Everlasting Life or Eternal Damnation,
c. 1830 (Pa. Dutch), woodcut & stencil, 9⅞" x 13⅝".
Phila. Mus.   # 20.71.9   GB 169

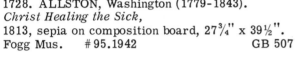

    1728. ALLSTON, Washington (1779-1843).
    Christ Healing the Sick,
    1813, sepia on composition board, 27¾" x 39½".
    Fogg Mus.   # 95.1942   GB 507

1729. BENECKE, Thomas (act. 1855-56) (aft. BENECKE, D.).
Sleighing in New York,
1855, col. lith., 21½" x 30½". J. C. Davies Coll., Mus.
City N.Y.   # 29.100.2408   GB 6

    1730. BENNETT, William James (1777-1844).
    Boston, from City Point Near Sea Street,
    c. 1832, col. aqua., 24⁵⁄₁₆" x 15¹²⁄₁₆". Stokes Coll.,
    N.Y. Pub. Lib.   GB 7

1731. —— (aft. HILL, J. W.).
New York, from Brooklyn Heights,
c. 1836, col. aqua., 31¹²⁄₁₆" x 19⁸⁄₁₆". Stokes Coll.,
N.Y. Pub. Lib.   GB 11

    1732. ——.
    West Point, from Phillipstown,
    c. 1830, col. aqua., 22⁵⁄₁₆" x 15¹³⁄₁₆". Stokes Coll.
    N.Y. Pub. Lib.   GB 10

1733. BIRCH, William Russell (1755-1844) and son
Thomas (1779-1851).
Bank of the United States, Philadelphia,
1799, engr., 11" x 13¼". Phila. Mus.   # 45.31.1 GB 20

    1734. ——.
    Congress Hall and New Theatre,
    1800, engr., 11" x 13¼". Phila. Mus.   # 45.31.1
                                            GB 19

1735. BLUM, Robert Frederick (1857-1903).
Scene at a Fair,
1885, etch., 4" x 5¼". Boston Mus.   # 20558   GB 22

    1736. BLYTHE, David Gilmour (1815-65).
    President Lincoln Writing the Proclamation of
    Freedom,
    1864, col. lith., 14" x 18¾". Lib. of Congress.
                                            GB 23

1737. BODMER, Karl (1809-93).
Indians Hunting the Bison,
1843-44, col. aqua., 11⅞" x 17⅛". Rare Book
Div., N.Y. Pub. Lib.   GB 24

　　　　1738. BOETTICHER, Major Otto (c. 1816- ?).
　　　　Union Prisoners at Salisbury, N.C.,
　　　　c. 1862, col. lith., 37⁹⁄₁₆" x 20¹⁴⁄₁₆". Stokes Coll.,
　　　　N.Y. Pub. Lib.   GB 25

1739. BROWN, M. E. D. (act. 1832-96).
Blue Jay and Ruby Crowned Wren,
1832, col. lith., 6⅜" x 8¼". Am. Antiq. Soc.   GB 31

　　　　1740. BROWN, William Henry (1808-83).
　　　　John Marshall,
　　　　1844, lith., 13½" x 10". Phila. Mus.   #45.52.1
　　　　　　　　　　　　　　　　　　　　　　GB 32

1741. ——.
John Randolph,
1844, lith., 13½" x 10". Phila. Mus.   #45.52.1   GB 33

　　　　1742. BUFFORD, John H. (act. 1835-71).
　　　　College of Princeton, N.J.,
　　　　c. 1836, lith., 17⁹⁄₁₆" x 11⁴⁄₁₆". Stokes Coll., N.Y.
　　　　Pub. Lib.   GB 34

1743. BURGIS, William (act. 1716-31).
*A Prospect of the Colleges in Cambridge, New
England (Harvard),*
1726, col. engr. 18¼" x 24½". Mass. Hist. Soc.   GB 35

　　　　1744. BURT, Charles K. (1823-92) (aft. MOUNT,
　　　　W. S.).
　　　　Bargaining for a Horse,
　　　　1851, engr. and etch., 7¾" x 10". Boston Mus.
　　　　　　　　　　　　　　　　　　　　　　GB 36

1745. BUTTERSWORTH, James (1817-94).
Clipper Ship Flying Cloud, 1851,
lith., 1852, 16⅛" x 23⅛". McKAY, Donald (ship
builder). Marine Hist. Assoc.   #49.3184   GB 37

　　　　1746. CAMERON, John (c. 1828- ?).
　　　　*Life of a Fireman: The Metropolitan System,
　　　　New York,*
　　　　1866, col. lith. pub: by Currier & Ives, 17" x 26".
　　　　Davies Coll., Mus. City N.Y.   #29.100.2471
　　　　　　　　　　　　　　　　　　　　　　GB 38

1747. ——.
*Taking the Back Track, A Dangerous
Neighborhood,*
1866, col. lith. pub: Currier & Ives, 17⅛" x 26¼".
Peters Coll., Mus. City N.Y.   #1572   GB 38B

　　　　1748. CASSATT, Mary (1845-1926).
　　　　The Coiffure,
　　　　1891, drpt, soft-ground & aqua., 10¼" x 14¼".
　　　　Rosenwald Coll., Nat'l Gall. Art.   GB 45

1749. ——.
The Fitting,
1891, drpt, soft-ground & aqua., 14¾" x 10⅛".
Rosenwald Coll., Nat'l Gall. Art.   GB 43

　　　　1750. ——.
　　　　The Map,
　　　　1890, drpt, 6⅛" x 8⅜". Prints Div., N.Y. Pub.
　　　　Lib.   GB 40

1751. CASSATT, Mary (1845-1926).
The Stocking,
1890, drpt, 10⅛" x 7¼". Phila Mus. #49.89.11   GB 41

    1752. CATLIN, George (1796-1872).
    Buffalo Hunt: Chasing Back,
    1844, col. lith., 12¾" x 18¼". Rare Books Div.,
    N.Y. Pub. Lib.   GB 48

1753. ——.
Osceola of Florida,
1838, lith., 26⅜" x 19⅝". Lib. of Congress.   GB 47

    1754. CHASE, William Merritt (1849-1916).
    Seated Woman,
    c. 1880, dwg, 15½" x 11". Cooper Union Mus.
    #1933-8-1   GB 49

1755. CHURCH, Frederick E. (1826-1900).
Niagara Falls,
1856, pencil, wash and Chinese white, 12"x 17½".
Cooper Union Mus.   #1917-4-144   GB 508

    1756. COLE, J. F. A. (1837-92).
    New Bedford, Mass.
    c. 1858-60, col. lith., 32⁶⁄₁₆" x 16³⁄₁₆". Stokes
    Coll., N.Y. Pub. Lib.   GB 51

1757. COLE, Thomas (1801-48).
The Good Shepherd,
1849, col. lith., 11½" x 16½". Phila. Mus.
#47.59.4   GB 54

    1758. ——.
    Study for Trees,
    c. 1825, pen and bistre ink, 13½" x 9⅞". Detroit
    Inst.   #39.162   GB 509

1759. COPLEY, John Singleton (1738-1815).
Study for Gen. Heathfield's Horse,
n.d., crayon & white chalk, 13"x 10". Addison
Gall.   #1935.21   GB 510

    1760. ——.
    Watson and the Shark,
    c. 1778, dwg, 19⅛" x 23½". Mus. Hist. Art,
    Princeton.   #9   GB 510A

1761. ——.
Portrait of Mrs. John Scollay,
1764, dwg, pastel, 21¾" x 17". Fogg Mus.
#1943.570   GB 56

    1762. ——.
    Portrait of Rev. William Welsteed,
    1753, mezzotint, 13¾" x 9¾". Boston Mus.
    GB 55

1763. CROPSEY, Jasper Francis (1823-1910).
A View from Bald Mountain,
1843, pen & ink, sepia wash, 14¼" x 19¼".
Cleveland Mus.   #33.401   GB 511

    1764. CURRIER & IVES.
    The American National Game of Baseball,
    1866, col. lith., 19⅝" x 29¾". Peters Coll., Mus.
    City N.Y.   #3214   GB 58B

1765. CURRIER & IVES.
The Great Fire at Chicago, Oct. 8th, 1871,
1871, col. lith., 16¼" x 24¼". Peters Coll., Mus.
City N.Y. #3917   GB 58C

    1766. DARLEY, Felix O. C. (1822-88).
    Conestoga Wagon and Coaching Inn,
    1874, wash, 10" x 14".. Hist. Soc. Pa.   ARP.07
                                     GB 500

1767. DAVIS, Alexander Jackson (1803-92).
Yale College and State House,
c. 1832, col. lith., 12¹/₁₆" x 8³/₁₆". Stokes Coll.,
N.Y. Pub. Lib.   GB 63

    1768. DAWKINS, Henry (act. 1753-, d. 1786?).
    The Paxton Expedition,
    1764, engr., 13¹¹/₁₆" x 7⁵/₁₆". Stokes Coll., N.Y.
    Pub. Lib.   GB 64

1769. DELATTRE, Henri (1801/02-67).
Mac and Zachary Taylor,
1851, col. lith. by CURRIER, N., 12½" x 20¾".
Peters Coll., Mus. City N.Y.   #3645   GB 64B

    1770. DONEY, Thomas (act. c. 1844-49) (aft.
    BINGHAM, G. C.).
    The Jolly Flat Boat Men,
    1847, engr., 23¼" x 27". Phila. Mus.
    #47.59.19   GB 65

1771. DOOLITTLE, Amos (1754-1832) (aft.
EARLE, Ralph).
Engagement at the North Bridge in Concord,
1775, col. engr., 17⁴/₁₆" x 11³/₁₆". Stokes Coll.,
N.Y. Pub. Lib.   GB 66

    1772. —— (aft. LACOUR, Peter).
    Federal Hall, the Seat of Congress,
    (view showing Inauguration of Washington),
    April 30, 1789, engr., 12¹³/₁₆" x 16⁹/₁₆". Stokes
    Coll., N.Y. Pub. Lib.   GB 67

1773. DURAND, Asher B. (1796-1886) (aft.
VANDERLYN, John).
Ariadne,
1835, etch. and engr., 14⅛" x 17¾". Boston Mus.
                                       GB 71

    1774. DURRIE, George H. (1820-63).
    Home to Thanksgiving,
    1867, col. lith., pub: Currier & Ives, 14½" x 25".
    Peters Coll., Mus. City N.Y.   #2388   GB 73B

1775. ——.
Winter in the Country, Getting Ice,
1864, lith., 18½" x 27". Coll. H. H. Kynett,
Philadelphia, Pa.   GB 72

    1776. DUVENECK, Frank (1848-1919).
    Riva Degli Schiavoni II,
    1880, etch., 13⅛" x 8½". Cincinnati Art Mus.
    #1913.860   GB 75

1777. EAKINS, Thomas (1844-1916).
The Gross Clinic,
1875, India ink dwg, 23⅝" x 19⅛". Met. Mus.
#23.94   Rogers Fund, 1923.   GB 501

    1778. ——.
    Masked Woman Seated,
    c. 1865, dwg, 24" x 18". Phila. Mus.
    #29.184.49   GB 78

1779. FORBES, Edwin (1839-95).
Going into Camp at Night,
1876, etch., 11" x $15\frac{7}{8}$". Lib. of Congress. GB 80

1780. FOSTER, John (1648-81).
Portrait of Richard Mather,
c. 1670, wood engr., 6" x 5". Mass. Hist. Soc. GB 81

1781. FROST, Arthur B. (1851-1928).
Brer B'ar Finds Brer Rabbit Caught in a Trap Set by Brer Fox,
c. 1895, pen & ink, 13" x $11\frac{1}{4}$". Coll. Philip Hofer, Cambridge, Mass. GB 513

1782. FULLER, George (1822-84).
Landscape with Two Women and Dog,
n.d., charcoal dwg, $9\frac{3}{8}$" x $12\frac{1}{2}$". M. & M. Karolik Coll., Boston Mus. GB 82B

1783. GEISTWEITE, George.
The Thirty-Fourth Psalm: "Ich will den Herrn Loben...",
1801, (Pa. Dutch), fraktur, 12" x $14\frac{3}{4}$". Phila. Mus. # 54.85.7 GB 167

1784. GREENWOOD, John (1727-92).
Jersey Nanny,
1748, mezzotint, 8" x 10". Coll. Henry L. Shattuck, Boston, Mass. GB 83B

1785. GROZELIER, Leopold (1830-65) (aft. WIMAR, Charles).
On the Prairie,
1860, col. lith., 26" x $17\frac{1}{4}$". St. Louis Mus. # 239.50 GB 84

1786. HARNETT, William Michael (1848-92).
Head of a Woman,
1881, dwg, $19\frac{1}{2}$" x $16\frac{1}{4}$". Fogg Mus. # 10.1947 GB 85

1787. HAVELL, Robert, Jr. (1793-1878) (aft. AUDUBON, J. J.).
American Goldfinch, with Common Thistle,
1827-38, col. aqua., 12" x $19\frac{1}{2}$". N.Y. Hist. Soc. GB 86

1788. —— (aft. AUDUBON, J. J.).
Herring Gull, with View of Entrance to St. Augustine,
1827-38, col. aqua., $23\frac{3}{4}$" x $34\frac{3}{4}$". N.Y. Hist. Soc. GB 91

1789. ——.
Niagara Falls, from the Chinese Garden,
1845, col. aqua., $27\frac{5}{16}$" x $17\frac{11}{16}$". Stokes Coll., N.Y. Pub. Lib. GB 95

1790. —— (aft. AUDUBON, J. J.).
Ruby-Throated Hummingbird, with Trumpet Flower,
1827-38, col. aqua., $20\frac{1}{2}$" x 26". N.Y. Hist. Soc. GB 88

1791. HEADE, Martin Johnson (1819-1904).
Newburyport Marshes, Twilight,
n.d., charcoal on paper touched with white chalk, 11" x $21\frac{5}{8}$". M. & M. Karolik Coll., Boston Mus. GB 94B

1792. HILL, John William (1812-79).
Broadway and Trinity Church,
1830, w.c. dwg, $13\frac{10}{16}$" x $9\frac{10}{16}$". Stokes Coll., N.Y. Pub. Lib. GB 101

1793. HILL, John (1770-1850) (aft. DOUGHTY, T.).
Fairmount Water Works,
c. 1825, col. aqua., 15⅝" x 23¾". Phila. Mus.
43.71.1   GB 98

    1794. —— (aft. WALL, W. G.).
    View Near Fishkill,
    c. 1820, aqua., 13¾" x 20¾". Prints Div., N.Y.
    Pub. Lib.   GB 99

1795. HOFFY, Alfred (1790-aft. 1860).
Lieutenant, U.S. Navy,
1840, col. lith., 10½" x 8". N.Y. Hist. Soc.   GB 102

    1796. HOMER, Winslow (1836-1910).
    A Bivouac Fire on the Potomac,
    wood engr., 13¾" x 20". "Harper's Weekly,"
    Dec. 21, 1861. N.Y. Pub. Lib.   GB 520

1797. ——.
Flamborough Head, England,
1882, dwg, 17¹³⁄₁₆" x 24". Art. Inst. Chicago.
33.1240   GB 504

    1798. ——.
    The Letter for Home,
    1862, lith., 10⅝" x 8½". Phila. Mus. # 41.53.3
                                            GB 106

1799. ——.
The Life Boat,
c. 1881, dwg, 11⅝" x 18½". Cooper Union Mus.
1912-12-130   GB 503

    1800. ——.
    The Life Line,
    1884, etch., 12¼" x 17¼". Prints Div., N.Y. Pub.
    Lib.   GB 516

1801. ——.
On the Bluff at Long Branch, at the Bathing Hour,
wood engr., 8¾" x 14". "Harper's Weekly,"
Aug. 6, 1870. N.Y. Pub. Lib.   GB 517

    1802. ——.
    Raid on a Sand-Swallow Colony—"How Many
    Eggs?"
    wood engr., 9" x 13½". "Harper's Weekly,"
    June 13, 1874. N.Y. Pub. Lib.   GB 519

1803. ——.
Shepherdess,
1877, dwg, pencil, 7¼" x 17". Addison Gall.
1936.46   GB 502

    1804. ——.
    Shepherdess Lying in a Field,
    c. 1878, dwg, 14¼" x 22". Cooper Union Mus.
                                            GB 103

1805. ——.
A Winter Morning—Shovelling Out,
wood engr., 9¾" x 12½". "Every Saturday,"
Jan. 14, 1871. N.Y. Pub. Lib.   GB 518

    1806. HORNOR, Thomas (act. 1828-44).
    Broadway, New York,
    c. 1835, col. aqua. by HILL, J., 27⁴⁄₁₆" x 17¹²⁄₁₆".
    Stokes Coll., N.Y. Pub. Lib.   GB 116

1807. HUDDY, William H. (act. 1837-47).
To the Ancient and Honorable Artillery of Boston,
1839, col. lith., 10½" x 8". Phila. Mus.   GB 117

    1808. HUNT, William Morris (1824-79).
    Woman at Well,
    c. 1856, lith. with tint stone, 9⅝" x 7⅜". Phila.
    Mus.   GB 119

1809. ——.
Portrait of Louis Agassiz,
c. 1860s, dwg, 18" x 14". Fogg Mus.   #1955.6
          GB 118

    1810. INMAN, Henry (1801-1846).
    Portrait of Artist's Wife (?),
    1831, lith., 9½" x 9". Prints Div., N.Y. Pub.
    Lib.   GB 121

1811. INNESS, George (1825-94).
June,
1886, dwg, w.c., 6⅝" x 8⅝". Addison Gall.
#1934.40   GB 123

    1812. JOHNSON, Eastman (1824-1906).
    Marguerite,
    c. 1865, lith., 10⅞" x 8¾". Am. Antiq. Soc.
              GB 126B

1813. ——.
Study for the Boy Lincoln,
n.d., charcoal, chalk, Chinese white, 15½" x 13½".
Detroit Inst.   #47.364   GB 505

    1814. JONES, Alfred (1819-1900) (aft.
    WOODVILLE, R. C.).
    Mexican News,
    1853, engr., 20½" x 18¼". Lib. of Congress.
    #46.23.68   GB 127

1815. KNIRSCH, Otto (act. c. 1853-60).
The Road—Winter,
1853, col. lith., pub: N. Currier; on stone by O.
Knirsh, 17½" x 26⅜". Peters Coll., Mus. City
N.Y.   #2473   GB 127B

    1816. LAWSON, Alexander (1773-1846) (aft.
    WILSON, A.).
    Blue Jay, Goldfinch and Oriole,
    1808, col. engr., 12" x 8". Stuart Coll., N.Y. Pub.
    Lib.   GB 131

1817. —— (aft. KRIMMEL, J. L.).
Election Day at Independence Hall 1815,
c. 1846, engr., 16½" x 24¾". Hist. Soc. Pa.
ARP 521   GB 130A

    1818. LEHMAN, George (? -1870) (aft.
    KRIMMEL, J. L.).
    Dance in a Country Tavern,
    c. 1833-34, col. lith., 7⅞" x 10⅞". Hist. Soc.
    Pa.   ARP 5222   GB 133

1819. ——.
Merchants' Exchange,
1835, lith., 7" x 10¾". Hist. Soc. Pa.   ARP 277
          GB 132

    1820. LEHMAN & DUVAL (aft. KING, G. B.).
    Se-Quo-Yah, Inventor of Cherokee Alphabet,
    1833, col. lith., 11" x 8¾". Phila. Mus.
    #37.40.1   GB 134

1821. LEWIS, James Otto (1799-1858), (aft. HARDING, Chester).
Col. Daniel Boone,
1820, stipple engr., 11¾" x 8". St. Louis Mus.
#71.43   GB 135

    1822. LONGACRE, James Barton (1794-1869), (aft. SULLY, T.).
    Portrait of Andrew Jackson,
    1820, stipple engr., 14¾" x 11¾". Phila. Mus.
    #47.59.35   GB 136

1823. MAURER, Louis (1832-1932).
Life of a Fireman: The Night Alarm, "Start her lively boys!"
1854, col. lith., pub: N. Currier, 16⅞" x 25⅞".
Davies Coll., Mus. City N.Y.   #34.3912   GB 137

    1824. ——.
    Life in the Woods, Starting Out,
    1860, col. lith., pub: Currier & Ives. Peters Coll.,
    Mus. City N.Y.   #3312   GB 138B

1825. ——.
Preparing for Market,
1856, lith., 18⅞" x 27¼". Coll. H. H. Kynett,
Philadelphia, Pa.   GB 138

    1826. MAVERICK, Peter, Jr., (aft. REINAGLE, Hugh).
    View from Trinity Church, Looking Down Wall Street...,
    1834, lith., 18¾" x 14". Arnold Coll., Met. Mus.
    on loan at Mus. City N.Y.   #L1400.18 GB 144B

1827. MILLER, Alfred Jacob (1810-74).
Pawnee Running Buffalo,
c. 1859, dwg, 8" x 11½". Walters Art.Gall.
#37.1940.121   GB 140

    1828. MORAN, Thomas (1837-1926).
    Solitude,
    1869, lith., 20½" x 16". Prints Div., N.Y. Pub.
    Lib.   GB 142

1829. NEWSAM, Albert (1809-64), (aft. FRANCIS, J. F.).
Joseph Ritner,
1838, lith., 14⅞" x 12¼". Hist. Soc. Pa.   GB 145

    1830. OTIS, Bass (1784-1861).
    The Mill,
    1819, lith., 3⅜" x 4⅝". Prints Div., N.Y. Pub.
    Lib.   GB 147

1831. PALMER, Frances Flora Bond (c. 1812-76), (aft. IVES, J. M.).
Across the Continent. "Westward the Course of Empire Takes Its Way,"
1868, col. lith., pub: Currier & Ives, 17¾" x 27⅛".
Peters Coll., Mus. City N.Y.   #2085   GB 150C

    1832. ——.
    American Express Train,
    1864, col. lith., pub: Currier & Ives, 18" x 31".
    Peters Coll., Mus. City N.Y.   #2088   GB 149C

1833. ——.
American Farm Scenes #1: Spring,
1853, col. lith., pub: N. Currier, c. 17" x 24".
Peters Coll., Mus. City N.Y.   #2306   GB 148B

    1834. ——.
    The "Lightning Express" Trains, "Leaving the Junction,"
    1863, col. lith., pub: Currier & Ives, 17⅞" x
    27⅞". Peters Coll., Mus. City N.Y.   #2103
                                     GB 149B

1835. PALMER, Frances Flora Bond (c. 1812-76).
Low Water in the Mississippi,
1868, col. lith., pub: Currier & Ives, 18⅛" x 28⅛".
Peters Coll., Mus. City N.Y.   #3946   GB 150D

1836. ——, (aft. MANNING, H. D.).
A Midnight Race on the Mississippi,
1860, col. lith., 18⅛" x 27⅛". Coll. H. H. Kynett,
Philadelphia, Pa.   GB 151

1837. ——.
*The Rocky Mountains. Emigrants Crossing the
Plains,*
1866, col. lith., pub: Currier & Ives, 17⅜" x 25¾".
Peters Coll., Mus. City N.Y.   #1568   GB 150B

1838. ——.
Trolling for Blue Fish,
1866, lith., pub: Currier & Ives, 18½" x 27¾".
Lib. of Congress.   GB 150

1839. ——.
The Trout Stream,
1852, col. lith., N. Currier; pub: Currier & Ives,
14⅝" x 20⅛". Peters Coll., Mus. City N.Y.   #3247
                                               GB 147B

1840. PARSONS, Charles (1821-1910), (aft. TAIT,
A. F.).
American Field Sports. Flush'd,
1857, col. lith., pub: Currier & Ives, 18½" x 26¾".
Peters Coll., Mus. City N.Y.   #3260   GB 155B

1841. ——.
Central Park, Winter: the Skating Pond,
1862, col. lith., 18" x 26⅝". N. Y. Hist. Soc.   GB 155C

1842. ——, (aft. McFARLANE, D.).
Clipper Ship Dreadnought off Tuskar Light,
1856, lith., 16" x 24⅜", pub: N. Currier. Marine
Hist. Assoc.   #49.3192   GB 155

1843. ——, (aft. BUTTERSWORTH, J. E.).
Clipper Ship Nightingale off the Battery, N.Y.,
1854, col. lith., 16¼" x 24", pub: N. Currier.
Marine Hist. Assoc.   #49.3189   GB 153

1844. ——, (aft. SMITH, J. B.).
*Clipper Ship Red Jacket...In the Ice off Cape
Horn,*
1855, lith., 16¼" x 23¾", pub: Currier & Ives.
Marine Hist. Assoc.   #49.3185   GB 154

1845. PEALE, Charles Willson (1741-1827).
Benjamin Franklin,
1787, mezzotint, 6" x 5½" (oval). Library Co.
Philadelphia, Pa.   GB 157

1846. ——.
George Washington,
1780, mezzotint, 9½" x 13¼". Prints Div., N.Y.
Pub. Lib.   GB 156

1847. PEALE, Rembrandt (1778-1860).
Jefferson's Rock Near Harpers Ferry,
c. 1826, lith., 9½" x 7¾". Prints Div., N.Y.
Pub. Lib.   GB 159

1848. ——.
Washington,
1827, lith., 19" x 15¼". Phila. Mus.
#41.53.466   GB 160

1849. PELHAM, Henry (1749-1806).
Boston Massacre,
1770, col. engr., 9³⁄₁₆" x 8¾". Am. Antiq. Soc.　GB 161

　　1850. PELHAM, Peter (1684-1751).
　　Portrait of Cotton Mather,
　　1727, mezzotint, 11⅞" x 9¾". Am. Antiq. Soc.
　　　　　　　　　　　　　　　　　　GB 162

1851. PENDLETON, (aft. REINAGLE, Hugh).
*View of St. Paul's Church, and the Broadway
Stages, N.Y.,*
1828, lith., 18" x 23½". Arnold Coll., Met. Mus.
on loan at Mus. City N.Y.　# L1400-19　GB 165

　　1852. PLATT, Charles Adams (1861-1933).
　　Buttermilk Channel,
　　1889, etch., 7" x 11¼". Phila. Mus.
　　# 50.103.159　　　　　　　　　　GB 173

1853. ——.
Three Fishermen,
1886, etch., 4½" x 6⅞". Addison Gall.　# 1930.178
　　　　　　　　　　　　　　　　　　GB 172

　　1854. RANGER, Henry W. (1858-1916).
　　View on the Seine,
　　c. 1896, lith., 9⅞" x 13¾". Phila. Mus.
　　# 42.30.218　　　　　　　　　　　GB 174

1855. REVERE, Paul (1735-1818), (aft.
PELHAM, H.).
Boston Massacre,
1770, col. engr., 7⅝" x 8⅝". Am. Antiq. Soc.　GB 176

　　1856. ——.
　　*View of Part of the Town of Boston and
　　British Ships of War Landing Their Troops,*
　　1770, engr., 9¾" x 15½". Elkins Coll., Free
　　Library, Philadelphia　　　　　GB 175

1857. RIMMER, William (1816-79).
The Call to Arms,
n.d., pencil dwg. Boston Mus.　　　GB 515

　　1858. ——.
　　Doing the Mountains on Foot,
　　1875, dwg, pencil, 9" x 15". Fogg Mus.
　　# 1936.10.47　　　　　　　　　GB 177B

1859. ——.
Female Figure on a Couch,
c. 1859, lith., 10¼" x 10⅞". Boston Mus.　GB 177

　　1860. ——
　　Warriors against Slavery,
　　1863, dwg, 17½" x 24½". Boston Mus.　GB 514

1861. SACHSE & CO. (c. 1840-late 70's).
Baltimore & Calvert Sts., Baltimore,
c. 1853, chromo, 14¹⁄₁₆" x 19¹³⁄₁₆". Stokes Coll.,
N.Y. Pub. Lib.　　　　　　　　　GB 178

　　1862. SAINT MEMIN, C. B. J. Fevret de
　　(1770-1852).
　　Cachasunghia, an Osage Warrior,
　　1807, dwg, 21¼" x 15¼". N.Y. Hist. Soc.
　　# 1860.90　　　　　　　　　　GB 180

1863. SAINT MEMIN, C.B.J. Fevret de
(1770-1852).
View of West Point and Clermont,
aft. 1815, hand col. lith., 8½" x 12⅝". M. & M.
Karolik Coll., Boston Mus.   GB 181

     1864. ——.
     Portrait of Thomas Jefferson,
     c. 1804, dwg, 23¾" x 17". Worcester Art Mus.
     #1954.82   GB 179

1865. SARGENT, John Singer (1856-1925).
Study of Seated Man,
1895, lith., 11⅝" x 8⅝". Phila. Mus.   #41.53.57
                                  GB 182

     1866. SAVAGE, Edward (1761-1817).
     The Washington Family,
     1798, col. stipple engr., 18¼" x 24¼". Hist.
     Soc. Pa.   ST 2754   GB 187

1867. SEVERIN, Charles (act. in N.Y. 1845), (aft.
JOHNSON, Eastman).
Husking,
1861, col. lith., pub: Currier & Ives, 21" x 27⅜". Peters
Coll., Mus. City N.Y.   #2392   GB 189B

     1868. ——.
     Peytona and Fashion. In Their Great Match for
     $20,000...,
     c. 1845, lith., 18" x 28½". Coll. H. H. Kynett,
     Philadelphia, Pa.   GB 189

1869. SMITH, John Rubens (c. 1770-1849).
Sanderson's Franklin House,
c. 1842, col. aqua., 11½" x 18⅛". Coll. H. H.
Kynett, Philadelphia, Pa.   GB 190

     1870. STRENGE, Christian.
     Biblical Quotation: "Halted euch nicht selbst
     for Klug....,"
     1798, (Pa. Dutch), fraktur, 15¼" x 12½". Phila.
     Mus.   #17.150   GB 170

1871. SULLY, Thomas (1783-1872).
Portrait of Capt. Jacob Jones,
c. 1817, dwg, 13¼" x 8½". Phila. Mus.
#40.32.111   GB 192

     1872. TAIT, Arthur Fitzwilliam (1819-1905).
     American Forest Scene, Maple Sugaring,
     1855, col. lith., 18⅝" x 27". Coll. H. H. Kynett,
     Philadelphia, Pa.   GB 195

1873. ——.
Catching a Trout. "We Hab You Now, Sar,"
1854, col. lith., pub: N. Currier, 18¼" x 25¾".
Peters Coll., Mus. City N.Y.   #3232   GB 194B

     1874. ——.
     Life on the Prairie,
     1862, col. lith., 18⅜" x 27⅛". Coll. H. H. Kynett,
     Philadelphia, Pa.   GB 194

1875. TANNER, Benj. (1775-1848), (aft.
REINAGLE, H.).
MacDonough's Victory,
1814, engr., 24⁹⁄₁₆" x 17²⁄₁₆". Stokes Coll.,
N.Y. Pub. Lib.   GB 197

     1876. THOMPSON, Thomas (1775/6-1852).
     The Battery and Harbor, N.Y.,
     1829, col. lith., 25" x 62". Arnold Coll., Met.
     Mus. on loan at Mus. City N.Y.   #L1400.109
                                      GB 198

1877. TIEBOUT, Cornelius (c. 1773-1832), (aft. BIRCH, Thomas).
The U.S. Frigate Constitution Capturing...Frigate Guerrière..., August 19, 1812,
1813, engr., 17¾" x 26⅜". Lib. of Congress.   GB 199

1878. TRUMBULL, John (1756-1843).
Reclining Nude,
c. 1787, dwg, 14⅛" x 24⅛". Yale U. Gall.
1938.273   GB 200

1879. ———.
Study for the Battle of Princeton,
1786. Princeton U. Lib.   GB 516A

1880. TWACHTMAN, John Henry (1853-1902).
Fishing Boats, Holland,
c. 1888, etch., 12½" x 17¾". Phila. Mus.
52.80.12   GB 201

1881. VOLCK, Adalbert John (1829-1912).
Caricature Portrait: Horace Greeley,
c. 1861, pencil dwg, 7⁹⁄₁₆" x 4¹¹⁄₁₆". M. & M.
Karolik Coll., Boston Mus.   GB 204B

1882. ———.
Passage Through Baltimore,
c. 1861, pencil dwg, 7¾" x 4³⁄₁₆". M. & M.
Karolik Coll., Boston Mus.   GB 204A

1883. WALTON, Henry (act. 1836-50).
East View of Ithaca, New York,
1837, col. lith., 11¾" x 25⅝". Brooklyn Mus.
45.144   GB 205

1884. WAUD, William (?-1878).
Signaling by Torches from General Butler's Headquarters,
1864, wash dwg, 5¾" x 10½". Lib. of Congress.
          GB 206

1885. WEIR, J. Alden (1852-1919).
Christmas Greens,
c. 1888, etch. & drpt, 7⅞" x 5⅞". Prints Div.,
N.Y. Pub. Lib.   GB 209

1886. ———.
Woman Sewing,
c. 1890, lith., 12¼" x 9". Prints Div., N.Y. Pub.
Lib.   GB 208

1887. WEST, Benjamin (1738-1820).
Angel of the Resurrection,
1801, lith., 12⅜" x 8⅞". Rosenwald Coll., Nat'l
Gall. Art.   GB 213

1888. WHISTLER, James Abbott McNeill
(1834-1903).
Annie Haden,
1860, drpt, 13¾" x 8⅜". Rosenwald Coll., Nat'l
Gall. Art.   GB 218

1889. ———.
Black Lion Wharf,
1859, etch., 5⅞" x 8⅞". Phila. Mus.   # 53.12.1
          GB 216

1890. ———.
Nocturne,
etch., 7⅞" x 11⅝". Prints Div., N.Y. Pub. Lib.
          GB 221

1891. WHISTLER, James Abbott McNeill
(1834-1903).
Riault, the Engraver,
1860, drpt, 8¾" x 5⅞". Prints Div., N.Y. Pub.
Lib.   GB 219

    1892. ——.
    St. Giles-in-the-Fields,
    1896, lith., 8½ x 5½ . Phila. Mus.   #46.71.6
                                         GB 227

1893. ——.
Tall Bridge,
1878, lith., 10⅞" x 7⅛". Rosenwald Coll., Nat'l
Gall. Art.   GB 225

    1894. YEAGER, Joseph (aft. KRIMMEL, J. L.).
    Victualers' Procession,
    1821, col. aqua., 14⅜" x 23¾". Coll. H. H. Kynett,
    Philadelphia, Pa.   GB 229

GRAPHIC ARTS OF THE TWENTIETH CENTURY

CARL ZIGROSSER

1895. ALBERS, Josef (1888-   ).
Aquarium,
1934, woodcut, 7⅛" x 10¼". Phila. Mus.
#47.37.13   GC 81

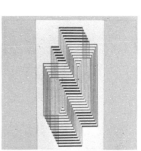

    *1896. ——.
    Ascension,
    1942, lith., 17¼" x 8³⁄₁₆". Mus. Mod. Art.
    #215.51   Purchase.   GC 1

1897. ALBRIGHT, Ivan LeLorraine (1897-   ).
Self-portrait - 55 Division Street,
1947, lith., 14¼" x 10¼". Mus. Mod. Art.
#429.53   Purchase.   GC 2

    1898. ALPS, Glen.
    Cliff Dwellings II,
    1954, col. serigraph, 16" x 25". Phila. Mus.
    #57.38.1   GC 82

1899. ARMS, John Taylor (1887-1953).
The Gothic Spirit,
1922, etch., 11¾" x 7⅛". Mus. Mod. Art.   #560.54
Purchase.   GC 3

    1900. BACON, Peggy (1895-   ).
    The Patroness,
    1927, etch., 10" x 7¹⁵⁄₁₆". Mus. Mod. Art.
    #613.40   Gift of Mrs. John D. Rockefeller, Jr.
                                       GC 4

1901. BARNET, Will (1911-   ).
Enfant,
1951, col. lith., 16¾" x 14". Mus. Mod. Art.
#87.52   Purchase.   GC 5

    1902. BASKIN, Leonard (1922-   ).
    Man of Peace,
    1952, woodcut, 59½" x 30⅝". Mus. Mod. Art.
    #430.53   GC 83A

* Items marked with an asterisk were not selected by
Mr. Zigrosser.

1903. BASKIN, Leonard (1922-   ).
Mantegna at Eremitani,
1952, wood engr., 14" x 23⅝". Phila. Mus.
#53.47.28   GC 83

    1904. BECKER, Fred (1913-   ).
    Encounter,
    1956, col. woodcut, 35¾" x 47¾". Phila. Mus.
    #56.44.1   GC 84

1905. BELLOWS, George (1882-1925).
Dempsey and Firpo,
1924, lith., 18⅛" x 22⅜". Mus. Mod. Art.
#556.51   Mrs. John D. Rockefeller, Jr., Fund   GC 6

    1906. ——.
    In the Park,
    1916, lith. (1st state), 16" x 21³⁄₁₆". Mus. Mod.
    Art.   #646.40   Gift of Mrs. John D.
    Rockefeller, Jr.   GC 7

1907. BENSON, Frank W. (1862-1951).
Broad Bills,
1919, etch. & drpt, 10" x 8". Phila. Mus.
#50.103.9   GC 85

    1908. BENTON, Thomas Hart (1889-   ).
    Going West,
    1929, lith., 12¼" x 23¼". Phila. Mus.
    #52.80.28   GC 86

1909. BERMAN, Eugene (1899-   ).
Nocturnal Cathedral,
1951, col. lith., 12⅞" x 9¼". Phila. Mus.
#52.31.39   GC 87

    1910. BIDDLE, George (1885-   ).
    Cows and Sugar Cane,
    1928, lith., 11½" x 7¾". Phila. Mus.   #43.2.48
                                                     GC 88

1911. BISHOP, Isabel (1902-   ).
Encounter,
1940, etch., 8¼" x 5½". Phila. Mus.   #41.99.112
                                                       GC 89

    1912. BLUME, Peter (1906-   ).
    Study for "Eternal City,"
    1933, pencil, 11¾" x 9⅜". Mus. Mod. Art.
    #242.54   Gift of Edgar Kaufmann, Jr.   GC 157

*1913. BRONER, Robert (1922-   ).
Blind Subway Minstrel: Harmonica Player,
1955, monotype, 35⅝" x 17⅝". Mus. Mod. Art.
#207.55   Purchase.   GC 8

    1914. CADMUS, Paul (1904-   ).
    Polo Game,
    c. 1936, etch., 7" x 9¹¹⁄₁₆". Mus. Mod. Art.   GC 9

1915. CALDER, Alexander (1898-   ).
Tightrope Artist,
1932, pen & ink, 9¾" x 18⅞". Phila. Mus.
#41.53.131   GC 148

    1916. CASTELLON, Federico (1914-   ).
    "Frustration of Little Things...,"
    1932, pen & ink, 10¾" x 15⅞". Phila. Mus.
                                                     GC 149

1917. CASTELLON, Federico (1914-   ).
Rendezvous in a Landscape,
1939, lith., 9 9/16" x 15 1/8". Mus. Mod. Art.
#642.39   Purchase.   GC 10

    1918. CHAMBERLAIN, Samuel (1895-   ).
    Dentelles Gothiques, Clamecy,
    1930, etch., 15" x 10". Phila. Mus.   #42.52.52
                               GC 90

1919. CHARLOT, Jean (1898-   ).
Mother and Child,
1941, col. lith., 12 1/2" x 18 5/8". Mus. Mod. Art.
#360.49   Gift of Albert Carman.   GC 11

    1920. CHESNEY, Lee (1920-   ).
    Pierced and Beset,
    1952, col. etch., engr. & aqua., 15 13/16" x 23 5/8".
    Mus. Mod. Art.   #582.54   Purchase.   GC 12

1921. CLOAR, Carroll (1913-   ).
Portrait (the Artist's Mother),
1940, lith., 14 7/8" x 10". Mus. Mod. Art.   #280.48
Purchase.   GC 13

    1922. COLE, Timothy (1852-1931)(aft.
    CONSTABLE, John).
    The Hay Wain,
    1899, wood engr., 5" x 7 3/4". Phila. Mus.
    #39.56.40   GC 91

1923. COLEMAN, Glenn O. (1887-1932).
Minetta Lane,
1928, lith., 11 1/4" x 11. Mus. Mod. Art.   #724.40
Gift of Mrs. John D. Rockefeller, Jr.   GC 14

    1924. CONSTANT, George (1892-   ).
    Girl at Window,
    c. 1938, etch. Phila. Mus.   #42.30.17   GC 92

1925. COOK, Howard (1901-   ).
Lower Manhattan,
1930, lith., 14" x 10". Phila. Mus.   #43.2.154   GC 93

    1926. ——.
    New England Church,
    1931, wood engr., 11 3/8" x 8 3/8". Phila. Mus.
    #43.2.136   GC 94

1927. CRAWFORD, Ralston (1906-   ).
Nets, Croix de Vie,
1955, lith., 23" x 18". Mus. Mod. Art.   #27.58
Purchase.   GC 15

    1928. CURRY, John Steuart (1897-1946).
    Line Storm,
    1935, lith., 9 3/4" x 14". Phila. Mus.   #41.53.15
                               GC 95

*1929. DAVIES, Arthur B. (1862-1928).
Doorway to Illusion,
1922, etch. & aqua., 7 11/16" x 6 9/16". Mus. Mod. Art.
#842.40   Gift of Mrs. John D. Rockefeller, Jr.   GC 16

    1930. ——.
    Uprising,
    1919, col. aqua., 6" x 9". Phila. Mus.   GC 96

1931. DAVIES, Arthur B. (1862-1928).
The Spring,
1895, lith., 8⅜" x 5⅝". Phila. Mus.   GC 95A

     1932. DAVIS, Stuart (1894-   ).
     Barber Shop Chord,
     1931, lith., 14" x 19". Mus. Mod. Art.   #738.40
     Gift of Mrs. John D. Rockefeller, Jr.   GC 17

1933. ——.
Detail Study for Cliché,
1957, col. lith., 12½" x 14⅝". Phila. Mus.   #58.53.7
                                         GC 97

     1934. ——.
     Windshield Mirror,
     c. 1932, gouache & ink, 21⅝" x 30¼". Phila. Mus.
     #55.61.1   GC 150

1935. DEHN, Adolf (1895-   ).
Garden of the Gods,
1940, lith., 13½" x 16½". Phila. Mus.
#41.53.476   GC 98

     1936. ——.
     Die Walküre,
     1930, lith., 13⁷⁄₁₆" x 17⅞". Mus. Mod. Art.
     #747.40   Gift of Mrs. John D. Rockefeller, Jr.
                                     GC 18

1937. ——.
Wintry Sun,
1930, pen & wash, 14⅞" x 22". Phila. Mus.
#54.78.43   GC 151

     *1938. DESHAIES, Arthur (1920-   ).
     The Alchemists,
     1953, wood engr., 20" x 11⅞". Mus. Mod. Art.
     #355.56   Purchase.   GC 19

1939. DURIEUX, Caroline (1896-   ).
Impasse,
1954, electron print, 12⅜" x 7¼". Phila. Mus.   GC 99

     1940. DWIGHT, Mabel (1876-1955).
     Aquarium,
     1928, col. lith., 10¼" x 10¾". Phila. Mus.
     #42.30.149   GC 100

*1941. FEININGER, Lyonel (1871-1956).
The Disparagers,
1911, etch., 8⅝" x 10¼". Mus. Mod. Art.
#218.55   Gift of Mrs. Lyonel Feininger.   GC 20

     1942. ——.
     Manhattan I,
     1951, lith., 10¾" x 8½". Phila. Mus.
     #52.31.68   GC 101

1943. ——.
The Old Locomotive,
1906, lith., 6¼" x 12⅝". Mus. Mod. Art.
#217.55   Gift of Mrs. Lyonel Feininger.   GC 21

     1944. FLANNAGAN, John B. (1895-1942).
     Recumbent Nude,
     c. 1936, brush & India ink, 10¼" x 10½". Phila.
     Mus.   #52.80.2   GC 152

*1945. FORNAS, Leander (1925-   ).
The Devil's Funeral,
1955, etch. & aqua., 11⁹⁄₁₆" x 17⁵⁄₈". Mus. Mod.
Art.   #80.56   Gift of Mr. & Mrs. Peter A.
Rubel.   GC 22

1946. FORSBERG, James (1919-   ).
The Family,
1953, cardboard & woodcut, 19⁷⁄₈" x 31¼". Mus.
Mod. Art.   #620.56   Gift of Bertha M.
Slattery.   GC 23

1947. FRASCONI, Antonio (1919-   ).
The Fulton Fish Market,
1952, col. woodcut in four panels, 23¾" x 11¾"
each panel. Mus. Mod. Art.   #84.54 A-D
Inter-American Fund.   GC 24

*1948. ——.
Self-portrait,
1951, woodcut, 21⁷⁄₈" x 6⁵⁄₈". Mus. Mod. Art.
#256.52   Inter-American Fund.   GC 25

1949. FRUEH, Alfred (1898-   ).
Lillian Russell,
c. 1920, col. linoleum cut, 14" x 10". Phila. Mus.
#43.56.9   GC 102

1950. FULLER, Sue (1914-   ).
Hen,
1945, engr. & soft ground etch., 14⁵⁄₈" x 11⁷⁄₈".
Mus. Mod. Art.   #86.49   Mrs. John D.
Rockefeller Fund.   GC 26

1951. GAG, Wanda (1893-1946).
Elevated Station,
1925, lith., 13³⁄₈" x 15¹⁵⁄₁₆". Mus. Mod. Art.
#257.52   Mrs. John D. Rockefeller Fund.   GC 27

1952. ——.
Philodendron,
1944, lith., 13" x 9½". Phila. Mus.   #52.32.19
                                             GC 103

1953. GANSO, Emil (1895-1941).
Nude with Mirror,
1930, etch. & aqua., 12" x 8". Phila. Mus.   GC 104

1954. GLACKENS, William (1870-1938).
Washington Square (a Holiday in the Park),
1913, pencil, 29" x 22". Mus. Mod. Art.
#138.40   Gift of Mrs. John D. Rockefeller, Jr.
                                             GC 158

1955. GOLDSTEIN, Milton (1914-   ).
The Sun,
1956, etch. & aqua., 17" x 13". Phila. Mus.
#57.38.8   GC 105

1956. GORKY, Arshile (1904-48).
Crayon Drawing,
1943, 19¾" x 27½". Wadsworth Atheneum.
#1953.275   GC 166

1957. GRAVES, Morris (1910-   ).
English Nightfall Piece,
1938, pencil & red ink, 24⅛" x 20½". Mus. Mod.
Art.   #16.42   Purchase.   GC 160

1958. GROPPER, William (1897-   ).
For the Record,
1936, lith., 11½" x 15¾". Phila. Mus.
#42.30.197   GC 106

1959. GWATHMEY, Robert (1903-   ).
Hitchhiker,
1943, serigraph, 16¾" x 13⅛". Mus. Mod. Art.
#27.48   Purchase.   GC 28

1960. HART, George Overbury ("Pops"),
(1868-1933).
Orchestra at Cock Fight,
1929, col. lith., 17⅞" x 24 1/16". Mus. Mod. Art.
#1040.40   Gift of Mrs. John D. Rockefeller, Jr.
                                                            GC 29

1961. HASKELL, Ernest (1876-1925).
Mirror of the Goddess,
1920, etch., 8⅞" x 11⅞". Phila. Mus.
#43.38.22   GC 107

*1962. HASSAM, Childe (1859-1935).
The Avenue of the Allies,
1918, drpt., 14¾" x 9 11/16". Mus. Mod. Art.
#937.40   Gift of Mrs. John D. Rockefeller, Jr.
                                                            GC 30

1963. ——.
House on Main Street, Easthampton,
1922, etch., 6 1/16" x 12⅛". Mus. Mod. Art.
#87.56   Mrs. John D. Rockefeller, Jr., Fund.   GC 31

1964. HILL, Clinton (1922-   ).
First Page,
1955, col. woodcut, 34½" x 11½". Mus. Mod. Art.
#45.58   GC 31A

1965. HOPPER, Edward (1882-   ).
The Evening Wind,
1921, etch., 6 15/16" x 8 5/16". Mus. Mod. Art.
#962.40   Gift of Mrs. John D. Rockefeller, Jr.   GC 32

1966. ——.
Night Shadows,
1921, etch., 6 15/16" x 8 3/16". Mus. Mod. Art.
#959.40   Gift of Mrs. John D. Rockefeller, Jr.
                                                            GC 33

1967. HORTER, Earle (1884-1940).
Rainy Night Chinatown,
c. 1925, aqua., 10¼" x 11⅛". Phila. Mus.   GC 108

1968. JACKSON, Martin (1919-   ).
Evening Song,
1952, lith., 12¾" x 18¼". Phila. Mus.
#52.31.92   GC 109

1969. JONES, John Paul (1924-   ).
Self-portrait,
1950, soft & hard ground etch., engr., aqua.,
16 1/16" x 10⅛". Mus. Mod. Art.   #97.52
Mrs. John D. Rockefeller, Jr., Fund.   GC 34

*1970. JORDAN, Raymond (1898-   ).
Black Rhythm,
1949, engr. & etch., 13 11/16" x 17⅞". Mus. Mod.
Art.   #367.56   Purchase.   GC 35

1971. KAHN, Max (1903-   ).
Lithographer Contemplating a Roller,
1939, col. lith., 25¼" x 18¾". Phila. Mus.
#44.41.21   GC 110

1972. KENT, Rockwell (1882-   ).
The End,
1927, wood engr., 5" x 7". Phila. Mus.
#44.26.17   GC 111

1973. KENT, Rockwell (1882-   ).
The Pinnacle,
1928, lith., 11$^{15}\!/_{16}$" x 7$^5\!/_{16}$". Mus. Mod. Art.
#1064.40   Gift of Mrs. John D. Rockefeller,
Jr.   GC 36

1974. KOHN, Misch (1916-   ).
Tiger,
1949, wood engr., 16$^5\!/_{16}$" x 23$^5\!/_8$". Mus. Mod. Art.
#433.49   Spaeth Foundation.   GC 37

*1975. KOPPELMAN, Chaim.
On Meeting Beauty,
1957, aqua. & roulette, 14$^7\!/_8$" x 17$^7\!/_8$". Mus. Mod.
Art.   #281.57   Purchase.   GC 38

1976. KUHN, Walter (1880-1949).
Trapeze Performer,
c. 1927, lith., 10$^1\!/_4$" x 8$^1\!/_2$". Phila. Mus.   GC 112

1977. KUNIYOSHI, Yasuo (1893-1953).
Interior with Dress Form,
1928, lith., 12$^9\!/_{16}$" x 8$^1\!/_2$". Mus. Mod. Art.
#1150.40   Gift of Mrs. John D. Rockefeller,
Jr.   GC 39

1978. KUPFERMAN, Lawrence (1909-   ).
Victorian Mansion,
1939, drpt, 14$^1\!/_{16}$" x 12$^7\!/_8$". Mus. Mod. Art.
#87.49   Mrs. John D. Rockefeller, Jr., Fund
                                                       GC 40

1979. LACHAISE, Gaston (1882-1935).
Nude,
1929, brush & ink, 17$^3\!/_4$" x 11$^5\!/_8$". Phila. Mus.
#43.36.2   GC 153

1980. LANDACRE, Paul (1893-   ).
The Press,
c. 1935, wood engr., 8$^1\!/_4$" x 8$^1\!/_4$". Phila. Mus.
#42.30.76   GC 113

*1981. LANDECK, Armin (1905-   ).
Alleyway,
1948, drpt, 13$^7\!/_8$" x 6$^{15}\!/_{16}$". Mus. Mod. Art.
#88.49   Mrs. John D. Rockefeller, Jr., Fund.   GC 41

1982. ——.
Stairhall,
1951, etch. & engr., 12" x 14$^3\!/_8$". Phila. Mus.
#52.31.71   GC 114

1983. LASANSKY, Mauricio (1914-   ).
Self-portrait,
1947, col. etch., aqua. & engr., 23$^{13}\!/_{16}$" x 15$^7\!/_8$".
Mus. Mod. Art.   #458.49   Inter-American
Fund.   GC 42

1984. LEBRUN, Rico (1900-   ).
Rabbit,
1945, lith., 14$^7\!/_{16}$" x 12$^5\!/_{16}$". Mus. Mod. Art.
#435.49   Spaeth Foundation.   GC 43

*1985. LEVINE, Arthur (1928-   ).
Cityscape,
1950, etch., 22" x 30$^1\!/_8$". Mus. Mod. Art.   #82.55
Gift of Mr. & Mrs. Irving Schugan.   GC 44

*1986. LEWIS, Martin.
The Glow of the City,
1930, etch., 11$^7\!/_{16}$" x 14$^3\!/_8$". Mus. Mod. Art.
#609.54   Purchase.   GC 45

1987. LEWIS, Martin.
Night, Greenwich Village,
1930, etch., 9⅞" x 12⅜". Phila. Mus.   # 32.15.1
                                                    GC 115

1988. LIMBACH, Russell (1904-   ).
Blues Singer,
1939, col. lith., 15" x 10". Phila. Mus.
2.43.56   GC 116

1989. LIPCHITZ, Jacques (1891-   ).
Study for Prometheus,
c. 1950, brush & ink, 16½" x 12⅝". Phila. Mus.
51.65.3   GC 154

*1990. LOZOWICK, Louis (1892-   ).
Still Life,
1929, lith., 10¼" x 13³⁄₁₆". Mus. Mod. Art.
#1216.40   Gift of Mrs. John D. Rockefeller, Jr.
                                                    GC 46

1991. ——.
Tanks,
1929, lith., 14" x 8". Phila. Mus.   # 43.2.183   GC 117

1992. MARGO, Boris (1902-   ).
The Sea,
1949, col. cellocut, 16⁹⁄₁₆" x 16⁹⁄₁₆". Mus. Mod.
Art.   # 502.49   Purchase.   GC 47

1993. MARIN, John (1870-1953).
Brooklyn Bridge,
1913, etch., 11¼" x 8⅞". Mus. Mod. Art.
1231.40   Gift of Mrs. John D. Rockefeller, Jr.   GC 48

*1994. ——.
St. Paul's, New York,
1930, etch., 9⅝" x 6¹³⁄₁₆". Mus. Mod. Art.
1233.40   Gift of Mrs. John D. Rockefeller, Jr.
                                                    GC 49

1995. ——.
Woolworth Building, New York,
1913, etch., 12¹³⁄₁₆" x 10⁷⁄₁₆". Mus. Mod. Art.
#1237.40   Gift of Mrs. John D. Rockefeller, Jr.   GC 50

1996. MARSH, Reginald (1898-1954).
Tattoo, Haircut and Shave,
1932, etch., 9¾" x 9¾". Phila. Mus.
41.53.486   GC 118

1997. MARTINELLI, Ezio (1913-   ).
Bog,
1952, col. etch. & aqua., 17¾" x 12". Phila. Mus.
52.31.25   GC 119

1998. MILLER, Kenneth Hayes (1876-1952).
Woman with Palm Leaf Fan,
1928, etch., 10" x 5". Phila. Mus.   # 43.2.107
                                                    GC 120

1999. MORGAN, Norma (1928-   ).
David in the Wilderness,
1955-56, engr., 34⅝" x 17½". Mus. Mod. Art.
372.56   Mrs. John D. Rockefeller, Jr., Fund.   GC 51

2000. MOY, Seong (1921-   ).
Chinese Actor,
1948, col. woodcut, 22¾" x 13¼". Mus. Mod. Art.
436.49   Spaeth Foundation.   GC 52

2001. MURPHY, John J. A.
Wild Horses,
1921, wood engr., 4⅜" x 5¼". Phila. Mus.   GC 121

2002. NASON, Thomas W. (1889-   ).
Leaning Silo,
1932, wood engr., 3⅜" x 8⅝". Phila. Mus.
          GC 122

2003. PARIS, Harold Persico (1925-   ).
The Innocents,
1956-57, col. engr. on lucite, 17¾" x 23⅞".
Phila. Mus.   GC 123

2004. PASCIN, Jules (1885-1930).
Nude,
c. 1925, crayon, 19¾" x 14⅛". Phila. Mus.
          GC 155

2005. PENNELL, Joseph (1857-1926).
The Gates of Pedro Miguel Lock,
1912, lith., 22" x 16⅞". Pa. Acad.   GC 124

2006. ——.
San Gimignano,
1883, etch., 10⅜" x 8". Lib. of Congress.
          GC 123A

2007. ——.
Timber Mills, Zaandam,
1897, lith., 8½" x 10½". Phila. Mus.   GC 123B

2008. PETERDI, Gabor (1915-   ).
Germination,
1952, col. aqua., etch. & engr., 19¾" x 23¹³⁄₁₆".
Mus. Mod. Art.   #469.53   Gift of Mrs.
Walter Barciss.   GC 53

*2009. ——.
Price of Glory,
1947, engr., 10⅞" x 17¾". Mus. Mod. Art.
#150.49   Mrs. John D. Rockefeller, Jr., Fund.   GC 54

*2010. PIERCE, Leona (1922-   ).
Strange Bird,
1952, col. woodcut, 10¾" x 27⅝". Mus. Mod. Art.
#292.52   Mrs. John D. Rockefeller, Jr., Fund.
          GC 55

2011. POZZATTI, Rudy (1925-   ).
Duomo,
1952, engr., 15⁷⁄₁₆" x 18¾". Mus. Mod. Art.
#380.56   Purchase.   GC 56

2012. PYTLAK, Leonard (1910-   ).
Night Skaters,
1941, col. serigraph, 13½" x 16⅛". Phila. Mus.
#42.52.30   GC 125

2013. RACZ, André (1916-   ).
Perseus Beheading Medusa, IV,
1945, engr. & soft ground etch., 21⁹⁄₁₆" x 14¹³⁄₁₆".
Mus. Mod. Art.   #439.49   Spaeth Foundation.   GC 57

2014. REDER, Bernard (1897-   ).
Lady of the Middle Ages,
1949, col. woodcut, 18³⁄₁₆" x 11⅞". Mus. Mod.
Art.   #196.50   Mrs. John D. Rockefeller, Jr.,
Fund.   GC 58

2015. RIGGS, Robert (1896-   ).
Psychopathic Ward,
1941, lith., 14¼" x 18¹³⁄₁₆". Mus. Mod. Art.
#627.54   Purchase.   GC 59

2016. ROBINSON, Boardman (1876-1952).
Turkish Cafe,
1918, lith., 14¼" x 10". Phila. Mus.   GC 126

2017. ROGALSKI, Walter R. (1923-   ).
Scorpion and Crab,
1951, engr., 14⅞" x 17¹³⁄₁₆". Mus. Mod. Art.
#25.52   Purchase.   GC 60

2018. RUZICKA, Rudolph (1883-   ).
Louisburg Square, Boston,
1914, col. woodcut, 5¼" x 3⅝". Phila. Mus.
                                           GC 127

*2019. SCHANKER, Louis (1903-   ).
Arrangement of Forms,
1949, col. woodcut, 22⅝" x 14³⁄₁₆". Mus. Mod. Art.
#445.49   Spaeth Foundation.   GC 61

2020. ——.
Carnival,
1945, col. woodcut, 14⁵⁄₁₆" x 21¹⁄₁₆". Mus. Mod.
Art.   #444.49   Spaeth Foundation.   GC 62

2021. SCHRAG, Karl (1912-   ).
Falling Night,
1949, col. etch. & engr., 17⅞" x 12". Mus. Mod.
Art.   #102.52   Mrs. John D. Rockefeller, Jr.,
Fund.   GC 63

2022. SCHWARTZ, Aubrey (1928-   ).
Predatory Bird,
1957, lith., 22½" x 30". Phila. Mus.   GC 128

2023. SELIGMANN, Kurt (1900-   ).
Oedipus and the Sphinx,
1944, etch., 17⅝" x 11¾". Mus. Mod. Art.
#14.44.1   Gift of Henry Church.   GC 64

2024. SHAHN, Ben (1898-   ).
Phoenix,
1952, serigraph & w.c., 22¾" x 21½". Mus. Mod.
Art.   #383.56   Mrs. John D. Rockefeller,
Jr., Fund.   GC 65

2025. ——.
"Where there is a sword there is no book,"
1950, serigraph, 13⅞" x 11⅝". Mus. Mod. Art.
#299.55   Purchase.   GC 66

*2026. SHEELER, Charles (1883-   ).
Barn Abstraction,
1918, lith., 8¼" x 18½". Mus. Mod. Art.
#385.56   Mrs. John D. Rockefeller, Jr., Fund.
                                           GC 67

*2027. ——.
Delmonico Building,
1926, lith., 9¾" x 6¹¹⁄₁₆". Mus. Mod. Art.
#1267.40   Gift of Mrs. John D. Rockefeller, Jr. GC 68

2028. ——.
Yachts,
1924, lith., 9¼" x 11". Phila. Mus.
#50.134.C.913   GC 129

2029. SLOAN, John (1871-1951).
Nude on Stairs,
1930, etch., 9⅞" x 7¾". Phila. Mus.
#56.35.156   GC 130

*2030. ———.
Roofs, Summer Night,
1906, etch., 5¼" x 7". Mus. Mod. Art.
#1304.40   Mrs. John D. Rockefeller, Jr.,
Kraushaar 23.   GC 69

2031. ———.
Turning Out the Light,
1905, etch., 4⅞" x 6⅞". Mus. Mod. Art.
#1297.40   Gift of Mrs. John D. Rockefeller, Jr.
Kraushaar 16.   GC 70

2032. SMITH, Charles (1893-   ).
Cocks,
1939, col. monoprint, printed from movable
forms, 10¼" x 18¼". Mus. Mod. Art.   #366.41
Purchase.   GC 71

2033. SOYER, Raphael (1899-   ).
The Mission,
1935, lith., 12⅛" x 17¼". Mus. Mod. Art.
#454.54   Gift of Mrs. Bertha M. Slattery.   GC 72

2034. SPENCER, Niles (1893-1952).
White Factories,
1928, lith., 10½" x 13½". Phila. Mus.   GC 131

2035. SPRUANCE, Benton (1909-   ).
Anabasis,
1957, col. lith., 17¼" x 23¼". Phila. Mus.
#58.41.27   GC 132

2036. STERNBERG, Harry (1904-   ).
Steel,
1941, lith., 11¾" x 20¾". Phila. Mus.
#41.53.333   GC 133

2037. STERNER, Albert (1863-1946).
Amour Mort,
1915, lith., 12½" x 21⅛". Phila. Mus.
#41.53.67   GC 134

2038. SUMMERS, Carol (1925-   ).
Construction,
1951, col. woodcut, 29⅞" x 13¾". Mus. Mod. Art.
#33.52   Purchase.   GC 73

2039. VELONIS, Anthony (1911-   ).
Decoration Empire,
1939, col. serigraph, 11½" x 13¾". Phila. Mus.
#41.53.272b   GC 135

2040. WALD, Sylvia (1914-   ).
Spirit's Constellation,
1952, serigraph, 15⅛" x 20½". Mus. Mod. Art.
#642.54   Purchase   GC 74

2041. WALKOWITZ, Abraham (1880-   ).
Abstraction: City,
1927, lith., 14" x 7½". Phila. Mus.   #41.114.64
                                            GC 136

2042. WARSAGER, Hyman (1909-   ).
Manhattan Night,
1939, col. woodcut, 17¼" x 14¼". Phila. Mus.
                                            GC 137

2043. WASHBURN, Cadwallader.
Buddhist Priest,
1904, drpt, 6" x 4½". Phila. Mus.   #41.85.38   GC 138

2044. WATKINS, Franklin C. (1894-   ).
Softly, Softly,
1951, woodcut, 17⅞" x 31⅞". Phila. Mus.
#51.59.12   GC 139

2045. WAYNE, June (1918-   ).
Last Chance,
1955, lith., 22⅜" x 28". Phila. Mus.   #56.98.3 GC 140

2046. WEBER, Max (1881-   ).
Beautification,
1947, lith., 15¼" x 18". Phila. Mus.   #54.40.8
                                                   GC 141

2047. ——.
The Feast of the Passover,
1918, col. woodcut, 5" x 5¹⁵⁄₁₆". Mus. Mod. Art.
#1464.40   Gift of Mrs. John D. Rockefeller, Jr.
                                                   GC 76

*2048. ——.
Primitive Man,
1918, col. woodcut, 9¹⁵⁄₁₆" x 3⅛". Mus. Mod. Art.
#1472.40   Gift of Mrs. John D. Rockefeller, Jr.
                                                   GC 77

2049. WENGENROTH, Stow (1906-   ).
Serenity,
1951, lith., 11¹¹⁄₁₆" x 17¹³⁄₁₆". Mus. Mod. Art.
#643.54   Purchase.   GC 78

2050. WHITE, Charles Henry (1878-1918).
St. James Church, Richmond,
1906, etch., 7¼" x 9". Phila. Mus.   GC 142

2051. WICKEY, Harry (1892-   ).
Sultry August Afternoon,
1936, lith., 11⅜" x 12⅛". Phila. Mus.
#41.53.147   GC 143

2052. WOOD, Grant (1892-1942).
Honorary Degree,
1937, lith., 11⅞" x 6¹⁵⁄₁₆". Mus. Mod. Art.
#377.49   Purchase.   GC 79

2053. WRIGHT, Stanton MacDonald (1890-   ).
Gaviota Pass,
1937, lith., 18" x 15". Phila. Mus.   GC 144

2054. YOUNG, Mahonri M. (1877-1957).
Navajo Watering Place,
1915, etch., 5" x 10¼". Phila. Mus.   #43.2.167
                                                   GC 145

2055. YUNKERS, Adja (1900-   ).
Magnificat,
1953, col. woodcut, 44" x 48". Phila. Mus.
#53.52.3   GC 146

2056. ——.
Ostia Antiqua VI,
1955, col. woodcut, 21" x 35⅜". Phila. Mus.
#56.71.1   GC 147

INDIAN ARTS AND ARTIFACTS
FREDERICK J. DOCKSTADER

PREHISTORIC

2057. *Maul,*
Mass. or Conn., 1000-1700. Carved stone, may
represent a fish head, L. 6". Cranbrook Inst.
Sci.　#1872　　　　　　　　　　　　IN 286

2058. *Crouching Figure,*
MISSISSIPPI Culture, Ill., c. 1200-1600. Stone,
H. 12". Chicago Nat. Hist. Mus.　#55500
　　　　　　　　　　　　　　　　　IN 308

2059. *Gorget* (spider),
MISSISSIPPI Culture, Ill., 1200-1600. Shell,
D. 3½". Chicago Nat. Hist. Mus.　#55034　　IN 309

2060. *Effigy Bird Pipe* (swan),
WOODLAND Culture, Barton Co., Ill., c. 1200-
1500. Steatite (?), L. 9". Chicago Nat. Hist. Mus.
#54960　　　　　　　　　　　　　　IN 302

2061. *Effigy Pipe,*
WOODLAND Culture, Ind., c. 1200-1500. Steatite
(?), L. 15". Chicago Nat. Hist. Mus.　#55518　IN 303

2062. *Seated Human Figure,*
MOUND BUILDER, Ohio, c. 1200-1600. Carved
stone, H. 9½". Smithsonian Institution.
#248285　　　　　　　　　　　　　IN 395

2063. *Human Head,*
INTRUSIVE MOUND Culture, Heinisch Mound,
Ohio, c. 1200-1500. Carved stone, H. 6". Ohio
State Mus.　#154/2　　　　　　　　IN 400

2064. *Human Head,*
HOPEWELL Culture, Seip Mound, Ohio, 1000-
1300. Pottery, H. 3". Ohio State Mus.　　IN 401

2065. *Effigy Pipe* (feeding crane),
Ohio, 1000-1300. Carved catlinite, H. 3½". Mus.
Am. Indian.　#16/3595　　　　　　　IN 72

2066. *Effigy Pipe* (spoonbill duck on fish),
HOPEWELL Mound, Ohio, 1000-1300. Stone,
4" x 2". Chicago Nat. Hist. Mus.　#56750
　　　　　　　　　　　　　　　　　IN 338

2067. *Effigy Pipe* (bear),
HOPEWELL Culture, Seip Mound, Ross Co., Ohio,
1000-1300. Carved stone, L. 13". Ohio State Mus.
　　　　　　　　　　　　　　　　　IN 408

2068. *Effigy Pipe* (toad),
HOPEWELL Culture, Mound City Group, Ohio,
1000-1300. Carved stone, partial restoration,
L. 3½". Ohio State Mus.　#260/35　IN 405

2069. *Spear-thrower Weights,*
HOPEWELL Mound, Ohio, 1000-1300. Stone,
L. 3½" to 4". Chicago Nat. Hist. Mus.   #56407;
#56408; #56466; #56467; #56746   IN 312

2070. *Carved Human Finger,*
HOPEWELL Mound, Ohio, 1000-1300. Carved
cannel coal, L. c. 6½". Chicago Nat. Hist. Mus.
#56401   IN 337

2071. *Heads* (2), deer antler, H. c. 4";
Human Figure, fossil mammoth ivory, H. c. 2½",
HOPEWELL Mound, Ohio, 1000-1300. Chicago
Nat. Hist. Mus.   #56735; #56736; #56737   IN 335

2072. *Headdress* (deer antler),
HOPEWELL Mound, Ohio, 1000-1300. Copper,
H. c. 16". Chicago Nat. Hist. Mus.   #56080
                                          IN 317

2073. *Bird Claw,*
HOPEWELL Mound, Ohio, 1000-1300. Cut sheet
mica, L. c. 11". Chicago Nat. Hist. Mus.
#110131   IN 318

2074. *Human Figure,*
HOPEWELL Mound, Ohio, 1000-1300. Cut sheet
mica, L. 13". Chicago Nat. Hist. Mus.   #110133
                                          IN 319

2075. *Human Hand* (silhouette),
HOPEWELL Mound, Ohio, 1000-1300. Cut sheet
mica, L. 10". Chicago Nat. Hist. Mus.   #110132
                                          IN 320

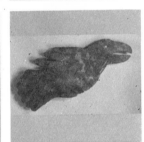

2076. *Bird Effigy,*
HOPEWELL Mound, Ohio, 1000-1300. Sheet
copper, inlaid pearl, L. 15". Chicago Nat. Hist.
Mus.   #56356   IN 321

2077. *Fish Effigy,*
HOPEWELL Mound, Ohio, 1000-1300. Sheet
copper, L. c. 8". Chicago Nat. Hist. Mus.
#56177   IN 322

2078. *Head of Serpent,*
HOPEWELL Mound, Ohio, 1000-1300. Sheet
copper, L. c. 20". Chicago Nat. Hist. Mus.
#56165   IN 333

2079. *Ornaments,*
HOPEWELL Mound, Ohio, 1000-1300. Cut copper
sheet, c. 6". Chicago Nat. Hist. Mus.
#56188/56191; #56164; #56163   IN 314

2080. *Duck Hawk* (ornament),
HOPEWELL Culture, Mound City Group, Ohio,
1000-1300. Copper, 8" x 12". Ohio State Mus.
#260/125   IN 399

2081. *Effigy Pipe* (human face),
MOUND BUILDER Culture, near Fort Atkinson,
Wis., 1300-1600. Carved steatite, H. 12".
Dartmouth College Mus.   #49.25.12209   IN 252

2082. *Wilmington, or Richardson Tablet,*
ADENA Culture, Clinton Co., Ohio, 500-1000.
Sandstone, bas-relief, 4¾" x 5¾". Ohio State
Mus.   #3490/210   IN 398

2083. *Bird Stones,*
MOUND BUILDER, Ind. & Ohio, 1300-1600.
Carved slate, largest L. 5". Mus. Am. Indian.
4/6985; # 19/5052; # 9/2544   IN 104

    2084. *Effigy Jar* (female figure),
MIDDLE MISSISSIPPI Culture, found at St. Louis,
Mo., 1300-1700. Pottery, H. 9". Mus. Am.
Indian.   # 7386   IN 75

2085. *Effigy Pipe* (warrior executing victim),
SPIRO Mound, LeFlore Co., Okla., 1200-1600.
Stone, H. 9½". Mus. Am. Indian.   # 21/4088   IN 90

    2086. *Human Effigy Pipe, or "Lucifer Pipe,"*
SPIRO Mound, Okla., 1200-1600. Stone,
representing man & deer, H. 8". Stovall Mus.
Sci. & Hist., U. Okla.   # B99-2   IN 200

2087. *Human Effigy Head,*
SPIRO Mound, Okla., 1200-1600. Carved wood
flecked with copper, H. 2". Cranbrook Inst. Sci.
6071   IN 272

    2088. *Button,*
SPIRO Mound, Okla., 1200-1600. Shell, carved
as human face, D. 1½". Cranbrook Inst. Sci.
5869   IN 273

2089. *Ceremonial Maces,*
TEMPLE Mound, LeFlore Co., Okla., 1200-1600.
Flaked stone, traces of paint, L. 14". Mus. Am.
Indian.   # 18/9334-5   IN 107

    2090. *Effigy Jar* (frog),
MOUND BUILDER, Blytheville, Mississippi Co.,
Ark., 1200-1600. Pottery, H. 7¾". Mus. Am.
Indian.   # 5/6528   IN 79

2091. *Effigy Jar* (human head),
MOUND BUILDER, Blytheville, Mississippi Co.,
Ark., 1200-1600. Painted & incised clay, H. 6".
Mus. Am. Indian.   # 5/2981   IN 85

    2092. *Human Effigy Jar,*
MOUND BUILDER, Ark., 1200-1600. Red & tan
polychrome painted pottery, H. 10½". Smithsonian
Institution.   # 63107   IN 389

2093. *Effigy Pot* (cat),
MIDDLE MISSISSIPPI Culture, White River, Ark.,
1200-1600. Pottery, 11" x 9". Chicago Nat. Hist. Mus.
50664   IN 304

    2094. *Water Bottle,*
MIDDLE MISSISSIPPI Culture, Ark., 1200-1600.
Incised black pottery, H. 6¼". Mus. Am. Indian.
21/5859   IN 78

2095. *Water Bottle,*
MOUND BUILDER, Lee Co., Ark., 1200-1600.
Painted clay, H. 11½". Mus. Am. Indian.
17/4296   IN 86

    2096. *Ear Ornament,*
MIDDLE MISSISSIPPI Culture, White River, Ark.,
1200-1600. Stone, D. 3½". Chicago Nat. Hist.
Mus.   # 45420   IN 305

2097. *Effigy Bowl,*
CADDOAN, Ouachita Parish, La., 1300-1700.
Pottery, H. 3". Mus. Am. Indian.   #17/3247   IN 88

   2098. *Jar,*
   square-base, CADDOAN, Ouachita Parish, La.,
   1300-1700. Pottery, H. 5½". Mus. Am. Indian.
   #17/3248   IN 89

2099. *Paint Disk (?),*
MIDDLE MISSISSIPPI Culture, Issaquena Co.,
Miss., 1200-1600. Carved stone, incised design,
D. 8½". Ohio State Mus.   #14/24   IN 407

   2100. *Pipe* (figure holding pipe),
   MOUND BUILDER, Jefferson Co., Miss.,
   1200-1600. Carved sandstone, H. 5½".
   University Mus.   #14328   IN 369

2101. *Gorget* (human figure),
MIDDLE MISSISSIPPI Culture, Miss. Valley,
1200-1600. Shell, D. c. 7". Chicago Nat. Hist.
Mus.   #68554   IN 311

   2102. *Bowl* (crested wood duck),
   Moundville, Ala., c. 1400-1600. Diorite, 10" x 12".
   Mus. Am. Indian.   #16/5232   IN 92

2103. *Effigy Pipe* (squatting man),
Moundville, Ala., 1400-1600. Sandstone, 4" x 8".
Mus. Am. Indian.   #17/2810   IN 91

   2104. *Monolithic Axe,*
   Hale Co., Ala., 1400-1600. Carved stone, L. 12".
   Mus. Am. Indian.   #17/891   IN 105

2105. *Jar,*
CADDOAN, Yell Co., Ark., 1300-1700. Pottery,
incised, 5" x 7". Mus. Am. Indian.   #5/6318   IN 77

   2106. *Effigy Jar* (human head),
   FORTUNE Mound, Ala., 1200-1600. Pottery,
   H. 7¼". Peabody Mus., Harvard U.   #21542
   IN 266

2107. *Human Figure with Folded Arms,*
MIDDLE MISSISSIPPI Culture, Ala., 1200-1600.
Ceramic jar, c. 12". Chicago Nat. Hist. Mus.
#50639   IN 306

   2108. *Ornament* (spider),
   MIDDLE MISSISSIPPI Culture, Ala., 1200-1600.
   Wood, c. 5" x 2½". Chicago Nat. Hist. Mus.
   #51425   IN 307

2109. *Effigy* (male),
MOUND Culture, Cumberland Valley, Tenn.,
1200-1600. Stone, H. 13½". Mus. Am. Indian.
#7277   IN 97

   2110. *Kneeling Human Figure,*
   TEMPLE MOUND BUILDER, Wilson Co., Tenn.,
   1200-1600. Carved stone, 18". U. Tenn.
   #1/1Wil   IN 385

2111. *Figure of a Kneeling Man,*
MOUND BUILDER, Shiloh, Tenn., 1200-1600.
Carved limestone, H. 10". Smithsonian
Institution.   #271570   IN 387

 2112. *Kneeling Male Figure,*
 MIDDLE MISSISSIPPI Culture, Duck River,
 Humphreys Co., Tenn., 1200-1600. Carved
 sandstone, H. 26¼". Mus. of Primitive Art.
 #57.1   IN 254

2113. *Effigy Pipe* (bird's head & 4 rattlesnakes),
Tenn., 1200-1600. Carved calcite, L. 11". Mus.
Am. Indian.   #10/3596   IN 76

 2114. *Bird Effigy Pipe,*
 MOUND CULTURE, Murfreesboro, Tenn.,
 1200-1600. Steatite, L. 12¼".   #7759   IN 93

2115. *Disk Gorgets,*
MOUND BUILDER, Ala. & Tenn., 1200-1600.
Incised shell, D. 3½". Mus. Am. Indian.
#17/929; #15/855   IN 100

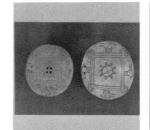

 2116. *Gorget,*
 CASTALIAN SPRINGS Mound, Sumner Co., Tenn.,
 1200-1600. Incised shell, D. 4". Mus. Am. Indian.
 #15/853   IN 99

2117. *Gorget,*
MOUND BUILDER, Hamilton Co., Tenn.,
1200-1600. Incised shell, D. 6½". Mus. Am.
Indian.   #17/2920   IN 98

 2118. *Effigy Jar* (dog),
 MOUND BUILDER, Tenn., 1200-1600. Pottery,
 H. 9". Peabody Mus., Harvard U.   #13998
          IN 265

2119. *Effigy Pipe Bowl* (bird),
MOUND BUILDER, Jackson Co., N.C., 1200-1600.
Steatite, 4" x 9". Mus. Am. Indian.   #15/1085   IN 80

 2120. *Effigy Pipe* (duck),
 Cherokee Co., N.C., 1200-1600. Steatite, L. 8".
 Mus. Am. Indian.   #4/4251   IN 81

2121. *Effigy Figure* (seated),
TUMLIN Mound, Bartow Co., Ga., 1200-1600. Stone,
traces of original paint, H. 15½". Mus. Am. Indian.
#14/1455   IN 82

 2122. *Seated Human Figure,*
 ETOWAH MOUNDS, Cartersville, Ga. (Etowah III
 or IV), 1400-1700. Carved stone, H. 18".
 Peabody, Phillips Acad.   #82/R113   IN 287

2123. *Male and Female Figures,*
ETOWAH MOUNDS, Cartersville, Ga., 1400-1700.
Marble, 24" x 22¼". Ga. State Hist. Comm.
#424   IN 380

 2124. *Effigy Pipes* (male & female),
 ETOWAH MOUNDS, Cartersville, Ga., 1400-1700.
 Stone, H. 3"; H. 2". Ga. State Hist. Comm.
 #676; #675   IN 382

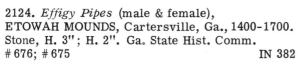

2125. *Gorget,*
ETOWAH MOUNDS, Cartersville, Ga., 1400-1700.
Shell, anthropomorphized eagle figure, incised
lines filled with black pigment, D. 3⅝". Ga. State
Hist. Comm.   IN 383

2126. *Hair Ornament,*
ETOWAH MOUNDS, Cartersville, Ga., 1400-1700.
Embossed & cut-out sheet copper eagle, H. 7¼".
Ga. State Hist. Comm.   IN 384

2127. *Vessel,*
ETOWAH MOUNDS, Cartersville, Ga., 1400-1700.
Pottery, impressed pattern, H. 8½". Ga. State
Hist. Comm.   #716   IN 381A

2128. *Gourd-effigy Pot,*
ETOWAH MOUNDS, Cartersville, Ga., 1400-1700.
Negative painted pottery, H. 8⅜". Ga. State Hist.
Comm.   #483   IN 381

2129. *Turtle Head,*
KEY DWELLER, Key Marco, Fla., c. 1000-1600.
Carved wood painted, H. 4". University Mus.
#40715   IN 371

2130. *Bird Head,*
KEY DWELLER, Key Marco, Fla., c. 1000-1600.
Carved wood, 4⅛" x 2⅝". University Mus.
#41240   IN 372

2131. *Figure Head* (deer),
KEY DWELLER, Key Marco, Fla., c. 1000-1600.
Carved wood, life size. University Mus.   #40707
                                                     IN 373

2132. *Alligator Head,*
KEY DWELLER, Key Marco, Fla., c. 1000-1600.
Carved wood painted, 9½" x 4½". University Mus.
#40718   IN 375

2133. *Seated Cat Figure,*
KEY DWELLER, Key Marco, Fla., c. 1000-1600.
Carved wood, H. 6". Smithsonian Institution.
#240915   IN 393

2134. *Dancer,*
KEY DWELLER, Key Marco, Fla., c. 1000-1600.
Painted on sun shell valve, L. 3¾". University
Mus.   #40796   IN 374

2135. *Effigy Jar* (human),
Gadsden Co., Fla., 1300-1700. Pottery, H. 13".
Mus. Am. Indian.   #17/3410   IN 96

2136. *Decorated Bowl: Two Men and Blanket,*
MIMBRES, New Mex., 1100-1300. Painted
pottery, H. 9". Peabody Mus., Harvard U.
#95.815   IN 267

2137. *Ceremonial Mortar,*
PUEBLO BONITO, New Mex., 900-1200.
Polychrome painted sandstone, 4" x 8". Mus.
Am. Indian.   #5/1364   IN 87

2138. *Effigy Jar* (bird),
ANASAZI Culture, Socorro Co., New Mex.,
1000-1300. Painted pottery, H. 9". Mus. Am.
Indian.   #18/6406   IN 74

2139. *Etched Shell,*
HOHOKAM, 900-1100. Ariz. State Mus.   #6550   IN 201

2140. *Plate,*
HOHOKAM, Snaketown Ruin, Ariz., 900-1100. Red
on buff, D. 10¾". Ariz. State Mus.   #43855
IN 202

2141. *Plate,*
HOHOKAM, c. 900-1100. Pottery, red on buff.
D. 12". Ariz. State Mus.   #21150   IN 257

2142. *Burden Basket,*
BASKET MAKER, Canyon del Muerto, Ariz.,
c. 500-900. Polychrome weave, yucca fiber,
oval, 32" x 29". U. Colo. Mus.   #2558   IN 220

2143. *Sandals,*
BASKET MAKER, Canyon del Muerto, Ariz.,
c. 500-900. Polychrome weave, yucca fiber,
10" x 3¾". U. Colo. Mus.   #2463A   IN 219

2144. *Carrying Strap,*
ANASAZI Culture, Pueblo Southwest, c. 500-900.
Woven, painted cotton, 3⅛" x 18⅓". Chicago Nat.
Hist. Mus.   #165170   IN 340

2145. *Butterfly Bowl,*
HOPI, Sikyatki Village, Ariz., 1300-1700. Painted
pottery, D. 10". Chicago Nat. Hist. Mus.   #80942
IN 342A

2146. CLIFF DWELLINGS.
Montezuma's Well,
across well, 900-1100. Sedona, Ariz.   IN 261

2147. ——. Ibid. Det.   IN 262

2148. CLIFF DWELLINGS.
Montezuma's Castle,
900-1100. Sedona, Ariz.   IN 264

2149. *Pueblo,*
TAOS, n.d., Taos, New Mex. Gen. view.   IN 259

2150. ——. Ibid. A street.   IN 260

2151. *Oil Lamp,*
ESKIMO, Kenai, Alaska, 500-1100. Carved stone,
H. 5½". University Mus.   #NA 9251   IN 361

HISTORIC

2152. *Mask,*
ESKIMO, Kuskokwim River, Alaska, c. 1875-1900.
Carved wood, painted, H. 11". Cranbrook Inst.
Sci.   #3225   IN 268

2153. *Ceremonial Effigy Mask* (fish),
ESKIMO, Kuskokwim River, Alaska, c. 1940.
Carved & painted wood, L. 17¼". Portland Art
Mus.   # 48.3.379   IN 221

2154. *Basket,*
ESKIMO, Alaska, c. 1880-1900. Sewn leather,
H. 6". Chicago Nat. Hist. Mus.   # 27727
                                                 IN 290

2155. *Fur Parka and Boots,*
ESKIMO, Bering Straits, Alaska, c. 1900.
Caribou fur, H. 58". Brooklyn Mus.   # 36.42;
36.32   IN 235

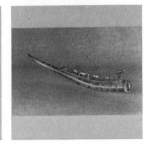

2156. *Pipe,*
ESKIMO, Alaska, 1850-75. Carved bone
(scrimshaw), L. 10¼". Cranbrook Inst. Sci.
4542   IN 269

2157. *Spirit Mask,*
TLINGIT, Point Lena, Alaska, 1875. Carved &
painted wood, L. 13". Mus. Am. Indian.
9/8032   IN 69

2158. *"Sky Man" Mask,*
TLINGIT, Sitka, Alaska, c. 1850-75. Carved &
painted wood, H. 7¾". Mus. Am. Indian.
9/8034   IN 83

2159. *Mask,*
TLINGIT, Chichagof Is., Alaska, 1835. Carved &
painted cedar, H. 13". Mus. Am. Indian.   # 9/7989
                                                 IN 84

2160. *Mask* (spirit of brown bear),
TLINGIT, Alaska, 1875. Wood, 7" x 11½". Mus.
Am. Indian.   # 9/8030   IN 67

2161. *Human Mask,*
TLINGIT, Prince of Wales Is., Alaska, 1865.
Wood, mice carved over eyebrow areas & cheeks,
7" x 10½". Mus. Am. Indian.   # 9/8036   IN 59

2162. *Ceremonial Mask* (mosquito),
TLINGIT, Alaska, 1860's. Hammered & incised
copper, inlaid eyes, 8½" x 14". Mus. Am. Indian.
6981   IN 68

2163. *Kneeling Male Effigy* (canoe figurehead),
TLINGIT, Alaska, 1860, Wood, inlaid with
haliotis, 14" x 21". Mus. Am. Indian.   # 1/6713   IN 71

2164. *Carved Human Figure,*
TLINGIT, Sitka, Alaska, 1850. Red cedar wood,
16". Wash. State Mus.   # 2216   IN 215

2165. *Owl Man Statuette,*
TLINGIT, Yakutat, Alaska, 1850-75. Wood
carving, painted, H. 17½". Portland Art Mus.
48.3.354   IN 213

2166. *Guardian from Medicine Man's Grave,*
TLINGIT, Alaska, before 1910. Diseased wood or
fungus, H. 22". Wash. State Mus.   # 1056
                                                 IN 238

2167. *Ceremonial Headdress,*
TLINGIT, Ketchikan, Alaska, c. 1875. Worked
copper, inlaid with abalone, H. 6⅝". Portland Art
Mus.   #48.3.440   IN 212

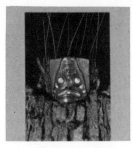

2168. *Ceremonial Hat,*
TLINGIT, Alaska, 1850-1900. Carved & painted
cedar wood, H. 10¾". University Mus.
#NA 11741   IN 363

2169. *Shaman's Hat,*
TLINGIT, 1850-1900. Quillwork, H. 9". Chicago Nat.
Hist. Mus.   #79722   IN 298

2170. *Chief's Hat,*
TLINGIT, Sitka, Alaska, 1860. Painted cedar
bark basketry, H. 14". Mus. Am. Indian.
#17/6251   IN 95

2171. *War Helmet,*
TLINGIT, Chilkoot, Alaska, 1850. Carved &
painted wood, H. 9". Am. Mus. Nat. Hist.
#E/453   IN 227

2172. *Box Front,*
TLINGIT, Chilkat River, Alaska, 1880. Carved &
painted cedar, 11½" x 27½". Mus. Am. Indian.
#20/3895   IN 109

2173. *House Posts,*
TLINGIT, Kluckwan, Alaska, 1850-1900. Carved
& painted wood, H. 91". University Mus.
#NA 31-29-14   IN 365B

2174. *Fish-killer Club,*
TLINGIT, Kluckwan, Alaska, 1855. Wood, L. 20".
Mus. Am. Indian.   #5/6897   IN 65

2175. *Ceremonial Staff,*
TLINGIT, Haines, Alaska, c. 1875. Carved &
painted wood, L. 10'9⅛". Portland Art Mus.
#48.3.465   IN 210

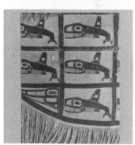

2176. *Ceremonial Blanket* (killer-whale repeat
design),
TLINGIT, Chilkat, Alaska, c. 1850. Woven
mountain goat hair, W. 5'2". Chicago Nat. Hist.
Mus.   #19571   IN 297

2177. *Buckskin Dance Apron,*
TLINGIT, Cape Fox, Alaska, 1875. Painted hide,
flannel trim, 27" x 40". Wash. State Mus.
#1956   IN 217

2178. *Dance Kilt,*
TLINGIT, Alaska, 1850-75. Woven textile,
c. 28" x 22". Chicago Nat. Hist. Mus.   #79304
                                                IN 299

2179. *Fighting Knives,*
TLINGIT, Alaska, 1840-60. Steel, bone, ivory,
wood, greatest L. 21". Mus. Am. Indian.
#1/2504; #8/1841; #2/8702   IN 108

2180. *Box Drum,*
TLINGIT, Alaska, 1850-75. Carved &
painted cedar wood, H. 35½". University Mus.
#NA 6828   IN 362

2181. *Effigy Pipe* (squatting man),
TLINGIT, Kluckwan, Alaska, 1850. Carved walrus
ivory, inlaid with abalone, H. 2½". Mus. Am.
Indian.   #9204   IN 103

 2182. *Pipe Bowl,*
 TLINGIT, Alaska, 1855. Cedar, H. 8½". Mus.
 Am. Indian.   #1/2927   IN 64

2183. *Pipe Bowl,*
TLINGIT, Alaska, 1875. Cedar, H. 3". Mus. Am.
Indian.   #9247   IN 66

 2184. *Shaman's Charms,*
 TLINGIT, Alaska, 1855-65. Carved ivory, largest
 L. 5". Mus. Am. Indian.   #4/1669; #1/2154;
 #11/1816   IN 102

2185. *Shaman's Charms,*
TLINGIT, Sitka and Wrangell, Alaska, 1860's.
Carved & inlaid ivory, largest L. 5". Mus. Am.
Indian.   #9/7948; #2/2089   IN 101

 2186. *Comb,*
 TLINGIT, Alaska, 1875. Carved wood, inlaid,
 5½" x 2¾". University Mus.   #NA 4265   IN 364

2187. *Grease Dish,*
TLINGIT, S. Eastern Alaska, late 1800's.
Mountain sheep horn, 8½" x 5½". Wash. State
Mus.   #L.1666   IN 239

 2188. *Spoon,*
 TLINGIT, Wrangell Is., Alaska, 1880. Wood,
 L. 23½". Mus. Am. Indian.   #2/6103   IN 63

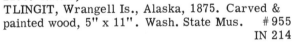

2189. *Rattle,*
TLINGIT, 1880. Hammered copper, abalone shell
inlay, H. 9½". Southwest Mus.   #980-9-131   IN 207

 2190. *Rattle,*
 TLINGIT, Wrangell Is., Alaska, 1875. Carved &
 painted wood, 5" x 11". Wash. State Mus.   #955
                                         IN 214

2191. *Ornamental Carving,*
TLINGIT, 1880. Maple, 4" x 16". Wash. State
Mus.   #2288   IN 216

 2192. *Ceremonial Headdress* (frog),
 HAIDA, Prince of Wales Is., Alaska, 1890. Carved
 & painted wood, 8½" x 5¼". Portland Art Mus.
 #48.3.241   IN 222

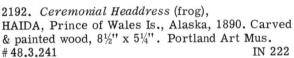

2193. *Dance Kilt,*
HAIDA, c. 1850. Decorated cloth, 20" x 30". Am.
Mus. Nat. Hist.   #16/344   IN 225

 2194. *Figure of a Woman,*
 HAIDA, c. 1900. Carved cedar, painted, H. 8".
 Cranbrook Inst. Sci.   #3224   IN 270

2195. *Mother and Child,*
HAIDA, late 19th C. Carved cedar, inlaid eyes,
H. 23". Mus. Primitive Art.   #56.335   IN 253

    2196. *The Bear Mother,*
    HAIDA, Alaska, c. 1900. Carved stone, H. 7".
    Cranbrook Inst. Sci.   #1763   IN 271

2197. *"Bear Mother" Effigy Statuette,*
HAIDA, Skidegate, Queen Charlotte Is., 1880.
Carved argillite, H. 5½". Smithsonian Institution.
#73117   IN 391

    2198. *Coffin Front,*
    HAIDA, Skidegate, Queen Charlotte Is.,
    1850-1900. Carved wood, 4'8" x 20½". Chicago
    Nat. Hist. Mus.   #85040   IN 292

2199. *Ornate Pipe,*
HAIDA, Skidegate, Queen Charlotte Is., collected
1853 by George Catlin. Carved argillite, L. 13½".
Mus. Am. Indian.   #1/9272   IN 106

    2200. *Shaman's Rattle,*
    HAIDA, Alaska, 1890. Carved & painted cedar,
    L. 13". Mus. Am. Indian.   #1/8028   IN 73

2201. *Bowl,*
HAIDA, c. 1875. Carved wood, abalone shell inlay.
Southwest Mus.   #611 G 701   IN 203

    2202. *Seal Oil Dish,*
    HAIDA, Sitka, Alaska, c. 1880. Carved cedar,
    6" x 14". Dartmouth College Mus.
    #46.17-9576   IN 251

2203. *Grease Dish* (2 cranes),
HAIDA, 1850-1900. Wood, c. 12". Chicago Nat.
Hist. Mus.   #14407   IN 294A

    2204. *Grease Dish* (otter),
    HAIDA, 1850-1900. Wood, 12". Chicago Nat. Hist.
    Mus.   #14412   IN 294

2205. *Feast Ladle,*
HAIDA, Alaska, 1855. Carved mountain sheep
horn, L. 15½". Mus. Am. Indian.   #9/8065   IN 61

    2206. *Dance Leader's Staff,*
    HAIDA, Alaska, 1885. Wood, L. 36". Mus. Am.
    Indian.   #21/8504   IN 70

2207. *Club,*
HAIDA, Queen Charlotte Is., 1850-75. Carved
antler, L. 15". University Mus.   #NA 3360   IN 415

    2208. *Carved Wooden Club,*
    HAIDA, Alaska, 1875. Wood, L. 26½". Mus. Am.
    Indian.   #6/9458   IN 62

2209. *Copper "Money" Shield,*
HAIDA (?), c. 1850. Painted & incised sheet
copper, H. 30". Brooklyn Mus.   # 05.260   IN 237

 2210. *Memorial Statue* (human figure),
 SALISH, 1876. Painted wood, carved, 6' 6" x 28".
 Am. Mus. Nat. Hist.   # 16/6946   IN 226

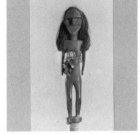

2211. *Ceremonial Figure,*
WASCO, 1800-50. Wood, H. 12". Chicago Nat.
Hist. Mus.   # 87603   IN 301

 2212. *Figure on Shaman's Staff,*
 QUINAULT, Washington, 1850-1900. Carved &
 painted wood, 15½" x 7½". Am. Mus. Nat. Hist.
 # 16A/4921   IN 413

2213. *Harvest Mask,*
ONONDAGA, c. 1875. Basswood, decorated with
feather & corn husks, L. 34". Mus. Am. Indian.
6/1103   IN 1

 2214. *Whirlwind Mask,*
 CAYUGA, 1900. Carved & painted basswood,
 H. 10½". Mus. Am. Indian.   # 19/8335   IN 4

2215. *False Face Society Mask,*
ONONDAGA, 1860. Basswood, H. 12". Mus. Am.
Indian.   # 21/6509   IN 5

 2216. *False Face Society Mask,*
 CAYUGA, N.Y., 1860. Wood, L. 11½". Mus. Am.
 Indian.   # 21/8246   IN 14

2217. *Mask* ("Old Broken Nose"),
ONONDAGA, Tonawanda, N.Y., 1937. Carved &
painted basswood with horsehair. Cranbrook
Inst. Sci.   # 3754   IN 285

 2218. *False Face Mask,*
 SENECA, N.Y., early 20th C. Carved wood,
 L. 10". Denver Art Mus.   # N.Sen. 8-P
 IN 224

2219. *Miniature False Face Medicine Masks,*
SENECA, Cattaraugus Reservation, N.Y., 1915-20.
Wood, painted, largest L. 4½". Mus. Am. Indian.
2/9809; # 20/6598; # 20/1870; # 2/6341   IN 16

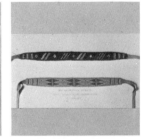

 2220. *Burden Straps,*
 ONEIDA, c. 1800. Dyed moose hair, woven on elm
 bark. L. 20"; 24". Chicago Nat. Hist. Mus.
 # 92071-72   IN 358

2221. *Effigy Spoons,*
ONEIDA, Wis., 1850-1900. Carved wood, animal
handles (squirrel, woodcock, grouse, swan), longest
8". Cranbrook Inst. Sci.   # 2123-2125; # 2242   IN 284

 2222. *Feast Spoon,*
 IROQUOIS, c. 1875. Carved wood, man reading
 book. Chicago Nat. Hist. Mus.   # 92093   IN 357

2223. *Garters*,
MOHEGAN, Conn., 1870. Beadwork on woven
textile, 3" x 12½". Mus. Am. Indian.   # 10/9724   IN 25

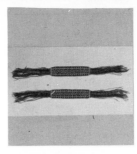 

  2224. *Shoulder Bag and Strap*,
  MOHEGAN, Conn., 1800-50. Beadwork on cloth
  & buckskin, 9½" x 10". Mus. Am. Indian.
  # 10/9723   IN 21

2225. *Leggings and Cap*,
PENOBSCOT, Maine, 1900. Silk work on red
flannel, decorated with beads, 23½" x 9½";
16½" x 9½". University Mus.   # NA 3619-20   IN 368

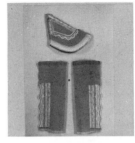 

  2226. *Baby Carrier*,
  PENOBSCOT, Maine, 1825-75. Carved wood,
  H. 29½". Mus. Am. Indian.   # 9628   IN 11

2227. *Coat Collar and Cuffs*,
PENOBSCOT, Maine, 1875-1900. Beaded cloth,
collar, max. W. 20"; L. c. 16". Chicago Nat.
Hist. Mus.   # 176487   IN 359

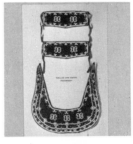 

  2228. *"Solid Face" Mask*,
  DELAWARE, Okla., 1890's. Carved & painted
  wood, L. 28". Mus. Am. Indian.   # 2/814
                                             IN 6

2229. *Wampum Belt*,
DELAWARE, Pa. Given to William Penn at the
Treaty of Shackamaxon, 1682. Quahog shell
woven on buckskin, 5½" x 24½". Mus. Am. Indian.
5/3150   IN 26

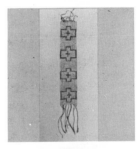 

  2230. *Booger Mask*,
  CHEROKEE, N.C., 1925. Wood, painted, H. 10½".
  Mus. Am. Indian.   # 8/7800   IN 12

2231. *Bag and Shoulder Strap*,
SEMINOLE, Fla., 1830's. Beadwork on strouding,
bag 7½" x 8½", strap 3" x 24". Mus. Am. Indian.
8/4299   IN 20

  2232. *Woven Sash*,
  SEMINOLE, Fla., 1860. Wool, 3" x 30½". Mus.
  Am. Indian.   # 2/5650   IN 22

2233. *Storage Basket and Lid*,
CHITIMACHA, La., 1890. Dyed cane, polychrome
design, 6" x 6". Mus. Am. Indian.   # 9557   IN 7

  2234. *Polychrome Basket*,
  CHITIMACHA, La., 1890. Woven cane, H. 5½".
  Mus. Am. Indian.   # 22/5207   IN 3

2235. *Wooden Bowl*,
KASKASKIA, Ill., 1750-75. Carved wood, beaver
design, L. 19¼". University Mus.   # L-83-6   IN 367

  2236. *Man's Moccasins*,
  HURON, Mich., 1830. Dyed moose hair on black-
  dyed deerhide, L. 9". Mus. Am. Indian.
  # 19/6346   IN 15

2237. *Blanket Shawl,*
MIAMI, Wabash, Ind., 1850-75. Silk appliqué &
beadwork on cloth, 55½" x 51½"· Cranbrook
Inst. Sci. #2208   IN 281

    2238. *Man's Leggings,*
    MIAMI, Wabash, Ind., 1850-75. Silk appliqué &
    beadwork on broadcloth, 14½" x 35½";
    24" x 9". Cranbrook Inst. Sci.   #2209; #2210
                             IN 282

2239. *Man's Moccasins,*
MIAMI, Wabash, Ind., 1850-75. Silk appliqué on
flaps, beadwork on buckskin, L. 9½". Cranbrook
Inst. Sci. #2207   IN 283

    2240. *Weaving Heddle,*
    POTAWATOMI, Skunk Hill, Wis., 1875-1900.
    Carved wood, 11½" x 9⅞". Cranbrook Inst. Sci.
    #3053   IN 277

2241. *Box for Storing Feathers,*
POTAWATOMI, Wis., 1850-75. Wood, incised,
L. 16½", W. 3¾", Depth 1½". Cranbrook Inst. Sci.
#3125   IN 276

    2242. *Roach Spreader,*
    POTAWATOMI, Cassian, Wis., 1850-75. Carved
    bone, L. 6½". Cranbrook Inst. Sci.   #2389
                             IN 274

2243. *Roach,*
POTAWATOMI, Blackwell, Wis., 1850-75. Dyed
deer hair & turkey beard, L. 10½". Cranbrook
Inst. Sci. #3063   IN 275

    2244. *Man's Shirt,*
    MENOMINI (Great Lakes), c. 1890. Beadwork
    trimming on black trade cloth, W. 18" x L. 36".
    Am. Mus. Nat. Hist.   IN 231

2245. *Belt,*
MENOMINI (Great Lakes), c. 1880. Woven wool,
L. 100" x W. 15". Am. Mus. Nat. Hist.
#50/9797   IN 230

    2246. *Pouch,*
    OTTAWA, Cross Village, Mich., 1825-50. Quilled
    buckskin dyed black, 6½" sq. Cranbrook Inst. Sci.
    #3690   IN 278

2247. *Effigy of Man* (doll squatting with crossed legs),
CHIPPEWA, c. 1875. Carved wood, 4¾". Am.
Mus. Nat. Hist.   #50/3722   IN 229

    2248. *Man's Coat,*
    CHIPPEWA, c. 1850. Beadwork trim on hide,
    W. (shoulder) 12½", L. 40". Am. Mus. Nat. Hist.
                             IN 228

2249. *Knife Sheath,*
CHIPPEWA, Turtle Mt., N. Dak., 1900. Beadwork
on rawhide, L. 16½". Mus. Am. Indian.
#20/4607   IN 34

    2250. *Pipe,*
    CHIPPEWA, Minn., 1850's. Wood, incised
    decoration, L. 24". Mus. Am. Indian.
    #15/2826   IN 29

2251. *Woven Mat,*
CHIPPEWA, c. 1850. Dyed grass, 7' 7" x 3' 3".
Am. Mus. Nat. Hist.   IN 232

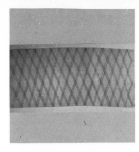

    2252. *Leggings,*
    PONCA, Okla., 1900. Silk appliqué & beadwork
    decoration, L. 33". Mus. Am. Indian.
    #19/3263   IN 50

2253. *Woman's Shawl,*
WINNEBAGO, Nebr., 1900. Ribbon work appliqué
on cloth, 18" x 34". Mus. Am. Indian.   #21/2688
                                                       IN 37

    2254. *Medicine Bowl* (bird effigy),
    WINNEBAGO, Sioux City, Iowa, 1875-1900.
    Carved wood, D. 3⅜", H. 2¼". Cranbrook Inst.
    Sci.   #2249   IN 280

2255. *Medicine Bowl* (turtle effigy on base),
WINNEBAGO, Sioux City, Iowa, 1850-75. Carved
wood, D. 2⅝", H. 1¼". Cranbrook Inst. Sci.
#2246   IN 279

    2256. *Pipe and Stem,*
    WINNEBAGO, Nebr., 1890. Quillwork & wood,
    L. 17½". Mus. Am. Indian.   #2/3268   IN 53

2257. *Pipe,*
WINNEBAGO, 1850-1900. Wood, L. c. 4½".
Chicago Nat. Hist. Mus.   #15161   IN 356

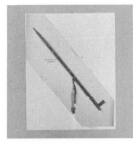

    2258. *Ceremonial Midewiwin Bowl,*
    SAC & FOX, 1860. Wood, 6" x 14". Mus. Am.
    Indian.   #2/6544   IN 42

2259. *Drum Holders* (horse heads),
OTO, c. 1850-75. Wood, H. c. 2½'. Chicago Nat.
Hist. Mus.   #71706   IN 354

    2260. *War Club,*
    OTO, 1850's. Wood, L. 23½". Mus. Am. Indian.
    #3/3555   IN 28

2261. *Shield Cover,*
OSAGE, Okla., c. 1900. Painted buffalo hide, D.
16". Mus. Am. Indian.   #4/5261   IN 31

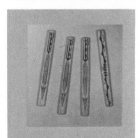

    2262. *Game Sticks* (4),
    KIOWA, 1875-1900. Wood, L. 6⅝". Chicago Nat.
    Hist. Mus.   #67841   IN 355

2263. *Woman's Dress,*
KIOWA, Okla., 1890. Buckskin painted & beaded,
L. 44". Mus. Am. Indian.   #20/3885   IN 57

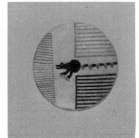

    2264. *Shield Cover,*
    KIOWA, c. 1900. Painted hide, D. 20".
    Smithsonian Institution.   #154349-A   IN 388

2265. *Dance Shield,*
COMANCHE, Okla., 1870. Buckskin, D. 17½".
Mus. Am. Indian.   # 2/1883   IN 35

2266. *Girl's Robe,*
CHEYENNE, 1850-90. Buckskin, painted,
45" x 36". Chicago Nat. Hist. Mus.   # 96847
                                            IN 349

2267. *Parfleche,*
CHEYENNE, c. 1875-1900. Painted hide,
c. 42" x 18". Chicago Nat. Hist. Mus.   # 97120 IN 351

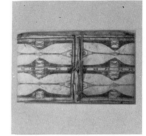 

2268. *Woman's Robe,*
ARAPAHO, c. 1850. Painted hide, 96" x 69".
University Mus.   # 45-15-706   IN 376

2269. *Eyeshade,*
ARAPAHO, 1850-75. Painted rawhide, L. 14".
Chicago Nat. Hist. Mus.   # 23469   IN 347

2270. *Sun Dance Skull of Buffalo,*
ARAPAHO, Wyo., 1870. Painted, decorated with
grass, 16½" x 24".   Mus. Am. Indian.
13/5098   IN 10

2271. *Horse Bridle Ornament,*
CROW, c. 1875. Buckskin, beaded, L. 12¾".
Carnegie Mus.   # 2418/97   IN 411

 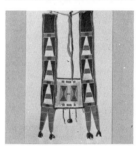

2272. *Horse Neck Ornament,*
CROW, c. 1875. Buckskin, beaded, 33" x 16".
Carnegie Mus.   # 2418/98   IN 409

2273. *Crupper,*
CROW, c. 1875. Painted rawhide, L. 32".
Carnegie Mus.   # 2418/91   IN 410

2274. *Baby Carrier,*
CROW, Mont., 1910. Beadwork, L. 42". Mus.
Am. Indian.   # 2/3140   IN 32

2275. *Girl's Robe,*
CROW, 1850-70. Beaded buckskin, c. 30" x 42".
Chicago Nat. Hist. Mus.   # 69412   IN 352

2276. *Shield Cover,*
CROW, Mont., 1845. Painted buffalo hide, D. 24".
Mus. Am. Indian.   # 20/7130   IN 33

2277. *Parfleche,*
BLACKFOOT, 1875-1900. Painted hide, c. 16" x
24". Chicago Nat. Hist. Mus.   # 51651   IN 348

2278. *Baby Carrier Hood,*
SIOUX, S. Dak., 1900. Bead & quillwork on cloth,
L. 33". Mus. Am. Indian.   # 22/4423   IN 36

2279. *Ceremonial Pipe*,
SIOUX, S. Dak., 1875-1900. Catlinite bowl, L. 30".
Mus. Am. Indian.   # 8756   IN 54

2280. *Image of Sacred Guardian*,
SIOUX, c. 1850 (?). Wood, H. c.12". Chicago Nat.
Hist. Mus.   # 67625   IN 353

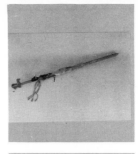

2281. *Decorated Robe*,
SIOUX, c. 1850. Quillwork on buffalo hide.
Southwest Mus.   # 630-6-82   IN 208

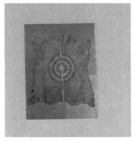

2282. *Man's Ghost Dance Shirt*,
WAHPETON SIOUX, S. Dak., 1890. Painted
cotton with beadwork strip, L. 30". Mus. Am.
Indian.   # 19/6762   IN 56

2283. *Man's Shirt*,
MANDAN, 1800-50. Buckskin with quillwork
decoration, H. 43". University Mus.   # 38252   IN 379

2284. *Man's Leggings*,
MANDAN, 1800-50. Quillwork on buckskin,
L. 50". University Mus.   # 38251   IN 378

2285. *Shield*,
MANDAN, N. Dak., 1865. Painted buffalo hide,
D. 19". Mus. Am. Indian.   # 21/4017   IN 40

2286. *Man's Shirt*,
ASSINIBOIN, Mont., 1900. Quillwork on buckskin,
H. 29½". Mus. Am. Indian.   # 20/928   IN 47

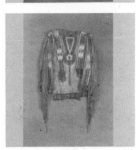

2287. *Man's Shirt*,
ASSINIBOIN, Mont., 1880. Quillwork & horsehair
on buckskin, L. 31½". Mus. Am. Indian.
20/1456   IN 49

2288. *Man's Shirt*,
ASSINIBOIN, Mont., 1900. Beadwork on buckskin,
17" x 20½". Mus. Am. Indian.   # 22/2727
                                                       IN 27

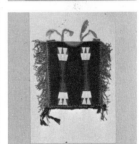

2289. *Parfleche*,
PLAINS, c. 1875. Painted rawhide, 21" x 14".
University Mus.   # 29-47-184   IN 370

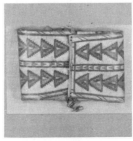

2290. *Robe*,
NEZ PERCÉ, c. 1850-70. Beaded & painted
buckskin, 5' x 4'. Chicago Nat. Hist. Mus.
69143   IN 346

2291. *Baby Carrier*,
NEZ PERCÉ, Idaho, 1880. Beaded buckskin,
L. 37½". Mus. Am. Indian.   # 18/9171   IN 38

2292. *Shield*,
UTE, Colo., 1875. Painted rawhide, D. 22½".
Mus. Am. Indian.   # 19/7329   IN 48

2293. *Sheath for Knife,*
UTE, Utah, 1900. Beadwork, L. 25½". Mus. Am.
Indian.   #2/5135   IN 24

 2294. *Boots,*
 UTE, Colo., 1880-1900. Beaded buckskin, 10"
 heel to toe. Mus. Am. Indian.   #6986   IN 39

2295. *Shoulder Sash,*
ALIBAMU, Tex., c. 1875. Beadwork on cloth,
5" x 24". Mus. Am. Indian.   #2/6757   IN 18

 2296. *Shoulder Sash,*
 KOASATI, Tex., c. 1875. Beadwork on cloth,
 6" x 24". Mus. Am. Indian.   #1/8587   IN 19

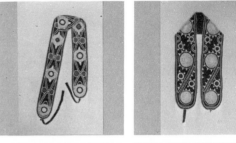

2297. *Basketry Plaque,*
HOPI, Ariz., c. 1900. Wicker weave, D. 24".
Chicago Nat. Hist. Mus.   #103531   IN 343

 2298. *Jar,*
 HOPI, Ariz., 1915. Painted pottery, H. 20". Mus.
 Am. Indian.   #19/2701   IN 44

2299. *Jar,*
ACOMA PUEBLO, New Mex., 1910. Polychromed
pottery, H. 9½". Mus. Am. Indian.   #19/4333   IN 55

 2300. *Woman's Dress,*
 ACOMA PUEBLO, c. 1875. Embroidered on wool,
 46" x 56". Am. Mus. Nat. Hist.   IN 234

2301. *Shield,*
TESUQUE PUEBLO, New Mex., c. 1850. Painted
buffalo hide, D. 20". Southwest Mus.
#491 G 1058   IN 205

 2302. *Shield,*
 SANTA CLARA PUEBLO, New Mex., c. 1850.
 Painted buffalo hide, D. 20". Southwest Mus.
 #491 G 1057   IN 204

2303. *Woman's Headdress* (used in Corn Dance),
ZUÑI, New Mex., 1900. Wood painted & decorated
with feathers, H. 35". Mus. Am. Indian.
#10/8739   IN 41

 2304. *Mask of Thlasiskwa Kachina,*
 ZUÑI, New Mex., c. 1900. Painted leather,
 feathers, wood, H. c. 18". Brooklyn Mus.
 #04.219   IN 236

2305. *Fetish Jar and 2 Fetishes,*
ZUÑI, New Mex., 1915. Pottery, H. 9½".
Mus. Am. Indian.   #20/3696   IN 8

 2306. *Shield,*
 PIMA, Southern Ariz., c. 1850. Painted rawhide,
 D. 20". Smithsonian Institution.   IN 396

2307. *Shield,*
APACHE, 1870. Painted buffalo hide, D. 20".
Southwest Mus.   #630 G 166   IN 204A

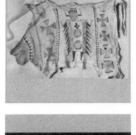

2308. *Fiddle and Bow,*
WHITE MOUNTAIN APACHE, Ariz., 1920's.
Painted yucca stalk, L. 24". Mus. Am. Indian.
#20/7147   IN 43

2309. *Saddle Bag,*
CHIRICAHUA APACHE, Ariz., 1910. Cut leather,
rawhide, 19½" x 44". Mus. Am. Indian.
#2/1199   IN 46

2310. *Devil Dance Headdress,*
SAN CARLOS APACHE, Ariz., 1915. Painted
wood, L. 37". Mus. Am. Indian.   #8/9949
                                             IN 45

2311. *Medicine Man's Shirt,*
APACHE, c. 1860-80. Painted buckskin, H. 26",
W. 35". Smithsonian Institution.   IN 394

2312. *War Shirt,*
CHIRICAHUA APACHE, Ariz., 1880. Painted
buckskin, scalplock fringe, L. 31". Mus. Am.
Indian.   #8/8017   IN 58

2313. *Basket,*
PANAMINT, 1900's. Woven grasses, H. 8".
University Mus.   #NA 8279   IN 255

2314. *Gambling Tray,*
TULARE, Calif., 1890-1910. Basketry, D. 31".
University Mus.   #NA 8307   IN 366

2315. *Basket,*
CHEMEHUEVI, Calif., 1900's. Woven grasses,
H. c. 5½". University Mus.   #NA 8804   IN 377

2316. DATSOLALI (weaver), WASHO, Nev.
Basket,
1918, H. 13". Philbrook Art Center.
#3169-3199   IN 250

2317. DATSOLALI (weaver), WASHO, Nev.
Basket,
c. 1910, H. 7". University Mus.   #38-26-1   IN 256

2318. *Baskets* (3),
POMO, 1850-1900. Feathers interwoven. Chicago
Nat. Hist. Mus.   IN 341

CONTEMPORARY PAINTING

2319. JAKE, Albin R., PAWNEE.
Pawnee Women Preserving Corn,
1949, w.c. & tempera, 30" x 22". Philbrook Art
Center.   #1211: IPC 360   IN 242

2320. MOMADAY, Al, KIOWA.
Apache Fire Dance,
1955, tempera, 20" x 21". Philbrook Art
Center.   #1698: IPC 386   IN 245

2321. BOSIN, Blackbear, KIOWA-COMANCHE.
Prairie Fire,
1953, w.c., 34" x 23¾". Philbrook Art Center.
#1564: IPC 381   IN 240

2322. BLUE EAGLE, Acee (d. 1959), CREEK-
PAWNEE.
Oklahoma War Dancers,
1951, w.c., 37" x 24". Philbrook Art Center.
#1393: IPC 168   IN 243

2323. WEST, Richard, CHEYENNE.
Viewing the Medicine Arrows,
1951, w.c., 23" x 24". Philbrook Art Center.
#2033: IPC 398   IN 248

2324. HOWE, Oscar, SIOUX.
Sioux Sun Dance,
n.d., w.c., 22" x 32¼". Philbrook Art Center.
#1224: IPC 370   IN 247

2325. HERRERA, Velino, ZIA.
Ceremonial Buffalo Dance,
1948, w.c., 28" x 21". Philbrook Art Center.
#817: IPC 522   IN 246

2326. HOUSER, Allen, APACHE.
Fresh Trail Apache War Party,
1952, w.c., 22" x 35". Philbrook Art Center.
#1468: IPC 575   IN 244

2327. TSIHNAJINNIE, Andrew, NAVAJO.
Navajo Woman Weaver,
1952, w.c., 39½" x 30½". Philbrook Art Center.
#1465: IPC 574   IN 241

2328. BEAVER, Fred, CREEK.
Muskogee Polecat Dance,
1949, tempera, 24½" x 16". Philbrook Art
Center.   #1208: IPC 154   IN 249

2329. BESODY, Hosteen, NAVAJO.
The Mountain Chant,
1902, sand painting, 40" x 36". Taylor Mus.
#3272   IN 258

PAINTING OF THE SEVENTEENTH AND
EIGHTEENTH CENTURIES
VIRGIL BARKER

2331. ANON.
Abraham and Isaac,
mid-18th C., fresco. Warner House, Portsmouth,
N.H.   PA 132

    2332. ANON.
    Landscape,
    aft. 1789, oil on wood panel, 27¼" x 51¼".
    Worcester Art Mus.   #1947.18   PA 130

2333. ANON.
Terrace of a Mansion,
1775-1800, oil on wood panel, Met. Mus. (wall
panel in room from "Marmion," King George Co.,
Va.)   #16.112   Rogers Fund, 1916   PA 131

    2334. ANON.
    Two Indian Chiefs,
    mid-18th C., fresco. Warner House, Portsmouth,
    N.H.   PA 133

2335. ANON.
Thomas Van Alstyne,
1721, o.c., 39¼" x 30". N.Y. Hist. Soc.   PA 22

    2336. ANON.
    Mrs. Thomas Van Alstyne,
    1721, o.c., 39¼" x 30". N.Y. Hist. Soc.   PA 23

2337. ANON.
John Van Cortlandt,
1720-30, o.c., 57" x 41". Brooklyn Mus.
#41.152   PA 42

    2338. ANON.
    Portrait of Elizabeth Eggington,
    1664, o.c., 36⁷⁄₁₆" x 29⅝". Wadsworth Atheneum.
    #1956.93   PA 152

2339. ANON.
Robert Gibbs,
1670, o.c., 40" x 33". Coll. Theron J. Damon, on
loan to Boston Mus.   #249.35   PA 16B

    2340. ANON.
    Edward Jaquelin II as a Child,
    c. 1722, o.c., 31¼" x 26". Ambler Family, on
    loan to Virginia Mus. Fine Arts.   #L1.39.6
                                      PA 26A

2341. ANON.
David, Joanna and Abigail Mason,
1670, o.c., 39½" x 42⅝". Nathaniel Hamlen,
Wayland, Mass.   PA 13

    2342. ANON.
    James A. dePeyster (?),
    1720-30, o.c., 50¼" x 41". N.Y. Hist. Soc.
                                      PA 41

285

2343. ANON.
Rev. James Pierpont,
1711, o.c., 31½" x 25". Lent by Allen Evarts
Foster to Yale U. Gall.   #101.1929   PA 17

2344. ANON.
Mrs. James Pierpont (Mary Hooker),
1711, o.c., 31" x 25". Lent by Allen Evarts
Foster to Yale U. Gall.   #102.1929   PA 18

2345. ANON.
Mrs. Anne Pollard,
1721, o.c., 28¾" x24". Mass. Hist. Soc.   PA 7

2346. ANON.
Nicolas William Stuyvesant,
1666, o.c., 35" x 25⅝". N.Y. Hist. Soc.   PA 19

2347. ANON.
Elisabeth Paddy (Mrs. John Wensley),
1670-80, o.c., 42¼" x 33¾". Pilgrim Hall,
Plymouth, Mass.   #296   PA 8

2348. ANON.
Thomas Thacher (?),
c. 1670-78, o.c., 29½" x 24⅞". Old South Assoc.,
Boston, Mass.   #1661   PA 6

2349. ALEXANDER, Cosmo John (c. 1724-72).
Alexander Grant,
1770, o.c., 50" x 40". Stonington Hist. Soc.,
Conn.   PA 64

2350. BADGER, Joseph (1708-65).
James Badger (1757-1817, artist's grandson),
c. 1760, o.c., 42½" x 33⅛". Met. Mus.   #29.85
Rogers Fund, 1929.   PA 73

2351. ———.
Mrs. John Edwards (Abigail Fowle),
1750-60, o.c., 36½" x 25½". Boston Mus.
#24.421   PA 50B

2352. ———.
Portrait of Hannah Upham Haskins,
1759, o.c., 35⅞" x 28⅜". Brooklyn Mus.
#52.43   PA 72A

2353. ———.
Captain John Larrabee,
c. 1760, o.c., 83½" x 51⅛". Worcester Art Mus.
#1920.53   PA 51B

2354. BENBRIDGE, Henry (1743-1812).
Hartley Family Group,
n.d., o.c., 77" x 60". Coll. Maitland Armstrong,
Newport, R.I.   PA 139

2355. BLACKBURN, Joseph (act. in U.S. 1754-63).
Theodore Atkinson,
1760, o.c., 50" x 40¼". Worcester Art Mus.
#1918.13   PA 58

2356. ———.
Mrs. Theodore Atkinson (Hannah Wentworth),
1760, o.c., 49⅛" x 39⅛". Cleveland Mus.
#563.19   PA 59A

2357. BLACKBURN, Joseph (act. in U.S. 1754-63).
Elizabeth and James Bowdoin,
1760, o.c., 36½" x 57½". Bowdoin College Mus.
Fine Arts.　　#1826.11　　　　　　　　PA 39B

　　　　2358. ——.
　　　　Isaac Winslow and His Family,
　　　　1755, o.c., 54½" x 79½". Boston Mus.
　　　　#42.684　　　　　　　　　　　　PA 57

2359. BLYTH, Benjamin (1746-aft. 1787).
Samuel Curwen,
1772, pastel on canvas, 22" x 17". Essex Inst.
#4,134.7　　　　　　　　　　　　　PA 125

　　　　2360. ——.
　　　　Sarah Curwen,
　　　　1772, pastel on canvas, 22" x 17". Essex Inst.
　　　　#4,134.12　　　　　　　　　　PA 126

2361. BRIDGES, Charles (act. 1735-40).
Mrs. Maria Taylor Byrd of Westover, Virginia
(1674-1744, second wife of William Byrd),
1724(?), o.c. 49½" x 40". Met. Mus.　#25.108
Fletcher Fund, 1925.　　　　　　　　PA 37

　　　　2362. BROWN, Mather (1761-1831).
　　　　Charles Bulfinch,
　　　　1786, o.c., 30¹/₁₆" x 25⅛". Fogg Mus.　#H428
　　　　　　　　　　　　　　　　　　PA 93B

2363. CHANDLER, Winthrop (1747-90).
Rev. Ebenezer Devotion,
1770, o.c., 55" x 43¾". Brookline Hist. Soc.　PA 95B

　　　　2364. ——.
　　　　Mrs. Ebenezer Devotion,
　　　　1770, o.c., 55" x 43¾". Brookline Hist. Soc.
　　　　　　　　　　　　　　　　　　PA 96B

2365. COPLEY, John Singleton (1738-1815).
Arrest of Monmouth before James II,
n.d., o.c., sketch, 24¾" x 29½". Fogg Mus.
#1957.225　　　　　　　　　　　　PA 106A

　　　　2366. ——.
　　　　Charles I Demanding Impeachment of Five
　　　　Members of House of Commons,
　　　　c. 1785-91, o.c., sketch, 24¼" x 29". Fogg Mus.
　　　　#1957.224　　　　　　　　　　PA 106

2367. ——.
Galatea,
c. 1754, o.c., 37" x 52". Boston Mus.　#12.45　PA 85

　　　　2368. ——.
　　　　Watson and the Shark,
　　　　1778, o.c., 72" x 90¼". Boston Mus.　#89.481
　　　　　　　　　　　　　　　　　　PA 109

2369. ——.
Self-portrait,
1770, pastel on paper, 23" x 17¼". Winterthur. PA 104A

　　　　2370. ——.
　　　　Joseph Barrell,
　　　　c. 1765, pastel on paper, 23⅜" x 18¼". Worcester
　　　　Art Mus.　#1915.81　　　　　　PA 92

2371. COPLEY, John Singleton (1738-1815).
Mrs. Jerathmiel Bowers (Mary Sherburne, 1735-99),
c. 1765, o.c., 49⅞" x 39¾". Met. Mus.
#15.128   Rogers Fund, 1915.   PA 89

2372. ——.
Mrs. Seymour Fort,
c. 1776, o.c., 50" x 40". Wadsworth Atheneum.
#1901.34   PA 100

2373. ——.
Ezekiel Goldthwait,
1771, o.c., 50" x 40". Boston Mus.   #41.85   PA 102

2374. ——.
Mrs. Ezekiel Goldthwait (Elizabeth Lewis),
1771, o.c., 50" x 40". Boston Mus.   #41.84
PA 103

2375. ——.
The Gore Children,
c. 1753, o.c., 40½" x 56¼". Winterthur.   PA 84A

2376. ——.
Nathaniel Hurd, Portrait A,
1765-70, o.c., 30½" x 25½". Cleveland Mus.
#350.15   PA 98

2377. ——. Ibid. Det. hand and book.   PA 99

2378. ——.
Jeremiah Lee,
1769, o.c., 95" x 59". Wadsworth Atheneum.
#1945.58   PA 72B

2379. ——.
Mrs. Jeremiah Lee,
1769, o.c., 95" x 59". Wadsworth Atheneum.
#1945.59   PA 73B

2380. ——.
Mr. & Mrs. Thomas Mifflin,
1773, o.c., 60½" x 48". Hist. Soc. Pa.   PA 105

2381. ——.
Henry Pelham (the Boy with the Squirrel),
c. 1765, o.c., 30¼" x 25". Private Coll., Boston,
Mass.   PA 96

2382. ——. Ibid. Det., still-life and squirrel.
PA 97

2383. ——.
Paul Revere,
1765-70, o.c., 35" x 28½". Boston Mus.
#30.781   PA 66B

2384. ——. Ibid. Det., hand and tea pot.
PA 67B

2385. COPLEY, John Singleton (1738-1815).
Epes Sargent,
c. 1760, o.c., 49⅞" x 40". Nat'l Gall. of Art.
#1533   PA 87

     2386. ——. Ibid. Det., face, approx. 10". PA 87A

2387. ——. Ibid. Det., hand on chest, approx.
6".   PA 87B

    2388. ——.
    Deborah Scollay,
    c. 1762, miniature, w.c. on ivory, 1¼" x 1¹⁄₃₂".
    Worcester Art Mus.   #1917.184   PA 88

2389. ——.
Isaac Smith,
1769, o.c., 40⅛" x 50½". Yale U. Gall.
#1941.73   PA 94

    2390. ——.
    Mrs. Isaac Smith,
    1769, o.c., 40⅛" x 50⅛". Yale U. Gall.
    #1941.74   PA 95

2391. ——.
Ann Tyng (Mrs. Thomas Smelt),
1756, o.c., 50" x 40¼". Boston Mus.   #39.646   PA 86

    2392. DELANOY, Abraham, Jr. (1742-95).
    Benjamin West,
    1766, o.c., 24" x 20". N.Y. Hist. Soc.   PA 134

2393. DURAND, John (act. 1766-82).
The Rapalje Children,
c. 1769, o.c., 50¾" x 39¾". N.Y. Hist. Soc.   PA 127

    2394. DUYCKINCK, Gerret (1660-c. 1710).
    Self-portrait,
    c. 1700, oil on wood panel, 30" x 25". N.Y. Hist.
    Soc.   PA 20

2395. ——.
Mrs. Gerret Duyckinck,
c. 1700, oil on wood panel, 30¼" x 24⅞". N.Y.
Hist. Soc.   PA 21

    2396. FEKE, Robert (act. 1741-50).
    James Bowdoin II,
    1748, o.c., 48¾" x 39¼". Bowdoin College Mus.
    Fine Arts.   PA 45B

2397. ——.
Mrs. James Bowdoin II (Elizabeth Erwin),
1748, o.c., 48¾" x 39". Bowdoin College Mus.
Fine Arts.   #1826.7   PA 46B

    2398. ——.
    Mrs. William Bowdoin (Phoebe Murdock),
    1748, o.c., 49⅛" x 38⅞". Bowdoin College Mus.
    Fine Arts.   #1826.9   PA 48B

2399. FEKE, Robert (act. c. 1741-50).
Self-portrait (early),
c. 1730, o.c., 30" x 26". Coll. Rev. Henry Wilder
Foote, Cambridge, Mass.   PA 65

    2400. ——.
    Self-portrait (late),
    c. 1750, o.c., 40" x 32". Rhode Island Hist. Soc.
                                       PA 66

2401. ——.
Rev. Thomas Hiscox,
1745, o.c., 28¾" x 24¼". Coll. Countess Lazlo
Szechenyi, New York, N.Y.   PA 68

    2402. ——.
    Isaac Royall and Family,
    1741, o.c., 54⅝" x 77¹¹⁄₁₆". Law School, Harvard
    U. #H 159   PA 67

2403. ——.
Brigadier-General Samuel Waldo,
1748-50(?), o.c., 96" x 59¼". Bowdoin College
Mus. Fine Arts. #1855.3   PA 70

    2404. ——.
    Isaac Winslow,
    c. 1748, o.c., 50" x 40". Boston Mus. #42.424
                                      PA 49B

2405. ——.
Unknown Woman (Mrs. John Vinal?),
c. 1748-50, o.c., 50" x 40". Brooklyn Mus.
#43.229   PA 69

    2406. FOSTER, John (?)(1648-81).
    John Davenport,
    1670, o.c., 27¼" x 23". Yale U. Gall. #1750.1
                                       PA 9

2407. FURNESS, John Mason (1763-1804).
John Vinal,
1780-90, o.c., 50" x 45⅝". Brooklyn Mus.
#41.878   PA 141

    2408. GREENWOOD, John (1727-92).
    Sea Captains Carousing at Surinam,
    c. 1755, oil, 56½" x 73¾". St. Louis Mus.
    #256.48   PA 76

2409. ——.
The Greenwood-Lee Family Group,
c. 1747, o.c., 56" x 68". Coll. Henry L. Shattuck,
Brookline, Mass.   PA 74

    2410. HESSELIUS, Gustavus (1682-1755).
    Bacchus and Ariadne,
    n.d., o.c., 24½" x 32⅜". Detroit Inst. #48.1
                                       PA 50

2411. ——.
Self-portrait,
c. 1740, o.c., 36" x 28". Hist. Soc. Pa.   PA 53

    2412. ——.
    Mrs. Lydia Hesselius,
    c. 1740, o.c., 36" x 27¾". Hist. Soc. Pa. PA 54

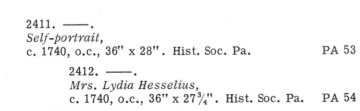

2413. HESSELIUS, Gustavus (1682-1775).
Lapowinska,
1735, o.c., 33" x 25". Hist. Soc. Pa.   PA 52

2414. ———.
Charles Calvert and Colored Slave,
1761, o.c., 50" x 40". Baltimore Mus.   PA 80

2415. ———.
Mrs. Richard Galloway, Jr., of Cedar Park,
Maryland (Sophia Richardson, 1697-1781),
1764, o.c., 36¾" x 30". Met. Mus.   #22.206
Maria DeWitt Jesup Fund, 1922.   PA 81

2416. ———.
Rev. Abraham Keteltas,
1758, o.c. Coll. Miss Edith Wetmore, New York,
N.Y.   PA 78

2417. ———.
Mrs. Abraham Keteltas (Sarah Smith),
1758, o.c., Coll. Miss Edith Wetmore, New York,
N.Y.   PA 79

2418. JOHNSTON, Henrietta (1705-1728/9).
Col. William Rhett,
c. 1710, pastel on paper, 12" x 9". Carolina Art
Assoc., Gibbes Art Gall.   #20.1.1   PA 28

2419. ———.
Mrs. Samuel Wragg (Mary du Bosc),
1708, pastel on paper, 11½" x 8½". Carolina Art
Assoc., Gibbes Art Gall.   #43.5.1   PA 27

2420. KING, Samuel (1748/9-1819).
Rev. John Eliot,
1779, o.c., 18" x 16". Mass. Hist. Soc.   PA 142

2421. KUHN, Justus Engelhardt (?-1717).
Henry Darnall III,
c. 1710, o.c., 52½" x 43". Maryland Hist. Soc.
#315.128.2   PA 21B

2422. ———.
Eleanor Darnall,
c. 1710, o.c., 53¾" x 44". Maryland Hist. Soc.
                                        PA 20B

2423. MARE, John (c. 1739-?).
John Keteltas,
1767, o.c., 30" x 25". Coll. Miss Edith Wetmore,
New York, N.Y.   PA 82

2424. ———. Ibid. Det., lower right center,
sleeve ruff with fly.   PA 83

2425. OTTO, Heinrich (n.d.).
Hand-painted Fractur, Birth and Baptismal
Certificate,
1782, w.c., 15¾" x 12⅝". Met. Mus.   #34.100.66
Gift of Mrs. Robert W. deForest, 1933.   PA 147

2426. PELHAM, Peter (1697-1751).
Rev. Cotton Mather,
1727, o.c., 30" x 25". Am. Antiq. Soc.   PA 32

2427. PORTZLINE, Francis (n.d.).
Birth and Baptismal Certificate,
c. 1838, w.c., 11¾" x 15¼". Phila. Mus. PA 148

  2428. PRATT, Matthew (1734-1805).
  The American School,
  1765, o.c., 36" x 50¼". Met. Mus. # 97.29.3
  Gift of Samuel P. Avery, 1897. PA 138

2429. ——.
Benjamin West,
c. 1765, o.c., 30" x 25". Pa. Acad. # A-206 PA 135

  2430. ——.
  Mrs. Benjamin West (Eliz. Shewell),
  c. 1765, o.c., 30" x 25". Pa. Acad. # A-205
            PA 136

2431. SMIBERT, John (1688-1751).
Dean George Berkeley and His Entourage,
1729, o.c., 70¾" x 94½". Yale U. Gall.
1808.1   PA 34

  2432. ——. Ibid. Det., self-portrait, upper left.
            PA 26B

2433. ——.
Nathaniel Byfield,
1730, o.c., 30" x 25". Met. Mus. # 24.109.87.
Bequest of Charles Allen Munn, 1924. PA 36

  2434. ——.
  Jane Clark,
  1739(?), o.c., 50" x 40". Mass. Hist. Soc.
            PA 37B

2435. ——.
Daniel, Peter and Andrew Oliver,
c. 1730, o.c., 40" x 57½". Boston Mus.
53.952   PA 35

  2436. SMIBERT, Nathaniel (1735-56).
  Ezra Stiles,
  1756, o.c., 28¾" x 25". Yale U. Gall.
  # 1919.11   PA 77

2437. SMITH, Thomas (attr.) (act. last quarter
17th C.).
Maj. Thomas Savage,
c. 1679, o.c., 40½" x 35¾". Coll. Henry L. Shattuck,
Brookline, Mass.   PA 14

  2438. ——. Ibid. Det.   PA 15

2439. ——.
Self-portrait,
c. 1690, o.c., 24½" x 23¾". Worcester Art. Mus.
1948.19   PA 16

  2440. THEUS, Jeremiah (c. 1719-74).
  Mrs. Peter Manigault (Elizabeth Wragg),
  1757, o.c., 50" x 40". Charleston Mus. PA 56

2441. THEUS, Jeremiah (c. 1719-74).
Elizabeth Rothmaler,
1757, o.c., 29⅞" x 25". Brooklyn Mus.   # 23.61
PA 55

2442. WATSON, John (1685-1768).
Governor Lewis Morris,
1726, o.c., 30 1/16" x 25". Brooklyn Mus.
43.196   PA 44A

2443. ——. (attr.).
Capt. and Mrs. Johannes Schuyler,
early 18th C., o.c., 54" x 71". N.Y. Hist. Soc.   PA 24

2444. WEST, Benjamin (1738-1820).
Conference of the Treaty of Peace with England,
1783, o.c., 28½" x 36½". Winterthur.   PA 151

2445. ——.
Death on the Pale Horse,
1802, o.c., 21" x 36". Phila. Mus.   PA 120

2446. ——.
Landscape with Cow,
1749-52, oil on wood panel, 26¾" x 50¼". Pa.
Hospital, Philadelphia, Pa.   PA 113

2447. ——.
Penn's Treaty with the Indians,
c. 1771, o.c., 75½" x 108¾". Pa. Acad.   PA 119

2448. ——.
The Adrian Hope Family Group,
1802, o.c., 70" x 100¾". Boston Mus.
06.2362   PA 124

2449. ——.
Self-portrait,
1756, miniature, w.c. on ivory, 2 9/16" x 1 15/16".
Yale U. Gall.   # 1940.529   PA 115

2450. ——.
Thomas Mifflin,
c. 1758-59, o.c., 51½" x 38½". Hist. Soc. Pa.
PA 114

2451. WILLIAMS, William (d. c. 1790).
John Wiley, His Mother and Sisters,
1771, o.c., 35½" x 46½". Coll. Mrs. W. O. Wiley,
New York, N.Y.   PA 49

2452. ——.
William Hall,
1766, o.c., 71" x 46". Winterthur.   PA 36B

2453. ——.
Deborah Hall,
1766, o.c., 71¼" x 46½". Brooklyn Mus.
42.45   PA 48

2454. WOLLASTON, John (act. in U.S. c. 1749-58
& 1766-67).
Warner Lewis,
c. 1756, o.c., 50" x 40". College William &
Mary.   # 82   PA 60A

2455. WOLLASTON, John (act. in U.S. c. 1749-58
& 1766-67).
Mrs. Warner Lewis,
c. 1756, o.c., 50" x 40". College William & Mary.
#86   PA 61A

 2456. ——.
 Warner Lewis II & Rebecca,
 c. 1756, o.c., 50" x 40". College William & Mary.
 #80   PA 62A

SPANISH COLONIAL

2457. ANON.
Flight into Egypt,
19th C. N. Mex., tempera(?) on wood panel,
19½" x 16½". Brooklyn Mus.   #40.128   PA 2

 2458. ANON.
 Holy Family (horizontally),
 the Holy Trinity (vertically),
 19th C., tempera on wood, 21" x 16". Taylor
 Mus.   #399   PA 155

2459. ANON.
Nuestra Señora de Guadalupe,
n.d., tempera on wood, 23" x 19". Taylor Mus.
#1554   PA 156

 2460. ANON.
 Reredos,
 1798, carved, pine, gesso, tempera, 22' x 10½'.
 San Miguel Church, Santa Fe, N. Mex.   PA 153

2461. ANON.
San Juan Nepomuceno,
1st half 19th C., tempera on wood, 16½" x 25".
Taylor Mus.   #1559   PA 157

 2462. ANON.
 Santo Niño de Atocha,
 1st half 19th C., retablo, tempera on gesso on pine.
 Bequest of Cady Wells, Mus. N. Mex.
 #CW-R-112   PA 160

2463. ANON.
Veronica's Veil,
1st half 19th C. Rio Grande Valley, retablo, wood,
gesso, tempera, 19⅛" x 13¾". Denver Art Mus.
#A-107   PA 154

 2464. ARAGON, José (of Chamisal).
 Retablo,
 1824-35, pine, 21" x 30". Bequest of Cady Wells,
 Mus. N. Mex.   #A9.54-11-R   PA 159

2465. ——.
Alma de la Virgen,
2nd q. 19th C., retablo, gesso over wood, tempera
on gesso, 8¼" x 10¾". Mus. N. Mex.   #L5.54-55
                                                PA 158

 2466. ARAGON, José Rafael (of Cordova)(act.
 1829-55).
 Reredos,
 2nd q. 19th C., tempera (?) on gesso on pine panel,
 6'6" x 8'4". Mus. N. Mex.   PA 3

2467. ——.
St. Cajetan,
2nd q. 19th C., retablo, tempera, gesso, pine,
8" x 11". Mus. N. Mex.   #L.5.54-54   PA 161

PAINTING OF THE FEDERAL PERIOD AND NINETEENTH CENTURY

E. P. RICHARDSON

PRIMITIVES

2469. ANON.
Girl in Garden,
c. 1840, o.c., 39¾" x 27⅛". Rockefeller Folk
Art Coll.   #100.98   PB 11A

    2470. ANON.
    Meditation by the Sea,
    1850-60, o.c., 13½" x 19½". M. & M. Karolik Coll.,
    Boston Mus.   #45.892   PB 504

2471. ANON.
A Street in Brooklyn,
c. 1840-60, o.c., 30" x 44½". Detroit Inst.
#34.21   PB 9

    2472. ANON.
    The Quilting Party,
    n.d., oil on paper mounted on wood, 13¼" x 25¼".
    Rockefeller Folk Art Coll.   #101.40   PB 2

2473. ANON.
Venus Drawn by Doves,
c. 1815, w.c. on silk, 15" x 15½". Rockefeller
Folk Art Coll.   #401.12   PB 506

    2474. ANON.
    The Water Color Class,
    c. 1820, w.c., 14⅝" x 23⅝". Art. Inst., Chicago.
    #51.202   PB 56

2475. ANON.
Miss Tweedy of Brooklyn,
2nd quarter 19th C., o.c., 41" x 33". Detroit Inst.
#53.107   PB 7

    2476. ANON.
    Portrait of a Young Lady,
    c. 1830, oil on wood panel, 17" x 13⅛". Art Inst.,
    Chicago.   #42.294   PB 8

2477. BRADLEY, I.
The Cellist,
1832, oil. Phillips Coll.   PB 12

    2478. BRADLEY, Mary.
    Basket of Fruit,
    c. 1840, w.c. on velvet, 12" x 15". Rockefeller
    Folk Art Coll.   #T58.403.1   PB 5

2479. COHOON, Hannah.
Tree of Life,
Shaker inspirational painting, 1854, 18" x 23".
Coll. Mr. & Mrs. Edward Deming Andrews, New
Haven, Conn.   PB 704

    2480. DAVIS, Joseph (act. 1832-37).
    James and Sarah Tuttle,
    1836, w.c., 9¾" x 14⅞". N.Y. Hist. Soc.   PB 14

2481. EMORY, Ella.
Alice Cushing in the West Parlor of Peter Cushing House, Hingham, Mass.,
c. 1878, o.c., 12¾" x 17½". Coll. Mrs. Nina Fletcher Little, Brookline, Mass.   PB 15

2482. ——.
East Parlor of Peter Cushing House, Hingham, Mass.,
c. 1878, o.c., 15½" x 21½". Coll. Mrs. Nina Fletcher Little, Brookline, Mass.   PB 15A

2483. FATHER JAMES (drawn by, for Jane Blanchard).
A Type of Mother Hannah's Pocket Handkerchief,
Shaker inspirational dwg., 1851, ink & w.c., 14" x 17". Coll. Mr. & Mrs. Edward Deming Andrews, New Haven, Conn.   PB 702

2484. FERRILL, M. E. (act. 1873).
Sleighing Scene,
o.c., 18⅛" x 24¼". Detroit Inst.   #43.28   PB 16

2485. FIELD, Erastus Salisbury (1805-1900).
The Garden of Eden,
1860's, o.c., 34¾" x 46". M. & M. Karolik Coll., Boston Mus.   #48.1027   PB 18

2486. ——. (attr.)
Girl Holding Rattle,
c. 1835, o.c., 34¾" x 25⅜". Rockefeller Folk Art Coll.   #100.4   PB 17

2487. ——.
Historical Monument of the American Republic,
c. 1876, o.c., 9'3" x 13'1". The Morgan Wesson Mem. Coll. Fine Arts.   #01.42.22   PB 19

2488. ——.
Portrait of Mrs. Joseph Moore, neé Almira Gallond,
c. 1840, o.c., 34" x 28½". Anon. loan, Boston Mus.   PB 700

2489. ——.
Joseph Moore & His Family,
c. 1840, o.c., 82¾" x 93⅜". M. & M. Karolik Coll., Boston Mus.   #58.25   PB 694

2490. ——. Ibid. Det. Mrs. Moore.   PB 695

2491. "Mr." FREEMAN.
Elizabeth Fenimore Cooper,
1816, w.c., 17½" x 21½". N.Y. State Hist. Assoc., Cooperstown.   #N343.55   PB 4

2492. MOTHER ANN (a Gift from).
An Emblem of the Heavenly Sphere,
Shaker inspirational painting, 1854, w.c., 18¼" x 23¾". Coll. Mr. & Mrs. Edward Deming Andrews, New Haven, Conn.   PB 703

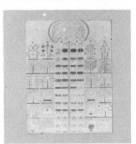

2493. HICKS, Edward (1780-1849).
The Peaceable Kingdom,
c. 1835, oil, 17¾" x 23½". Coll. Mr. & Mrs. Holger Cahill, New York, N.Y.   PB 21

2494. ——.
Residence of David Twining, 1787,
c. 1845-48, o.c., 27" x 32". Rockefeller Folk Art Coll.   #101.20   PB 20

2495. LEAVITT, Joseph Warren.
House of Moses Morse, Loudon, N.H.,
c. 1825, w.c., 7" x 9". Coll. Mrs. Nina Fletcher
Little, Brookline, Mass.   PB 22

2496. LEE, Joseph.
Oak Knoll, Napa,
c. 1880, 47½" x 72". de Young Mem. Mus.
45227   PB 23

2497. PINNEY, Eunice (1770-1849).
Two Women,
c. 1810, w.c. on paper, 9½" x 11¾". N.Y. State
Hist. Assoc., Cooperstown.   # N-40.50 L   PB 29

2498. STOCK, Joseph Whiting (1815-55).
Portrait of Jasper Raymond Rand,
c. 1845, o.c., 46" x 40". Newark Mus.
U.S. 35.40   PB 10

2499. TILLES, J. A.
Watch and Fob,
1829, w.c., 9" x 6¾". Rockefeller Folk Art Coll.
303.16   PB 6

2500. WETHERBY, Isaac Augustus (1819-1904).
Mary Eliza Jenkins,
1843, o.c., 39¾" x 31½". Fruitlands Mus.,
Harvard, Mass.   PB 37

2501. WHITNEY, L.
American Landscape,
19th C., o.c., 17¾" x 28". Newark Mus.
U.S.31:149B   PB 38

2502. WYLIE, Theophilus Adam.
Political Scene in Early Bloomington,
1837, oil, 27¾" x 20⅛". Indiana U.   PB 40

PROFESSIONALS

2503. ANON.
Rafting Downstream,
c. 1840-50, o.c., 22" x 27⅜". Indiana U.   PB 57

2504. ANON.
Suspension Bridge at Niagara Falls,
n.d., o.c., 30¼" x 39". Coll. Maxim Karolik,
Newport, R.I.   PB 505

2505. ANON.
Capt. Nicholson Broughton,
n.d., o.c., 28½" x 20½". Peabody Mus., Salem,
Mass.   # 4145   PB 55

2506. ALEXANDER, Francis (1800-80).
Mrs. Jared Sparks,
c. 1830, oil, 30¼" x 24⅞". Fogg Mus.   # 60.1953
                                             PB 42

2507. ALLSTON, Washington (1779-1843).
The Deluge,
1804, o.c., 48¼" x 66". Met. Mus.   # 09.14
Gift of William Merritt Chase, 1909.   PB 44

2508. ———.
Diana in the Chase,
1805, o.c., 64¾" x 95½". Fogg Mus.   # 1956.62
                                             PB 46

2509. ALLSTON, Washington (1779-1843).
Elijah in the Desert,
1818, o.c., 48¾" x 72½". Boston Mus.   #70.1   PB 50

    2510. ——.
    Flight of Florimell,
    1819, o.c., 35¾" x 28½". Detroit Inst.   #44.165
    PB 51

2511. ——.
Moonlit Landscape,
1819, o.c., 24" x 35". Boston Mus.   #21.1429   PB 53

    2512. ——.
    Rising of a Thunderstorm at Sea,
    1804, o.c., 38½" x 51". Boston Mus.   #78.46
    PB 43

2513. ——.
Self-portrait,
1805, o.c., 31½" x 26½". Boston Mus.   #84.301 PB 45

    2514. ——.
    Samuel T. Coleridge,
    1814, o.c., unfinished sketch, 44" x 33½". Fogg
    Mus.   #6.1955   PB 49

2515. ANSHUTZ, Thomas P. (1851-1912).
Steelworkers' Noontime,
c. 1890, o.c., 17" x 24". Coll. Lawrence H.
Fleischman, Detroit, Mich.   PB 59

    2516. AUDUBON, John James (1785-1851).
    American Porcupine,
    1842, 4' x 2½'. Am. Mus. Nat. Hist.   PB 63

2517. ——.
Black-billed Cuckoo,
publ. 1827-38, w.c., 24¼" x 19⅜". N.Y. Hist.
Soc.   PB 60

    2518. ——.
    Gyrfalcon,
    n.d., w.c., 38½" x 25⅝". N.Y. Hist. Soc.   PB 61

2519. ——.
Natchez, Mississippi in 1822,
1822, oil, 48¼" x 29¼". Coll. Mrs. George
M. D. Kelly, Natchez, Miss.   PB 64

    2520. ——.
    Purple Grackle,
    n.d., w.c., 23⅞" x 18½". N.Y. Hist. Soc.   PB 62

2521. ——.
Virginia Deer,
1838-51, o.c., 37¾" x 60¼". Brooklyn Mus.
#05.85   PB 65

    2522. BARD, James (1815-97).
    Hudson River Steamboat: Rip Van Winkle,
    1854, o.c., 31¼" x 53". M. & M. Karolik Coll.,
    Boston Mus.   #47.1212   PB 67

2523. BIERSTADT, Albert (1830-1902).
Bombardment of Fort Sumter,
1861, oil, 26" x 68". Union League, Philadelphia,
Pa.   # 8   PB 73

    2524. ——.
    The Burning Ship,
    1869, o.c., 30¼" x 50". Coll. Maxim Karolik,
    Newport, R.I.   PB 511

2525. ——.
Last of the Buffalo,
n.d., o.c., 72" x 119". Corcoran Gall.   # 09.12   PB 69

    2526. ——.
    The Rocky Mountains,
    1863, o.c., 73¼" x 120¾". Met. Mus.   # 07.123
    Rogers Fund, 1907   PB 75

2527. ——.
The St. Lawrence River from the Citadel, Quebec,
aft. 1880, oil on paper on canvas, 22" x 30½".
M. & M. Karolik Coll., Boston Mus.   # 47.1258   PB 510

    2528. ——.
    Thunderstorm in the Rocky Mountains,
    1859, o.c., 19" x 29". Boston Mus.   # 43.134
                                                  PB 71

2529. BINGHAM, George Caleb (1811-79).
The County Election,
1851-52, o.c., 35 7/16" x 48¾". City Art Mus.,
St. Louis.   # 124.44   PB 81

    2530. ——.
    Daniel Boone Escorting a Band of Pioneers,
    c. 1851, o.c., 39½" x 50". Washington U.,
    St. Louis, Mo.   # WU2171   PB 83

2531. ——.
Fur Traders Descending the Missouri,
c. 1845, o.c., 29" x 36½". Met. Mus.   # 33.61
Morris K. Jesup Fund, 1933.   PB 76

    2532. ——.
    Jolly Flatboatmen, No. 2,
    1857, o.c., 46¼" x 69". City Art Mus., St. Louis.
    # 123.44   PB 85

2533. ——.
Raftsmen Playing Cards,
1851, o.c., 17" x 21". Lent by Rev. Paul Moore,
Jr., Yale U. Gall.   # 1.4.1951   PB 79

    2534. ——.
    Shooting for the Beef,
    1850, o.c., 33½" x 49½". Brooklyn Mus.
    # 40.342   PB 78

2535. ——.
The Trappers' Return,
1851, o.c., 26¼" x 36¼". Detroit Inst.   # 50.138 PB 80

    2536. BIRCH, Thomas (1779-1851).
    The Fairmount Water Works,
    1821, o.c., 20" x 30". Pa. Acad.   PB 88

2537. BIRCH, Thomas (1779-1851).
Penn's Treaty Tree,
n.d., o.c., 39¼" x 50". Hist. Soc. Pa.   PB 87

2538. ——.
United States and the Macedonian,
n.d., o.c., 27½" x 34½". Hist. Soc. Pa.   PB 86

2539. BLAKELOCK, Ralph Albert (1847-1919).
Indian Encampment,
n.d., o.c., 37⅜" x 40¼". Met. Mus.   # 06.1269
Gift of George A. Hearn, 1906   PB 514

2540. ——.
Moonlight,
c. 1885, o.c., 27¼" x 32¼". Brooklyn Mus.
42.171   PB 512

2541. ——.
The Vision of Life,
c. 1895, o.c., 21⅛" x 39⅜". Art Inst. Chicago
47.55   PB 513

2542. BLASHFIELD, Edwin Howland (1848-1936).
The Power of the Law,
1899, mural. Appellate Div., Supreme Court,
New York, N.Y.   PB 515

2543. BLYTHE, David (1815-65).
Art Versus Law,
n.d., o.c., 24" x 20". Brooklyn Mus.   # 40.907   PB 90

2544. ——.
*General Doubleday Watching His Troops Cross the
Potomac,*
1863, o.c., 30¼" x 40". Baseball Hall of Fame,
Cooperstown, N.Y.   # B159.37   PB 92

2545. BROWN, John George (1831-1913).
The Country Gallants,
1876, o.c., 30" x 46". Toledo Mus. Art.   # 49.23 PB 93

2546. BUNTING, J. D.
Darby, Pa., after the Burning of Lord's Mill,
1840-50(?), o.c., 42" x 51¼". Coll. Maxim
Karolik, Newport, R.I.   PB 517

2547. BURNHAM, Thomas M. (1818-66).
First State Election in Michigan,
1837, o.c., 24½" x 30¾". Detroit Inst.   # 57.267   PB 94

2548. CASSATT, Mary (1845-1926).
After the Bath,
c. 1901, pastel, 25¾" x 39¼". Cleveland Mus.
20.379   PB 100

2549. ——.
The Bath,
c. 1891, o.c., 39½" x 26". Art Inst. Chicago
10.2   PB 99

2550. ——.
Mother and Child,
1890, oil, 35½" x 25¼". Roland P. Murdock Coll.,
Wichita Art Mus.   # M-109   PB 95A

2551. CASSATT, Mary (1845-1926).
Woman and Child Driving,
1881, o.c., 35¼" x 51½". Phila. Mus.   PB 95

2552. ———.
Woman Arranging Her Veil,
c. 1890, pastel, 25½" x 21½". Phila. Mus.   PB 97

2553. ———.
Women Picking Fruit,
1891, o.c., 51½" x 36". Carnegie Inst.   PB 98

2554. CATLIN, George (1796-1872).
Buffalo Chase in Snowdrift,
late 1830's, o.c., 23" x 27¾". Smithsonian
Institution.   #416   PB 518

2555. ———.
One Horn. A Dakota (Sioux) Chief,
1832, oil, 27⅞" x 23". Chicago Nat. Hist. Mus.   PB 102

2556. ———.
The Upper Missouri: The Grand Detour,
c. 1832, oil on paper, 22" x 16½". Am. Mus. Nat.
Hist.   PB 103

2557. CHAPMAN, Conrad Wise.
The Confederate Submarine Torpedo Boat H. L.
Hunley,
1863, oil, 10" x 14". Confederate Mem. Lit. Soc.
Coll., Confederate Mus., Richmond, Va.   PB 106

2558. ———.
Fort Sumter, Dec. 8, 1863,
1863, oil, 10" x 14". Confederate Mem. L:. Soc.
Coll., Confederate Mus., Richmond, Va.   PB 105

2559. ———.
Panorama: the Valley of Mexico
(part 3 of four parts), 1865, oil on panel, 14⅜"
x 20⅛". Valentine Mus., Richmond, Va.   PB 108

2560. CHASE, William Merritt (1849-1916).
A Friendly Call,
1895, o.c., 30¼" x 48¼". Chester Dale Coll.,
Nat'l Gall. of Art.   #703   Gift.   PB 520

2561. ———.
In the Studio,
n.d., o.c., 28½" x 40⅜". Brooklyn Mus.   #13.50 PB 114

2562. ———.
Lady with the White Shawl,
1893, o.c., 76" x 52". Pa. Acad.   PB 117

2563. ———.
Near the Beach, Shinnecock,
c. 1895, o.c., 30" x 48". Toledo Mus. Art.
#24.58   PB 522

2564. ———.
The Open Air Breakfast,
c. 1888, o.c., 37½" x 56¾". Toledo Mus. Art.
#53.136   PB 523

2565. CHASE, William Merritt (1849-1916).
Miss Dora Wheeler,
1881-83, o.c., 62½" x 65¼". Cleveland Mus.
#21.1239   PB 521

2566. CHURCH, Frederick E. (1826-1900).
Grand Manan, Sunrise off the Maine Coast,
1863, oil, 21" x 31½". Wadsworth Atheneum.
                                            PB 710

2567. ——.
Hooker's Party Coming to Hartford,
1846, o.c., 40¼" x 60". Wadsworth Atheneum.
#1850.9   PB 126

2568. ——.
The Mountains of Ecuador,
1855, o.c., 24⅜" x 36¾". Wadsworth Atheneum.
#1948-177   PB 524

2569. ——.
Niagara,
1857, o.c., 42" x 89". Corcoran Gall.   #76.15   PB 123

2570. ——.
Scene in the Catskills,
1851, o.c., 35¼" x 51¾". Smith Art Mus. PB 119

2571. ——.
View of Cotopaxi,
1857, o.c., 24½" x 36½". Art Inst. Chicago.
#19.753   PB 125

2572. CHURCH, Frederick (1826-1900), HEALY,
George P. A. (1813-94) & McENTEE, Jervis
(1828-1891).
Arch of Titus, Rome,
1871, o.c., 73½" x 49". Newark Mus.   #26.1260
                                            PB 220

2573. CLONNEY, James Goodwyn (1812-67).
The Happy Moment,
1847, o.c., 27" x 22". M. & M. Karolik Coll.,
Boston Mus.   #47.1222   PB 525

2574. COLE, Thomas (1801-48).
The Architect's Dream,
1840, o.c., 54" x 84". Toledo Mus. Art.
#49.162   PB 138

2575. ——.
The Catskill Mountains,
1833, o.c., 39⅜" x 63". Cleveland Mus.
#1335.17   PB 526

2576. ——.
Course of Empire: Destruction,
1836, o.c., 38½" x 62½". N.Y. Hist. Soc. PB 128

2577. ——.
Expulsion from the Garden of Eden,
1827, o.c., 39" x 54". M. & M. Karolik Coll.,
Boston Mus.   #47.1188   PB 134

2578. ——.
In the Catskills,
1837, o.c., 39" x 63". Met. Mus.   #95.13.3
Gift in memory of Jonathan Sturges by his
children, 1895   PB 137

2579. COLE, Thomas (1801-48).
Landscape with Tree Trunks,
n.d., o.c., 26¼" x 32⅛". Rhode Island Mus.
#30.063   PB 132

   2580. ——.
   Mountain Landscape with Waterfall,
   1847, o.c., 51" x 39". Rhode Island Mus.
   #38.054   PB 527

2581. ——.
The Oxbow (the Connecticut River near Northampton),
1846, o.c., 51½" x 76". Met. Mus.   #08.228
Gift of Mrs. Russell Sage, 1908.   PB 528

   2582. ——.
   Voyage of Life: Childhood,
   1842, o.c., 52" x 78". Munson-Williams-Proctor
   Inst.   PB 133

2583. ——.
Voyage of Life: Youth,
1842, o.c., 52" x 78". Munson-Williams-Proctor
Inst.   PB 139

   2584. ——.
   Voyage of Life: Manhood,
   1842, o.c., 52" x 78". Munson-Williams-Proctor
   Inst.   PB 140

2585. ——.
Voyage of Life: Old Age,
1842, o.c., 52" x 78". Munson-Williams-Proctor
Inst.   PB 141

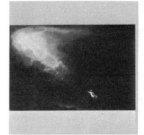

   2586. COLMAN, Samuel (1832-1920).
   Ships of the Plains,
   1872, oil, 48" x 96¼". The Union League Club,
   New York, N.Y.   PB 529

2587. COX, Kenyon (1856-1919).
The Light of Learning,
1910-13, mural, c. 20' x 12'. Pub. Lib., Winona,
Minn.   PB 530

   2588. ——.
   Augustus Saint-Gaudens,
   1908, o.c., 33½" x 46⅞". Met. Mus.   #08.130
   Gift of friends of the Sculptor, 1908   PB 531A

2589. CROPSEY, Jasper Francis (1823-1900).
Eagle Cliff, New Hampshire,
1851, o.c., 37" x 53". M. & M. Karolik Coll.,
Boston Mus.   #47.1190   PB 532

   2590. ——.
   Starrucca Viaduct, Susquehanna Valley,
   1865, o.c., 22⅛" x 36⅜". Toledo Mus. Art.
   #47.58   PB 533

2591. ——.
View of the Kaaterskill House,
1855, o.c., 29" x 44". Minn. Inst.   #31.47   PB 145

   2592. DEAS, Charles (1818-67).
   The Death Struggle,
   1845, o.c., 30" x 25". Coll. Maxim Karolik,
   Newport, R.I.   PB 534

2593. DEAS, Charles (1818-67).
Prairie Fire,
1847, o.c., 29" x 35⅞". Brooklyn Mus.   # 48.195 PB 535

2594. DEWING, Thomas W. (1851-1938).
The Recitation,
1891, o.c., 30" x 55". Detroit Inst.   # 08.9
PB 146

2595. ——.
The Spinet,
n.d., oil on wood, 15½" x 20". Nat'l Coll. Fine
Arts.   PB 536

2596. DOUGHTY, Thomas (1793-1856).
In the Catskills,
1836, o.c., 30" x 42". Addison Gall.   # 1943.39
PB 538

2597. ——.
In Nature's Wonderland,
1835, o.c., 24¼" x 30". Detroit Inst.   # 35.119   PB 150

2598. ——.
Landscape, House on Cliff above Pool,
n.d., oil, 18¾" x 25½". Pa. Acad.   PB 148

2599. DUNCANSON, Robert S. (1821-71).
Blue Hole, Flood Waters, Little Miami River,
1851, o.c., 29¼" x 42¼". Cincinnati Mus.
1926.18   PB 540

2600. DUNLAP, William (1766-1839).
The Dunlap Family,
1788, o.c., 42¼" x 49". N.Y. Hist. Soc.   PB 153

2601. ——.
Major David VanHorne,
n.d., o.c., 30¼" x 24¼". Detroit Inst.   # 54.233   PB 151

2602. DURAND, Asher B. (1796-1886).
Capture of Major Andre.
1833, o.c., 25⅛" x 30½". Worcester Art Mus.
1933.161   PB 156

2603. ——.
Catskill Clove,
1866, o.c., 39" x 60". The Century Assoc., New
York, N.Y.   PB 158

2604. ——.
Kindred Spirits,
1849, o.c., 44" x 36". N.Y. Pub. Lib.   PB 157

2605. ——.
The Old Oak,
1844, oil, 36" x 48". N.Y. Hist. Soc.   PB 154

2606. ——.
Portrait of Mrs. Durand and Her Sister,
1831, o.c., 36" x 29⅛". Newark Mus.   # 35.32B
PB 155

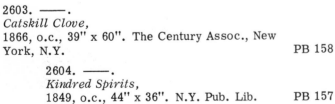

2607. DURRIE, George Henry (1820-63).
Farmyard, Winter,
1862, o.c., 26" x 36". R. L. Stuart Coll., N.Y.
Hist. Soc.   PB 541

    2608. ——.
    Wood for Winter,
    1860, o.c., 36" x 54". R. L. Stuart Coll., N.Y. Hist.
    Soc.   PB 541B

2609. Du SIMITIERE, Pierre Eugene (c. 1736-84).
Unknown Man,
n.d., pastel on paper, 19" x 14½". N.Y. Hist. Soc. PB 159

    2610. DUVENECK, Frank (1848-1919).
    The Turkish Page,
    1876, o.c., 43" x 59¾". Pa. Acad.   PB 161

2611. ——.
Whistling Boy,
1872, o.c., 28" x 21½". Cincinnati Mus.
#1904.196   PB 542

    2612. ——.
    Woman with Forget-Me-Nots,
    c. 1876, o.c., 32¾" x 40". Cincinnati Mus.
    #1904.195   PB 160

2613. ——.
Mary Cabot Wheelwright,
1882, o.c., 50" x 33". Brooklyn Mus.   #40.87   PB 543

    2614. EAKINS, Thomas (1844-1916).
    The Agnew Clinic,
    1889, o.c., 74½" x 130½". Medical School, U. of
    Pa., Philadelphia, Pa.   PB 178

2615. ——. Ibid. Det. of Dr. Agnew.   PB 178A

    2616. ——. Ibid. Det. of operation.   PB 178B

2617. ——.
Between Rounds,
1899, o.c., 50¼" x 40". Phila. Mus.   #29.184.16 PB 551

    2618. ——.
    Chess Players,
    1881, oil on wood, 11¾" x 16¾". Met. Mus.
    #81.14   Gift of the Artist, 1881.   PB 172

2619. ——.
The Concert Singer,
1892, o.c., 75" x 54". Phila. Mus.   PA 549

    2620. ——.
    The Gross Clinic,
    1875, o.c., 96" x 78". Jefferson Medical College,
    Philadelphia, Pa.   PB 171

2621. EAKINS, Thomas (1844-1916).
The Gross Clinic,
det. head of Dr. Gross.   PB 171A

    2622. ——. Ibid. Det. operation.   PB 171B

2623. ——.
A Lady with a Setter (Mrs. Eakins),
1885, o.c., 30" x 23". Met. Mus.   #23.139
Fletcher Fund, 1923.   PB 546

    2624. ——.
Max Schmitt in a Single Scull,
1871, o.c., 32¼" x 46¼". Met. Mus.   #34.92
Alfred N. Punnett Fund and gift of George D.
Pratt, 1934.   PB 163

2625. ——. Ibid. Det. small boat in front of
bridge, center.   PB 163A

    2626. ——. Ibid. Det. man in single scull, in
front of bridge, right.   PB 163B

2627. ——.
The Pathetic Song,
1881, o.c., 45¼" x 32½". Corcoran Gall.   #19.26
                 PB 175

    2628. ——.
Salutat,
1898, o.c., 50" x 40". Addison Gall.   #1928.39
                 PB 550

2629. ——.
Starting out after Rail,
n.d., w.c., 20" x 25". Roland P. Murdock Coll.,
Wichita Art Mus.   #M-26   PB 544

    2630. ——.
The Swimming Hole,
1883, o.c., 27" x 36". Fort Worth Art Center,
Texas.   #1925.3.P.P.   PB 545

2631. ——.
The Thinker (Louis N. Kenton),
1900, o.c., 82" x 42". Met. Mus.   #17.172
Kennedy Fund, 1917.   PB 552

    2632. ——.
Turning Stake-Boat,
1873, o.c., 40¼" x 60¼". Cleveland Mus.
#1984.27   PB 165

2633. ——.
*William Rush Carving the Allegorical Figure of
the Schuylkill,*
1877, o.c., 20⅛" x 26½". Phila. Mus.   PB 173

    2634. ——. Ibid. Det. of nude girl.   PB 173A

2635. EAKINS, Thomas (1844-1916).
William Rush Carving His Allegorical Figure of the Schuylkill River,
1908, o.c., 36" x 48". Brooklyn Mus.   # 39.461   PB 553

    2636. ——.
    Letitia Wilson Jordan Bacon,
    1888, o.c., 59½" x 40½". Brooklyn Mus.   # 27.50
    PB 177

2637. ——.
Professor Rowland,
1891, o.c., 82½" x 54". Addison Gall.
#1931.5   PB 548

    2638. ——.
    Miss Van Buren,
    c. 1891, o.c., 45" x 32". Phillips Coll.   PB 547

2639. ——.
Walt Whitman,
1887, o.c., 30" x 24". Pa. Acad.   PB 174

    2640. EARL, Ralph (1751-1801).
    Landscape: Looking East from Denny Hill,
    1790's(?), o.c., 45¾" x 79½". Worcester Art Mus.
    #1916.97   PB 182

2641. ——.
Major General Friedrich Wilhelm August,
Baron von Steuben,
c. 1786, o.c., 49¾" x 41¼". Yale U. Gall.
#1939.14   PB 560

    2642. ——.
    William Carpenter,
    1779, o.c., 47⅞" x 35⅝". Worcester Art Mus.
    #1916.1   PB 555

2643. ——.
Justice Oliver Ellsworth and Wife,
1792, o.c., 75¹⁵⁄₁₆" x 86¾". Wadsworth Atheneum.
#1903.7   PB 181

    2644. ——.
    Mrs. William Moseley and Her Son Charles,
    1791, o.c., 86¾" x 68¼". Yale U. Gall.
    #1942.64   PB 558

2645. ——.
Roger Sherman,
n.d., o.c., 64¾" x 49½". Yale U. Gall.   #1918.3
PB 179

    2646. ——.
    Benjamin Tallmadge and His Son William,
    1790, o.c., 78¼" x 54⅛". Litchfield Hist. Soc.,
    Conn.   #I329-2043   PB 556

2647. ——.
Mrs. Benjamin Tallmadge with Her Son Henry
and Daughter Maria,
1790, o.c., 78⅜" x 54". Litchfield Hist. Soc.,
Conn.   #I330-2044   PB 557

    2648. ——.
    William Taylor,
    1790, o.c., 48½" x 38". Albright Gall.   #35:14.1
    PB 561

2649. EARL, Ralph (1751-1801).
Mrs. William Taylor and Her Son Daniel,
1790, o.c., 48⅜" x 38". Albright Gall.
ACQ35.14.2   PB 562

    2650. EASTMAN, Seth (1808-75).
    Lacrosse Playing Among Sioux Indians,
    1857, o.c., 28" x 40". Corcoran Gall.   # 69.63
                                          PB 186

2651. ———.
Mourning for the Dead,
1849, w.c., 5½" x 7". Hill Lib., St. Paul, Minn.
15   PB 184

    2652. ———.
    Sioux Indians Breaking Up Camp,
    c. 1848, o.c., 25½" x 35". M. & M. Karolik Coll.,
    Boston Mus.   # 46:850   PB 565

2653. ———.
Squaws Playing Ball on the Prairie,
n.d., o.c., 25" x 34". Peabody Mus., Harvard U.
41.72   PB 563

    2654. EICHHOLTZ, Jacob (1776-1842).
    Self-portrait,
    c. 1810, o.c., 23¼" x 28½". Coll. Mrs. James H.
    Beal, Pittsburgh, Pa.   PB 188

2655. ELLIOT, Charles Loring (1812-68).
Mrs. Thomas Goulding,
1858, o.c., 34" x 27". Nat'l Academy of Design,
New York, N.Y.   # 862   PB 190

    2656. FISHER, Alvan (1792-1863).
    Niagara,
    n.d., o.c., 34" x 48". Coll. Arthur Fleischman,
    Detroit, Mich.   PB 191

2657. FULLER, George (1822-84).
Ideal Head,
n.d., o.c., 24" x 20". Phillips Coll.   PB 192

    2658. ———.
    The Tomato Patch,
    n.d., o.c., 20¼" x 30". Detroit Inst.   # 53.471
                                          PB 193

2659. ———.
Winifred Dysart,
1881, o.c., 50½" x 40½". Worcester Art Mus.
1910-31   PB 570

    2660. GIFFORD, Sanford Robinson (1823-80).
    In the Wilderness,
    1860, o.c., 30" x 54". Toledo Mus. Art.
    # 51.403   PB 194

2661. ———.
Kaaterskill Falls,
1862, o.c., 48" x 39⅞". Met. Mus.   # 15.30.62
Bequest of Maria DeWitt Jesup, 1915.   PB 195

    2662. GROOMBRIDGE, William (1748-1811).
    Fairmount and Schuylkill River,
    1800, oil, 25" x 36". Hist. Soc. Pa.   PB 196

2663. GUY, Francis (1760-1820).
Tontine Coffee House,
c. 1797, o.c., 42¼" x 64¼". N.Y. Hist. Soc.   PB 197

2664. ———.
Winter Scene in Brooklyn,
1817-20, o.c., 58⅝" x 75". Brooklyn Mus.
#97.13   PB 572

2665. GUYOL de GUIRAN, François-Marie.
Marie Elise Provenchere,
c. 1815, w.c., miniature, 4"x 5". Missouri Hist.
Soc.   #Bx72-1   PB 696

2666. HABERLE, John (1856-1933).
Grandma's Hearthstone,
1890, o.c., 96" x 66". Detroit Inst.   #50.31
    PB 200

2667. ———. Ibid. Det. objects on mantel.   PB 200A

2668. ———.
Time and Eternity,
c. 1890, o.c., New Britain Mus. American Art.
    PB 199

2669. HARDING, Chester (1792-1866).
Mrs. John Ball Brown (Rebecca Warren),
n.d., o.c., 30" x 25". Boston Mus.   #14.425   PB 576

2670. ———.
Amos Lawrence,
c. 1845, o.c., 84⅝" x 54". Nat'l Gall. of Art.
#764   Gift of the Children of the Rt. Rev.
William Lawrence   PB 202

2671. HARDY, Jeremiah P. (1800-88).
Catherine Wheeler Hardy and Her Daughter,
c. 1842, o.c., 29¼" x 36". M. & M. Karolik Coll., Boston
Mus.   #47.1146   PB 204

2672. HARNETT, William M. (1848-92).
After the Hunt,
1885, o.c., 70½" x 47½". Mildred Anna Williams
Coll., Calif. Palace Legion of Honor.   PB 206

2673. ———.
Emblems of Peace,
1890, o.c., 28½" x 33¾". Springfield Mus. Fine
Arts.   #38.03   PB 209

2674. ———.
The Faithful Colt,
1890, o.c., 22½" x 18½". Wadsworth Atheneum.
#1935.236   PB 210

2675. ———.
Old Models,
1892, o.c., 54" x 28". Boston Mus.   #39.761   PB 211

2676. ———.
The Old Violin,
1886, o.c., 38"x 24". Coll. W. J. Williams,
Cincinnati, Ohio.   PB 208

2677. HARVEY, George (c. 1800-78).
*Spring: Burning up Fallen Trees, A Girdled
Clearing, Canada,*
n.d., w.c., 13⅞" x 10¼". Brooklyn Mus.
#46.49   PB 577

2678. HASSAM, Childe (1859-1935).
Columbus Avenue, Boston: Rainy Day,
1885, o.c., 17⅛" x 21⅛". Worcester Art Mus.
#1935.36   PB 212

2679. ——.
Little Cobbler's Shop,
c. 1912, o.c., 30½" x 16½". Addison Gall.
#1936.27   PB 580

2680. ——.
Rainy Day, Boston,
1885, o.c., 26¼" x 48¼". Toledo Mus. Art.
#56.53   PB 578

2681. ——.
Southwest Wind,
1905, o.c., 25" x 30". Worcester Art Mus.
#1940.69   PB 213

2682. HEADE, Martin J. (1819-1904).
Approaching Storm: Beach near Newport,
c. 1860's, o.c., 28" x 58¼". M. & M. Karolik Coll.,
Boston Mus.   #45.889   PB 582

2683. ——.
Humming Birds and Orchids,
o.c., 14¼" x 22¼". Detroit Inst.   #47.36   PB 214

2684. ——.
South American River,
1868, o.c., 26" x 22½". M. & M. Karolik Coll.,
Boston Mus.   #47.1153   PB 216

2685. ——.
Spring Shower, Connecticut Valley,
1868, o.c., 20" x 40". M. & M. Karolik Coll.,
Boston Mus.   #47.1173   PB 583

2686. HEALY, George P. A. (1813-94).
John Tyler,
1864, o.c., 62" x 47". The White House,
Washington, D.C.   PB 586

2687. HENRY, Edward Lamson (1841-1919).
The 9:45 Accommodation, Stratford, Connecticut,
1867, o.c., 16" x 30⅝". Met. Mus.   #39.47.1
Bequest of Moses Tanenbaum, 1937.   PB 588

2688. HOMER, Winslow (1836-1910).
Adirondacks,
1892, w.c., 13⅜" x 19½". Fogg Mus.   #1939.230
                                              PB 236

2689. ——.
The Adirondack Guide,
1894, w.c., 15" x 21¼". Boston Mus.   PB 238

2690. ——.
After the Hurricane, Bahamas,
1899, w.c., 14¹⁵⁄₁₆" x 29⅜". Ryerson Coll., Art
Inst. Chicago.   #33.1235   PB 242

2691. HOMER, Winslow (1836-1910).
The Bridle Path, White Mountains,
1868, o.c., 24" x 38". Clark Art Inst.   PB 591A

    2692. ——.
    Canoe in Rapids,
    1897, w.c. on paper, 13⅜" x 20½". Fogg Mus.
    #1924.30   PB 593

2693. ——.
Children on a Fence,
1874, w.c., 6½" x 11⅜". Lawrence Art Mus.   PB 222A

    2694. ——.
    Country School,
    1871, o.c., 21" x 38". City Art Mus., St. Louis.
    #123.46   PB 226

2695. ——.
Croquet Scene,
1866, o.c., 15⅞" x 26¹⁄₁₆". Art Inst. Chicago.
#42.35   PB 589

    2696. ——.
    Eight Bells,
    1886, o.c., 25" x 30". Addison Gall.   #1930.379
                                                                 PB 233

2697. ——.
Fox Hunt,
1893, o.c., 38" x 68". Pa. Acad.   PB 237

    2698. ——.
    The Green Dory, Gloucester,
    prob. 1880, w.c., 13¾" x 19¾". Boston Mus.
                                                                 PB 227A

2699. ——.
The Gulf Stream,
1899, o.c., 28⅛" x 49⅛". Met. Mus.   #06.1234
Wolfe Fund, 1906   PB 243

    2700. ——.
    Huntsman and Dogs,
    1891, o.c., 28¼" x 48". Phila. Mus.   PB 235

2701. ——.
Inside the Bar, Tynemouth,
1883, w.c. on paper, 15⅜" x 28½". Met. Mus.
#54.183   Gift of Louise Ryals Arkell, 1954, in
memory of her husband, Bartlett Arkell.   PB 592

    2702. ——.
    Life Line,
    1884, o.c., 28¾" x 41⅝". Phila. Mus.   PB 231

2703. ——.
Long Branch, New Jersey,
1869, o.c., 15" x 21½". Boston Mus.   #41.631 PB 225

    2704. ——. Ibid. Det. woman on right, full
    length.   PB 225B

2705. HOMER, Winslow (1836-1910).
Long Branch, New Jersey,
det. woman on left, full length, 1869, o.c. Boston
Mus.   # 41.631   PB 225A

    2706. ———. Ibid. Det. face of woman at right.
                                                    PB 225C

2707. ———.
Northeaster,
1895, o.c., 34⅜" x 50¼". Met. Mus.   # 0.64.5
Gift of George A. Hearn, 1910.   PB 240

    2708. ———.
    Prisoners from the Front,
    1866, o.c., 24" x 38". Met. Mus.   # 22.207
    Gift of Mrs. Frank B. Porter, 1922.   PB 224

2709. ———.
Searchlight, Harbor Entrance, Santiago de Cuba,
1901, o.c., 30⅝" x 50½". Met. Mus.   # 06.1282
Gift of George A. Hearn, 1906.   PB 245

    2710. ———.
    Snap the Whip,
    1872, o.c., 22" x 36½". Butler Art. Inst.   PB 590

2711. ———.
The Turtle Pound,
1898, w.c. on paper, 15" x 21⅜". Brooklyn Mus.
23.98   PB 594

    2712. ———.
    The Two Guides,
    1876, o.c., 24" x 38½". Clark Art Inst.   PB 591

2713. ———.
West Point, Prout's Neck,
1900, o.c., 30" x 48". Clark Art Inst.   PB 595

    2714. HUBARD, William James (1807-62).
    Horatio Greenough in His Studio in Florence,
    c. 1838-39, o.c., 36" x 29". Valentine Mus.
                                             PB 247

2715. HUNT, William Morris (1824-79).
Anahita, The Flight of Night,
c. 1878, o.c., 62" x 99". Study for Albany Mural,
Boston Mus.   # 44.48   PB 251A

    2716. ———.
    Flight of Night,
    c. 1878, pastel, 62" x 99". Pa. Acad.   PB 251

2717. ———.
Gloucester Harbor,
1877, o.c., 21" x 31¼". Boston Mus.   # 44.47   PB 597

    2718. ———.
    Self-portrait,
    1866, o.c., 30" x 25". Boston Mus.   # 97.63
                                             PB 601

2719. HUNT, William Morris (1824-79).
Mrs. Richard Morris Hunt and Child,
n.d., o.c., 56" x 36". Estate of Louisa D. Hunt,
loaned to Boston Mus.   # 2116-13   PB 596

    2720. ———.
Marguerite,
1870, o.c., 50" x 38". Boston Mus.   # 26.63
                                      PB 598

2721. ———.
Miss Ida Mason,
1878, o.c., 42" x 30¼". Boston Mus.   # 32.127 PB 600

    2722. ———.
Chief Justice Lemuel Shaw,
1859, o.c., 79" x 50". Court House, prop. of
Essex Co. Bar Assoc., Salem, Mass.   PB 599

2723. INMAN, Henry (1801-46).
Picnic in the Catskills,
c. 1840, o.c., 48⅛" x 34¼". Brooklyn Mus.
13.73   PB 254

    2724. ———.
Georgianna Buckham and Her Mother,
1839, o.c., 34¼" x 27¼". Boston Mus.
19.1370   PB 252

2725. INNESS, George (1825-94).
Autumn Oaks,
c. 1875, o.c., 21⅛" x 30¼". Met. Mus.   #87.8.8
Gift of George I. Seney, 1887   PB 602

    2726. ———.
The Clouded Sun,
1891, o.c., 30" x 45". Carnegie Inst.   # 29
                                        PB 605

2727. ———.
The Coming Storm,
c. 1880, o.c., 27½" x 42¼". Addison Gall.
1928.25   PB 603

    2728. ———.
Delaware Water Gap,
1861, o.c., 36" x 50⅛". Met. Mus.   # 32.151
Morris K. Jesup Fund, 1932.   PB 258

2729. ———.
Grey Day, Goochland,
1884, oil on wood panel, 18" x 24". Phillips
Coll.   PB 263

    2730. ———.
The Home of the Heron,
1893, o.c., 30" x 45". Art Inst. Chicago.
11.31   PB 264

2731. ———.
June,
1882, o.c., 31¼" x 45". Brooklyn Mus.
41.776   PB 261

    2732. ———.
The Lackawanna Valley,
1855, o.c., 33⅞" x 50³⁄₁₆". Nat'l Gall. of Art.
779   Gift of Mrs. Huttleston Rogers.   PB 256

2733. INNESS, George (1825-94).
The Monk,
1873, o.c., 38½" x 64½". Addison Gall.
#1956.6   PB 262

     2734. ———.
     Peace and Plenty,
     1865, o.c., 77⅝" x 112⅜". Met. Mus.   #94.27
     Gift of George A. Hearn, 1894.   PB 260

2735. ———.
Venice: S. Giorgio Maggiore,
n.d., w.c., 5" x 9". Lawrence Art Mus.   PB 261A

     2736. JARVIS, John Wesley (1780-1840).
     Jacob Houseman,
     1809, oil on panel, 34" x 26½". Detroit Inst.
     #41.55   PB 265

2737. ———.
Oliver Hazard Perry,
1816, o.c., 96" x 60". Art Commission of the
City of New York.   PB 266

     2738. JENNYS, William (act. 1800-10).
     Gentleman of the Brewer Family (also known as
     The Man in the Coonskin Hat),
     c. 1800, o.c., 29" x 24". Shelburne Mus.
     #27-394   PB 606B

2739. ———.
Major Reuben Hatch,
n.d., o.c., 30" x 25¼". Lyman Allyn Mus.
#1947.8   PB 606

     2740. ———.
     Mrs. Reuben Hatch (Eunice Denison),
     n.d., o.c., 30" x 25¼". Lyman Allyn Mus.
     #1947.9   PB 606A

2741. ———.
Col. Constant Storrs,
1802, o.c., 29½" x 24½". Pa. Acad.   #A.198   PB 268

     2742. ———.
     Mrs. Constant Storrs,
     1802, o.c., 30" x 24½". Pa. Acad.   PB 267

2743. JOHNSON, Eastman (1824-1906).
Corn Husking,
1860, o.c., 26" x 30". Syracuse Mus.
#PC 116   PB 607

     2744. ———.
     In the Fields,
     1870s, oil on academy board, 17¾" x 27½".
     Detroit Inst.   #38.1   PB 272

2745. ———.
Old Kentucky Home,
1859, o.c., 36" x 45". R. L. Stuart Coll., N.Y.
Hist. Soc.   PB 270

     2746. ———.
     Family Group (the Hatch Family),
     1871, o.c., 48" x 73⅜". Met. Mus.   #26.97
     Gift of Frederick H. Hatch, 1926.   PB 273

2747. JOHNSON, Eastman (1824-1906).
Two Men,
portraits of Samuel W. Rowse and Robert W.
Rutherford, 1881, o.c., 60½" x 78¼". Met. Mus.
#98.14   Gift of Robert Gordon, 1898.   PB 274

2748. JOHNSTON, David C. (1797-1865).
The Militia Muster,
1822-29, w.c., 10¹/₁₆" x 15". Am. Antiq. Soc.
                                                 PB 276

2749. ———.
Termination of a Militia Sham Fight,
1833, w.c., 10¾" x 15⅛". Am. Antiq. Soc.   PB 277

2750. KENSETT, John F. (1818-72).
Cascade in the Forest,
1852, o.c., 29½" x 26". Detroit Inst.   #27.598
                                                 PB 278

2751. ———.
Coast Scene with Figures,
1869, o.c., 36¹/₁₆" x 60¼". Wadsworth Atheneum.
#1942.345   PB 609

2752. ———.
River Scene,
1870, o.c., 24⅛" x 36⅜". Met. Mus.
#25.110.5   Bequest of Collis P. Huntington,
1925.   PB 282

2753. ———.
Third Beach, Newport,
1869, oil, 11⅝" x 24¼". Art Inst. Chicago.
#44.686   PB 281

2754. KING, Charles B. (1785-1862).
The Vanity of an Artist's Dream,
c. 1830, oil, 35¼" x 29½". Fogg Mus.
#1942.193   PB 285

2755. ———.
*Young Omahaw, War Eagle, Little Missouri and
Pawnees,*
1821, oil, 27¾" x 35¾". Smithsonian Institution.
                                                 PB 283

2756. KRIMMEL, John Lewis (1789-1821).
Election Day at the State House,
1816, w.c. & ink, 8½" x 12½". Hist. Soc. Pa.
                                                 PB 705

2757. ———.
Fourth of July in Centre Square,
c. 1810-12, o.c., 23" x 29". Pa. Acad.   PB 287

2758. ———.
*Fourth of July Celebration in Center Square
Philadelphia, 1819,*
1819, India ink & w.c. on paper, 12" x 18". Hist.
Soc. Pa.   PB 287A

2759. ———.
Interior of an American Inn,
c. 1813, o.c., 16⅞" x 22½". Toledo Mus. Art.   #54.13
                                                 PB 288

2760. ———.
The Quilting Party,
1813, oil, 21½" x 16". Winterthur.   PB 286

2761. LaFARGE, John (1835-1910).
Athens,
1898, oil, 12' radius. Bowdoin College Mus. Fine
Arts.   PB 294

2762. ———.
Bridle Path, Tahiti,
c. 1890, w.c., 29½" x 33". Fogg Mus.   #1917.4
                                                 PB 611

2763. ———.
Christ and Nicodemus,
19th C., mural painting. Trinity Church, Boston,
Mass.   PB 612

2764. ———.
Halt of the Wise Men,
prob. aft. 1868, o.c., 32¾" x 42". Boston Mus.
#90.151   PB 610

2765. ———.
Magnolia Grandiflora,
1870, oil on panel, 36" x 17¾". Lawrence Art
Mus.   #PA 54   PB 291

2766. ———.
The Strange Thing Little Kiosai Saw in the River,
1897, w.c., 12¾" x 18½". Met. Mus.
#17.180.2   Rogers Fund, 1917.   PB 293

2767. ———.
Window Welcome (8 panels),
1909, stained glass, 13' x 8'. Met. Mus.   #44.90
Anonymous Gift, 1944.   PB 698

2768. ———.
Portrait of the Artist, 1859,
o.c., 16¹/₁₆" x 11½". Met. Mus.   #34.134
Samuel D. Lee Fund, 1934.   PB 289

2769. ———.
"Maua" - Our Boatman,
1891, o.c., 47" x 38". Addison Gall.   #1931.8   PB 614

2770. LANE, Fitz Hugh (1804-65).
Fresh Water Cove from Dolliver's Neck,
n.d., o.c., 24" x 36". M. & M. Karolik Coll.,
Boston Mus.   #48.445   PB 616

2771. ———.
A Maine Inlet,
n.d., o.c., 16½" x 25". M. & M. Karolik Coll.,
Boston Mus.   #48.443   PB 615

2772. ———.
Ships in Ice off Ten Pound Island, Gloucester,
1850's, o.c., 12" x 19¾". M. & M. Karolik Coll.,
Boston Mus.   #48.447   PB 295

2773. LE CLEAR, Thomas (1818-82).
Buffalo Newsboy,
1853, o.c., 24" x 20". Albright Gall.   PB 297

2774. LEUTZE, Emanuel (1816-68).
Westward the Course of Empire Takes Its Way,
1861, oil, 33¼" x 43¼". Nat'l Coll. Fine Arts.
                                                 PB 618

2775. MacKAY (act. 1788-91).
Hannah Bush (Mrs. John Bush),
1791, oil, 36" x 29". Am. Antiq. Soc.　　　PB 299

　　2776. ——.
　　John Bush,
　　1791, oil, 36" x 29". Am. Antiq. Soc.　　PB 300

2777. MALBONE, Edward Greene (1777-1807).
Washington Allston,
c. 1800, w.c. on ivory, miniature, 3⅜" x 2⅞".
Boston Mus.　#97.599　　　　　　　PB 301

　　2778. MARTENS, J. W.
　　Brooklyn Navy Yard (Frigate USS United States),
　　1836, w.c., 19½" x 30". Marine Hist. Assoc.
　　　　　　　　　　　　　　　　　PB 701

2779. MARTIN, Homer Dodge (1836-97).
The Harp of the Winds: View of the Seine,
1895, o.c., 28¾" x 40¾". Met. Mus.　#97.32
Gift of Several Gentlemen, 1897.　　　PB 619

　　2780. ——.
　　Lake Sanford in the Adirondacks,
　　1870, o.c., 24½" x 39½". The Century Assoc.,
　　New York, N.Y.　　　　　　　　PB 303

2781. ——.
The Logging Camp,
n.d., o.c., 20" x 30¼". Boston Mus.　#225.48
Anon. loan.　　　　　　　　　　　PB 620

　　2782. ——.
　　Sand Dunes, Lake Ontario,
　　1887, o.c., 36" x 60½". Met. Mus.　#06.1287
　　Gift of George A. Hearn, 1906.　　PB 622

2783. MEEKER, Joseph Rusling (1827-89).
The Land of Evangeline,
1874, o.c., 33" x 45½". City Art Mus., St. Louis.
#163.46　　　　　　　　　　　　PB 624

　　2784. MILLER, Alfred Jacob (1810-74).
　　Beating a Retreat,
　　n.d., o.c., 29" x 36". M. & M. Karolik Coll.,
　　Boston Mus.　#48.454　　　　　PB 699

2785. MORAN, Thomas (1837-1926).
*Cliffs on the Upper Colorado River, Wyoming
Territory,*
1882, o.c., 16" x 24⅛". Nat'l Coll. Fine Arts.
　　　　　　　　　　　　　　　　PB 627

　　2786. ——.
　　Grand Canyon of the Yellowstone River,
　　1893-1901, oil, 96" x 168". Nat'l Coll. Fine
　　Arts.　　　　　　　　　　　　PB 627A

2787. MORSE, Samuel F. B. (1791-1872).
Congress Hall: Old House of Representatives,
1821, o.c., 87" x 131¼". Corcoran Gall.
#11.14　　　　　　　　　　　　PB 307

　　2788. ——.
　　Exhibition Gallery of the Louvre,
　　1833, oil, 76" x 106½". Art Coll., Syracuse U.
　　　　　　　　　　　　　　　　PB 311

2789. MORSE, Samuel F. B. (1791-1872).
Niagara Falls from Table Rock,
1835, o.c., 24" x 30". M. & M. Karolik Coll.,
Boston Mus.   #48.456   PB 312

2790. ———.
View from Apple Hill, Cooperstown,
1828-29, o.c., 22⅜" x 29½". Coll. Stephen C.
Clark, New York, N.Y.   PB 310

2791. ———.
Marquis de Lafayette,
1824, o.c., 96" x 64". Art Commission of the
City of New York.   PB 308

2792. ———.
The Muse: Susan Walker Morse,
c. 1835-37, o.c., 73¾" x 57⅞". Met. Mus.
#45.62.1   Bequest of Herbert L. Pratt, 1945.
                                     PB 628

2793. MOULTHROP, Reuben (1763-1814).
Bradford Hubbard,
c. 1790-91, o.c., 30" x 25¾". New Haven Colony
Hist. Soc.   #1   PB 313

2794. ———.
The Rev. Ammi Ruhamah Robbins,
1812, o.c., 58⅛" x 59⅛". Yale U. Gall.
#1943.104   PB 629

2795. MOUNT, William Sidney (1807-68).
Banjo Player,
c. 1858, o.c., 25" x 30". Detroit Inst.   #38.60   PB 321

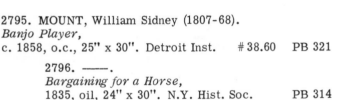

2796. ———.
Bargaining for a Horse,
1835, oil, 24" x 30". N.Y. Hist. Soc.   PB 314

2797. ———.
Boys Caught Napping in a Field,
1848, o.c., 29⅛" x 36⅛". Brooklyn Mus.
#39.608   PB 630

2798. ———.
Eel Spearing at Setauket,
1845, o.c., 29" x 36". N.Y. State Hist. Assoc.,
Cooperstown.   PB 317

2799. ———.
Landscape with Figures,
Nov. 26, 1851, o.c., 19" x 28½". Pa. Acad.   PB 319

2800. ———.
Long Island Farmhouse,
aft. 1854, o.c., 21⅞" x 29⅞". Met. Mus.
#28.104   Gift of Louise F. Wickham in memory
of her father, William H. Wickham, 1928. PB 320

2801. ———.
The Painter's Triumph,
1838, oil on panel, 20" x 24". Pa. Acad.   PB 316

2802. ———.
The Power of Music,
1847, o.c., 17" x 21". The Century Assoc., New
York, N.Y.   PB 318

2803. NEAGLE, John (1796-1865).
View of the Schuylkill,
1827, oil, 25" x 30". Art Inst. Chicago.
#34.388   PB 324

2804. ———.
Henry Clay,
1843, o.c., 111¼" x 72½". Union League,
Philadelphia, Pa.   #83   PB 631

2805. ———.
Matilda Washington Dawson,
1829, o.c., 56" x 41". Pa. Acad.   PB 325

2806. ———.
Pat Lyon,
1829, o.c., 69" x 95". Pa. Acad.   PB 326

2807. ———.
William Strickland, Esq.,
1829, o.c., 25¼" x 30". Yale U. Gall.
#1950.731   PB 322

2808. ———.
Gilbert Stuart,
1825, oil, 27⅜" x 22½". Boston Athenaeum.
                                           PB 323

2809. NEWMAN, Robert Loftin (1827-1912).
Landscape with Figures,
1903, o.c., Brooklyn Mus.   #18.34   PB 635

2810. ———.
Madonna and Child,
n.d., o.c., 43½" x 22½". Coll. St. Thomas
Seminary, Hartford, Conn.   PB 634

2811. PAGE, William (1811-85).
Cupid and Psyche,
1843, o.c., 10¹³⁄₁₆" x 14¹¹⁄₁₆". Coll. Lawrence A.
Fleischman, Detroit, Mich.   PB 330

2812. ———.
The Young Merchants,
n.d., o.c., 42" x 36". Pa. Acad.   #B-308
                                           PB 327

2813. ———.
Mrs. William Page,
c. 1860, o.c., 60¼" x 36¼". Detroit Inst.
#37.61   PB 332

2814. PEALE, Charles Willson (1741-1827).
Exhuming the Mastodon,
1806, o.c., 50" x 62½". Peale Mus.   PB 345

2815. ———.
The Artist in His Museum,
1822, o.c., 103½" x 80". Pa. Acad.   PB 636

2816. ———.
William Buckland,
1774, o.c., 48" x 36½". Yale U. Garvan Coll.
#1934.303   PB 342

2817. PEALE, Charles Willson (1741-1827).
Family Group,
1773, o.c., 56½" x 89½". N.Y. Hist. Soc.   PB 338

    2818. ——.
    Benjamin Franklin,
    1785, o.c., 36" x 27". Hist. Soc. Pa.   PB 341

2819. ——.
Thomas Jefferson,
c. 1791, o.c., 23¼" x 19". Independence Nat'l
Hist. Park, Philadelphia.   PB 343

    2820. ——.
    Lamplight Portrait of James Peale,
    1822, o.c., 24½" x 36". Detroit Inst.   # 50.58
    PB 346

2821. ——.
The Staircase Group,
1795, o.c., 89" x 39½". Phila. Mus.   PB 344

    2822. ——.
    Washington,
    1779, o.c., 94" x 59". Pa. Acad.   PB 339

2823. ——.
*Washington, Gen. LaFayette and Gen. Tilghman
at Yorktown,*
1781, o.c., 96" x 63½". House of Delegates,
Annapolis, Md.   PB 340

    2824. PEALE, James (1749-1831).
    Still Life,
    1828, oil, 24¾" x 18¾". Winterthur.   PB 348

2825. ——.
Self-portrait with His Family,
c. 1795, o.c., 31" x 33". Pa. Acad.   PB 351

    2826. ——.
    *The Ramsay-Polk Family at Carpenter's Point,
    Maryland,*
    c. 1793, o.c., 50" x 40". Coll. Lawrence A.
    Fleischman, Detroit, Mich.   PB 350

2827. ——.
Washington and His Generals at Yorktown,
c. 1786, o.c., 21" x 29½". Maryland Hist. Soc.
51.3   PB 349

    2828. PEALE, Raphaelle (1774-1825).
    After the Bath,
    1823, o.c., 28" x 23". Nelson Gall.   # 34-149
    PB 354

2829. ——.
Still Life,
c. 1820, oil on panel, 18½" x 22½". Toledo
Mus. Art.   # 51.498   PB 353

    2830. PEALE, Rembrandt (1778-1860).
    Self-portrait,
    1828, o.c., 19" x 14¼". Detroit Inst.   # 45.469
    PB 361

2831. PEALE, Rembrandt (1778-1860).
Robert Fulton,
c. 1806-10, o.c., 27½" x 22". Detroit Inst.
47.118   PB 358

2832. ———.
Thomas Jefferson,
1805, o.c., 29" x 24". N.Y. Hist. Soc.   PB 356

2833. ———.
George Washington
(porthole portrait), n.d., o.c., 72" x 54". Pa.
Acad.   # B-6   PB 355

2834. PEALE, Rubens (1784-1865).
Two Grouse in an Underbrush of Laurel,
1864, o.c., 19¼" x 27¼". Detroit Inst.   # 43.41
                                                  PB 363

2835. PETO, John F. (1854-1907).
After Night's Study,
n.d., o.c., 14¼" x 20". Detroit Inst.   # 48.386   PB 364

2836. ———.
The Poor Man's Store,
1885, o.c., 35½" x 25½". Coll. Maxim Karolik,
Newport, R.I., on loan to Boston Mus.   # 148.54
                                                  PB 365

2837. PINE, Robert Edge (1730(?)-88) and
SAVAGE, Edward (1761-1817).
Congress Voting Independence,
1785, o.c., 19¾" x 26½". Hist. Soc. Pa.   PB 368

2838. QUIDOR, John (1801-81).
*Battle Scene from Knickerbocker's History of
New York,*
1838, o.c., 27" x 34½". M. & M. Karolik Coll.,
Boston Mus.   # 48.468   PB 637

2839. ———.
The Money Diggers,
1832, o.c., 16¾" x 21½". Brooklyn Mus.
48.171   PB 638

2840. ———.
Voyage to Hell Gate from Communipaw,
1866-67, o.c., 27" x 34". Roland P. Murdock
Coll., Wichita Art Mus.   # M-115   PB 372

2841. ———.
Wolfert's Will,
1856, o.c., 27" x 34". Brooklyn Mus.   # 40.46   PB 371

2842. RIMMER, William (1816-79).
Flight and Pursuit,
1872, o.c., 18" x 26¼". Boston Mus.
56.119   PB 373

2843. ROBINSON, Theodore.
The Vale of Arconville,
c. 1888, o.c., 18" x 21⅞". Art Inst. Chicago.
41.11   PB 639

2844. ———.
The Watering Pots,
1890, o.c., 22" x 18⅛". Brooklyn Mus.   # 21.47
                                                  PB 640

2845. RYDER, Albert Pinkham (1847-1917).
Constance,
o.c., 28¼"x 36". Boston Mus.   #45.770   PB 642

2846. ——.
Dead Bird,
1890-1900, oil on wood, 4¼" x 9⅝". Phillips
Coll.   PB 382

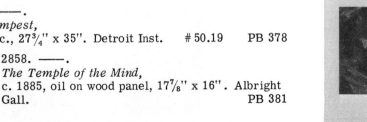

2847. ——.
The Flying Dutchman,
bef. 1890, o.c., 13⅝" x 16⅝". Nat'l Coll. Fine
Fine Arts.   PB 645

2848. ——.
The Forest of Arden,
1897, o.c., 19" x 15". Coll. Stephen C. Clark,
New York, N.Y.   PB 644

2849. ——.
Grazing Horse,
1914, o.c., 10¼" x 14¼". Brooklyn Mus.
#14.554   PB 643A

2850. ——.
Jonah,
n.d., o.c., 26½" x 33¾". Nat'l Coll. Fine
Arts.   PB 376

2851. ——.
Macbeth and the Witches,
1890; finished 1908, o.c., 28⅛" x 35¾". Phillips
Coll.   PB 383

2852. ——.
Moonlit Cove,
late 1880s or 1890s, o.c., 14" x 17". Phillips
Coll.   PB 380

2853. ——.
Moonlight Marine,
n.d., o.c., 11⅜" x 12". Met. Mus.   #34.55
Samuel D. Lee Fund, 1934.   PB 643

2854. ——.
Pastoral Study,
n.d., oil, 23¾" x 29". Nat'l Coll. Fine Arts.
                                               PB 375

2855. ——.
The Race Track,
c. 1910, o.c., 28¼" x 35¼". Cleveland Mus.
#28.8   PB 385

2856. ——.
Siegfried and the Rhine Maidens,
1875-91, o.c., 19⅞" x 20½". Mellon Coll., Nat'l
Gall. of Art.   #886   PB 384

2857. ——.
The Tempest,
n.d., o.c., 27¾" x 35". Detroit Inst.   #50.19   PB 378

2858. ——.
The Temple of the Mind,
c. 1885, oil on wood panel, 17⅞" x 16". Albright
Gall.   PB 381

2859. RYDER, Albert Pinkham (1847-1917).
Toilers of the Sea,
bef. 1884, oil on wood, 11½" x 12". Met. Mus.
#15.32   George A. Hearn Fund, 1915.   PB 641

    2860. SALMON, Robert (bef. 1800-aft. 1840).
    Boston Harbor from Constitution Wharf,
    c. 1829, oil, 32½" x 47¹/₁₆". U.S. Naval Acad.
    Mus.   #1282   PB 646

2861. ——.
South Sea Whale Fishing,
1831 or 1835, oil on panel, 16½" x 23¾". Boston
Mus.   #27.356   PB 392

    2862. SARGENT, Henry (1770-1845).
    The Dinner Party,
    c. 1825, o.c., 59½" x 48". Boston Mus.   #19.13
    PB 394

2863. ——.
The Tea Party,
c. 1820, o.c., 64¼" x 52½". Boston Mus.
#19.12   PB 393

    2864. SARGENT, John Singer (1856-1925).
    Decorations in the Dome,
    1916-21, o.c., bas-relief. Boston Mus.
    #21.10508 - 21.10515   PB 402

2865. ——.
Doctrine of the Trinity,
1895-1916, mural (lunette). Boston Pub. Lib.   PB 400

    2866. ——.
    El Jaleo,
    1882, o.c., 7' 7½" x 11' 8". Gardner Mus.
    PB 407

2867. ——.
Luxembourg Gardens at Twilight,
1879, o.c., 29" x 36½". Minn. Inst.   #16.20   PB 404

    2868. ——.
    Muddy Alligators,
    1917, w.c., 13½" x 20¾". Worcester Art Mus.
    #1917.86   PB 411

2869. ——.
The Daughters of Edward Darley Boit,
1882, o.c., 87" x 87". Boston Mus.   #19.124   PB 409

    2870. ——.
    Mrs. Charles Gifford Dyer,
    1880, o.c., 24⅝" x 17¼". Art Inst. Chicago.
    #15.592   PB 405

2871. ——.
Mr. and Mrs. John W. Field,
1882, o.c., 44" x 32½". Pa. Acad.   #B-128   PB 650

    2872. ——.
    Madame X (Mme. Pierre Gautreau),
    1884, o.c., 82⅛" x 43¼". Met. Mus.   #16.53
    Arthur H. Hearn Fund, 1937   PB 395

2873. SARGENT, John Singer (1856-1925).
Mr. & Mrs. Isaac Newton Phelps Stokes,
1897, o.c., 84¼" x 39¾". Met. Mus.   #38.104
Bequest of Edith Minturn Stokes, 1938.   PB 649

2874. SHARPLES, James (c. 1750-1811).
*Médéric Louis Elie Moreau de Saint-Mery
(1750-1819),*
1794-98, pastel on paper, 9⅞" x 8⅛". Met. Mus.
#24.109.89   Bequest of Charles Allen Munn,
1924.   PB 412

2875. STANLEY, John Mix (1814-72).
Indians Playing Cards,
1866, o.c., 16¼" x 26". Detroit Inst.   #43.60   PB 413

2876. STEARNS, Junius Brutus (1810-85).
Fisherman's Still Life,
1853, o.c., 22" x 32". Toledo Mus. Art.
#51.410   PB 414

2877. STUART, Gilbert (1755-1828).
John Adams,
n.d., o.c., 30" x 25". Coll. C. F. Adams, Jr.,
Dover, Mass.   PB 416

2878. ——.
Mrs. John Bannister and Her Son,
c. 1774, o.c., 36" x 30". Redwood Lib., Newport,
R.I.   PB 656

2879. ——.
Joseph de Jaudenes y Nebot,
c. 1795, o.c., 50¼" x 39½". Met. Mus.   #07.75
Rogers Fund, 1907   PB 653

2880. ——.
Matilde Stoughton de Jaudenes,
c. 1795, o.c., 50⅛" x 39½". Met. Mus.   #07.76
Rogers Fund, 1907.   PB 654

2881. ——.
Mrs. Perez Morton,
c. 1802, o.c., 29⅛" x 24⅛". Worcester Art Mus.
#1899.2   PB 655

2882. ——.
The Skater,
1782, o.c., 96⅝" x 58⅛". Mellon Coll., Nat'l
Gall. of Art.   #1051   PB 418

2883. ——.
George Washington (Vaughan),
1795, o.c., 29" x 23¾". Mellon Coll., Nat'l Gall.
of Art.   #580   PB 420

2884. ——.
George Washington (Athenaeum),
1796, o.c., 39½" x 34½". Boston Athenaeum, on
loan to Boston Mus.   #ATH 1   PB 421

2885. ——.
George Washington (Landsdowne),
1796, o.c., 60" x 96". Pa. Acad.   PB 422

2886. ——.
Mrs. Richard Yates,
1793, o.c., 30¼" x 25". Mellon Coll., Nat'l Gall.
of Art.   #490   PB 419

2887. SULLY, Thomas (1783-1872).
Samuel Coates,
1812, o.c., 64" x 94". Pa. Hospital, Philadelphia,
Pa.   PB 424

    2888. ——.
    Mother and Son (Mrs. William H. W. Darley and
    Francis Thomas Sully Darley),
    1840, o.c., 57" x 45⅜". Met. Mus.   #14.126.5
    Bequest of Francis T. S. Darley, 1914.   PB 659

2889. ——.
Captain Jean T. David,
1813, o.c., 35¼" x 27¼". Cleveland Mus.
#1416.16   PB 425

    2890. ——.
    Mary Sicard David,
    1813, o.c., 27½" x 35¼". Cleveland Mus.
    #1417.16   PB 426

2891. ——.
Col. Thomas Handasyd Perkins,
1832, o.c., 58" x 94". Boston Athenaeum.   PB 429

    2892. ——.
    Lady with a Harp: Eliza Ridgely,
    1818, o.c., 84⅜" x 56⅛". Nat'l Gall. of Art.
    #831   Gift of Maude Monell Vetlesen.   PB 658

2893. ——.
Captain Charles Stewart,
1811-12, o.c., 93¼" x 58¾". Nat'l Gall. of Art.
#893   Gift of Maude Monell Vetlesen   PB 660

    2894. ——.
    The Passage of the Delaware,
    1819, o.c., 146½" x 207". Boston Mus.
    #03.1079   PB 428

2895. THAYER, Abbott Henderson (1849-1921).
Florence Protecting the Arts,
c. 1894, mural. Bowdoin College Mus. Fine Arts.
                                           PB 662

    2896. ——.
    Stevenson Memorial Angel,
    1903, o.c., 80¼" x 59¼". Nat'l Coll. Fine
    Arts.   PB 661

2897. THOMPSON, A. E. (?) (act. 1847).
Wetumpka Bridge, Alabama,
1847, o.c., 42¾" x 58¼". M. & M. Karolik Coll.,
Boston Mus.   #48.482   PB 663

    2898. THOMPSON, Jerome B. (1814-86).
    A "Pic Nick" in the Woods of New England,
    n.d., o.c., 41" x 62". M. & M. Karolik Coll.,
    Boston Mus.   #46.852   PB 431

2899. ——.
The Picnic. Near Mount Mansfield, Vermont,
n.d., 40½" x 56⅛". de Young Mem. Mus.
#TL 28   PB 432

    2900. TIRRELL, George (act. c. 1860).
    *View of Sacramento, California, from across the
    Sacramento River,*
    1855-60, o.c., 27" x 48". Coll. Maxim Karolik,
    Newport, R.I.   PB 664

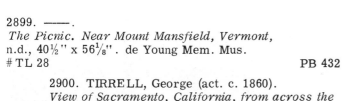

2901. TRUMBULL, John (1756-1843).
Battle of Bunker's Hill,
1786, o.c., 25" x 34". Yale U. Gall.   #1832.1   PB 439

    2902. ——.
    Death of Montgomery in the Attack on Quebec,
    1786, o.c., 20" x 30". Yale U. Gall.   #1832.2
    PB 440

2903. ——.
The Declaration of Independence,
1786-97, o.c., 21⅛" x 31⅛". Yale U. Gall.
#1832.3   PB 665

    2904. ——.
    Sortie of the British Garrison at Gibraltar,
    1788, o.c., 20" x 30". J. J. Emery Coll.,
    Cincinnati Mus.   PB 435

2905. ——.
View of Niagara, from Upper Bank on British Side,
c. 1807, o.c., 24¼" x 36⅞". Wadsworth Atheneum.
#1848-4   PB 443

    2906. ——.
    Alexander Hamilton,
    1792, o.c., 30" x 24". Essex Inst.   #106,821
    PB 441

2907. ——.
Jonathan Trumbull, Jr., and Family,
1777, oil, 38½" x 48⅛". Yale U. Gall.   #1920.2   PB 438

    2908. ——.
    John Vernet and Family,
    1806, o.c., 40" x 50⅛". Yale U. Gall.   #1943.1
    PB 444

2909. ——.
Jeremiah and His Son Daniel Wadsworth,
1784, o.c., 34½" x 26½". Coll. Faneuil Adams, on
loan to Wadsworth Atheneum.   Loan #725   PB 437

    2910. TWACHTMAN, John H. (1853-1902).
    Hemlock Pool,
    c. 1902, o.c., 30" x 25". Addison Gall.
    #1928.34   PB 666

2911. ——.
Holly House, Cos Cob, Conn.,
n.d., o.c., 14½" x 20". Lawrence Art Mus.
PA 88   PB 667

    2912. ——.
    Sailing in the Mist,
    n.d., o.c., 30½" x 30½". Pa. Acad.   PB 445

2913. ——.
Snowbound,
1885, o.c., 25¼" x 30⅛". Art Inst. Chicago.
#17.200   PB 446

    2914. ——.
    Summer,
    n.d., o.c., 30" x 53". Phillips Coll.   PB 668

2915. VANDERLYN, John (1775-1852).
Ariadne,
1814, o.c., 69" x 88". Pa. Acad.   PB 453

    2916. ——.
    Death of Jane McCrea,
    1804, o.c., 32½" x 26½". Wadsworth Atheneum.
    #1855.4   PB 451

2917. ——.
Marius amidst the Ruins of Carthage,
n.d., o.c., 87" x 68½". de Young Mem. Mus.   PB 448

    2918. ——.
    Panorama: Palace and Gardens of Versailles,
    first hemicycle, gen. view, c. 1820, o.c.,
    12' x 165'. Met. Mus.   #52.184   Gift of the
    Senate House Assoc., Kingston, N.Y., 1952.
                 PB 454

2919. ——. Ibid. Det.   PB 455

    2920. ——. Ibid. Det.   PB 456

2921. ——. Ibid. Second hemicycle, gen. view.   PB 457

    2922. ——.
    View of Niagara Falls,
    1827, o.c., 54¼" x 90½". Senate House Mus.,
    Kingston, N.Y.   #1000   PB 458

2923. ——.
View in Rome,
n.d., w.c., 18½" x 13½". Senate House Mus.,
Kingston, N.Y.   #A1168   PB 447

    2924. ——.
    A Lady and Her Son,
    1800, w.c., 12¾" x 12". Senate House Mus.,
    Kingston, N.Y.   #A1166   PB 449

2925. ——.
Robert R. Livingston,
1804, o.c., 46¼" x 35¼". N.Y. Hist. Soc.   PB 452

    2926. VEDDER, Elihu (1836-1923).
    Lair of the Sea Serpent,
    1864, o.c., 21" x 36". Boston Mus.   #84.283
                 PB 460

2927. ——.
The Lost Mind,
1864-65, o.c., 39⅛" x 23¼". Met. Mus.
#21.132.1   Bequest of Helen L. Bullard in
memory of Laura C. Bullard, 1921.
             PB 461

    2928. ——.
    Rome,
    1894, oil, radius 12'. Bowdoin College Mus. Fine
    Arts.   PB 465

2929. VEDDER, Elihu (1836-1923).
Ideal Head,
1872, o.c., 14½" x 14". Coll. Edgar P. Richardson,
Detroit, Mich.   PB 462

2930. WALDO, Samuel Lovett (1783-1861).
James Gould,
c. 1817, o.c., 30" x 25". Yale U. Gall.   #1872.3
                                           PB 467

2931. WALDO, Samuel Lovett (1783-1861) and
JEWETT, William (1795-1873).
John Trumbull,
c. 1821, o.c., 33" x 26". Yale U. Gall.
#1920.23   PB 669

2932. WEIR, John Ferguson (1841-1926).
Forging the Shaft: a Welding Heat,
1877, o.c., 52¹/₁₆" x 73¼". Met. Mus.   #01.7
Gift of Lyman G. Bloomingdale, 1901.   PB 674

2933. WEIR, Julian Alden (1852-1919).
The Red Bridge,
n.d., o.c., 24¼" x 33¾". Met. Mus.   #14.141
Gift of Mrs. John A. Rutherford, 1914.   PB 673

2934. ——.
Visiting Neighbors,
1900-09, o.c., 24½" x 34". Phillips Coll.   PB 671

2935. WHISTLER, James A. McNeill (1834-1903).
Alone with the Tide: Coast of Brittany,
1861, oil, 34¾" x 46¾". Wadsworth Atheneum.
#1925.393   PB 472

2936. ——.
*Arrangement in Flesh Color and Black: Portrait
of Theodore Duret,*
1883, oil, 76⅛" x 35¾". Met. Mus.   #13.20
Wolfe Fund, 1913.   PB 484

2937. ——.
Lady of the Lange Lijsen,
1864, o.c., 36¼" x 24¼". Johnson Coll.,
Philadelphia, Pa.   PB 677

2938. ——.
The Last of Old Westminster,
1862, o.c., 24" x 30½". Boston Mus.   #39.44
                                         PB 475

2939. ——.
Music Room,
1860, o.c., 37⅝" x 27⅞". Freer Gall. Art.   PB 471

2940. ——.
Nocturne in Black and Gold: The Falling Rocket,
c. 1874, oil on panel, 24¾" x 18⅜". Detroit Inst.
#46.309   PB 481

2941. ——.
*Old Battersea Bridge: Symphony in Brown and
Silver,*
c. 1865, o.c., 29" x 34". Addison Gall.
#1928.55   PB 678

2942. ——.
La Princesse du Pays de la Porcelaine,
1864, o.c., 78¾" x 45¾". Freer Gall. Art.
                                         PB 679

2943. WHISTLER, James A. McNeill (1834-1903).
The White Girl,
1861-62, o.c., 84½" x 42½". Harris Whittemore
Coll., Nat'l Gall. of Art.   #750   PB 474

2944. WHITTREDGE, Worthington (1820-1910).
The Crow's Nest,
1848, o.c., 39¾" x 56". Detroit Inst.   #41.12
                                          PB 487

2945. ——.
Deer, Mount Storm Park, Cincinnati,
bef. 1850, o.c., 28⅜" x 40 3/16". Worcester Art
Mus.   #1943.3   PB 489

2946. ——.
Home by the Sea,
1872, o.c., 35½" x 53½". Addison Gall.
#1943.41.a   PB 491

2947. WIMAR, Charles (1828-62).
The Buffalo Dance,
1860, o.c., 24¾" x 48". City Art Mus., St. Louis.
#164.46   PB 682

2948. WOOD, Thomas Waterman (1823-1903).
The Village Post Office,
1873, oil, 36" x 47". N.Y. State Hist. Assoc.,
Cooperstown.   #N.393.55   PB 495

2949. WOODVILLE, Richard Caton (1825-56).
The Card Players,
1846, o.c., 18½" x 25". Detroit Inst.   #55.175 PB 496

2950. ——.
Politics in an Oyster House,
1848, o.c., 16" x 13". Coll. Morgan Marshall,
Walters Art Gall.   #37.1944   PB 497

2951. ——.
War News from Mexico,
1848, o.c., 27" x 25". Nat'l Academy of Design,
New York, N.Y.   #26   PB 684

2952. WRIGHT, Joseph (1756-93).
Self-portrait of the Artist with His Family,
c. 1793, o.c., 32" x 38". Pa. Acad.   PB 500

2953. ——.
George Washington,
1783, oil on wood panel, 14⅛" x 12". Hist. Soc.
Pa.   PB 499

2954. WYANT, Alexander Helwig (1836-92).
The Mohawk Valley,
1866, o.c., 34¾" x 53¾". Met. Mus.   #13.53
Gift of Mrs. George E. Schanck in memory of
Arthur Hoppock Hearn, 1913.   PB 502

2955. ——.
An Old Clearing,
1881, o.c., 49¼" x 37". Met. Mus.   #12.205.2
Gift of Robert Gordon, 1912.   PB 686

PAINTING OF THE TWENTIETH CENTURY

JOHN I. H. BAUR

2957. ADLER, Samuel (1898-   ).
Invocation,
1952, oil on composition board, 42" x 30".
Whitney Mus.   #53.1   PC 500

    2958. ALBERS, Josef (1888-   ).
    The Gate,
    1936, oil, 18¾" x 20⅝". Société Anonyme Coll.,
    Yale U. Gall.   #1941.325   PC 501

2959. ——.
Homage to the Square: "Ascending,"
1953, oil on composition board, 43½" x 43½".
Whitney Mus.   #54.34   PC 3

    2960. ALBRIGHT, Ivan Le Lorraine (1897-   ).
    Into the World There Came a Soul Called Ida,
    1927-30, oil, 56¼" x 47". Coll. Artist, Chicago.
                                        PC 4

2961. ——.
That Which I Should Have Done I Did Not Do,
1931-41, oil, 97" x 36". Art Inst. Chicago.
#340.45   PC 6

    2962. ARONSON, David (1923-   ).
    Coronation of the Virgin,
    1945, encaustic, 41¾" x 35". Virginia
    Mus. Fine Arts.   PC 8

2963. ATHERTON, John (1900-52).
Christmas Eve,
1941, o.c., 30¼" x 35". Mus. Mod. Art.
#136.42   Purchase.   PC 508

    2964. AUSTIN, Darrel (1907-   ).
    Catamount,
    1940, o.c., 20" x 24". Mus. Mod. Art.   #312.41
    Mrs. John D. Rockefeller, Jr., Fund.   PC 510

2965. AVERY, Milton (1893-   ).
Gaspé Landscape,
1943, oil, 36" x 48". Coll. Mr. & Mrs. Roy R.
Neuberger, New York, N.Y.   PC 9

    2966. ——.
    Two Figures at Desk,
    1944, oil, 48" x 32". Coll. Mr. & Mrs. Roy R.
    Neuberger, New York, N.Y.   PC 10

2967. BACON, Peggy (1895-   ).
The Untilled Field,
1937, pastel, 19⅛" x 25¼". Whitney Mus.
#52.29   PC 11

    2968. BAZIOTES, William (1912-   ).
    Dwarf,
    1947, o.c., 42" x 36⅛". Mus. Mod. Art.
    #229.47   A. Conger Goodyear Fund.   PC 12

2969. BAZIOTES, William (1912-   ).
Pompeii,
1955, o.c., 60" x 48". Mus. Mod. Art.   #189.55
Mrs. Louise Smith Fund.   PC 15

2970. BEAL, Gifford (1879-1956).
The Albany Boat,
1915, oil, 36⅜" x 60¼". Met. Mus.   #17.48.1
George A. Hearn Fund, 1917   PC 16

2971. BEAUX, Cecilia (1855-1942).
Man in White (Dr. Henry S. Drinker),
1902, oil, 48" x 34". Nat'l Coll. Fine Arts.   PC 518

2972. BECK, Rosemarie (1923-   ).
No. 3, 1954,
1954, o.c., 49¾" x 45¾". Whitney Mus.   #55.51
Anonymous gift.   PC 520

2973. BELLOWS, George (1882-1925).
Both Members of This Club,
1909, o.c., 45¼" x 63⅛". Chester Dale Coll.,
Nat'l Gall. of Art.   #775   Gift.   PC 18

2974. ——.
The Cliff Dwellers,
1913, oil, 40" x 42". Los Angeles County Mus.
P.146.16-1   PC 20

2975. ——.
Forty-two Kids,
1907, oil, 42" x 60". Corcoran Gall.   #31.12   PC 17

2976. ——.
Elinor, Jean and Anna,
1920, oil, 59" x 66". Albright Gall.   PC 19

2977. BENN, Ben (1884-   ).
Mother and Child,
1915, o.c., 36" x 27". Whitney Mus.   #31.98   PC 21

2978. BENTON, Thomas H. (1889-   ).
Arts of the West (mural #2),
1932, tempera & oil, 7'10" x 13'3". New Britain
Mus.   PC 527

2979. ——.
Boom Town,
1928, oil, 45" x 54". Rochester Mem. Art Gall.
#51.1   PC 22

2980. ——.
July Hay,
1943, egg tempera & oil, 38" x 26¾". Met. Mus.
#43.159.1   George A. Hearn Fund, 1943   PC 24

2981. BEN-ZION (1898-   ).
Moses,
1955, o.c., 52" x 63". Coll. Artist, New York,
N.Y.   PC 22A

2982. BERMAN, Eugene (1899-   ).
The Gates of the City, Nightfall,
1937, o.c., 30¼" x 40¼". Mus. Mod. Art.
#224.47   Gift of James Thrall Soby.   PC 26

2983. BERMAN, Eugene (1899-   ).
The Muse of the Western World,
1942, oil, 50⅞" x 37¾". Met. Mus.   #43.159.2
George A. Hearn Fund, 1943.   PC 27

2984. BIDDLE, George (1885-   ).
A Woman with a Letter (Marguerite Zorach),
1933, oil, 32" x 26". Met. Mus.   #37.71
Arthur H. Hearn Fund, 1937.   PC 531

2985. BISHOP, Isabel (1902-   ).
Homeward,
1951, oil & tempera, 26" x 20". Coll. Mr. & Mrs.
Stanley J. Wolf, Great Neck, L.I., N.Y.   PC 30

2986. ———.
Waiting,
1938, oil, 29" x 22⅛". Newark Mus.   #44.41
                                          PC 29

2987. BLANCH, Arnold (1896-   ).
Four Ships,
1951, o.c., 30" x 48". Whitney Mus.   #53.9   PC 32

2988. ———.
Swamp Folk,
1939-40, o.c., 20" x 29¹⁵⁄₁₆". Brooklyn Mus.
#40.304   PC 31

2989. BLOOM, Hyman (1913-   ).
The Anatomist,
1953, o.c., 70½" x 40½". Whitney Mus.   #54.17
                                          PC 541

2990. ———.
Corpse of an Elderly Female,
1945, o.c., 70½" x 42". Swetzoff Gall., Boston,
Mass.   PC 36

2991. ———.
Synagogue,
c. 1940, o.c., 65¼" x 46¾". Mus. Mod. Art.
#611.43   Acquired through the Lillie P. Bliss
Bequest.   PC 34

2992. ———.
Treasure Map,
1945, o.c., 42" x 32". Addison Gall.   #53.2529
                                          PC 35

2993. BLUEMNER, Oscar Florianus (1867-1938).
Old Canal Port,
1914, oil, 30¼" x 40¼". Whitney Mus.   #31.114
                                          PC 38

2994. ———.
Radiant Night,
1933, o.c., 34" x 47". Addison Gall.   #1957.48
                                          PC 997

2995. ———.
Silktown on the Passaic,
1915, oil. Graham Galleries, New York, N.Y.   PC 39

2996. BLUME, Peter (1906-   ).
The Eternal City,
1934-37, oil on composition board, 34" x 47⅞".
Mus. Mod. Art.   #574.42   Mrs. Simon
Guggenheim Fund.   PC 42

2997. BLUME, Peter (1906-   ).
Man of Sorrows,
1951, tempera on canvas, 28" x 24". Whitney
Mus.   #51.5   PC 544

2998. ——.
Parade,
1930, oil, 49¼" x 56⅜". Mus. Mod. Art.
#29.35   Gift of Mrs. John D. Rockefeller, Jr.
                                                 PC 41

2999. ——.
Passage to Etna,
1954-56, oil, 78"x 39". Fogg Mus.   PC 996

3000. ——.
The Rock,
1948, oil, 58" x 74". Art Inst. Chicago.
#56.338   PC 44

3001. ——.
White Factory,
1928, oil, 30" x 20". Nebraska Art Assoc., U. of
Nebr.   PC 44A

3002. BOHROD, Aaron (1907-   ).
Landscape near Chicago,
1934, oil on composition board, 24" x 32".
Whitney Mus.   #34.13   PC 45

3003. BOLOTOWSKY, Ilya (1907-   ).
Blue Rectangles,
1953, oil, 34" x 42". Whitney Mus.   #56.1   PC 47

3004. BOSA, Louis (1905-   ).
My Family Reunion,
1950, o.c., 42¼"x 62". Whitney Mus.   #54.55
Gift of Mr. & Mrs. Alfred Jaretzki, Jr.   PC 48

3005. BOUCHÉ, Louis (1896-   ).
Ten Cents a Ride,
1942, oil, 45" x 30". Met. Mus.   #42.157
George A. Hearn Fund, 1942.   PC 549

3006. BOYNTON, James (1928-   ).
Limestone Edge,
1953, o.c., 34" x 48". Dallas Mus. Fine Arts.
#1953.24   PC 998A

3007. BREININ, Raymond (1909-   ).
The Night,
1941, gouache, 20¼ " x 28¾". Boston Mus.   PC 550

3008. BROOK, Alexander (1898-   ).
The Sentinels,
1934, o.c., 32" x 48¼". Whitney Mus.   #34.15
                                                 PC 49

3009. ——.
Peggy Bacon and Metaphysics,
1935, oil, 26" x 36". F. M. Hall Coll., U. of
Nebr.   #H-198   PC 50

3010. BROOKS, James (1906-   ).
Ainlee,
1957, oil, 87⅞" x 66⅛". Met. Mus.   #57.48
George A. Hearn Fund, 1957.   PC 53A

3011. BROWN, Carlyle (1919-   ).
The Red Cabinet,
1954, oil, 50¾" x 36¼". Whitney Mus.   # 55.21
PC 55

3012. ——.
Still Life with Glasses and Roses,
1951, oil, 36¼" x 40. U. of Ill.   # 163437
PC 54

3013. BROWNE, Byron (1907-   ).
Woman with Bird,
1948, o.c., 38" x 30". Whitney Mus.   # 49.1
Gift of Mr. & Mrs. Roy R. Neuberger.   PC 559

3014. BRUCE, Patrick Henry (1880-1937).
Composition II,
bef. 1919, oil, 38¼" x 51". Société Anonyme Coll.,
Yale U. Gall.   # 1941.369   PC 56

3015. ——.
Painting,
c. 1930, o.c., 35" x 45¾". Whitney Mus.   # 54.20
Anonymous gift.   PC 57

3016. BRUSH, George de Forest (1855-1941).
In the Garden,
1906, oil, 37" x 16¾". Met. Mus.   # 06.1218
Gift of George A. Hearn, 1906.   PC 58

3017. BURCHFIELD, Charles (1893-   ).
An April Mood,
1946-55, w.c., 40" x 54". Whitney Mus.   # 55.39
Gift of Mr. & Mrs. Laurence Fleischman (and
purchase).   PC 569

3018. ——.
Black Iron,
1935, w.c., 29" x 41". Coll. Lawrence A.
Fleischman, Detroit, Mich.   PC 61

3019. ——.
Church Bells Ringing, Rainy Winter Night,
1917, w.c., 30" x 19". Cleveland Mus.   # 49.544
PC 59

3020. ——.
House of Mystery,
1924, tempera & oil glaze, 29½" x 24½". Art.
Inst. Chicago.   # 41.501   PC 567

3021. ——.
Insects at Twilight,
1917, w.c., 14" x 19¾". Mus. Mod. Art.   # 3-36
Gift of Mrs. John D. Rockefeller, Jr.   PC 565

3022. ——.
Song in the Rain,
1947, w.c., 39" x 27½". Wadsworth Atheneum.
1957.16   PC 565A

3023. ——.
The Sphinx and the Milky Way,
1946, w.c., 52⅝" x 44¾". Munson-Williams-
Proctor Inst.   PC 62

3024. ——.
Sun and Rocks,
1918-50, w.c., 40" x 56". Albright Gall.,
292.85   PC 63

3025. BURLIN, Paul (1886-   ).
Homunculus,
1946, oil, 42" x 30". Coll. Mr. & Mrs. Milton
Lowenthal, New York, N.Y.   PC 65

  3026. BURLIUK, David (1882-   ).
  Harlem River Bridge,
  1926, oil, 29" x 33⅞". Société Anonyme Coll.,
  Yale U. Gall.   #1941.377   PC 66

3027. ——.
The White Cow,
c. 1936, o.c., 36" x 54". Whitney Mus.   #49.24
Gift of Samuel N. Tompkin.   PC 67

  3028. CADMUS, Paul (1904-   ).
  Bar Italia,
  1952-55, tempera, 37½" x 45½". Midtown
  Galleries, New York, N.Y.   PC 70

3029. ——.
Playground,
1948, oil, 24" x 18". Midtown Galleries, New
York, N.Y.   PC 69

  3030. CALLAHAN, Kenneth (1906-   ).
  Transition,
  1956, gouache, 19¼" x 25". Whitney Mus.
  #57.50   Living Arts Foundation Fund.   PC 71

3031. CANDELL, Victor (1903-   ).
Ascendant,
1952, o.c., 60" x 32". Whitney Mus.   #53.4   PC 72

  3032. CARLES, Arthur B. (1882-1952).
  Arrangement,
  bef. 1928, oil, 46¾" x 40⅛". Art Inst. Chicago.
  #28.1185   PC 576

3033. ——.
Bouquet Abstraction,
c. 1930, o.c., 31¾" x 36". Whitney Mus.
#53.41   PC 73

  3034. CARROLL, John (1892-   ).
  White Lace,
  1935, oil, 40¼" x 30". Toledo Mus. Art.
  #36.71   PC 74

3035. CARTER, Clarence (1904-   ).
Jane Reed and Dora Hunt,
1941, o.c., 36" x 45". Mus. Mod. Art.   #334.42
Mrs. Simon Guggenheim Fund.   PC 577

  3036. CASTELLON, Federico (1914-   ).
  The Dark Figure,
  1938, o.c., 17" x 26⅛". Whitney Mus.   #42.3
                                         PC 75

3037. COLEMAN, Glenn O. (1887-1932).
Angelo's Place,
1929, o.c., 25¼" x 34¼". Mus. Mod. Art.
#47.35   Gift of Mrs. John D. Rockefeller, Jr.   PC 579

  3038. ——.
  Downtown Street,
  1926, o.c., 33" x 44". Whitney Mus.   #31.154
                                         PC 77

3039. COLEMAN, Glenn O. (1887-1932).
Fort Lee Ferry,
1923, o.c., 25" x 30". Brooklyn Mus.   # 30.1153
PC 578

3040. CONGDON, William (1912-   ).
St. Germain,
1954, oil on composition board, 48" x 54".
Whitney Mus.   # 54.59   Gift of Miss Katherine
Ordway.   PC 80

3041. CORBETT, Edward (1919-   ).
Number 15,
1951, chalk & casein, 28" x 15". Mus. Mod. Art.
43.52   Purchase.   PC 81

3042. CORBINO, Jon (1905-   ).
Flood Refugees,
1938, oil, 40" x 64". Met. Mus.   # 50.93
Arthur H. Hearn Fund, 1950.   PC 82

3043. ———.
Stampeding Bulls,
1937, oil, 28" x 42". Toledo Mus. Art.   # 37.19   PC 83

3044. CORCOS, Lucille (1908-   ).
Afternoon at the Zoo,
1937, gouache, 11⅛" x 15½". Whitney Mus.
38.14   PC 583

3045. COVERT, John R. (1882-   ).
Temptation of St. Anthony,
1916, oil, 25¾" x 23¾". Société Anonyme Coll.,
Yale U. Gall.   # 1941.416   PC 84

3046. ———.
Brass Band,
1919, oil & string, 26" x 24". Société Anonyme
Coll., Yale U. Gall.   # 1941.411   PC 85

3047. CRAMER, Konrad (1888-   ).
Improvisation Number 2,
1913, oil, 28" x 24". Coll. Artist, Woodstock
(Bearsville Flats), N.Y.   PC 86

3048. CRAWFORD, Ralston (1906-   ).
Whitestone Bridge,
1939, oil, 40" x 32". Rochester Mem. Art Gall.
51.2   PC 87

3049. CURRY, John Steuart (1897-1946).
Hogs Killing Rattlesnake,
1930, oil, 30⅜" x 38⁵⁄₁₆". Art Inst. Chicago.   # 47.392
PC 89

3050. ———.
Tornado over Kansas,
1929, oil, 48" x 63". Hackley Art Gall.   # 35.4
PC 90

3051. DASBURG, Andrew M. (1887-   ).
Apples,
1929, o.c., 16⅛" 24¼". Whitney Mus.   # 31.163
PC 94

3052. ———.
Autumn Fruit,
1934, oil, 39" x 23". Coll. Hardwood Fdn., Taos,
N. Mex.   PC 93

3053. DAVIES, Arthur B. (1862-1928).
Dancers,
n.d., oil, 84" x 150". Detroit Inst.   #27.158   PC 97

    3054. ——.
    Dream,
    bef. 1909, oil, 18" x 30". Met. Mus.   #09.72.4
    Gift of George A. Hearn, 1909.   PC 96

3055. ——.
The Flood,
bef. 1909, o.c., 18" x 30". Phillips Coll.   PC 618

    3056. ——.
    Unicorns,
    1906, oil, 18¼" x 40¼". Met. Mus.   #31.67.12
    Bequest of Lizzie P. Bliss, 1931.   PC 95

3057. DAVIS, Stuart (1894-   ).
Bass Rocks, No. 1,
1939, oil, 33" x 43". Roland P. Murdock Coll.,
Wichita Art Mus.   #M-49   PC 616

    3058. ——.
    Egg Beater No. 1,
    1927, o.c., 27" x 38⅛". Phillips Coll.   PC 99

3059. ——.
Lucky Strike,
1921, o.c., 33¼" x 18". Mus. Mod. Art.   #132.51
Gift of The American Tobacco Co., Inc.   PC 98

    3060. ——.
    Mural,
    1955, oil, 8' x 30'. Drake Univ., Des Moines,
    Iowa.   PC 615

3061. ——.
Owh! In San Pao,
1951, o.c., 52¼" x 41¾". Whitney Mus.   #52.2
                            PC 999

    3062. ——.
    Place Pasdeloup,
    1928, o.c., 36¼" x 28¾". Whitney Mus.
    #31.170   PC 100

3063. ——.
Report from Rockport,
1940, oil, 24" x 30". Coll. Mr. & Mrs. Milton
Lowenthal, New York, N.Y.   PC 101

    3064. ——.
    Something on the Eight Ball,
    1953-54, oil, 56" x 45". Phila. Mus.   PC 102

3065. DEHN, Adolph (1895-   ).
Beauty Is Where You Find It,
1943, w.c., 19⅛" x 27⅝". Whitney Mus.
#43.13   PC 104A

    3066. ——.
    Jimmy Savo and Rope,
    1944, gouache, 14⅜" x 21⅜". Whitney Mus.
    #45.12   PC 103

3067. DE MARTINI, Joseph (1896-   ).
Crotch Island Derricks,
1938, oil, 33" x 22". Walker Art Center. #43.15   PC 600

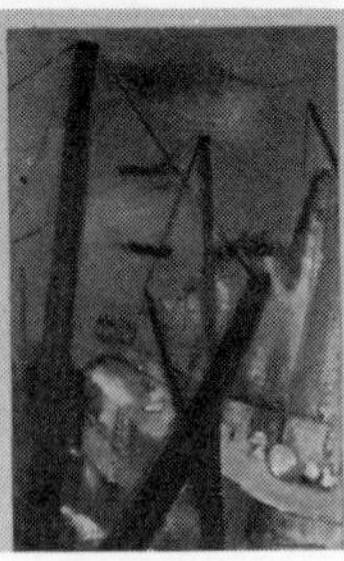

3068. DEMUTH, Charles (1883-1935).
Acrobats,
1919, w.c., 13" x 7⅞". Mus. Mod. Art.   #51.35
Gift of Mrs. John D. Rockefeller, Jr.   PC 602

3069. ——.
The Circus,
1917, w.c., 8" x 10⅝". Ferdinand Howald Coll.,
Columbus Gall.   PC 110

3070. ——.
At a House in Harley Street,
1918, w.c., 8" x 11". Mus. Mod. Art.   #56.35
Gift of Mrs. John D. Rockefeller, Jr.   PC 111

3071. ——.
I Saw the Figure 5 in Gold,
1928, oil, 36" x 29¾". Stieglitz Coll., Met. Mus.
#49.59.1   The Alfred Stieglitz Coll., 1949.   PC 606

3072. ——.
My Egypt,
1927, oil on composition board, 35¾" x 30".
Whitney Mus.   #31.172   PC 113

3073. ——.
Paquebot Paris,
n.d., oil, 24½" x 19⁷⁄₁₆". Ferdinand Howald Coll.,
Columbus Gall.   PC 112

3074. ——.
Poppies,
1929, w.c., 14" x 20". Coll. Edith G. Halpert,
Downtown Gallery, New York, N.Y.   PC 114

3075. ——.
Trees and Barns: Bermuda,
1917, w.c., 9½" x 13½". Lawrence Art Mus.
#57.8   PC 110A

3076. DICKINSON, Edwin (1891-   ).
Woodland Scene,
1933-35, oil, 71⅜" x 68½". White Art Mus.,
Cornell U.   #52.143   PC 115

3077. DICKINSON, Preston (1891-1930).
Industry,
bef. 1924, o.c., 30" x 24¼". Whitney Mus.
#31.173   PC 118

3078. ——.
Still Life with Yellow-green Chair,
1928, oil, 15" x 21". Ferdinand Howald Coll.,
Columbus Gall.   PC 119

3079. DODD, Lamar (1909-   ).
Monhegan Theme,
1949, o.c., 24" x 36". Met. Mus.   #51.98
George A. Hearn Fund, 1951.   PC 123

3080. DOVE, Arthur G. (1880-1946).
Fog Horns,
1929, oil, 19" x 27". Colorado Springs Fine Arts
Center.   PC 189

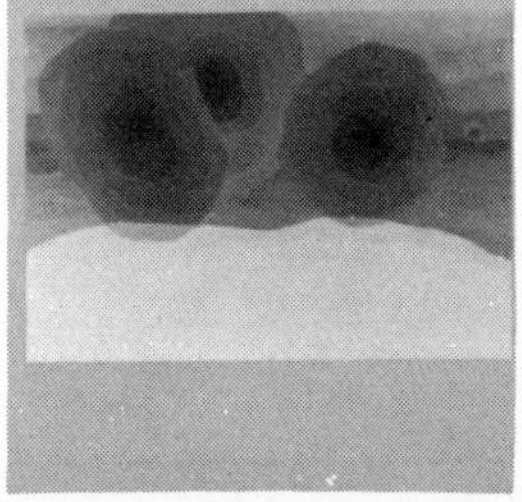

3081. DOVE, Arthur G. (1880-1946).
Goin' Fishin',
1925, collage, 19½" x 24". Phillips Coll.   PC 188

    3082. ——.
    Green, Gold and Brown,
    1941, oil, 18" x 27". Phillips Coll.   PC 190

3083. ——.
Nature Symbolized, No. 2,
1914, pastel, 17⅞" x 21½". Art Inst. Chicago.
#49.533   PC 187

    3084. ——.
    Rain or Snow,
    1934-44, o.c., 35" x 25". Phillips Coll.   PC 191

3085. DOZIER, Otis (1904-   ).
Summer,
1935, oil on wood, 19½" x 21½". Dallas Mus.
Fine Arts.   #1953.3   PC 124

    3086. DU BOIS, Guy Pène (1884-1958).
    The Doll and the Monster,
    1914, oil, 20" x 15". Met. Mus.   #21.147
    Gift of Mrs. Harry Payne Whitney, 1921. PC 125

3087. ——.
Morning, Paris Café,
1926, o.c., 36¼" x 28¾". Whitney Mus.
#31.182   PC 631

    3088. EILSHEMIUS, Louis M. (1864-1941).
    Afternoon Wind,
    1899, o.c., 20" x 36". Mus. Mod. Art.   #394.41
    Anonymous gift.   PC 127

3089. ——.
Bridge for Fishing,
c. 1905, oil, 18" x 35". Phillips Coll.   PC 632

    3090. ——.
    Tragedy,
    1916, oil, 39½" x 60½". Miss Adelaide M.
    de Groot Coll., Met. Mus.   #L.52.24.154   Lent
    by Adelaide Milton de Groot, 1952.   PC 633

3091. ERNST, Jimmy (1920-   ).
Personal History,
1949, o.c., 46" x 40". Whitney Mus.   #50.10
Juliana Force Purchase.   PC 130

    3092. ——.
    Timescape,
    1956, oil, 36" x 48". Roby Fdn c/o Whitney Mus.
            PC 131

3093. EVERGOOD, Philip (1901-   ).
Dream Catch,
1946, oil, 29¼" x 20". Coll. Joseph H. Hirshhorn,
New York, N.Y.   PC 137

    3094. ——.
    Lily and the Sparrows,
    1939, oil on composition board, 30" x 24".
    Whitney Mus.   #41.42   PC 136

3095. EVERGOOD, Phillip (1901-   ).
The New Lazarus,
1927-54, o.c., 48" x 83¼". Whitney Mus.
#54.60   Gift of Joseph H. Hirshhorn.   PC 139

3096. FEININGER, Lyonel (1871-1956).
Church of the Minorites, II,
1926, oil, 42¾" x 43". Walker Art Center.
#43.20   PC 141

3097. ——.
City at Night,
1941, oil, 36" x 24". Coll. Mr. & Mrs. Stanley J.
Wolf, Great Neck, L.I., N.Y.   PC 143

3098.
Glorious Victory of the Sloop Maria,
1926, oil, 21¼" x 33¼". City Art Mus., St. Louis.
#848.40   PC 142

3099. ——.
The River,
1940, w.c., 13" x 20". Worcester Art Mus.
#1942.48   PC 648

3100. ——.
Side Wheeler,
1913, oil, 31¾" x 39⅝". Detroit Inst.   #21.208
                                                 PC 140

3101. ——.
Yacht,
1952, w.c., 12¼" x 17½". Coll. Mr. & Mrs. Roy
R. Neuberger, New York, N.Y.   PC 144

3102. FEITELSON, Lorser (1898-   ).
Genesis, First Version,
1934, oil, 24" x 30". San Francisco Mus.
#37.2978   Gift of Miss Helen Klokke.   PC 145

3103. FERREN, John (1905-   ).
The Garden,
1954, o.c., 82" x 65¼". Whitney Mus.   #55.53
                                                 PC 147

3104. FIENE, Ernest (1894-   ).
Hudson Navigation Boat,
1927, oil on composition board, 38" x 40".
Whitney Mus.   #31.199   PC 148

3105. ——.
Variations on a Theme: "The Wreck, No. 2,"
1948, o.c., 34" x 44". Whitney Mus.   #53.39   PC 651

3106. FOGEL, Seymour (1911-   ).
Cosmos,
1951, mural, ethyl silicate, 15'3" x 12'6".
Petroleum Club, Houston, Tex.   PC 653

3107. FRENCH, Jared (1905-   ).
The Rope,
1954, egg tempera on paper, 13½" x 14¼".
Whitney Mus.   #56.3   Charles F. Williams
Fund.   PC 151

3108. FRIEDMAN, Arnold (1879-1946).
Sawtooth Falls,
1945, o.c., 36⅛" x 29⅞". Mus. Mod. Art.
#119.46   Purchase Fund & gift of Dr.
Nathaniel S. Wolff.   PC 149

3109. GATCH, Lee (1902-   ).
Gothic Night,
1957, o.c., 42¼" x 46¼". Boston Mus.
57.666   PC 659

3110. ——.
Greenhouse,
1950, oil, 44" x 36". Coll. Mr. & Mrs. Roy R.
Neuberger, New York, N.Y.   PC 152

3111. ——.
Pennsylvania Farm,
c. 1936, oil, 45" x 14". City Art Mus., St. Louis.
45.42   PC 153

3112. GLACKENS, William J. (1870-1938).
Chez Mouquin,
1905, oil, 48³/₁₆" x 36¼". Art Inst. Chicago.
25.295   PC 156

3113. ——.
Hammerstein's Roof Garden,
c. 1901, o.c., 30" x 25". Whitney Mus.   # 53.46
                                           PC 155

3114. ——.
The Soda Fountain,
1935, oil, 49" x 38". Pa. Acad.   PC 158

3115. GLARNER, Fritz (1899-   ).
Relational Painting,
1949-51, o.c., 65" x 52". Whitney Mus.   # 52.3
                                           PC 159

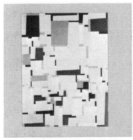

3116. ——.
Tondo No. 15,
1950, oil, D. 22". Saidie A. May Coll., Baltimore
Mus.   # 51.303   PC 160

3117. GLASCO, Joseph (1925-   ).
Portrait of a Poet,
1951, o.c., 68" x 46". Whitney Mus.   # 52.4   PC 161

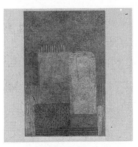

3118. ——.
Salome,
1955, oil, 80" x 67". Coll. Stanley Seeger, Jr.,
on loan to Whitney Mus.   # 3.56   PC 163

3119. ——.
Sleeping Figure,
1958, oil, 48" x 72". Coll. Artist, Ottsville, Pa.   PC 162

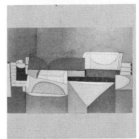

3120. GONZALEZ, Xavier (1898-   ).
Landscape No. 9,
1950, w.c. & casein, 21½" x 30". Whitney Mus.
51.23   PC 671

3121. GORKY, Arshile (1904-48).
Agony,
1947, o.c., 40" x 50½". Mus. Mod. Art.
88.50   A. Conger Goodyear Fund.   PC 168

3122. ——.
The Betrothal II,
1947, o.c., 50¾" x 38". Whitney Mus.   # 50.3
                                           PC 167

3123. GORKY, Arshile (1904-48).
Enigmatic Combat,
c. 1936, oil, 36" x 48". San Francisco
Mus. Art.   #41.3763   PC 164

    3124. ——.
    The Liver Is the Cock's Comb,
    1944, oil, 73" x 98". Albright Gall. Gift of
    Seymour H. Knox.   PC 166

3125. GOTTLIEB, Adolph (1903-   ).
Evil Omen,
1946, oil, 38" x 30". Coll. Mr. & Mrs. Roy R.
Neuberger, New York, N.Y.   PC 169

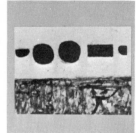

    3126. ——.
    The Frozen Sounds, No. 1,
    1951, o.c., 36" x 48". Whitney Mus.   #57.3
    Gift of Mr. & Mrs. Samuel M. Kootz.   PC 170

3127. ——.
Hot Horizon,
1956, oil, 50" x 72". Coll. Artist, New York,
N.Y.   PC 171

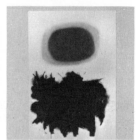

    3128. ——.
    Transfiguration #2,
    1958, oil, 58" x 40". Coll. Artist, New York,
    N.Y.   PC 678A

3129. GRAVES, Morris (1910-   ).
Bird Maddened by the Long Winter,
1945, tempera, 28½" x 59½". Coll. Mr. & Mrs.
Stanley J. Wolf, Great Neck, L.I., N.Y.   PC 175

    3130. ——.
    Bird Singing in the Moonlight,
    1938-39, gouache, 26¾" x 30⅛". Mus. Mod. Art.
    #14.42   Purchase.   PC 172

3131. ——.
Flight of Plover,
1955, oil on composition board, 36" x 48".
Whitney Mus.   #56.4   Gift of Mr. & Mrs.
Roy R. Neuberger.   PC 174

    3132. GREENE, Balcomb (1904-   ).
    The Ancient Form,
    1940, o.c., 20" x 30". Mus. Mod. Art.   #326.41
    Purchase.   PC 176

3133. ——.
Composition: the Storm,
1953-54, oil, 36¼" x 48". Whitney Mus.   #55.4
                                        PC 177

    3134. GREENE, Stephen (1918-   ).
    The Deposition,
    1947, oil, 59" x 34". City Art Mus., St. Louis.
    #529:57   Gift of Louise & Joseph Pulitzer, Jr.
                                        PC 178

3135. GROPPER, William (1897-   ).
Homeless,
1938, oil, 20" x 28". Met. Mus.   #39.49
Arthur H. Hearn Fund, 1939.   PC 181

    3136. ——.
    The Senate,
    1935, o.c., 25⅛" x 33⅛". Mus. Mod. Art.
    #108.36   Gift of A. Conger Goodyear.   PC 180

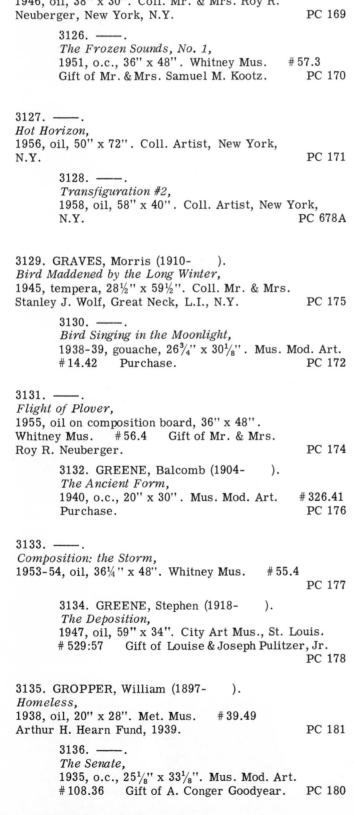

3137. GROSZ, George (1893-1959).
Couple,
1934, w.c., 25¼" x 17¾". Whitney Mus.
#36.18   PC 182

    3138. ——.
    The Pit,
    1946, oil, 60¼" x 37¼". Roland P. Murdock Coll.,
    Wichita Art Mus.   #M-72   PC 185

3139. ——.
The Survivor,
1944, oil, 31" x 39". Coll. Marc J. Sandler,
Pittsburgh, Pa.   PC 184

    3140. ——.
    Waving the Flag,
    1947-48, w.c., 25" x 18". Whitney Mus.   #54.9
                                       PC 186

3141. GUGLIELMI, Louis (1906-   ).
The River,
1942, oil, 34" x 30". Art Inst. Chicago.   #45.6
                                           PC 193

    3142. ——.
    Terror in Brooklyn,
    1941, oil, 34" x 30". Whitney Mus.   #42.5
                                       PC 192

3143. GUSTON, Philip (1903-   ).
Martial Memory,
1941, oil, 39¾" x 31½". City Art Mus., St. Louis.
#115.42   PC 194

    3144. ——.
    The Street,
    1956, oil, 76" x 72". Courtesy Sidney Janis
    Gallery, New York, N.Y.   PC 195

3145. GWATHMEY, Robert (1903-   ).
Bread and Circuses,
1945, o.c., 28" x 40". Mus. Fine Arts,
Springfield, Mass.   #46.04   PC 196

    3146. ——.
    Painting of a Smile,
    c. 1951, oil, 41" x 60". Nebr. Art Assoc., U. of
    Nebr.   #N-81   PC 198A

3147. ——.
Vacationist,
1946, oil, 50" x 30". Coll. Mr. & Mrs. Milton Lowenthal,
New York, N.Y.   PC 197

    3148. HALPERT, Samuel (1884-1930).
    Brooklyn Bridge,
    1913, o.c., 34" x 42". Whitney Mus.   #54.2
    Gift of Mr. & Mrs. Benjamin Halpert.   PC 199

3149. HART, George Overbury ("Pop")(1868-1933).
The Bahamas,
c. 1918, w.c., 13½" x 21½". Whitney Mus.   #32.7
                                           PC 201

    3150. ——.
    Cockfight, Mexico,
    1926, w.c., 15½" x 21¼". Newark Mus.
    #U.S. 281759   PC 202

3151. HARTIGAN, Grace (1922-   ).
Grand Street Brides,
1954, o.c., 72" x 102½". Whitney Mus.   #55.27
Anonymous gift.   PC 703

    3152. HARTLEY, Marsden (1877-1943).
    Fisherman's Last Supper,
    1940-41, oil, 30" x 41". Coll. Mr. & Mrs. Roy R.
    Neuberger, New York, N.Y.   PC 206

3153. ——.
Mt. Katahdin, Autumn, No. 1,
1939-40, oil, 30⅛" x 40". F. M. Hall Coll., U. of
Nebr.   #H-232   PC 205

    3154. ——.
    Painting No. 5,
    1914-15, oil, 39½" x 31¾". Whitney Mus.
    #58.65   Anonymous gift.   PC 704

3155. ——.
Portrait of a German Officer,
1914, oil, 68¼" x 41⅜". Met. Mus.   #49.70.42
The Alfred Stieglitz Coll., 1949.   PC 203

    3156. ——.
    The Wave,
    1940, oil on fiberboard, 30¼" x 40⅞". Worcester
    Art Mus.   #1942.1   PC 207

3157. HELIKER, John (1909-   ).
Monreale,
1950, oil, 28" x 22". Phila. Mus.   PC 209

    3158. ——.
    White Rocks, Nova Scotia,
    1955, oil, 13½" x 24½". Roby Fdn c/o Whitney
    Mus.   PC 210

3159. HENRI, Robert (1865-1929).
Eva Green,
1907, oil, 24" x 20⅛". Roland P. Murdock Coll.,
Wichita Art Mus.   #M-59   PC 212

    3160. ——.
    Fifty-Seventh Street,
    1902, oil, 26" x 32". Yale U., Garvan Coll.
    #1947.185   PC 211

3161. ——.
Portrait of George Luks,
1904, oil, 77" x 38¼". Coll. Miss Violet Organ,
New York, N.Y.   PC 713

    3162. HIGGINS, Eugene (1874-   ).
    The Gamblers,
    1907, oil, 16" x 12". Met. Mus.   #35.33
    George A. Hearn Fund, 1935.   PC 213

3163. HIRSCH, Joseph (1910-   ).
The Senator,
1941, o.c., 16" x 32". Whitney Mus.   #42.6   PC 214

    3164. HIRSCH, Stefan (1899-   ).
    Pic of Orizaba,
    1932, o.c., 29¼" x 39¼". Whitney Mus.   #33.14
                                            PC 715

3165. HIRSHFIELD, Morris (1872-1946).
Girl in a Mirror,
1940, o.c., 40⅛" x 22¼". Mus. Mod. Art.
#327.41   Purchase.   PC 215

   3166. HOFMANN, Hans (1880-   ).
   Magenta and Blue,
   1950, o.c., 48" x 58". Whitney Mus.   #50.20
                                              PC 218

3167. HOGUE, Alexandre (1898-   ).
Drought-Stricken Area,
1934, oil, 30" x 42¾". Dallas Mus. Fine Arts.
#1945.6   PC 220

   3168. HOLTY, Carl R. (1900-   ).
   Carousel,
   1945, oil, 48½" x 40". Coll. Mr. & Mrs. Roy R.
   Neuberger, New York, N.Y.   PC 221

3169. HOPKINSON, Charles (1869-   ).
Afternoon Light,
1932, w.c., 14½" x 21¼". Boston Mus.   PC 222

   3170. HOPPER, Edward (1882-   ).
   Corner Saloon,
   1913, o.c., 24" x 24". Mus. Mod. Art.   #329.41
   Mrs. John D. Rockefeller, Jr., Fund.   PC 720

3171. ——.
Early Sunday Morning,
1930, o.c., 35" x 60". Whitney Mus.   #31.426   PC 226

   3172. ——.
   Gas,
   1940, o.c., 26¼" x 40¼". Mus. Mod. Art.
   #577.43   Mrs. Simon Guggenheim
   Fund.   PC 722

3173. ——.
House on Pamet River,
1934, w.c., 19¾" x 24⅞". Whitney Mus.
#36.20   PC 224A

   3174. ——.
   House by the Railroad,
   1925, o.c., 24" x 29½". Mus. Mod. Art.   #3.30
   Anonymous gift.   PC 223

3175. ——.
Nighthawks,
1942, oil, 33³⁄₁₆" x 60⅛". Art Inst. Chicago.   #42.51
                                              PC 227

   3176. ——.
   Pennsylvania Coal Town,
   1947, oil, 28" x 40". Butler Art Inst.   PC 724

3177. ——.
White River at Sharon,
1937, w.c., 19⅜" x 27⅜". Roby Fdn c/o Whitney Mus.
                                              PC 723

   3178. HOWARD, Charles (1899-   ).
   Prescience,
   1942, oil, 28¼" x 40½". Met. Mus.   #42.163
   Arthur H. Hearn Fund, 1942.   PC 229

3179. HULTBERG, John (1922-   ).
Night Still Life,
1954, o.c., 38¼" x 51". Whitney Mus.   # 55.5   PC 228

3180. HURD, Peter (1904-   ).
The Boy from the Plains,
1938, tempera, 24½" x 24". Coll. Mr. & Mrs.
Roy R. Neuberger, New York, N.Y.   PC 231

3181. JOHNSTON, Ynez (1902-   ).
Breakwater,
1952, casein & ink, 16⅜" x 28⅜". Whitney Mus.
52.20   PC 1001

3182. JONES, Joe (1909-   ).
American Farm,
1936, oil & tempera on canvas, 30" x 40".
Whitney Mus.   # 36.144   PC 1002

3183. KANE, John (1860-1934).
Scotch Day at Kennywood,
1933, o.c., 19⅞" x 27⅛". Mus. Mod. Art.
504.53   Gift of Mr. & Mrs. Albert Lewin.   PC 235

3184. ———.
Turtle Creek Valley,
1922, oil, 34¼" x 44". Roland P. Murdock Coll.,
Wichita Art Mus.   # M-74   PC 233

3185. ———.
Self-portrait,
1929, o.c. over composition board, 36⅛" x 27⅛".
Mus. Mod. Art.   # 6.39   Mrs. John D.
Rockefeller, Jr., Fund.   PC 234

3186. KANTOR, Morris (1896-   ).
Haunted House,
1930, oil, 37⅛" x 33½". Art Inst. Chicago.
31.707   PC 731

3187. ———.
Storm,
1944, oil & egg tempera on composition board,
27⅞" x 36". Whitney Mus.   # 52.9   PC 237

3188. KARFIOL, Bernard (1886-1952).
Boy Bathers,
1916, o.c., 28" x 36". Whitney Mus.   # 54.19
PC 241

3189. ———.
Christina,
1936, oil, 34" x 26". Carnegie Inst.   # 290   PC 243

3190. ———.
Cuban Nude,
n.d., o.c., 36" x 50". Met. Mus.   # 37.76
George A. Hearn Fund, 1937   PC 734

3191. KATZMAN, Herbert (1923-   ).
Two Nudes before Japanese Screen,
1952, oil on composition board, 76" x 43".
Whitney Mus.   # 53.5   Juliana Force Purchase
PC 238

3192. ———.
Zinnias,
1953, o.c., 36" x 28½". Lawrence Art Mus.
57.42   Gift of Mr. & Mrs. Roy R. Neuberger.
PC 240

3193. KENT, Rockwell (1882-   ).
Mount Equinox, Winter,
1921, oil, 34³/₁₆" x 44³/₁₆". Art Inst. Chicago.
#23.51   PC 245

    3194. ———.
    Shadows of Evening,
    1921-23, o.c., 38" x 44". Whitney Mus.
    #31.257   PC 739

3195. KIENBUSCH, William (1914-   ).
Barns and Fences, No. 1,
1948, casein, 22½" x 31". New Britain Mus.   PC 246

    3196. ———.
    Black Bush, Autumn, Dogtown,
    1954, gouache, 30" x 40". Coll. Mr. & Mrs. Roy
    R. Neuberger, New York, N.Y.   PC 247

3197. KINGMAN, Dong (1911-   ).
The El and Snow,
1946, w.c., 21" x 29³/₈". Whitney Mus.   #47.9   PC 249

    3198. KLINE, Franz (1910-   ).
    Mahoning,
    1956, o.c., 80" x 100". Whitney Mus.   #57.10
    Gift of the Friends of the Whitney Museum of
    American Art.   PC 250

3199. ———.
Painting, No. 7,
1952, oil, 57½" x 81¾". Guggenheim Mus.
F. N. 1403   PC 251

    3200. KNATHS, Karl (1891-   ).
    Autumn Leaves,
    1948, o.c., 36½" x 42½". Brooklyn Mus.
    #50.58   PC 254

3201. ———.
Cock and Glove,
c. 1927-28, o.c., 36" x 26". Phillips Coll.   PC 252

    3202. ———.
    Duck Flight,
    1948, o.c., 40" x 30". Whitney Mus.   #49.18
                                               PC 253

3203. KOERNER, Henry (1915-   ).
Vanity Fair,
1946, oil on composition board, 36" x 42".
Whitney Mus.   #48.2   PC 255

    3204. de KOONING, Willem (1904-   ).
    Asheville,
    1949, o.c., 25⁵/₈" x 31⁷/₈". Phillips Coll.   PC 107

3205. ———.
Woman, I,
1950-52, o.c., 75⁷/₈" x 58". Mus. Mod. Art.
#478.53   Purchase.   PC 108

    3206. KOPMAN, Benjamin (1887-   ).
    Portrait—Bear,
    1928, oil, 25" x 24". Fisk U.   #41   PC 256

3207. KROLL, Leon (1884-   ).
In the Country,
1916, oil, 46" x 52". Detroit Inst.   #19.35   PC 258

3208. ——.
Nude,
1933-34, oil, 48" x 36". Met. Mus.   #49.127
Arthur H. Hearn Fund, 1949.   PC 259

3209. KUHN, Walt (1880-1949).
Apples in the Hay,
1932, o.c., 30" x 40". Mus. Mod. Art.   #14.36
Anonymous gift.   PC 262

3210. ——.
The Blue Clown,
1931, o.c., 30" x 25". Whitney Mus.   #32.25
    PC 261

3211. ——.
A Girl in White and Silver,
1943, oil, 40" x 30¼". Met. Mus.   #50.28.4
George A. Hearn Fund, 1950.   PC 758

3212. ——.
Clown in His Dressing Room,
1943, o.c., 72" x 32". Whitney Mus.   #50.1
Anonymous gift.   PC 263

3213. ——.
Dressing Room,
1926, o.c., 45" x 33". Brooklyn Mus.   #27.860
    PC 260

3214. KUNIYOSHI, Yasuo (1893-1953).
The Amazing Juggler,
1952, oil, 65" x 40". Des Moines Art Center.
    PC 268

3215. ——.
Headless Horse Who Wants to Jump,
1945, oil, 57" x 35". Mus. Cranbrook Academy of
Art, Bloomfield Hills, Mich.   #1946.10   PC 266

3216. ——.
I'm Tired,
1938, o.c., 40¼" x 31". Whitney Mus.   #39.12
    PC 265

3217. ——.
Little Joe with Cow,
1923, oil, 28" x 42". Coll. Edith G. Halpert,
Downtown Gallery, New York, N.Y.   PC 264

3218. ——.
Look, It Flies,
oil, 30" x 40". Coll. Joseph H. Hirshhorn, New
York, N.Y.   PC 762

3219. ——.
Revelation,
1949, oil, 70" x 46". Roland P. Murdock Coll.,
Wichita Art Mus.   #M-80   PC 267

3220. ——.
Strong Woman and Child,
1925, o.c., 57" x 45". Roby Fdn c/o Whitney Mus.
    PC 763A

3221. LAWRENCE, Jacob (1917-   ).
Sedation,
1950, casein, 31" x 22⅞". Mus. Mod. Art.
#15.51   Gift of Mr. & Mrs. Hugo Kastor.   PC 272

3222. ——.
Tombstones,
1942, gouache, 28¾" x 20½". Whitney Mus.
#43.14   PC 270

3223. ——.
War Series: Another Patrol,
1946, tempera, 16" x 20". Whitney Mus.   #51.7
                                                  PC 767

3224. LAWSON, Ernest (1873-1939).
Early Summer, Vermont,
n.d., oil, 24" x 30". Ferdinand Howald Coll.,
Columbus Gall. Fine Arts.   PC 275

3225. ——.
Spring Night, Harlem River,
1913, oil, 25" x 30". Phillips Coll.   PC 274

3226. ——.
Winter on the River,
1907, o.c., 33" x 40". Whitney Mus.   #31.280
                                                  PC 764

3227. LE BRUN, Rico (1900-   ).
Wood of the Holy Cross,
1948, oil & casein, 80" x 30". Whitney Mus.
#53.10   PC 277

3228. LEONID (1896-   ).
Entretat, le Cabestan Capstan,
1931, o.c., 19⁹⁄₁₆" x 31¾". Wadsworth Atheneum.
#1935.255   PC 773A

3229. ——.
Malamocco,
1948, o.c., 36" x 28". Mus. Mod. Art.   #10.50
Purchase.   PC 773

3230. LEVI, Julian E. (1900-   ).
Last of the Lighthouse,
1941, oil, 43" x 35". Newark Mus.
#U.S. 146.129A   PC 280

3231. LEVINE, Jack (1915-   ).
Gangster Funeral,
1952-53, o.c., 63" x 72". Whitney Mus.   #53.42
                                                  PC 284

3232. ——.
The Street,
1938, oil tempera & o.c., 59½" x 83". Lent by
W.P.A. Art Program to Mus. Mod. Art.
#E.L.41.2378   PC 281

3233. ——.
The Trial,
1953-54, oil, 72" x 63". Art Inst. Chicago.
#54.438   PC 777

3234. ——.
Welcome Home,
1946, o.c., 40" x 60". Brooklyn Mus.   #46.124
                                                  PC 282

3235. LIE, Jonas (1880-1940).
The Old Ships Draw to Home Again,
1920, o.c., 40" x 50". Brooklyn Mus.   #21.24   PC 779

    3236. LOCKWOOD, Ward (1894-   ).
    Southwest, Number 4,
    1954, casein on cardboard, 24¾" x 30¾".
    Whitney Mus.   #54.31   PC 780

3237. LUKS, George (1867-1933).
Armistice Night,
1918, o.c., 37" x 68¾". Whitney Mus.   #54.58
Anonymous gift.   PC 783

    3238. ——.
    The Old Duchess,
    1905, oil, 30" x 25". Met. Mus.   #21.41.1
    George A. Hearn Fund, 1921.   PC 287

3239. ——.
The Spielers,
1905, o.c., 36" x 26". Addison Gall.   #1931.9   PC 288

    3240. ——.
    The Wrestlers,
    1905, o.c., 48¼" x 66¼". Boston Mus.   #45.9
        PC 289

3241. MACDONALD-WRIGHT, Stanton (1890-   ).
"Conception" Synchromy,
1915, o.c., 30" x 24". Whitney Mus.   #52.40
Gift of George F. Of.   PC 290

    3242. ——.
    "Oriental" Synchromy in Blue-Green,
    1918, o.c., 36" x 50". Whitney Mus.   #52.8
        PC 291

3243. McFEE, Henry L. (1886-1953).
Crow with Peaches,
1928, o.c., 30¼" x 24⅛". Whitney Mus.
#31.301   PC 293

    3244. MacIVER, Loren (1909-   ).
    Hopscotch,
    1940, o.c., 27" x 35⅞". Mus. Mod. Art.
    #1649.40   Purchase.   PC 294

3245. ——.
Venice,
1949, o.c., 59" x 93". Whitney Mus.   #49.19   PC 296

    3246. ——.
    Emmett Kelly,
    1947, oil, 40" x 32". Coll. Mr. & Mrs. Roy R.
    Neuberger, New York, N.Y.   PC 295

3247. McLAUCHLIN, Gerald (1925-   ).
The Host,
1955, oil, 45" x 99". Art. Inst. Chicago.   #56.8
    PC 1003

    3248. MANGRAVITE, Peppino (1896-   ).
    City People in the Country,
    1936, o.c., 25½" x 39½". Whitney Mus.
    #36.145   PC 298

3249. MANIGAULT, Middleton (1887-1922).
Procession,
1911, oil, 20" x 24". Ferdinand Howald Coll.,
Columbus Gall.   PC 793

    3250. MAN RAY (1890-   ).
*Admiration of the Orchestrelle for the
Cinematograph,*
1919, airbrush, 26" x 21½". Mus. Mod. Art.
#231.37   Gift of A. Conger Goodyear.   PC 380

3251. ——.
*The Rope Dancer Accompanies Herself with Her
Shadows,*
1916, o.c., 52" x 73⅜". Mus. Mod. Art.
#33.54   Gift of G. David Thompson.   PC 379

    3252. MARCA-RELLI, Corrado (1913-   ).
Sleeping Figure,
1953-54, collage of painted canvas, 52⅛" x 77⅝".
Mus. Mod. Art.   #337.55   Mr. & Mrs.
Walter Bareiss Fund.   PC 300

3253. MARGO, Boris (1901-   ).
Winter Evening,
1955, lacquer on aluminum, 29⅝" x 35⅝".
Brooklyn Mus.   #55.158   PC 302

    3254. MARIN, John (1870-1953).
From the Bridge, New York,
1933, w.c., 27" x 22". Wadsworth Atheneum.
#1948.479   PC 305A

3255. ——.
Lower Manhattan,
1922, w.c., 21⅝" x 26⅞". Mus. Mod. Art.
#143.45   Acquired through the Lillie P. Bliss
Bequest.   PC 305

    3256. ——.
Maine Islands,
1922, w.c., 16¾" x 20". Phillips Coll.   PC 795

3257. ——.
Movement, Fifth Avenue,
1912, w.c., 16¹⁵⁄₁₆" x 13¾". Art Inst. Chicago.
#49.554   PC 303

    3258. ——.
Movement—Sea and Sky,
1946, o.c., 22" x 28". Lane Foundation,
Leominster, Mass.   PC 799

3259. ——.
Pertaining to Stonington Harbor, Maine, No. 4,
1926, w.c., 15⅝" x 21¾". Met. Mus.   #49.70.134
The Alfred Stieglitz Collection, 1949.   PC 306

    3260. ——.
Pine Tree, Small Point, Maine,
1926, w.c., 17¼" x 22". Art Inst. Chicago.
#49.565   PC 307A

3261. ——.
Region of Brooklyn Bridge Fantasy,
1932, w.c., 18¾" x 22¼". Whitney Mus.   #49.8
     PC 798

    3262. ——.
Storm Over Taos,
1930, w.c., 16⅞" x 21¾". Alfred Stieglitz Coll.,
Nat'l Gall. of Art.   #B15.867   PC 797

3263. MARIN, John (1870-1953).
Sunset,
1922, w.c., 17¾" x 22¼". Coll. Edith G. Halpert,
Downtown Gallery, New York, N.Y.   PC 304

    3264. ——.
    Tunk Mountains, Autumn, Maine,
    1945, o.c., 25" x 30". Phillips Coll.   PC 307

3265. MARSH, Reginald (1898-1954).
The Bowl,
1933, egg tempera, pressed wood panel,
35⅞" x 59⅞". Brooklyn Mus.   #42.404   PC 309

    3266. ——.
    Discharge of Cargo at Pier,
    1937, fresco secco. Section of Mural, Customs
    House, New York, N.Y.   PC 1005

3267. ——.
Swimming off West Washington Market,
1940, w.c., 26¾" x 40¼". Albright Gall.   PC 311

    3268. ——.
    Tattoo and Haircut,
    1932, tempera, 46½" x 47⅞". Art Inst. Chicago.
    #47.39   PC 308

3269. MARTIN, Fletcher (1904-   ).
Cherry Twice,
1946, o.c., 72" x 40". Whitney Mus.   #55.48
Artists and Students Assistance Fund.   PC 805

    3270. ——.
    Trouble in Frisco,
    1938, o.c., 30" x 36". Mus. Mod. Art.   #10.39
    Mrs. John D. Rockefeller, Jr., Fund.   PC 313

3271. MATTSON, Henry E. (1887-   ).
Moonlit Landscape,
1934, o.c., 25" x 30". Whitney Mus.   #34.19   PC 315

    3272. ——.
    Wings of the Morning,
    1937, oil, 36" x 50". Met. Mus.   #37.79
    Arthur H. Hearn Fund, 1937.   PC 316

3273. MAURER, Alfred H. (1868-1932).
Landscape—in the Vineyard,
c. 1912, oil, 31½" x 25". Weyhe Gallery, New
York, N.Y.   PC 809

    3274. ——.
    Still Life with Doily,
    c. 1930, oil on composition panel, 17¾" x 21½".
    Phillips Coll.   PC 318

3275. ——.
Twin Heads,
c. 1930, o.c., 26⅜" x 18". Whitney Mus.   #53.28
Gift of Mr. & Mrs. Hudson D. Walker (and
exchange).   PC 319

    3276. ——.
    Self-portrait,
    c. 1927-28, oil, 39" x 23⅞". Walker Art Center.
    #46.50   PC 317

3277. MELCHERS, Gari (1860-1932).
The Fencing Master,
c. 1901, oil, 80¼" x 39½". Detroit Inst.   #13.9
PC 320

3278. MENKES, Zygmunt (1896-   ).
The Painter,
1954, o.c., 44¾" x 37". Whitney Mus.   #55.41
Gift of Mr. & Mrs. Alfred Jaretzki, Jr.   PC 812

3279. MILLER, Kenneth Hayes (1876-1952).
Box Party,
1936, oil & tempera on cardboard, 60" x 46".
Whitney Mus.   #36.147   PC 328

3280. ———.
The Fitting Room,
1931, oil, 28" x 34". Met. Mus.   #31.117
Arthur H. Hearn Fund, 1931.   PC 327

3281. MOHOLY-NAGY, Lászlo (1895-1946).
Space Modulator,
1938-40, o.c., 47" x 47". Whitney Mus.   #55.31
Gift of Mrs. Sibyl Moholy-Nagy.   PC 816

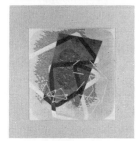

3282. ———.
Space Modulator L3,
1936, perforated zinc over painting on
composition board with glass-headed pins, 17¼"
x 19⅛". Mus. Mod. Art.   #223.47   Purchase.
PC 329

3283. MOLLER, Hans (1905-   ).
Crown of Thorns,
1958, o.c., 30" x 40". Coll. Artist, Fine Arts
Associates, New York, N.Y.   PC 1014

3284. MORGAN, Randall (1920-   ).
Port at Night,
1954, oil on composition board, 28" x 44".
Whitney Mus.   #55.19   Charles F. Williams
Fund.   PC 331

3285. MORRIS, Carl (1911-   ).
Autumn No. 3,
1954, gouache & Chinese ink, 24⅜" x 17¼". Coll.
Mrs. James H. Beal, Pittsburgh, Pa.   PC 817

3286. MORRIS, George L. K. (1905-   ).
Nautical Composition,
1937-42, o.c., 51" x 35". Whitney Mus.   #43.11
PC 332

3287. MOTHERWELL, Robert B. (1915-   ).
Elegy to the Spanish Republic XXXIV,
1953-54, oil, 80" x 100". Albright Gall. Gift of
Seymour H. Knox.   PC 1013

3288. ———.
The Voyage,
1949, oil & tempera on paper, 48" x 94". Mus.
Mod. Art.   #339.55   Gift of Mrs. John D.
Rockefeller, 3rd.

3289. MUELLER, George (1929-   ).
The Study,
1955, egg tempera, casein & enamel on
composition board, 56¾" x 48". Whitney Mus.
#55.25   Gift of Mr. & Mrs. Roy R. Neuberger.   PC 336

3290. MURCH, Walter (1907-   ).
The Bulb,
1951, oil, 21" x 17". Roby Fdn c/o Whitney Mus.
PC 337

3291. MURCH, Walter (1907-   ).
Governor II,
1952, oil on paper, 40⅜" x 17⅜". Whitney Mus.
#53.11   Wildenstein Benefit Purchase Fund.   PC 338

3292. MYERS, Jerome (1867-1940).
End of the Street,
1922, oil, 24½" x 29½". Art Inst. Chicago.
#23.974   PC 340

3293. ——.
Summer Night, East Side Park,
1919, o.c., 25" x 30". Whitney Mus.   #31.313   PC 339

3294. OKADA, Kenzo (1902-   ).
Tanabata,
1956, o.c., 43" x 37". Boston Mus.   #58.20
                                        PC 341A

3295. O'KEEFFE, Georgia (1887-   ).
Black Iris,
1926, o.c., 36" x 29⅞". Met. Mus.   #L.49.37.4
The Alfred Stieglitz Collection.   PC 344

3296. ——.
Blue and Green Music,
1919, oil, 23" x 19". Lent by the artist. Art Inst.
Chicago.   PC 343

3297. ——.
Cow's Skull, Red, White and Blue,
1931, oil, 39⅞" x 35⅞". Met. Mus.   #52.203
The Alfred Stieglitz Collection, 1949.   PC 345

3298. ——.
The White Place in Shadow,
1940, oil, 30" x 24". Phillips Coll.   PC 346

3299. OSVER, Arthur (1912-   ).
Two Ventilators,
1947, oil, 39¾" x 27⅞". Met. Mus.   #50.35
Arthur H. Hearn Fund, 1950.   PC 347

3300. PALMER, William (1906-   ).
Dust, Drought and Destruction,
1934, egg tempera on composition board,
24" x 30". Whitney Mus.   #34.22   PC 349

3301. ——.
The Last Snow,
1956, oil, 40" x 44". Roby Fdn c/o Whitney Mus.
                                        PC 350A

3302. PARKER, Robert Andrew (1927-   ).
Marseilles, Night,
1955, w.c. & ink, 28½" x 17¼". Whitney Mus.
#56.40   Gift of the New York Foundation.
                                        PC 1006

3303. PASCIN, Jules (1885-1930).
Reclining Model,
n.d., o.c., 28¾" x 36¼". Mus. Mod. Art.
#564.41   Gift of A. Conger Goodyear.   PC 352

3304. PEIRCE, Waldo (1884-   ).
Haircut by the Sea,
1933, oil, 51" x 35". Met. Mus.   #37.152
George A. Hearn Fund, 1937.   PC 841

3305. PEREIRA, I. Rice (1907-   ).
Evaporating Night,
1951, oil, 36" x 30". Dallas Mus. Fine Arts.
1953.18   PC 355

    3306. ——.
    Landscape of the Absolute,
    1955, o.c., 40" x 50". Whitney Mus.   # 56.15
    Gift of Richard Adler.   PC 356

3307. ——.
Undulating Arrangement,
n.d., glass, plastic & oil, 23⅜" x 17¼".
Wadsworth Atheneum.   # 1948.6   PC 353A

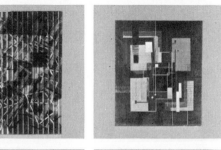

    3308. ——.
    White Lines,
    1942, oil on vellum, 25⅞" x 21⅞". Mus. Mod. Art.
    # 341.42   Gift of Edgar Kaufmann, Jr.   PC 353

3309. PERLIN, Bernard (1918-   ).
The Farewell,
1952, casein tempera, 34¼" x 47⅛". Roby Fdn
c/o Whitney Mus.   PC 357

    3310. ——.
    The Lovers,
    1946, gouache, 30" x 37¾". Mus. Mod. Art.
    # 269.48   Purchase.   PC 840

3311. PETERDI, Gabor (1915-   ).
The Misty Ocean,
1954, o.c., 49¾" x 82⅛". Brooklyn Mus.
55.212   PC 359

    3312. PICKENS, Alton (1917-   ).
    The Blue Doll,
    1942, o.c., 42⅞" x 35". Mus. Mod. Art.
    # 622.43   James Thrall Soby Fund.   PC 360

3313. PICKETT, Joseph (1848-1918).
Coryell's Ferry, 1776,
prob. 1914-18, o.c., 37½" x 48¼". Whitney Mus.
31.316   PC 362

    3314. ——.
    Manchester Valley,
    1914-18(?), oil with sand on canvas, 45" x 60".
    Mus. Mod. Art.   # 541.39   Gift of Mrs. John
    D. Rockefeller, Jr.   PC 847

3315. ——.
Washington under the Council Tree, Coryell's
Ferry, New Hope, Pa.,
n.d., oil, 35" x 37½". Newark Mus.
U.S.31,152A   PC 363

    3316. PIPPIN, Horace (1888-1946).
    The Buffalo Hunt,
    1933, o.c., 21¼" x 31". Whitney Mus.   # 41.27
                                       PC 848

3317. PLEISSNER, Ogden Minton (1905-   ).
Along the Arno,
1945, w.c., 22¼" x 30¼". Met. Mus.   # 46.75.1
George A. Hearn Fund, 1946   PC 364

    3318. POLLOCK, Jackson (1912-56).
    Autumn Rhythm,
    1950, o.c., 105" x 207". Met. Mus.   # 57.92
    George A. Hearn Fund, 1957.   PC 367A

3319. POLLOCK, Jackson (1912-1956).
Convergence,
1952, oil, 94" x 156". Albright Gall. Gift of
Seymour H. Knox.   PC 1011

> 3320. ———.
> *Number 1, 1948,*
> 1948, o.c., 68" x 104". Mus. Mod. Art.   #77.50
> Purchase.   PC 366

3321. POOR, Henry Varnum (1888-   ).
The Pink Tablecloth,
1933, oil, 35⅞" x 45¹³⁄₁₆". Cleveland Mus.
#2197.35   PC 369

> 3322. POUSETTE-DART, Richard (1916-   ).
> *The Magnificent,*
> 1950-51, o.c., 86¼" x 44". Whitney Mus.
> #53.43   Gift of Mrs. Ethel K. Schwabacher.
>   PC 323

3323. PRENDERGAST, Maurice (1859-1924).
April Snow, Salem,
1906-07, w.c., 14¾" x 21⅝". Mus. Mod. Art.
#129.35   Gift of Mrs. John D. Rockefeller, Jr.
                                          PC 371A

> 3324. ———.
> *Autumn Festival,*
> 1917-18, oil, 24" x 28". Phillips Coll.   PC 371

3325. ———.
Central Park,
1901, w.c., 14⅛" x 21¾". Whitney Mus.
#32.41   PC 326

> 3326. ———.
> *Ponte della Paglia,*
> 1899, o.c., 28" x 23". Phillips Coll.   PC 325

3327. ———.
Sunset and Sea Fog,
1915, oil, 18" x 29". Butler Art Inst.   PC 370

> 3328. PRESTOPINO, Gregorio (1907-   ).
> *Glitter, No. 3,*
> 1951, w.c., pastel, crayon & ink, 29⅞" x 26".
> Whitney Mus.   #52.21   PC 373

3329. ———.
Winter,
1945, o.c., 20¼" x 30¼". Whitney Mus.   #46.3 PC 372

> 3330. PRICE, Clayton S. (1874-   ).
> *Fisherman,*
> c. 1941, oil, 34" x 42". Detroit Inst.   #43.432
>   PC 374

3331. QUIRT, Walter (1902-   ).
Mutation,
1940, o.c., 30" x 40". Whitney Mus.   #42.34   PC 375

> 3332. RATTNER, Abraham (1898-   ).
> *April Showers,*
> 1939, oil, 32" x 39½". Coll. Mr. & Mrs. Roy R.
> Neuberger, New York, N.Y.   PC 376

3333. RATTNER, Abraham (1898-   ).
The Emperor,
1944, o.c., 28¾" x 23¾". Whitney Mus.   #45.6

PC 377

    3334. ——.
    Figure and Mask,
    c. 1948, oil, 36¼" x 28¾". U. of Ill.   #67122

PC 378

3335. REFREGIER, Anton (1905-   ).
Shipbuilding in the 18th Century,
1951, mural, o.c., 4' x 4'8". Dining room,
S.S. Constitution, American Export Lines, New
York, N.Y.

PC 381

    3336. ——.
    The Staircase,
    1949, tempera on canvas, 45" x 28¼". Whitney
    Mus.   #49.20

PC 382

3337. REINHARDT, Ad (1913-   ).
No. 18, 1948-49,
1949, o.c., 40" x 60". Whitney Mus.   #53.13   PC 383

    3338. ——.
    No. 24, 1954,
    1954, oil, 20" x 50". Betty Parsons Gallery,
    New York, N.Y.

PC 875

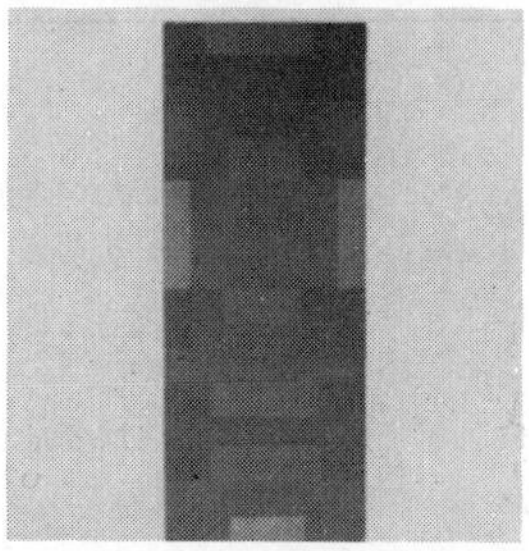

3339. REYNAL, Jeanne (1903-   ).
Ogo,
1952-53, mosaic, 52" x 60". Whitney Mus.
#54.45

PC 385

    3340. RIVERS, Larry (1923-   ).
    Double Portrait of Birdie,
    1955, o.c., 70¾" x 82½". Whitney Mus.   #56.9
    Anonymous gift.

PC 386

3341. ROBINSON, Boardman (1876-1952).
Richard Bone,
c. 1942, tempera, 13¾" x 10¾". Art Inst.
Chicago.   #43.756

PC 879

    3342. ROSE, Herman (1909-   ).
    Manhattan Tops,
    1946, oil, 16" x 17⅞". Coll. Joseph H. Hirshhorn,
    New York, N.Y.

PC 387

3343. ROTHKO, Mark (1903-   ).
No. 10, 1950,
1950, o.c., 90⅜" x 57⅛". Mus. Mod. Art.
#38.52   Gift of Philip C. Johnson.

PC 389

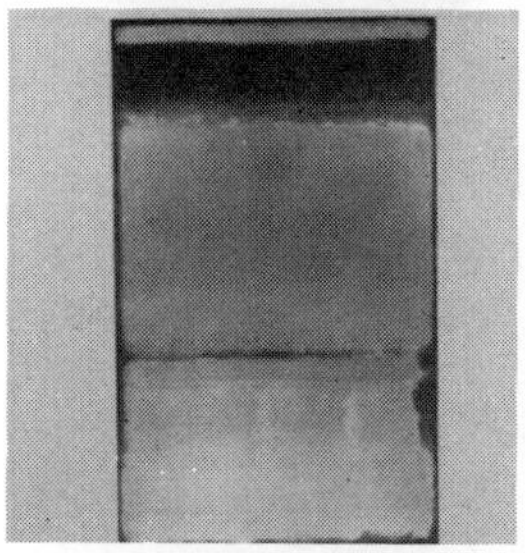

    3344. ——.
    Painting,
    1953-54, oil, 104½" x 117½". Art Inst. Chicago.
    #54.1308

PC 390

3345. ——.
Vessels of Magic,
c. 1947, w.c., 38¾" x 25¾". Brooklyn Mus.
#47.106

PC 388

    3346. RUSSELL, Morgan (1886-1953).
    Synchromy No. 3, Color Counterpoint,
    1913, o.c., mounted on cardboard, 10¼" x 11⅞".
    Mus. Mod. Art.   #149.51   Anonymous gift.

PC 391

3347. SAGE, Kay (1898-   ).
No Passing,
1954, o.c., 51¼" x 38". Whitney Mus.   #55.10   PC 395

    3348. ——.
    The Unicorns Came Down to the Sea,
    1948, oil, 36" x 28". Viviano Gallery, New York,
    N.Y.   PC 394

3349. SALEMME, Attilio (1911-55).
Caught in the Equinox,
1953, oil, 52" x 80". Met. Mus.   #53.184
Arthur H. Hearn Fund, 1953.   PC 398

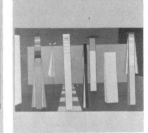

    3350. ——.
    Inquisition,
    1952, o.c., 40" x 63". Whitney Mus.   #53.26
    PC 397

3351. SAMPLE, Paul Starrett (1896-   ).
Janitor's Holiday,
1936, oil, 26" x 40". Met. Mus.   #37.60.1
Arthur H. Hearn Fund, 1937.   PC 890

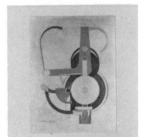

    3352. SCHAMBERG, Morton L. (1882-1918).
    Machine,
    1916, oil, 30⅛" x 22¾". Société Anonyme Coll.,
    Yale U. Gall.   #1941.673   PC 399

3353. ——.
Telephone,
1916, oil, 24" x 20". Ferdinand Howald Coll.,
Columbus Gall. Fine Arts.   PC 400

    3354. SCHMIDT, Katherine (1898-   ).
    Broe and McDonald Listen In,
    1937, o.c., 30" x 24". Whitney Mus.   #50.15
    PC 401

3355. SCHUCKER, Charles (1914-   ).
The Bridge,
1954, o.c., 26" x 83½". Whitney Mus.   #55.11   PC 402

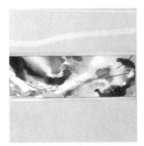

    3356. SELIGMANN, Kurt (1900-   ).
    The Balcony, I,
    1949-50, o.c., 33" x 48". Whitney Mus.   #53.52
    PC 403

3357. ——.
Fallen Angels,
1955, oil, 64" x 85". Coll. Artist, New York,
N.Y.   PC 406

    3358. SEPESHY, Zoltan (1898-   ).
    On Deck,
    1952, tempera, 33" x 45". Midtown Galleries,
    New York, N.Y.   PC 902

3359. SHAHN, Ben (1898-   ).
The Blind Botanist,
1955, oil, 52" x 31". Roland P. Murdock Coll.,
Wichita Art Mus.   #M-137   PC 409A

    3360. ——.
    Everyman,
    1954, tempera on composition board. 72" x 24".
    Whitney Mus.   #56.5   PC 412A

3361. SHAHN, Ben (1898-   ).
The Passion of Sacco and Vanzetti,
1931-32, tempera on canvas, 84½" x 48".
Whitney Mus.   #49.22   Gift of Edith & Milton
Lowenthal in memory of Juliana Force.   PC 409

 3362. ——.
 Reconstruction,
 1945, tempera on composition board, 26" x 39".
 Whitney Mus.   #46.4   PC 905

3363. ——.
The Red Stairway,
1944, tempera, 18" x 24". City Art Mus., St. Louis.
#25.45   PC 904

 3364. ——.
 Vacant Lot,
 1939, tempera, 19" x 23". Wadsworth Atheneum.
 #1941.390   PC 410

3365. ——.
Welders,
1943, tempera on cardboard, 22" x 39¾". Mus.
Mod. Art.   #264.44   Purchase.   PC 411

 3366. SHARRER, Honoré D. (1920-   ).
 Workers and Paintings,
 1943, oil on composition board, 11⅝" x 37". Mus.
 Mod. Art.   #17.44   Gift of Lincoln Kirstein.
 PC 908

3367. SHEELER, Charles (1883-   ).
Architectural Cadences,
1954, o.c., 25" x 35". Whitney Mus.   #54.35   PC 418

 3368. ——.
 City Interior,
 1936, oil on fiberboard, 22⅛" x 27". Worcester
 Art Mus.   #1937.3   PC 417

3369. ——.
Classic Landscape,
1931, oil, 25" x 32¼". Coll. Mrs. Edsel B. Ford,
Dearborn, Mich.   PC 416

 3370. ——.
 Pertaining to Yachts and Yachting,
 c. 1922, crayon, 19" x 24¼". Whitney Mus.
 #48.4   PC 414A

3371. ——.
Upper Deck,
1929, oil, 29" x 21¾". Fogg Mus.   #1933.97   PC 415

 3372. SHEETS, Millard (1907-   ).
 Black Horse,
 1934, w.c., 14½" x 22". Whitney Mus.   #36.24
 PC 915

3373. SHINN, Everett (1876-1953).
Early Morning, Paris,
1901, pastel, 21" x 29⅛". Art Inst. Chicago.
#39.181   PC 419

 3374. ——.
 London Hippodrome,
 1902, oil, 26⅜" x 34¼". Art Inst. Chicago.
 #28.197   PC 420

3375. SIPORIN, Mitchell (1910-   ).
Dancers by the Clock,
1949, o.c., 40½" x 60⅛". Whitney Mus.
50.22   PC 422

    3376. ——.
    The Refugees,
    1939, oil on composition board, 30" x 36". Mus.
    Mod. Art.   # 573.39   Purchase.   PC 421

3377. SLOAN, John (1871-1951).
Backyards, Greenwich Village,
1914, o.c., 26" x 32". Whitney Mus.   # 36.153   PC 423

    3378. ——.
    The Picnic Grounds,
    1906-07, o.c., 24" x 36". Whitney Mus.   # 41.34
    PC 424

3379. ——.
Sixth Avenue Elevated at Third Street,
1928, o.c., 30" x 40". Whitney Mus.   # 36.154   PC 427

    3380. ——.
    South Beach Bathers,
    1908, oil, 25⅞" x 31⅞". Walker Art Center.
    # 48.27   PC 425

3381. ——.
Three A.M.,
1909, oil, 32" x 26". Phila. Mus.   PC 426

    3382. ——.
    The Wake of the Ferry,
    1907, o.c., 26" x 32". Phillips Coll.   PC 920

3383. ——.
Yeats at Petitpas,
1910, oil, 26⅜" x 32¼". Corcoran Gall.
32.9   PC 922

    3384. SOYER, Isaac (1907-   ).
    Employment Agency,
    1937, o.c., 34¼" x 45". Whitney Mus.   # 37.44
    PC 428

3385. SOYER, Moses (1899-   ).
Girl in Orange Sweater,
1953, o.c., 30" x 24". Whitney Mus.   # 54.5   PC 429

    3386. SOYER, Raphael (1899-   ).
    The Brown Sweater,
    1952, o.c., 50" x 34". Whitney Mus.   # 53.53
    PC 432

3387. ——.
Office Girls,
1936, o.c., 26" x 24". Whitney Mus.   # 36.149   PC 430

    3388. ——.
    Waiting Room,
    n.d., oil, 34¼" x 45¼". Corcoran Gall.   # 43.4
    PC 431

3389. SPEICHER, Eugene (1883-   ).
The Mountaineer,
1929, oil, 54" x 42". Coll. Stephen C. Clark, New
York, N.Y.   PC 435

    3390. ——.
    Katherine Cornell as Candida,
    1925-26, oil, 84" x 44½". Albright Gall.
    #299.38   PC 434

3391. SPENCER, Niles (1893-1952).
City Walls,
1921, o.c., 39⅜" x 28¾". Mus. Mod. Art.
#25.36   Anonymous gift.   PC 436

    3392. ——.
    The Green Table,
    1930, o.c., 50" x 40". Whitney Mus.   #31.361
                                                     PC 437

3393. ——.
In Fairmont,
1951, o.c., 65½" x 41½". Mus. Mod. Art.   #6.56
Edward Joseph Gallagher, III, Memorial Coll.   PC 439

    3394. SPRUCE, Everett (1907-   ).
    The Hawk,
    1939, oil, 19⅜" x 23½". Mus. Mod. Art.
    #574.39   Purchase.   PC 440

3395. STAMOS, Theodoros (1922-   ).
Greek Orison,
1952, o.c., 67" x 27". Whitney Mus.   #53.15   PC 444

    3396. ——.
    Sounds in the Rock,
    1946, oil on composition board, 48⅛" x 28⅜".
    Mus. Mod. Art.   #27.47   Gift of Edward Root.
                                                     PC 442

3397. STELLA, Joseph (1877-1946).
Battle of Light, Coney Island,
1913, oil, 75¾" x 84". Société Anonyme Coll.,
Yale U. Gall.   #1941.689   PC 445

    3398. ——.
    The Bridge,
    1922, oil, 88¼" x 54". (One of a series of five
    panels entitled "New York Interpreted.") Newark
    Mus.   PC 940

3399. ——.
Brooklyn Bridge,
1917-18, oil, 84" x 76". Société Anonyme Coll.,
Yale U. Gall.   #1941.690   PC 447

    3400. ——.
    Spring,
    1914, oil, 75" x 40⅛". Société Anonyme Coll.,
    Yale U. Gall.   #1941.692   PC 446

3401. STERNE, Maurice (1878-1957).
Bali Bazaar,
1913-14, o.c., 36½" x 39". Whitney Mus.   #54.13
                                                     PC 448

    3402. ——.
    Breadmakers,
    1923, oil on panel, 48" x 32¼". Boston Mus.
    #44.581   PC 449

3403. STETTHEIMER, Florine (1871-1944).
Family Portrait, No. 2,
1933, o.c., 46¼" x 64⅝". Mus. Mod. Art.   #8.56
Gift of Miss Ettie Stettheimer.   PC 452

3404. STILL, Clyfford (1904-   ).
Painting,
1951, o.c., 7'10" x 6'10". Mus. Mod. Art.
#277.54   Blanchette Rockefeller Fund.   PC 453

3405. STUEMPFIG, Walter (1914-   ).
Thunderstorm II,
1948, oil, 36" x 48". Met. Mus.   #49.164
George A. Hearn Fund, 1949.   PC 456

3406. TAM, Ruben (1916-   ).
Moon and Shoals,
1949, o.c., 30" x 34⅞". Mus. Mod. Art.
#289.49   Gift of Sam A. Lewisohn.   PC 457

3407. TANGUY, Yves (1900-55).
Fear,
1949, o.c., 60⅛" x 40". Whitney Mus.   #49.21   PC 460

3408. ——.
Indefinite Divisibility,
1942, oil, 40" x 35". Albright Gall. Room of
Contemporary Art.   PC 458

3409. ——.
Multiplication of the Arcs,
1954, o.c., 40" x 60". Mus. Mod. Art.   #559.54
Mrs. Simon Guggenheim Fund.   PC 461

3410. ——.
The Rapidity of Sleep,
1945, oil, 50" x 40". Art Inst. Chicago.   #46.46
                                                       PC 459

3411. TARBELL, Edmund C. (1862-1938).
Girl Crocheting,
n.d., oil, 29¾" x 25". Canajoharie Lib. Art Gall.,
N.Y.   PC 462

3412. THOMAS, Howard (-1959).
Fernandina,
1954, gouache, 14½" x 20¾". Coll. Estate of
Howard Thomas, Athens, Ga.   PC 462A

3413. THON, William (1906-   ).
Midnight Quarry,
1952, w.c., 26½"x 40". Whitney Mus.   #53.16
Wildenstein Benefit Purchase Fund.   PC 464

3414. ——.
Seabirds,
1953, oil, 28⅜" x 44". Met. Mus.   #54.98
Gift of Mr. & Mrs. Morris W. Haft, 1954. PC 463

3415. TOBEY, Mark (1890-   ).
Broadway,
1936, tempera, 26" x 19¼". Met. Mus.   #42.170
Arthur H. Hearn Fund, 1942.   PC 465

3416. ——.
Fountains of Europe,
1955, tempera, 17½" x 22". Boston Mus.
#56.312   PC 466

3417. TOBEY, Mark (1890-   ).
Universal Field,
1949, tempera & pastel on cardboard, 28" x 44".
Whitney Mus.   #50.24   PC 467

       3418. TOMLIN, Bradley Walker (1899-1953).
Number 13, 1952-53,
1953, o.c., 46" x 35". Betty Parsons Gallery,
New York, N.Y.   PC 472

3419. ——.
No. 20,
1949, o.c., 7'2" x 6'8¼". Mus. Mod. Art.   #58.52
Gift of Philip C. Johnson.   PC 473

       3420. ——.
Still Life,
1939, o.c., 34" x 46". Whitney Mus.   #42.10
                                          PC 470

3421. TOOKER, George (1920-   ).
Government Bureau,
1956, tempera, 19⅝" x 29⅝". Met. Mus.   #56.78
George H. Hearn Fund, 1956.   PC 475

       3422. ——.
The Subway,
1950, egg tempera on composition board, 18⅛" x
36⅛". Whitney Mus.   #50.23   Juliana Force
Purchase.   PC 964

3423. TUCKER, Allen (1866-1939).
Washington Crossing the Delaware,
1931, o.c., 20" x 36". Whitney Mus.   #33.35   PC 476

       3424. TWORKOV, Jack (1900-   ).
The Wheel,
1953, o.c., 54" x 50". Mus. Mod. Art.   #31.54
Gift of the Gramercy Park Foundation, Inc.
                                          PC 477

3425. VICKREY, Robert (1926-   ).
Fear,
1954, egg tempera, 34¾" x 58½". Roby Fdn
c/o Whitney Mus.   PC 479

       3426. VYTLACIL, Vaclav (1892-   ).
Wood Interior,
1949, oil on composition panel, 32" x 40".
Phillips Coll.   PC 480

3427. WALKOWITZ, Abraham (1880-   ).
New York,
1917, w.c., ink & pencil, 30⅝" x 21¾". Whitney
Mus.   #51.35   Gift of the artist in memory
of Juliana Force.   PC 481

       3428. WATKINS, Franklin C. (1894-   ).
The Fire Eater,
1933-34, oil, 60¾" x 39". Phila. Mus.   PC 482

3429. ——.
Soliloquy,
1932, o.c., 25¼" x 30¼". Whitney Mus.   #34.26
                                          PC 484A

       3430. ——.
Justice Owen J. Roberts,
1947, oil, 50" x 40". Law School, U. of Pa.
                                          PC 483

3431. WEBER, Max (1881-).
Adoration of the Moon,
1944, o.c., 48" x 32". Whitney Mus.   #46.5   PC 489

    3432. ——.
    Chinese Restaurant,
    1915, o.c., 40" x 48". Whitney Mus.   #31.382
                                    PC 486

3433. ——.
The Geranium,
1911, o.c., 39⅞" x 32¼". Mus. Mod. Art.
#18.44   Acquired through the Lillie P. Bliss
Bequest.   PC 485

    3434. ——.
    Hasidic Dance,
    1940, oil, 32" x 40". Coll. Mr. & Mrs. Milton
    Lowenthal, New York, N.Y.   PC 488

3435. ——.
Rush Hour, New York,
1915, oil, 36¼" x 30¼". Coll. Artist, Great Neck,
L.I., N.Y.   PC 976

    3436. ——.
    Three Literary Gentlemen,
    1945, o.c., 29" x 36". Lane Foundation,
    Leominster, Mass.   PC 980

3437. ——.
Tranquility,
1929, oil, 32" x 40⅛". Coll. Artist, Great Neck,
L.I., N.Y.   PC 487

    3438. ——.
    Winter Twilight,
    1938, oil, 29" x 39". Santa Barbara Mus. Art.
    #Pt-1059-BH-43   Buell Hammett Memorial
    Gift.   PC 978

3439. WENTZ, Harry (1876-).
Rocks in the Sea,
1929, w.c., 14½" x 11". Portland Art Mus.
#29.3   PC 1009

    3440. WILDE, John (1919-).
    The Apotheosis of Marie-Henri Beyle,
    1953, oil, 33½" x 17½". Robert Isaacson Gallery,
    New York, N.Y.   PC 490

3441. WILLIAMS, Walter (1920-).
Poultry Market,
1953, o.c., 46" x 38". Whitney Mus.   #55.29   PC 982

    3442. WOELLFER, Emerson (1914-).
    Birds and Orange Sky,
    1956, o.c., 6' x 4'. Paul Kantor Gallery, Beverly
    Hills, Calif.   PC 1010

3443. WOOD, Grant (1892-1942).
American Gothic,
1930, oil, 29⅞" x 24⅞". Art Inst. Chicago.
#30.934   PC 491

    3444. ——.
    Midnight Ride of Paul Revere,
    1931, oil, 30" x 40". Met. Mus.   #50.117
    George A. Hearn Fund, 1950.   PC 986

3445. WYETH, Andrew (1917-   ).
Christina's World,
1948, tempera on gesso panel, 32¼" x 47¾". Mus.
Mod. Art.   #16.49   Purchase.   PC 496

      3446. ——.
      Soaring,
      1950, tempera on panel, 48" x 87". Anon. loan,
      Boston Mus.   #1.51   PC 990

3447. ——.
Karl,
1948, tempera, 30⅝" x 23⅝". Coll. Mrs. John D.
Rockefeller, III, New York, N.Y.   PC 495

      3448. ZERBE, Karl (1903-   ).
      Harlem,
      1952, polymer tempera on canvas over
      composition board, 44½" x 24". Mus. Mod. Art.
      #483.53   Gift of Mr. & Mrs. Roy R. Neuberger.
                                   PC 499

3449. ——.
Harlequin,
1944, encaustic on canvas, 44" x 34". Whitney
Mus.   #45.8   PC 498

3451. ANON.
Carriage with Young Couples,
c. 1885, tintype. Coll. B. & N. Newhall, Rochester,
N.Y.   F 5

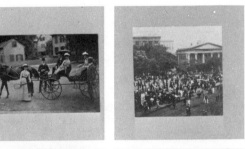

    3452. ANON.
    Crowds Breaking up after Parade in New York,
    July 4, 1860,
    1860, stereograph. Coll. G. L. Howe, M.D.,
    Rochester, N.Y.   F 3

3453. ANON.
Asher B. Durand, American Painter,
c. 1850, daguerreotype. N.Y. Hist. Soc.
36759 A   F 1

    3454. ANON.
    New York: Looking up Broadway from Broome St.,
    c. 1860, stereograph. Coll. Eastman House,
    Rochester, N.Y.   F 4

3455. ANON.
A Windy Day,
c. 1888, snapshot taken with Model I, Kodak.
Coll. Eastman House, Rochester, N.Y.   F 6

    3456. ANON.
    Woman and Child,
    c. 1850, daguerreotype. SPNEA, Boston, Mass.
                                                 F 2

3457. ADAMS, Ansel.
Aspens, Dawn, Colorado,
1938. Coll. B. & N. Newhall, Rochester, N.Y.   F 9

    3458. ——.
    Courthouse, Bridgeport, California,
    1938. Coll. B. & N. Newhall, Rochester, N.Y.
                                                 F 10

3459. ——.
Grass and Burned Tree,
1934. Coll. B. & N. Newhall, Rochester, N.Y.   F 7

    3460. ——.
    Mono Lake, California,
    1947. Coll. B. & N. Newhall, Rochester, N.Y.
                                                 F 14

3461. ——.
Moonrise, Hernandez, N.M.,
1941. Coll. B. & N. Newhall, Rochester, N.Y.   F 11

    3462. ——.
    Mt. Williamson, from Manzanar,
    1943. Coll. B. & N. Newhall, Rochester, N.Y.
                                                 F 13

3463. ADAMS, Ansel.
Refugio Beach, California,
1936. Coll. B. & N. Newhall, Rochester, N.Y.   F 8

     3464. ——.
     Sierra Nevada from Lone Pine, Calif.,
     1943. Coll. B. & N. Newhall, Rochester, N.Y.
                                             F 12

3465. BEMIS, Samuel A.
King's Chapel, Boston,
1840, daguerreotype. Coll. Eastman House,
Rochester, N.Y.   F 15

     3466. BOURKE-WHITE, Margaret.
     Construction of Fort Peck Dam,
     1936. Coll. Eastman House, Rochester, N.Y.
                                             F 16

3467. ——.
Contour plowing; Walsh, Colo.,
1954. Coll. Eastman House, Rochester, N.Y.   F 18

     3468. ——.
     Mahatma Gandhi,
     1946. Coll. Eastman House, Rochester, N.Y.
                                             F 17

3469. BRADY, Mathew B. (c. 1823-1896).
The Ruins of Richmond, Va.,
1865, 6" x 8¼". Mus. Mod. Art.   # 373.38   F 21

     3470. ——.
     Portrait of Robert E. Lee,
     1869. Coll. John W. Childress, Washington, D.C.
                                           F 22A

3471. ——.
Abraham Lincoln,
c. 1863, carte de visite. Coll. Eastman House,
Rochester, N.Y.   F 20

     3472. ——.
     Portrait of a Woman,
     c. 1860, ambrotype. Coll. Eastman House,
     Rochester, N.Y.   F 19

3473. BRUGUIERE, Francis.
Light Abstraction,
1920's. Coll. Eastman House, Rochester, N.Y.   F 23

     3474. EAKINS, Thomas (1844-1916).
     Pole Vaulter,
     1884-85, multiple exposure on glass plate. Met.
     Mus.   # MM 28626   Gift of Charles Bregler,
     1941.   F 24

3475. EVANS, Walker.
Connecticut Frame House,
1933, 4½" x 5¾". Mus. Mod. Art.   # 38.2411   F 27

     3476. ——.
     Country Store and Gas Station, Alabama,
     1936. Coll. B. & N. Newhall, Rochester, N.Y.
                                             F 29

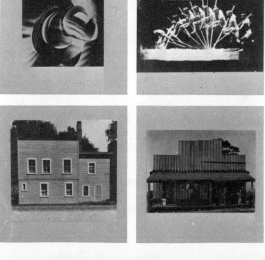

3477. EVANS, Walker.
Maine Pump,
1933, 5½" x 7¾". Mus. Mod. Art.   #41.33   F 26

3478. FITZ, Henry, Jr.
Self-portrait,
1839-40, daguerreotype. Smithsonian Institution.
#4114   F 30

3479. GARDNER, Alexander.
Home of a Rebel Sharpshooter, Gettysburg,
1863. Coll. Eastman House, Rochester, N.Y. (Plate
41 of "Gardner's Sketch Book.")   F 33

3480. ——.
Scouts and Guides of the Army of the Potomac,
1862. Coll. Eastman House, Rochester, N.Y.
(Plate 28 of "Gardner's Sketch Book.")   F 32

3481. HILLERS, John K.
John Wesley Powell and Tau-Gu,
c. 1872, stereograph. Coll. Eastman House,
Rochester, N.Y.   F 34

3482. HINE, Lewis W.
Carolina Cotton Mill,
1908. Coll. Eastman House, Rochester, N.Y.
                                                F 36

3483. ——.
Italian Family, Ellis Island,
1905. Coll. Eastman House, Rochester, N.Y.   F 35

3484. JACKSON, William Henry.
*Yellowstone National Park: Mammoth Hot
Springs on Gardiner's River,*
1871. Coll. Eastman House, Rochester, N.Y.
                                                F 37

3485. KASEBIER, Gertrude.
"Blessed Art Thou Among Women,"
c. 1900, photogravure. Coll. B. & N. Newhall,
Rochester, N.Y. (From "Camera Notes.")   F 38

3486. LANGE, Dorothea.
Bread-Line,
1933. Coll. Eastman House, Rochester, N.Y.
                                                F 39

3487. ——.
Hoe Culture, Alabama,
1937. Coll. Eastman House, Rochester, N.Y.   F 41

3488. ——.
In a Camp of Migratory Pea Pickers,
1936. Coll. Eastman House, Rochester, N.Y.
                                                F 40

3489. LANGENHEIM, W. & F.
Philadelphia Exchange,
c. 1849, calotype. Coll. Eastman House,
Rochester, N.Y.   F 42

3490. MAN RAY.
Rayograph,
1923. Mus. Mod. Art.   #625.41   F 51

3491. MAN RAY.
Solarization,
1929. Coll. Eastman House, Rochester, N.Y.   F 52

    3492. ——.
    Portrait of Pablo Picasso,
    1933. Coll. Eastman House, Rochester, N.Y.
                                     F 53

3493. MORGAN, Barbara.
Martha Graham in "Letter to the World,"
1941. Coll. B. & N. Newhall, Rochester, N.Y.   F 43

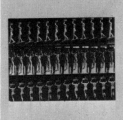
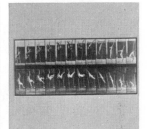

    3494. MUYBRIDGE, Eadweard.
    Galloping Horse (Sallie Gardner running),
    1878. Coll. Eastman House, Rochester, N.Y.
                                     F 44

3495. ——.
Nude Woman, Basket on Head,
1885, albumen print. Coll. Eastman House,
Rochester, N.Y.   F 45

    3496. ——.
    Dr. Shell Pole Vaulting,
    1885, sequence photos. Coll. Eastman House,
    Rochester, N.Y.   F 46

3497. O'SULLIVAN, T. H.
Canyon de Chelly, Arizona,
1873. Coll. B. & N. Newhall, Rochester, N.Y.   F 49

    3498. ——.
    Gen. U. S. Grant and Staff Officers; Massapomax
    Church, Va.,
    1864, stereograph. Coll. B. & N. Newhall,
    Rochester, N.Y.   F 48

3499. ——.
A Harvest of Death, Gettysburg, Pa.,
1863. Coll. Eastman House, Rochester, N.Y.
(Plate 36 of "Gardner's Sketch Book.")   F 47

    3500. PREVOST, Victor.
    Gori's Marble-working Establishment,
    (Broadway at 20th St.), 1853, calotype, N.Y. Hist.
    Soc.   F 50

3501. RIIS, Jacob A.
Bandits' Roost,
1888, New York (59½ Mulberry St.), N.Y. Jacob
A. Riis Coll., Mus. City N.Y.   Neg. #101   F 55

    3502. ——.
    Home of an Italian Ragpicker,
    1888-89, New York (Jersey St.), N.Y. Jacob
    A. Riis Coll., Mus. City N.Y.   Neg. #157   F 54

3503. ROTHSTEIN, Arthur.
Father and Son Walking in Face of Dust Storm,
1936. Coll. Eastman House, Rochester, N.Y.   F 56

    3504. SARONY, Napoleon.
    Joe Jefferson as "Rip Van Winkle,"
    1869. Coll. Eastman House, Rochester, N.Y.
                                       F 57

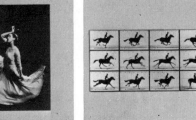

3505. SAVAGE (?).
Meeting of the Rails, Promontory, Utah,
1869. Coll. Union Pacific R.R., Omaha, Neb.   F 58

3506. SAXTON, Joseph.
*Old Arsenal and Cupola of the Old Philadelphia
High School,*
1839, daguerreotype, 1¾" x 2¼". Hist. Soc. Pa.
F 59

3507. SHEELER, Charles.
Ford Plant,
1927. Coll. Photographer, Irvington-on-Hudson,
N.Y.   F 62

3508. ——.
Stair Well,
1914. Coll. Photographer, Irvington-on-Hudson,
N.Y.   F 60

3509. ——.
White Barn,
1916. Coll. Eastman House, Rochester, N.Y.   F 61

3510. SMITH, W. Eugene.
Spinner,
1952. Coll. Photographer, Croton-on-Hudson,
N.Y.   F 64

3511. SOUTHWORTH, Albert Sands, and HAWES,
Josiah Johnson.
Classroom,
c. 1850, daguerreotype. Met. Mus.   # MM 8974
37.14.22   Gift of I. N. Phelps Stokes, Edward S.
Hawes, Alice Mary Hawes and Marion Augusta
Hawes, 1937.   F 68

3512. ——.
Cunard Liner "Niagara" in Dry Dock, Boston,
c. 1850, daguerreotype. Coll. Richard Parker,
Marblehead, Mass.   F 67

3513. ——.
*Operating Room of the Massachusetts General Hospital,
Boston,*
c. 1850. Coll. Holman Print Shop, Boston, Mass.   F 66

3514. ——.
John Quincy Adams,
daguerreotype. Met. Mus.   # MM 8980
37.14.34   Gift of I. N. Phelps Stokes, Edward
S. Hawes, Alice Mary Hawes and Marion Augusta
Hawes, 1937.   F 65

3515. ——.
Lemuel Shaw, Chief Justice,
daguerreotype. Met. Mus.   # MM 8978   38.34
Gift of Edward S. Hawes, Alice M. Hawes and
Marion A. Hawes, 1938.   F 69

3516. STEICHEN, Edward.
Portrait of Henri Matisse,
c. 1913, photogravure, Coll. Eastman House,
Rochester, N.Y. (From "Camera Work.")   F 72

3517. ——.
J. Pierpont Morgan,
1903, photogravure. Coll. B. & N. Newhall,
Rochester, N.Y. (From "Camera Work.")   F 71

3518. ——.
Rodin—The Thinker,
1902, photogravure. Coll. B. & N. Newhall,
Rochester, N.Y. (From "Camera Work.")   F 70

3519. STIEGLITZ, Alfred.
Equivalent No. 149-A,
1931. Coll. Eastman House, Rochester, N.Y.   F 80

3520. ——.
Hands of Georgia O'Keeffe,
1918. Coll. Eastman House, Rochester, N.Y.
                                                    F 78

3521. ——.
New York: R.C.A. Building,
1935(?). Coll. Eastman House, Rochester, N.Y.   F 81

3522. ——.
Paula,
1889. Coll. Eastman House, Rochester, N.Y.
                                                    F 75

3523. ——.
The Steerage,
1907, photogravure. Coll. Eastman House,
Rochester, N.Y.   F 77

3524. ——.
The Terminal,
1893, lantern slide. Coll. Eastman House,
Rochester, N.Y.   F 76

3525. ——.
Venetian Gamin,
1887(?). Coll. Eastman House, Rochester, N.Y.   F 74

3526. ——.
Portrait of Georgia O'Keeffe,
1922. Coll. Eastman House, Rochester, N.Y.
                                                    F 79

3527. STRAND, Paul.
Early Morning,
1927. Coll. B. & N. Newhall, Rochester, N.Y.   F 84

3528. ——.
Latch,
1944. Coll. Photographer, Orgeval, S/O, France.
                                                    F 86

3529. ——.
New England Town Hall,
1946. Coll. Photographer, Orgeval, S/O, France.   F 87

3530. ——.
White Fence,
1917, photogravure. Coll. B. & N. Newhall,
Rochester, N.Y. (From "Camera Work.")   F 83

3531. ——.
Young Boy, Charente,
1951. Coll. Eastman House, Rochester, N.Y.   F 88

3532. ——.
Portrait, New York,
1915, photogravure. Coll. B. & N. Newhall,
Rochester, N.Y. (From "Camera Work.")   F 82

3533. WESTON, Brett.
Brooklyn Bridge,
1946. Coll. B. & N. Newhall, Rochester, N.Y.   F 97

    3534. ——.
    Shattered Plastic,
    1951. Coll. B. & N. Newhall, Rochester, N.Y.
                                      F 98

3535. WESTON, Edward.
Armco, Ohio,
1922. Coll. Eastman House, Rochester, N.Y.   F 89

    3536. ——.
    Artichoke, Halved,
    1930. Coll. Eastman House, Rochester, N.Y.
                                        F 92

3537. ——.
Belle Grove, Louisiana,
1941. Coll. B. & N. Newhall, Rochester, N.Y.   F 96

    3538. ——.
    Guadalupe de Rivera, Mexico, D.F.,
    1924. Coll. Eastman House, Rochester, N.Y.
                                        F 90

3539. ——.
Nude,
1936. Coll. Eastman House, Rochester, N.Y.   F 93

    3540. ——.
    Shell,
    1927. Coll. Eastman House, Rochester, N.Y.
                                        F 91

3541. ——.
White Door,
1940. Coll. Eastman House, Rochester, N.Y.   F 95

    3542. ——.
    White Dune, Oceano,
    1936. Coll. B. & N. Newhall, Rochester, N.Y.
                                        F 94

3543. WHITE, Clarence, Sr.
In the Orchard, Newark, Ohio,
1902, platinum print. Mus. Mod. Art.   # 443.41   F 99

    3544. WHITE, Minor.
    Point Lobos,
    c. 1947. Coll. Photographer, Rochester, N.Y.
                                        F 100

3545. ——.
Side of Barn with Windows,
1957. Coll. Photographer, Rochester, N.Y.   F 101

SCULPTURE OF THE SEVENTEENTH, EIGHTEENTH, AND NINETEENTH CENTURIES

GEORGE HEARD HAMILTON

FOLK SCULPTURE

3547. ANON.
Cigar Store Indian,
1st q. 19th C., painted wood, H. 45½".
N.Y. State Hist. Assoc., Cooperstown.   #178.50L
SB 11A

3548. ANON.
Cigar Store Indian, Chief Black Hawk,
19th C., wood. N.Y. Hist. Soc.   #1956.86
SB 216

3549. ANON.
Cigar Store Figure, Lady of Fashion,
late 19th C., wood, H. 57½". Rockefeller Folk
Art Coll.   #57.705.3   SB 101D

3550. ANON.
Cigar Store Figure, Sailor,
2nd half 19th C., painted wood, H. c. 6'. N.Y.
Hist. Soc.   SB 20

3551. ANON.
Ship Figurehead, "Asia,"
1855, from Bath, Maine, white oak, oil-painted.
Marine Hist. Assoc., Mystic Seaport, Conn.   SB 144

3552. ANON.
Ship Figurehead, Classical Figure,
c. 1830, wood, originally painted, H. 5'.
Shelburne Mus., Inc.   # F 517   SB 202

3553. ANON.
Ship Figurehead, Commodore Perry,
early 19th C., wood, originally painted, H. 35".
Mariners' Mus., Newport News, Va.   # OF 72   SB 7

3554. ANON.
Ship Figurehead, Twin Girls,
c. 1860, white oak, house paint. Marine Hist.
Assoc., Mystic Seaport, Conn.   SB 143

3555. ANON.
Ship Figurehead, Woman in Yellow,
c. 1835, polychrome wood, H. 38½". N.Y. State
Hist. Assoc., Cooperstown.   #N-246.50L   SB 215

3556. ANON.
The Grim Reaper,
n.d., cast iron relief (possibly from cemetery
vault), H. 52½". Nadelman Coll., Shelburne Mus.,
Inc.   # FM 41   SB 200

3557. ANON.
The Holmes Children,
1795, brownstone. Cemetery, East Glastonbury,
Conn.   SB 6

3558. ANON. (poss. Daniel Hastings).
Gravestone of John Holyoke,
1775, stone. Centre St. Burying Ground, Newton,
Mass.   SB 4

3559. ANON. (poss. "J.N.").
Gravestone of Thaddeus MacCarty,
1705, stone. Granary Burying Ground, Boston,
Mass.   SB 2

    3560. ANON.
    Gravestone of David Thurston,
    1777, stone, above ground 29½" x 27½".
    Cemetery, Auburn, Mass.   SB 5

3561. ANON.
Gravestone of Rebekah Row,
1680, stone. Phipps St. Burying Ground,
Charlestown, Boston, Mass.   SB 1

    3562. ANON.
    Canada Goose,
    19th C., wood, 29" x 15¾". N.Y. State Hist.
    Assoc., Cooperstown.   #N-156 50L   SB 102

3563. ANON.
Cocks, Rabbit and Goat,
1850-85 (Pa. Dutch), plaster painted, H. 8"; 7½";
8⅛"; 6¼". Phila. Mus.   #54.85.84; 54.85.85;
54.85.87; 54.85.93   SB 221

    3564. ANON.
    Christopher Columbus,
    c. 1850, wood, originally painted, probably one of
    a pair for circus wagon, H. 58½". Shelburne
    Mus., Inc.   # FC 10   SB 201

3565. ANON.
Dancing Negro,
1825-50, painted wood, 3'11". N.Y. State Hist.
Assoc., Cooperstown.   #N33.48   Three-
quarter view.   SB 210

    3566. ——. Ibid. Full view.   SB 210A

3567. ANON.
Eagle (in action),
19th C., wood, carved in sections, H. 28½".
Shelburne Mus., Inc.   # FE 20   SB 206

    3568. ANON.
    Eagle,
    19th C., found in Portsmouth, N.H., laminated
    wood, H. including rope base 4'6". Shelburne
    Mus., Inc.   # FE 1   SB 13

3569. ANON.
Eagle, Rooster and Two Hens,
19th C. (Pa. Dutch), toys, wood, painted. N.Y.
Hist. Soc.   SB 222

    3570. ANON.
    Goat, Figure from Merry-go-round,
    187-, oil on pine. Shelburne Mus., Inc.   SB 209

3571. ANON.
Relief of Mt. Vernon, Paddle Box Decoration,
c. 1846, wood, 77" x 25". N.Y. Hist. Assoc.,
Cooperstown.   #N-226.50L   SB 214

    3572. ANON.
    Peacock,
    mid-19th C., painted wood, H. 10". N.Y. State
    Hist. Assoc., Cooperstown.   #N1-52.L

SB 212

3573. ANON.
The Reverend Campbell,
1880-85, painted wood, 7'(?). N.Y. State Hist.
Assoc., Cooperstown.   #N-180.50L   SB 213

3574. ANON.
Benjamin Franklin,
early 19th C., bust, wood. Yale U. Gall.
#1947.181   SB 12

3575. ANON. Aft. CERACCHI, Giuseppe (1751-1801).
Alexander Hamilton,
aft. 1804, marble, H. 19". Mus. City N.Y.
#35.214 A-B   SB 114

3576. ANON.
Clog Dancer "Jim Crow,"
n.d., wood, painted, H. 57". Represents
Mr. T. Rice,"The original Jim Crow." Shelburne
Mus., Inc.   # FM 80   SB 205

3577. ANON.
George Washington,
early 1800's, terra cotta bust, H. 26". Shelburne
Mus., Inc.   #1954-514   SB 203

3578. ANON. Lancaster Co., Pa.
Eagle,
1st q. 19th C., wood, H. 32⅜". Met. Mus.
#45.52   Rogers Fund, 1945.   SB 16

3579. ANON.
Kent County Jail Sign, East Greenwich,
early 19th C., painted wood, H. 34". Rhode Island
Hist. Soc.   SB 8

3580. ANON.
Mariner with Sextant, Ship Chandler's Sign,
1830-40, painted wood, 26". N.Y. State Hist.
Assoc., Cooperstown.   #115B-N   SB 211

3581. ANON.
Navigator, Shop Sign,
c. 1815, painted wood, H. 25". Old Dartmouth Hist.
Soc. & Whaling Mus., New Bedford, Mass.   SB 10

3582. ANON.
Pheasant, Trade Sign,
early 19th C., sheet iron, L. 30¾". Coll. Edith G.
Halpert, Downtown Gall., New York, N.Y.   SB 9

3583. ANON.
Weathervane, Bull,
19th C.(?), wood, 44" x 31". N.Y. State Hist.
Assoc., Cooperstown.   #N-12.54   SB 105

3584. ANON.
Weathervane, Cockerel,
c. 1830, wood, 25" x 46". Rockefeller Folk Art
Coll.   #57.700.4   SB 101B

3585. ANON.
Weathervane, Indian Hunter,
c. 1810, sheet-iron, silhouette painted, H. 51".
Shelburne Mus., Inc.   # FW 4   SB 208

3586. ANON.
Weathervane, Indian with Bow and Arrow,
late 19th C., H. 2'6¼". Shelburne Mus., Inc.
FW 80   SB 204

3587. ANON.
Weathervane, Rooster,
mid-19th C., cast-iron with sheet-iron tail
painted red & white, L. 32¾". Rhode Island
Mus.   #39.120   SB 18

    3588. ANON.
    Weathervane, Sea Serpent,
    19th C.(?), wood, 54" x 24". N.Y. State Hist.
    Assoc., Cooperstown.   #N152L   SB 104

3589. ANON.
Weathervane, Snake,
c. 1830, iron, L. 29¾". Rockefeller Folk Art Coll.
#800.8   SB 101A

    3590. AMES, Alexander.
    Bust of a Woman,
    c. 1840, wood, H. 21¼". Rockefeller Folk Art
    Coll.   #57.701.3   SB 101C

3591. ——.
Head of a Boy,
1847, wood, 18". N.Y. State Hist. Assoc.,
Cooperstown.   #N-402.55   SB 107

    3592. BEECHER, Laban S.
    Andrew Jackson, Figurehead from the U.S.
    Frigate Constitution,
    1834, painted wood, H. c. 10'. Marine Mus. City
    N.Y.   #M52.11AB   SB 14

3593. CORBIN (attr.).
Henry Ward Beecher,
c. 1840, wood, H. 21½". Rockefeller Folk Art
Coll.   #701.11   SB 101

    3594. LAMSON, Joseph.
    Gravestone of John Fowle,
    1711, stone. Phipps St. Burying Ground,
    Charlestown, Boston, Mass.   SB 3

3595. REBER of Lehighton.
Stag,
n.d.,(Pa. Dutch), carved wood, H. 10¾". Phila.
Mus.   #55.94.4   SB 223

    3596. SKILLIN, Simeon, Jr.
    Head of Apollo,
    c. 1800, wood, 24". N.Y. State Hist. Assoc.,
    Cooperstown.   #64   SB 108

3597. ——.
Head of Ceres,
c. 1800, wood, 24". N.Y. State Hist. Assoc.,
Cooperstown.   #65   SB 108B

SPANISH COLONIAL SCULPTURE

    3598. ANON.
    Bishop,
    1st half 19th C., cottonwood root, gesso &
    tempera, H. 24". Mus. N. Mex.   #L5.56-90
                                        SB 153

3599. ANON.
Holy Trinity,
c. 1800, gesso, cloth, tempera & cottonwood root,
H. 11½". Archdiocese Santa Fe, lent to Mus.
N. Mex.   #L.1.56-15   SB 151

    3600. ANON.
    Nuestra Señora de Guadalupe,
    1st half 19th C., cottonwood root, gesso, tempera,
    H. 24½". Bequest of Cady Wells, Mus. N. Mex.
    #CW-B-11   SB 219

3601. ANON.
Nuestra Señora de la Luz,
c. 1760-80, plaster relief on pine, 32" x 18½".
Taylor Mus., Colorado Springs.   #396   SB 220

3602. ANON.
St. Antonio of Padua,
1st half 19th C., cottonwood root, gesso &
tempera, H. 17". Bequest of Cady Wells, Mus. N.
Mex.   #CW.B.6   SB 152

3603. ANON.
St. Francis of Assisi,
c. 1875, wood, gesso, tempera, H. 33½". Denver
Art Mus.   #A-126   SB 147

3604. ANON.
San Rafael Archangel,
c. 1825-35, bulto, wood, tempera. El Santuario,
Chimayo, N. Mex.   SB 157

3605. ANON.
Santiago,
1st q. 19th C., gesso, tempera, cottonwood root,
H. 14". Cornelia G. Thompson Coll., Mus.
N. Mex.   SB 149

3606. ANON.
Santo Niño Perdido, in wooden shrine,
1st half 19th C., pine box: painted tempera over
gesso, H. 17", W. 7"; figure: cottonwood root,
gesso & tempera, H. 12" without base. Bequest
of Cady Wells, Mus. N. Mex.   #A.9.54-17a &
17b   SB 150

3607. ANON.
Stone Altar Piece,
1763, limestone polychromed, H. 28' x W. 18'. Cristo
Rey Church, Santa Fe, N. Mex.   SB 158

3608. GALLEGOS, Celso (1857-1943).
Rooster,
n.d., pine, H. 11". Mus. N. Mex.   #L.5.52-17
                                         SB 156

3609. VELASQUEZ, Juan Ramon (-1901).
Crucifix,
late 19th C., pine, gesso, tempera, H. 31".
Mus. N. Mex.   #A9.54-61   SB 155

PROFESSIONAL SCULPTURE

3610. AUGUR, Hezekiah (1791-1858).
Jephthah and His Daughter,
1828-32, marble, Yale U. Gall.   #1835-11A-B
                                         SB 42

3611. ——.
Alexander Fisher,
(bust sculptured posthumously from S. F. B.
Morse's *Portrait of Professor Fisher*),
marble. Yale U. Gall.   #1827.3   SB 41

3612. BALL, Thomas (1819-1911).
Lincoln Freeing the Slaves,
1876, bronze. Lincoln Park, Washington, D.C.
                                         SB 74

3613. ——.
George Washington (equestrian),
1864 (cast 1869), bronze. Public Gardens,
Boston, Mass.   SB 73

3614. BLYTHE, David G. (1815-65).
Lafayette,
1845, walnut, 8' 4". Fayette County Court House,
Uniontown, Pa.   SB 37

3615. BRACKETT, Edward A. (1818-1908).
Washington Allston (1779-1843),
1844, bust, marble, H. without base 26½". Met.
Mus.   #95.8.2   Gift of the Children of
Jonathan Sturges, 1895.   SB 69

3616. BROWERE, John H. I. (1792-1834).
Life Mask of John Adams, Aged 90,
1824, bronze, H. 30". N.Y. State Hist. Assoc.,
Cooperstown.   #N-2.57L   SB 35

3617. ——.
Life Mask of James Madison, Aged 74,
1825, bronze, H. 29". N.Y. State Hist. Assoc.,
Cooperstown.   #N-12.57L   SB 36

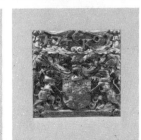

3618. BROWN, Henry Kirke (1814-86).
Abraham Lincoln,
1868, bronze. Union Square, New York, N.Y.
                                       SB 113

3619. ——.
George Washington (equestrian),
1853-56, bronze. Union Square, New York, N.Y.   SB 72

3620. CHILD, Thomas (1658-1706).
Sign,
(for his painting shop), used in London 1697,
Boston 1701, oil on carved wood panel, 35½"
x 35½". Bostonian Society.   SB 218

3621. CLEVENGER, Shobal Vail (1812-43).
Henry Clay (bust),
1842, marble, H. 30¼". Met. Mus.   #36.17
Gift of the Empire Trust Company, Trustee of the
Estate of J. Hampden Robb, 1936.   SB 70

3622. CRAWFORD, Thomas (1813-57).
The Progress of American Civilization,
1850-56, pediment sculpture, U.S. Senate, marble.
The Capitol, Washington, D.C.   SB 58

3623. ——.
Seated Indian Chief,
1850-56, marble, H. 7'7". N.Y. Hist. Soc.   SB 54

3624. ——.
Beethoven,
1854, bronze, H. 8'. New England Conservatory
of Music, Boston, Mass.   SB 53

3625. ——.
Washington Monument,
1858, bronze & stone. Richmond, Va.   SB 115

3626. CRAWFORD, Thomas (1813-57) and
RINEHART, William H. (1825-74).
The Senate Doors,
c. 1850-66, bronze, U.S. Senate, Washington, D.C.
                                       SB 57

3627. DALLIN, Cyrus E. (1861-1944).
The Medicine Man,
1899, bronze, life-sized equestrian figure.
Fairmount Park, Philadelphia.   SB 96

3628. DODGE, Charles J. (1806-86).
Bust of Jeremiah Dodge,
19th C., wood. N.Y. Hist. Soc.   SB 217

3629. EAKINS, Thomas (1844-1916).
General Grant's Horse,
1893-94, bronze, high relief, life-size. Brooklyn
Memorial Arch, N.Y.   SB 119

    3630. ——.
    Knitting,
    bronze relief, 18½" x 15". Phila. Mus.
    #30-32-22   SB 91A

3631. ——.
Spinning,
bronze relief, 18¼" x 14½". Phila. Mus.
#30-32-21   SB 91

    3632. FRAZEE, John (1790-1852).
    Self-portrait,
    1829, bronze, life-size. Pa. Acad.   SB 116

3633. ——.
Thomas H. Perkins,
1834, bust, marble, H. 31". Boston Athenaeum.   SB 39

    3634. ——.
    John Wells,
    1824, bust, marble. St. Paul's Chapel, New York,
    N.Y.   SB 40

3635. FRENCH, Daniel Chester (1850-1931).
Alma Mater,
1902-03, bronze, H. c. 7'. Columbia U., N.Y.   SB 90

    3636. ——.
    The Angel of Death Staying the Hand of the
    Sculptor,
    1893, bronze, c. 90" x 98". Forest Hills Cem.,
    Boston, Mass.   SB 88

3637. ——.
The Minute Man,
1874-75, bronze. Concord, Mass.   SB 89

    3638. GREENOUGH, Horatio (1805-1852).
    Castor and Pollux,
    1831, marble, 34¾" x 45". Boston Mus.
    #92.2642   SB 43

3639. ——.
The Rescue,
1837, marble, H. c. 10'. The Capitol, Washington,
D.C.   SB 44

    3640. ——.
    George Washington,
    1833-41, marble, H. 11' 6". Smithsonian
    Institution.   SB 45

3641. HOSMER, Harriet Goodhue (1830-1908).
Beatrice Cenci,
1854, marble 5' x 2'. Mercantile Lib., St. Louis,
Mo.   SB 64

    3642. HUNT, William Morris (1824-79).
    A Plaster Study for the Flight of Night,
    n.d., 18½" x 28½". Met. Mus.   #80.12
    Gift of Richard Morris Hunt, 1880.   SB 80

3643. KITSON, Henry (1865-1947).
The Minute Man,
c. 1900, bronze, H. c. 10'. Lexington, Mass.   SB 95

    3644. McINTIRE, Samuel (1757-1811).
    Medallion of George Washington,
    c. 1805, wood, 56'' x 38''. Essex Inst.   #110728
                                       SB 28

3645. ———.
Governor Winthrop,
1798, bust, wood, H. 15½''. Am. Antiq. Soc.   SB 29

    3646. MacMONNIES, Frederick (1863-1937).
    Nathan Hale,
    1889, bronze. City Hall Park, New York, N.Y.
                                         SB 123

3647. ———.
Washington, at the Battle of Princeton,
n.d., marble, approx. H. 40'. Princeton, N.J.   SB 122

    3648. MILLS, Clark (1810-83).
    Andrew Jackson,
    1848-53, bronze. Washington, D.C.   SB 71

3649. MILMORE, Martin (1844-83).
Soldiers' and Sailors' Monument,
1871-77, bronze & stone. The Common, Boston,
Mass.   SB 75

    3650. ———. Ibid. Det.   SB 75A

3651. PALMER, Erastus Dow (1817-1904).
The White Captive,
1859, marble, H. 66''. Met. Mus.   #94.9.3
Gift of Hamilton Fish, 1894.   SB 61

    3652. POWERS, Hiram (1805-73).
    California,
    April 3, 1858, marble. Met. Mus.   #72.3
    Gift of William B. Astor, 1872.   SB 46

3653. ———.
The Greek Slave,
1843, marble, H. 67''. Corcoran Gall.   #73.4   SB 48

    3654. ———.
    Benjamin Franklin,
    bef. 1863, H. approx. 10'. The Capitol,
    Washington, D.C.   SB 49

3655. ———.
General Andrew Jackson (1767-1845),
bust, marble, H. 34¼''. Met. Mus.   #94.14
Gift of Mrs. Frances V. Nash, 1894.   SB 47

    3656. REMINGTON, Frederic (1861-1909).
    The Bronco Buster,
    1895, bronze, 24'' x 21''. Joslyn Art Mus.,
    Omaha, Nebr.   SB 94A

3657. RIMMER, William (1816-79).
Despair, Seated Youth,
1830, gypsum, H. 10 1/16". Boston Mus.
#20.210   SB 127

    3658. ——.
    The Dying Centaur,
    1871, statuette, bronze, H. 21 1/2". Met. Mus.
    #06.146   Gift of Edward Holbrook, 1906. SB 52

3659. ——.
Falling Gladiator,
1861 (cast 1900), bronze, H. 62 3/4". Boston Mus.
#08.74   SB 50

    3660. ——.
    Fighting Lions,
    c. 1871, bronze, cast in 1907 from original
    plaster, H. 16 1/2", L. 24". Met. Mus.   #07.223
    Gift of Daniel Chester French, 1907.   SB 51

3661. ——.
Alexander Hamilton Monument,
n.d., granite, 9' 4" (?). Boston (Commonwealth
Ave.), Mass.   SB 126

    3662. RINEHART, William H. (1825-74).
    Clytie,
    1872, marble, H. 60". Peabody Institute,
    Baltimore, Md.   #8-C   SB 67

3663. ——.
Latona and Her Children,
1874, marble, H. 46". Met. Mus.   #05.12
Rogers Fund, 1905.   SB 65

    3664. ——.
    Roger Brooke Taney,
    1871 (cast 1872), bronze, H. 7 1/2'. State of
    Maryland, Annapolis.   SB 66

3665. ROGERS, John (1829-1904).
Checkers up at the Farm,
1877, plaster, H. 20". N.Y. Hist. Soc.   SB 79

    3666. ——.
    Wounded to the Rear,
    1864, plaster, H. 23 1/2". N.Y. Hist. Soc.   SB 78

3667. ROGERS, Randolph (1825-92).
Nydia,
1859, marble, H. 55". Met. Mus.   #99.7.2
Gift of James Douglas, 1899.   SB 59

    3668. RUSH, William (1756-1833).
    Charity,
    c. 1811, painted wood, life-size. Committee on
    Masonic Culture of the R.W. Grand Lodge
    F. & A.M. of Philadelphia.   SB 33

3669. ——.
Comedy, and *Tragedy* (two figures),
1808, pine, over life-size. Pa. Acad.   #187
& 188   SB 129

    3670. ——.
    The Schuylkill Chained,
    c. 1828, wood, life-size. Fairmount Park,
    Philadelphia, Pa.   SB 132

3671. RUSH, William (1756-1833).
Self-portrait, "pine-knot portrait,"
c. 1822, bronze, H. 19¾". Pa. Acad.   SB 30

   3672. ——.
   Marquis de Lafayette,
   1824, plaster, H. 24½". Pa. Acad.   SB 131

3673. ——.
Elisabeth Rush,
c. 1816, head, life-size, terra cotta. Phila.
Mus.   SB 34

   3674. ——.
   George Washington,
   1814, painted wood (pine), H. 81½". Coll.
   Independence Nat. Hist. Park, Phila.   SB 32

3675. SAINT-GAUDENS, Augustus (1848-1907).
Diana,
1892, bronze, H. 102". Phila. Mus.   SB 83

   3676. ——.
   Adams Memorial,
   1891, bronze, H. 70". Rock Creek Cemetery,
   Washington, D.C.   SB 85

3677. ——.
Memorial to Deacon Samuel Chapin,
1887, bronze, H. 8'5½". City of Springfield,
Mass.   SB 135

   3678. ——.
   Admiral David Glasgow Farragut Monument,
   1881, bronze & stone. Madison Square, New
   York, N.Y.   SB 134

3679. ——.
Lincoln,
1887, bronze. Lincoln Park, Chicago, Ill.   SB 84

   3680. ——.
   Shaw Memorial,
   1884-97, bronze, H. c. 10'. The Common, Boston,
   Mass.   SB 86

3681. ——.
General William Tecumseh Sherman Memorial,
1892-1903, (equestrian), bronze, 12' x 14'.
Central Park, 5th Ave. at 59th St., New York, N.Y. SB 82

   3682. WARD, J. Q. A. (1830-1910).
   Indian Hunter,
   1868, bronze. Central Park, New York,
   N.Y.   SB 77

3683. ——.
Henry Ward Beecher,
1891, bronze figure, c. 7'. Borough Hall Park,
Brooklyn, N.Y.   SB 76

   3684. ——.
   Horace Greeley,
   1890, bronze. Greeley Square, New York, N.Y.
                                                      SB 139

3685. WARD, J. Q. A. (1830-1910).
Washington,
1883, bronze. Sub-Treasury, Wall Street, New
York, N.Y.   SB 138

    3686. WARNER, Olin Levi (1844-96).
    "Oral Tradition" Door,
    1896, bronze. Lib. of Congress.   SB 142

3687. ——.
William Lloyd Garrison,
1885, bronze, H. c. 6'. Boston (Commonwealth
Ave.), Mass.   SB 140

SCULPTURE OF THE TWENTIETH CENTURY

ANDREW CARNDUFF RITCHIE

Assisted by Eleanor Barton and Rosalind Irvine

3689. ALBRIZIO, Humbert (1901-   ).
Head of Athlete,
1955, blue marble, H. 18". Kraushaar Galleries,
New York, N.Y.   SC 2

    3690. AMINO, Leo (1911-   ).
    Zoophite No. 1,
    1952, plastic, wire, colored mesh & threads,
    L. 14". Sculpture Center, New York, N.Y.   SC 3

3691. ARCHIPENKO, Alexander (1887-   ).
The Spirit of This Century, "Modeling of Light,"
1947, carved plastic illuminated from within,
H. 22½". Coll. Artist, New York, N.Y.   SC 178A

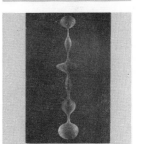

    3692. ASAWA, Ruth (1926-   ).
    Number 9-1956,
    brass wire, H. 66". Peridot Gallery, New York,
    N.Y.   SC 124

3693. BAIZERMAN, Saul (1889-1957).
Slumber,
1948, hammered copper, L. 40". Whitney Mus.
#48.20   SC 8

    3694. BARNARD, George Grey (1863-1938).
    The Refugee,
    c. 1930, marble, H. 4'. Coll. Stephen C. Clark,
    New York, N.Y.   SC 6

3695. ——.
Abraham Lincoln: Head,
20th C., white marble, H. 21¼". Met. Mus.
#29.161   Morris K. Jesup Fund, 1929.   SC 8A

    3696. BARTLETT, Paul Wayland (1865-1925).
    Democracy Protecting the Arts of Peace,
    1909-16, marble. Pedimental sculpture, House of
    Representatives, The Capitol, Washington, D.C.
                                           SC 181

3697. BARTLETT, Paul Wayland (1865-1925).
History, Philosophy, Romance, Religion, Poetry,
Drama,
c. 1905, marble, above main entr. of N.Y. Pub.
Lib.   SC 180

    3698. BASKIN, Leonard (1922-   ).
    Man with Dead Bird,
    1954, walnut, H. 64". Mus. Mod. Art.   # 25.57
    A. Conger Goodyear Fund.   SC 125

3699. BEN-SCHMUEL, Aaron (1903-   ).
Torso of a Boy,
1930, black granite, H. 28¾". Mus. Mod. Art.
314.41   Anonymous gift.   SC 9

    3700. BERTOIA, Harry (1915-   ).
    Sculptured and Metal Screen,
    1954, steel, brass, copper & nickel, H. 16' x 70' x
    2'. Manufacturers Trust Co., New York, N.Y.
                                           SC 10

3701. BOURGEOIS, Louise (1911-   ).
Sleeping Figure,
1950, balsa wood, H. 74½". Mus. Mod. Art.
3.51   Katharine Cornell Fund.   SC 12

    3702. CAESAR, Doris.
    Torso,
    1953, bronze, H. 58". Whitney Mus.   # 43.30
                                           SC 13

3703. CALDER, Alexander (1898-   ).
The Horse,
1928, walnut, L. 34¾". Mus. Mod. Art.
747.43   Acquired through the Lillie P. Bliss
Bequest.   SC 15

    3704. ———.
    The Hostess,
    1928, wire construction, H. 11½". Mus. Mod. Art.
    # 319.41   Gift of Edward M. M. Warburg. SC 16

3705. ———.
Red Gongs,
20th C., mobile, sheet aluminum, sheet brass,
steel rod and wire, red paint, L. c. 12'. Met. Mus.
55.181   Fletcher Fund, 1955.   SC 19

    3706. ———.
    Spiny,
    1942, stabile, sheet aluminum, H. 26". Private
    Coll., New York, N.Y.   SC 17

3707. CALDER, Alexander Stirling (1870-1945).
Washington as President,
bef. 1918. West pier of Washington Arch, New
York, N.Y.   SC 14

    3708. CALLERY, Mary (1903-   ).
    Composition of Birds,
    1954, aluminum, 3 large birds, each 12' x 12'.
    Alcoa Bldg., Pittsburgh, Pa.   SC 21

3709. CAPARN, Rhys (1909-   ).
A Gathering of Birds,
1954, cast stone, 20½" x 20". Whitney Mus.
55.18   Gift of George Claiborne Royall through
Fed. of Mod. Painters & Sculptors, Inc.   SC 23

    3710. COOK, Robert.
    Job,
    1955, bronze, 39" x 56" x 30". Sculpture Center,
    New York, N.Y.   SC 126

3711. CORNELL, Joseph (1903-   ).
Construction: Hotel du Nord,
c. 1953, wood, glass & paper, 19" x 13¼" x 5½".
Whitney Mus.   #57.6   SC 24A

    3712. de CREEFT, José (1884-   ).
    Cloud,
    1939, green stone, H. 13½". Whitney Mus.
    #41.17   SC 29

3713. ——.
Maya,
1937(?), black Belgian granite. Roland P.
Murdock Coll., Wichita Art Mus.   #M-42   SC 127

    3714. ——. Ibid. Profile.   SC 127A

3715. ——.
Saturnia,
1939, hammered lead relief, 61" x 38". Mus.
Mod. Art.   #591.39   Gift of Mrs. George E.
Barstow.   SC 28

    3716. DAVIDSON, Jo (1883-1952).
    Gertrude Stein,
    1920, bronze, H. 31". Whitney Mus.   #54.10
                                            SC 26

3717. DAVIS, Emma Lu (1905-   ).
Cosmic Presence,
1934, wood, painted, L. 66¼". Mus. Mod. Art.
#9.42   Purchase.   SC 27

    3718. DIEDERICH, W. Hunt (1884-1953).
    The Jockey,
    1924, bronze, H. 23¼". Newark Mus.
    #27.1073   SC 33

3719. DUBLE, Lu (1896-   ).
Cain,
1953, hydrocal, H. 38". Whitney Mus.   #53.35   SC 34

    3720. EPSTEIN, Jacob (1880-1959).
    Mother and Child,
    1913, marble, H. 17¼". Mus. Mod. Art.   #5.38
    Gift of A. Conger Goodyear.   SC 35

3721. ——.
Madonna and Child,
1927, bronze, H. 67". Coll. Miss Sally Ryan,
Georgetown, Conn.   SC 36

    3722. ——.
    Social Consciousness,
    1955, bronze, H. 16'. Fairmount Park Art Assoc.,
    Philadelphia, Pa.   SC 38

3723. ——.
Portrait of Oriel Ross,
1931, bronze, H. 26¼". Mus. Mod. Art.   #2.33
Gift of Edward M. M. Warburg.   SC 37

    3724. ESHERICK, Wharton (1887-   ).
    Reverence,
    1942, wood, H. 12'. Fairmount Park Art Assoc.,
    Philadelphia, Pa.   SC 128

3725. FAGGI, Alfeo (1885-   ).
Saint Francis,
1915, bronze, H. 53". Albright Gall.   #720.40   SC 39

3726. FERBER, Herbert (1906-   ).
"and the bush was not consumed,"
1951, metals, H. 12' 8". Congr. B'nai Israel,
Millburn, N.J.   SC 44

3727. ——.
The Flame,
1949, brass, lead, and soft solder, H. 65½".
Whitney Mus.   #51.30   SC 43

3728. ——.
Sun Wheel,
1956, brass, copper, silver solder, H. 56¼".
Whitney Mus.   #56.18   SC 129

3729. FLANNAGAN, John (1898-1942).
Design for a Skyscraper Court: Mother and Child,
1934-35, red sandstone, H. 41". Fogg Mus.
#1940.51   SC 41

3730. ——.
Figure of Dignity—Irish Mountain Goat,
20th C., granite and cast aluminum. Met. Mus.
#41.47   Gift of the Alexander Shilling Fund,
1941.   SC 130

3731. ——.
Jonah and the Whale: Rebirth Motif,
1937, bluestone, H. 30½". Coll. Mr. & Mrs.
Milton Lowenthal, New York, N.Y.   SC 40A

3732. ——.
Triumph of the Egg, I,
1937, granite, L. 16". Mus. Mod. Art.   #296.38
Purchase.   SC 42

3733. FRASER, James Earle (1876-1953).
End of the Trail,
1915, plaster & wire. Mooney Grove Park,
Tulare Co., California.   SC 131

3734. FULLER, Sue (1914-   ).
String Construction, Number 51,
1953, plastic thread, aluminum, 33½" x 45½".
Whitney Mus.   #54.23   SC 132

3735. GABO, Naum (1890-   ).
Construction,
1951-52, plastic & wire, L. 15'. Saidie A. May
Coll., Baltimore Mus.   SC 45

3736. ——.
Construction,
1956, lucite, plastic & metals, D. 10'. U.S.
Rubber Co. Bldg., Rockefeller Center, New York,
N.Y.   SC 47

3737. ——.
Construction in Space,
1953, plastic, H. 28". Private Coll., New York,
N.Y.   SC 46

3738. GLASCO, Joseph (1925-   ).
Man Walking,
1955, bronze, H. 17½". Mus. Mod. Art.
#190.56   Purchase.   SC 133

3739. GLENNY, Anna (1888-   ).
The Jewess,
1934-35, red concrete, cast, H. 24". Albright
Gall.   #S-146   SC 48

    3740. GORDIN, Sidney (1918-   ).
    Construction Number 10,
    1955, painted steel, 36" x 41¼". Whitney Mus.
    #56.10   SC 49

3741. GOTO, Joseph (1916-   ).
Organic Form #1,
1951, welded steel, H. 11'4¼". Mus. Mod. Art.
#175.52   Purchase.   SC 50A

    3742. GRAFLY, Charles (1862-1929).
    Frank Duveneck,
    1915, bronze bust, H. 26". Carnegie Inst.   #7
                                                SC 182

3743. ———.
General Meade Memorial,
1915-25, marble, H. c. 20'. Washington, D.C.   SC 183

    3744. GREENBAUM, Dorothea S. (1893-   ).
    Drowned Girl,
    1950, Tennessee marble, H. 10". Sculpture
    Center, New York, N.Y.   SC 134

3745. GRIPPE, Peter (1912-   ).
The City,
1942, terra cotta, H. 9½". Mus. Mod. Art.
#20.43   Anonymous gift.   SC 51

    3746. GROSS, Chaim (1904-   ).
    Handlebar Riders,
    1935, lignum vitae, H. 41¼". Mus. Mod. Art.
    #156.37   Gift of A. Conger Goodyear.   SC 52

3747. ———.
Reflection,
1954, pink alabaster, H. 17". Coll. Artist,
New York, N.Y.   SC 135

    3748. HADZI, Dimitri (1921-   ).
    Bird Woman,
    1956, bronze, H. 29". Coll. Mrs. John D.
    Rockefeller, III, New York, N.Y.   SC 53

3749. HAGUE, Raoul (1905-   ).
Ohayo Wormy Butternut (title and medium),
1947-48, H. 66½". Mus. Mod. Art.   #248.56
Katharine Cornell Fund.   SC 54

    3750. HARDY, Tom (1921-   ).
    Bison,
    1954, welded steel, L. 40½". Kraushaar
    Galleries, New York, N.Y.   SC 136

3751. HARE, David (1917-   ).
Crab,
1951, welded bronze, H. 23¾". Mus. Mod. Art.
#136.51   Purchase.   SC 56

    3752. ———.
    Head of an Animal,
    1955, steel & iron, H. 65½". Whitney Mus.
    #57.45   SC 56A

3753. HARE, David (1917-   ).
Juggler,
1950-51, steel, H. 80¼". Whitney Mus.
#51.34   SC 55

    3754. ——.
    Sunrise,
    1954-55, bronze & steel, H. 84". Albright Gall.
                                     SC 137

3755. HARKAVY, Minna R. (1895-   ).
American Miner's Family,
1931, bronze, H. 27". Mus. Mod. Art.   #303.38
Mrs. John D. Rockefeller, Jr., Fund.   SC 57

    3756. Der HAROOTIAN, Koren (1909-   ).
    Eagles of Ararat,
    1955-56, marble, H. 58". Whitney Mus.
    #56.22   SC 30

3757. HEBALD, Milton (1917-   ).
Group of Figures,
1952, bronze, 16'. Bronx Municipal Hospital
Group, N.Y.   SC 58

    3758. HOFFMAN, Malvina (1887-   ).
    Paderewski, the Artist: Head,
    1923, bronze, H. 16". Met. Mus.   #40.99
    Francis Lathrop Fund, 1940.   SC 59

3759. HOWARD, Robert B. (1896-   ).
The Miscreant,
1950, composite, 31" x 98". Addison Gall.
#1951.18   SC 139

    3760. KAZ, Nathaniel (1917-   ).
    Cyrano,
    1950, bronze, H. 34¼". Whitney Mus.   #53.17
    Wildenstein Benefit Purchase Fund.   SC 60

3761. KENT, Adaline (1900-57).
Figment,
1953, magnesite, H. 65". Betty Parsons Gallery,
New York, N.Y.   SC 61

    3762. KING, William (1925-   ).
    Venus,
    1956, bronze, H. 62½". Coll. Joseph H.
    Hirshhorn, New York, N.Y.   SC 62A

3763. KREIS, Henry (1899-   ).
Reclining Half-nude,
1942, limestone, L. 31". Wadsworth Atheneum,
#1955.262   SC 64

    3764. KRUGER, Louise (1924-   ).
    Man,
    1955, polychromed pine, H. 49". Martha Jackson
    Gallery, New York, N.Y.   SC 65

3765. LACHAISE, Gaston (1882-1935).
Dolphin Fountain,
1924, bronze, L. 39". Whitney Mus.   #31.41   SC 141

    3766. ——.
    Floating Figure,
    1927 (cast 1935), bronze, H. 51¾". Mus. Mod.
    Art.   #3.37   Anonymous gift in memory of
    the artist.   SC 66

3767. LACHAISE, Gaston (1882-1935).
Head,
1928, bronze, nickel-plated, H. 13¼". Whitney
Mus.   #31.42   SC 142

    3768. ——.
    Standing Woman,
    1912-27, bronze, H. 70". Whitney Mus.   #36.91
                                  SC 68

3769. ——.
Torso,
1930, bronze, H. 13½". Whitney Mus.   #58.4   SC 143

    3770. ——.
    John Marin,
    1928, bronze, H. 12½". Mus. Mod. Art.
    #154.34   Gift of Mrs. John D. Rockefeller, Jr.
                                  SC 67

3771. LASSAW, Ibram (1913-   ).
Kwannon,
1952, welded bronze with silver, H. 6'. Mus.
Mod. Art.   #196.52   Katharine Cornell Fund.   SC 70

    3772. ——.
    Procession,
    1955-56, wire, copper, bronze & silver, L. 40".
    Whitney Mus.   #56.19   SC 71A

3773. LAURENT, Robert (1890-   ).
Kneeling Figure,
1935, bronze, H. 23½". Whitney Mus.   #36.2   SC 144

    3774. ——.
    The Wave,
    1926, alabaster, L. 22⅞". Brooklyn Mus.
    #28.275   SC 72

3775. LEE, Arthur (1881-   ).
Rhythm,
bef. 1930, bronze, H. 73½". Whitney Mus.
#33.59   SC 145

    3776. LIPCHITZ, Jacques (1891-   ).
    Birth of the Muses,
    1944-50, bronze. Coll. Mrs. John D. Rockefeller,
    III, New York, N.Y.   SC 146

3777. ——.
Mother and Child, II,
1941-45, bronze, H. 50". Mus. Mod. Art.
#508.51   Mrs. Simon Guggenheim Fund.   SC 73

    3778. ——.
    Prometheus Strangling the Vulture,
    1952-53, bronze, H. 7' 9". Phila. Mus.   SC 147

3779. ——.
Sacrifice, II,
1948-52, bronze, H. 49¼". Whitney Mus.
#52.27   SC 75

    3780. ——.
    Sketch for a Portrait of Marsden Hartley,
    1942, terra cotta, H. 14¼". Met. Mus.   #42.142
    Anonymous gift, 1942.   SC 74

3781. LIPMAN-WULF, Peter (1905-   ).
The Dancing Couple,
1949, ebony, H. 68". Whitney Mus.   # 55.50
Gift of Paul Gourary.   SC 148

3782. LIPPOLD, Richard (1915-   ).
Variation No. 7—Full Moon,
1949-50, brass rods, nickel-chromium and
stainless steel wire, H. 10'. Mus. Mod. Art.
241.50   Mrs. Simon Guggenheim Fund   SC 80

3783. ——.
Variation within a Sphere, No. 10: The Sun,
1953-56, 22 carat gold-filled wire, H. c. 11',
W. c. 22'. Met. Mus.   # 56.106   Fletcher
Fund, 1956.   SC 149

3784. LIPTON, Seymour (1903-   ).
Menorah,
1954, nickel-silver on steel, H. 48". Temple
Israel, Tulsa, Okla.   SC 77

3785. ——.
Prophet,
1956, nickel-silver on monel metal, H. 87".
Betty Parsons Gallery, New York, N.Y.   SC 78

3786. MALDARELLI, Oronzio (1892-   ).
Gemini No. 1,
1942-43, bronze, H. c. 40". Fairmount Park
Assoc., Philadelphia, Pa.   SC 81

3787. MANSHIP, Paul (1885-   ).
Dancer and Gazelles,
1916, bronze, H. 70". Corcoran Gall.   SC 82

3788. ——.
Prometheus,
1933, fountain figure, 18' x 15'. Lower Plaza of
Rockefeller Center, New York, N.Y.   SC 83

3789. MARGOULIES, Berta (1907-   ).
Mine Disaster,
1942, bronze, L. 28½". Whitney Mus.   # 45.10   SC 150

3790. MESTROVIC, Ivan (1883-   ).
Jacob's Well,
1957, bronze, 8' x 7½'. Coll. Artist, South Bend,
Ind.   SC 151

3791. MILLES, Carl (1875-1955).
Meeting of the Waters,
1940, fountain, bronze, 200' x 35'. St. Louis, Mo.   SC 152

3792. ——. Ibid., det. male figure.   SC 152A

3793. ——. Ibid., det. central figures.   SC 152B

3794. MONROE, Keith (1917-   ).
Political Prisoner,
1953, H. 17". Coll. Artist, San Francisco, Calif.
                                                SC 84A

3795. MUNDT, Ernst (1905-   ).
Tradition and Progress,
1955, 2' 11" x 1'6". Purchase Prize, Art
Commission—City & County of San Francisco,
Calif.   SC 153

3796. NADELMAN, Elie (1882-1946).
Man in the Open Air,
c. 1915, bronze, H. 54½". Mus. Mod. Art.
#259.48   Gift of William S. Paley.   SC 85

3797. ———.
Sur La Plage,
c. 1917, marble & bronze, 26¼" x 23⅜". Roby
Fdn. c/o Whitney Mus.   SC 154

3798. ———.
Wounded Bull,
1915, bronze, L. 11½". Mus. Mod. Art.
#226.27   Gift of Mrs. Elie Nadelman.   SC 86

3799. NAKIAN, Reuben (1897-   ).
Young Calf,
1929, Georgia pink marble, H. 15". Mus. Mod.
Art.   #297.38   Purchase.   SC 155

3800. NEVELSON, Louise (1904-   ).
First Personage,
1956 or 57, wood, H. 94"; pine tree, H. 73¹¹⁄₁₆".
Brooklyn Mus.   #57.23   SC 156

3801. NICKFORD, Juan (1926-   ).
Aggression,
1951, welded steel, L. 32". Sculpture Center,
New York, N.Y.   SC 157

3802. NIVOLA, Costantino (1911-   ).
Deus,
1953, sand and plaster, 63¾" x 34½". Whitney
Mus.   #55.12   SC 158

3803. NOGUCHI, Isamu (1904-   ).
Cronos,
1949, balsa wood, H. 85". Stable Gallery, New
York, N.Y.   SC 92

3804. ———.
Even the Centipede,
1952, Kasama ware in 11 pieces, each c. 18" L.,
mounted on wood pole 14' H. Mus. Mod. Art.
#1.55 a-k   A. Conger Goodyear Fund.   SC 93

3805. ———.
Kouros,
1944-45, pink Georgia marble, slate base, H. 9' 9".
Met. Mus.   #53.87 a-i   Fletcher Fund, 1953.   SC 90

3806. ———.
Night Voyage,
c. 1949, York marble, H. 14". Stable Gallery,
New York, N.Y.   SC 91

3807. ———.
Plaque (symbolic of "News"),
1940, stainless steel, 17' x 22'. Associated Press
Bldg., Rockefeller Center, New York, N.Y.   SC 89

3808. O'CONNOR, Andrew (1874-1941).
Abraham Lincoln,
c. 1916, bronze, H. 12'. Springfield, Ill.   SC 159

3809. O'CONNOR, Andrew (1874-1941).
Head of Lincoln,
c. 1916, bronze, H. 27½". Whitney Mus.
#31.60   SC 159A

    3810. O'HANLON, Richard (1906-   ).
    Small Monument,
    1957, 17" x 8". Willard Gallery, New York,
    N.Y.   SC 94A

3811. PINEDA, Marianna (1925-   ).
Sleepwalker,
c. 1951, bronze, H. 39⅜". Swetzoff Gallery,
Boston, Mass.   SC 95

    3812. RAEMISCH, Waldemar (1888-1955).
    Young Mother,
    1947, marble, H. 37½". Lent by Mrs. Waldemar
    Raemisch, Rhode Island Mus.   SC 161

3813. REDER, Bernard (1897-   ).
Torso,
1938, limestone, H. 45". Mus. Mod. Art.
#187.52   Gift of J. Von Straaten.   SC 96

    3814. de RIVERA, José (1904-   ).
    Construction Blue and Black,
    1951, painted aluminum, L. 47". Whitney Mus.
    #52.16   SC 31A

3815. ——.
Homage to the World of Minkowski,
1955, chrome, nickel and stainless steel, H. 14⅞".
Met. Mus.   #55.204   Fletcher Fund, 1955.   SC 32

    3816. ROBUS, Hugo (1885-   ).
    Girl Washing Her Hair,
    1933, marble, H. 17". Mus. Mod. Art.   #659.39
    Mrs. John D. Rockefeller, Jr., Fund.   SC 97

3817. ——.
One and Another,
1934, bronze, 27" x 41". Roby Fdn. c/o Whitney
Mus.   SC 163

    3818. ROSENTHAL, Bernard.
    Ark of Wisdom,
    1956, red brass, H. 47". Viviano Gallery, New
    York, N.Y.   SC 98

3819. ——.
Wall of Thebes,
1957, red brass, H. 27". Viviano Gallery, New
York, N.Y.   SC 98A

    3820. ROSENWALD, Robert (1920-   ).
    The Womb,
    1954, marble, H. 35". Coll. Mr. & Mrs. Max J.
    Pincus, Pleasant Ridge, Mich.   SC 164

3821. ROSZAK, Theodore J. (1907-   ).
Sea Sentinel,
1956, steel brazed with bronze, H. 105". Whitney
Mus.   #56.26   SC 166

    3822. ——.
    Spectre of Kitty Hawk,
    1946-47, welded and hammered steel brazed with
    bronze and brass, H. 40¼". Mus. Mod. Art.
    #16.50   Purchase.   SC 99

3823. ROSZAK, Theodore J. (1907-   ).
Spire and Bell Tower,
1954-55, aluminum, H. 45". M.I.T., Cambridge,
Mass.   SC 101

    3824. ———.
    Vertical Construction,
    1943, painted wood & plastic, H. 74". Whitney
    Mus.   #57.7   Gift of the Artist.   SC 165A

3825. ROX, Henry.
Arise!
1951, terra cotta, H. 44". Coll. Artist, South
Hadley, Mass.   SC 167

    3826. RUDY, Charles (1904-   ).
    Reclining Figure,
    1940, marble, 17½" x 10¼". Pa. Acad.   SC 168

3827. RUMSEY, Charles Cary (1879-1922).
Pagan Kin,
n.d., bronze (plaster dated 1921), H. 12⅝". Whitney
Mus.   #31.72   SC 169

    3828. SALERNO, Charles (1916-   ).
    Torso in the Clouds,
    1951, Mexican onyx, H. 22¼". Weyhe Gallery,
    New York, N.Y.   SC 170

3829. SCHNABEL, Day (1905-   ).
Transformations,
1956, marble, H. 19¾". Whitney Mus.
#57.24   SC 104

    3830. SIMKHOVITCH, Helena (1908-   ).
    Isabel Bolton,
    1951, brass, H. 14½". Whitney Mus.   #56.13
    Gift through Fed. of Mod. Painters & Sculptors,
    Inc.   SC 105

3831. SMITH, David (1912-   ).
Forgings VII, X, VIII,
1955, steel, H. 87⅛"; 90". Coll. Artist,
Bolton's Landing, N.Y.   SC 109

    3832. ———.
    History of Le Roy Borton,
    1956, steel, H. 88¼". Mus. Mod. Art.   #159.37
    Mrs. Simon Guggenheim Fund.   SC 106A

3833. ———.
Hudson River Landscape,
1951, steel, 50¼" x 74¼" x 18⅜". Whitney Mus.
#54.14   SC 108

    3834. ———.
    Iron Woman,
    1955-57, steel. Coll. Artist, Bolton's Landing,
    N.Y.   SC 110

3835. ———.
The Letter,
1950, welded steel, 37⅝" x 25⅛". Munson-Williams-
Proctor Inst.   #51.37   SC 107

    3836. ———.
    Personage of May,
    1957, bronze, H. 71¾" x 32" x 14¼". Coll.
    Artist, Bolton's Landing, N.Y.   SC 110A

3837. SQUIER, Jack (1927-   ).
Caged Creature,
1956, bronze, H. 18". Alan Gallery, New York,
N.Y.   SC 111

    3838. STANKIEWICZ, Richard (1922-   ).
    Secretary,
    1953, steel, H. 30". Coll. Mrs. Martin Cannon,
    Jr., Charlotte, N.C.   SC 112

3839. STERNE, Maurice (1878-1957).
The Bomb Thrower,
1910/14, bronze, H. 12". Whitney Mus.   #54.51
Bequest of Mrs. Sam A. Lewisohn.   SC 171

    3840. ——.
    Monument to the Early Settlers,
    1927-29, bronze & stone, H. of bronze 12½';
    base: H. 26' x L. 28'. Elm Park, Worcester,
    Mass.   SC 172

3841. TOVISH, Harold (1921-   ).
Blind,
1950, bronze, moonstone & quartz. H. 8½".
Walker Art Center.   #51.27   SC 113

    3842. TOWNLEY, Hugh (1923-   ).
    Forms in Compression,
    1952-53, oak, H. 36". Private Coll., New York,
    N.Y.   SC 114

3843. UMLAUF, Charles (1911-   ).
The Prophet,
n.d., bronze, H. 36". Dallas Mus. Fine Arts.
#1950.23   SC 115A

    3844. VAGIS, Polygnotos (1894-   ).
    Revelation,
    1951, granite, H. 16⅛". Mus. Mod. Art.
    #583.56   Gift of Mr. & Mrs. John de Menil.
                                                SC 116

3845. WALTERS, Carl (1883-1955).
Ella,
1927, glazed ceramic, H. 16¾". Mus. Mod. Art.
#373.41   Purchase.   SC 173

    3846. WARING, Pegot (1910-   ).
    Hippopotamus,
    n.d., stone. Coll. Bruno Adriani, Carmel, Calif.
                                                SC 117

3847. WARNEKE, Heinz (1895-   ).
Wild Boars,
1929, Belgian granite, 12½" x 15" x 8¾". Art
Inst. Chicago.   #31.570   SC 174A

    3848. WEINBERG, Elbert (1928-   ).
    Ritual Figure,
    1953, beechwood, H. 60¼". Mus. Mod. Art.
    #35.55   A. Conger Goodyear Fund.   SC 118

3849. WERNER, Nat (1907-   ).
Conquistador,
1949, black walnut, H. 28½". Whitney Mus.
#54.7   Gift of Mr. & Mrs. Jack I. Poses.   SC 173A

    3850. YOUNG, Mahonri M. (1877-1957).
    Groggy,
    1926, bronze, H. 14¼". Whitney Mus.   #31.82
                                                SC 174

3851. YOUNG, Mahonri M. (1877-1957).
Man with Pick,
1915, bronze, H. 28½". Met. Mus.   #18.107
Gift of Mrs. Edward H. Harriman, 1918.   SC 119

3852. ZORACH, William (1887-   ).
Floating Figure,
1922, African mahogany, H. 9" x L. 33¼".
Albright Gall.   #32.836   SC 121

3853. ——.
The Future Generation,
1942-47, Botticini marble, H. 40". Whitney Mus.
#51.32   SC 175

3854. ——.
Head of Moses,
1953, granite, H. 27". Earl Hall, Columbia U.,
New York, N.Y.   SC 177

3855. ——.
Mother and Child,
1927-30, Spanish marble, H. 65". Met. Mus.
#52.143   Fletcher Fund, 1952.   SC 122

3856. ——.
Torso,
1932, Labrador granite, H. 33". Roby Fdn c/o
Whitney Mus.   SC 176

3857. ——.
Victory,
1945, French marble, H. 43". Downtown Gallery,
New York, N.Y.   SC 123

STAGE DESIGN

DONALD OENSLAGER

3859. ANON.
*A Mid-19th C. Melodrama with Frank
Mayo as Davy Crockett:*
"Wolves! What Can Save Us?" poster, n.d.
Theatre Div., N.Y. Pub. Lib.   T 203

    3860. ANON.
    Palace Throne Room,
    c. 1900, photo, 5½" x 4¼". Theatre Div., N.Y.
    Pub. Lib.   T 207

3861. ANON. (designed & built in Italy).
Girl of the Golden West,
1910, print, 4¼" x 7½". Theatre Div., N.Y.
Pub. Lib.   T 199

    3862. ARMISTEAD, Horace.
    The Medium,
    1947, w.c. Coll. Artist, Boston, Mass.   T 4

3863. ——. Ibid. Seance scene.   T 4A

    3864. ARONSON, Boris.
    The Crucible:
    Room Interior, 1953, w.c., 10¾" x 21". Coll.
    Artist, New York, N.Y.   T 10A

3865. ——.
The Diary of Anne Frank,
1955, w.c., 13½" x 23". Coll. Artist, New York,
N.Y.   T 11

    3866. ——.
    The First Born,
    1940, oil on cardboard, 14¾" x 24". Coll. Artist,
    New York, N.Y.   T 7

3867. ——.
The Gentle People:
The Pier, 1939, tempera, 9" x 14½". Coll. Artist,
New York, N.Y.   T 6

    3868. ——.
    J. B.,
    1958, oil on cardboard, 19⅞" x 29⅞". Coll.
    Artist, New York, N.Y.   T 219

3869. AYERS, Lemuel.
Camino Real,
1953, ink & w.c., 11⅞" x 16". Coll. Mrs. Martin
Poll, New York, N.Y.   T 19

    3870. ——.
    Kismet,
    1953, w.c., 11⅝" x 20¾". Coll. Mrs. Martin Poll,
    New York, N.Y.   T 220

3871. AYERS, Lemuel.
Kiss Me, Kate:
Set Design, 1948, tempera, 8" x 11". Coll. Mrs.
Lemuel Ayers, New York, N.Y.   T 17

3872. ——.
Oklahoma,
1943, tempera, 15" x 21". Coll. Miss Selma
Tamber, New York, N.Y.   T 14

3873. ——.
The Pirate:
Act I, Scene 2, 1942, tempera, 29⅝" x 39⅝".
Coll. Mrs. Lemuel Ayers, New York, N.Y.   T 13

3874. BAY, Howard.
One-third of a Nation,
1938, half-tone engraving, 4⅞" x 6½". Coll.
Artist, New York, N.Y.   T 21

3875. ——.
Up in Central Park:
Times Office, 1945, ink & w.c., 13" x 20". Coll.
Artist, New York, N.Y.   T 23

3876. BEL GEDDES, Norman.
Dead End,
1935, b. & w. photo, 10½" x 13¼". U. of Texas,
Austin.   T 34

3877. ——.
The Divine Comedy,
1921, w.c., 20" x 22½". U. of Texas, Austin.   T 31

3878. ——. Ibid. Dwg. in sanguine, 20" x 23".
        T 31C

3879. ——.
Iphigenia in Aulis,
1935, b. & w. photo of charcoal sketch, 8" x 10".
U. of Texas, Austin.   T 35

3880. ——.
The Miracle,
1924, charcoal & pastel, 19¼" x 29¼". U. of
Texas, Austin.   T 32A

3881. ——. Ibid. Inquisition Scene, charcoal,
20" x 29⅞".   T 32

3882. BELL, E. Hamilton.
Strife:
Board of Directors Room, 1909, photo, 6" x 11".
Theatre Div., N.Y. Pub. Lib.   T 38

3883. BERMAN, Eugene.
Amahl and the Night Visitors,
1952, w.c. & gouache. Coll. Knoedler, New
York, N.Y.   T 39A

3884. ——.
Don Giovanni,
1957, w.c. & gouache. Coll. Knoedler, New York,
N.Y.   T 39B

3885. BERMAN, Eugene.
La Forza del Destino,
1952, w.c. & gouache. Coll. Knoedler, New
York, N.Y.   T 39D

   3886. BERNSTEIN, Aline.
   The Little Clay Cart,
   1925, photo, 7" x 9". Brugiere Coll., Theatre
   Div., N.Y. Pub. Lib.   T 42

3887. BRAGDON, Claude.
Hamlet:
Act I, Scene 1, 1919, ink & wash, 8⅛" x 11⅞".
Coll. Henry W. Bragdon, Exeter, N.H.   T 46

   3888. ———. Ibid. Act V, Scene 1, 8⅛" x 11⅞".
                                               T 46B

3889. CHANEY, Stewart.
The House of Bernarda Alba,
1951, ink & wash, 10⅛" x 17¼". Coll. Artist,
New York, N.Y.   T 54

   3890. ———.
   Life with Father,
   1939, w.c. & pencil, 8" x 19¼". Coll. Artist,
   New York, N.Y.   T 51

3891. ———.
The Old Maid:
The School Room, 1935, ink & w.c., 5¾" x 12⅝".
Coll. Artist, New York, N.Y.   T 49A

   3892. ———.
   Twelfth Night,
   1940, ink & w.c., 4¼" x 9¼". Coll. Artist, New
   York, N.Y.   T 52

3893. DREYFUSS, Henry.
The Last Mile,
1930, b. & w. photo, 7" x 9". Coll. Artist, New
York, N.Y.   T 59

   3894. du Bois, Raoul.
   Plain and Fancy:
   Gas Station Drop, w.c., 13½" x 23". Coll. Artist,
   New York, N.Y.   T 64A

3895. ———. Ibid. 7 sketches, montage,
7" x 11¾" plus 4 details.   T 64C

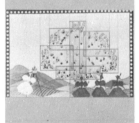

   3896. ECKART, William and Jean.
   The Golden Apple:
   The Orchard, 1954, w.c., 10" x 15". Coll.
   Artists, New York, N.Y.   T 65

3897. ———. Ibid. Helen's House.   T 65A

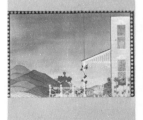

   3898. EDWARDS, Ben.
   The Ponder Heart,
   1956, ink & wash, 7½" x 12". Coll. Artist,
   New York, N.Y.   T 68

3899. ELDER, Eldon.
Legend of Lovers:
Railway Station, 1951, b. & w. photo, 7½" x 9½".
Coll. Artist, New York, N.Y.   T 69

   3900. ELSON, Charles.
   Lohengrin:
   Act II, 1953, 18" x 11". Coll. Artist, Armonk
   Village, N.Y.   T 71

3901. EMENS, Homer (with MILLER, Henry).
The Great Divide,
1906. Theatre Coll., N.Y. Pub. Lib.   T 73

   3902. GATES, Frank.
   Becky Sharp,
   1899, photo, 9½" x 12". Theatre Div., N.Y. Pub.
   Lib.   T 79

3903. GORELIK, Mordecai.
Casey Jones:
Permanent Set, 1939, w.c., 6" x 11". Coll.
Artist, New York, N.Y.   T 84

   3904. ———.
   The Flowering Peach,
   1954, w.c. & col. pencil, 14½" x 10½". Coll.
   Artist, New York, N.Y.   T 87

3905. ———.
Processional:
Act I, 1925, ink & w.c., 12" x 23½". Coll.
Artist, New York, N.Y.   T 82

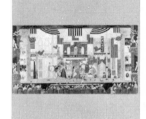

   3906. ———.
   They Shall Not Die:
   Act III, Scene 2, 1933, tempera & photographs,
   19½" x 29½". Coll. Artist, New York, N.Y.
                                                T 85

3907. GROS, Ernest.
The Return of Peter Grimm,
1911, photo, 7" x 9½". Theatre Div., N.Y. Pub.
Lib.   T 88

   3908. HORNER, Harry.
   Dialogue of the Carmelites:
   Act I, Scene 2, 1957. Coll. Artist, Los Angeles,
   Calif.   T 218

3909. ———. Ibid. Act II, Last Scene.   T 218A

   3910. ———.
   The Magic Flute,
   1956. Coll. Artist, Los Angeles, Calif.   T 93

3911. JENKINS, George.
I Remember Mama:
Kitchen, 1944, w.c., 16" x 24½". Coll. Artist,
New York, N.Y.   T 94

   3912. ———.
   Lost in the Stars:
   Stephen Kumalo's Hut, 1949, w.c., 11" x 20".
   Coll. Artist, New York, N.Y.   T 96

3913. JOHNSON, Albert.
The Chase,
1952, w.c., 5¼" x 8¾". Coll. Artist, New York,
N.Y.   T 97

      3914. ——.
      Of Thee I Sing (Revival),
      1952, w.c., 6⅛" x 10½". Coll. Artist, New York,
      N.Y.   T 98

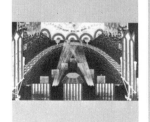 

3915. ——. Ibid.   T 98C

      3916. JONES, Robert Edmond.
      Desire Under the Elms:
      The Cabot Homestead, 1925. Coll. Mrs. Walter
      Huston, New York, N.Y.   T 105

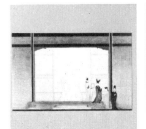 

3917. ——.
Lute Song:
The Blue Pavilion, 1946, w.c. Theatre Arts Coll.,
Mus. Mod. Art.   T 110

      3918. ——.
      Hamlet:
      The Burial of Ophelia, 1922. Coll. Mrs. William
      E. Pennington, Milford, Conn.   T 112

3919. ——.
Macbeth:
Act III, Scene 4, 1921. Mrs. H. L. Luttgen,
Westport, Conn.   T 104

      3920. ——.
      The Man Who Married a Dumb Wife,
      1915. Jones Estate, New York, N.Y.   T 103

3921. ——.
Skyscrapers:
Steel Girders, 1926. Coll. B. L. Webster,
Woodstock, N.Y.   T 106

      3922. KERZ, Leo.
      Antony and Cleopatra:
      Cleopatra's Palace, 1947, w.c., 11" x 20". Coll.
      Artist, New York, N.Y.   T 117

 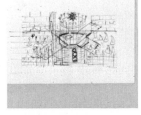

3923. ——.
Parsifal:
Design for Projection Effect, 1956, w.c.,
11½" x 15". Coll. Artist, New York, N.Y.   T 119

      3924. KIESLER, Frederic J.
      The Prisoner,
      1951, ink & wash, 15" x 32". Coll. Artist, New
      York, N.Y.   T 121

3925. LARKIN, Peter.
Inherit the Wind,
1955, ink & wash, 15" x 22½". Coll. Herman
Shumlin, New York, N.Y.   T 124

      3926. ——.
      Teahouse of the August Moon:
      Chinaman, 1953, w.c., 10" x 16". Coll. Henry
      Hewes, New York, N.Y.   T 122

3927. MacKAYE, Steele.
Anarchy or Paul Kauvar:
Act V, 1887, 2½" x 4". Repro. of dwg. by
MORGAN, Matt. Theatre Div., N.Y. Pub. Lib.   T 205

3928. ——.
Madison Square Garden Theatre,
double stage, 1879, print, 4" x 4½". Theatre Div.,
N.Y. Pub. Lib.   T 204

3929. MIELZINER, Jo.
Death of a Salesman:
Scene 1, 1949, tempera, 13" x 24". Coll. Artist,
New York, N.Y. Copyr. Jo Mielziner, 1949.   T 136

3930. ——.
The Innocents:
Children's Masquerade, 1950, w.c., 13½" x 22½".
Coll. Artist, New York, N.Y. Copyr. Jo
Mielziner, 1950.   T 227

3931. ——.
The Lark:
Court at Chinon, 1955, w.c. & ink, 17½" x 23½".
Coll. Artist, New York, N.Y. Copyr. Jo
Mielziner, 1955.   T 139

3932. ——. Ibid. Prison Set, Joan in jail.
          T 139A

3933. ——.
Look Homeward, Angel:
Summer Night, 1957, w.c., 13" x 20". Coll.
Edward F. Kook, New York, N.Y.   T 228

3934. MORRISON, Paul.
View from the Bridge,
1958, w.c., 6⅛" x 11¼". Coll. Artist, New York,
N.Y.   T 226

3935. OENSLAGER, Donald.
The Ballad of Baby Doe:
Act II, Scene 1, 1956, collage, 17" x 26". Coll.
Artist, New York, N.Y.   T 153

3936. ——.
Coriolanus,
1954, 20" x 13½". Coll. Phoenix Theatre, New
York, N.Y.   T 152

3937. ——.
The Fabulous Invalid:
Alexandria Theatre, Opening Night, 1900, 1938,
w.c., 19" x 20". Coll. Artist, New York, N.Y.   T 150

3938. ——.
Of Mice and Men:
The Bank of the Salinas River, 1937, w.c.,
12" x 16". Coll. Artist, New York, N.Y.   T 148

3939. ——.
Tristan and Isolde:
Act I, 1939, w.c., 15" x 22". Coll. Artist, New
York, N.Y.   T 151

3940. ——. Ibid. Act I, Finale.   T 151A

3941. PARRISH, Maxfield.
A Kiss for Cinderella,
1916. Theatre Coll., N.Y. Pub. Lib.   T 154

  3942. ROTH, Wolfgang.
  Porgy and Bess:
  Picnic Scene, Kittinah Island, 1953, w.c.,
  14" x 24". Coll. Artist, New York, N.Y.   T 161

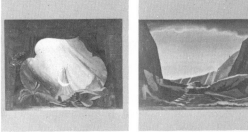

3943. RYCHTARIK, Richard.
Magic Flute:
Queen of the Night, Act I, Scene 2, 1940, w.c.,
12¼" x 16¾". Coll. Artist, New York, N.Y.   T 211A

  3944. ——.
  Die Walküre:
  Rocky Pass, Act II, 1947, w.c., 12½" x 18".
  Coll. Artist, New York, N.Y.   T 215B

3945..SIMONSON, Lee.
The Adding Machine,
1923, 8" x 10". Photo: Vandamm, New York,
N.Y.   T 168

  3946. ——.
  Amphitryon:
  Porch, 1937, 8" x 10". Photo: Vandamm, New
  York, N.Y.   T 172

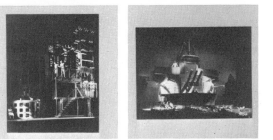

3947. ——.
Dynamo:
Dynamo Set. Photo: Vandamm, New York, N.Y.   T 170A

  3948. ——.
  Roar China!
  Battleship, 1930, 8" x 10". Photo: Vandamm, New
  York, N.Y.   T 171

3949. ——.
The Tidings Brought to Mary:
Two Stage Figures, 1922. Photo: Vandamm, New
York, N.Y.   T 167

  3950. SMITH, Oliver.
  Brigadoon:
  Church Ruins, 1947, w.c., 13½" x 19½". Coll.
  Miss Cheryl Crawford, New York, N.Y.   T 217

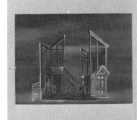

3951. ——.
Facsimile,
1946, w.c., 14" x 20½". Coll. Jerome Robbins,
New York, N.Y.   T 176

  3952. ——.
  Fall River Legend,
  1948, w.c., 12⅜" x 16½". Coll. Miss Lucia
  Chase, New York, N.Y.   T 178

3953. ——.
Fancy Free,
1944, w.c., 9" x 14". Coll. Jerome Robbins,
New York, N.Y.   T 175

  3954. ——.
  Rodeo:
  Farm Kitchen, 1950, w.c., 12¼" x 18¼". Coll.
  Miss Lucia Chase, New York, N.Y.   T 179A

3955. SOVEY, Raymond.
Green Grow the Lilacs:
Bedroom & Back Porch, 1934, b. & w. photo,
8" x 10". Photo: Vandamm, New York, N.Y.   T 182

3956. TCHELICHEW, Pavel.
The Cave of Sleep,
1942, gouache, 19⅜" x 32⅞". Theatre Arts Coll.,
Mus. Mod. Art.   #64.42.11   T 186

3957. THOMPSON, Woodman.
Iolanthe,
1926. Brander Matthews Dramatic Mus.,
Columbia U.   T 188

3958. THROCKMORTON, Cleon.
Noah:
Animals Outside the Ark, 1935, b. & w. photo,
8" x 10". Photo: Vandamm, New York, N.Y. T 190

3959. URBAN, Joseph.
Little Miss Springtime:
Village, 1916, tempera, 10¾" x 7". Brander
Matthews Dramatic Mus., Columbia U.   T 193

3960. ——.
Norma:
Act IV, Scene 1, 1927-28, w.c., 8" x 5½".
Brander Matthews Dramatic Mus., Columbia U.
T 192

3961. ——.
Show Boat:
Curtain, 1928, tempera, 10½" x 6½". Brander
Matthews Dramatic Mus., Columbia U.   T 194

3963. ANON.
*The Providential Detection (A Caricature
of Jefferson),*
1800, etch., 13½" x 15½". Library Co.,
Philadelphia, Pa.   V 7B

    3964. ANON.
    The Square Dance,
    cartoon, 8⁵⁄₁₆" x 4⅛". "Port Folio," August,
    1817. N.Y. Hist. Soc.   V 154

3965. ANON.
Mr. Vilallave's Company,
Aug. 15, 1818, det. broadside, 4¾" x 8⅛". Am.
Antiq. Soc.   V 155

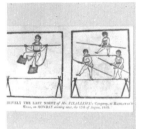

    3966. ANON.
    Crockett Delivering War Speech,
    1847, engr., 3⅞" x 3⅜". Am. Antiq. Soc.   V 156

3967. ANON.
Advertisement for South Side R. R., Long Island,
1873, lith., 13" x 19½". Landauer Coll., N.Y.
Hist. Soc.   V 204

    3968. ACKOFF, Milton (1915-   ).
    Polio Care Open to All,
    1949, poster for National Foundation for Infantile
    Paralysis, 44½" x 29". Study Coll., Mus. Mod.
    Art.   V 2

3969. ———.
Wipe Out Discrimination,
1949, poster for CIO National Labor Service,
32¾" x 44". Study Coll., Mus. Mod. Art.   V 1

    3970. ALLNER, Walter (1909-   ).
    Mighty Engine Power,
    1955, advertisement for AVCO. Mus. Mod. Art.
                                             V 4

3971. ———.
*Great Ideas of Western Man — Declaration
of Rights of Man,*
n.d., advertisement for Container Corporation of
America, 13" x 16". Study Coll., Mus. Mod. Art.   V 3

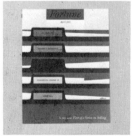

    3972. ———.
    Fortune, April, 1952,
    magazine cover, 10⅛" x 13". Study Coll., Mus.
    Mod. Art. Courtesy of "Fortune" magazine,
    copyr. 1952, Time, Inc.   V 5

3973. ———.
Fortune, October, 1952,
magazine cover, 10⅛" x 13". Study Coll., Mus.
Mod. Art. Courtesy of "Fortune" magazine,
copyr. 1952, Time, Inc.   V 5B

    3974. ———.
    Fortune, March, 1954,
    magazine cover, 10⅛" x 13". Study Coll., Mus.
    Mod. Art. Courtesy of "Fortune" magazine,
    copyr. 1954, Time, Inc.   V 5A

3975. ANCONA, Victor, and KOEHLER, Karl.
This is the Enemy,
poster. Study Coll., Mus. Mod. Art.   V 6

    3976. ANDERSON, Alexander (1775-1870).
    To the Grave Go Sham Protectors of
    "Free Trade and Sailors' Rights,"
    1814, engr., 4¾" x 7⅜". Prints Div., N.Y.
    Pub. Lib.   V 7

3977. ARNO, Peter (1902-   ).
Aw Shucks!
cartoon, 9½" x 7". "The New Yorker," Aug. 12,
1933, New York, N.Y. Copyr. 1933, The New
Yorker Magazine, Inc.   V 8

    3978. ———.
    But I Distinctly Said Whistlers,
    cartoon, 9" x 7". "The New Yorker," Nov. 17,
    1934, New York, N.Y. Copyr. 1934, The New
    Yorker Magazine, Inc.   V 9

3979. ARNOLD, A. F. (1921-   ).
Form Follows Function,
1949, poster for Workshop School of Advertising
Art, 51" x 30". Study Coll., Mus. Mod. Art.   V 10

    3980. ———.
    Music Under the Stars,
    1949, poster for American Fund for Palestinian
    Institutions, 60" x 45". Study Coll., Mus. Mod.
    Art.   V 11

3981. ATHERTON, John (1900-   ).
A Careless Word—Another Cross,
poster for Office of War Information, 29" x 20⅛".
Mus. Mod. Art.   #87.44   V 12

    3982. BAKER, John.
    Trade Card for Fisher and Bird's
    Marble Yard, 287 Bowery, New York,
    c. 1837, engr. 9" x 7⅞". Edward W. C.
    Arnold Coll., Met. Mus. on loan at Mus. City N.Y.
    # L1400.53   V 13A

3983. BASS, Saul (1920-   ).
The Man with the Golden Arm,
1955, poster, 40½" x 27". Mus. Mod. Art.
#202.56   V 13B

    3984. BASSFORD, F.
    Ad for American Line, S.S. New York,
    1893, lith., 11½" x 9½". Mus. City N.Y.
    # L4796.56   V 205

3985. BAYER, Herbert (1900-   ).
Can Our Cities Survive?
1942, bookjacket, pub. Harvard University
Press, 12½" x 9¼". Study Coll., Mus. Mod. Art.   V 15

    3986. ———.
    Merry Christmas,
    1949, greeting card, 3⁹⁄₁₆" x 8⁵⁄₁₆". Study Coll.,
    Mus. Mod. Art.   V 16

3987. ———.
Our Allies Need Eggs,
1941, poster for Rural Electrification
Administration, USA, 20¼" x 30". Study Coll.,
Mus. Mod. Art.   V 14

    3988. ———.
    Polio Research—a Light Is Beginning to Dawn,
    1949, poster for the National Foundation for
    Infantile Paralysis, 44½" x 29". Study Coll.,
    Mus. Mod. Art.   V 17

3989. BEALL, Lester (1903-   ).
Don't Let Him Down!
1941, poster for Division of Information, Office
of Emergency Management, USA, 40" x 30".
Study Coll., Mus. Mod. Art.   V 22

3990. ——.
Farm Work,
1937, poster for Rural Electrification
Administration, 40" x 30". Study Coll., Mus.
Mod. Art.   V 20

3991. ——.
Photoengraving No. 1,
c. 1948, brochure cover for Sterling Engraving
Co., N.Y., 8½" x 10½". Study Coll., Mus. Mod.
Art.   V 23

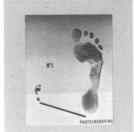

3992. ——.
Radio,
1937, poster, 40" x 30". Mus. Mod. Art.
#A218.37   V 21

3993. ——.
Rural Electrification Administration,
1937, poster for U. S. Dept. of Agriculture,
40" x 30". Mus. Mod. Art.   #90.44   V 19

3994. ——.
Uncorking the Facts about Fine Liquors,
1936, magazine cover for Hiram Walker & Sons,
Inc., 10¾" x 14". Study Coll., Mus. Mod. Art.
                                               V 18

3995. BEGG, John (1903-   ).
Mechanization Takes Command,
1948, bookjacket, 8¾" x 9⅞". Study Coll., Mus.
Mod. Art.   V 24

3996. BELLEW, Frank H. T. (1828-88).
"She twined herself around the strong,
resolute man as the tender vine clings to
the mighty oak for protection and support,"
cartoon, 1½" x 2½". "Life," Feb. 16, 1888.
N.Y. Hist. Soc.   V 24B

3997. BENEKER, G. A. (1882-1934).
SURE! We'll Finish the Job,
1918, poster, Liberty Loan, 25½" x 37½". Mus.
Mod. Art.   #1569.40   V 25A

3998. BIRCH, Thomas (1779-1851).
Business Card of Thomas Birch,
c. 1815, wood-engr., 2½" x 3⅞". Worcester Art
Mus.   #G436   V 25B

3999. BRADLEY, Will (1868-   ).
Victor Bicycles,
1890's, poster printed by Forbes Co., Boston,
Mass., 26¾" x 41". "Les Maîtres de l'affiche,"
Paris, Imprimerie Chaix, 1898. Mus. Mod. Art. V 26

4000. BURTIN, Will (1908-   ).
The Architectural Forum, Design Decade,
1940, magazine cover. Study Coll., Mus. Mod.
Art.   V 29

4001. ——.
Terapia, January, 1955,
journal cover, pub. in Quito, Ecuador, 9½" x 12".
Study Coll., Mus. Mod. Art.   V 31

4002. ——.
Strathmore Paper Company,
1953, catalogue, 8½" x 11". Study Coll., Mus.
Mod. Art.   V 30

4003. CASSIERS, H. (1858-?).
American Line, New York Southampton,
c. 1908, poster. "Les Maîtres de l'affiche,"
Paris, Imprimerie Chaix, 1898. Mus. Mod. Art. V 35

 4004. CHARLES, William H. (1776-1820).
 Modern Spectacles Easily Seen Through,
 1806, etch., 11⅞" x 8⅜". Prints Div., N.Y. Pub.
 Lib. V 36

4005. CHILDS and INMAN (aft. JOHNSTON, D.C.)
The Trollope Family,
1832, lith., 8½" x 10½". Hist. Soc. Pa. V 36B

 4006. CHRISTY, Howard Chandler (1873-?).
 Fight or Buy Bonds,
 1917, poster, Third Liberty Loan, 30" x 40".
 Mus. Mod. Art.   #1577.40 V 37

4007. COINER, Charles (1898-   ).
Give It Your Best!
1942, poster, Division of Information, Office for
Emergency Management, 16" x 20"; 20" x 28½".
Study Coll., Mus. Mod. Art. V 38A

 4008. CURRIER, Nathaniel (1813-88).
 The Bloomer Costume,
 1851, lith., 11⅝" x 8¼". Lib. of Congress.
 V 38B

4009. DE HARAK, Rudolph (1924-   ).
Ralph Sutton at the Piano,
1953, record album cover, 10" x 10". Study Coll.,
Mus. Mod. Art. V 40

 4010. DOW, Arthur W. (1857-1922).
 Modern Art,
 1890's, poster for magazine published in Boston,
 Mass., 21¼" x 15⅜". "Les Maîtres de l'affiche,"
 Paris, Imprimerie Chaix, 1898. Mus. Mod. Art.
 V 41

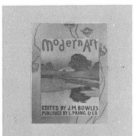

4011. DREXLER, Arthur (1926-   ).
*Exhibition, Ten Automobiles, The Museum of
Modern Art,*
September, 1953, brochure cover, 7½" x 10".
Study Coll., Mus. Mod. Art. V 42

 4012. DURAND, Asher B. (1796-1886), (aft.
 MORSE, S. F. B.).
 The Wife,
 engr., 3⅝" x 2⅞". "Godey's Lady's Book,"
 December, 1831. Prints Div., N.Y. Pub. Lib.
 V 42B

4013. EAMES, Charles (1907-   ).
Christmas Card,
1948, photograph, 6¾" x 4⅝". Study Coll., Mus.
Mod. Art. V 43

 4014. EHRHART.
 *"And this is how the workingman enjoys
 the (Metropolitan) Museum on his only
 day of liberty,"*
 cartoon, 9" x 9½". "Puck," Jan. 2, 1889. N.Y.
 Hist. Soc. V 157

4015. FAIRMAN'S JOB PRINTING, Elmira.
Advertisement for Oysters,
1853, with cut, 10½" x 13½". Landauer Coll.,
N.Y. Hist. Soc. V 198

 4016. FEDERICO, Gene (1918-   ).
 Call to Printing for Commerce,
 1955, mailing piece & poster, 23¼" x 16¼".
 Study Coll., Mus. Mod. Art. V 45

4017. FEDERICO, Gene (1918-   ).
We Invite You to Join Cinema 16,
1950, post card, 7" x 11". Study Coll., Mus. Mod.
Art.   V 44

4018. FRANKLIN, Benjamin (attr.)(1706-90).
Join or Die,
cartoon, 2" x 2⅞". "Pennsylvania Gazette,"
May 9, 1754. Rare Book Div., N.Y. Pub. Lib.
                                                        V 46B

4019. FRASCONI, Antonio (1919-   ).
Happy Greetings,
1956, Christmas card, 17" x 22". Study Coll., Mus.
Mod. Art.   V 48

4020. ———.
Woodcuts by Antonio Frasconi,
1954, poster, exhibit at Weyhe Galleries, N.Y.,
22" x 17". Mus. Mod. Art.   #515.54   V 47

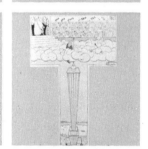

4021. FROST, Arthur B. (1851-1928).
The Democratic Trojan Horse,
cartoon, 9¼" x 11". "Harper's Weekly," July 31,
1880. N.Y. Hist. Soc.   V 48B

4022. FRUEH, Alfred (1898-   ).
Onward and Upward Forever,
cartoon, 10" x 6¾", "The New Yorker," May 7,
1927, New York, N.Y. Copyr. 1927, The New
Yorker Magazine, Inc.   V 50

4023. ———.
700,000 Years of Progress,
cartoon, 5¼" x 6", "The New Yorker," July 25,
1925, New York, N.Y. Copyr. 1925, The New
Yorker Magazine, Inc.   V 49

4024. GÁG, Wanda (1893-1946).
New Masses,
December, 1927, cover design, 9¼" x 12". Mus.
Mod. Art.   V 50B

4025. GAGE, Robert (1921-   ).
Levy's Bread—Any Way You Slice It,
1954, subway poster for Levy's Bread, 30" x 46".
Mus. Mod. Art.   #516.54   V 52

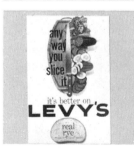

4026. ———.
New York Is Eating It Up,
1953, subway poster for Levy's Bread, 30" x 46".
Mus. Mod. Art.   #299.53   V 51

4027. GANGEL, Richard (1918-   ).
The Weekly Newsmagazine—Time,
1953, poster, 28" x 44". Mus. Mod. Art.
#303.53   Courtesy of "Time" Magazine, copyr.
1953, Time, Inc.   V 53

4028. GELLERT, Hugo (1892-   ).
The Dial,
cartoon, 7⅝" x 10⅝". "New Masses,"
September, 1929. Mus. Mod. Art.   V 54

4029. ———.
Poison,
cartoon, 4" x 5", "New Masses," 1927. Mus.
Mod. Art.   V 53B

4030. GIUSTI, George (1908-   ).
Fortune,
May, 1948, magazine cover, 10¼" x 13". Study
Coll., Mus. Mod. Art. Courtesy of "Fortune"
magazine, copyr. 1948, Time, Inc.   V 55

4031. GLANZMAN, Martin (1923-   ).
See Hockey at the Garden,
1951, poster for Madison Square Garden, N.Y.,
42" x 84". Study Coll., Mus. Mod. Art.   V 56

4032. GLENNY, Alice R. (1858-   ).
Women's Edition (Buffalo) Courier,
1890's, poster for Courier Lithograph Co.,
Buffalo, N.Y., 14¼" x 24⅜". "Les Maîtres de
l'affiche," Paris, Imprimerie Chaix, 1898. Mus.
Mod. Art.   V 57

4033. GODEY'S LADY'S BOOK.
A Magenta-colored Dress, Spring Fashions 1861,
1861, wood engr., 6½" x 4⅞". Free Library,
Philadelphia, Pa.   V 7C

4034. GOLDEN, William (1911-   ).
Get That Man,
1954, brochure cover for Columbia Broadcasting
Co. Television Film Sales, 9" x 11⅜". Study
Coll., Mus. Mod. Art.   V 59

4035. ———.
Network Identification,
1954, advertisement for Columbia Broadcasting
System Television Network, 17½" x 11½".
Study Coll., Mus. Mod. Art.   V 60

4036. GOTO, Byron (1919-   ).
Omnibus,
1956, brochure cover for Omnibus, TV Radio
Workshop of the Ford Foundation, 11" x 11¼".
Study Coll., Mus. Mod. Art.   V 61

4037. GROPPER, William (1897-   ).
The Great American Individualist,
cartoon, 7½" x 11⅜", "New Masses," April,
1930. Mus. Mod. Art.   V 62

4038. ———.
The Noble Senator,
cartoon, 10" x 12¾", "New Masses," August,
1926. Mus. Mod. Art.   V 61B

4039. HAAK, Kenneth (1923-   ) and SMITH,
Paul (1907-   ).
Get All the News and Get It Right,
1950, poster for "The New York Times,"
45" x 60". Mus. Mod. Art.   #604.51   V 64

4040. HARPER, Irving (1916-   ).
*America's Foremost Collection of Modern
Furniture,*
1952, magazine advertisement for Herman Miller
Furniture Co., 8½" x 11⅞". Study Coll., Mus.
Mod. Art.   V 66

4041. ———.
Chairs,
1951, advertisement, 12" x 8½". Study Coll.,
Mus. Mod. Art.   V 65

4042. HELD, John Jr. (1889-1958).
Teaching Old Dogs New Tricks,
cartoon, 8½" x 10¾". "Life," Feb. 18, 1926.
N.Y. Hist. Soc.   V 67

4043. HERRIMAN, George.
Krazy Kat—Over with It,
1924, comic strip cartoon, 5" x 5¾". N.Y. Pub.
Lib.   V 67C

4044. HOMER, Winslow (1836-1910).
The Morning Bell,
wood engr., 9⅛" x 13½", "Harper's Weekly,"
Dec. 13, 1873. Phila. Mus.   #41-53-104
        V 68B

4045. HOMER, Winslow (1836-1910)..
Sea-Side Sketches—A Clam-Bake,
wood engr., 9¼" x 14", "Harper's Weekly,"
Aug. 23, 1873. Phila. Mus.   #41-53-101   V 68C

   4046. ——.
   Ship-Building, Gloucester Harbor,
   wood engr., 9¼" x 13⅝", "Harper's Weekly,"
   Oct. 11, 1873. Phila. Mus.   #41-53-58

                                                 V 68D

4047. ——.
Waiting for a Bite,
wood engr., 9⅛" x 13¾", "Harper's Weekly,"
Aug. 22, 1874. Phila. Mus.   #41-53-113   V 68E

   4048. ——.
   The Wheelbarrow Polka,
   1856, sheet music cover, lith., 9½" x 13". Music
   Div., N.Y. Pub. Lib.   V 68

4049. IRVIN, Rea (1881-   ).
Aut Cesar,
cartoon, 9½" x 14". "The New Yorker," Nov. 13,
1937, New York, N.Y. Copyr. 1937, The New
Yorker Magazine, Inc.   V 69A

   4050. JOHNSTON, David Claypoole (1797-1865).
   The Ice Cream Quick Step,
   1841, sheet music cover for Thayer & Co., lith.,
   5⅝" x 9"(size of illus.). Lib. of Congress. V 69C

4051. ——.
A Militia Drill Thirty Years Ago,
1862, lith., 10¾" x 16". Am. Antiq. Soc.   V 69B

   4052. JONES, Robert M. (1913-   ).
   mood ellington,
   1948, record album cover for Columbia records,
   N.Y., 10½" x 10⅜". Study Coll., Mus. Mod. Art.
                                                 V 70

4053. KAUFFER, E. McKnight (1891-   ).
Civil Airways,
1943, poster, 28½" x 40". Mus. Mod. Art.
#94.44   V 71

   4054. ——.
   Greece Fights On,
   1942, poster, 24" x 32". Mus. Mod. Art.
   #95.44   V 72

4055. ——.
*Subway Posters Perform Daily before
5,000,000 Pairs of Eyes,*
1947, poster for New York Subway Advertising
Co., 44" x 29". Study Coll., Mus. Mod. Art.   V 71B

   4056. KEPPLER, Joseph (1855-1945).
   The Bosses of the Senate,
   cartoon, 18½" x 11⅛". "Puck," Jan. 23, 1889.
   N.Y. Hist. Soc.   V 72C

4057. ——.
A Telephonic Suggestion,
cartoon, 8¾" x 12". "Puck," March, 1877. N.Y.
Pub. Lib.   V 72B

   4058. KETTERLINUS, & Co., Phila.
   Calendar for 1855,
   1854, embossed lith., 16½" x 20¾". Landauer
   Coll., N.Y. Hist. Soc.   V 199

4059. KLEIN, David (1918-   ).
New York, Fly TWA,
1956, poster. Mus. Mod. Art.   # 329.57   V 73

    4060. KOERNER, Henry (1915-   ).
    Someone Talked,
    1942, poster, 23¼" x 33⅜". Mus. Mod. Art.
    # P 316   V 74

4061. KOMAI, Ray (1918-   ).
Gotham Lighting Corporation,
1951, brochure cover for Gotham Lighting Corp.,
8½" x 10⅛". Study Coll., Mus. Mod. Art.   V 75

    4062. KRIKORIAN, George (1914-   ).
    Cross Word Puzzle ... New York Times,
    1949, poster, 45" x 60". Study Coll., Mus. Mod.
    Art.   V 76

4063. KRONE, Helmut (1925-   ).
The Clearest Road into New York,
advertisement in the "New York Herald-Tribune,"
Tues., Mar. 20, 1956, 3¼" x 21¼". Study Coll.,
Mus. Mod. Art.   V 77

    4064. LEYENDECKER, F. X. (1877-1924).
    U.S.A. Bonds Weapons for Liberty,
    World War I, poster, 26" x 38". Mus. Mod. Art.
    # 134.43   V 78

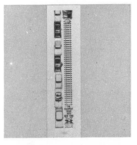

4065. LIE, Jonas (1880-1940).
On the Job for Victory,
World War I, poster, 26" x 38". Mus. Mod.
Art.   # 1600.40   V 79

    4066. LIONNI, Leo (1910-   ).
    8 Automobiles,
    1951, poster & catalogue cover for Mus. Mod.
    Art exhib., 26" x 10". Mus. Mod. Art.   # 613.51
    V 81

4067. ——.
Fortune,
Jan. 1955, magazine cover, 10³⁄₁₆" x 13". Study
Coll., Mus. Mod. Art. Courtesy of "Fortune"
magazine, copyr. 1955, Time, Inc.   V 84

    4068. ——.
    Olivetti, Lettera 22 (a series of four),
    1954, poster, 19" x 26¾". Mus. Mod. Art.
    # 524.54a, b, c, d   V 82

4069. ——.
Which Way Out?
1956, poster for Family Service Assoc. of
America, 30" x 46". Mus. Mod. Art.   # 333.57   V 85

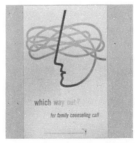

    4070. ——.
    *The World of Modern Art—Twenty-fifth
    Anniversary,*
    1954, car card poster for Mus. Mod. Art,
    20¹⁵⁄₁₆" x 11". Mus. Mod. Art.   # 173.55   V 83

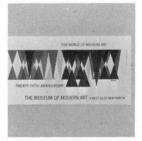

4071. LUBALIN, Herb (1918-   ).
Design and Printing for Commerce 1956,
catalogue pub. by American Institute of Graphic
Arts, page size 11⅝" x 11¼".   V 86

    4072. LUKS, George B. (1867-1933).
    Hanna: That Man Clay Was an Ass...,
    cartoon. "The Verdict," Mar. 13, 1889. N.Y.
    Pub. Lib.   V 86B

4073. LUSTIG, Alvin (1915-55).
J. S. Bach,
1953, record album cover for The Haydn Society,
Boston, 12½" x 12⅜". Study Coll., Mus. Mod.
Art.   V 89

    4074. ———.
    J. S. Bach; Vivaldi,
    1953, record album cover for The Haydn Society,
    Boston, 12¼" x 12⅜". Study Coll., Mus. Mod.
    Art.   V 90

4075. ———.
Fortune, September, 1952,
magazine cover, 10¼" x 12⅞". Study Coll., Mus.
Mod. Art. Courtesy of ''Fortune'' magazine,
copyr. 1952, Time, Inc.   V 88

    4076. ———.
    Industrial Design in America,
    1954, bookjacket, 9" x 12¼". Study Coll., Mus.
    Mod. Art.   V 93

4077. ———.
Monsieur Test,
1947, bookjacket, pub. Alfred A. Knopf, 6¼" x 9½".
Study Coll., Mus. Mod. Art.   V 87

    4078. ———.
    Noonday—New Books from the Noonday Press,
    Fall, 1953, brochure cover, 4" x 9". Study Coll.,
    Mus. Mod. Art.   V 91

4079. ———.
375 Park Avenue,
November, 1955, brochure cover for the Seagram
Bldg., 12" x 14". Study Coll., Mus. Mod. Art.   V 94

    4080. ———.
    375 Park Avenue,
    advertisement in the ''New York Herald-Tribune,''
    Tues., Apr. 24, 1956, for the House of Seagram,
    14⅝" x 22¼". Study Coll., Mus. Mod. Art.   V 95

4081. ———.
Vivaldi,
1953, record album cover for The Haydn Society,
Boston, 12⅜" x 12⅜". Study Coll., Mus. Mod.
Art.   V 92

    4082. LUSTIG, Elaine (1927-   ).
    Museu de Arte Moderna, Rio de Janeiro,
    1958, catalogue cover. Study Coll., Mus. Mod.
    Art.   V 96A

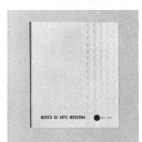

4083. ———.
A Type Specimen Page,
1952, 14" x 12½". Study Coll., Mus. Mod. Art.   V 96

    4084. McLEAN, Alexander.
    Music Cover: Bayard Waltz,
    1870, lith., 14" x 10¾". Mariners Mus.   V 96B

4085. MARSH, Reginald (1898-1954).
The Angelus,
cartoon, 9½" x 15". ''The New Yorker,'' Jan. 3,
1931. New York, N.Y. Copyr. 1931, The New
Yorker Magazine, Inc.   V 97B

    4086. ———.
    Where Men Accumulate and Wealth Decays,
    cartoon, 9¾" x 7". ''The New Yorker,'' Jan. 31,
    1932. New York, N.Y. Copyr. 1932, The New
    Yorker Magazine, Inc.   V 97

4087. MARTIN, Noel (1924-   ).
In the Flat and Round,
1952, catalogue cover for the Cincinnati Mod.
Art Soc., Cincinnati Art Mus., 7" x 8½". Study
Coll., Mus. Mod. Art.   V 100

    4088. ——.
    R. K. LeBlond Machine Tool Co.,
    1953, brochure cover, 9⅞" x 13". Study Coll.,
    Mus. Mod. Art.   V 101

4089. MARTIN, David Stone (1910-   ).
Roy Eldridge Collates,
1947, record album cover for Mercury Records,
10½" x 10½". Study Coll., Mus. Mod. Art.   V 99

    4090. ——.
    Strong in the Strength of the Lord, We Who
    Fight in the People's Cause Will Never
    Stop until That Cause Is Won,
    1942, poster for Office of War Information,
    20" x 27¾". Study Coll., Mus. Mod. Art.   V 98

4091. MATTER, Herbert (1907-   ).
Advertisement,
for Knoll Associates, N.Y., 9⅜" x 12⅜". Study
Coll., Mus. Mod. Art.   V 103

    4092. ——.
    America Calling,
    1941, poster for Office of Civilian Defense,
    40" x 29½". Mus. Mod. Art.   #118.44   V 104

4093. ——.
Fortune, July, 1948,
magazine cover, 10⅜" x 12⅞". Study Coll., Mus.
Mod. Art. Courtesy of "Fortune" magazine,
copyr. 1948, Time, Inc.   V 106

    4094. ——.
    4-Story Groceries,
    1942, magazine advertisement for Container
    Corporation of America, 8" x 10". Study Coll.,
    Mus. Mod. Art.   V 102

4095. ——.
How to Combine Architecture, Painting,
Sculpture, 1951,
announcement for Mus. Mod. Art, 10" x 17¾".
Study Coll., Mus. Mod. Art.   V 108

    4096. ——.
    Knoll Office Planned Furniture,
    1956, brochure cover for Knoll Associates,
    8¾" x 12". Study Coll., Mus. Mod. Art.   V 109

4097. ——.
One of Them Had Polio,
1949, poster for National Foundation for Infantile
Paralysis, 30" x 46". Study Coll., Mus. Mod.
Art.   V 107

    4098. ——.
    Paperboard Fills the Soldier's Pack!
    Jan. 11, 1943, advertisement for the Container
    Corp. of America, 8¼" x 11½". Study Coll.,
    Mus. Mod. Art.   V 105

4099. MINOR, Robert (1884-1951).
"at last a perfect soldier,"
1915, cartoon. N.Y. Pub. Lib.   V 109B

    4100. NARDIN, Warren (1920-   ).
    The Mouse with Red Eyes,
    1950, bookjacket, 5¼" x 7¹³⁄₁₆". Study Coll., Mus.
    Mod. Art.   V 110

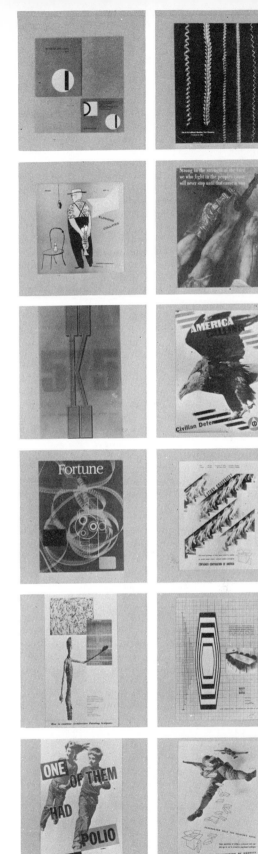

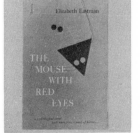

4101. NAST, Thomas (1840-1902).
The "Brains,"
cartoon, engr., 5" x 5". "Harper's Weekly,"
Oct. 21, 1871. N.Y. Pub. Lib.   V 112

   4102. ——.
   *A Group of Vultures Waiting for the
   Storm to "blow over"—"Let Us Prey,"*
   cartoon. "Harper's Weekly," Sept. 30, 1871.
   N.Y. Pub. Lib.   V 111B

4103. ——.
Peace Party No Go,
1863, engr. 12" x 18⅞". Phila. Mus.
#43.99.33   V 111C

   4104. ——.
   Too Thin,
   caricature, wood engr., 9⅛" x 11". "Harper's
   Weekly," Sept. 30, 1871. N.Y. Pub. Lib.   V 111

4105. NITSCHE, Erik (1908-   ).
Atoms for Peace,
1955, poster for the Atomic Energy Conference,
Geneva, 1955, by General Dynamics Corp.,
50" x 35½". Mus. Mod. Art.   #218.56   V 117

   4106. ——.
   The Boeing B17,
   page in "Air Tech," February, 1944,
   7¹³⁄₁₆" x 11". Study Coll., Mus. Mod. Art.   V 113

4107. ——.
No Way Out,
1950, advertisement for 20th Century-Fox movie,
13⅛" x 10". Study Coll., Mus. Mod. Art.   V 115

   4108. ——.
   Say it Fast...Often...in Color,
   1947, poster for the N.Y. Subway Advertising Co.,
   47" x 29". Study Coll., Mus. Mod. Art.   V 114

4109. OSBORN, Robert (1904-   ).
"Who Goes There?"
cartoon, "Scope," Winter, 1955, 5½" x 4".
Study Coll., Mus. Mod. Art.   V 117B

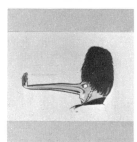

   4110. PARSONS, Charles (1821-1910), for
   ENDICOTT & Co.
   *Advertisement for Wheeler and Wilson's
   Sewing Machines,*
   c. 1860, col. lith., 29" x 22". Landauer Coll.,
   N.Y. Hist. Soc.   V 202

4111. PENFIELD, Edward (1866-1925).
Harper's March,
1894, poster for "Harper's Magazine,"
7½" x 10". Les Maîtres de l'affiche, Paris,
Imprimerie Chaix, 1898. Mus. Mod. Art.   V 118A

   4112. ——.
   Harper's May,
   1894, poster for "Harper's Magazine,"
   19¼" x 13¾". Les Maîtres de l'affiche, Paris,
   Imprimerie Chaix, 1898. Mus. Mod. Art.   V 118

4113. PENNELL, Joseph (1860-1926).
*That Liberty Shall Not Perish from the Earth
Buy Liberty Bonds,*
poster, Fourth Liberty Loan, 22" x 33". Mus.
Mod. Art.   #A 1605.40   V 119

   4114. RAND, Paul (1914-   ).
   "AD,"
   March, 1941, magazine cover, black & pink
   montage, 5½" x 8". Coll. The Composing Room,
   New York, N.Y.

4115. RAND, Paul (1914-   ).
Dada Painters,
1951, bookjacket, pub. Wittenborn & Co. Study
Coll., Mus. Mod. Art. V 123

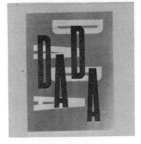

4116. ——.
Guide to the New York World's Fair,
1939, booklet cover, 5¼" x 8". Study Coll., Mus.
Mod. Art. V 120

4117. ——.
*Of All the Advertising Agencies in the United
States William H. Weintraub Ranks Second in
Total Hours of Network Television,*
Advertisement in "The New York Times," Jan. 4,
1951, 9⁹⁄₁₆" x 14¾". Study Coll., Mus. Mod. Art. V 124

4118. ——.
*To the Executives and Management of the
Radio Corporation of America,*
Newspaper Advertisement for William H.
Weintraub & Co., Jan. 28, 1954, 15¼" x 26¾".
Study Coll., Mus. Mod. Art. V 126

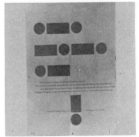

4119. RAYNOR, R. J., for ENDICOTT & Co.
Advertisement for Tucker, Crawford and Rector,
c. 1855, lith., 4½" x 7". Landauer Coll., N.Y.
Hist. Soc. V 200

4120. REIS, Henry (1917-   ).
Alert Executives Keep Up with the Times,
1953, poster for "The New York Times,"
45" x 60". Study Coll., Mus. Mod. Art. V 127

4121. ——.
Poster,
for Family Service Assoc. of America, 1956,
30" x 46". Mus. Mod. Art.   # 339.57 V 128

4122. RHEAD, Louis J. (1857-1926).
Advertising in the Sun gives best results,
1890's, poster, 39⅜" x 30¹⁵⁄₁₆". "Les Maîtres de
l'affiche," Paris, Imprimerie Chaix, 1898. Mus.
Mod. Art. V 129

4123. ROBINSON, Boardman (1876-1952).
Signed,
cartoon. "The Liberator," June 28, 1919. N.Y.
Pub. Lib. V 129B

4124. SARONY and MAJOR.
*Autumn & Winter Fashions, 1849 & 1850 by
A. Wheeler,*
1849, advertisement, lith., 19¾" x 25⅞". J. C.
Davies Coll., Mus. City N.Y.   # 29.100.2496
V 129C

4125. ——.
Christy's Melodies,
1848, sheet music cover, col. lith., 12¼" x 9½". Ph
Phila. Mus. V 129D

4126. SEMENOICK; Alexander (1917-   ).
Fortune, August, 1945,
magazine cover, 10½" x 13". Courtesy of
"Fortune" magazine, copyr. 1945, Time, Inc.
V 130

4127. SHAHN, Ben (1898-   ).
Break Reaction's Grip—Register—Vote,
c. 1946. Mus. Mod. Art.   # 96.47   Courtesy of
Committee on Political Education, AFL-CIO. V 134A

4128. ——.
The empty studio,
1948, advertisement for Columbia Broadcasting
System, N.Y. Study Coll., Mus. Mod. Art. V 135

4129. SHAHN, Ben (1898-   ).
For All These Rights We've Just Begun to Fight,
1946, poster for Political Action Committee,
CIO, 30" x 39". Mus. Mod. Art.   #97.47   V 132

4130. ——.
A Partridge in a Pear Tree,
1951, brochure cover & 1st page for Mus. Mod.
Art, 8½" x 7⅜". Study Coll., Mus. Mod. Art.
V 137

4131. ——.
See the '52 Republican Convention,
July 6, 1952, advertisement in "The New York
Times" for CBS Television Network, 14¾" x 22¾".
Study Coll., Mus. Mod. Art.   V 138

4132. ——.
Two Turtle Doves,
1952, Christmas card published & sold by Mus.
Mod. Art, 5⅛" x 6½". Study Coll., Mus. Mod.
Art.   V 139

4133. ——.
The Untouchables,
May, 1949, brochure cover, 6" x 18". Study Coll.,
Mus. Mod. Art.   V 136

4134. ——.
We French Workers Warn You...,
1942, poster for War Production Board,
39⅛" x 28½". Mus. Mod. Art.   #108.44   V 131

4135. ——.
We Want Peace—Register Vote,
1946, poster for CIO, 27½" x 41½". Mus. Mod.
Art.   #100.47   V 134

4136. SMITH, David (1912-   ).
Poster,
1951-52, for artists' exhibition, 20⁵⁄₁₆" x 15⅝".
Mus. Mod. Art.   #168.52   V 140B

4137. ——.
Poster,
1953-54, for artists' exhibition at the Willard
Gallery, 15½" x 20". Study Coll., Mus. Mod.
Art.   V 140

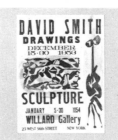 

4138. SMITH, Paul (1907-   ).
A Triumph in Metallurgy and Prosthetic Beauty,
1931, brochure cover for Coe Laboratories, Inc.,
Chicago, Ill., 8½" x 11". Study Coll., Mus. Mod.
Art.   V 141

4139. ——.
X Marks the Spot Where Your Customers Are Looking,
1947, poster for N.Y. Subway Advertising Co.,
44" x 29". Study Coll., Mus. Mod. Art.   V 142A

4140. SMITHER, James (1741-97).
Benjamin Randolph, Cabinet Maker,
c. 1770, furniture label, engr., 9⅛" x 7⅛".
Library Co. Philadelphia, Pa.   B 142B

4141. SNYDER, Jerome (1916-   ).
Speaking of Allergy, Let's Get Down to Cases...,
1950, folder for Ciba Pharmaceutical Products,
N.J. Study Coll., Mus. Mod. Art.   V 143

4142. STEINBERG, Saul (1914-   ).
And She Did It All by Herself,
1955, advertisement, 10" x 5½". Simplicity
Patterns, New York, N.Y.   V 143B

4143. STEINBERG, Saul (1914-   ).
Untitled cartoon (man carrying sign), 4" x 5¼".
"The New Yorker," Jan. 15, 1949. New York,
N.Y. Copyr. 1949, The New Yorker Magazine, Inc.   V 144

    4144. ——.
    Untitled cartoon (woman writing under water),
    6" x 5½". "The New Yorker," June 15, 1946.
    Copyr. 1946, The New Yorker Magazine, Inc.
                                 V 145

4145. STEINWEISS, Alex (1917-   ).
Boogie Woogie,
1941, record album cover for Columbia Records,
10½" x 10⅜". Study Coll., Mus. Mod. Art.   V 146

    4146. STEPHENS, Henry L. (1824-82).
    Giraffe,
    1851, col. engr., 5¾" x 9½". Prints Div., N.Y.
    Pub. Lib.   V 147

4147. SUTNAR, Ladislav (1897-   ).
*Catalog Design, New Patterns in Product
Information,*
1944, catalogue cover for Sweet's Catalog
Service, F. W. Dodge Corp., N.Y., 5⅞ x 8⅜".
Study Coll., Mus. Mod. Art.   V 149

    4148. THURBER, James (1894-   ).
    *Well, Who Made the Magic Go out of
    Our Marriage, You or Me?*
    cartoon, 4" x 6". "The New Yorker," Apr. 13,
    1940. New York, N.Y. Copyr. 1940, The New
    Yorker Magazine, Inc.   V 152

4149. TISDALE, Elkanah (1771-?).
Gerrymander,
1812, cartoon. Prints Div., N.Y. Pub. Lib.   V 152B

    4150. TSCHERNY, George (1924-   ).
    Interiors,
    February, 1951, magazine cover, 9⅛" x 12⅛".
    Study Coll., Mus. Mod. Art.   V 153

4151. WHISTLER, James Abbott McNeill
(1834-1903).
Song of the Graduates—U.S. Military Academy,
1852, sheet music cover, 9½" x 13". Music Div.,
N.Y. Pub. Lib.   V 159

    4152. WILLIAMS, Gluyas (1888-?).
    Fellow Citizens Club Library,
    cartoon, 6½" x 9½". "The New Yorker," June 6,
    1933. New York, N.Y. Copyr. 1933, The New
    Yorker Magazine, Inc.   V 160

4153. WOODBURY, Charles H. (1864-1940).
The July Century,
1890's, poster, 18⅞" x 11¾". "Les Maîtres de
l'affiche. Paris, Imprimerie Chaix, 1898. Mus.
Mod. Art.   V 161

    4154. WYNNE, Milton.
    Time and Tools Influence Art,
    1950, poster for Workshop School of Advertising
    Art, 46" x 30". Mus. Mod. Art.   #171.52
                                  V 162

4155. YOUNG, Art (1866-1943).
The Greater Inferno,
cartoon, 6½" x 8". "Life," Apr. 22, 1926. N.Y.
Hist. Soc.   V 164

    4156. ——.
    Having Their Fling,
    cartoon. "New Masses," September, 1917. N.Y.
    Pub. Lib.   V 163

APPENDIX A

Paintings Useful as Supplements to the Costume List

2337. ANON.	*John van Cortland*	PA 42	2397. FEKE, Robert	*Mrs. James Bowdoin II*	PA 46B
2339. ANON.	*Robert Gibbs*	PA 16B	2401. ——.	*Rev. Thomas Hiscox*	PA 68
2341. ANON.	*David, Joanna and Abigail Mason*	PA 13	2402. ——.	*Isaac Royall and Family*	PA 67
2342. ANON.	*James A. De Peyster*	PA 41	2403. ——.	*Brigadier-general Samuel Waldo*	PA 70
2345. ANON.	*Mrs. Anne Pollard at Age 100*	PA 7	2404. ——.	*Isaac Winslow*	PA 49B
2335. ANON.	*Thomas Van Alstyne*	PA 22	2405. ——.	*Unknown Woman*	PA 69
2350. BADGER, Joseph	*James Badger*	PA 73	2406. FOSTER, John	*John Davenport*	PA 9
2352. ——.	*Hannah Upham Haskins*	PA 72A	2414. HESSELIUS, John	*Charles Calvert and Colored Slave*	PA 80
2356. BLACKBURN, Joseph	*Mrs. Theodore Atkinson*	PA 59A	2415. ——.	*Mrs. Richard Galloway*	PA 81
2357. ——.	*Elizabeth and James Bowdoin*	PA 39B	2422. KÜHN, Justus Englehardt	*Eleanor Darnall*	PA 20B
2358. ——.	*The Winslow Family*	PA 57	2421. ——.	*Henry Darnall III*	PA 21B
2374. COPLEY, John Singleton	*Mrs. Ezekiel Goldthwait*	PA 103	2440. THEUS, Jeremiah	*Mrs. Peter Manigault*	PA 56
2376. ——.	*Nathaniel Hurd*	PA 98	2442. WEST, Benjamin	*Penn's Treaty with the Indians*	PA 119
2378. ——.	*Jeremiah Lee*	PA 72B	2453. WILLIAMS, William	*Deborah Hall*	PA 48
2379. ——.	*Mrs. Jeremiah Lee*	PA 73B	2530. BINGHAM, George Caleb	*Daniel Boone Escorting a Band of Pioneers*	PB 83
2380. ——.	*Mr. and Mrs. Thomas Mifflin*	PA 105	2531. ——.	*Fur Traders Descending the Missouri*	PB 76
2383. ——.	*Paul Revere*	PA 66B	2532. ——.	*Jolly Flatboatman, No. 2*	PB 85
2385. ——.	*Epes Sargent*	PA 87	2560. CHASE, William Merritt	*A Friendly Call*	PB 520
2389. ——.	*Isaac Smith*	PA 94	2562. ——.	*Lady with the White Shawl*	PB 117
2390. ——.	*Mrs. Isaac Smith*	PA 95	2565. ——.	*Miss Dora Wheeler*	PB 521
2396. FEKE, Robert	*James Bowdoin II*	PA 45B	2619. EAKINS, Thomas	*The Concert Singer*	PB 549
			2631. ——.	*The Thinker*	PB 552

2636. EAKINS, Thomas *Letitia Wilson Jordan Bacon*	PB 177	
2638. ——. *Miss Van Buren*	PB 547	

2641. EARL, Ralph
      Major-general Frederick William August,
      Baron von Steuben
	PB 560	

2643. ——. *Justice Oliver Ellsworth and Wife*	PB 181	
2644. ——. *Mrs. William Moseley and Her Son Charles*	PB 558	
2645. ——. *Roger Sherman*	PB 179	

2647. ——.
      Mrs. Benjamin Tallmadge with Her Son Henry
      and Daughter Maria
	PB 557	

2655. ELLIOT, Charles Loring *Mrs. Thomas Goulding*	PB 190	
2489. FIELD, Erastus Salisbury *Joseph Moore and His Family*	PB 694	
2669. HARDING, Chester *Mrs. John Ball Brown*	PB 576	
2670. ——. *Amos Lawrence*	PB 202	
2695. HOMER, Winslow *Croquet Scene*	PB 589	

2704. ——.
      Long Branch, New Jersey
      detail
	PB 225B	

2705. ——.
      Long Branch, New Jersey
      detail
	PB 225A	

2708. ——. *Prisoners from the Front*	PB 224	
2710. ——. *Snap the Whip*	PB 590	
2719. HUNT, William Morris *Mrs. Richard Morris Hunt and Child*	PB 596	
2720. ——. *Marguerite*	PB 598	
2721. ——. *Ida Mason*	PB 600	
2722. ——. *Chief Justice Lemuel Shaw*	PB 599	
2736. JARVIS, John Wesley *Jacob Houseman*	PB 265	
2737. ——. *Oliver Hazard Perry*	PB 266	

2738. JENNYS, William *Gentleman of the Brewer Family*	PB 606B	
2740. ——. *Mrs. Reuben Hatch*	PB 606A	
2741. ——. *Col. Constant Storrs*	PB 268	
2742. ——. *Mrs. Constant Storrs*	PB 267	
2746. JOHNSON, Eastman *Family Group*	PB 273	
2775. MacKAY *Mrs. Hannah Bush*	PB 299	
2776. ——. *John Bush*	PB 300	
2792. MORSE, Samuel F. B. *The Muse, Susan Walker Morse*	PB 628	
2796. MOUNT, William Sidney *Bargaining for a Horse*	PB 314	
2798. ——. *Eel Spearing at Setauket*	PB 317	
2801. ——. *The Painter's Triumph*	PB 316	
2806. NEAGLE, John *Pat Lyon*	PB 326	
2807. ——. *William Strickland, Esq.*	PB 322	
2817. PEALE, Charles Willson *Family Group*	PB 338	
2818. ——. *Benjamin Franklin*	PB 341	
2821. ——. *The Staircase Group*	PB 344	
2823. ——. *Washington, Lafayette and Tilghman at Yorktown*	PB 340	
2869. SARGENT, John Singer *The Daughters of Edward D. Boit*	PB 409	
2873. ——. *Mr. and Mrs. Isaac Newton Phelps Stokes*	PB 649	
2882. STUART, Gilbert *William Grant (The Skater)*	PB 418	
2886. ——. *Mrs. Richard Yates*	PB 419	
2887. SULLY, Thomas *Samuel Coates*	PB 424	

2889.	SULLY, Thomas *Captain Jean T. David*	PB 425
2890.	——. *Mary Sicard David*	PB 426
2892.	——. *Lady with a Harp*	PB 658
2888.	——. *Mother and Son*	PB 659
2891.	——. *Col. Thomas Handasyd Perkins*	PB 429
2893.	——. *Commodore Charles Stewart*	PB 660
2500.	WETHERBY, Isaac Augustus *Mary Eliza Jenkins*	PB 37
4008.	CURRIER, Nathaniel *The Bloomer Costume*	V 38B
4033.	GODEY'S LADY'S BOOK *A Magenta-colored Dress*	V 7C

APPENDIX B

The original architects for Rockefeller Center were: Reinhard & Hofmeister; Corbett, Harrison and MacMurray; and Hood and Fouilhoux. From 1931 to 1937 the first eleven buildings were constructed. By 1940 three more had been added and the original concept of Rockefeller Center was completed. The Center's fifteenth structure, the 33-story Esso Building, designed by Carson & Lundin, was built in 1947, after World War II. In 1954 the Center Theater was demolished. Early in 1955 construction was started on the site for a 19-story addition to the United States Rubber Company Building. Designed by Harrison and Abramovitz, it was opened in December, 1955.

INDEX

Numbers in *italic* type refer to pages. Other numbers refer to the catalogue numbers of the illustrations.